MW00835134

HOMERIC GRAMMAR

D. B. MONRO

A GRAMMAR

OF THE

HOMERIC DIALECT

BY

D. B. MONRO, M.A.

PROVOST OF ORIEL COLLEGE, OXFORD

SECOND EDITION, REVISED AND ENLARGED

L'objet de cette science est de rechercher dans l'esprit de l'homme
la cause de la transformation des idiomes

M. BRÉAL

WIPF & STOCK · Eugene, Oregon

Wipf and Stock Publishers
199 W 8th Ave, Suite 3
Eugene, OR 97401

A Grammar of the Homeric Dialect, Second Edition, Revised and Enlarged
By Monro, D. B.
Softcover ISBN-13: 978-1-6667-6465-9
Hardcover ISBN-13: 978-1-6667-6466-6
eBook ISBN-13: 978-1-6667-6467-3
Publication date 11/10/2022
Previously published by Oxford, 1891

This edition is a scanned facsimile of the original edition published in 1891.

DEDICATED TO THE MEMORY

OF THE REV.

JAMES RIDDELL

LATE FELLOW AND TUTOR OF BALLIOL

PREFACE TO THE FIRST EDITION.

IT may be said, without fear of giving offence, that a new Grammar of the Homeric dialect is sorely wanted. The admirable *Griechische Formenlehre* of the late H. L. Ahrens is now just thirty years old, and is confined, as its title indicates, to the inflexions. Not only has the course of discovery been going on since Ahrens wrote (and with hardly less rapidity than in the first years of the new science), but the historical method has been carried into the field of syntax. And apart from 'comparative philology,' the researches of Bekker, Cobet, La Roche, and many other students have brought together a wealth of material that only needs careful analysis and arrangement to make it accessible to the general body of learners.

The plan of this book has sufficient novelty to call for some explanation. I have not attempted to write a Comparative Grammar, or even a Grammar that would deserve the epithet 'historical:' but I have kept in view two principles of arrangement which belong to the historical or genetic method. These are, that grammar should proceed from the simple to the complex types of the Sentence, and that the form and the meaning should as far as possible be treated together. Now the simplest possible Sentence—apart from mere exclamations—consists of a *Verb*, or word containing in itself the two elements of all rational utterance, a Subject and a Predicate. We begin, therefore, by analysing the Verb, and classifying (1) the Endings, which express the Person and Number of the Subject (§§ 1–7), and serve also to distinguish the 'Middle' or Reflexive use (§ 8), and (2) the modifications of the Stem which yield the several Tenses and Moods. These modifications, we at once perceive, are more numerous than the meanings which they serve to express, and we have therefore to choose between classifying according to *formation*—i. e. according to the process by which each Tense-Stem and Mood-Stem is derived from the simple Verb-Stem or Root,—and the ordinary classification according to meaning (Present, Future, Perfect, Aorist, &c.). The former course seemed preferable because it answers to the historical order. The problem is to find how pre-existing forms—common to Greek and Sanscrit, and therefore part of an original 'Indo-European' grammar—were adapted to the specifically Greek system of Tense-meanings. I have therefore taken the different formations in turn, beginning with the simplest (§§ 9–20, 22–27, 29–69, 79–83), and introducing an account of the meaning of each as soon as possible (§§ 21, 28, 70–78). This part of the subject naturally includes the accentuation of the different forms of the Verb (§§ 87–89).

The next great division of the subject is concerned with the first enlargement of the Sentence. A word may be added which taken by itself says nothing—contains no Subject and Predicate—but which combines with and qualifies the primitive one-word Sentence. The elements which may gather in this way round the basis or nucleus formed by the Verb are ultimately of two kinds, Nouns and Pronouns; and the relations in which they may stand to the Verb are also two-fold. A Noun or Pronoun may stand as a Subject—limiting or explaining the Subject already contained in the Person-Ending—or may qualify the Predicate given by the Stem of the Verb. These relations are shown by the Ending, which again may be either a Case-Ending or an adverbial Ending. We begin accordingly by an account of the *Declensions*, supplemented by a list of the chief groups of *Adverbs* (Chapter V).

When we pass from the Endings to the Stems of Nouns and Pronouns, we find that they are essentially different. A 'Nominal Stem' consists in general of two parts, (1) a *predicative* part, usually identical with a Verb-Stem, and (2) a Suffix. Each of these two elements, again, may be complex. The addition of a further Suffix yields a fresh Stem, with a corresponding derivative meaning; and thus we have the distinction between *Primitive* or Verbal and *Secondary* or Denominative Nouns. The Suffixes employed in these two classes are generally distinct, and deserve a more careful enumeration than is usually given in elementary grammars. The predicative part, again, may be enlarged by a second Nominal Stem, prefixed to the other, and qualifying it nearly as a Case-form or Adverb qualifies the Verb. The Compounds thus formed are of especial interest for the poetical dialect of Homer. The analysis which I have given of the chief forms which they present must be taken to be provisional only, as the subject is still full of doubt. With respect to the meaning I have attempted no complete classification. It is always unsafe to insist on distinctions which may be clear to us, but only because we mark them by distinct forms of expression.

The chapter on the formation of Nouns should perhaps have been followed by one on the formation of Pronouns. The material for such a chapter, however, lies for the most part beyond the scope of a grammar. It is represented in this book by a section on Heteroclite Pronouns (§ 108), which notices some traces of composite Pronominal Stems, and in some degree by another on the Numerals (§ 130).

When we come to examine the syntactical use of the Cases, we find ourselves sometimes dealing with sentences which contain at least two members besides the Verb. Along with the constructions which may be called 'adverbial' (using the term *Adverb* in a wide sense, to include all words directly construed with the Verb), we have the constructions in which the governing word is a Noun or Preposition. And in these again we must distinguish between the government of a Case *apparently* by a Noun or Preposition, really by the combined result of the Noun or Preposition and the Verb, and the true government by a Noun alone, of which the dependent Genitive and the Adjective are the main types. These distinctions, however, though of great importance in reference to the development of the use of Cases, cannot well be followed exclusively in the order of treatment. I have therefore taken the Cases in succession, and along with them the chief points which have to be noticed regarding the 'concords' of Gender (§§ 166–168) and Number (§§ 169–173).

In the Infinitive and Participle (Chapter X) we have the first step from the simple to the complex Sentence. The predicative element in the Verbal Noun is treated syntactically like the same element in a true or 'finite' Verb; that is to say, it takes 'adverbial' constructions. Thus while retaining the character of a Noun it becomes the nucleus of a new imperfect Sentence, without a grammatical Subject properly so called (though the Infinitive in Greek acquired a quasi-Subject in the use of the Accusative before it), and standing to the main Sentence as an adverb or adjective.

While the Infinitival and Participial Clauses may thus be described as Nouns which have expanded into dependent Sentences, the true Subordinate Clause shows the opposite process. In many instances, especially in Homeric syntax, we can trace the steps by which originally independent Sentences have come to stand in an adverbial or adjectival relation. The change is generally brought about, as we shall see, by means of Pronouns, or Adverbs formed from Prono-minal stems. Hence it is convenient that the account of the uses of the Pronouns (Chapter XI) should hold the place of an introduction to the part in which we have to do with the relations of Clauses to each other.

The next chapter, however, does not treat directly of sub-ordinate Clauses, but of the uses of the Moods in them. It seemed best to bring these uses into immediate connexion with the uses which are found in simple Sentences. In this way the original character of Subordinate Clauses comes into a clearer light. If anything remains to be said of them, it finds its place in the account of the Particles (Chapter XIII); in which also we examine the relations of independent Sentences, so far at least as these are expressed by grammatical forms.

The last chapter contains a discussion of the Metre of Homer (Chapter XIV), and of some points of 'phonology' which (for us at least) are ultimately metrical questions. Chief among these is the famous question of the Digamma. I have endeavoured to state the main issues which have been raised on this subject as fully as possible: but without much hope of bringing them to a satisfactory decision.

A book of this kind is necessarily to a great extent a compilation, and from sources so numerous that it is scarcely possible to make a sufficient acknowledgment of indebtedness. The earlier chapters are mainly founded on the great work of G. Curtius on the Greek Verb. More recent writers have cleared up some difficulties, especially in the phonology. I have learned very much from M. de Saussure's *Mémoire sur le système primitif des voyelles*, and from several articles by K. Brugmann and Joh. Schmidt, especially the last. I would mention also, as valuable on single points, the papers of J. Paech (Vratisl. 1861) and H. Stier (*Curt. Stud.* II) on the Subjunctive, B. Mangold on the 'diectasis' of Verbs in -άω (*Curt. Stud.* VI), F. D. Allen on the same subject (*Trans. of the American Phil. Assoc.* 1873), Leskien on σσ in the Fut. and Aor. (*Curt. Stud.* II), and K. Koch on the Augment (Brunsvici 1868). On the subject of Nominal Composition I may name a paper by W. Clemm in *Curt. Stud.* VII, which gives references to the earlier literature of the subject, and one by F. Stolz (Klagenfurt 1874). On the forms of the Personal Pronouns there is a valuable dissertation by P. Cauer (*Curt. Stud.* VII): on the Numerals by Joh. Baunack (*K. Z.* XXV): on the Comparative and Superlative by Fr. Weihrich (*De Gradibus*, &c. Gissae 1869). Going on to the syntax of the Cases, I would place first the dissertation of B. Delbrück, *Ablativ Localis Instrumentalis, &c.* (Berlin 1867), and next the excellent work of Hübschmann, *Zur Casuslehre* (München 1875). On the Accusative I have obtained the greatest help from La Roche, *Der Accusativ im Homer* (Wien 1861): on the Dual from Bieber, *De Duali Numero* (Jena 1864). On the Prepositions I have used the papers of C. A. J. Hoffmann (Lüneburg 1857–60, Clausthal 1858–59), T. Mommsen (see § 221), Giseke, *Die allmäliche Entstehung der Gesänge der Ilias* (Göttingen 1853), La Roche, especially on ὑπό (Wien 1861) and ἐπί (in the *Z. f. öst. Gymn.*), Rau on παρά (*Curt. Stud.* III), and the articles in Ebeling's *Lexicon*. On this part of syntax the fourth volume of Delbrück's *Forschungen* is especially instructive. Of the literature on the Infinitive I would mention J. Jolly's *Geschichte des Infinitivs im Indogermanischen* (München 1873), also a paper by Albrecht (*Curt. Stud.* IV), and a note in Max Müller's *Chips from a German Workshop* (IV. p. 49 ff.). The use of the Participle has been admirably treated by Classen, in his *Beobachtungen über den homerischen Sprachgebrauch*

(Frankfurt 1867). A paper by Jolly in the collection of *Sprachwissenschaftliche Abhandlungen* (Leipzig 1874) is also suggestive. On the subject of the Pronouns* the chief source is a dissertation by E. Windisch in *Curt. Stud.* II. On the Article almost everything will be found in H. Foerstemann's *Bemerkungen über den Gebrauch des Artikels bei Homer* (Magdeburg 1861). The controversy on the Reflexive Pronoun is referred to in § 255. On the Homeric uses of the Moods, besides Delbrück's great work, I would mention Jolly's monograph entitled *Ein Kapitel vergleichender Syntax* (München 1872), and L. Lange's elaborate papers on εἰ (Leipzig 1872–73). It is to be regretted that they have not yet been carried to the point of forming a complete book on the Homeric use of εἰ. For the general theory of the subject Prof. Goodwin's *Greek Moods and Tenses* is of the very highest value. Regarding the cognate question of the uses of ἄν and κεν the main principles have been laid down by Delbrück. It is worth while to mention that they were clearly stated as long ago as 1832, in a paper in the Philological Museum (Vol. I. p. 96), written in opposition to the then reigning method of Hermann. For the other Particles little has been done by Homeric students since Nägelsbach and Hartung. I have cited three valuable papers; on τε by Wentzel, on ἤ (ἠέ) by Praetorius, and on μή by A. R. Vierke. I would add here a paper on the syntax of Causal Sentences in Homer, by E. Pfudel (Liegnitz 1871). On all syntactical matters use has been made of the abundant stores of Kühner's *Ausführliche Grammatik*. And it is impossible to say too much of the guidance and inspiration (as I may almost call it) which I have derived from the *Digest of Platonic Idioms* left behind by the lamented friend to whose memory I have ventured to dedicate this book.

On the collateral subjects of Metre I have profited most by Hartel's *Homerische Studien*, La Roche, *Homerische Untersuchungen* (Leipzig 1869), Knös, *De digammo Homerico* (Upsaliae 1872–79), and Tudeer, *De dialectorum Graecarum digammo* (Helsingforsiae 1879).

OXFORD, *July* 18, 1882.

PREFACE TO THE SECOND EDITION.

THE rapid progress of linguistic science during the nine years that have passed since this Grammar was first published has necessitated considerable alteration and enlargement in a new edition. Much has been discovered in the interval; much that was then new and speculative has been accepted on all sides; and much has been done in sifting and combining the results attained. The *Morphologischen Untersuchungen* of Osthoff and Brugmann have been followed by Brugmann's admirable summary of Greek grammar (in Iwan Müller's *Handbuch*), and his comprehensive *Grundriss der vergleichenden Grammatik der indogermanischen Sprachen.* Of three portions of this work that have already appeared (Strassburg 1886–90–91), the last (treating chiefly of the Declensions) came too late to be of service to the present book. The part which deals with the Verb has not yet been published : and the volume on Comparative Syntax, promised by Delbrück—the first complete work on this part of the subject—is also still to come. It will doubtless be a worthy sequel to the *Altindische Syntax,* which now forms the fifth volume of his *Syntaktische Forschungen.* Among other books which have appeared since the publication of this Grammar, or which were not sufficiently made use of for the first edition, I would mention Joh. Schmidt's *Pluralbildungen der indogermanischen Neutra* (Weimar 1889), G. Meyer's *Griechische Grammatik* (second edition, Leipzig 1886), the new edition of Mr. Goodwin's *Moods and Tenses* (London 1889), the treatises in Schanz's series of *Beiträge zur historischen Syntax der griechischen Sprache,* Aug. Fick's two books (see Appendix F), articles by Wackernagel, Fröhde and others in *Kuhn's Zeitschrift* and *Bezzenberger's Beiträge,* the long series of papers by Aug.

Nauck collected in the *Mélanges gréco-romains* (St. Petersburg 1855–88)—a book not often seen in this country,—and the dissertations of J. van Leeuwen in the *Mnemosyne*. The two writers last mentioned are chiefly concerned with the restoration of the Homeric text to its original or prehistoric form. Their method, which is philological rather than linguistic, may lead to some further results when the numerous MSS. of the Iliad have been examined and have furnished us with an adequate *apparatus criticus*.

Although very much has been re-written, the numbering of the sections has been retained, with a few exceptions; so that the references made to the first edition will generally still hold good. The new sections are distinguished by an asterisk.

I will not attempt to enumerate the points on which new matter has been added, or former views recalled or modified. The increase in the size of the book is largely due to the fuller treatment of the morphology. Additions bearing on questions of syntax will be found in §§ 238, 248, 267, 270*, 362, 365. On the whole I have become more sceptical about the theories which seek to explain the forms of the Subordinate Clause from parataxis, or the mere juxta-position of independent clauses. In general it may be admitted that the complex arose in the first instance by the amalgamation of simpler elements: but we must beware of leaving out of sight the effect of 'contamination' in extending syntactical types once created. The neglect of this consideration is in reality another and more insidious form of the error from which recent writers on morphology have delivered us, viz. that of explaining grammatical forms as the result of direct amalgamation of a stem with a suffix or ending, without duly allowing for the working of analogy.

OXFORD, *March* 21, 1891.

TABLE OF CONTENTS.

———◆◆———

b

CHAPTER X. The Verbal Nouns.

CHAPTER XIII.   The Particles.

CHAPTER XIV.   Metre and Quantity.

ERRATA.

Page 70, line 6, *for* γνώς *read* γνῶς
,, 83, ,, 23, *for* κρηόεντος *read* κρυόεντος
,, 93, ,, 30, *for* θήρηθι *read* θύρηθι
,, 149, ,, 38, *before* 18. 305 *insert* Il.
,, 185, ,, 1, *for* Il. *read* Od.
,, 223, ,, 32, *for* οἶος *read* οἷος
,, 245, ,, 36, *for* three *read* two, *and dele* 16. 131.,
,, 259, ,, 12, *for* govering *read* governing
,, 309, ,, 12, *for* 22. 280 *read* 16. 61
,, 329, ,, 10, *for* φίλην *read* φίλον

HOMERIC GRAMMAR.

CHAPTER I.

INTRODUCTORY.—THE PERSON-ENDINGS.

1.] ALL language of which grammar takes cognisance consists of SENTENCES. The simplest complete Sentence expresses the combination of a SUBJECT—that about which we speak (or think); and a PREDICATE—that which we say (or think) about the Subject. On the sentences which are (apparently or really) without a Subject, see §§ 161, 163.

2.] In Greek (and generally in languages whose structure resembles that of Greek) every Verb is a complete Sentence, consisting of two parts, the *Stem*, which expresses the Predicate, and the *Ending*, which expresses the Subject. Thus ἔσ-τι *he* (or *it*) *is*, φα-θί *say thou*, ἤλθο-μεν *we came*, are Sentences; the several Predicates are expressed by the Stems ἐσ-, φα-, ἤλθο-, and the Subjects by the Endings -τι, -θι, -μεν. As the Endings of a Verb may always be translated by Personal Pronouns they are called the *Person-Endings*.

It may happen that the ending has been lost by phonetic corruption, as in ἔλαβε (for ἔλαβε-τ) *he took*. This however does not form a real exception, because in Greek such words are used exactly as if the lost ending were still sounded. In English it is different: *took* can only be used to express a Predicate. The original Subject is lost to the mind as well as to the ear.

It should be noticed that the term 'Verb' is used in Grammars with a double meaning, sometimes of a single form—as when we say that ἐτύπτο-μεν is 'a Verb'—sometimes collectively, as when we say that ἐτύπτο-μεν is a 'part' of 'the Verb τύπτω.' Here 'a Verb' means a group of forms, derived from a common root.

3.] There are three main sets of Person-Endings :—

1. Those used in the Tenses called 'Principal' (the Present, Perfect, and Future Indicative), and in the Subjunctive; these are called the *Primary* Endings.

2. Those used in the 'Historical Tenses' (the Imperfect, Aorist, and Pluperfect), and in the Optative; these are called the *Secondary* Endings.

3. The Endings of the Imperative.

B

4.] The further modifications which the Endings undergo depend chiefly upon the final letter of the Stem.

In certain forms the Ending is preceded by O or E : that is to say, O before the nasals μ, ν, and E before other letters; e. g. τύπτO-μεν, τύπτE-τε, τύπτO-ντι (older and Dor. form of τύπτουσι). We shall call this the *Thematic* Vowel,* and the Stems which contain it *Thematic Stems*. The term will naturally include the corresponding Subjunctives, in which the final letter of the Stem varies in the same way between η and ω, as τύπτω-μεν, τύπτη-τε, &c. and the 1 Sing. in -ω. These long vowels doubtless represent a primitive contraction of the Thematic vowel with some other element : but the exact process can hardly be determined.

The forms which do not contain this variable ε or ο are called *Non-Thematic*. Among these, again, we have to distinguish a group of Tenses with Stems ending in -ă, viz. the Perfect, the First Aorist, and some forms peculiar to the Ionic Dialect, as the Plpf. (e. g. ᾔδεα *I knew*), the Impf. ἦα *I was*, ᾔα *I went*. In these Stems the -ă changes in the 3 Sing. to -ε(ν).†

The distinction between Thematic and Non-Thematic applies in strictness only to *forms*, but may generally be extended to Tenses and Moods. Thus the Pres. and Impf. of τύπτω are Thematic, the same Tenses of φημί are Non-Thematic. In every Verb the Future is Thematic, the Optative is Non-Thematic, &c. But the distinction does not apply to 'Verbs' (in the collective sense of the term), because almost every Verb is made up of forms of both kinds.

5.] In the following Table of the Person-Endings found in Homer the Endings distinguished by larger type are those of the Non-Thematic Tenses. The Endings in smaller type are, first, those of the forms with -ă, and, under them again, those of the Thematic forms. In the Dual and Plural (except the 3 Plur.) the Endings are the same throughout.

---

* This vowel has also been termed the ' Connecting ' or 'Auxiliary' Vowel— names given on the supposition that it is originally euphonic, inserted in order to allow the Stem and the Ending to be distinctly heard in pronunciation. The name 'Thematic' implies a different theory, viz. that it serves to form a ' Theme ' from a simpler element or 'Root,' as λεγ-ε from the Root λεγ- ; see Curt. *Chron.* p. 40. On this theory the Stem λεγ-ε, λεγ-ο is originally the same as the Theme or Stem of the Noun λόγο-s. See the remarks of Brugmann, *Grundriss*, ii. § 8, *n.* 1.

In the former edition the -ω of the 1 Sing. was explained as -ο-μι (Sanscr. -*ā*-*mi*). It is now generally thought that -ω and -μι are originally distinct, and represent respectively the Thematic and Non-Thematic Endings of the primitive Indo-European Verb. If so, the Sanscrit -*āmi* has extended from the Non-Thematic to the Thematic conjugation ; and similarly the -ομαι of Greek φέρομαι (Sanscr. *bhare*). See Meyer, *G. G.* p. 404.

† The ă of these Stems is of course quite different from the final vowel of the Stem in such forms as φα-μέν, ἴστα-μαι, τέτλα-θι, where it is part of the Verb-Stem or 'Root.'

	PRIMARY		SECONDARY		IMPERATIVE	
	ACT.	**MID.**	**ACT.**	**MID.**	**ACT.**	**MID.**
1 Sing.	-μι -ᾰ -ω, Subj. -ω, -ωμι	-μαι -ομαι, S. -ωμαι	-ν -ᾰ -ον	-μην ᾰ-μην -όμην	—	—
2 Sing.	-σι, -ς, -σθᾰ -σᾰ -εις, S. -ῃς, -ῃσι	-σαι, -αι -εαι, S. -ῃαι	-ς -σᾰ -ες	-σο, -ο -ᾰο -εο	-θι, -ς -ον -ε, -ες	-σο, -ο -ᾰσο, -αο -εο
3 Sing.	-τι(ν), -σι(ν) -ε(ν) -ει, S. -ῃ, -ῃσι	-ται -εται, S. -ηται	-(τ) -ε(ν) -ε(ν)	-το -ᾰτο -ετο	-τω -ᾰτω -ετω	-σθω -ᾰσθω -εσθω
1 Dual	—	-μεθον	-τον	-σθον	—	—
2 ...	-τον	-σθον	-την, -τον	-σθον	-τον	-σθον
3 ...	-τον	-σθον	-την, -τον -σθην	-σθην	-των	-σθων
1 Plur.	-μεν	-μεσθα, -μεθα	-μεν	-μεσθα, -μεθα	—	—
2 ...	-τε	-σθε	-τε	-σθε	-τε -θε	-σθε
3 ...	-νσι(ν), -ασι(ν), -ᾱσι(ν) -ουσι(ν), S. -ωσι(ν)	-νται, -ᾰται -ονται, S. -ωνται	-ν, -σαν -ᾱν -ον	-ντο, -ᾰτο -αντο -οντο	-ντων -ᾰντων -όντων	-σθων -ᾰσθων -εσθων

Remarks on the Table of Person-Endings.

1 Sing. On the Subj. in -ω-μι see § 82, and on the Optatives which take -μι in the 1 Sing. see § 83.

2 Sing. The original -σι remains only in ἐσ-σί *thou art.*

The form εἶs (or enclitic εἰs) is read in nine places, but there is only one (Od. 17. 388) in which the metre does not allow ἔσσ' to be read instead. Probably, therefore, ἐσσί is the genuine Homeric form. The Attic εἶ is not found in Homer.

The Ending -σθα occurs in the Pf. οἶσθα *thou knowest* (οἶδαs in Od. 1. 337, is a very doubtful reading), Plpf. ῄδησθα (Od. 19. 93), the Impf. ῆσθα and ἔησθα *thou wast,* ἔφησθα *thou saidst,* and the Pres. εἶσθα *thou wilt go,* τίθησθα (Od. 9. 404., 24. 476), διδοῖσθα (Il. 19. 270), perhaps φῆσθα (Od. 14. 149) : also in some Subjunctives, ἐθέλῃσθα, εἴπῃσθα, βουλεύῃσθα (Il. 9. 99), ἴῃσθα (Il. 10. 67) ; and in the Optatives βάλοισθα (Il. 15. 571), κλαίοισθα (Il. 24. 619), and προφύγοισθα (Od. 22. 325).

The history of this -σθα can still be traced. Originally -θα (Sanscr. -tha) was the Ending of the 2 Sing. Pf. Ind. : hence οἶσθα for οἶδ-θα (Sanscr. vettha for ved-tha), and ῆσ-θα (Sanscr. ásitha) properly Pf. from the root ἐσ-. Having in these cases appeared accidentally an ending -σθα, it was transferred in this form to other Tenses and Moods.*

The forms ῆσθas, οἶσθαs which appear in some MSS are due to the common 2 Sing. in -ăs. Aristarchus rejected them in Homer.

In the Middle the σ of -σαι, -σο when it follows a vowel is generally lost : so always in the Secondary Tenses, as ἐμάρνα-ο, δαίνυ-ο, ἔσσυ-ο, ἐείσα-ο, contracted ἐκρέμω (Il. 15. 18), ἐπεφράσω (Il. 21. 410), ἐκτήσω (Od. 24. 193)—for which, however, the metre allows us to write ἐκρέμα', &c.—and the Opt. -οι-ο. In the Pres. and Pf. Indic. and the Imper. the usage is not uniform : δύνα-σαι (Il. 1. 393), ὄνο-σαι (Od. 17. 378), παρ-ίστα-σαι (Il. 10. 279., Od. 17. 450), ὑπο-δάμνα-σαι (Od. 16. 95), δαίνυ-σαι (Od. 21. 290), μέμνη-σαι (Il. 23. 648), Imper. ἴστα-σο (seven times), ὄνη-σο (Od. 19. 68), κεῖ-σο (Il. 21. 122) : but μέμνη-αι (Il. 21. 442), μέμνῃ (Il. 15. 18, where we may read μέμνῃ'), βέβλῃαι (three places in the Iliad), δίζη-αι (Od. 11. 100), Imper. θέ-ο (Od. 10. 333), φά-ο (Od. 18. 171), μάρνα-ο (Il. 15. 475), παρ-ίστα-ο (Il. 10. 291, according to Aristarchus, παρ-ίστα-σο MSS.).

The loss of σ was in accordance with Greek phonetic law, and originally universal ; but new forms in -σαι, -σο were produced on the analogy of forms such as λέξο (for λεχ-σο), ῆσο (for ῆσ-σο), πέπυσσαι (for πεπυθ-σαι), τέτυξο, &c., in which the σ is preserved by the preceding consonant.

Verbs in -εω, which would properly form -εεαι, -εεο, sometimes

---

* On this point recent writers have gone back to the explanation given by Bopp, *Vergl. Gr.* II. pp. 292, 498.

suffer Hyphaeresis (cp. § 105, 4), and drop one ε; as μύθεαι (Od. 2. 202), ἀπο-αίρεο, ἔκλεο. But we find also μυθεῖαι (Od. 8. 180), νεῖαι (Od. 11. 114., 12. 141)—where it is possible to substitute the uncontracted μυθέεαι, νέεαι—and αἰδεῖο (Il. 24. 503).

In the Imper. the Ending -θι is common in Non-Thematic Tenses : ἴ-θι, στῆ-θι, κλῦ-θι, κέκλυ-θι, ἔστα-θι, ὄρνν-θι, φάνη-θι (Il. 18. 198), δίδω-θι (Od. 3. 380), ἐμπίπλη-θι (Il. 23. 311). We find -ς in θέ-ς, δό-ς, πρόε-ς (προ-ίημι), and the thematic ἐνί-σπε-ς tell (cp. Attic σχέ-ς).

In the forms ἴστη (Il. 21. 313), δαίνῦ (Il. 9. 70), δείκνῦ (Hes. Th. 526), the long final vowel probably comes by analogy from the Pres. and Impf. Singular forms (by the 'proportion' Impf. ἔλεγε-ς, ἔλεγε : Imper. λέγε : : ἴστης, ἴστη : ἴστη). For the forms καθ-ίστα, τίθει, δίδου, &c., see § 18.

3 Sing. The original -τι remains only in ἔσ-τι(ν), in which the phonetic change of -τι to -σι is prevented by the preceding σ. On the Subjunctives in -ῃ-σι see § 82.

3 Plur. The Ending -ᾱσι (for -αντι) is found in ἔ-ᾱσι (for *ἔσ-αστι) they are and ἴ-ᾱσι they go.

Stems in α, ε, ο, υ form -ᾱσι, -εισι, -ουσι, -ῦσι (for -α-ντι, &c.), as φασί, ἱστᾶσι, τιθεῖσι, διδοῦσι, ζευγνῦσι (not τιθέ-ασι, &c., as in Attic). On the accent of these forms, see § 87, 2.

The Perfect Act. has -ᾱσι and -ᾰσι. The latter occurs only twice in Homer, πεφύκ-ᾰσι (Od. 7. 114), λελόγχᾱσιν (Od. 11. 304); for other examples in Ionic see Curt. Verb. ii. 166. In these forms the ᾰ belongs to the Ending, since -ασι is for -ατι, which corresponds to the -ντι of the Doric φα-ντί, λέγο-ντι (as -ᾰται in the Mid. to -νται). The forms with -ασι belong to two essentially distinct groups ; see § 7.

The secondary -ᾰν (for -αντ) is found in all Aorists which form the 1 Sing. in -ᾰ. It may also be traced in the Impf. of εἰμί, in the form ἦν (Hes. Th. 321, 825), for ἦαν (Sanscr. âsan).

Non-Thematic -ν occurs in the forms ἔφᾰ-ν, ἔβᾰ-ν, ἔστᾰ-ν, φθᾰ-ν, ἔδῠ-ν (Il. 11. 263), ἐφῦ-ν (Od. 10. 397), ἔκτᾰ-ν, Impf. ἴε-ν (in ξύν-ιεν, μέθ-ιεν), πρό-τιθε-ν (read by Aristarchus in Od. 1. 112), ἔδιδο-ν (H. Cer. 327), and many Passive Aorists, as ἔβλα-βε-ν, δι-έτμαγε-ν, ἄγε-ν, ἄλε-ν, δάμε-ν, πάγε-ν, ἤγερθε-ν, κόσμηθε-ν, κατ-έκταθε-ν. On the form μιάνθην (Il. 4. 146) see § 40. In these tenses -ν is commoner in Homer than -σᾰν. But -σᾰν is the only Ending found in the two Imperfects ἦ-σαν and ἤϊ-σαν, ἴ-σαν, and in the Pluperfect : see § 68.

In the Middle, the forms -ᾰται, -ᾰτο are regular after consonants and the vowel ι (including the diphthongs ει, ῃ, οι, &c.); the forms -νται, -ντο after ᾰ, ε, ο. After υ, η both forms are found : e.g. εἰρύ-αται, εἰρύ-ατο, but λέλυ-νται, κέχυ-νται ; βεβλή-αται (Il. 11. 656), but μέμνη-ντο, ξύμβλη-ντο ; even ἦντο (Il. 3. 153) as well as ἦ-ατο (for *ἦσ-ατο).

The Imper. Endings -τωσαν, -σθωσαν are post-Homeric.

1 Dual. -μεθον occurs only once, in περιδώμεθον, Il. 23. 485. Elmsley (on Ar. Ach. 733) maintained that this form was a fiction of the grammarians. It is defended by G. Curtius (*Verb.* I. 97 f.), and there seems no valid reason for rejecting it.

2 and 3 Dual. In the Historical Tenses, according to the ancient grammarians, the regular Endings are—

2 Dual Act. -τον, Mid. -σθον.

3 ,, ,, -την, ,, -σθην.

This scheme, however, is open to some doubt ; for—

(1) Homer has three instances of the 3 Dual Impf. in -τον, where the metre does not admit of -την, viz. διώκε-τον (Il. 10. 363), ἐτεύχε-τον (Il. 13. 345), λαφύσσετον (Il. 18. 583). Three others in -σθον occur as various readings, where the metre admits of either -σθον or -σθην, viz. ἀφίκε-σθον, read by some ancient critics (probably Zenodotus) in Il. 13. 613 : θωρήσσε-σθον, the reading of A. (the Cod. Venetus) and Eust. in Il. 16. 218 : πέτε-σθον, a marginal variant of A. in Il. 23. 506.

(2) Three forms of the 2 Dual in -την were read in the text of Zenodotus, viz. καμέ-την (Il. 8. 448), λαβέ-την (Il. 10. 545), ἠθελέ-την (Il. 11. 782). Aristarchus read κάμε-τον, λάβε-τον, ἠθέλε-τον. The metre gives no help to a decision.

(3) In Attic the examples of the 2 Dual in -την, -σθην are so common that Elmsley (on Ar. Ach. 733) held these to be the only correct forms, thus making the Dual of Historical Tenses uniformly end in -ην, as the Dual of the Principal Tenses ends in -ον. Cobet maintains the same view (*Misc. Crit.* pp. 279 ff.). But the account of the Greek grammarians is strikingly borne out by the forms of the Sanscrit Dual. In Sanscrit we find that in the Historical Tenses the 2 Dual ends in -tam, 3 Dual in -tâm, answering perfectly to the Greek -τον, -την. This therefore is to be regarded as the original rule. The exceptions which have been quoted are evidently due to the tendency towards uniformity : and it is to be noticed that this tendency seems to have acted in Homer in the direction of making all Duals end in -τον, -σθον, whereas in Attic the tendency was to extend the Endings -την, -σθην to the Second Person.

The Imper. Ending -των is found in ἔστων (Il. 1. 338) and κομείτων (Il. 8. 109). As to ἔστων in Od. 1. 273, where it is usually taken as a Plural, see § 173.

Variation of the Stem.

6.] In Thematic Stems it is plain that the Ending influences only the final ε(ο), leaving the rest of the Stem unaffected. Non-Thematic forms, on the other hand, are liable to variations in *quantity* which affect the main vowel of the Stem. These variations are governed by the general rule that *when there are two forms of a Stem the longer is found with the Endings of the*

Sing. Indic. Act., the shorter with all other Endings, viz. those of
the Dual and Plural, the Imperative, and the Middle. Thus :—

(1) ἄ, ε, ο interchange with the corresponding long vowels
ᾱ (in Ionic η), η, ω ; as φη-μί, ἔ-φη-ν, but 1 Plur. φᾰ-μέν, Imper.
φᾰ-θί, Mid. ἔ-φα-το; τίθη-μι, Mid. τίθε-μαι; δίδω-μι, Mid.
δίδο-μαι.

(2) ι with ει and οι: as εἶ-μι, 1 Plur. ἴ-μεν, Imper. ἴ-θι; οἶδα,
1 Plur. ἴδ-μεν.

(3) ῠ with ευ and ῡ: as ἔ-χευα, Mid. χύ-το (§ 15); δείκνῡ-μι,
1 Plur. δείκνῠ-μεν. Sometimes with ου, as εἰλήλουθα, stem
ἐλῠθ-.

Note however that all vowels are liable to be shortened before
the combination ντ, as in the 3 Plur. ἔστᾰν (but ἔστη-μεν), &c.,
and the Participle, στάντ-ος, γνόντ-ος. Also before ι of the
Optative, σταίην, γνοίην.

The same law governs the interchange of—

(4) ᾰ with εν and ον: as γέγονα (γένος), 1 Plur. γέγᾰ-μεν;
πέπονθα (πένθ-ος), Part. Fem. πεπᾰθ-υῖα.*

(5) ᾰρ with ερ and ορ: as ἔφθορα, Mid. ἔφθαρ-ται (Pres.
φθείρω for φθερ-ϳω); and, with Metathesis (ρα for αρ, &c.),
τέτροφε, Mid. τέθραπ-ται (τρέφ-ω).*

The combinations ᾰρ(ρᾰ) and ᾰλ(λᾰ) represent the primitive 'liquid
vowels,' ρ̥ and ḷ. They appear in place of the consonantal ρ and λ when
these are phonetically impossible : e. g. ἔφθαρται is for ἐ-φθρ-ται,—the ερ
of the root φθερ- passing into αρ where Sanscr. ar would pass into ρ̥.
Similarly, ᾰ represents the 'nasal vowels' m̥ and n̥ : thus πᾰθ- is for πνθ-.
Before another vowel εμ, εν sometimes pass into ᾰμ, ᾰν, as in ἔκτανον for
ἔ-κτν-ον (root κτεν-), in the same way that u and i before a vowel may appear
as uv, iy.

Sometimes the longer Stem contains an additional consonant,
viz. in the Perfects and Aorists in -κᾰ, as ἔστηκα, 1 Plur. ἔστᾰ-
μεν; ἔθηκα, 1 Plur. ἔθε-μεν.

These are the principal variations which can be exemplified
within the limits of a single Tense. When we compare one Tense
with another, we observe further the interchange of—

(6) Stems with the vowel ε or ο and Stems in which the vowel
is lost; as ἔχ-ω (for *σέχ-ω), ἔ-σχ-ον; πέτ-εσθαι, Aor. πτ-έσθαι
(cp. ποτ-άομαι).

This definition will cover the reduction of ερ, ελ, εμ, εν to ρ, λ, μ, ν (instead
of ᾰρ, ᾰλ, ᾰ); as in ἔγρ-ετο (ἐγερ- in ἐγείρω), ἔ-πλ-ετο (πέλ-ω), ἔ-τε-τμ-ον (τεμ-

---

* Similarly, ᾰλ(λᾰ) with ελ and ολ : but it is difficult to find examples in
Greek. The form πί-πλᾰ-μεν perhaps answers to an original Sing. *πί-πελ-μι
(cp. Sanscr. *piparmi*, Pl. *pipṛ-mas*, Brugmann, *M. U.* I. p. 44), and the form
τέ-τλᾰ-μεν to *τέ-τολ-α (Lat. *tetuli*).

νω), ἔ-πε-φν-ον (φεν-, cp. φόν-os). Thus we have an apparent interchange of two short Stems, as φν- in ἔπε-φν-ον with φᾰ- in πέ-φᾰ-ται, &c.

When loss of ε would make the word unpronounceable, it is sometimes retained in the short form, as in ἔ-τεκ-ον, τεκ-εῖν (Stems τεκ-, τοκ-).

Again, there are in general two longer forms of each Stem, one marked by the predominance of the sounds ε, η, the other by that of o, ω. The chief interchanges which are due to this cause are—

(7) ε and o, including the combinations ει, ευ, ερ, ελ, εμ, εν and οι, ου, ορ, ολ, ομ, ον. It is needless to give further examples.

(8) ᾱ (Ionic η) and ω: ἔ-πτη *flew*, πτήσσω *cower*, and πέ-πτω-κα; cp. φη-μί and φω-νή, ὁδ-ηγός and ἀγ-ωγ-ή.

(9) η and ω: ῥήγ-νυμι and ἔρ-ρωγα; cp. ἀρήγω and ἀρωγ-ός, ἦθος and εἴωθα.

(10) In a certain number of Stems the only variation is between ω and o: δί-δω-μι (δο-), ὄδ-ωδα, ὄλ-ωλα.

The Endings which are found with the long Stem have been called the *Light*, the others the *Heavy* Endings.

The short form of the Stem is usually called the *Weak* Stem. Of the longer forms that which contains the vowel o (οι, ου, ον, ορ, ολ) may be distinguished as the *O-form* : the other will be simply called the *Strong* form.

The different variations may be represented in a tabular form:—

Strong	ᾱ(η)	η	ω	ει	ευ	ερ(ρε)	ελ	εμ	εν	ε
O-form	ω	ω	ω	οι	ου	ορ(ρο)	ολ	ομ	ον	o
Weak	ᾰ	ε	o	ῐ	ῠ	ρ ἀρ(ρᾰ)	λ ἀλ	μ ᾰ ᾰμ	ν ᾰ ᾰν	nil

7.] The 3 Plur. offers some exceptions to the general rule:—

(1) The Ending -ᾰσι (for -ᾰτι, -NTI) is used with the long Stem of the Pf., as λελόγχ-ᾰσι, πεφύκ-ᾰσι. Cp. Mid. τετεύχ-ᾰται, ἐ-τετεύχ-ᾰτο (§ 22, 5).

(2) The long Stem is also found in a few forms of the Pf. with the Ending -ᾱσι, as πεποίθᾱσι, ἑστήκᾱσι (§ 24), and of the Aor. in -α, as ἔχεναν, ἔθηκαν, ἔδωκαν (§ 15).

(3) The Endings -(σ)ᾱσι, -σαν (for -ΣΑΝΤΙ, -ΣΑΝΤ) are found with the weak Stem. The leading examples are:—

With Simple Stems: ἴ-σαν, ἔ-φα-σαν, ἔ-θε-σαν, ἔ-δο-σαν, &c.
Presents : τιθέ-ασι, διδό-ασι (Att.); ἐ-τίθε-σαν, ἐ-δίδο-σαν, &c.
Perfects : ἴσασι (ἰδ-σασι), ἴσαν; εἴξασι (Att. 3 Plur. of ἔοικα).
βεβά-ασι, γεγά-ασι, μεμά-ασι; Plpf. βέβα-σαν, μέμα-σαν.
ἑστᾶσι (for ἑστά-ασι), τεθνᾶσι; ἔστα-σαν, τέθνα-σαν.
πεφύ-ασι, δεδί-ασι; δείδι-σαν.

The hiatus shows that -ᾱσι is for -σᾱσι, the Primary Ending

answering to -σάν. The corresponding Mid. -σᾶται is found in Doric (γεγράψαται, *Tab. Heracl.* i. 121, in *C. I.* 5774).

The contraction in ἑστᾶσι, τεθνᾶσι is evidently due to the impossibility of ἑστά-ασι, τεθνά-ασι in the hexameter. Brugmann regards them as wrongly accented, and would write ἕστασι, τέθνασι, i. e. ἕστα-ντι, τέθνα-ντι (Curt. *Stud.* ix. 296). This is open to the objection (1) that it separates them from βεβά-ασι, γεγά-ασι, μεμά-ασι; and (2) that in all other Stems which form a Pf. or Aor. in -κα the Endings -ντι and -ν are confined in Homer to the forms with -κ : thus we find—

πεφύκ-ᾶσι	and	πεφύ-ᾶσι,	but not	πέφυσι
ἑστήκᾶσι, &c.	,,	βεβά-ασι,	,,	βέβασι
(οἴδασι Hdt.)	,,	ἴσασι	,,	ἴδ-ασι
ἔθηκα-ν	,,	ἔθε-σαν	,,	ἔθε-ν
ἔδωκα-ν	,,	ἔδο-σαν	,,	ἔδο-ν (Hesiod).

The weak form with -ντι, -ν is therefore confined to Verb-Stems ending in a vowel, as in φασί, τιθεῖσι (for φαντί, τίθε-ντι). And in these the short vowel is due to the (original) following -ΝΤ, as in ἔ-σταν, ἤγερθεν, ἀλό-ντες, &c.

For a plausible hypothesis as to the origin of the Ending -σαν see § 40. Regarding -(σ)ᾶσι (i. e. the Ending -ᾶσι preceded by hiatus) no satisfactory view has been put forward.

Meaning of the Middle.

8.] The original force of the Middle Person-Endings is 'Reflexive;' that is to say, they denote that the action of the Verb is directed towards the agent.

Greek has no Passive Endings distinct from those of the Active and Middle : it is desirable therefore to speak, not of Passive *forms*, but of the Passive *meaning* or *use* of a form.

The chief uses of the Middle are —

(1) The use to signify that the agent is also the *indirect object* of the action—that the action is done by some one *for* or *toward* himself, or in his own interest : ἕννυ-μαι *I put* (clothes, &c.) *on myself*; δέχο-μαι *I take to myself*; ἄορ ὀξὺ ἐρυσσάμενος *having drawn him his sharp sword*; ἡρεῖτο τόξον *took his bow with him*; φερέσθω *let him bear away* (*as his prize*).

(2) The use in which the agent is the direct object of the action, as λούο-μαι *I wash myself*. This is comparatively rare.

(3) The Intransitive use, in which the reflexive sense is faint, as φαίνε-ται *appears* (but φαίνει ἑαυτόν *he shows himself*). So, generally, when the action centres in the agent; as in Verbs of *bodily action* (ἔρχομαι, πέτομαι, ἄλλομαι, οἴχομαι, &c.), and in such uses as λαβέσθαι *to gain a hold* (not *to take* a thing), δεδραγμένος *clutching*; ἐχεύατο *threw her arms*; also in Verbs of *feeling* and *thinking* (αἰσθάνομαι, αἰδέομαι, βούλομαι, οἴομαι, μέμνημαι, ἐπίσταμαι, μέλομαι, μέμφομαι, &c.). So in French, 'je m'aperçois' *I perceive*, 'je me doute' *I suspect*, 'il se peut' *it may be*.

(4) The Reciprocal use ; ἀμειβόμενος *taking his turn* ; λέγεσθαι *to tell over* (in talk); ἀρέσκεσθαι *to make friends with*; νυσσομένων (Il. 14. 26) *as they pierced each other*; ἐρείδεσθον (Il. 23. 735) *push each other, strive.* Hence the Middle form of μάχομαι, Fr. *se battre* and its equivalents, ἀγωνίζομαι, ἀμιλλάομαι, δικάζομαι.

(5) The Passive use, as ἔχε-ται *is possessed,* ἔβλη-το *was struck,* δέδε-το *was bound,* ἐκ-πέπο-ται *is drunk up.* This is not a very common use of the Middle. It may be illustrated from the similar use of some Reflexive Verbs in French, as 'je me trouve' *I am found,* 'il se mange' *it is eaten.*

The Middle is rather more common in Homer than in later Greek. For example, in the class of Verbs of *feeling* and *thinking* we may add the Homeric ἔραμαι, γάνυμαι, ἔλδομαι, ἔλπομαι, ὄθομαι, ὄνομαι, στένομαι, κεχάροντο, ὀδύσασθαι. And the use is extended to Verbs of *seeing* and *hearing,* as ὁρῶ-μαι (Aor. ἰδέ-σθαι), ἀκούο-μαι (used as well as ὁρῶ, ἰδεῖν, ἀκούω), δέρκομαι, ὄσσομαι, σκέπτομαι, φράζομαι; cp. the Attic σκοποῦ-μαι *I consider.*

Conversely, Homer has the Act. ὀΐω *I think, expect,* as well as the Mid. ὀΐο-μαι *I harbour the thought, suspect* (cp. the distinction in French between *je doute* and *je me doute*).

Sometimes (esp. in Homer) the Middle appears to be used because the Verb implies acting *arbitrarily, as a superior,* &c. ; e. g. βιάζομαι *I use force towards,* σίνομαι, δηλέομαι, &c. *I do mischief for pleasure*; ἐφίλατο *made a favourite of*; δίε-νται *run in a race,* δίεσθαι *to chase* (but δίον *I fled*); δειδίσσεσθαι *to terrify*; κέκλετο *shouted in command.**

A use intermediate between the Reflexive and the Passive (pointed out by Riddell, *Dig.* § 88) may be exemplified in ἀπήχθετο *got himself hated, incurred hatred,* κτείνονται (Il. 13. 110) *let themselves be slain,* λείπεσθε (Il. 23. 409) *get left behind* : cp. Il. 13. 525., 15. 645, Od. 3. 284.

On the Futures only used in the Mid., see § 66.

CHAPTER II.

THE TENSES.

9.] Verb-Stem and Tense-Stem. A comparison of the different forms of a Greek VERB usually enables us to see that some one syllable or group of syllables is present in them all : as τυπ- in the forms of τύπτω, or βουλευ- in those of βουλεύω.

---

* Cp. Icelandic '*heita*' *I promise,* '*heitaz*' *I threaten.*

This we shall call the *Verb-Stem*. A Verb-Stem not derived from more primitive elements is called a *Root*.

Again, the different forms belonging to any one TENSE are based upon a common part, which we shall call the *Tense-Stem*. This part may be the same as the Verb-Stem ; or it may contain an additional element, as δι- in δί-δο-μεν, δι-δο-ίη-ν, &c. ; -τε, -το in τύπ-τε-τε, τύπ-το-μεν, ἔ-τυπ-το-ν, τύπ-το-ι-μι, &c.

The Subjunctive and Optative, again, are distinguished by a Suffix to the Tense-Stem : e.g. δο-ίη-ν, διδο-ίη-ν, τύπτο-ι-μι, στήσα-ι-μι. The new Stems so formed may be called *Mood-Stems*.

Finally, the Stems used in the 'Historical' Tenses—the Impf., Aor., and Plpf.—are formed from the Tense-Stem by prefixing the *Augment*.

The Stems of the augmented forms are therefore parallel to the Mood-Stems, the only difference being that they are formed by a prefix, while the Mood-Stems are formed by a suffix. They may be described as Time-Moods of the several Tenses,—combining the notion of Past Time, which is expressed by the Augment, with the meaning contained in the Tense-Stem.

Each Tense-Stem furnishes an *Infinitive* and a *Participle*.

Thus we have (supplying one or two links by analogy) from the three Tense-Stems βαλλε (or -ο), βαλε (or -ο), βεβληκα.

	PRES.	AOR.	PERF.
Principal Tense	βάλλε-τε	wanting	βεβλήκα-τε.
Historical	ἐ-βάλλε-τε	ἐ-βάλε-τε	ἐ-βεβλήκε-α.
Subjunctive	βάλλη-τε	βάλη-τε	βεβλήκη-τε.
Optative	βάλλο-ι-τε	βάλο-ι-τε	βεβλήκο-ι-τε.
Imperative	βάλλε-τε	βάλε-τε	βεβλήκα-τε.
Infinitive	βαλλέ-μεναι	βαλέ-ειν	βεβληκ-έναι.
Participle	βάλλο-ντος	βαλό-ντος	βεβληκ-ότος.

It is evident that there might have been a Future 'Time-Mood' as well as a Past for each Tense-Stem. In English indeed we can distinguish progressive action in the future as well as in the present and past : *I shall be writing* as well as *I am writing* and *I was writing*. See Goodwin's *Moods and Tenses*, § 65 ; Driver's *Use of the Tenses in Hebrew*, § 4. Modern Greek has two such Futures, θὰ γράφω *I will be writing* and θὰ γράψω *I will write*, related to each other as ἔγραφον and ἔγραψα.

10.] **Formation of Tense-Stems.** Leaving out of sight the meanings of the several Tenses, and looking to the mode of their formation, we may distinguish the following groups :—

(1) With the Verb-Stem serving as Tense-Stem—

The Simple Non-Thematic Present, as φη-μί.

The Simple Non-Thematic Aorist, as ἔ-βη-ν.

The Aorist in -ă, as ἔ-χευ-α.

(2) With Tense-Stem enlarged from Verb-Stem—
The Non-Thematic Reduplicated Present, as τί-θη-μι.
The Present in -νη-μι and -νῡ-μι, as σκίδ-νη-μι, δείκ-νῡ-μι.
The Perfect.

(3) With the Thematic Vowel—
The ordinary Thematic Present, as λέγω.
The Present with short Stem, as ἄγω.
The Simple Thematic Aorist, as ἔ-λᾰβ-ο-ν.

(4) With Reduplication (Thematic)—
The Thematic Reduplicated Present, as γί-γν-ο-μαι.
The Thematic Reduplicated Aorist, as ἤγ-ᾰγ-ο-ν.

(5) With other Suffixes (Non-Thematic)—
The Aorist in -σᾰ, and in -σε, -σο.
The Aorist in -η-ν (Aor. II Pass.).
The Aorist in -θη-ν (Aor. I Pass.).

(6) With other Suffixes (Thematic)—
The Present in -τω (T-Class of Curtius).
The Present in -νω (Nasal Class).
The Present in -σκω, and the Iterative forms.
The Present in -ιω (I-Class).
The Future in -σω, -(σ)ω.

The Non-Thematic Present and Aorist.

11.] The Simple Non-Thematic Present. The chief Presents
in which the Tense-Stem is the same as the Verb-Stem are—
εἰ-μί (for ἐσ-μί) I am, εἶ-μι I go, φη-μί I say, ἦ he said, κεῖ-ται
lies, ἦσ-ται sits (3 Plur. εἴ-αται, properly ἤ-αται, for *ἦσ-αται),
ἐπί-στα-μαι I know, ἄγα-μαι I wonder, ἔρα-μαι I love, δύνα-μαι I
am able, ἐ-κρέμω (for ἐ-κρέμα-ο) didst hang, δέα-το seemed, δίε-νται
race (ἐν-δίε-σαν tried to scare), ὄνο-σαι dost blame (ὤνα-το Il. 17.
25), ἄη-τον blow, κιχή-την caught, ἔρῡ-το protected, στεῦ-ται is
ready, threatens, ἔδ-μεναι to eat : also ἵετο desired (ἱέμενος eager),
if it is to be separated from ἵημι and referred to Ϝίεμαι, Sanscr.
vî (see § 397). For ἵληθι see § 16.

On the Non-Thematic forms of Contracted Verbs (such as φορή-μενος),
see § 19.

12.] Variation of the Stem according to the 'weight' of the
ending is carried out consistently in φη-μί and εἰ-μι. Thus—
Pres. φη-μί, φή-s, φη-σί, Plur. φᾰ-μέν, φᾰ-τέ, φασί.
Impf. ἔ-φη-ν, ἔ-φη-s and ἔ-φη-σθα, ἔ-φη, 1 Plur. φᾰ-μεν (for
ἐ-φᾰμεν), 3 Plur. ἔ-φᾰ-σαν and ἔφαν, Part. φάς.

Mid. 2 Plur. φά-σθε, Impf. ἐ-φά̆-μην, ἔ-φά̆-το, Imper. φά-ο,
φά-σθω, Inf. φά-σθαι, Part. φά̆-μενος.

And similarly—

Pres. εἶ-μι, εἶ-σθα, εἶ-σι, 3 Du. ἴ-τον, Plur. ἴ-μεν, ἴ-τε, ἴασι.
Impf. 3 Du. ἴ-την, 3 Plur. ἴσαν, Imper. ἴ-θι, ἴ-τω, ἴ-τε, Inf.
ἴ-μεναι (once ἴ), and ἰέναι.

The 1 Sing. ἤϊα does not represent the original form of the Impf., which
would be ἦα (for ἦι̯α, Sanscr. áyam). Hence ἤϊα with the 3 Sing. ἤει and 3 Plur.
ἤϊσαν, ᾖσαν must be formed like ᾔδεα and other Pluperfects in -εα (§ 68, 2) ;
the ε of the original ἤεα, ἤεσαν being changed to ι under the influence of ἴ-μεν,
&c. (Wackernagel, K. Z. xxv. 266). For -σαν see § 40.
    The forms ἤϊον (1 Sing. and 3 Plur.), ἴεν, Part. ἰών, are evidently produced
by confusion with the Thematic conjugation (§ 30, cp. also § 18).

The Verb εἰμί *I am* is inflected as follows :—

		Sing.	Dual.	Plur.
	1.	εἰμί	——	εἰμέν (for ἐσ-μέν)
Pres.	2.	ἐσ-σί, εἶς (§ 5)	ἐσ-τόν	ἐσ-τέ
	3.	ἐσ-τι(ν)	ἐσ-τόν	εἰσί (Dor. ἐντί), ἔ-ασι.
	1.	ἦα, ἔα (Th. ἔον)	——	ἦμεν
Impf.	2.	ἦσθα, ἔησθα	——	ἦτε
	3.	ἦεν, ἦν, ἔην, ἤην	ἤσ-την	ἦσαν, ἔσαν, ἦν (Hes.).
		(Dor. ἦς)		

Imper. ἐσ-τω, ἔσ-τε, ἔσ-των; Inf. ἔμμεναι, ἔμεναι, ἔμεν, εἶναι; Imper. Mid.
ἔσ-σο (Od. 1. 302).

The root ἐσ- is not reduced before Heavy Endings, as in the
corresponding Sanscr. forms (Dual *s-vas, s-thas, s-tas*, Plur. *s-mas,
-tha, s-anti*, Opt. *syám*), and the Lat. *sumus, sunt, sīm*. The loss of
σ in εἰμί, εἰμέν, ἦμεν (for ἐσ-μί, &c.) is according to Greek phonetic
law : the Attic ἐσ-μέν is a new formation, due to the analogy of
ἔσ-τι, ἐσ-τέ, &c. On the other hand ἦτε (Il. 16. 557) follows
ἦμεν ; the older ἦσ-τε survives in Attic. The σ of ἦσαν belongs
to the ending -σαν (§ 40), not to the root.

In the Impf. it is probable that we have an admixture of
forms from the original Perfect : thus ἦσ-θα (Sanscr. *ásitha*) is
Pf., ἦα, for *ἦσα, is both Pf. (Sanscr. *ása*) and Impf. (Sanscr.
ásam), ἦεν may be Pf. (Sanscr. *ása*) or thematic Impf. (answering
to the Homeric 1 Sing. ἔον) ; the original 3 Sing. Impf. survives
in the Dor. ἦς (Vedic *ás*). Again, the 2 Sing. ἔησθα and 3 Sing.
ἔην, ἤην seem to require a stem (ἐ)ση-, found also in Lat. *e-rām*
(Brugmann, *M. U.* i. p. 35), The -ν of the 3 Sing. is unexplained : it does not appear to be the ν ἐφελκυστικόν, for we find
no form *ἦε alongside of ἦεν.
    Note that the 1 Sing. ἦν is not found in Homer.

The Homeric forms of εἰμί were discussed some years ago by L. Meyer
(K. Z. ix. pp. 385, 423). He maintained that the Homeric 3 Sing. Impf.
was ἦεν or (without augment) ἔεν : the forms ἦν, ἔην and ἤην being due to

corruption or misreading. The facts certainly give much countenance to this view, which has been adopted by Curtius (*Stud.* i. 2, 292) and Nauck. It can hardly be accidental that out of 54 places in which ἦν occurs in the *thesis* or second half of the foot, there are 50 in which it is followed by a vowel, as—

Il. 2. 77 Νέστωρ ὅς ῥα Πύλοιο ἄναξ ἦν ἠμαθόεντος.
Od. 17. 208 ἀμφὶ δ' ἄρ' αἰγείρων ὑδατοτρεφέων ἦν ἄλσος.

Moreover, out of 72 instances of ἔην there are 63 in which it is followed by a consonant (including ϝ). On the other hand, in 26 places ἦν occurs in the first half of the foot, and in 2 places it ends the line (in the phrase οὐδ' ἄρα πως ἦν); and it is not easy to correct many of these so as to admit ἦεν or ἔεν. Again, ἦν and ἔην have some support in the 2 Sing. forms ἦσθα, ἔησθα. (For ἔησθα Curtius proposed ἔεσθα, but there is no good reason for this.) And ἔην is found on an Ionic inscription of the 5th century (Röhl, no. 382). On the whole it seems that the argument for ἔεν is stronger than the argument against ἦν and ἔην. Perhaps we must recognise two Stems, giving four forms : a Stem ἐσ-, whence ἦεν, without augment ἔεν, and a Stem (ἐ)ση- (Lat. *e-rām*), whence ἔ-ην, without augment ἦν. The rare ἤην occurs followed by a vowel (so that we cannot read ἦεν) in 3 places only, viz. Od. 19. 283 (al. εἴη, ἤειν), 23. 316., 24. 343. It may be due to mere 'contamination' of ἦεν and ἔην. But no theory can be accepted as satisfactory that does not account for the fixed -ν of all these forms.

The α of ἔα is treated as long in 3 places, Il. 4. 321., 5. 887., Od. 14. 352. In Od. 14. 222 τοῖος ἔ' ἐν πολέμῳ it is elided ; but perhaps the ἐν may be omitted.

The vowel remains long before Heavy Endings in the Stems—
ἀη-, 3 Du. ἄη-τον, Inf. ἀή-μεναι, Mid. ἄη-το, Part. ἀή-μενος,
κιχη-, 3 Du. Impf. κιχή-την, 1 Plur. ἐ-κίχη-μεν, Inf. κιχή-μεναι,
  Part. κιχή-μενος,
except that it is shortened before -ντ and -ι (§ 6), as in the Part. ἀέντες *blowing*, 3 Plur. ἄεισι (for ἄε-ντι, in Hes. Th. 875), and the Opt. κιχε-ίη *may find*. The vowel is also long in ἔρῡ-το *protected*, Inf. ῥῦ-σθαι ; and in all forms of κεῖμαι, ἦμαι, στεῦμαι.

A similar Non-thematic inflexion, in which the final vowel of the Stem is long except before -ντ and -ι, appears in the Æolic conjugation of verbs in -μι, as γέλαι-μι *I laugh*, αἴνη-μι *I praise* (Hes. Op. 681), φίλη-μι *I love* (1 Plur. φίλη-μεν, 3 Plur. φίλεισι, Part. φιλή-μενος), σάω-μι *I save*. See § 19.

13.] The Simple Non-Thematic Aorist. This term includes the 'Second Aorists,' such as ἔ-βη-ν ἔ-στη-ν &c., and also those so-called First Aorists in which the -ἄ of the 1 Sing. Active is added directly to the Verb-stem, as in ἔ-χευ-α.

Variation of quantity is rare in the Active, but the Stem is usually shortened in the Middle. The chief forms are :—ἔ-βη-ν *I went*, 3 Du. βᾰ-την (but also ἐ-βήτην), 3 Plur. ὑπέρ-βᾰ-σαν, Imper. μετά-βηθι, Inf. βή-μεναι : ἔ-στη-ν *I stood*, Du. στή-την, Plur. ἔ-στη-μεν, ἔ-στη-τε, ἔ-στη-σαν, Imper. στῆ-θι, στῆ-τε, Inf. στή-μεναι ; ἔ-φθη *came before*, Part. φθά-μενος : ἐξ-έ-πτη *flew out*

(Hes. Op. 98), 3 Du. κατα-πτή-την *cowered*, Mid. ἔ-πτα-το *flew*: ἔ-σβη *was quenched*; ἔ-τλη-ν *I endured*, Plur. ἔ-τλη-μεν, ἔ-τλη-τε, Imper. τλή-τω, τλῆ-τε ; ἔ-γνω-ν *I knew*, 3 Du. γνώ-την, 3 Plur. ἔ-γνω-σαν ; ἐπ-έ-πλω-ς *didst sail over*, Part. ἐπι-πλώς ; βιώ-τω *let him live*, Inf. βιῶ-ναι ; ἁλῶ-ναι *to be taken*, Part. ἁλούς : ἔ-φθι-το *perished*; κτί-μενος *built* ; ἔ-δῡ *sank under*, 3 Du. ἐ-δύ-την, 2 Plur. ἔ-δῡ-τε, Imper. δῦ-θι, Inf. δύ-μεναι ; ἔ-φῦ *grew*, 3 Plur. ἔ-φῦ-σαν (H. Ven. 265) : λύ-το *was loosed* (once λῦ-το, Il. 24. 1). κλῦ-θι *hear*, Plur. κλῦ-τε (Part. κλύ-μενος as a Proper Name in Homer). On the forms ἔσσῦ-το, ἔ-χῦ-το see § 15.

The vowel is invariably long in ξυμ-βλή-την *the two encountered*, Mid. βλῆ-το *was struck* ; πλῆ-το *was filled*; πλῆ-το *came near* ; ἀπ-όνη-το *profited*, Imper. ὄνη-σο, Part. ὀνή-μενος ; ἄμ-πνῦ-το *recovered breath* ; ἔ-στρω-το *was strewed* : see § 14.

On the other hand the vowel is short throughout in κατ-έ-κτᾰ-ν (Il. 4. 319, where some ancient critics read κατέκτᾱ), 3 Sing. ἔ-κτᾰ (the quantity is proved by Od. 11. 410 ἔκτα σὺν οὐλομένῃ κ. τ. λ.), 1 Plur. ἔ-κτᾰ-μεν, Part. κατα-κτάς, Mid. ἔ-κτᾰ-το, Inf. κτά-σθαι, Part. κτά-μενος. The longer form of the root is κτεν- (Pres. κτείνω for κτεν-ι̯ω). A similarly irregular 3 Sing. in -ᾰ is found in οὖτα *he wounded*, Inf. οὐτά-μεναι, Part. Mid. οὐτά-μενος : perhaps also in ἀπ-ηύρα-ς, ἀπ-ηύρα. For, comparing the Part. ἀπο-ύρας, Mid. ἀπο-υρά-μενος (Hes. Sc. 173), we may conjecture that the Indic. should be written ἀπ-εῦρα-ς, ἀπ-εῦρα (or ἀπ-έ-ϝρᾰ-ς, ἀπ-έ-ϝρᾰ), where ϝρᾰ- is the weak form of a root ϝερ- (Meyer, G. G. § 524). We have -ᾰ for -εν also in ἀπ-έ-φα-το *died* (Hesych.), from the root φεν- (Pf. πέφᾰ-ται).

On the Non-Thematic Aorists with Stems ending in a consonant, such as ἆλτο, ἔ-παλτο, ὦρτο, δέκτο, λέκτο, μίκτο, &c., with the Inf. πέρθαι and the Participles ἄρμενος, ἴκμενος, ἄσμενος, see § 40.

14.] Metathesis. This term has been employed to explain a number of forms in which a short vowel is lost before a liquid, and the corresponding long vowel follows the two consonants thus brought together: as ξυμ-βλή-την *met*, Mid. βλῆ-το *was struck* (βᾰλ-, βέλ-ος), ἔ-τλη *endured* (τάλα-ς), πλῆ-το *drew near* (πέλα-ς), πλῆ-το *was filled* (Sanscr. *par*-), ἔ-στρω-το *was scattered* (στορε-), κλη-τός *called* (καλ-έω, κέλ-ομαι), κασί-γνη-τος *kinsman* (γεν-), μέ-μνη-μαι (μεν-), δμη-τός *tamed* (δᾰμᾰ-), &c. But this long vowel— ᾱ, η, or ω—is clearly of the same nature as the η of σχή-σω (σεχ-), ἐνι-σπή-σω (σεπ-), πε-πτη-ώς (πετ-, πί-πτ-ω), ἄημι (root *av* in αὔρα), or the ω of πέ-πτω-κα (πετ-), ἔ-γνω-ν (root *gan*), ζω-ός (root *gi*, hence Greek ζη- and ζω-, for γι̯-η, γι̯-ω). In these and many similar cases 'metathesis' is out of the question. Moreover we find several Stems of the same character with the long vowel ῡ, as ῥῦ-σθαι *to shield* (Ϝρῦ-), ῥῦ-τός *drawn* (Ϝερῦ-, Ϝρῦ-), τρύ-ω (cp. τρ-η-, root *tar*). Hence it is probable that the long vowel is of the nature of a suffix, by which a new verbal stem is formed from the primitive stem or ' root.' This vowel usually does not vary with the Person-endings, but is long in all forms of the Tense. It cannot be an accident, however, that the same Stems appear also as disyllables with a *short* final vowel : τᾰλ-ᾰ, πελ-ᾰ, στορ-ε, καλ-ε (in καλέ-σαι), γεν-ε (in γένε-σις), δᾰμ-ᾰ, πετ-ᾰ, Ϝερ-ῠ in ἐρύ-σαι, and many others. What then is the relation between these forms and the monosyllabic τλ-η, πλ-η, στρ-ω, κλ-η, γν-η, δμ-η, πτ-η? Apparently the difference is ultimately one of accent. The same disyllable would become τάλ-α or τλ-ή as the stress fell upon the first or the second syllable*.

15.] **Aorists in -ᾰ and -κᾰ.** These consist of (1) four Aorists from stems ending in -υ, (2) three Aorists in -κᾰ, and (3) the isolated forms ἤνεικα and εἶπα.

The four Aorists ἔσσευ-ά (weak stem σῠ-) *I urged*, ἔ-χευ-α or ἔ-χε-α *I poured*, ἔ-κη-α (weak stem κᾰυ-) *I burned*, ἠλεύ-ατο *avoided* (Opt. ἀλέ-αιτο, Inf. ἀλέ-ασθαι) form the 1 Sing. with -ᾰ instead of -ν. Thus ἔ-χευ-α is formed like ἔ-φη-ν, except that, after the diphthong ευ the final -*m* of the ending passed into -ᾰ, as in the Impf. ἦα (for ἦσ-α). So too in the Accusative of Nouns we have -ν after a single vowel (λόγο-ν, πόλι-ν, ἰχθύ-ν), but -ᾰ after ηυ, ευ or a consonant : νῆ-α (for νηῦ-α or νῆϝ-α), πόδ-α, as in Latin *nāv-em, ped-em*. The forms without υ, as ἔχεα, ἔκηα, are obtained by υ passing into the semi-vowel (ἔχε-α for ἔχεϝα). The original inflexion then was ἔ-χευ-α (ἔ-χεϝ-α), ἔ-χευ-ς, ἔ-χευ(-τ), Plur. ἔ-χῠ-μεν, ἔ-χυ-τε (cp. ἔ-κτᾰ-μεν, § 13), ἔ-χευ-αν, Mid. ἔ-χῠ-το (like ἔ-φᾰ-το, ἔ-κτᾰ-το), &c. Thus ἔχυτο and ἔσσυτο are primitive forms, standing to ἔχενα, ἔσσευα as ἔ-φᾰ-το to ἔ-φη-ν.

How then are we to account for such forms as ἐ-χεύα-μεν, ἐ-χεύα-το, σευά-μενος, ἠλεύα-το? They are obtained from the 1 Sing. and 3 Plur. by treating the stem *plus* the -ᾰ as a new stem or base, to which the Person-endings are then attached. Thus ἔ-χευα-ς, ἐ-χεύα-μεν, ἐ-χεύα-το are duplicate forms, related to ἔ-χευ-ς, ἔ-χῠ-μεν, ἔ-χυ-το as the later οἶδα-ς, οἰδᾰ-μεν to οἶσθα,

---

* Joh. Schmidt, *K. Z.* xxiii. 277 ; Brugmann, *M. U.* i. 1-68 ; Fröhde, *B. B.* ix. 119. The whole subject, as Brugmann has recently warned us (*Grundriss*, ii. § 8, *n*. 1), is full of uncertainty, and it is possible that forms such as *pelē*- represent the 'root' or primitive word, from which not only *plē*- (πλη-, Lat. *plē-nus*) and *pele*-, but also *pel*- (Sanscr. *pi-par-ti*) and *pl*- (πί-πλᾰ-μεν), are derived. We are dealing here, not with the derivation of Greek, &c. from Indo-European,— where the comparison of other languages, such as Sanscrit, may give us help,— but with the formation of Indo-European itself, to which the comparative method is *ex hypothesi* inapplicable.

ἴδ-μεν. The 3 Sing. in -ε(ν), follows the analogy of the Thematic conjugation (ἔχευε like ἔλεγε).

The three Aorists in -κἄ, ἔ-θηκα *I put*, ἔ-ηκα *I sent forth*, ἔ-δωκα *I gave*, are inflected as follows :—

1 Sing.	ἔ-θηκα		1 Plur.	ἔ-θε-μεν
2 ,,	ἔ-θηκα-s	2 Du. ἔ-θε-τον	2 ,,	ἔ-θε-τε
3 ,,	ἔ-θηκε(ν)	3 ,, ἐ-θέ-την	3 ,,	{ ἔ-θε-σαν / ἔ-θηκα-ν.

Imper. θέ-s, θέ-τω, Plur. θέ-τε, θέ-ντων.
Inf. θέ-μεναι, θέ-μεν, θεῖναι, Part. θείς, θέ-ντος, &c.
Mid. ἐ-θέ-μην &c. with θε- as stem throughout.

Thus θηκα-, ἠκα-, δωκα- alternate with θε-, ἑ-, δο- as long and short Stems respectively. The only forms in Homer which do not conform to this scheme are the 1 Plur. ἐν-ήκα-μεν (Od. 12. 401), and the 3 Sing. Mid. θήκα-το (Il. 10. 31., 14. 187, also Hes. Th. 175). The primitive 3 Plur. ἔ-δο-ν occurs in Hes. Th. 30, and in Doric : ἔ-θε-ν only on inscriptions (C. I. 29).

The Homeric forms with the stem ἑ- do not take the augment: in Attic we have (e. g.) εἷ-μεν εἷ-τε (for ἐ-ἑ-μεν ἐ-ἑ-τε).

In respect of the -ἄ of the Stem the 2 Sing. ἔ-θηκα-s is formed like ἔ-χευα-s, and the occasional examples of the type ἐ-θήκα-μεν, ἐ-θήκα-το are parallel to ἐ-χεύα-μεν, ἐ-χεύα-το. That is to say, the -ἄ comes from ἔ-θηκα, ἔ-θηκα-ν. The relation of ἐ-θήκα-μεν, ἐ-θήκα-το to ἔ-θε-μεν, ἔ-θε-το, is complicated by the use of a new Verb-Stem (θη-κ- instead of θη-). Thus it is the same as the relation of ἑστήκα-μεν to ἑστἄ-μεν (§ 22).

The Aorist ἤνεικα (without augment ἔνεικα) shows no variation of stem ; 1 Plur. ἐνείκα-μεν, 3 Plur. ἤνεικα-ν and ἔνεικα-ν, Imper. ἐνείκα-τε, Mid. 3 Plur. ἠνείκα-ντο.
On the Aorist εἷπα see § 37.

16.] The Non-Thematic Reduplicated Present. These Presents are formed by Reduplication, usually of the initial consonant with ἴ; τίθη-σι *puts*, δίδω-μι *I give*, ἵη-σι (for σίση-σι?) *sends*, ἱστᾶσι (σι-στᾰ-) *they set*, πιμπλᾶσι *they fill* (the μ is euphonic: it is dropped after μ in ἐμ-πίπλη-θι), δίδη *bound*, βιβά-s *striding*; with Attic Reduplication, ὀνίνη-σι (for ὀν-ονη-) *benefits* : perhaps also ἵλη-θι *be appeased* (ἵλα-μαι *I propitiate*, Hom. H. xxi. 5: Stem ἱλα for σι-σλᾰ, Meyer, G. G. p. 437).

In these Present Stems the quantity of the vowel in the Stem regularly varies under the rules laid down in § 6 (1).

The vowel is long in ἐμ-πίπλη-θι (Il. 21. 311), ἵλη-θι, δίδω-θι (Od. 3. 380)*, and the Inf. τιθή-μεναι (Il. 23. 83, 247) and Part.

---

* The variation is perhaps less regular in the Imper.; cp. κλῦ-θι. In Sanscr. the 3 Sing. Imper. has the strong Stem.

τιθή-μενος (Il. 10. 34). Also in δίζη-μαι I seek (for *δι-δίη-), the Homeric Verb answering to Attic ζη-τέω.

ἵημι is now generally connected with Lat. sero (for si-so, cp. ἵστημι sisto). Earlier scholars (as Bopp) derived it from the root yā (Lat. ja-c-io). Possibly it represents both σί-σημι (sā-) and ἱ-ιημι (yā-). In meaning it is much nearer to jacio than to sero.

17.] **Present Stems in -νη (-νᾰ) and -νυ.** The Tense-Stems of this class—which may be called the Non-Thematic Nasal class—form the Present-Stem from the Verb-Stem by the Suffixes -νη, -νῡ (which with Heavy Endings regularly become -νᾰ, -νῠ).

The Presents with -νη (-νᾰ) are nearly all peculiar to Homer, δάμ-νη-μι I subdue, κίρ-νη mixed, πέρ-να-s selling, σκίδ-να-ται is scattered, πίλ-να-ται comes near, μάρ-να-ται fights. Note ι for ε in κιρ-, σκιδ-, πιλ-; cp. the later Verbs πίτ-νω, κτίν-νυμι.

A few Presents with -νυ are common to all periods of Greek, δείκ-νυ-μι I show, ὄμ-νυ-μι I swear, ζεύγ-νυ-μι I join, ὄλλυμι (for ὄλ-νυ-μι) I destroy; but they are mainly Homeric or poetical; ὄρ-νῠ-θι arouse, δαί-νῡ feasted, ἄγ-νυ-τον break, στορ-νῦσα spreading, ἀπ-ομόργ-νῠ wiped away, ἐέργ-νυ shut in, ῥηγ-νῦσι they break, γά-νυ-ται is gladdened, τά-νυ-ται is stretched, ἤ-νυ-το was finished, κί-νυ-ντο were moved, τί-νυ-νται punish, αἴ-νυ-ται takes, ἐ-καί-νυ-το surpassed, ἀρ-νύ-σθην won, ἄχ-νυ-μαι I am vexed, ὤιγ-νυ-ντο were opened, ἔννυτο (for ἐσ-νυ-το) put on, ζώννυ-το (for ζωσ-νυ-) girded himself, ὀρεγ-νύ-s stretching out, σβεννυ-μενάων (Hes. Op. 590).

In the Verbs in -νημι the Verb-Stem is nearly always disyllabic : cp. δαμά-σαι (παν-δαμά-τωρ, &c.), κερά-σαι, πετά-σαι, περά-σαι, σκεδά-σαι, πέλα-s. So in some Verbs in -νῡμι ; cp. ὁμό-σαι, ὀλέ-σαι, στορέ-σαι. Thus we may regard δαμ-α and δαμ-νη, ὀμ-ο and ὀμ-νῡ, &c., as twin forms obtained by the addition of a different suffix to the same original root δαμ-, ὀμ-, &c. (§ 14). It is to be observed also that Presents in -νημι are often found along with forms in -αζω and -αω : δάμ-νημι, Attic δαμ-άζω ; κίρ-νημι, κερ-άω : πέρ-νημι, περ-άω : σκίδ-νημι, σκεδ-άω : πίλ-νημι, πελ-άζω. Cp. κάμ-νω, κάμα-τος (§ 47).

The Verb-Stem, it will be seen, has most commonly its weak form (note especially τά-νυ-ται, Pf. τέ-τᾰ-ται), sometimes the strong form, as in δείκ-νυ-μι, ζεύγ-νυ-μι, ῥήγ-νυ-μι.

The forms in -αννυμι and -εννυμι are post-Homeric.

18.] **Thematic forms.** Some forms of Non-Thematic Tenses follow the conjugation of the corresponding Contracted Verbs in -αω, -εω, -οω (§ 56); especially in the Impf. Indic. and the Imperative. Thus we find :—

ἐδάμνα (as if from *δαμνάω), ἐκίρνα (Od. 7. 182, &c.), πίτνα : Imper. καθ-ίστα (Il. 9. 202).

ἐτίθει, ἵει (ἀφ-ίει, προ-ίει, &c.), ἄει (v. l. ἄη) blew, κίχεις : Imper. τίθει, ἵει (ξυν-ίει).

ἐδίδους, ἐδίδου : Imper. δίδου (Od. 3. 58).

Examples occur also in the Pres. Indic.; δαμνᾷ (3 Sing. Act.) in Od. 11. 221 (with v. l. δάμνατ'); δαμνᾷ (2 Sing. Mid.) in Il. 14. 199 (with v. l. δάμνᾳ, for δάμνα-αι); ἀν-ιεῖς (Il. 5. 880), μεθ-ιεῖς (Il. 6. 523, Od. 4. 372), μεθ-ιεῖ (Il. 10. 121), τιθεῖ (Il. 13. 732), παρ-τιθεῖ (Od. 1. 192), for which the MSS. usually have ἀνίεις, &c. : διδοῖς (Il. 9. 164), διδοῖ (Il. 9. 519, Od. 4. 237). So for προίει in Il. 2. 752 we should read προιεῖ.

Add the Part. βιβῶντα (Il. 3. 22, cp. 13. 807., 16. 609), Fem. βιβῶσα (Od. 11. 539); for which Bekk. writes βιβάντα, βιβᾶσα.

Editors differ in their manner of dealing with these forms. Bekker in his second edition (1858) restored the 2 Sing. Pres. τίθης, ἵης, δίδως, and Impf. ἐτίθη, ἵη, ἐδίδω, but left the 3 Sing. τιθεῖ, διδοῖ and Imper. τίθει, ἵει, δίδου. Nauck proposes to restore καθίστη (Imper.) and the Impf. ἐδάμνη, πίτνη, ἐκίρνη. In the case of τίθημι, ἵημι, δίδωμι the weight of authority seems to be for the spelling which follows the Thematic conjugation, viz. -εῖς, -οῖς in the 2 Sing. Pres., and -εις, -ει, -ους, -ου in the Impf. (Cobet, Misc. Crit. p. 281, is extremely positive on this side). But Verbs which have η in the Dual and Plural (ἄη-τον, κιχή-την) should follow the analogy of the Passive Aorists : hence ἄη, κίχης. And we may leave undisturbed the form δίδη he bound (Il. 11. 105), for which no one has proposed to read δίδει.

The 1 Sing. προ-ίειν (Od. 9. 88., 10. 100., 12. 9) stands alone, and is doubtless a mere error for προίην (Bekker, ed. 1858).

Porson (in his note on Eur. Or. 141) condemns ξυνιεῖς, τιθεῖς, &c. on the ground that if τιθεῖς were right we ought also to have τιθῶ, τιθεῖ, τιθοῦμεν, τιθεῖτε. It is possible, however, that a form like τιθεῖς may have crept in through the analogy of the Verbs in -εω, although no 'Verb' τιθέω was in use. It is characteristic of the working of analogy to be partial and gradual. In Homer we find the corresponding 3 Sing. Pres. δαμνᾷ, τιθεῖ, μεθιεῖ, διδοῖ—forms which are guaranteed by the metre. The forms so guaranteed are indeed few, and perhaps were not found in the oldest text of the poems; but they are supported by similar forms in Herodotus and other Ionic writers*.

Similarly, in the Presents formed with -νυ there is evidence of a tendency to introduce the Thematic -νυε(ο). The instances are:— ὄρ-νυ-ον (Il. 12. 142), ὤμνυε (Il. 14. 278), ζεύγνυον (Il. 19. 393), ὀμνυ-έτω (Il. 19. 175), τανύ-ουσι, τανύ-οντο (four times),

---

* In considering this and similar questions it should be remembered (1) that we do not know when the Homeric poems were first written down ; (2) that we do not know of any systematic attention having been paid to spelling, accentuation, &c. before the time of the Alexandrian grammarians ; (3) that the tendency of oral recitation must have been to substitute later for earlier forms, unless the metre stood in the way ; (4) that this modernising process went on in different parts of Greece, and therefore need not represent the exclusive influence of any one dialect ; (5) that the older Ionic alphabet confused ε, ει, η and ο, ου, ω.

ταυύ-ειν (Il. 17. 391), ἀνύω (Il. 4. 56, but may be Fut.). As to δαινύ-ῃ (2 Sing. Subj. Mid.) see § 80.

Also, the Verb ῥύομαι *protect, save*, is for the most part Non-Thematic (ἔρῡ-σο, ἔρῡ-το, 3 Plur. ρῦ-ατο, Inf. ῥῦ-σθαι), but partly Thematic (ῥύε-ται, ῥύε-το, ῥύο-νται, &c.), see § 11. And the Aor. ἔ-κλυ-ον is Thematic, except the Imper. κλῦ-θι, κλῦ-τε.

It should be observed that in all the foregoing cases the Thematic form is obtained by combining thematic endings with the final vowel of the Stem. In other cases the original final vowel is lost, as κίχε(ν) for ἐ-κίχη, δίζω for δίζη-μαι, and the like.

19.] Non - Thematic Contracted Verbs. The following Homeric forms are usually regarded as instances of 'irregular Contraction' of Verbs in -αω, -εω, -οω :—

(-αω): συναντή-την *met*, συλή-την *spoiled*, προσαυδή-την *spoke to*, φοιτή-την *went about*, κνῆ *scraped*, ἀρή-μεναι *to pray*, γοή-μεναι *to bewail*, πεινή-μεναι *to hunger*, θῆ-σθαι *to milk*.

(-εω): ἀπειλή-την *threatened*, ὁμαρτή-την *met*, καλή-μεναι *to call*, πενθή-μεναι *to mourn*, ποθή-μεναι *to regret*, φιλή-μεναι *to love*, φορή-μεναι, φορῆ-ναι *to carry*, ἀλιτή-μενος *sinning*, τερσή-μεναι *to get dry* (§ 42).

(-οω): σάω 3 Sing. Impf. and also 2 Sing. Imper of σαόω *I keep safe*.

These forms cannot be explained by the ordinary contraction with the Thematic ε or ο : e. g. φοιτή-την cannot come from *φοιταέτην, φορῆ-ναι from *φορεέ-ναι, ἀλιτή-μενος from *ἀλιτεό-μενος, σάω from σάοε, &c. On the other hand, as Curtius has shown (*Stud.* iii. 377–401, *Verb.* i. 352 ff.), they agree exactly with those Non-Thematic forms in which *the vowel before the Ending is long except before -ντ and -ι*, such as the Pres. κιχή-μεναι, ἀή-μεναι (§ 12), the Aor. στή-μεναι, τλῆ-ναι, γνώ-μεναι, &c. and (as we may add by anticipation) the Passive Aorists in -ην and -θην.

Moreover, the same type of inflexion appears in the peculiar 'Verbs in -μι' of the Æolic dialect, as φίλη-μι, 1 Plur. φίλη-μεν, 3 Plur. φίλεισι (for φίλε-ντι), Part. φιλή-μενος; and also in the Latin Verbs in -*āre* and -*ēre*, except in the 1 Sing.; e. g. *amā-mini* is parallel to ἀρή-μεναι, *docēmini* to φορή-μεναι, *docemus*, *doce-nt* to φίλη-μεν, φίλεισι.

Further traces of this formation may be seen in those Attic verbs in -αω and -οω which take η and ω instead of ᾱ and ου respectively (as ζάω, ζῇς, ζῇ, &c., ῥιγόω, Inf. ῥιγῶν), and in the Opt. in -ῳην, -οιην (for which however in the case of verbs in -εω we expect -ειην, as in κιχείην and Æolic φιλείη).

These facts seem to show that the formation now in question is of high antiquity, and Curtius even maintained that it was older than the ordinary conjugation of the verbs in -άω, -εω, -οω.

In these verbs, as he pointed out, there is evidence to show that the vowel before the thematic ending was originally long (e.g. in Homeric διψάων, πεινάων, ὑπνώοντες, Æolic ποθήω, ἀδικήει, &c.). The forms in -άω, -ηω, -ωω, again, may represent an older (and Æolic) -ᾱμι, -ημι, -ωμι, just as δεικνύω is for older δείκνῡμι: and these again may be explained by contraction from -ᾱͺημι, -ηͺημι, -ωͺημι, the Greek representatives of the Sanscrit -ayámi. The Latin amo, doceo, Pl. amāmus, docēmus, would fall into this scheme, if we suppose that they belong to the stage at which the thematic endings had not extended beyond the 1 Sing.

Against this theory it is urged by Brugmann (M. U. i. 86) that the thematic conjugation of these verbs is found also in Sanscrit, Zend, Slavo-Lithuanian and Germanic—all which members of the Indo-European family, if Curtius is right, must have recast their derivative verbs on the same thematic model. It is more probable therefore that these verbs were originally thematic, and according to the final vowel of the base appeared as verbs in -αω (as νικά-ω), -εω (as ποθέ-ω), or -οω (as δηϊό-ω). On this assumption, again, the Homeric forms now in question may be variously explained. Where we find η for εε or αε, as in φιλήμεναι, γοήμεναι (instead of the ει, ᾱ required by the ordinary rules), we may suppose, with Wackernagel (K. Z. xxvii. 84), that the contraction belongs to an earlier (pre-Hellenic) period. The existence of such a period is proved (e. g.) by the temporal augment, as in ἦ(σ)α for an original ἐ-εσα. Then the participles ἀλιτήμενος, φιλήμενος and the like may be explained by supposing a form in -εμενος, cp. Lat. leg-imini, docēmini, so that φιλήμενος would be a primitive contraction from φιλε-έμενος (φιλε-ͺε-μενος). The solution however is confessedly incomplete. It does not (directly at least) explain Æolic φίλημεν, φίλεισι, Lat. amāmus, docēmus, amant, docent. It only explains the long vowel of φιλή-σω, ἐφίλη-σα, φιλητός, &c., if we also suppose that the -ͺε of the Present was carried through all the tenses. And it does not give any satisfactory account of the common contracted forms, νικᾶτε, φιλεῖτε, δηλοῦτε, &c., since these must have come from νικάετε, φιλέετε, δηλόετε, &c. at a period in which the ordinary Greek rules of contraction were in force.

A wholly different explanation is proposed by Brugmann himself (l. c.). He shows, as we have seen (§ 14), that there is a large class of non-thematic forms with stems ending in a long vowel—ᾱ, η, ω—which is of the nature of a suffix. Such are ἔ-βλη-η-ν (βᾰλ-, βλη-η), ἔ-πτη-ν (πετ-, πτ-η), ἔ-γνω-ν (γεν-, γν-ω-), and many others, which have their representatives in all languages of the Indo-European family. By an extension of this type has been formed the specifically Greek class of the Passive aorists in -ην, as ἔ-φανη-ν, ἐ-τύπη-ν and one or two in -ων, as ἐ-άλω-ν.

Similarly, again, the analogy of the 'verbs in -μι,' and especially
of those tenses which do not vary the quantity of the stem (as
κίχημι, ἄημι, πλῆ-το, ἔγνων) has affected the derivative verbs, and
has thus produced the non-thematic forms in question—φιλήμεναι
like ἀήμεναι, ἀλιτήμενος like κιχήμενος, and so on. The forms
τιθή-μεναι (Il. 23. 83, 247), τιθή-μενον (Il. 10. 34) are probably
due to the influence of the same group of Verbs. A similar
process explains the Æolic conjugation of verbs in -μι (γέλαιμι,
φίλημι, δοκίμωμι), the difference being that in Æolic it was carried
much further. In Homer we have nothing answering to the
1 Sing. φίλημι, the 1 Plur. φίλημεν, the 3 Plur. φίλεισι, or the
corresponding Imperfect forms.

We cannot be sure, however, that all the examples of this type which
appeared in the original text of Homer have been preserved. Wackernagel
has observed that nearly all the words now in question are forms which
would be unfamiliar in the Greece of classical times. The list is made up
chiefly of duals (προσαυδήτην, φοιτήτην, &c.) and Infinitives in -μεναι. It is not
improbable (e.g.) that the familiar form προσηύδα has supplanted an original
Non-Thematic προσηύδη. On the other hand in Il. 11. 638 ἐπὶ δ' αἴγειον κνῆ
τυρόν the metre points rather to the uncontracted κνάε.

20.] Aorists. Of the Aorist Stems noticed in § 13, several
are probably derived from Nouns, and do not differ in formation
from the Presents discussed in the preceding section : e.g. ἐ-γήρα
(γῆρα-s), βιώ-τω (βίο-s), ἐπ-έπλω-s (πλόο-s), ἀλῶ-ναι, perhaps
ἀπ-όνη-το. Regarding the Passive Aorists, see §§ 42-44.

21.] Meaning of the Non-Thematic Pres. and Aor. The
Presents formed by Reduplication, and by the Suffixes -νη and
-νυ, are nearly always Transitive or 'Causative' in meaning, as
ἵστη-μι, σκίδ-νη-μι, ὄρ-νυ-μι : whereas the simpler Verbs, whether
Present or Aorist, are usually Intransitive as ἔστη-ν, ἔσβη.

Regarding the Tense-meaning, it is enough to point out here
that the difference of the Present and Aorist is not given by the
form of the Tense : thus the Impf. ἔ-φη-ν is the same in formation as the Aor. ἔ-βη-ν, ἔ-στη-ν.

The Perfect.

22.] The Perfect-Stem is formed by Reduplication, and is
liable to vary with the Person-Endings (§ 6). This variation is
the rule in the Homeric Perfect. In Attic it survives in a few
forms only; it is regular in οἶδα and ἕστηκα.

The weak form of the Stem is the same (except for the Reduplication) as in the Tenses already discussed. The long Stem
is often different, showing a predilection for the O-form.

The variation appears in the interchange of—

(1) η (ā) and ă : as τεθήλ-ει *bloomed*, Part. Fem. τεθᾰλ-υῖα; ἄρηρε *is fitting*, ἀρᾰρ-υῖα; λελ ηκ-ώς, λελᾱκ-υῖα *yelling*, μεμηκ-ώς, μεμᾱκ-υῖα *bleating*; λέλασται (λελαθ-ται, λήθ-ω) *has forgotten*, ἀκαχ-μένος *sharpened*, πέφαν-ται *has appeared*; σέσηπε *is rotten* (σαπρός), τέτηκα (τήκ-ω), τέθηπα (Aor. Part. ταφ-ών), πέπηγε (πάγ-η), κεχην-ότα, κεκληγ-ώς, πεπληγ-ώς, τετρήχ-ει (τᾰρᾰχ-); πεπάσ-μην *I had eaten* (πατ-έομαι), κεκασμένος (κᾰδ-) *excelling*, ἐρράδ-αται *are sprinkled*, δέδασ-ται *is divided* (but 3 Plur. δεδαί-αται, from δαι-, § 51, 2). In the last four cases the strong form does not actually occur.

δέδηε *is on fire* is for *δέδηνε (δεδηϝ-ε) : the weak Stem is δᾰυ-(δαίω for δαϝ-ιω, cp. καίω, ἔκηα). Similarly γέγηθε *rejoices* is for *γέγηνθε (Lat. *gaud-eo*).

ā for η occurs in ἔαγε *is broken* (Hes. Op. 534 : ἐάγῃ as Subj. is only Bekker's conj. in Il. 11. 558, see § 67) : also in ἐᾱδ-ότα *pleasing*, as to which see § 26, 2.

ω and ă : this interchange cannot be exemplified from Homer : cp. Attic ἔρρωγα (ῥᾰγ-, Mid. συν-έρρηκ-ται). ω is also found in ἄνωγα *I bid*, γέγωνε *calls aloud*, but the corresponding weak Stems are unknown.

(2) ω and ε : εἴωθε *is accustomed* (cp. ἔθων, ἦθος, root σϝηθ-) : ἐπ-ώχ-ατο *were shut to* (of gates), from ἐπ-έχω : συν-οχωκ-ότε (better perhaps συν-οκωχότε, see Cobet, *Misc. Crit.* p. 303) *leaning together*, from συν-έχω (cp. ὀκωχή a *stay* or *buttress*, ἀν-οκωχή = ἀνοχή *staying*, *cessation*).

η and ε : in μέμηλε *is a care*, ἐδ-ηδ-ώς *having eaten*.

(3) ω and ο : in δέδο-ται (δω-), ἐκ-πέπο-ται *is drunk up*, ὄλωλε *is lost*, ὄρωρε *is aroused*, ὄπωπα *I have seen*, ὀδώδ-ει *smelt* : perhaps also ὀρώρει *watched* (Il. 23. 112 ἐπὶ δ' ἀνὴρ ἐσθλὸς ὀρώρει = *was the ἐπί-ουρος*), cp. § 30.

προ-βέβουλα (Il. 1. 113) seems to follow the Pres. βούλομαι : we expect *βέβωλα (βολ-, § 30).

(4) οι and ῐ : οἶδα, 1 Plur. ἴδ-μεν; πέποιθα, 1 Plur. Plpf. ἐ-πέπιθ-μεν; ἔοικα, Dual ἔϊκ-τον, Part. Fem. ἐϊκ-υῖα; λέλοιπα, Aor. ἔ-λῐπ-ον; δείδω *I fear*, for δέδϝοια (by loss of ι and contraction), 1 Plur. δείδι-μεν (for δέδϝι-μεν).

This account of the isolated 1 Sing. δείδω was given by G. Mahlow (*K. Z.* xxiv. 295), and has been adopted by most scholars. The original Homeric form was probably δείδοα (or δέδϝοα), which can be restored in all the passages where the word occurs. Others (as Cobet) would substitute δείδια, a form which is found in several places, sometimes as an ancient v. l. for δείδω. But it is difficult on his view to account for the change from δείδια. Rather, an original δείδοα (or δέδϝοα) was altered in two ways, (1) by contraction, which gave it the appearance of a Present in -ω, and (2) by change of ο to ῐ under the influence of δείδῐ-μεν, &c.

(5) ευ and ὔ: πεφευγ-ώς *having escaped*, Mid. πεφυγ-μένος; τετεύχ-αται *are made*, 3 Sing. τέτυκ-ται; κέκευθε *hides* (Aor. κύθε); ἐζευγ-μένοι *joined* (ζυγ-όν). Other weak Stems: κέχΰ-ται, ἔσσΰται (§ 15), πέπυσ-μαι (πΰθ-), κέκλΰ-θι *listen*.

ου interchanging with υ is much less common: εἰλήλουθα *I am come* (ἐλΰθ-), perhaps δεδουπ-ότος (cp. κτύπ-ος).

ῡ appears in μέμῡκε (Aor. μύκε), βέβρῡχεν *roars*, as in the Pres. μυκάομαι, βρύχω.

(6) op (po), oλ and ἄρ (ρἄ), ἄλ (for ṛ, ḷ, § 6, 5): δι-έφθορας *art destroyed* (φθἄρ-); ἔμμορε *has a share*, Mid. εἵμαρ-το *was apportioned*; τέτροφε *is thickened* (τρἄφ-); ἐπι-δέδρομε *runs over*; δέδορκε *sees*; ἔοργας *hast done*; ἔολπα *I hope*. Weak forms: πεπαρ-μένος *pierced*, τέτραπ-το (τρέπ-ω), ἐ-τέταλ-το (τέλλω).

But ερ, ελ in ἐερ-μένος *strung* (Lat. *sero*), ἔρχ-αται *are packed in*, Part. ἐεργ-μέναι (Fέργ-ω), and ἐελ-μένος *cooped in*: cp. § 31, 6.

ρῑ appears in βέβρῑθε *is heavy*, ἔρρῑγα *I dread*, πεφρῑκ-υῖαι *bristling*, τετρῑγ-υῖαι *chirping*, with no corresponding weak Stem. In these words ρῑ seems to come from original ερ, ρ, or ṛ; cp. § 29, 4.

(7) ον and ἄ (for ṇ): γέγονε *is born*, 1 Plur. γέγἄ-μεν; πέπονθα *I suffer*, 2 Plur. πέπασθε (for πεπαθ-τε), Part. πεπἄθ-υῖα; μέμονας *art eager*, 2 Plur. μέμἄ-τε; λελόγχ-ἄσι *have as portion* (Aor. ἔλἄχ-ον); πέφἄ-ται *is slain* (φόν-ος), τέτἄ-ται *is stretched* (τόν-ος), δεδαώς (§ 31, 5). But we find αν in κεχανδ-ώς *containing* (Aor. ἔχἄδε).

(8) ο and ε: as in τέτοκα (Hes. Op. 591, cp. Aor. ἔ-τεκ-ον); δέδεγ-μαι *I await* (cp. προ-δοκ-αί *ambush*); ἔσ-σαι *art clothed*; ἀνήνοθεν *mounted up* (of a stream of blood, Il. 11. 266), ἐπ-ενήνοθε *is upon*: ἀγηγέρ-ατο *were assembled* (cp. ἀγορ-ή): κεκοπ-ώς *striking*. Properly the form with ο should interchange with a form without a vowel (τοκ- with τκ-, &c.), but when this is impossible ε remains in the weak Stem: see § 6, 6.

ἀνήνοθε answers in meaning to the Attic ἀνθέω, *to be on the surface, come forth upon*: the Pres. would be ἀνέθ-ω (related to ἄνθ-ος as ἀλέγ-ω to ἄλγ-ος). So ἐν-ήνοθε supposes ἐνέθ-ω, weak form ἐνθ-.

(9) Stems which take the suffix κ*.

---

* A word may be said here on the origin of the Perfects in -κἄ. They may be regarded as formed in the ordinary way from Stems in which a Root has been lengthened by a suffixed κ, as in ὀλέ-κ-ω, ἐρύ-κ-ω (§ 45), πτήσσω (for πτη-κ-ϳω, cp. ἔ-πτα-κ-ον), δειδίσσομαι (for δει-δϝικ-ϳο-μαι). Thus ὀλώλεκα is the regular Pf. of ὀλέκω, and πέπτωκα, δείδοικα, answer to the weak stems πτἄ-κ-, δϝῑ-κ-. So βέβηκα, ἔστηκα answer to (possible) Presents *βή-κω (cp. βάκ-τρον), *στή-κω. It is not necessary to suppose an actual Stem in κ in each case; a few instances would serve to create the type. The reason for the use of the longer Stems βη-κ, στη-κ, &c., was probably that the forms given by the original Stems were too unlike other Perfects. The characteristic -ἄ would be lost by contraction with the preceding vowels.

When the Stem ends in a vowel, certain forms of the Pf. Act. take κ, thus filling the hiatus which would otherwise be made between the Stem and the Ending: as in ἕστη-κ-ας, δείδοι-κ-α, τεθαρσή-κ-ᾱσι. The Perfects of this type—including those of which no forms with κ are actually found—may be divided again into—

(a) Perfects with variable root-vowel : ἕστηκα *I stand*, 1 Plur. ἕστᾰ-μεν ; δείδοικα *I fear*, 1 Plur. δείδῐ-μεν ; πέφυκε, 3 Plur. πεφύ-ᾱσι : βέβηκα, Inf. βεβᾰ-μεν ; τέθνηκα, Imper. τέθνᾰ-θι ; τέτληκα, Imper. τέτλᾰ-θι. Add also μέμῡ-κε *is closed* (of a wound), δέδῡ-κε *is sunk in*, though the short form is not found.

(b) Perfects with invariable long vowel, especially η and ω (discussed in § 14) : βεβλή-κ-ει *struck*, Mid. βέβλη-ται (cp. ξυμ-βλή-την, βλή-μενος) ; κέκμη-κ-ας *art weary* ; πεπλη-μένος *brought near*, κέκλη-μαι, εἴρη-ται, μέμνη-μαι, τετμη-μένος ; βεβρω-κ-ώς *having eaten* (Fut. Mid. βεβρώ-σεται), μέμβλω-κ-ε *is gone*, πεπρω-μένος *fated*.

Similarly, from disyllabic Stems, δεδάη-κε (Aor. ἐ-δάη-ν) *has learned* (Od. 8. 134), τετύχη-κε (Od. 10. 88), and the Participles κεχαρη-ότα (ἐ-χάρη-ν), βεβαρη-ότα, κεκαφη-ότα, τετιη-ότες.

To this class belong the Perfects of derivative Verbs in -αω, -εω, -οω, -υω, as βεβίη-κ-εν (Il. 10. 145, 172., 16. 22), ὑπ-εμνήμυ-κε (Il. 22. 491), δεδειπνή-κει (Od. 17. 359), τεθαρσή-κ-ᾱσι (Il. 9. 420, 687) : κεκοτη-ότα, κεκορη-ότα, ἀκ-άχη-μαι, ἀλ-άλη-μαι, ἀλα-λύκτη-μαι.

παρ-ῴχη-κεν (Il. 10. 252, with v. l. παρῴχωκεν) is formed as if from *παρ-οιχέω, for παρ-οίχομαι.

ἀδη-κ-ότες (Od. 12. 281, and four times in Il. 10) means *displeased, disgusted*, and should probably be written ἀαδηκότες, from ἀαδέω (for ἀ-σϝᾰδ-εω).

The Subj. ἱλήκῃσι (Od. 21. 36), Opt. ἱλήκοι (H. Apoll. 165) point to a Pf. ἵληκα or Pres. ἱλή-κω.

(10) A Perfect in -θα may be recognised in ἐγρηγόρ-θᾱσι *keep awake* (Il. 10. 419) : perhaps in the Opt. βεβρώθοις (Il. 4. 35).

In general the Perfects of derivative Verbs are formed with an

---

It is a confirmation of this view that the Stem with -κα is in the same form as the Present Stems with a suffixed κ, γ, θ (§ 45), or σκ (§ 48).

A similar theory may be formed of the Perfects in -θα, of which the germs have been mentioned above. βέβρω-θα is related to a Part. βεβρω-ώς (§ 26, 4) as τέθνη-κα to τεθνη-ώς, and to a Mid. *βέβρω-μαι (cp βεβρώ-σεται) as βέβλη-κα to βέβλη-μαι. If in a few more cases, such as βέβρῑ-θα (βρῑ-), εἴωθα (suē-tus), γέγη-θα (γαϝ-ι̯ω), we had had short forms of the Stem without θ, the suffix -θα would have been felt to characterise the Pf. Act. ; that is to say, the *type* of the ' Pf. in -θα' would have been created, and might have spread as the Pf. in -κα has done.

The Aorists in -κᾰ are to be accounted for in the same way. The κ may be traced in the Pres. δώκω (on the inscription of Idalion, see Curt. *Stud.* vii. 243) and in the Noun θήκ-η, which points to a Verb-Stem θη-κ-.

invariable Stem : as κεκορυθ-μένος, πεπόλισ-το, ὀδώδυσ-ται, κεκονῑμένος. But no such Perfects are used in the Active.

23.] The Reduplication takes the following forms :—

(1) An initial consonant is repeated with ε. This is the general rule : we need only notice the Perfects in which an original consonant has been lost, viz. :—

A labial semi-vowel (ϝ) in ἐ-ελ-μένος *cooped in* (for ϝε-ϝελμένος), εἰρύαται (ϝερυ-) *are drawn up*, εἴλυ-το (ϝελυ-, *volvo*), ἔ-οργα (ϝέργ-ον), ἔ-ολπα, ἔοικα, Mid. ἤϊκ-το (unless this comes from ἔϊσκω).

A sibilant (σ) in ἔ-στηκα (for *σέ-στηκα), ἐ-ερ-μένος *strung together* (Lat. *sero*). But the σ is retained in σέσηπε.

(2) Stems beginning with two consonants (except when the second is ρ λ μ or ν), or with ζ, usually prefix ε only : as δι-έφθορας, ἐ-φθίατο, ἐ-κτῆσθαι (but κέκτημαι, Hes. Op. 437), ἐ-ζευγμέναι. But we find πε-πτηώς, πέ-πτανται. And in ἔστηκα the rough breathing represents original σ-.

The group σϝ has been lost in ἐ-άδώς (either σε-σϝάδώς or ἐ-σϝάδώς) *pleasing*, and εἴωθα, ἔωθα (Lat. *suē-sco*).

The group δϝ has the effect of lengthening the vowel of the reduplication in δείδοικα, δείδι-μεν, &c., which represent original δέ-δϝοι-κα, δέ-δϝϊ-μεν, &c.

Initial ρ, which generally stands for ϝρ (sometimes σρ), gives ἐρρ-, as in ἔρρηκται (ϝρηγ-), ἐρρίζωται. Sometimes εἰρ-, as εἴρηται (ϝρη-, cp. *ver-bum*), and εἰρύαται (ῥύομαι, ϝρῡ- *protect*). One Stem reduplicates ρ, viz. ῥε-ρυπωμένα, from ῥυπόω.

Similarly we have ἔμμορε, Mid. εἴμαρ-ται (σμαρ-), and ἔσσυται (σεύω, root κιευ- : also εἴληφα (post. Hom., cp. ἔλλαβον, § 67.)

We must distinguish between (1) phonetic loss, as of σ or ϝ, and (2) *substitution* of initial ἐ- for the reduplication. The latter may be seen (*e. g.*) in ἐ-κτῆσθαι, which cannot be derived by phonetic decay from κε-κτῆσθαι. The distinction will serve to explain the difference between εἴμαρται, which is the proper representative of an original σέ-σμαρ-ται, and ἔμμορε, which follows the general tendency to double an initial μ, ν, λ or ρ after the augment.

(3) **Attic Reduplication**; as ὄπ-ωπα *I have seen*, ἐλ-ήλα-το *was driven*, ἐγρ-ήγορα *I am awake*.

The syllable which follows the Attic Reduplication may vary in quantity, as ἄρηρε, Fem. Part. ἀρᾰρυῖα; ἐρήριπε, Mid. ἐρέριπτο. Usually it is long, as ἐλήλαται, ἀρηρομένος, ἀκηχεμένος, ὀδώδυσται, ἠρήρειστο, ἐρήρισται (Hes. fr. 219), 3 Plur. ἀγηγέρατο, ἐρηρέδαται, ὀρωρέχαται. But it is short in ἀκάχημαι, ἀλάλημαι.

(4) Temporal Augment (see § 67): e.g. ἐφ-ῆπ-ται (ἅπτω), κατ-ῄκισ-ται (αἰκίζω), ἤσκη-ται (ἀσκέω), ἤσχυμμένος·

(5) In a few cases there is no Reduplication :—
οἶδα, for Ϝοῖδα, Sanscr. *veda.*
ἔρχ-αται are *shut in* (Ϝεργ-), Plpf. ἔρχ-ατο and (with augment) ἐέρχατο.
εἷμαι I *am clothed with* (Ϝεσ-), ἔσ-σαι, Plpf. ἔσ-σο, ἔσ-το and (with augment) ἔ-εσ-το, Du. ἔσ-θην, 3 Plur. εἵατο, Part. εἱμένος. Reduplication is not to be found in the ει of εἷμαι, εἱμένος, since these are for Ϝέσ-μαι, Ϝεσ-μένος (as εἷμα for Ϝέσμα). The 3 Sing. Pf. occurs once in Homer, in Od. 11. 191, where the best MSS. have ἧσται, others εἷσται and εἷται. The true form is probably ἔσται, preserved in an oracle in Hdt. 1. 47 (cp. ἔσσαι).

ἀμφιαχυῖα (Il. 2. 316) *crying around* can hardly be divided ἀμφ-ιαχυῖα, since the Stem ἰάχ- has initial Ϝ (§ 390). But a Stem Ϝηχ- (Ϝηχή *cry*), weak form Ϝάχ-, without Reduplication would give the Fem. Part. Ϝάχυῖα, whence ἀμφι-αχυῖα.

These examples make it doubtful whether initial Ϝ was originally reduplicated in the Pf. stem. In Sanscr. the roots which begin with *va* (answering to Gr. Ϝε-) take *u-*, as *uváca* (*vac-*, Gr. Ϝεπ-). Thus the Ϝε- of ϜέϜοικα, ϜεϜελμένος, &c. may be later, due to the analogy of other Perfects.

δέχ-αται *await* (Il. 12. 147), Plpf. ἐ-δέγμην (Od. 9. 513., 12. 230), Part. δέγμενος (Il. 2. 794., 9. 191., 18. 524., Od. 20. 385), with the same Pf. meaning that we have in δέδεγμαι (*await*, not *receive*, § 28) : while in other places ἔ-δεκτο, &c. are no less clearly Aorists. It seems that we must recognise a Pf. form *δέγμαι (Buttm. *G. G.* ii. 149., Curt. *Verb.* ii. 144), probably older than δέδεγμαι.

(6) The Reduplication in δει-δέχ-αται *they welcome*, seems to be that of the 'Intensive' forms, as in δει-δίσκομαι: see § 61. The form belongs to δείκ-νυμι, not δέχ-ομαι (see Veitch).

24.] In the 3 Plur.—

1. The long Stem with -ᾱσι (-α-ΝΤΙ) is comparatively rare :—
πεποίθᾱσι (Il. 4 325), ἑστήκᾱσι (Il. 4. 434, v. l. ἑστήκωσι), κατα-τεθνήκᾱσι (Il. 15. 664), τεθαρσήκασι (Il. 9. 420, 682), ἐγρηγόρθᾱσι (Il. 10. 419).

These forms evidently result from *generalising the Stem in* -α. So we have οἶδα-s (Od. 1. 337), οἶδᾰ-μεν, οἴδασι in Herodotus (and in Attic, see Veitch *s. v.*).

2. The final consonant of the Stem, if a labial or guttural, is aspirated before the -ᾰται, -ᾰτο of the Mid.; as ἐπι-τετράφ-αται *are entrusted*, τετράφ-ατο *were turned*, ἔρχ-αται (Ϝεργ-) *are shut in*, ὀρωρέχ-αται (ὀρέγ-ω) *are stretched out*, δειδέχ-αται (δείκ-νυμι)

welcome, κεκρύφ-αται (Hes. Op. 386). The aspirated forms of the Act., such as εἴληφα, κέκοφα, are entirely unknown to Homer.

It has been pointed out by Joh. Schmidt (*K. Z.* xxviii. 309) that the aspiration in these cases is due to the analogy of the forms in which a similar aspiration is caused by the ending : τετράφ-αται because of the 2 Plur. τέτραφ-θε, Inf. τετράφ-θαι. This explains why a final *dental* is not affected : for δ before θ passes into σ.

3. An anomalous ε for ῐ appears in δει-δέχ-αται (δε'.κ-νυμι, see § 23, 6), ἐρ-ηρέδ-αται (ἐρείδω, cp. ἠρισ-μένος Hesych.), and ἀκ-ηχέδ-αται (ἀκαχίζω).

4. A final δ of the Stem sometimes appears only in the 3 Plur. : as ἀκηχέδ-αται, ἐρράδ-αται (ῥαίνω, 1 Aor. ῥάσσατε), ἐληλάδ-ατο. But the last of these forms is doubtful; it occurs only in Od. 7. 86 χάλκεοι μὲν γὰρ τοῖχοι ἐληλάδατ', where some good MSS. have ἐρηρέδατ'.

25.] Interchange of Stems. The original variation between the Strong and the Weak form is disturbed by various causes.

1. The O-form of the Stem is found instead of the weak form in εἰλήλουθ-μεν *we are come* (for εἰλήλυθ-μεν), ἄωρτο *was hung aloft* (cp. ἄερ-θεν), ἐγρήγορθε *keep awake*, with the Inf. ἐγρήγορθαι (Il. 10. 67, cp. ἐγρηγορτί 10. 182); ἄνωγμεν (H. Apoll. 528); cp. ἔοιγμεν (in Tragedy), δέδοιγμεν (Et. M.).

2. The strong Stem of the Pres. takes the place of the weak Stem in συν-έρρηκται (Attic ἔρρωγα), λέλειπ-ται, ἐζευγ-μέναι, ἠρήρειστο (ἐρείδω); also in ἐερ-μένος, ἐελ-μένος, ἔρχ-αται (§ 22, 6). So κεχανδ-ώς (for κεχᾰδ-Fώς, χανδάνω).

ἔστητε, commonly read in Il. 4. 243, 246, is an error for ἔστητε : see § 76.

3. The influence of the Present may further be traced in the Perfects which take ῐ for ει (§ 22, 4), and ῡ, ευ for ου (§ 22, 5). So ἐδηδ-ώς (but ἐδωδή), προ-βέβουλα (βούλομαι).

In all these cases it is worth noticing that the change does not affect the metrical form of the word : e. g. we may read εἰλήλυθμεν, ἔρρακται, ἐζυγμέναι, ἠρήριστο, &c. and some of these may be the true Homeric forms.

The weak Stem appears to take the place of the O-form in δείδια (as to which see § 22, 4), and in ἀνα-βέβρῠχεν (Il. 17. 54) *gushes up*. For the latter Zenodotus read ἀναβέβροχεν—doubtless rightly, since this is the correct Pf. of ἀνα-βρέχω.

In Attic Reduplication the second vowel of a disyllabic Stem may be short, as in ἐλήλυθα (less common in Homer than εἰλήλουθα), and κατερήριπε (Il. 14. 55).

26.] The Perfect Participle was formed originally from the

weak Stem, but there are exceptions in Homer, due partly to
the ϝ of the Masc. and Neut. Suffix (-ϝώς, -υῖα, -ϝός), partly to
the general tendency to adopt the form of the Sing. Indic. as the
Stem. Thus the Homeric Pf. Part. is intermediate between the
primitive formation with the weak Stem (as in Sanscrit), and the
nearly uniform long Stem of Attic. In particular—

1. When the Ending -ώς (-ότος) follows a vowel, one or both
of the concurrent vowels may be long : μεμᾰ-ότε, μεμᾰ-ῶτε (both
for μεμᾰ-ϝότε). So γεγᾰ-ῶτας ; βεβᾰ-ῶτα ; πεφῠ-ῶτε ; κεκμη-ότας
and κεκμη-ῶτα ; τεθνη-ότος, τεθνη-ῶτα, also τεθνεῶτι ; πεπτη-ότα
and πεπτη-ῶτες (πτήσσω) : πεπτεῶτα (πίπτω). Both vowels are
short in ἑστᾰ-ότος.
ω also appears in τετρῑγ-ῶτας (Il. 2. 314), κεκληγ-ῶτας (Il. 16.
430). For the latter there is a v. l. κεκλήγοντας (see § 27) ; and
so perhaps we may read τετρίγοντας.

2. When -ώς (-ότος) follows a consonant, the Stem generally
takes the long form, as in the Sing. Ind. Act. : ἀρηρ-ώς, μεμηκώς, λεληκ-ώς, ἐοικ-ώς, πεποιθ-ώς, ἐοργ-ώς : except εἰδ-ώς (οἶδα),
εἰκ-ώς or ἔϊκ-ώς (Il. 21. 254), ἐᾱδ-ότα (ἀνδάνω, root σϝᾰδ-).

As these exceptions show, the strong form is not original : thus εἰδώς is for
ϝιδ-ϝώς, ἐᾱδότα for ἐσϝαδ-ϝότα. So we have μεμᾱώς (perhaps μεμανώς), not
μεμονώς. When ϝ was lost the original quantity of the *syllable* was preserved
by lengthening the vowel: and in determining the new long vowel the
analogy of the Sing. Ind. naturally had much influence.

3. A long vowel appears in the Feminine εἰδ-υῖα (Il. 17. 4,
elsewhere ἰδυῖα, Schol. Il. 20. 12), εἰοικ-υῖα (Il. 18. 418, elsewhere
ἔϊκ-υῖα)*, τεθνη-υῖα, πεπληγ-υῖα, τετρηχ-υῖα (as Plpf. τετρήχ-ει),
βεβρῑθ-υῖα, τετρῑγ-υῖα, πεφρῑκ-υῖα, κεκληγ-υῖα (Hes. Op. 449). Later
forms, ἀρηρ-υῖα (Hes. Th. 608), τεθηλ-υῖα (Hom. H. xlviii. 4).
The form βεβῶσα (Od. 20. 14) is an anomaly, apparently
formed from the Masc. βεβώς on the analogy of Participles in
-ούς, -οῦσα and -είς, -εῖσα.

4. The κ of the Indic. Act. (§ 22, 9) appears in τετυχη-κ-ώς
(Il. 17. 748), δεδαη-κ-ότες (Od. 2. 61), ἀδη-κ-ότες (Il. 10. 98,
312, 399, 471., Od. 12. 281), and βεβρω-κ-ώς (Il. 22. 94., Od.
22. 403). These instances are hardly sufficient to prove that
the form is Homeric, since we might read τετυχηώς, δεδαηότες,
&c. (like κεχαρηώς, κεκοτηώς, &c.) A form βεβρωώς is supported by Attic βεβρῶτες (Soph. Ant. 1022). τεθνη-κ-ώς (for

---

* The form ἐοικυῖα is found in—

καλὴ Κασσιέπεια θεοῖς δέμας ἐοικυῖα

quoted by Athenaeus xiv. p. 632 as an instance of a line defective in quantity.
It does not occur in the text of Homer, but seems to be a variant for Il. 8. 305—

καλὴ Καστιάνειρα δέμας ἔϊκυῖα θεῇσιν.

the Homeric τεθνη-ώς) is not earlier than Theognis. Similarly γεγον-ώς for γεγαώς first appears in H. Merc. 17.

5. The form πεφυζ-ότες *flying* (only in Il. 20 and 21), seems to be formed from the noun φύζα, without the intervention of any Tense-Stem. This account will apply also to—

κεκοπ-ώς (Il. 13. 60), from κόπ-ος *striking*.

δεδουπ-ότος (Il. 23. 679) *having fallen with a thud*. (The regular form would be δεδουπη-ώς, or rather perhaps ἐγδουπη-ώς, cp. ἐ-γδούπη-σαν.)

ἀρη-μένος, in which the α of ἄρη is retained, against analogy. It is in favour of this view that many Denominative Verbs form the Pf. Part. without the corresponding Indicative, as κεκοτη-ώς and the others given above (§ 22, 9). That is to say, the Participle is treated as a derivative *Adjective*, which may be formed independently of the corresponding verb.

27.] **Thematic Perfects.** By this term we understand the forms which arise when a Perfect is inflected like a Present in -ω. This change took place universally in Syracusan Doric, occasionally in other dialects. The chief Homeric instances are as follows:—

ἄνωγα : 3 Sing. ἀνώγει, which has a Present sense in several places (though more commonly it is a Plpf.), Dual ἀνώγε-τον ; also ἤνωγον, ἄνωγον, ἄνωγε, Opt. ἀνώγοιμι, Imper. ἀνωγέ-τω, ἀνώγε-τε. Such a form as ἤνωγον may be regarded either as a thematic Plpf. of ἄνωγα, or as Impf. of a new thematic Pres. ἀνώγω. This remark applies also to the next three cases.

γέγωνα : ἐγέγωνε, Inf. γεγωνέ-μεν (also γεγώνειν or γεγωνεῖν, Il. 12. 337).

πεπληγώς (only in the Part.): ἐπέπληγον and πέπληγον, Inf. πεπληγέ-μεν, Mid. πεπλήγε-το. Similarly—

μεμηκώς (Part.) : ἐμέμηκον.

κεκληγώς : Plur. κεκλήγοντες (Il. 12. 125., 16. 430., 17. 756, 759), perhaps τετρίγοντες (§ 26, 1), and κεκόπων (v. l. for κεκοπώς, Il. 13. 60., Od. 18. 335).

μέμνημαι : the Opt. μεμνέῳτο (Il. 23. 361) is apparently obtained by transference of quantity from a thematic μεμνή-οιτο ; but we may read μέμνητο, 3 Sing. of the regular Opt. μεμνή-μην (Il. 24. 745). For this, again, some MSS. have μεμνοίμην, as if from *μέμνο-μαι. The 2 Sing. Ind. μέμνη (Il. 15. 18) also points to μέμνομαι, but we may read μέμνη' (i. e. μέμνηαι).

μέμβλε-ται (Il. 19. 343) and μέμβλε-το (μέλ-ω) may be variously explained. Perhaps μεμελ-, the short Stem answering to μέμηλε, became by metathesis μεμλε-, μεμβλε- : cp. ἤμβροτον for ἤμαρτον.

ὀρώρε-ται (Od. 19. 377, 524, Subj. ὀρώρη-ται Il. 13. 271).

ἐδήδε-ται (v. l. in Od. 22. 56, see § 25, 3). We may add the

Pluperfects δείδιε *feared*, ἀνήνοθεν (Il. 11. 266), ἐπ-ενήνοθεν (Il. 2. 219., 10. 134): perhaps also the Optatives in -οιμι, -οις, &c. viz. βεβρώθ-οις (Il. 4. 35), βεβλήκοι (Il. 8. 270), πεφεύγοι (Il. 21. 609), ἰλήκοι (H. Apoll. 165); see § 83.

28.] Meaning of the Perfect. The Perfect denotes a lasting condition or attitude (ἕξις). If we compare the meaning of any Perfect with that of the corresponding Aorist or Present, we shall usually find that the Perfect denotes a permanent *state*, the Aor. or Pres. an *action* which brings about or constitutes that state. Thus, δαίω *I kindle*, δέδηε *blazes*, or (better) *is ablaze*; κύθε *hid*, κέκευθε *has in hiding*; ὄρ-νυ-ται *bestirs himself*, ὄρωρε *is astir*; ὤλε-το *was lost*, ὄλωλε *is undone*; ἤραρε *made to fit*, ἄρηρε *fits* (Intrans.); ταράσσω *I disturb*, τετρήχει *was in disorder*; μείρο-μαι *I divide*, ἔμμορε *has for his share*; ῥύομαι *I save, shelter*, εἰρύ-αται *keep safe*; τεύχω *I make*, τέ-τυκ-ται *is by making* (not *has been made*); ἔφυ *grew*, πέφυκε *is by growth*.

Thus the so-called *Perfecta praesentia*, βέβηκα, ἕστηκα, γέγηθα, μέμνημαι, πέποιθα, οἶδα, ἔοικα, κέκτημαι, &c., are merely the commonest instances of the rule.

Note the large number of Homeric Perfects denoting attitude, temper, &c. Besides those already mentioned we have—παρ-μέμβλωκε *is posted beside*, δέδορκε *is gazing*, ἔρριγε *shudders*, τέτηκα *I am wasting*, μέμυκε *is closed* (of wounds), δεδάκρυσαι *art in tears*, δέδεξο *be in waiting*, ὀρωρέχατο *were on the stretch*, πεποτή-αται *are on the wing*, κέκμηκα *I am weary*, προβέβουλα *I prefer*, δείδια *I fear*, ἔολπα *I hope*, τέθηπα *I am in amazement*, τέτληκα-s *thou hast heart*, πέπνυται *has his senses*, δειδέχ-αται *welcome* (in the *attitude* of holding out the hand, while δεικνύ-μενος denotes the *action*), together with many Participles—κεχηνώς *agape*, κεκαφηώς *panting*, πεπτηώς *cowering*, συν-οχωκότε *bent together*, κεκοτηώς *in wrath*, τετιηώς *vexed*, ἀδηκώς *disgusted*, μεμηλώς *in thought*, πεφυλαγμένος *on the watch*, δεδραγμένος *clutching*, λελιη-μένος *eager*, κεχολωμένος *enraged*, &c. So in later Greek; ἐξην-θηκός (Thuc. 2. 49) *in eruption*, ἐσπουδασμένος *in haste*.

Verbs expressing sustained sounds, esp. cries of animals, are usually in the Perfect: γέγωνε *shouts*, βέβρυχε *roars*, κεκληγώς, λεληκώς, μεμηκώς, μεμυκώς, τετριγώς, ἀμφιαχυῖα. So in Attic, βοῶν καὶ κεκραγώς (Dem.).

With Verbs of *striking* the Perfect seems to express con-tinuance, and so completeness: κεκοπώς, πεπληγώς, βεβολή-ατο *was tossed about*, βεβλήκει *made his hit*, ἠρήρειστο *was driven home*. (Cp. Ar. Av. 1350 ὃς ἂν πεπλήγῃ τὸν πατέρα νεοττὸς ὤν.)

Note the number of Imperatives of the Perfect in Homer: τέτλαθι, μέματε, δέδεξο, τέθναθι, δείδιθι, κέκλυθι, ἄνωχθι; Mid. τετύχθω *let it be ordered*, τετράφθω *let him keep himself turned*.

(In later Greek this use seems to be confined to the Middle : μὴ πεφόβησθε *do not be in alarm*, πέπαυσο *keep silence*.)

The number of Homeric Perfects which can be rendered by *have* is comparatively small. The chief instances in the Active are, ἔοργα-s *thou hast done*, ὄπωπα *I have seen*, λέλοιπε *has left*, πέπασθε *ye have suffered*, ἐδηδ-ώs, βεβρωκ-ώs *having eaten ;* they are somewhat commoner in the Middle. Yet in the use of these Perfects (and probably in the Perfect of every period of Greek) we always find some *continuing result* implied. There is nothing in Greek like the Latin idiom *fuit Ilium* (=*Ilium is no longer*), *vixi* (=*I have done with living*), &c.

The Intransitive meaning prevails in the Perfect, so that the Act. is hardly distinguishable from the Mid.: cp. τέτευχε and τέτυκται, πεφευγώς and πεφυγμένος, γέγονα and γεγένη-μαι. Compare also the Pf. Act. with the Pres. Mid. in such instances as ὄλωλα and ὄλλυμαι, πέποιθα and πείθομαι, βέβουλα and βούλομαι, ἔολπα and ἔλπομαι. The forms τέτροφα, ἔφθορα are Intrans. in Homer, but Trans. in Attic : and an Intrans. or almost Passive meaning is conspicuous in the Homeric group of Participles κεκοτηώς *enraged*, τετιηώς (=τετιη-μένος) *vexed*, κεκορηώς (=κεκορη-μένος) *satiated*, βεβαρηώς *heavy*, κεχαρηώς *rejoicing*, κεκαφηώς *panting* (§ 22, 9, *b*).

Thematic Tenses.

29.] The simple Thematic Present. The Stems which fall under this description generally contain the same vowels (or diphthongs) as the strong Stem of the Non-Thematic Present (§§ 6, 12). They may be classed according to the stem-vowel, as follows :—

(1) η, Ionic for ᾱ : λήθ-ε-το *forgot*, τήκομαι *I waste away*, θήγει *sharpens*, σήπεται *is rotted*, κήδει *vexes*.

η : ἀρήγει *helps*, λήγει *ceases*, μήδεται *devises*. The η of these Stems is 'pan-Hellenic,' *i. e.* answers to η, not ᾱ, in other dialects.

(2) ει : εἴδ-ε-ται *seems*, εἴκε *yield*, λείβειν *to pour*, λείπει *leaves*, πείθω *I persuade*, στεῖβον *trod*, στείχειν *to march*, πείκετε *comb*, εἴβει *drops*, φείδεο *spare*, ἄειδε *sing*, ἄλειφε *anointed*, ἄμειβε *exchanged*, ἐρεικόμενος *torn*, ἔρειδε *stayed*, ἔρειπε *knocked down*, νειφέμεν *to snow* (so to be read instead of νῑφέμεν in Il. 12. 280). For ἵκω *I come* the Doric form is εἴκω.

(3) ευ : φεύγ-ω *I fly*, πεύθομαι *I learn* (by hearing), ἐρεύγεται *belches*, ἐρεύθων *reddening*, σπεύδειν *to hasten*, ψεύδονται *play false*, εὐόμενοι *being singed*, ἐσσεύοντο *were urged on*, νεῦον *nodded*, δεύομαι *I need ;* also, with loss of υ before the Thematic vowel, ἔν-νεον *swam* (νεϝ-ον), θέει *runs*, πλέων *sailing*, πνέει *breathes*, ῥέει *flows*, χέει *pours*, κλέομαι *I am famed*.

The forms with ει for ε, as θεί-ειν, πλείειν, πνείων, ἐγ-χείῃ, (for θέ-ειν, &c.) should probably be written with ευ, θεύ-ειν, πλεύ-ειν, &c. See Appendix C.

(4) ερ (ρε) : δέρκ-ο-μαι *I behold*, τέρπειν *to rejoice*, πέρθετο *was sacked*, ἐέργει *confines*, τέρσεται *is dried*, ἕρπει *creeps*, σπέρχουσι *urge*, ἔρρων *sweeping*, δέρον *flayed*, θέρεσθαι *to be warmed*, ῥέπε *sank downwards*, ἔπρεπε *shone*, τρέπε *turned*, τρέφει *nurtures*, στρέφει *twists*.

ελ : ἔλπ-ο-μαι *I hope*, μέλπεσθαι *to play*, ἕλκει *draws*, ἄμελγε *milked*, κέλομαι *I command*, πέλει *turns*, ἐθέλω *I am willing*.

ρι from ερ appears in τρῖβ-έμεναι *to rub* (Lat. ter-o), χρῖ-ον *anointed* (Sanscr. gharsh-ati), βρῖθον *were heavy*.

ιρ (ρῐ, ρῑ) for ŗ appears in certain combinations : κίρ-νημι (§ 17), κρίνω, κρῐ-τός (cerno, certus), ῥίζα for ϝρδ-ϳα, δρί-ον for δρϝ-ον (δρῦ-s) : κρῑός (Lat. cervus), κριθή for κρσ-θη, hordeum, O. Germ. gersta (Meyer, G. G. p. 35 : Thurneysen, K. Z. xxx. 352).

(5) εν : πέν-ε-σθαι *to labour*, στένει *groans*, μένω *I wait*, φθέγγεο *call out*, ἐλέγχει *reproves*, σπένδων *making libation*.

εμ : πέμπω *I send*, ἐπι-μέμφομαι *I blame*, τέμει (Il. 13. 707) *cuts*, δέμον *built*, βρέμει *roars*, νέμει *apportions*, ἔ-τρεμε *trembled*.

(6) ε : λέγ-ε *told*, ἔχ-ω *I have*, ἔδει *eats*, ἕπεται *follows*, πέτεται *flies*, δέχομαι *I receive*, ἔνν-επε *say*, ἔ-στεφε *set as a covering* ; with loss of σ, τρεῖ (τρέει, for τρεσ-ει, cp. ἄ-τρεσ-τος) *trembles*, ζεῖ (ζέει) *boils*, νέομαι (cp. νόσ-τος) *I return*.

The Thematic forms of εἰμί, viz. ἔον, Opt. ἔοι, Part. ἐών, belong to this head, since ἐσ- is the *strong* stem. So too κέονται (for κει-ονται), 3 Plur. of κεῖ-μαι.

ω (instead of η) appears in τρώγ-ειν *to gnaw* (τρἄγ-), διώκειν *to chase*. Both forms appear to be derivative (with suffixed γ, κ, § 45) : τρώ-γω may be connected with τορ-εῖν (§ 31, 4). διώ-κω is related to δίε-μαι (§ 11) : it has been supposed to be a Thematic Perfect, with loss of reduplication (*i.e.* from *δε-δίω-κα).

ῡ appears in τρύχ-ουσι *waste away*, ἀνα-ψύχ-ειν *to cool*, ἐρύκ-ει *restrains*. These also are derivative (§ 45).

ο appears in λόε *washed* (Od. 10. 361, H. Apoll. 120), Inf. λοῦσθαι (Od. 6. 216). λο- is for λοϝ-, cp. Lat. lav-ere. A Pres. *λούω is inferred from the form λούεσθαι (Il. 6. 508 = 15. 265), for which we may read λοέεσθαι (from the derivative Pres. λοέω).

30.] Thematic Present with weak Stem.

Of this formation there are a few instances : ἄγ-ω *I drive*, *bring* (Aor. ἤγ-ἄγον), ἄχομαι *I am vexed* (Aor. ἤκ-ἄχε), μάχονται *fight*, βλάβεται *fails*, breaks down, βόλεται *wishes*, ὄρονται *watch*, ὄθομαι *I care*, ἀίεις *dost hear*, ἀπο-δρύφοι (Opt.) *tear off*, ἄρχει *leads*, ἄγχε *choked* ; also the Thematic forms of εἶμι, viz. Impf. ἤ-ϊον, Opt. ἴοι, Part. ἰών.

Note that γράφω is not found in Homer except in the Aor. ἔγραψα.

The forms βόλεται (Il. 11. 319), ἐβόλοντο (Od. 1. 234), βόλεσθε (Od. 16. 387) were restored by Wolf: see Buttmann's Lexil. s. v. The form βλάβεται (Il. 19. 82, 166, Od. 13. 34) occurs in gnomic passages only, where an Aorist would be equally in place (§ 78, 2).

ὄρονται (Od. 14. 104), ὄροντο (Od. 3. 471) occur in the phrase ἐπὶ δ' ἀνέρες ἐσθλοὶ ὄρονται, where ἐπὶ ὄρονται seems to be = ' act as ἐπίουροι,' 'are in charge.' ἀΐω only occurs as a Pres. in the phrase οὐκ ἀΐεις; = have you not heard ? Elsewhere ἄϊον is used as .in Aorist (Schulze, K. Z. xxix. 249). A Pres. δρύφω cannot be inferred with certainty from the Opt. ἀποδρύφοι (Il. 23. 187., 24. 21), which may be an Aorist.

The forms ἄρχω, ἄγχω are difficult because original ἀρχ-, ἀγχ- would shorten the vowel (before a semi-vowel and mute), and consequently the Stem would be indistinguishable from original ἀρχ-, ἀγχ-. That in ἀρχ-ω the Stem is *weak* may be inferred from the Nouns ἀρχ-ός, ἀρχ-ή (§ 109) : the O-form may be found in ὄρχαμος, the strong form possibly in ἔρχ-ομαι. Again ἀγχ-ω may be identified with Sanscr. áh-ati (for ńgh-ati) : the strong form being ἐγχ- in ἔγχ-ελυς (De Saussure, Mém. p. 276 ff.).

31.] The Thematic Aorist. The Verb-Stem is in the weak form : we may distinguish the following groups :—

(1) With ἄ as Stem vowel (the strong Stem with ā or η) : λάθε *was unseen by*, λάκε *crackled*, ἔλ-λαβε *took*, εὔαδε (for ἔ-σϝᾰδε) *pleased*, μακών *bellowing*, φάγον *ate*, δι-έ-τμαγον (τμήγω) *parted*, ἀν-έ-κραγον *cried aloud* (Attic Pf. κέκρᾱγα), ἄρετο *gained*, ἄληται (Subj.) *shall leap*, ἔ-χραε *assailed* (χρᾶυ-), δάηται (Subj.) *shall be burned* (δᾰυ-), φάε *shone* (φᾶυ-, cp. πιφαύσκω), λάε *seized, pinned* (λᾶυ-, cp. ἀπο-λαύω), ἄλθετο *was healed*, ἤλφον (Opt. ἄλφοι) *earned*, ἤντετο *met* (Part. ἀντ-όμενος).

The forms φάε (Od. 14. 502) and λάε, Part. λάων (Od. 19. 229, 230) are placed here provisionally. Each occurs once, in a context which does not decide between Aor. and Impf.

The existence of an Aor. ἔ-ϝαχ-ον has been made probable by W. Schulze (K. Z. xxix. 230). He shows that the form ἴαχον, generally taken as the Impf. of ἰάχω (§ 35), is an Aor. in meaning, and constantly occurs after elision (μέγ' ἴαχον, ἐπὶ δ' ἴαχον, ἐπ-ίαχον). Consequently we can always read ϝάχον (μέγα ϝάχον, ἐπὶ δὲ ϝάχον, ἐπί-ϝαχον), or with augment εὔαχον (cp. εὔαδε for ἔ-ϝαδε). In Il. 20. 62 καὶ ἴαχε would be read καὶ εὔαχε. The alternative is to suppose that ἐ-ϝίϝαχον became εἴαχον by loss of ϝ and contraction (Wackernagel, K. Z. xxv. 279): but contraction in such a case is very rare in Homer, and the Aor. *meaning* of ἴαχον has to be accounted for. On the other hand if we accept Schulze's view we have still to admit a Pres. (or Aor. ?) Participle ἰάχων (ϝιϝάχων).

(2) With ε (strong η) : ἔθων *doing as he is wont* (cp. ἤθ-ος for σϝηθ-ος), perhaps μέδ-οντο *bethought them* (μήδ-ομαι).

The forms μέδοντο, &c. are generally referred to a Verb μέδο-μαι : but no such Present is found, and the other Moods—Subj. Opt. Imper. and Inf.—always admit the Aor. meaning. As to ἔθων see § 243, 1. If an Aor. it should be accented ἐθών.

(3) With ι (strong ει): ἔ-στίχ-ον (στείχω) *marched*, ἐ-πίθοντο *obeyed*, ἱκέσθαι *to come to*, λιτέσθαι *to entreat*, ἤριπε (ἐρείπω) *fell down*, ἤρικε (ἐρείκω) *was torn*, ἤλιτεν *offended* (Mid. ἀλιτέσθαι), ἄϊον *heard*, δίε *feared* (δϝι-), δίον *ran*, ἔ-κιον *moved*, ἔ-πιον *drank*, ὄλισθε *slipped*, κρίκε *cracked*.

With αι, αἰθόμενον *burning*, αἴδετο *felt shame* (§ 32, 2); ἔχραισμε *availed* (§ 32, 3).

δίον *I ran* (Il. 22. 251) is not to be connected with δίε *feared*, but with ἐν-δίε-σαν, δίε-νται *chase*, of which we have the Thematic Subj. δίωμαι, Opt. δίοιτο, Inf. δίεσθαι. That they are Aorists appears (e.g.) from Il. 16. 246 ἐπεί κε δίηται *when he shall have chased*.

ἔκιον is probably an Aor., since *κίω does not occur. The accentuation of the Part. κιών is in favour of this, but not decisively (cp. ἐών, ἰών).

(4) With υ (strong ευ): κύθε *hid*, φύγον *fled*, τύχε *hit upon*, πυθόμην *I heard tell*, ἔστυγον *felt disgust*, ἔκτυπε *sounded*, ἤρυγε *bellowed*, ἤλυθον *I came*, ἔκλυον *heard*, ἄμ-πνυε *recovered breath*.

With αυ, αὖε *shouted*, αὔῃ (Subj.) *kindle*, ἐπ-αυρεῖν *to gain from*, *enjoy*. With ευ, εὗρε *found*.

ἔκλυον is clearly an Aor. in Homer. The Pres. κλύω, which occurs in Hesiod (Op. 726 οὐ γὰρ τοί γε κλύουσιν) and in Attic poets, is perhaps only a mistaken imitation of the Homeric style.

(5) With ἄρ, ρᾰ, ρ (strong ερ, ρε): ἐ-πράθ-ο-μεν (πέρθ-ω) *we sacked*, κατ-έδραθον *went to sleep*, ἔ-δρακον (δέρκομαι) *looked*, ἔδραμον (δρόμος) *ran*, ἔ-τραπον *turned*, ἔτραφε (τρέφω) *was nurtured*, ταρπώμεθα (τέρπω) *let us take our pleasure*, ἔβραχε *rattled*, ἄμαρτε (also ἤμβροτε) *missed*, ἔπταρε *sneezed*, ἔγρ-ετο (ἐγερ-) *was roused*, ἀγρόμενοι (ἀγερ-) *assembled* (§ 33).

With ἄλ, λ (strong ελ): ἔ-βαλ-ον (βέλ-ος), ἔ-πλ-εν, ἔπλετο *turned*, *came to be* (§ 33).

With ορ, ολ: ἔ-πορ-ον *furnished*, ἔθορε *leaped*, ἔτορε *pierced*, ὦρετο *was stirred up*, ἔκ-μολ-ε *came out*, ὀλέσθαι *to perish*.

The ε of the strong Stem appears in εἷλον, ἕλ-ον *took*, ἑρ-έσθαι *to ask* (cp. § 22, 6).

It will be seen that ἄρ, ρᾰ, ἄλ are generally placed between consonants, where ρ, λ would be unpronounceable. The only exceptions are, ἔπταρον and ἔβαλον. On the other hand ορ, ολ only appear before a vowel.

(6) With ᾰ (strong εν, εμ): ἔ-παθ-ον (πένθ-ος) *suffered*, μάθ-ον *learned*, ἔλαχον *obtained as share*, ἔχαδε (Fut. χείσομαι) *contained*, δακέειν *to bite*, δάηται *shall learn* (δἄσ-, strong form *δενσ-, cp. δέδαεν, § 36, 5).

ἄν, ἄμ (before a vowel): ἔ-κταν-ον *killed*, ἔθανε *died*, ἔ-καμ-ον *wearied*, τάμε *cut* (cp. ἐ-δάμ-η, § 42).

εν appears in γεν-έσθαι *to become*.

(7) With loss of ε: ἔ-σχ-ον *held* (ἔχ-ω for σέχ-ω), ἔσπετο *followed*, Inf. ἐπι-σπέσθαι (ἔπομαι for σεπ-ομαι), ἐπι-πτέσθαι (πετ-) *to fly over*, ἕζετο *sat* (for ἐ-σδ-ετο, Ahrens, *Gr. F.* § 95).

The ε is retained in ἔ-τεκ-ον *brought forth*, ἀπ-εχθ-έσθαι *to incur hatred*, ἔσχεθον *held* (?). In these cases loss of ε is phonetically impossible.

ἀπ-ήχθε-το is an Aor. in Homer (the Pres. being ἀπ-εχθάνο-μαι), although a Present ἔχθο-μαι is found in Attic. The simple ἤχθετο (Od. 14. 366, ἔχθεσθαι Od. 4. 756, ἐχθόμενος Od. 4. 502) is called Impf. by Veitch; but the meaning in the three places seems to be the same as in ἀπ-ήχθετο—not *was hateful*, but *came to be hated*.

The only ground for taking ἔσχεθον to be an Aor. is the Inf. σχεθέειν (Il. 23. 466, Od. 5. 320). Possibly this may be a Pres. Inf. in -εεν (§ 85, 2), preserved owing to the impossibility of σχίθειν in the hexameter.

32.] The foregoing list calls for some further remarks.

1. Comparing the Second Aorists of later Greek, we are struck by the number of instances in Homer in which the Thematic ε or ο follows another vowel.

In ἔχραε, φάε, λάε, δάηται (for ἔ-χραϝ-ε, φάϝ-ε, λάϝ-ε, δάϝ-ηται) the hiatus is due to the loss of ϝ. So in λύε (for λόϝε). Similarly σ is lost in δάηται (δάσ-) *shall learn*.

In several cases the Thematic inflexion is found intermingled with Non-thematic forms. Thus we have ἔκλυον, Imper. κλῦθι; ἄμ-πνυε, Mid. ἄμ-πνῦ-το; ἔπιον, Imper. πῖθι (Ar. Vesp. 1489); δίον *I ran*, ἐν-δίε-σαν *chased* (δίη-μι). The presumption is that the Non-thematic forms are older, the others being derived from them as ἔον *I was* and ἤιον *I went* from corresponding parts of εἰμί, εἶμι (cp. § 18). Similarly we may account for ἔκιον (κι- in Pres. κί-νυμαι), and perhaps δίε *feared*, ἄιον *heard*.

2. Another characteristic group is formed by the Aorist Stems in which we find initial α either entering into a diphthong (αἰ-, αὐ-) or followed by a double consonant: viz. αἰθ-, αἰδ-, αὐ- (in αὖε), αὐ- (in αὔη *kindle*), αὐρ-, ἀλθ-, ἀλφ-, ἀντ-. Some of these which are usually counted as Present Stems require separate notice:—

αἰθ- occurs in Homer only in the Part. αἰθόμενος *burning*: as to the adjectival use of Participles see § 244. The Stem is found in the Sanscr. *idh-ati burns*.

αἰδ- occurs in the Indic. αἴδετο, Imper. αἴδεο, Part. αἰδόμενος; the corresponding Pres. is always αἰδέομαι.

αὖε *shouted* may always be an Aor. (Il. 11. 461., 13. 477., 20.

48, 51). We may identify this αὐ- with *u* in Sanscr. *u-noti calls*.
The ἀ- is a distinct syllable in the Aor. αὖ-σε, cp. αὐτή.
αὔῃ (Od. 5. 490, v. l. αὔοι) makes good sense as an Aor., expressing the *act* of kindling. The Stem is weak (αὐσ- = Sanscr.
ush- in *ush-ás*, Æol. αὔως); the strong form appears in εὔ-ω,
Lat. *uro*.

ἐπ-αυρεῖν exhibits the Thematic form answering to ἀπ-ηύρα,
ἀπο-υράς (§ 13).

ἄλθ-ετο, found only in Il. 5. 417, is clearly an Aor.

ἀλφ- occurs in ἦλφον, Opt. ἄλφοι, with Aor. meaning.

ἀντ- in ἤντετο, συν-αντέσθην, Inf. ἄντεσθαι, Part. ἀντόμενος,
always with clear Aor. meaning. Accordingly ἄντεσθαι in Il. 15.
698 (the only place where it occurs) was accented by Tyrannio
ἀντέσθαι.

The ἀ- of αἰθ-, αὐσ-, &c. is discussed by De Saussure along with that of ἀρχ-,
ἀγχ- in a passage quoted above (§ 30 *note*). He regards it as 'prothetic,' so
that the Stems in which it appears are generally in the *weak* form. The -ὐ-
of αὐ- may answer to either ϝε or ευ in the strong form; thus αὐδ-ή : ἀϝειδ-ω
= αὔξω : ἀϝέξ-ω (Sanscr. *vaksh*-) = αὐχ-ή : εὔχ-ομαι, perhaps ἐπ-αυρεῖν : εὐρ-εῖν.
A similar ἀ- appears in ἀ-μείβω, ἀ-μέλγω, ἀείρω ; perhaps in ἀ-λιτέσθαι, ἀ-μαρτεῖν
(but in these it may be originally significant, *infra*, 3).

In ἀλθ-, ἀλφ-, ἀντ- the form is weak (perhaps ἀλθ- is to a strong ἀλεθ- as
ἄλγ-ος : ἀλέγ-ω or ἀλκ-ή : ἀλεκ- in ἀλέξω), or else the strong and weak forms
coincided (as in ἀρχ-, ἀγχ-, § 30).

It appears then that in the Tenses with which we are dealing the strong
Stem has generally disappeared, and the Present has been derived afresh from
the weak Stem, by means of one of the various Suffixes. Thus we have αἰδ-,
Pres. αἰδ-έομαι ; αὖε, Pres. αὔτέω ; αὐρ-, Pres. ἐπ-αυρ-ίσκω ; ἀντ-, Pres. ἀντιάω,
ἀντιάζω. The process has been the same in ἀλιτ-έσθαι and Pres. ἀλιτ-αίνω,
ἀμαρτ-εῖν and ἀμαρτ-άνω, εὐρ-εῖν and εὑρ-ίσκω, ἐχθέσθαι and ἀπ-εχθ-άνομαι, ὄλισθε
and ὀλισθ-άνω, also in Attic αἰσθ-έσθαι and αἰσθ-άνομαι. The last is interesting
as the only post-Homeric Second Aorist which is used in good Attic prose.

3. A few Thematic Aorists seem to be formed from the Stems
of Nouns of the O-declension. Thus ἔχραισμε *availed* is generally
derived from χρήσιμος *useful* (Curt. *Verb.* ii. 13). So, according
to Curtius, θέρμε-τε *warm ye*, θέρμε-το *grew warm*, from θερμός ;
ὅπλε-σθαι (Il. 19. 172., 23. 159) *to get ready*, from ὅπλον (ὁπλέ-ω);
γόον (Il. 6. 500) *bewailed*, from γόος (γο-άω); ἀμαρτ-εῖν *to miss*,
from ἀ-μαρ-το- *without part in*.

Some at least of these instances may be otherwise explained. For ὅπλεσθαι
we may read ὁπλεῖσθαι (the uncontracted ὁπλέεσθαι is impossible in the
hexameter). γόον in Il. 6. 500 αἱ μὲν ἔτι ζωὸν γόον Ἕκτορα κ. τ. λ. makes better
sense as an Impf. : Fick reads γόαν, 3 Plur. of an 'Æolic' γόημι. Possibly γόον
is for γόεον by hyphaeresis (§ 105, 4).

33.] In several cases it is difficult to say whether loss of ε is
characteristic of an Aor. Stem, or is merely phonetic, due to

'syncope.' Thus we have ἀγέροντο, Part. ἀγρόμενοι: ὤφελον *ought* and the Attic ὦφλον *owed*: πέλω and the syncopated forms ἔπλεν, ἔπλετο, Part. ἐπιπλόμενος, &c. (not ἔπελεν, ἐπέλετο, &c. in Homer).

ἀγέροντο *were assembled*, Inf. ἀγέρεσθαι (so accented in MSS.) imply a Pres. ἀγέρω; but the Part. ἀγρ-όμενοι seems to be an Aor. The ε is only lost in the Part., whereas in the undoubted Aor. ἔγρ-ετο the form ἐγερ- never occurs (Opt. ἔγροιτο, Inf. ἔγρεσθαι). In Il. 7. 434., 24. 789 ἀμφὶ πυρὴν . . . ἔγρετο λαός Cobet (*Misc. Crit.* p. 415) proposed to read ἤγρετο, from ἀγερ-. The emendation gives a good sense, but is not absolutely necessary.

ὤφελον *ought* (= *would that*) bears a different sense from the Aor. ὦφλον, but is indistinguishable from the Impf. ὤφελλον (Od. 8. 312 τὼ μὴ γείνασθαι ὄφελλον, so Il. 7. 390., 24. 764, Od. 14. 68., 18. 401). Hence ὤφελον is probably an older form of the Imperfect which has survived in this particular use.

ἔπλεν, ἔπλε-το, &c. must be Aorists, since—

(1) ἔπλετο occurs in the 'gnomic' use, e.g.—

Il. 2. 480 ἠΰτε βοῦς ἀγέληφι μέγ' ἔξοχος ἔπλετο πάντων·

and so in Il. 24. 94, Od. 7. 217. This use is not found with the Impf.

(2) ἔπλετο with the meaning of a Present can only be explained as an Aor. = the English Pf., *has turned out, has come to be*, (and so *is*): see § 78, and cp. Il. 12. 271 νῦν ἔπλετο ἔργον ἁπάντων *now it has become*: with another Aor. similarly used, Il. 15. 227 πολὺ κέρδιον ἔπλετο, ὅτι ὑπόειξεν *it is better that he has yielded*: also Il. 6. 434., 7. 31., 8. 552., 14. 337., 19. 57, Od. 20. 304, &c.

The Part. occurs in ἐπι-πλόμενον ἔτος (Od.) and περι-πλομένων ἐνιαυτῶν, with much the same force as the Pres. Part. in the equivalent phrase περιτελλομένων ἐνιαυτῶν. But, as we shall see, an Aor. Part. may have the meaning of an *adjective* (§ 244): cp. *volvenda dies*.

34.] Comparison of the Thematic 'Strong' Aorists found in Homer with those of other periods of Greek brings out strikingly the relation between the Homeric and the later dialect.

It may be assumed that the Strong Aorists, like the Strong Preterites in English, were a diminishing class, never added to (except by learned imitators of the Epic style), and gradually superseded by the more convenient forms in -σα. Hence the comparative frequency of these Aorists in an author indicates either an early date or (at least) the use of an archaic style.

Curtius enumerates altogether 117 Strong Aorists, of which 84 are found in Homer. Of these 84, again, about 30 occur also in prose, while as many more are used in the later poetical style (ἔλακον, ἔκιον, ἔκλυον, μολεῖν, πορεῖν, &c.). Of the non-Homeric examples only one, viz. αἰσθέσθαι, belongs to the language of prose; about 15 are found in good early poetry (e.g. δικεῖν, θιγεῖν, κανεῖν, βλαστεῖν, in Attic dramatists); most of the others are evidently figments of learned poets, imitated from actual Homeric forms, e.g. ἔδαεν (from Homeric δέδαεν), ἔμμορον (from μόρος and the Homeric Pf. ἔμμορε), ἔδουπε.

These facts seem to show both the high antiquity of the Homeric language and the position which it held as the chief though not the only source of the poetical vocabulary of historical times.

35.] The Reduplicated Thematic Present. This formation appears in a few instances only :—

μί-μν-ετε *await* (μέν-ω).

πίπτε *fell* (πετ-).

ἴσχει *holds*, for *σι-σχ-ει, from *σεχ-.

ἴζει *sits*, for *σι-σδ-ει, from σεδ-.

γίγνεται *becomes* (γεν-).

τίκτω, for τι-τκ-ω, from τεκ-.

νίσομαι *I go, pass*, for νι-νσ-ομαι, or νι-νσ-ι̯ο-μαι, from νεσ- : related to νέομαι (§ 29, 6) as ἴσχω to ἔχω.

δίζε *sought* (Thematic form answering to δίζη-μαι, § 16).

ἰαύ-εις *sleepest* (Aor. ἄεσα, for ἀϝε-σα, *I slept*, cp. αὔξω and ἀέξω).

In this group of Verbs the Root is in the weak form; the vowel of the reduplication is always ι.

ἰάχω (for ϝι-ϝάχω) is generally placed in this class. The Pres. Indic. does not occur, and the past Tense ἴαχον is an Aor. in Il. 5. 860., 14. 148., 18. 219 ὅτε τ' ἴαχε σάλπιγξ (§ 79), and *may* always be so in Homer. As to its original form see § 31, 1, *note*. Thus the evidence for ἰάχω is reduced to the Part. ἰάχων, and that is not used in a way that is decisive between the Pres. and the Aor.

36.] The Reduplicated Aorist. These Tenses are formed with the weak Stem, and either (1) reduplication of an initial consonant with ε, or (2) Attic Reduplication. The following are the chief examples :—

(1) ᾰ : ἐκ-λέλαθ-ον *made to forget*, λελαβέσθαι *to seize*, κεκαδών *severing*, κεκάδοντο *yielded*, κεχάροντο *rejoiced*, ἀμ-πεπαλών *brandishing on high*, τεταγών *grasping*, ἤγ-αγ-ον *led*, ἐξ-ήπαφε *deceived*, ἤραρε *fitted*, ἤκαχε *vexed*.

(2) ῐ : πεπίθ-οιμεν *may persuade*, πεφιδέσθαι *to spare*.

(3) ῠ : τετύκ-οντο *made for themselves*, πεπύθοιτο *may hear by report*, κεκύθωσι *shall hide*.

(4) ᾰρ (ρᾰ), ᾰλ, λ : τετάρπ-ετο *was pleased*, πέφραδε *showed forth*, ἀλ-αλκε *warded off*, ἐ-κέ-κλ-ετο *shouted* (κελ-).

(5) ᾰ, ν (for εν) : λελάχ-ητε (Subj.) *make to share*, δέδαεν *taught* (cp. § 31, 5); ἔ-πε-φν-ε *slew* (cp. πέ-φᾰ-ται *is slain*).

(6) Loss of ε : ἔ-τε-τμε *found, caught* (τεμ-?); ἔειπον *said* (perhaps for ἐ-ϝε-ϝεπ-ον)* ; also ἔσπετο *followed*, if it is taken to be for σέσπε-το.

---

* The difficulty in the way of this explanation is that in the old Attic inscriptions which distinguish the original diphthong ει (written EI) from the sound arising from contraction or 'compensatory' lengthening (written E), the word εἶπε is always written with EI (Cauer in *Curt. Stud.* viii. 257). In Sanscr. the corresponding form is *avocam*, for *a-va-vac-am* (*văc* becoming *uc*). Answering to this we expect in Greek ἔευπον (Vogrinz, *Gr. d. hom. Dial.* p. 123).

The forms which point to *σε-σπε-το, viz. ἔσπωνται (Od. 12. 349), ἐσποίμην (Od. 19. 579., 21. 77), ἐσπέσθω (Il. 12. 350, 363), ἐσπόμενος (Il. 10. 246., 12. 395., 13. 570), can be easily altered (*e.g.* by writing ἅμα σποίμην for ἅμ' ἐσποίμην). We always have ἐπι-σπέσθαι, ἐπι-σπόμενος, μετασπόμενος (never ἐφ-εσπόμενος, &c.) ; *i. e.* ἐσπ- only creeps in when a preceding final vowel can be elided without further change.

(7) A peculiar Reduplication is found in ἤρύκακε (Pres. ἐρύκ-ω) *checked*, and ἤνίπαπε (ἐνιπή) *rebuked*.

These Aorists are exclusively Homeric, except ἤγαγον and ἔειπον (Attic εἶπον). They are mostly Transitive or Causative in meaning; compare ἔ-λαχο-ν *I got for my share*, with λέλαχο-ν *I made to share;* ἄρηρε *is fitting*, with ἤραρε *made to fit*, &c.

The Inf. δεδάα-σθαι (Od. 16. 316) is not to be connected with the Perf. Part. δεδα-ώς, but is for δεδαέσθαι, Inf. Mid. of the Reduplicated Aorist δέδαεν *taught*. Thus the sense is *to have oneself taught*.

37.] Aorists in -ă. Besides the usual forms of ἔ-ειπο-ν (εἶ-πο-ν) we find a 2 Sing. εἶπα-s (Il. 1. 106, 108), or ἔ-ειπα-s (Il. 24. 379), 2 Plur. εἴπα-τε (Od. 3. 427). Answering to the Attic ἤνεγκον Homer has ἤνεικα, Opt. ἐνείκα-ι, &c. : but Inf. ἐνεικέ-μεν (Il. 19. 194). In these two cases the form in -ον is probably older.

Tenses with Suffix (Non-Thematic).

38.] The Tense-Stems which remain to be discussed are formed (like the Presents in -νημι and -νυμι) by means of a characteristic Suffix. Of these Tense-Stems three are Non-Thematic, viz. those of the Aorists formed by the Suffixes -σă, -η, and -θη.

It is important to notice the difference between these formations and the Perfect and Aorist Stems which take -κă. The Suffix -κă in such cases is not characteristic of the Tense-Stem. It is only found as a rule with certain Person-Endings.

39.] The Aorist in -σă (called ' Sigmatic ' and ' Weak* ' Aor.). The Suffix -σă is joined to the Verb-Stem (usually in its strong form), as ἔρρηξε (ῥηγ-), ἤλειψα-ν (ἀλειφ-), ἔ-πνευ-σα-ν (πνευ-), ἔδεισε (for ἔ-δϝει-σε) *feared*, ἔ-βη-σă-ν, ἔ-φϋ-σă.

The following are the chief varieties :—

1. Verb-Stems ending in a Dental or σ, preceded by a short vowel, form -σσă or -σă : thus we have ἤρεσσα and ἤρεσα (for ἤ-ρετ-σα, from ἐρετ-); ἔσ-σατο, ἔσασθαι (ϝεσ-); σβέσ-σαι, τρέσ-

---

* The term ' Weak ' implies formation by means of a Suffix. It was suggested by the analogy between the two Aorists and the Strong and Weak Preterites of the Teutonic languages.

σαι; ἔσας, ἐφ-έσσα-το (ἐδ- for *σεδ-); ἔ-θλασε and θλάσ-σε,
σπάσα-το, ἐ-δάσ-σα-το, ἐσ-ε-μάσ-σα-το, νάσ-τα (§ 51, 2); χάσσα-το
(cp. ἔ-χαδε), ἐ-φρασά-μην (φράδ-), ῥάσσα-τε (ῥάδ-), πασά-μην (πᾶτ-);
ἐλλισά-μην (λἴτ-), ὠδύσα-το (ὀδυσ-).

Verbs in -ζω form the Aorist in this way, as ὤπασα, ἐκόμισσα,
ξείνισεν, ἥρμοσε; or (less commonly) in -ξᾰ, as ἐξενάριξα, δαΐξαι,
μερμήριξε, ἐγγυάλιξε. ἁρπάζω forms ἥρπαξε and ἥρπασε.

2. Derivative Verbs in -αω, -εω, -οω, -υω usually form the Aor.
with a long vowel (in -ησα, -ωσα, -ῦσα). But the Verbs in -εω
often form the Aor. in -εσσα, -εσα; not only the Verbs derived
from Noun-Stems in -εσ, such as τελέω, νεικέω, ἀκηδέω, but also
several Verbs derived from Masc. Nouns in -o-ς; e.g. ἐκορέσ-σατο
was satiated (Pf. κεκορη-μένος), κοτέσ-σατο was enraged (κεκοτη-ώς),
πόθεσαν longed for (ποθή-μεναι), ἄλεσσαν ground.

Other examples of σσ in the Aor., though the Verb-Stem
cannot be shown to end in σ or a Dental, are : ἠγάσσατο (ἄγα-μαι)
was amazed, ἐτάλα-σσα endured, κέρα-σσε mixed, πέρα-σσα sold,
ἥλα-σσα drove, ἠρα-σάμην loved, ἐδάμα-σσα tamed, ἱλά-σσονται
(Subj.) shall appease, καλέ-σσαι to call, ὀλέ-σσαι to destroy, ἐτάνυ-
σσα stretched, ἐκάπυ-σσε panted, ἐρύ-σσαμεν drew, ἄε-σα slept, λοέ-
σσατο washed, ὀμό-σαι to swear, ὀνό-σσατο made light of; see § 51.
Note that when -σα is preceded by a short vowel there is always
a collateral form in -σσα : the only exceptions are στορέ-σαι
to strew and κρεμά-σαι to hang, and these are due to metrical
reasons.

Most of the Aorists in -ᾰσσα, -εσσα, &c; are evidently due to the analogy
of those in which -σα was originally preceded by a short vowel and a dental
or σ. That is to say, ἐτάλα-σσα, ἐκάλε-σσα, &c. do not follow the type of
ἔρρηξα, ἥλειψα (as ἔβη-σα, ἔφῦ-σα did), but the type of ἔθλασ-σα, ἐτέλεσ-σα. Thus
-σσᾰ becomes the Tense Suffix after a short vowel, just as -σᾰ is after a long
vowel or diphthong.

The forms λοῦσε, λοῦσαι, λούσαντο, λούσασθαι, &c., which suppose an Aor.
* ἔ-λου-σα can nearly always be written λοε-. The exceptions are, Il. 14. 7
θερμήνῃ καὶ λούσῃ ἄπο βρότον (read λοέσῃ τε ἀπὸ), Od. 6. 210 λούσατέ τ᾽ ἐν ποταμῷ,
6. 219 ἀπολούσομαι.

3. With Verb-Stems ending in μ, ν, ρ, λ, the σ is usually lost,
and the preceding vowel lengthened, ε becoming ει : as ἔ-γημα
(γαμ-), κρηῆναι (κρᾱαν-, § 55), ἐπ-έ-τειλα (τελ-), ἐ-φίλα-το (φῖλ-),
ἤγειρα (ἐγερ-), χῆρα-το (χαρ-)*. A few Stems retain σ : ὦρ-σα,
ἄρ-σαι, ἀπό-ερ-σε, ἔ-κερ-σε, κύρ-σα-ς, φύρ-σω, ἔλ-σα-ν, κέλ-σαι,
κένσαι. This is the rule when ρ or λ of the Stem is followed by
a dental, as in ἔ-περσε (for ἐ-περθ-σε), ἤμερσε (ἀμέρδω). But ν

---

* The form ἦρᾰ-το, which is usually taken to be an Aor. of ἄρ-νυ-μαι, may
stand to ἀρέσθαι as ἔ-πτᾰ-το to πτέσθαι, ὦνα-το to ὄνο-μαι, δίε-νται to δίε-σθαι (see
however Cobet, Misc. Crit. p. 400).

42   TENSES.   [40.

before δ is lost in ἔ-σπεισα (for ἐ-σπενδ-σα): cp. πείσομαι for πένθ-σομαι, &c. The form κένσαι (Il. 23. 337) is later. The Verb-Stem ὀφελ- makes an Aor. Opt. ὀφέλλειε : see § 53.

40.] Primitive Aorists with Suffix -σ-. Originally the Sigmatic Aorist was inflected like the Aorist in -ă already described (§ 15): that is to say, the α appeared in the 1 Sing. (perhaps also 3 Plur. -ᾰν) and the Stem was liable to variation between a strong and a weak form. Thus from a Stem τευκ-, τῠκ-, with the regular phonetic changes, we should have had—

Active, 1 Sing. ἔτευξα.
    2   ἔτευξ (for ἐ-τευκ-σ-ς).
    3   ἔτευξ (for ἐ-τευκ-σ-τ).
    1 Plur. ἔτευγμεν (or ἔτυγμεν).
    2   ἔτευκτε (or ἔτυκτε).
    3   ἔτευξαν.
Middle, 1 Sing. ἐτύγμην (for ἐ-τυκ-σ-μην).
    2   ἔτυξο (for ἐ-τυκ-σ-σο), Imper. τύξο.
    3   ἔτυκτο (for ἐ-τυκ-σ-το).
    3 Du. ἐτύχθην (for ἐ-τυκ-σ-σθην).
   Inf. τύχθαι (for τυκ-σ-σθαι or τυκ-σ-θαι).
   Part. τύγμενος (for τυκ-σ-μενος).

Several forms belonging to this scheme have survived in Homer:

ἔλεξα, Mid. ἐλέγμην, ἔλεκτο, Imper. λέξο, Inf. κατα-λέχθαι, Part. κατα-λέγμενος.
(ἐδεξά-μην), δέκτο, Imper. δέξο, Inf. δέχθαι.
ἔμιξα, Mid. ἔμικτο and μῖκτο.
ἔπηξα, Mid. κατ-έπηκτο (Il. 11. 378).
ἔπερσα, Mid. Inf. πέρθαι.
ἔπηλα, Mid. ἀν-έπαλτο, πάλτο.
(ἧλα-το), ἆλσο, ἆλτο (better ἄλσο, ἄλτο), Part. ἐπ-άλμενος.
ὦρσα, Mid. ὦρτο, Imper. ὄρσο, Inf. ὄρθαι, Part. ὄρμενος.
ἦρσα, Part. ἄρμενος.
(ἧσα-το), Part. ἄσμενος.
(ἐλελιξά-μενος), ἐλέλικτο (read Ϝελιξάμενος, ἐϜέλικτο, § 53).
γέντο *seized* (γεμ-).
ἐμίηνα, 3 Du. μιάνθην (cp. πέφανθε for πεφαν-σθε).
ἷκτο (Hes. Th. 481), Part. ἵκμενος *coming*.

Add εὖκτο (Thebais, fr. 3), κέντο (Alcm. fr. 141).

The 'regular' forms, such as ἐδέξατο, ἥλατο, ἥσατο, are to be explained like ἐχεύα-το, &c. (§ 15). On this view ἐδέξατο and ἥλατο are related to δέκτο and ἄλτο precisely as ἐχεύατο to χύτο, and similarly ἧσα-το to ἄσμενος as ἐχεύατο to χύμενος.

The form μιάνθην (Il. 4. 146) is now generally taken as 3 Plur., for ἐμίανθεν, or ἐμιάνθησαν. The 3 Plur. in -ην is found occa-

sionally on inscriptions in other dialects (Meyer, *G. G.* p. 468);
but that is very slight ground for admitting it in Homer. In
any case it is later than -εν, and due to the analogy of the other
Person-Endings*.

The Homeric forms of the Subj. also pre-suppose a Stem without final α:
e. g. the Subj. βήσ-ο-μεν points to an Indic. *ἔ-βησ-μεν (§ 80). The existence
of such Indicatives in an earlier period of the language is proved by the Sanscrit Aorists with *S*, many of which join the Person-Endings directly to the
Stem, without an 'auxiliary' *a* (except in the 1 Sing. and 3 Plur.) ; e. g. the
Root *ji* gives *ajaish-am*, 3 Sing. *ajais* (for *a-jai-s-t*), 1 Plur. *ajaish-ma*, &c.

Upon this stage of inflexion Joh. Schmidt has based a very probable
explanation of the 3 Plur. Ending -σαν (*K. Z.* xxvii. p. 323). It is evident
that owing to the loss of σ the Tense-Stem of such forms as ἔτευγμεν, ἔτευκτε,
ἔτυκτο appears as τευκ- or τυκ-, instead of τευξ-, τυξ-. Consequently the form
ἔτευξαν would be felt as ἔτευκ-σαν ; that is to say, -σαν would become in fact
the 3 Plur. Ending. Such an Ending would then be easily transferred to
other Tenses,—ἔδο-σαν, ἔστα-σαν, &c. The usual theory is that -σαν in these
forms comes from the regular Aor. in -σα. But this does not explain why it
is confined to the 3 Plur.—why we have (*e. g.*) ἔδο-σαν but not ἐδό-σαμεν.

41.] Aorist in -σε(ο). Several Stems form a Weak Aorist as
a thematic tense, with ε or ο instead of ἄ : viz. ἴξο-ν, ἐ-βήσε-το,
ἐ-δύσε-το (δυσό-μενος Od. 1. 24); Imper. πελάσσε-τον (Il. 10.
442), ἄξε-τε, οἴσε-τε, λέξε-ο, ὄρσε-ο; Inf. ἀξέ-μεναι (Il. 23. 50,
111), οἰσέμεναι (Il. 3. 120): perhaps also ἔ-πεσο-ν (πετ-).

The forms ἐβήσετο, ἐδύσετο were preferred by Aristarchus to
those in -σᾰτο: see Schol. A on Il. 2. 579., 3. 262., 10. 513.
They were regarded by ancient grammarians as Imperfects
(Schol. A on Il. 1. 496); and this view is supported by one or
two passages, esp. Od. 10. 107, where ἡ μὲν ἄρ' ἐς κρήνην κατεβή-
σετο must mean *she was going down to the spring* (when the mes-
sengers met her). So in the Part., Od. 1. 24 οἱ μὲν δυσομένου
Ὑπερίονος οἱ δ' ἀνιόντος, and Il. 5. 46 νύξ' ἵππων ἐπιβησόμενον
pierced as he was mounting his chariot, cp. 23. 379.

The forms ἴξο-ν, ἀξέ-μεναι, &c. answer closely to the Sanscr. Preterite
in -*sa-m*, as *á-diksha-m*. ἔπεσον is difficult to explain as ἔ-πετ-σον, both (1) because
it can hardly be accidental that we never have ἔπεσσον, and (2) because it
has to be separated from the Doric ἔπετον. Possibly there was a primitive
non-Thematic *ἔ-πετα, ἔ-πες, ἔπες (for ἐ-πετ-s, ἐ-πετ-τ), Du. ἐπεστον, &c., 3 Plur.
ἔ-πετ-αν, from which both ἔπετ-ον and ἔπεσ-ον might be derived in much the
same way as ἔ-κταν-ον from the primitive ἔ-κτενα, Plur. ἔ-κτᾰ-μεν (§ 13).

---

* One of the reviewers of the former edition (Cauer in the *Jahresb. d. philol.
Vereins*) objects that the Dual does not suit the context ('hier gar nicht in den
Zusammenhang passt'). The subject is μηροί, which is Dual in sense; and
the Dual might well be restored throughout the sentence (τοίω τοι, Μενέλαε,
μιάνθην αἵματι μηρὼ εὐφυέε, κνῆμαί τε κ. τ. λ.). The explanation of μιάνθην as
a Dual is due to Buttmann (*Ausf. Spr.* ii. 244, ed. 2).

42.] The Aorist in -η-ν. The Stem of this Tense is formed by suffixing η to the weak form of the Verb-Stem. This η becomes ε in the 3 Plur. (-εν for original -εντ), the Opt. and the Part. (*i. e.* before ι and ντ). The Person-Endings are those of the Active, but the meaning is either Intransitive or Passive: e. g. ἐ-χάρ-η *rejoiced*, ἐ-δάη *was taught*, ἐ-φάν-η *appeared*, τράφ-η *was nurtured*, ἐ-ἀλ-η *shrank* (Stem Fελ-), δι-έ-τμαγ-ε-ν *parted asunder*, ἐ-πάγ-η, ἐ-δάμ-η, ἐ-άγ-η, ἔ-βλαβ-εν, ἐ-μίγ-η, τάρπ-η-μεν and (with Metathesis) τραπ-ή-ομεν (τέρπ-ω), &c.

The Stem is long in ἐ-πλήγ-η (cp. ἐ-πέπληγ-ον, πληγ-ή), and once in ἐάγη (ᾱ in Il. 11. 559)*. The Inf. τερσή-μεναι (τερσῆναι), which occurs in Il. 16. 519, Od. 6. 98, need not be an Aorist: see the similar forms in § 19. The Part. ἀνα-βροχέν (Od. 11. 586) is not connected with ἀνα-βέβροχεν (§ 25); see Buttmann, *Lexil.*

There is evidently a close relation between these 'Passive' Aorists and the forms discussed in § 14 (such as ἔ-βλη-ν, ἔ-πτη-ν, ἔ-τλη, ἔ-σβη), and we can hardly doubt that they are nothing more than an extension by analogy of that older type (see Brugmann, *M. U.* i. 71). The chief difference is that (as in the Thematic Aorist) the Stem is usually disyllabic, retaining the short vowel of the root: thus we have ἐ-δάμη, but δμη- in δέ-δμη-ται, &c.

The Aorists with Stems in ᾱ and ω (§ 19) are parallel to the Aorists in -η. Thus γηρᾶ-ναι, βιῶ-ναι, ἀλῶ-ναι only differ in the quality of the vowel from δαῆ-ναι, ἀλῆ-ναι: and there might have been numerous Aorists in -ᾱν and -ων along with those in -ην, just as there are derivative Verbs in -αω, -οω as well as in -εω.

43.] The Aorist in -θη-ν. The Stem of this Tense is formed by the Suffix -θη. The Person-Endings are the same as those of the Aorist in -η, and the meaning is Reflexive or Passive.

In later Greek the Verb-Stem is mostly in the strong form, as ἐ-δήχ-θη-ν, ἐ-λείφ-θην, ἐ-ζεύχ-θην; but this does not seem to have been the original rule: e. g. Homer has ἐ-τύχ-θη *was made*, Attic ἐ-τεύχ-θη. So we find the weak Stem in κατ-έ-κτᾰ-θεν (κτεν-), τᾰ-θη (τεν-), τάρφ-θη (τέρπ-ω), τραφ-θῆ-ναι (τρέπω), ἐ-στᾰ-θη (Od. 17. 463), λύ-θη, ἐξ-ε-σύ-θη, ἔ-φθϊ-θεν.

The Stems of κλίνω and κρίνω vary in regard to the ν: we have ἐ-κλίν-θη and ἐ-κλῐ-θη, κριν-θέ-ντες and δι-έ-κρῐ-θε-ν.

44.] Meaning of the Passive Aorists. The Aorist in -η appears to have originally had an Intransitive sense, of which the Passive sense was a growth or adaptation. This transition is

---

* In the former edition Bekker's reading ἐάγῃ (Pf. Subj.) was given as the probable correction for this passage. But the sense required is rather that of the Aor.—*were* (i. e. *had been*) *broken*—than the Pf.—*are in a broken sta e.* Cp. Hes. Op. 534 οὖ τ' ἐπὶ νῶτα ἔαγε *whose back is broken down*, i. e. *bowed.* As to the ᾱ of ἐάγη see § 67, 3.

seen (*e.g.*) in ἐχάρη *rejoiced,* ἐδάη *learned,* ῥύη *flowed,* ἐφάνη
appeared. In these instances the Passive grows out of the
Intransitive meaning (as in the Middle forms it grows out of
the Reflexive meaning). Similar transitions of meaning may be
found in the Perfect (§ 28, *fin.*), the Aorist (ἔσβη *was quenched*),
and even in the Present, as ἐκπίπτειν *to be driven out,* κεῖται *is
laid down* (as Pf. Mid. of τίθημι), and πάσχω itself.

The Aorist in -θη-ν is often indistinguishable in meaning
from the Aor. Middle. There appears to be ground for distinguishing it from the Aor. in -ην as originally reflexive rather
than intransitive (Wackernagel, *K. Z.* xxx. 305.) In many cases
Middle forms are used in Homer interchangeably with those
in -θη-ν : thus we find ἀάσατο and ἀάσθη, αἴδετο ἠδέσατο and
αἰδέσθητε, ἀΐξασθαι and ἀϊχθῆναι, δυνήσατο and δυνάσθη, κορέσσατο
and κορέσθην, μνήσασθαι and μνησθῆναι, ἀπ-ενάσσατο and νάσθη,
ἐφρασάμην and ἐφράσθης, ὀΐσατο and ὠΐσθη, ἐχολώσατο and
ἐχολώθη, ἐρείσατο and ἐρείσθη, ὡρμήσατο and ὡρμήθη, &c.; also
ἔφθιτο and ἔφθιθεν, ἄμπνυτο and ἀμπνύνθη, λύτο and λύθη, ἔκτατο
and ἔκταθεν, λέκτο and ἐλέχθην, μῖκτο and ἐμίχθη.

This observation has recently suggested a very probable account of the
origin of the Aor. in -θη-ν. The 2 Sing. Mid. Ending in Sanscr. is -*thās*, to
which would correspond Greek -θης. Hence the original inflexion was (e.g.)
ἐ-λύ-μην, ἐ-λύ-θης, ἐ-λυ-το, &c. Then ἐλύθης was regarded as ἐ-λύθη-ς, that is to
say, λυθη- was taken as the Tense-Stem, and the inflexion was completed on
the model of the already formed Aorists in -ην (Wackernagel, *l. c.*).

The Aorists in -η-ν and -θη-ν are formations peculiar to Greek, and were
doubtless developed along with the separation of Present and Aorist forms
which had hardly been completed in the time of Homer (Curtius, *Verb.*
ii. 1 ff.). It is worth notice that the three Aorists that have a distinctive
Suffix agree in avoiding the Thematic Endings, while the Impf. tends to adopt
them, as in ἐτίθει, ἐδίδου, ὤμνυε, &c. The reason doubtless was that the
Thematic inflexion already prevailed in the Present. Thus a distinction of
form was gained which was especially needed for the Aorists in -η-ν. Forms
like ἐφίλει (which at first, as we see from φιλή-μεναι, subsisted side by side
with ἐφίλη) were adopted as Imperfects, while ἐμίγη &c. were retained as
Aorists.

Thematic Present (*with Suffix*).

45.] In the forms to which we now proceed the Verb-Stem
receives a suffix which serves to distinguish the Present Stem;
as τύπ-τω, κάμ-νω, βά-σκω, κτείνω (for κτεν-ι̯ω).

These suffixes may be compared with other elements used in
the same way, but not always confined to the Present; as κ in
ὀλέ-κω *I destroy,* ἐρύ-κω *I restrain,* διώ-κω *I chase,* γ in τμή-γω
I cut, χ in νη-χέ-μεναι *to swim,* τρύ-χουσι *they waste,* σμή-χειν *to
smear,* σ in αὔξω (*aug-eo*), θ in σχέ-θε *held,* ἔσθειν (ἐδ-θειν) *to eat,*

βρῖ-θο-ν *were heavy*, πλῆ-θεν *was full*, ἔρε-θε *provoke*, φλεγέ-θει *blazes*, μινύ-θει *diminishes*, φθινύ-θει *wastes*, ἔργα-θεν *kept off*, θαλέ-θο-ντες *blooming*, μετ-ε-κία-θον *moved after*, ἠερέ-θο-νται *flutter*, ἠγερέ-θο-ντο *were assembled* (ἀγερ-, in ἀγείρω), &c. These elements were called by Curtius Root-Determinatives (*Chron*. p. 22 ff.)—the name implying that they are of the nature of suffixes modifying or ʻdeterminingʼ the meaning of a simple Root. But their origin and primitive significance are quite unknown (Brugmann, *Grundriss*, ii. § 8, *n.* 2).

46.] **The T-Class.** The suffix -τε (ο) is usually found with a Verb-Stem ending in a *labial mute* (π, β, φ), as ἔνιπ-τε *rebuke* (ἐνῖπ-ή), χαλέπ-τει *annoys*, ἀστράπ-τει *lightens*, σκέπ-τεο *look out*, κλέπ-τε, κόπ-τε, τύπ-τε, ἔ-μαρπ-τε; ἅπτω (ἀφ-) *fasten*, κρύπτων (κρύφ-α) *hiding*, θάπτε (θάφ-) *bury*, ῥάπτειν *to sew*, *string together*; βλάπτει (βλάβ-) *harms*.

The Stem is in the weak form; the corresponding long forms are generally wanting.

This suffix is combined with Reduplication in ἰ-άπ-τω (for ἰ-ἰάπ-τω, cp. Lat. *jac-io*) *I hurl*, which occurs in Od. 2. 376 κατὰ χρόα καλὸν ἰάπτῃ *shall maltreat* (lit. *knock about*) *her fair flesh**.

πτ may be for π-ι-, and, if so, these Verbs would belong to the I-Class (§ 50). In some cases, however, the π represents an original guttural. Thus we find ἐνίσσω (ἐνικ-ιω), as well as ἐνίπτω (ἐνιπ-ή); πέσσω, later πέπτω (πέπ-ων); νίζω, later νίπτω (ἀπονίπτεσθαι in Od. 18. 179 is doubtful). Here ἐνίσσω, πέσσω, νίζω are formed by the suffix -ιε(ο), and consequently ἐνίπτω, πέπτω, νίπτω must be otherwise explained. So in σκέπτομαι, since σκεπ- is for σπεκ- (Lat. *spec-io*), the form with πτ must be at least later than the metathesis. Hence if we adhere to the supposition that -πτ- is for -πι- we must explain these four forms as due to the analogy of other Verbs in -πτε(ο) already in existence.

47.] **The Nasal Class.** The suffix is -νε (ο) after a vowel or μ : φθά-νει *comes first*, τί-νων *paying* (*a penalty*), δύ-νε *sank in*, θύ-νον *bustled*, κάμ-νε *grew weary*, τάμ-νε *cut*; -ανε(ο) after a mute, ἡμάρτ-ανε *missed*, ἤλδ-ανε *made fat*, ληθ-άνει *makes to forget*, οἰδ-άνει *swells*, κυδ-άνει *glorifies*, ἐ-κεύθ-ανον *hid*, ἀπ-εχθ-άνεαι *becomest hateful*: often with the weak Stem and ν inserted, ἁνδ-άνει *pleases* (ἁδ-), λανθ-ανόμην, ἐ-χάνδ-ανον, ἐ-λάγχ-ανον, τύγχ-ανε, πυνθ-άνομαι.

The suffix -ανε(ο) is combined with Reduplication (as in § 35)

---

* With ἰ-άπ-τω may be connected ἰ-άφ-θη, which occurs in the phrase ἐπὶ δ' ἀσπὶς ἰάφθη καὶ κόρυς (Il. 13. 543., 14. 419), of a warrior's shield, which falls with or after him. For the aspirate (ἰάφθη for ἰ-ιάφθη) compare ἕηκα, ἕεστο, &c. This explanation was given by Ebel, in *K. Z.* iv. 167. The scholar to whom I owe this reference, F. Froehde, derives it from Sanscr. *vapāmi*, ʻI throw, strew about:ʼ so ἀπτοεπής = ʻone whose words are thrown about at randomʼ (*Bezz. Beitr.* iii. 24). See Curtius, *Verb.* ii. 364 (2 ed.).

in πιμ-πλ-άνεται (Il. 9. 679), ἰσχάνω (for *σι-σχ-άνω), ἰζάνω (for
*σι-σδ-άνω).
The class of Verbs in -νω is derived from the Non-thematic
Verbs in -νυ-. Sometimes, as has been noticed (§ 18), -νυ takes
the Thematic ε or ο after it, as in ὀμ-νύω for ὄμνῡ-μι; but in
other cases, especially when -νυ follows a vowel, υ becomes ϝ and
is lost. Thus ἀ-νυ- gives ἀνύω 1 accomplish, and also ἄνεται (ᾱ)
draws to a close: so τίνυ-ται punishes and τίνω, φθίνυ- (in φθῑνύ-
θω) and φθίνω. The vowel of ἄνω, φθάνω, τίνω, φθίνω is long in
Homer, short in Attic (cp. Homeric ξεῖν-ος for ξέν-ϝος, Attic
ξέν-ος); whereas in κλίνω, κρίνω (for κλιν-ι̯ω, κριν-ι̯ω) it is
always long. Note also that -νε(ο) for -νϝε(ο) is confined to the
Present, while the ν of κλίνω, &c. appears in other Tenses
(Solmsen, K. Z. xxix. 78).
ἐλαύνω has been explained as *ἐλα-νυ-ω, but there is no parallel
for epenthesis of υ.
The ᾱ of ἱκάνω, κιχάνω points to -αν-ϝω, but the forms have
not been satisfactorily explained.

48.] Stems formed by -σκε(ο), the Iterative class of Curtius.

(1) Without Reduplication, as βά-σκε go, βό-σκει feeds, φά-σκε
said, ἱλά-σκο-νται propitiate, ἠλάσκουσι flit about, θνῆ-σκο-ν died,
θρώ-σκουσι leap, προ-βλω-σκέ-μεν to go before (βλω- for μλω-).

(2) With Reduplication, μι-μνή-σκε-ται is reminded, κί-κλη-σκεν
called, γι-γνώ-σκω 1 know, πί-φαυ-σκε showed.
Stems ending in a consonant sometimes insert ι, as ἀπ-αφ-ί-
σκει deceives, ἀρ-άρ-ι-σκε fitted, εὑρ-ίσκω I find (Od. 19. 158), ἐπ-
αυρ-ίσκονται get benefit from (Il. 13. 733). A final consonant is
lost before σκ in δι-δασκέ-μεν (for δι-δαχ-σκε-), ἴσκω and ἐΐσκω
(cp. ἴκ-ελος), τι-τύσκε-το (τῠκ- or τῠχ-), δει-δίσκετο welcomed (δῐκ-);
probably also in μίσγο-ν (for μιγ-σκο-ν) and πάσχω (for παθ-σκω).

49.] Iterative Tenses. The suffix -σκε(ο) is also used to
form a number of Past Tenses with Iterative meaning, as ἔσκε
(for ἐσ-σκε) used to be, ἔχε-σκε used to hold, καλέ-εσκε, πελέ-σκε-ο
(Il. 22. 433), νικά-σκο-μεν (Od. 11. 512), τρωπά-σκετο (Il. 11.
568), ῥίπτα-σκε, οἴχνε-σκε, πωλέ-σκε-το, ὦθε-σκε, &c.; and from
Aorist Stems, as στά-σκε, δό-σκο-ν, εἴπε-σκε, φάνε-σκε, ἐρητύ-σα-
σκε, δα-σά-σκε-το, ὦσα-σκε, &c. These formations differ from
the Present Stems described above (1) in carrying distinctly the
notion of repeated action and (2) in being confined to the Past
Indicative. They are peculiar to the Ionic dialect, and the
forms derived from Aorists in -σα are only found in Homer.

ἔ-φασκο-ν has sometimes a distinctly Iterative meaning in Homer, as
Od. 8. 565 Ναυσιθόου, ὃς ἔφασκε Ποσειδάων' ἀγάσασθαι, and the Pres. φάσκω does

not occur. It may be regarded as a link between the two groups of Stems with -σκ.

It is remarkable that in the Latin Verbs in -sco we may distinguish in the same way between the regular Inceptives, such as lique-sco, puer-a-sco, and the Presents, such as pa-sco, pro-fic-iscor, in which the Inceptive meaning is hardly, or not at all, perceptible. Originally, no doubt, there was a single group of derivative Stems in σκε(ο) with the meaning of continued or repeated action.

50.] The I-Class. The suffix was probably -ιͅε(ο) in a prehistoric period of Greek : it appears in Stems of the following forms :—

a. In -ιω, -αιω, -ειω, -υιω or -ῡω (for -ι-ιͅω, -α-ιͅω, &c.), the ιͅ blending with the final vowel of the Stem.

b. With epenthesis of ι, in -αινω, -αιρω (for -αν-ιͅω, -αρ-ιͅω).

c. With assimilation, in -λλω (for -λ-ιͅω), -σσω (for -κ-ιͅω, -τ-ιͅω), and -ζω (for -δ-ιͅω, -γ-ιͅω).

d. By compensatory lengthening in -εινω, -ειρω, -ῑνω, -ῡνω, -ῡρω (for -εν-ιͅω, -ερ-ιͅω, -ῐν-ιͅω, -ῠν-ιͅω, -ῠρ-ιͅω). That the ει of -εινω, -ειρω is not a true diphthong (and therefore not due to epenthesis) is shown by the corresponding Doric -ηνω, -ηρω.

e. In -αω, -εω, -οω, -αυω, -ευω, -ουω (for -α-ιͅω, &c.).

a. Verbs in -ιω, &c.

51.] The Verbs in which the original ιͅ becomes ι, thus forming -ιω, -αιω, -ειω, -υιω, are almost confined to the Homeric dialect. The chief examples are as follows :—

(1) -ιω : ἐσθίει eats, ἴδιον I sweated, μήνιε be angry, μάστιε whip, ἀνα-κήκιε gushed forth, κονίο-ντες raising dust. In these verbs (except perhaps the first two) the Verb-Stem ends in ι, so that (e. g.) κονίο-ντες is for κονι-ιͅο-ντες; so probably τίω I honour, φθίω I waste away, for τι-ιͅω, φθι-ιͅω. The ι therefore is naturally long, but may be shortened before a vowel; hence it is usually doubtful in quantity.

(2) -αω : usually with loss of σ or Ϝ, ναίουσι dwell (Aor. νάσ-σα, νάσ-θη), μαίεσθαι to feel one's way (Fut. μάσ-σεται), λιλαίεαι desirest (λι-λασ-); καίω (for κᾰϜ-ιͅω, cp. Aor. ἔκηα for ἔ-κηϜ-α), κλαίω (for κλᾱϜ-ιͅω), δαῖε kindled (δᾱυ-), ναῖον swam (cp. ναῦ-s), γαίων rejoicing (γαῦ-ρος, Lat. gau-deo); κέραιε mix, ἀγαιόμενος indignant (cp. ἐ-κέρασ-σα, ἠγάσ-σατο, but the σ in these words is not original, § 39, 2); perhaps also φθαίω (if παρα-φθαίῃσι in Il. 10. 346 is Pres. Subj., see K. Z. xxiii. 298).

δαίω divide forms its Tenses from two roots, (1) δαι-, 3 Plur. Pf. δεδαί-αται, cp. δαί-νυμι, δαί-s, δαι-τρός, and (2) δατ-, Pf. δέδασ-ται, Pres. δατ-έομαι (cp. πατ-έομαι, πεπάσμην).

(3) -ειω : πενθείε-τον (probably for πενθεσ-ιε-τον) *mourn*, μαχειό-
μενος *fighting*, οἰνοβαρείων *drunken*, τέλειο-ν *brought to pass*, κείων
splitting, ἀκειό-μενοι *being healed*, νεικείη-σι *shall quarrel*, ὀκνείω *I
shrink*, ὑμνείω (Hes.).

When the diphthongs αι, ει come before a vowel there is a
tendency to drop the ι; as ἀγα-ίο-μαι, 2 Plur. ἀγάα-σθε (for ἀγάε-σθε, § 55); κερα-ίω, 2 Plur. κεράα-σθε; τέλε-ιο-ν, also τέλε-ο-ν;
ναῖον *swam*, also νά-ει, νά-ουσι; perhaps also δάηται *shall be
destroyed* (root δαι- ; see Schulze, *K. Z.* xxix. p. 258). Where
this tendency does not show itself, as in παίω, πταίω, σείω, it
will usually be found that the diphthong belongs to the whole
Verb, not merely to the Present Stem.

So perhaps ἐράασθε *ye loved*, ἱλάονται *appease*, ἔλων *drove* (Part. ἐλάων), ἔκλων
broke : unless these forms are obtained by simple change from the Non-
Thematic ἔρα-μαι, &c. (§ 18).

For the Presents in -ειω from -εϝω (θείω, πλείω, &c.), see § 29, 3.

(4) -υιω : ὄπυιε *had to wife* (for ὀπυσ-ιω).

Most of the Presents in -υω are of this Class (original -υιω), as
φύω (Aeolic φυίω), θύω (ἔθυιεν Hesych.), λύω, δύω, ἰθύω, ἤπύω,
ὀϊζύω. The vowel is doubtful, but only because it comes before
another vowel (as was noticed in the case of Verbs in -ιω).

ἰθύω generally has ῠ; but ῡ in ἐπ-ιθύουσι (Il. 18. 175), which ought to be so
divided, not ἐπι-θύουσι. It is a Denominative from ἰθύς (ῡ) *aim*.

The Verbs in -ευω, -ουω are probably also of the I-Class (for
-ευιω, -ουιω). For, as Curtius points out (*Verb.* i. 360), they
are chiefly Denominatives, and it is contrary to analogy to form
a Verb by suffixing the Thematic ε (ο) to a Noun-Stem.

b. Epenthesis of ι.

52.] It will suffice to give a few examples :—

-νω : μαίνο-μαι, φαίνω, βαίνω (βαμ-ιω), and with reduplication,
τι-ταίνω, παμφαίνω.

-ρω : αἴρω, σκαίρω, ἀσπαίρω, μαρμαίρω, καρκαίρω, χαίρω.

αἴρω (for ἀρ-ιω) is distinct from ἀείρω, which by contraction would become
ᾄρω : cp. ἀείδω, ᾄδω (Brugmann, *K. Z.* xxvii. 196).

This Class includes also the numerous Denominatives in -αινω,
-αιρω : see § 120. The Stem is in the weak form.

c. Assimilation of ι.

53.] Examples : -λλω : ἄλλο-μαι, βάλλω, πάλλω, στέλλω, τέλλω;
from Nouns, ἀγγέλλω, ναυτίλλομαι; with Reduplication ἰάλλω,
ἀτιτάλλω *I rear, tend*, cp. ἀτάλλω *I cherish*.

Epenthesis (instead of Assimilation) is found in ὀφείλω *I owe*.

-σσω : ὄσσο-μαι (ὀκ-), πέσσω (πεκ-), ἐλίσσω (ἐλικ-), πτύσσω
(πτύχ-), λίσσο-μαι (λίτ-), κορύσσω (κορυθ-), πτώσσω (πτωκ-).

E

-ζω : for -δι̯ω in κλύζω, φράζω, χάζο-μαι; for -γι̯ω in ἄζο-μαι, ῥέζω, τρίζω; with reduplication, μιμνάζω *I loiter*, βιβάζω *I cause to go*, ἐλελίζω *I make to quiver* (Il. 1. 530)*.

d. Compensatory lengthening.

54.] Examples : -εινω (for -εν-ι̯ω), in τείνω, κτείνω, θείνω.
-ειρω (for -ερ-ι̯ω), in εἴρω, κείρω, μείρομαι, πείρω, σπείρω, τείρω, φθείρω, ἀγείρω, ἀείρω, ἐγείρω, ἐθείρω.
-ῑνω (for -ιν-ι̯ω), in κλίνω, κρίνω, ὀρίνω.
-ῡνω (for -υν-ι̯ω), in πλύνω, ἐντύνω.
-ῡρω (for -υρ-ι̯ω), in κύρω, μύρομαι, φύρω, ὀδύρομαι.

e. Verbs in -αω, -εω, -οω.

55.] **Assimilation.** This term is applied to certain forms of the Verbs in -αω, in which, instead of contraction, we find *assimilation* of one of two concurrent vowels to the other, as ὁρόω for ὁράω, ὁράᾳς for ὁράεις.

The chief varieties are as follows :—

(*a*) Forms with simple Assimilation, the vowel being long—

μνᾱό-μενοι	gives	μνωό-μενοι
ἠβάο-ντες	,,	ἠβώο-ντες
μενοινάω	,,	μενοινώω
ἠγά-εσθε	,,	ἠγάασθε
μνά-εσθε	,,	μνάασθε
μνάῃ	,,	μνάᾳ (2 Sing. Mid.).

(*b*) With shortening of the first vowel—

ὁράω	gives	ὁρόω
ἐάη-ς	,,	ἐάᾳ-ς
αἰτιάε-σθαι	,,	αἰτιάα-σθαι.

Cp. δεδάα-σθαι from δεδαέ-σθαι (§ 35) and ἀγάα-σθε from ἀγάε-σθε; Fut. ἐλόω, κρεμόω from ἐλάω, κρεμάω.

(*c*) With lengthened second vowel—

ὁράο-ντες	gives	ὁρόω-ντες
ὁράοι-τε	,,	ὁρόῳ-τε
ὁράει-ς	,,	ὁράᾳ-ς.

This is the commonest form of Assimilation : cp. δηϊόω-ντο, δηϊόω-εν from δηϊόω, ἀρόωσι (Od. 9. 108) from ἀρόω, κατ-ηπιόωντο (Il. 5. 417), ἐστρατόωντο (Il. 4. 378), ῥυπόωντα (Od.).

---

* Cobet (*Misc. Crit.*), following Bentley, has sought to show that the forms of ἐλελίζω belong in reality to ἐλίσσω (ϝελίσσω). He is doubtless right in substituting ϝελιχθέντες for ἐλελιχθέντες *wheeling about*: but it seems necessary to retain ἐλελίζω where the meaning is *to set trembling* (with intensive reduplication, like ἀκαχίζω, ὀλολύζω, &c.).

(*d*) With lengthened second vowel (the first being also long),
in very few forms—

δράουσι gives δρώωσι
μαιμάουσι „ μαιμώωσι
ἡβάουσα „ ἡβώωσα
μενοινάει „ μενοινάᾳ.

Other isolated examples are: μενοινήῃσι (Il. 15. 82); ἀλόω
(Od. 5. 377), 2 Sing. Imper. of ἀλάομαι (for ἀλάεο ἀλάου);
κεκράανται, κρηῆναι, κραιαίνω; φαάνθη (for φαέν-θη); σόωσι
(Subj.), σόῳς, σόῳ (Opt., cp. § 83), σώοντες (σαόω). Similar
phenomena may be seen in φόως for φάος (or φᾶος), σόος for
σάος, φαάντατος for φαέντατος, νηπιάας for νηπιέας, πρώονες (Il.)
for πρήονες, ἀστυβοώτης for ἀστυβοήτης : also in a form Αἰνείωο
(for Αἰνείαο) read by Zenodotus in Il. 5. 263, 323.

1. These forms were regarded by the older grammarians as
the result of a process called 'distraction,' (the exact reverse of
contraction), by which a long vowel, ᾱ or ω, could be separated
into two distinct vowels (ᾰᾱ, οω, &c.). The first attempt to
account for them in a more rational way was made by L.
Meyer (*K. Z.* x. 45 ff.). According to him they represent an
intermediate stage in the process of contraction. The order, he
argued, is ὁράω—ὁρόω—ὁρῶ: *i.e.* in ὁρόω the α has been assimilated
to the following ω, but is not yet uttered in one breath with it.
In the forms ὁρόωντες, ὁρόωσι, &c. he pointed out that the long
vowel is never wanted for the metre, and accordingly he wished
to read ὁρόοντες, ὁρόουσι, &c. To this last proposal exception
was taken by G. Curtius (*Erläuterungen*, p. 96), who made the
counter-supposition that, as the α of these Verbs was originally
long, the successive steps might be ὁράοντες, ὁρώοντες and
(by metathesis of quantity) ὁρόωντες. The stage -ωο- is
exemplified in μνωόμενος.

2. The main objection to this theory lies in the circumstance
that the forms ὁρόω, ὁράᾳς and the like are exclusively 'Epic,'
that is to say, they are confined to Homer, Hesiod, and their
direct imitators. If they had been created by any natural
development of Greek sounds, we should expect to find them
in other dialects. But neither in Ionic nor elsewhere is there
any trace of their existence in living speech. It must be
admitted, too, that neither Meyer nor Curtius has given a
satisfactory account of the long vowel in ὁρόωσι, ὁρόωντο,
ὁρόωντες, &c. A form ὁρόοντες, as Curtius pointed out, would
give ὁροῦντες, not ὁρῶντες. And if there has been metathesis
of quantity, why do we never find ὁρόωμεν for ὁράομεν, or ὁράᾱτε
for ὁράετε?

3. An entirely different theory was put forward by J. Wack-

ernagel (*Bezz. Beitr.* iv. 259). The true Homeric forms, in his
view, are the original uncontracted ὁράω, ὁράεις, &c. and these have
passed into the ὁρόω, ὁράᾳς, &c. of our Homer by a process of
textual corruption consisting of two stages : (1) contraction,
according to the ordinary rules of Attic, into ὁρῶ, ὁρᾷς, &c.—
which would obviously give forms of different metrical value
from the original words,—and then (2) restoration of the metre
by a kind of 'distraction' (in the old sense of the term), *i.e.*
the insertion of a short vowel before the new contracted -ῶ, -ᾷs,
&c. Thus οὐχ ὁράεις first became οὐχ ὁρᾷς, and then *metri
gratia* οὐχ ὁράᾳς*.

4. Paradoxical as this may seem, there can be little doubt
that it is substantially right. The forms in question, as Wackernagel justly argues, are not a genuine growth of language.
They are the result of literary tradition, that is to say, of the
modernising process which the language of Homer must have
undergone in the long period which elapsed before the poems
were cared for by scholars. The nature of this process is
excellently described and illustrated in his dissertation. In
many cases, too, he shows that when the later form of a word
ceased to fit the metre, some further change was made by
which the metrical defect was cured, or at least disguised.
Corruption of this latter kind may often be traced in the
various readings of MSS.

But must we suppose that ὁρόω, &c. went through the two
changes which Wackernagel postulates ?

5. The case is unique, not only from the large number of
forms involved, and the singularly thorough and systematic way
in which they have been introduced into the text, but also from
the circumstance which he has himself so well pointed out,
viz. their unreal conventional stamp. They are hardly more
'modern'—in the sense of being familiar through contemporary
speech—than the forms which they have displaced. Wackernagel has shown how ἕως and τέως supplanted the original ἦος
and τῆος, even where the result was absolute ruin to the verse;
as in Od. 19. 367, where nearly all the MSS. have ἕως ἵκοιο.
Similarly the loss of the old Gen. in -οο (§ 98) has produced
the forms Αἰόλου, Ἰφίτου, Ἰλίου, &c. scanned – – – . These
examples, however, prove too much; for if such unmetrical
forms could remain in the text without further change, why
do we never find the slightest trace of an unmetrical ὁρῶ ?

6. It is a further objection to this part of Wackernagel's
theory that in several words the original -αω, -αεις, -αουσα, &c.

---

* This theory was criticised by Curtius in the *Leipziger Studien*, iii. pp. 192 ff.

have been retained. The instances are, ναιετάω, -άει (Hes. Th. 775), -άουσι, -άων, -άοντα, ὑλάει, -άουσι, ἀοιδιάει, -άουσα, ὁμο-στιχάει, γοάοιμεν, -άοιεν, κραδάων, ἐλάων, ἱλάονται, τηλεθάοντας; with ᾱ, ἀναμαιμάει, πεινάων, -άοντα, διψάων. (The forms which have lost a ϝ, as λάε, φάε, ἔχραον, do not concern us now.) A third variety is exhibited by the form ναιετάωσαν (-σης, -ση, -σας), which occurs in MSS., usually as a variant along with -άουσαν and -όωσαν. These facts are enough to show that the causes which produced the Homeric -οω, -αϙς, &c. were not of universal efficacy.

7. Is there, then, any way from ὁράω, ὁράεις to ὁρόω, ὁράϙς except through the contracted ὁρῶ, ὁρᾷς? We have to deal with a time when ὁρῶ, ὁρᾷς were the forms of ordinary speech, while ὁράω, ὁράεις were only known from the recitation of epic poetry. Under such conditions it is surely possible that the poetical forms were *partially assimilated* to the colloquial forms—that ὁράω, ὁράεις were changed into ὁρόω, ὁράϙς *by the influence of* the familiar ὁρῶ, ὁρᾷς. Similarly ἑήνδανε for ἑάνδανε was doubtless due to the presence of the later ἥνδανε, not to any process of contraction and distraction. The principle is constantly exemplified in language; cp. the change of φρασί, the original Dat. Plur. of φρήν, into φρεσί through the association of the other Case-forms.

8. With this modification of Wackernagel's view it is easier to account for the occasional retention of the original -αω, -αεις, &c. If ὁρόω, ὁράϙς are due to the presence of ὁρῶ, ὁρᾷς in everyday language, we may expect to find a different treatment of words which went out of use in post-Homeric times. Thus ναιετάω does not pass into ναιετόω because there was no ναιετῶ alongside of it in common use. Similarly ἐλόω, ἐλάαν are accounted for by the Attic ἐλῶ, ἐλᾶν; but the Homeric Pres. Part. ἐλάων is unaffected. Two instances call for a different explanation, viz. πεινάω and διψάω, since they are not rare or poetical words. But these are exceptions which prove the rule. As is shown by the Attic contraction (πεινῆς, &c.), they are not really Verbs in -αω. Whatever may be the origin of the ᾱ in the Homeric πεινάων, διψάων, &c., they do not belong to the group with which we are now concerned.

9. An example of the process supposed by Wackernagel may be found in the Homeric τρωπάω, τρωχάω, στρωφάω, πωτάομαι (as to which see Nauck, *Mél. gr.-rom.* iv. 886). The forms which occur are always contracted, but in every instance except one (Il. 13. 557 στρωφᾶτ') the uncontracted form can be restored *if at the same time the root-vowel is shortened.* Thus in Il. 15. 666 μηδὲ τρωπᾶσθε φόβονδε we may read μηδὲ τρο-πάεσθε φόβονδε. The verb πωτάομαι only occurs once (Il. 12.

287 λίθοι πωτῶντο θαμειαί), while the form ποτάομαι is well attested. In the other cases the restoration is supported by etymology (τροπάω from τροπή, &c.), and by the considerable traces of τροπάω, τροχάω, στροφάω in our manuscripts (see Leaf on Il. 15. 666). The process must have been that (*e.g.*) original τροπάεσθε became τροπᾶσθε (which is also found in MSS.), and then τρωπᾶσθε.

10. In the Impf. Act. assimilation is unknown, mainly because the metre generally allows contraction. We find however (1) several uncontracted forms, viz. οὗταε (Od. 22. 356), πέραον (Il. 16. 367), ὕλαον (Od. 16. 5), κατεσκίαον (Od. 12. 436): ἐχράετε, ἔχραον (for ἐχράϝετε ἔχραϝον) do not belong to this head. Also (2) some verbs show the New Ionic -εο- for -αο-, viz. ὁμόκλεον, ὁμοκλέομεν, ποτέονται, μενοίνεον, ἤντεον, τρόπεον.

For φάος we find the two forms φόως and φώως (Il. 16. 188 ἐξάγαγεν φώωσδε), but never φόος or φῶς*. The exclusion of φῶος is remarkable, since it is related to φᾶος as μνωόμενος to μνάόμενος. The reason doubtless is that φᾶος came under the influence of φῶς (cp. ὁράᾳς and ὁρ-ᾷς). On the other hand σάος became σόος owing to the later σῶος. The change of πρηόνες to πρώονες is similarly due to πρῶνες. In the case of ἀστυβοώτης (for -βοήτης) there is no evidence of a form -βώτης, but such a form would be according to the rules of Ionic contraction (βώσας for βοήσας, &c.).

56.] Contraction. The extent to which contracted forms of verbs were admitted in the original text of Homer is a matter of much dispute. In this place we are properly concerned only with verbs of the I-Class (-αω, -εω, -οω, for -α-ι̯ω, -ε-ι̯ω, -ο-ι̯ω), not with those in which a different spirant has been lost (as τρέω for τρέσ-ω, πλέω for πλέϝ-ω).

1. In the verbs in -αω contraction is frequent. If the resolved form were written wherever the metre admits it, we should still find that in about half the whole number of cases the contraction must remain. It is worth notice too that contracted forms are often used in phrases of a fixed type, as ἔπεα πτερόεντα προσηύδα (or προσηύδων)—τόδ᾽ ὀφθαλμοῖσιν ὁρῶμαι— ὁρᾷ (ὁρᾶν) φάος ἠελίοιο—ἀνείρεαι ἠδὲ μεταλλᾷς—ἐξαύδα, μὴ κεῦθε, and the like†. It has indeed been noticed that there is an apparent preference for the resolved -αον of the 1 Sing. and 3 Plur. Impf. ‡; but this must be accidental. We must conclude then that contracted and uncontracted forms of verbs in -αω were used in the language of Homeric times with equal freedom: or at least—if this be thought improbable—that they subsisted together as alternative forms in the poetical dialect.

---

* φόως may represent an ancient Plur. φάως (Joh. Schmidt, *Pluralb.* p. 142).
† Mangold, *Curt. Stud.* vi. 194. ‡ Menrad, pp. 122-124.

2. Verbs in -εω rarely contract -εο or -εω, except in the Participle (-ευμενος for -εομενος). This rule is confirmed from New Ionic inscriptions (Erman, *Curt. Stud.* v. 292), as well as the MSS. of Herodotus. For ευ in ποιεύμην (Il. 9. 495), θηεῦντο (Il. 7. 444), ὀχλεῦνται (Il. 21. 261), ἐγεγώνευν (Od. 9. 47, &c.) and a few similar forms we should write -εο (see § 57).

The contraction of -εε, -εει is established by the large number of instances * in which it is required by the metre. Moreover it is not merely a *license*, necessary for the sake of admitting certain forms into the hexameter (such as ταρβεῖς, νεικεῖν, τελεῖται, ἡγεῖσθαι, σμαραγεῖ, ἐφίλει, οἰνοχόει). Among the instances of contraction in the last foot we find 29 of -ει for -εε (as χόλος δέ μιν ἄγριος ᾕρει), and 16 of -εῖ for -έει (as καί με γλυκὺς ἵμερος αἱρεῖ); also the forms φιλεῖ (Il. 2. 197 τιμὴ δ' ἐκ Διός ἐστι, φιλεῖ δέ ἑ μητίετα Ζεύς, also Il. 7. 280., 10. 245, 552., 16. 94, Od. 15. 74), δοκεῖ (Od. 2. 33, and six times in the phrase ὥς μοι δοκεῖ εἶναι ἄριστα), τελεῖ (Il. 4. 161), καλεῖ (Il. 3. 390, Od. 17. 382), φοβεῖ (Il. 17. 177). On the other hand the uncontracted form has the support of the metre in about a hundred places, and against the instances now quoted of φιλεῖ, &c. we have to set about thirty of the corresponding uncontracted φιλέει, δοκέεις, -ει, τελέει, καλέει, φοβέειν. The uncontracted form therefore seems to have a slight preference, when the metre allows either.

In the MSS. of Homer contraction is generally introduced as far as possible, according to the tendencies of Attic: but the open forms occasionally survive, chiefly in the fourth foot (in such forms as προσεφώνεε θεῖος ὄνειρος—καὶ ᾔτεε σῆμα ἰδέσθαι—κατὰ δ' ᾔρεε Πηλείωνα). And the metre clearly points to the open form in several other places: as—

Il. 11. 553 (= 17. 663) τάς τε τρέει ἐσσύμενός περ.

21. 362 ὡς δὲ λέβης ζέει ἔνδον κτλ.

16. 201 ἀπειλέετε Τρώεσσιν.

Od. 10. 548 ἀωτέετε γλυκὺν ὕπνον.

3. Verbs in -οω generally contract; χολοῦμαι, κορυφοῦται, γουνοῦμαι. For the 'assimilated' forms δηϊόωντο, κατηπιόωντο, ἐστρατόωντα, ῥυπόωντα (§ 55) we ought, on the analogy of the Verbs in -αω, to substitute δηϊόοντο, &c.

57.] Synizesis. The vowel ε sometimes coalesces with a following ο or ω, so as to form one syllable for the purpose of the metre; e. g. ἀελπτέοντες, ἠλάστεον, ἠγίνεον, ἐπόρθεον (at the end of a verse), οἰκέοιτο, εἰλέωσι, χρεώμενος. Whether the pronunciation of these words differed from that of the contracted forms is a question which perhaps there are no means of determining.

---

* About 160 according to the list in Menrad, pp. 132-142.

Meaning of Verbs of the I-Class.

58.] Verbs in -εω are mainly Intransitive, whether formed from Adjectives, as ἀπιστέω *I am unbelieving,* or abstract Nouns, as μοχθέω *I labour.* But there is also a group of Causatives in -εω, as φοβέω *I put to flight,* ὀχέω, φορέω.

Verbs in -οω are chiefly formed from Adjectives in -ος, and are Causative, as χηρόω *I make desolate.* Exceptions are, ὑπνώ-οντες *sleeping,* ῥιγόω *I shudder,* βιόω *I live.*

59.] **Desideratives.** One instance in -σειω is found in Homer, ὀψείοντες (Il. 14. 37) *going to see.* A suffix -ιε(ο) may be found in κακκείοντες *going to bed* (κατά-κει-μαι), πι-όμενα *going to drink,* δραίνεις (Il. 10. 96) *thou art for doing.*

60.] **Frequentatives,** expressing *habitual* action, in -ταω, -ταζω, -τεω : as εὐχετάο-μαι, ναιετάω, οἰνοπο-τάζω, ζη-τέω (δί-ζη-μαι), λαμ-πετόωντι, ἑλκυστάζων.

In -ιαω, κελευτιόων *shouting* (as if from an abstract Noun κελευ-τία), κυδιόων *glorying.*

In -ναω, as ἐρυκανόωσι *keep restraining,* ἰσχανόωσι.

In -θαω, as τηλεθόωσα *blooming* (θαλ-έθω).

61.] **Intensives,** expressing actions *intensified by repetition.* These are generally reduplicated Verbs of the I-Class, the reduplication containing either a diphthong or a second consonant, as δει-δίσσεσθαι *to terrify,* δαι-δάλλων *working curiously,* ἐκ-παι-φάσσειν *to rush in front,* παμ-φαίνων *gleaming,* βαμ-βαίνων *staggering,* μαρμαίροντες *glittering,* κάρ-καιρε *chattered,* πόρ-φυρε *was troubled* (lit. of water), πα-φλάζοντα *splashing,* πα-πταίνων *peeping round,* μαι-μάει *rages,* δενδίλλων (for δελδ-?) *winking.*

62.] **Collateral forms of the Present.** It is characteristic of the Homeric language that Present Stems formed in different ways from the same Verb-Stem often subsist together in actual use, as alternative forms expressing the same (or nearly the same) meaning. Thus we have λήθ-ω, ληθ-άνω, λανθάνω ; πεύθο-μαι, πυνθάνο-μαι ; βά-σκω, βαίνω, βιβά-s, βιβά-ζω, βιβάσθων ; ἵκω, ἱκάνω, ἱκ-νέ-ο-μαι ; ἔχω, ἴσχω, ἰσχάνω, ἰσχανάω ; ἐρύ-κο-μαι, ἐρυ-κ-άνω, ἐρυ-κ-ανό-ωσι ; ἀλεύ-ομαι, ἀλύσκω, ἀλυσκάνω, ἀλυσκάζω ; τά-νυ-μαι, τα-νύω, τείνω, τιταίνω ; τεύχω, τυγχάνω, τι-τύ-σκο-μαι ; μένω, μί-μνω, μι-μνά-ζω.

It may be conjectured that these different forms originally expressed corre-sponding shades of meaning. In some cases a more specific meaning may still be traced ; e.g. **φάσκω** *I allege* (i.e. *keep saying,* or perhaps *try to say*) has something of the Iterative force (cp. **ῥίπτασκε** *he kept flinging about*) which in θνήσκω, διδάσκω, &c. has been softened or generalised into the ordinary meaning of the Present. Similarly the reduplication in βίβας *striding*, μιμνάζω *I stay waiting*, τιταίνω *I stretch* is to be compared with that of the Intensive Verbs. The Perfect, too, may be regarded as a refined and generalised kind of Intensive; cp. the forms λέληκα, κέκρᾱγα, μέμῡκα, &c. with καρκαίρω, ὀλολύζω, παφλάζω, &c.

Future in -σω.

63.] The Stem of the Future is formed by suffixing -σε(ο) to the Verb-Stem (in the strong form); as φή-σει, δώ-σω, δείξω (δεικ-), ἐκ-πέρσω (περθ-), πείσομαι (πενθ-), χείσεται (χενδ-), δέξομαι (δεχ-), εἴ-σομαι (εἶ-μι).

The Stem ἐσ- gives ἔσ-σομαι and ἔσομαι (3 Sing. ἔσε-ται and ἔσ-ται); so ἔσ-σω (Ϝεσ-). The Futures φράσσο-μαι (or φράσο-μαι), μάσσε-ται, ἀπο-δάσσο-μαι (δάσο-νται), χάσσο-νται are formed like the corresponding Aorists in -σα; see § 39.

Other Verbs which have an Aorist in -σσᾰ (-σᾰ)—the Verb-stem ending in a *short* vowel (§ 39, 2)—usually form the Future without σ. Thus we find:—

Aor. τελέσσαι   Fut. τελέ-ω.
καλέσσαι   καλέ-ουσα (Il. 3. 383).
ὀλέσσαι   ὀλεῖται, ὀλέ-εσθε (also ὀλέσσεις, ὀλέσσει).
μαχέσασθαι   μαχέ-ονται, μαχεῖται.
κορέσασθαι   κορέ-εις.
κρεμάσαντες   κρεμόω (for κρεμά-ω).
ἐπέρασσε   περάαν (for περά-ειν).
ἐδάμασσα   δαμόω, δαμᾷ (for δαμά-ω, δαμά-ει).
ἤλασσα   ἐλόω, Inf. ἐλάαν (for ἐλά-ω, ἐλά-ειν).
ὤμοσα   ὀμοῦμαι (for ὀμό-ομαι: 3 Sing. ὀμεῖται,
                         on the analogy of ὀλεῖται, μαχεῖται).
ἐτάννσσε   τανύω.
ἀνύσας   ἀνύω.
ἔρυσσα   ἐρύω, ἐρύ-εσθαι.
ἐρρύσατο   ῥύεσθαι (Il. 20. 195).
ἀντιάσας   ἀντιόω (also ἀντιάσεις, Od. 22. 28).
ἐκόμισσα   κομιῶ.
ἀεικίσσασθαι   ἀεικιῶ.
κτερίσαιεν   κτεριοῦσι.
                        ἀγλαϊεῖσθαι.

It is not easy to determine (even approximately) the number of Future Stems formed like the Aorist in -σσᾰ. In several instances the reading is uncertain: e. g. between ἐρύσσεσθαι and ἐρύσασθαι (Il. 21. 176, Od. 21. 125), ἀγάσσεσθαι and ἀγάσασθαι (Od. 4. 181), ἀνύσσεσθαι and ἀνύσασθαι (Od. 16. 373), παρε-λάσσεις, παρελάσσαις and παρελάσσαι (Il. 23. 427), ἀπουρίσσουσι and ἀπουρήσουσι (Il. 22. 489). Several forms may be either

Fut. or Aor. Subj.: γουνάσομαι (Il. 1. 427), ὀπάσσομεν (Il. 24.
153), εὐνάσω (Od. 4. 408), ληΐσσομαι (Od. 23. 357), ἐρύσσεται
(Il. 10. 44), ὀλέσω (Od. 13. 399), ἀρεσσόμεθα. There remain:
ἀρκέσει (Il. 21. 131—in Od. 16. 261 we should read ἀρκέσῃ),
αἰδέσεται (Il. 22. 124., 24. 208), ὀνόσσεται (Il. 9. 55), γανύσσεται
(Il. 14. 504), ὀλέσσεις (Il. 12. 250), ὀλέσσει (Od. 2. 49), and a
few forms of derivative Verbs in -αζω, -ιζω, viz. αἰχμάσσουσι
(Il. 4. 324), θαυμάσσεται (Il. 18. 467), ἐφοπλίσσουσι (Od.
6. 69), ἀντιάσεις (Od. 22. 28). On the whole it would appear
that the Futures with σσ (or σ representing original σσ) are confined to the stems which ended in σ or a dental. In a very few
instances they are due to analogy, like the corresponding Aorists
in -σσᾰ. Distinct Stems are used in ἁρπάζω, Aor. ἥρπασεν and
ἁρπάξαι, Fut. ἁρπάξων; ἀφύσσω, Aor. ἀφυσσάμενος, Fut. ἀφύξειν.

From μάχο-μαι, besides Aor. μαχέσασθαι, Fut. μαχέ-ονται, the MSS. give an
Aor. μαχέσσατο, Fut. μαχήσομαι. The ancient critics were divided as to these
forms: Aristarchus wrote μαχήσατο, μαχήσομαι, others μαχέσσατο, μαχ-
έσσομαι. The form μαχέσσα-το is supported by μαχέσασθαι; on the other hand
μαχήσομαι is supported by μαχητής, μαχήμων, &c. Considering the number of
cases in which the language has avoided forming the First Aorist and the
Future in the same way, the probability would seem to be that the MSS. are
right.

For γυναῖκα γαμέσσεται αὐτός, which the MSS. give in Il. 9. 394, Aristarchus
read γυναῖκά γε μάσσεται αὐτός: doubtless rightly, the trochaic caesura in the
fourth foot being unknown in Homer (§ 367, 2 : Veitch, p. 130). The usual
Fut. is γαμέω.

Verb-Stems ending in a *liquid* (ρ, λ, μ, ν) insert ε and drop the
σ, as μεν-έ-ω, ἀγγελ-έων, κερ-έειν, κραν-έεσθαι, ὀτρῦν-έω, κτεν-έω*,
and (with contraction) ἐκ-φανεῖ (Il. 19. 104), κατα-κτενεῖ (Il. 23.
412). But some Stems in ρ form -ρσω, as δια-φθέρ-σει, ὄρ-σουσα
(Il. 21. 335), θερ-σόμενος (Od. 19. 507).
Similarly μάχομαι forms μαχέ-ονται (Il. 2. 366), and with contraction μαχεῖται (Il. 20. 26).
The derivative Verbs in -αω, -εω, -οω, -νω form -ησω, -ωσω,
-ῦσω, the vowel being invariably long.
Exceptional: διδώ-σομεν (Od. 13. 358), διδώσειν (Od. 24. 314).
On the anomalous Futures ἔδομαι, πίομαι, δήω, κείω, βείομαι, see
§§ 59, 80.

64.] **The Future in -σεω.** The Suffix -σεε(ο) is found in
ἐσ-σεῖται (Il. 2. 393., 13. 317, Od. 19. 302), and πεσέονται (Il. 11.
824) which is perhaps for *πετ-σεο-νται (but see § 41). Also,

---

* The forms κατα-κτανέουσι (Il. 6. 409) and κατακτανέεσθε (Il. 14. 481) are
probably corrupt (Cobet, V. L. p. 195). κτανέοντα (Il. 18. 309) involves a use
of the Fut. Part. which is hardly to be defended: see § 86.

the accent of the Futures κομι-ῶ, ἀεικι-ῶ, κτερι-οῦσι, ἀγλαϊ-εῖσθαι points to contamination of the forms in -σω and in -εω.

According to some ancient grammarians the Fut. of ἀνύω, ἐρύω, &c. should be written ἀνῶ, ἐρῶ, &c. ; see Schol. Il. 11. 454., 20. 452. This form in -σῶ is found in Attic (πλευσοῦμαι, &c. : see however Rutherford's *New Phrynichus*, pp. 91-95) ; it answers to the Doric Fut. in -σιω.

65.] Futures from Perfect and Aorist Stems. A Future Perfect meaning appears in μεμνή-σομαι *I shall remember*, κεκλή-σῃ *thou wilt bear the name*, εἰρή-σεται *will be said*, κεχολώ-σεται *he will be in wrath*, δεδέξομαι *I will await*, πεφή-σεται *will appear* (Il. 17. 155), πεφή-σεαι *thou wilt be slain*, τετεύξεται *will be made*, λελείψεται *will remain behind*, βεβρώσεται *will be devoured*. In these cases the Fut. answers to a Perfect in actual use.

For πεφήσεαι J. Wackernagel (*K. Z.* xxvii. 279) would read πεφείσεαι (for πε-φεν-σεαι, related to πεφᾰ-ται as τετεύξεται to τέτυκται). But the stem πεφεν-does not occur in the inflexion of the Verb, and there is no analogy to suggest it. More probably πεφήσεαι is formed from πέφαται on the analogy of ἐφᾰ-το and φή-σω, δύνα-μαι and δυνή-σομαι, &c.

Active Futures of the kind occur in Il. 15. 98 οὐδέ τί φημι πᾶσιν ὁμῶς θυμὸν κεχαρη-σέμεν *I do not suppose I shall gladden the heart of all alike* (cp. Od. 23. 266 οὐ μέν τοι θυμὸς κεχαρή-σεται *will not be gladdened*) : Il. 22. 223 πεπιθή-σω *I will persuade* : Od. 21. 153, 170 κεκαδή-σει *will deprive*. These forms may be either connected with the Perfect (κεχαρη-ότα *rejoicing*), or with the Reduplicated Aorist (κεχάρο-ντο *were gladdened*, πεπιθεῖν *to persuade*). The latter view is supported by two other Futures of the kind ; κεκαδη-σόμεθα *we will give way*, answering to the Aor. κεκαδών, Mid. κεκάδο-ντο ; and πεφιδή-σεται *will spare*, answering to πεφιδέ-σθαι *to spare*. It will be seen that the Active forms of this kind have a distinctly *causative* meaning, whereas (*e.g.*) χαιρήσω and πιθήσω are intransitive.

Futures from the Passive Aorists. Of this formation two examples at most can be found in Homer : μιγή-σε-σθαι (Il. 10. 365), and δαή-σε-αι (Od. 3. 187., 19. 325). It has been already noticed (§ 9) that there is nothing in the Greek Future answering to the distinction between the Aorist and the Imperfect, though à priori such a distinction is quite conceivable.

It is worth noticing that in the Doric dialect this group of Futures takes the Active endings : as φανήσω.

66.] The Fut. is sometimes found with Mid. Endings while the corresponding Pres. is Act. The examples in Homer are :—

εἰμί, ἔσομαι ; θέω, θεύσομαι; κλαίω, κλαύσομαι ; φεύγω, φεύξομαι ; ἀείδω, ἀείσομαι ; κατα-νεύω, κατα-νεύσομαι ; θαυμάζω, θαυμάσσεται.

With these are usually reckoned the Verbs in which the Pres.
is of a different formation, as ὀμοῦμαι (ὄμ-νυμι), πεσέονται (πίπτω),
τέξεσθαι(τίκτω), φθήσονται (φθάνω), βήσομαι (βαίνω), καμεῖται (κάμνω),
τεύξεσθαι (τυγχάνω), ἀμαρτήσεσθαι (ἀμαρτάνω), θανέεσθαι (θνῄσκω),
πείσομαι (πάσχω) : also the Futures to which no Pres. corresponds,
as εἴσομαι (οἶδα), δείσομαι (δείδια), ὄψομαι (ὀπ-).

It may help to explain these cases if we consider that the Fut.
Act. is apt to have a *Transitive* sense, as in στήσω, βήσω, φύσω.
Hence there was a tendency to have recourse to the Middle
whenever a distinctly intransitive sense was wanted.

Historical Tenses—the Augment.

67.] **The Augment** takes two forms, the *Syllabic* and the
Temporal.

The Syllabic Augment is the prefix ἐ-, and is used for Stems
beginning with a consonant. The Temporal Augment is a
simple lengthening of the initial vowel of a Stem, the vowels ἀ
and ε becoming η; as ἦγο-ν (ἄγο-), ἦλα-σα-ν (ἐλἄ-), ἵκε-το (ἴκε-),
ὦρ-το (ὀρ-), ἠλήλα-το (Pf. ἐλήλα-ται), ἤνεον (αἰνέω), ᾤχετο (οἴχομαι). So the Impf. ᾖα *I went* (Sanscr. *áyam*), from the stem
εἰ (εἰ-μι) : as to the form ἤϊα see § 12.

Many seeming exceptions are due to the loss of the original
initial consonants, ϝ, σ, ι. The loss of one of these consonants
may generally be presumed whenever we find the Syllabic instead
of the Temporal Augment. Thus—

ϝ has been lost in ἐ-άγη and ἔ-αξε (ἄγνυμι), ἐ-άλη (ϝελ-), ἔ-ειπε,
ἐ-έσ-σα-το (ἔννυμι), εἶδον (for ἔ-ϊδο-ν), ἐ-ώθεο-ν ; so perhaps, with
contraction of εε to ει, εἴρυ-σα (ϝερυ-), and εἴλο-ν.

For εἶδον there is an Æolic form εὔιδον (ἔ-ϝιδον, cp. εὔαδε), which should
perhaps be restored in some at least of the numerous places where the present
text of Homer has εἴσιδε (Nauck, *Mél. gr.-rom.* ii. 407).

σ in ἐ-έσσα-το (for ἐ-έσσα-, from σεδ-), and, with contraction,
εἷπε-το (σεπ-), εἷσα-ν (σεδ-), εἷχο-ν (σεχ-), εἷρπο-ν (σερπ-). In
these cases the σ passed into the rough breathing, which was
then thrown back on the Augment: but εἶχον has the smooth
breathing owing to the following χ. Also εἴα (ἐάω for σεϝάω).

ι (or *y*) perhaps in ἔηκα (for ἐ-ι̯ηκα) and, with contraction, εἷμεν
(ἐ-έ-μεν), and παρ-είθη (-ε-εθη). But see § 16.

Several Homeric forms have been supposed to point to a Syllabic Augment
ἠ- (instead of ἐ-). One of these—ἤϊα *I went*—has been already explained (§ 12).
As to the others we have to note as follows :

(1) ἤειρεν (Il. 10. 499) is not from εἴρω *to join together* (Lat. *sero*), but from
ἀείρω : for, as Cobet has shown (*Misc. Crit.* p. 326), ἀείρω is a technical word in
the sense required (cp. Il. 15. 680 συναείρεται ἵππους, also the words ξυνωρίς, for
ξυν-αορ-ίς, and παρ-ήορος).

(2) In several words (as usually written) the initial vowel of the Stem is lengthened after ἐ-ϝ-: ἤνδανε (for ἐ-'ϝανδανε), ἐ-ϣνοχόει (ϝοινοχοέω), ἀν-έ-ϣγεν, ἀν-έ-ϣξε (ἀνα-ϝοίγω), also ἐ-άγη (ϝάγ-νυμι), with ā in one place (Il. 11. 559), and the Plpf. forms ἐώλπει (ἔολπα, ϝελπ-), ἐώργει (ἔοργα, ϝεργ-), ἐώκει (ἔοικα, ϝικ-). In some of these there may be merely confusion with the later use of the Temporal Augment: e. g. ἐήνδανε is doubtless due to the Attic ἤνδανε, a form which arose after the loss of ϝ. Hence recent editors write ἐάνδανε, ἐοινοχόει, ἀνέοιγον, also ἐόλπει, ἐύργει, ἐοίκει.

(3) A different explanation is required for ἐάγη (ā), supported as it is by Attic ἐώρων (ὁράω) and ἐάλων (ă in ἀλῶναι, &c.)*. These point to an Augment ἠ-, the combinations ηϝο, ηϝă passing into εω, εā (as in βασιλέως, -εā for -ηϝος, -ηϝα). Such an Augment is also found in ἠείδης, ἠείδει (Plpf. of οἶδα), and ἠΐσκε. There is much probability in the suggestion of G. Meyer (G. G. p. 423) that this ἠ- is a Temporal Augment obtained from the prothetic ἐ- so often found before ϝ: e. g. in ἐ-εισάμενος (ϝειδ-). Thus ἠΐσκε would be the augmented form of ἐΐσκω, not of ἴσκω.

(4) The forms ἀνέϣγε, ἀνέϣξε are peculiarly difficult on account of the Homeric Pres. ὀΐγ-νυμι, Aor. ὤϊξα, and Lesbian ὀείγω (Pres. Inf. ὀείγην, Coll. 214, 43). We might read ἀν-όειγε, &c., but the ordinary forms οἴγω (Hes. Op. 817), ἀν-οίγω, &c. would still be unexplained.

Initial ρ is nearly always doubled, initial λ, μ, ν, σ very often. This may often be explained as the assimilation of an original initial ϝ or σ : thus ἔρρηξα is for ἔ-ϝρηξα, and so ἔρρεξε (ϝεργ-) and ϝρεγ-), ἐρρίγησε (ϝρῑγ-). Again ἔρρεεν is for ἔ-σρεεν, ἔννεον for ἔ-σνεον, ἔλλαβε perhaps for ἔ-σλαβε (Joh. Schmidt, Pluralb. p. 434). So ἔδδεισεν (which Ar. wrote ἔδεισεν) is for ἔ-δϝεισεν : and ἔσσευα probably for ἐ-κιενα(Sanscr. root ϛyu). So too in ἐ-γδούπησαν the γ reappears which is lost in the unaugmented δούπησεν.

There are instances, however, to which this explanation does not apply, as ἔμμαθε. These are probably due to the influence of forms such as those already mentioned upon the traditional poetic dialect (Curtius, Stud. iv. 479 ff.; for a different view see Hartel's Homerische Studien). Cp. § 371.

68.] The Pluperfect. The Perfect Stem forms the corresponding Historical or Past Tense—the Pluperfect—in two ways :—

1. Simply, with the Augment (often omitted) and the Secondary Person-Endings. All Middle forms of the Tense are of this kind, as ἐ-τέτυκ-το, ἐφ-ῆπτο, τετά-σθην, ἠλήλα-το. In the Active the examples are comparatively few, viz. δείδιε (Il. 18. 34), ἀνήνοθεν (Il. 11. 266), and ἐπ-ενήνοθε (Il. 2. 219); Plur. ἐ-πέπιθ-μεν, ἐ-δείδι-μεν, ἐ-δείδι-σαν, ἔστα-σαν, βέβα-σαν, μέμα-σαν, ἀπο-τέθνα-σαν; Dual ἐΐκ-την, ἐκ-γεγά-την.

---

* ἥλω was taken (Od. 22. 230 σῇ δ' ἥλω βουλῇ κτλ.) should perhaps be written ἐάλω. The Stem 'ϝᾰλω- appears in the Moods (ἀλώω, ἀλῴην, ἀλῶναι, ἀλούς), except in the form ἀλόντε (Il. 5. 487), where the metre requires ā.

With these may be placed the Thematic forms ἐ-γέγωνε (Il.
14. 469), ἄνωγο-ν, ἄνωγε, ἐ-πέπληγο-ν, πεπλήγε-το, ἐμέμηκον, in
Hesiod ἐπέφυκον : see § 27.

2. By Composition, with the Augment and the Suffix -εα
(probably for -εσα), joined to the longer form of the Stem : e.g.
ἐ-τεθήπ-εα, πεποίθεα, ἠνώγ-εα. The 3 Sing. usually has -εε(ν)
contracted -ει(ν), as ἐ-πεποίθει, ἠνώγειν, δεδήει, ἠρήρει, βεβήκει.
The Plur. occurs only once in Homer, in ἐοίκ-εσαν (Il. 13. 102) :
the Dual never.

To this group belongs ᾔδεα I knew, 2 Sing. ἠείδης (for ἐ-ϝείδεας),
also ᾔδησθα, 3 Sing. ἠείδει, ᾔδει (or, as Aristarchus read, ἠείδη,
ᾔδη). As to the augment ἠ- see § 67. In respect of form ᾔδεα
is a Sigmatic Aorist, standing for ἐ-ϝείδεσα, Sanscr. ávedisham,
and is only a Pluperfect because it is used as the past tense
answering to οἶδα (M. U. iii. p. 16).

69.] Loss of Augment. The Augment is so often dropped in
Homer that the augmented and the unaugmented forms are
almost equally numerous. It has been observed however * that
the forms without the Augment are comparatively rare in the
speeches, the proportion of augmented to unaugmented forms
(excluding speeches which mainly consist of narrative matter)
being about 10 to 3, whereas in narrative it is about 5 to 7. It
would appear therefore that the Augment is chiefly omitted
where the context shows that past time is meant ; and this is
confirmed by the remarkable fact that the Iteratives, which are
only used as Historical Tenses, do not take the Augment.

The only clear instance of an Iterative form with the Augm. is ἐ-μισγέσ-
κοντο (Od. 20. 7). On the forms ἐ-φασκο-ν, ἐ-φασκε see § 49.

Meaning of the Present and Aorist Stems.

70.] **The forms which contain the Present Stem** (the Present and Imperfect Indic., with the Moods of the Present)
denote *progressive* action (incipient, continued, repeated, &c.), as
opposed to a *single* fact or event.

It is easy to understand why a language which distinguished these two
kinds of action should have no Aorist for present time (*βῆμι, *λάβω, &c.).
The present is not a space of time, but a point ; what is present therefore is
not (generally speaking) a whole action or event, but the fact that it is in
course of happening. So in English we usually say, not *I write now*, but *I am
writing now*. The mere effort of regarding an action as in present time almost
obliges us to give it a progressive character.

The forms εἰμί, εἶμι, φημί, ἄγω, γράφω, &c., in which the Stem has the form
generally found only in Aorists (§ 11, § 30), may be regarded as surviving

---

* Konrad Koch, *De Augmento apud Homerum omisso*, Brunswick, 1868.

instances of the 'Present Aorist,' *i.e.* of a Present not conveying the notion of progress. We may compare the English use of *I am, I go* (now archaic in the sense of *I am going*), *I say* (*says he*), &c. In these cases the use of a distinctly progressive form has not been felt to be necessary.

A past action may usually be regarded, if we choose, as a single fact, irrespective of its duration (ἐβασίλευσεν ἔτη τριάκοντα *he reigned*, not *he continued reigning*). But an action which is thought of as contemporary with some other event is almost necessarily regarded as progressive. Accordingly, answering to the Present *I am writing* (*now*), we have the Past Tense *I was writing* (*when he came*).

It follows from what has been said that a Pres. or Impf. may be used either (1) because the action intended is essentially progressive, or (2) because the time is fixed by reference (a) to the moment of speaking, or (β) to a point of time in the past. *E. g.* δίδωμι may mean either *I seek to give, I offer,* or *I am giving;* ἐδίδου either *he offered* or *he was giving.* In the second of these uses the notion of progress is only *relative*, arising from the relation of time under which the action is thought of *.

71.] From the relative notion of progress or continuance is derived the general rule that the Impf. is used of a *subordinate* action or circumstance : Il. 8. 87 ὄφρ' ὁ γέρων ἀπέταμνε τόφρ' Ἕκτορος ὠκέες ἵπποι ἦλθον *while he was cutting the chariot came.*

Some varieties of this use may be noticed :—

(1) The Impf. shows that a Verb stands in a special connexion with the Verb of another clause ; Il. 1. 3–5 ψυχὰς Ἄϊδι προΐαψεν ἡρώων, αὐτοὺς δὲ ἑλώρια τεῦχε κύνεσσιν *sent down the souls of heroes to Hades,* while *it made themselves a prey to dogs.*

Od. 8. 532 ἔνθ' ἄλλους μὲν πάντας ἐλάνθανε δάκρυα λείβων, Ἀλκίνοος δέ μιν οἶος ἐπεφράσατ' ἠδ' ἐνόησε while *he was unobserved by the others, Alcinous observed him.*

So Il. 7. 303 ὡς ἄρα φωνήσας δῶκε ξίφος ἀργυρόηλον, Αἴας δὲ ζωστῆρα δίδου (gave in exchange).

Od. 8. 63 τὸν περὶ Μοῦσ' ἐφίλησε, δίδου δ' ἀγαθόν τε κακόν τε, ὀφθαλμῶν μὲν ἄμερσε, δίδου δ' ἡδεῖαν ἀοιδήν.

(2) In *oratio obliqua,* as Il. 22. 439 ἤγγειλ' ὅττι ῥά οἱ πόσις ἔκτοθι μίμνε πυλάων.

(3) The action or point of time to which the Verb in the Impf. is subordinate may be merely implied :—

Il. 4. 155 θάνατόν νύ τοι ὅρκι' ἔταμνον *it was death then to you that I made* (*in making the treaty*).

So in the common use with ἄρα : as σὺ δ' οὐκ ἄρα τοῖος ἔησθα *you were not as I thought* (=you are not, it now seems).

---

* Aken, *Hauptdata,* p. 9.

72.] **Essentially progressive** action (incomplete or continuous) is exemplified—

(1) In the Verbs which form the Aor. from a different Verb-Stem: ὁράω *I watch* (Lat. *tueor*, whereas εἶδον means *I descried*); λέγω *I relate, set forth* (but εἶπον *I said*); φέρω *I carry* (but ἤνεγκον *I brought*); so τρέχω, ἔρχομαι (expressing different kinds of motion).

(2) In other Verbs of motion, esp. βαίνω and ἵστημι, as Il. 21. 313 ἵστη δὲ μέγα κῦμα *raise up a great wave*, and often in the Mid., as Il. 2. 473 ἐν πεδίῳ ἵσταντο *were drawn up in the plain*, παρίστατο *came and stood beside*, &c.

Note 1. We should read ἵστασαν (not ἔστᾰσαν as a First Aor.) in—
Il. 2. 525 στίχας ἵστασαν (Bekk., La R., from the best MS.).
12. 56 τοὺς ἵστασαν υἷες ᾿Αχαιῶν *which the Greeks had planted*; see § 73.
Od. 3. 180 τέτρατον ἦμαρ ἔην ὅτ᾽ ἐν ᾿Αργεϊ νῆας ἐΐσας
Τυδεΐδεω ἕταροι ... ἵστασαν (see Ameis *a. l.*).
8. 435 αἱ δὲ λοετροχόον τρίποδ᾽ ἵστασαν }
18. 307 αὐτίκα λαμπτῆρας τρεῖς ἵστασαν } Bekk., La Roche.

2. The Verb ἄγω is often so used: Il. 1. 367 τὴν δὲ διεπράθομέν τε καὶ ἤγομεν ἐνθάδε πάντα; Il. 7. 363 κτήματα δ᾽ ὅσσ᾽ ἀγόμην *the treasures which I brought* (=*have brought*); Il. 9. 664 τὴν Λεσβόθεν ἦγε *whom he had brought*. In this Verb, however, the Aorist meaning appears distinctly in the Participle; Il. 6. 87 ἣ δὲ ξυνάγουσα γεραιάς *assembling* (=*having assembled*); Il. 1. 311 εἷσεν ἄγων *brought and seated* (cp. 3. 48., 4. 392., 11. 827., 22. 350). Perhaps these uses should be connected with the Aoristic form of the Stem (§ 70).

(3) In Verbs expressing the *beginning* of a motion, as ὤρνυτο *bestirred himself* (but ὦρτο *arose*); ἀφίει, προΐει, ἔπεμπε; μύθων ἦρχε *began speech*.

This usage extends to all words which imply a continuous result; κελεύει, ἐκέλευε, ἐπέτελλε, ἤτεε; οὐκ ἐᾷ *will not allow*; λείπω (*to leave=to keep at home*).

(4) ἀκούω and πεύθομαι sometimes mean *to know by hearing*; as Il. 11. 497 οὐδέ πω ῞Εκτωρ πεύθετο *Hector was not yet aware*: 14. 125 τὰ δὲ μέλλετ᾽ ἀκονέμεν *ye are like to have heard it*; Od. 3. 87, 187, 193. So in Attic μανθάνω *I understand*, αἰσθάνομαι *I am aware*, πυνθάνομαι *I learn* (Goodwin, § 28).

73.] A process thought of in relation to the present time, or to a point in the past, is expressed by the Impf. (=Engl. *I have been doing, I had been doing*): *e. g.*—
Il. 6. 282 μέγα γάρ μιν ᾿Ολύμπιος ἔτρεφε πῆμα *has reared him up to be a mischief* (a process). Cp. Il. 1. 414 τί νύ σ᾽ ἔτρεφον; *why have I reared thee?* 9. 524 ἐπευθόμεθα *we have been accustomed to hear*. So the Participle, Il. 3. 44 φάντες *who have been saying*.

74.] The 'historical Present' is not found in Homer, but

somewhat the same effect is often given by the use which may
be called the *descriptive* Imperfect. *E. g.*—

Il. 2. 150 νῆας ἔπ᾽ ἐσσεύοντο, ποδῶν δ᾽ ὑπένερθε κονίη
    ἵστατ᾽ ἀειρομένη, τοὶ δ᾽ ἀλλήλοισι κέλευον
    ἅπτεσθαι νηῶν ἠδ᾽ ἑλκέμεν εἰς ἅλα δῖαν,
    οὐρούς τ᾽ ἐξεκάθαιρον κ.τ.λ.

The Impf. appears sometimes to be used in a description along
with Aorists for the sake of connexion and variety (*i. e.* in order
to avoid a series of detached assertions): *e. g.* in Il. 1. 437–439.,
2. 43–45., 4. 112–119, Od. 4. 577–580.

75.] **The Aorist** gives the meaning of a Verb without the
accessory notion of progress or continuance. It does not *describe*,
or transport us to a time in the past when the action was
present (as the Impf. does), but makes us think of it as *now past.*
Hence it asserts a *single* occurrence,—an action, or series of
actions, regarded as an undivided whole,—or *completion*, a *culminating point*, in which the action is summed up. Thus μογέω *I am
toiling*, ἐμόγησα (Il. 1. 162) *I have toiled ;* νοέω *I think of*, ἐνόησε
perceived, understood ; θαρσέω *I feel confident*, θαρσήσας *taking
courage*, and so δείσας, ἀλγήσας, μίσησε, νεμέσησε, &c., of the
access of a feeling; δηρινθήτην (Il. 16. 756) *joined in strife ;*
παπτήνας *casting a glance;* φωνήσας either *raising his voice* or
having spoken : ἐπ᾽ ἤματι δακρύσαντες (Il. 19. 229) *performing the
due weeping for the day.*

76.] **The Aorist** is often used in Homer of the immediate past
—that which in an especial sense is thought of as *now* past :—

Il. 2. 114 νῦν δὲ κακὴν ἀπάτην βουλεύσατο, καί με κελεύει
    δυσκλέα Ἄργος ἱκέσθαι.

Od. 1. 182 νῦν δ᾽ ὧδε ξὺν νηὶ κατήλυθον (cp. 23. 27).

Il. 20. 16 τίπτ᾽ αὖτ᾽, ἀργικέραυνε, θεοὺς ἀγορήνδε κάλεσσας ;

Sometimes the Aor. seems to give the question a tone of im-
patience: Il. 2. 323 τίπτ᾽ ἄνεω ἐγένεσθε ; 4. 243 τίφθ᾽ οὕτως
ἔστητε τεθηπότες ; (vulg. ἔστητε, an impossible form), cp. 20. 178
τί νυ τόσσον ὁμίλου πολλὸν ἐπελθὼν ἔστης ; 21. 562., 22. 122.,
Od. 4. 810., 10. 64. Cp. the Attic use of τί οὐ, as Soph. O. T.
1002 τί δῆτ᾽ ἐγὼ οὐχὶ . . . ἐξελυσάμην ; (Goodwin, § 62).

When the Aor. is used of an action which is subordinate to
another in the past, it implies completion before the main
action : Il. 2. 642 οὐδ᾽ ἄρ᾽ ἔτ᾽ αὐτὸς ἔην, θάνε δὲ ξανθὸς Μελέαγρος
he was no longer living, and yellow-haired Meleager had died.

A similar use of the Aor. is regular in the Subj., as Il. 1. 168
ἐπεί κε κάμω *when I have grown weary:* and in the Participle, as
ὡς εἰπών *having thus spoken.* The Aor. in these uses expresses,
not past time as such (with reference to the moment of speak-

ing), but *completion* with reference to (*i. e.* usually before) the time of the principal Verb.

77.] The Participle of the Aor. is sometimes used to express *exact coincidence* with the action of the principal Verb: as βῆ δὲ ἀίξασα *went with a spring,* ψευσαμένη προσηύδα *spoke a lie,* ἆλτο λαθών *leaped unseen.* Here a Pres. Part. would imply that there was a *distinct* subordinate action : the Aor. expresses something that *coincides* with, or is *part* of, the main action.

This is especially found with Verbs expressing the manner (tone, gesture, &c.) with which a thing is said or done: Il. 6. 54 ὁμοκλήσας ἔπος ηὔδα *shouted the words;* Il. 8. 219 ποιπνύσαντι θοῶς ὀτρῦναι Ἀχαιούς *to make hot haste in stirring up the Greeks;* Il. 13. 597 χεῖρα παρακρεμάσας : Il. 10. 139., 16. 474., 17. 334., 20. 161, Od. 2. 422., 17. 330 (cp. φεύγειν παρασείσαντι Arist. Eth. Nic. 4. 3. 15).

78.] The Aor. sometimes appears to be used of present time. (1) As in—

Il. 14. 95 νῦν δέ σευ ὠνοσάμην πάγχυ φρένας οἷον ἔειπες.

The Aor. here expresses a culminating point, reached in the immediate past, or rather at the moment of speaking: *I have been brought to the point of blaming,* i. e. *I blame.*

Il. 20. 306 ἤδη .. ἤχθηρε *has now come to hate.*

Il. 3. 415 τὼς δέ σ' ἀπεχθήρω ὡς νῦν ἔκπαγλ' ἐφίλησα *come to hate you as I now love you* (lit. *have got to love;* cp. Od. 8. 481).

So ἔπλετο *has come to be, is* (§ 32); Attic ἥσθην, ἐπήνεσα, &c. In these cases the Aor. is used because the stress is on the nature of the action as something completed, though the completion is in present time*.

By a slight boldness of expression the Aor. may even be used of an event completed in future time :—

Il. 9. 412 εἰ μέν κ' αὖθι μένων Τρώων πόλιν ἀμφιμάχωμαι,

ὤλετο μέν μοι νόστος, ἀτὰρ κλέος ἄφθιτον ἔσται·

= *my return will have been lost,* i. e. will be *ipso facto* lost. The

---

* So Eur. Med. 791 ᾤμωξα, I. A. 510 ἀπέπτυσα : where, as Aken observes, 'die Handlung geschieht erst mit dem Aussprechen' (*Grundz.* § 18). These Aorists are sometimes explained of the past time at which the action began. As a reviewer of the former edition put it, 'Greek speakers, in describing feelings excited by the previous remarks of other speakers, frequently refer those feelings to the time when they were felt, and not to the present time of the description' (*Saturday Rev.*, Feb. 17, 1883). That is to say, ἐπήνεσα means *I praised (when I heard).* But this kind of subordination to a past event is precisely what is expressed by the Impf., not the Aor. The reviewer goes on to explain ἔπλετο in Il. 19. 57 by the presence of the particle ἄρ (ἦ ἄρ τι τόδ' ἔπλετο *this was as we can now see*), 'as in the common ἦν ἄρα'. This would only be possible if ἔπλετο were an Impf. ; see § 33.

speaker puts himself at the (future) point of time given by the
context, and uses the Tense which then becomes appropriate.

(2) Again—
When an assertion is made irrespective of time, the Pres. or
Aor. is used—the Pres. for continuous and the Aor. for single or
momentary action.   Hence the use—
  In similes, as Il. 3. 23 ὥστε λέων ἐχάρη as a lion is gladdened
(but in v. 25 κατεσθίει goes on devouring) : Il. 4. 75 οἷον δ' ἀστέρα
ἧκε . . τοῦ δέ τε πολλοὶ ἀπὸ σπινθῆρες ἵενται.
  The only examples of the Impf. in a simile are Il. 15. 274.,
21. 495, in the phrase οὐδ' ἄρα . . αἴσιμον ἦεν, where it is vir-
tually a Present.
  Also in 'gnomic' passages, reflexions, general sayings, &c. :
  Il. 1. 218 ὅς κε θεοῖς ἐπιπείθηται μάλα τ' ἔκλυον αὐτοῦ.
  9. 320 κάτθαν' ὁμῶς ὅ τ' ἀεργὸς ἀνήρ, ὅ τε πολλὰ ἐοργώς.
These uses of the Aor. are very common in Homer.

The Impf. may possibly be found in a gnomic passage, Il. 13. 730–732—
      ἄλλῳ μὲν γὰρ ἔδωκε θεὸς πολεμήϊα ἔργα
      ἄλλῳ δ' ἐν στήθεσσι τιθεῖ νόον εὐρύοπα Ζεύς,
where the MS. reading τίθει may be defended as an Impf. marking subordination to the Aor. ἔδωκε : cp. the examples in § 71. 2.

Much light has been thrown upon the history of the Aorist by the comparison of the use in Sanscrit (Delbrück, S. F. ii, and A. S. p. 280). If the
result has not been to determine the original force of the Aorist, it has at
least shown that the question cannot be settled from the material furnished
by Greek alone.   The use which predominates in Greek, the historical use to
assert the happening of a single event in the past, is almost unknown to the
earliest Sanscrit.   In the Veda the Aor. is employed, as often in Homer (§ 74),
of what has happened in the immediate past.   In the early Sanscrit prose (the
Brāhmaṇas) the Aor. is used of what has happened to the speaker himself.
It is worth noticing that these uses, in which the Aor. answers approximately
to the English Pf. with have, are found in later Greek in the case of the verbs
whose Pf. retains its original meaning.   As Mr. Gildersleeve puts it, 'when
the Perfect is used as a Present, the Aorist is used as a Perfect.   So ἐκτησάμην
I have gained possession of, κέκτημαι I possess' (Am. Journ. of Phil. iv. 429). Hence,
if the Greek Perfect is originally a kind of present, there is a presumption
that the Aor. was originally akin in meaning to our Perfect. On this view the
ordinary historical Aor. is a derivative use.

CHAPTER III.

The Moods.

79.] The Moods of the Verb (properly so called) are the
Subjunctive, the *Optative*, and the *Imperative*.   It is convenient
however to rank the two Verbal Nouns, the *Infinitive* and the

Participle, along with them. The meanings of the Moods and Verbal Nouns cannot well be discussed until we come to the chapters dealing with Complex Sentences.

The Subjunctive.

80.] Non-Thematic Tense-Stems usually form the Subj. by taking the Thematic Vowel, with the Primary Endings; except that when the Thematic Vowel enters into a diphthong, or is followed by two consonants, it becomes η or ω instead of ε or ο. Thus the scheme is—

	Sing.		Dual.		Plur.	
Act.	*Mid.*	*Act.*	*Mid.*	*Act.*		*Mid.*
-ω	-ομαι			-ομεν	-όμεθα,	-όμεσθα
-ης	-εαι	-ετον	-ησθον	-ετε	-ησθε	
-η (-ησι ?)	-εται	-ετον	-ησθον	-ωσι(ν)	-ωνται.	

The long η or ω, it will be seen, comes in place of ε or ο *wherever it can do so without disturbing the metre.* Examples:—

Strong Aorists : ἔ-φθη, Subj. φθή-η :
ἔ-βη, Subj. βή-ω (or βείω), ὑπερ-βή-η, βή-ομεν (or βεί-ομεν):
ἔ-στη, Subj. στή-ης, στή-η, στή-ετον, στή-ομεν, στή-ωσι :
ἔ-γνω, Subj. γνώ-ω, γνώ-ομεν, γνώ-ωσι :
ἔ-δυ, Subj. δύω, δύ-ης, δύη :
ἔ-βλη-το, Subj. βλή-εται :
ἔ-φθι-το, Subj. φθί-εται, φθι-όμεσθα :
ἅλ-το, Subj. ἅλ-εται :
Stem θη-, Subj. θεί-ω (or θή-ω), θή-ης, θεί-ομεν (or θή-ομεν),
　　ἀπο-θεί-ομαι :
Stem ἡ-, Subj. ἐφ-εί-ω, ἀν-ή-η :
Stem δω-, Subj. δώ-η and δώ-ησι, δώ-ομεν, δώ-ωσι.
Presents : εἰμί, Subj. ἔ-ω (for ἔσ-ω), ἔ-ης, ἔ-η and ἔ-ησι, ἔ-ωσι :
εἶ-μι, Subj. ἴ-ω, ἴ-ησθα, ἴ-ησι, ἴ-ομεν (ἴ) :
φη-μί, Subj. φή-η :
κιχῆ-ναι, Subj. κιχεί-ω, κιχεί-ομεν (or κιχή-ω, κιχή-ομεν) :
so ἐρεί-ομεν as if from *ἔρη-μι.
Passive Aorists : ἐ-δάμην, Subj. δαμεί-ω, δαμή-ης, δαμή-ετε :
so δαεί-ω, ἁλώ-ω, ἁλώ-η, σαπή-η, φανή-η, τραπεί-ομεν.
For δαινύη, 2 Sing. Subj. Mid. (Od. 8. 243., 19. 328), we may read δαινύε', i. e. δαινύ-ε-αι.
Perfects : πέποιθα, Subj. πεποίθ-ης, πεποίθ-ομεν : ἔρριγε, Subj. ἐρρίγ-ησι : βέβηκε, Subj. προ-βεβήκ-η : so ἑστήκ-η, ἀρήρ-η, μεμήλ-η, ὀλώλ-η, ὀρώρ-η, βεβρύχ-η : also ἰλήκησι (Od. 21. 365.)—unless we assume a Pres. ἰλήκω (§ 45).
Pf. Mid. προσ-αρήρεται (Hes. Op. 431).
οἶδα, Subj. εἰδέω, εἰδῇς, εἰδῇ, εἴδομεν, εἴδετε, εἰδῶσι.

For εἰδέω, &c., Tyrannio wrote εἴδω, εἴδης, εἴδη, εἴδωσι (Schol. Od. 1. 174), uniform with εἴδομεν, εἴδετε. Both forms may be accounted for: εἰδέω is Subj. of ἐ-ϝεῖδεα (§ 68); εἴδω with the Plur. εἴδ-ο-μεν, εἴδ-ε-τε, is Subj. of a Non-Thematic * ϝεῖδ-μι, Sanscr. *ved-mi* (*M. U.* iii. 18). The form ἰδέω, read by most MSS. in Il. 14. 235, is a mere error for εἰδέω.

Aorists in -σᾰ: ἐ-βήσα-μεν, Subj. βήσ-ομεν: ἤγειρα, Subj. ἀγείρ-ομεν: ἔ-τισα, Subj. τίσ-ετε, τίσ-ωσι: ἠμείψα-το, Subj. ἀμείψ-εται: ἠλεύα-το, Subj. ἀλεύ-εται: and many more. These Subjunctives properly belong to the older inflexion of the Sigmatic Aorist without -ᾰ (§ 40).

To these should be added some forms used as Futures:—

ἔδ-ο-μαι, ἔδονται *shall eat* (cp. Sanscr. *ad-mi*, Lat. *est* for *ed-t*).

δή-εις, δή-ομεν, δή-ετε *shall find*, with the strong Stem answering to δᾰ(σ)- in δέδαεν, &c.

βεί-ο-μαι *shall live*, from the stem βιϝ-; also in the form βέομαι. Evidently βείομαι : βιῶναι : : δήω : δαῆναι.

It will be found that the Homeric uses of these words are all such as can be referred to the Subj. On πίομαι and κείω see § 59. The form δήεις may be a trace of an older inflexion, -ω, -εις, -ει, answering to -ομεν, -ετε.

It will be seen that the strong form of the Stem is found in the Subjunctive, as φή-ῃ, δώ-ομεν, ἑστήκ-ῃ. Apparent exceptions are, (1) the Subj. of εἶμι—in which the ῑ of ἴομεν (for εἴ-ομεν) is unexplained, while the forms ῐ-ω, ῐ-ῃσι may be Thematic, (as are Opt. ἴοι, Part. ἰών); and (2) the forms ἀφ-έ-ῃ (Aor. of ἀφ-ίη-μι), μιγέ-ωσι, φθέ-ωσι, στέ-ωμεν, κτέ-ωμεν, φθέ-ωμεν, θέ-ωμεν, ἔ-ωμεν. These forms are the result of transference of quantity, στε-ω- for στη-ο-, &c., and it is important to notice that the last six are always scanned as disyllables, thus forming the transition to the contracted φθῶσι, στῶμεν, &c.

Anomalous lengthening is found in μετ-είω (Il. 23. 47) for μετ-έ-ω.

On the ει for η in βεί-ω, θεί-ω, δαμεί-ω, &c. see Append. C.

81.] Subjunctives with lengthened Stem-vowel. The formation of the Subj. by means of the Thematic vowel must have been confined originally to Stems ending in a consonant, or in one of the vowels *i, u*. The hiatus in such forms as φή-ῃ, στή-ομεν, γνώ-ομεν is enough to prove that they are not primitive. In Vedic Sanscrit, accordingly, while *as-a-ti, han-a-ti* are Subj. of *as-ti, han-ti*, we find *sthá-ti, dá-ti* as the Subj. answering to the Aorists *á-sthā-t, á-dā-t*. These would become in Homer στῆ-σι, δῶ-σι or (with the usual ι of the 3 Sing.) στῆ-σι, δῷ-σι. Similarly we may infer an original Plural στήμεν, στῆτε, στῆντι (στῆσι); δῶμεν, δῶτε, δῶντι (δῶσι); and so on. The principle of the formation is that the Stem ends in a simple long vowel—not one that has arisen from specifically Greek contraction.

Traces of this type of Subj. are found in the Greek dialects :
δύνᾱ-μαι (for δύνωμαι), καθ-ίστᾱ-ται, προ-τίθηντι, &c. (Meyer, *G. G.*
p. 502). In Homer it may be recognised in the 3 Sing. forms
φῇσιν (Od. 1. 168), φθῇσι (Il. 23. 805), ᾖσι (Il. 15. 359), μεθ-ίῃσι
(Il. 13. 234), δῶσι ; perhaps in δῶ, δῷς, δῶμεν, δῶσι, περι-δώμεθον,
ἐπι-δώμεθα ; γνῷς, γνῶμεν, γνῶσι ; ἐπι-βῆτον, πειρηθῆτον, &c.—
which are usually regarded as contracted from the regular
Homeric δώω, δώῃς, δώομεν, &c.—and in δύνη-ται, ἐπί-στηται
(§ 87, 3).

How then did the Homeric forms of the type of φή-ῃ, στή-
ομεν, γνώ-ομεν arise ? Doubtless by a new application of the
process already familiar in ἴ-ο-μεν (εἶ-μι), φθί-ε-ται, χεύ-ε-ται,
πεποίθ-ο-μεν, &c. We may compare the extension of the Endings
-ᾰται, -ᾰτο to the Pf. βεβλή-αται, in imitation of κεκλί-αται,
εἰρύ-αται (§ 5).

Contraction appears in the 3 Sing. φῇ (Od. 19. 122), στῇ (Od.
18. 334), βῇ (Od. 2. 358), φανῇ (Il. 9. 707), γνῷ (Il. 1. 411., 16.
273)—unless we suppose that these are obtained by dropping the
-σι of φῇ-σι, &c. on the analogy of the Thematic -ῃ. Also in the
1 Plur. μεθ-ῶμεν (Il. 10. 449), συν-ώμεθα (Il. 13. 381), δαῶμεν
(Il. 2. 299), μεμν-ώμεθα (Od. 14. 168 ; and the 3 Plur. ὦσι (Il.
14. 274, Od. 24. 491), βῶσιν (Od. 14. 86); but it is probably
more correct to write these words with εω (like φθέωσι, ἔωμεν,
&c.), except when a vowel precedes (as in δαῶμεν).

The two forms of the Subj. present a certain analogy to the two kinds of
derivative Verbs—the Attic -αω, -εω, -οω, and the Æolic -ἁμι, -ημι, -ωμι. Thus
δύνᾱ-μαι, τίθη-ντι are related to δύνω-μαι, τιθέωσι nearly as φίλημεν, φίλεισι to
φιλέομεν, φιλέουσι.

κεῖται occurs as a Subj. in Il. 19. 32., 24. 554, Od. 2. 102., 19. 147. It has
been regarded as contracted from κεί-εται, the regular form answering to the
Non-Thematic κεῖ-ται (*Curt. Stud.* vii. 100). The best MS. (Ven. A of the
Iliad) gives κῆται. The true reading is probably κέεται (related to κείεται as
τελέω to τελείω).

ζώννυνται, construed with ὅτε κεν (Od. 24. 89) is regarded by Curtius as a
Subj. (*Verb.* ii. 67). But the example is uncertain ; the clause refers to past
time, so that ὅτε κεν with the Subj. is quite irregular (§ 298).

σόῳ and σόῳς or σοῷς (Il. 9. 424, 681) are probably Optatives ; see § 83.

82.] Thematic Tense-Stems form the Subj. by changing ε
into η and o into ω.

The Subjunctive of the Thematic Aor. and Pres. frequently
employs the Person-Endings -μι and -σι : e.g. ἐθέλ-ωμι, ἐθέλ-ῃσι ;
εἴπωμι, εἴπῃσι ; ἀγάγωμι, ἀγάγῃσι ; τύχωμι, τύχῃσι ; ἴδωμι, κτείνωμι ;
ἄγῃσι, ἀείδῃσι, ἄρχῃσι, ἀλάλκῃσι, βάλῃσι, ἔλῃσι, κάμῃσι, &c.
(Bekker, *H. B.* i. 218). These Endings are also found (but
rarely) with Non-Thematic Stems: Pres. ἔ-ῃσι, ἴ-ῃσι (which
however may be Thematic), Aor. δώ-ῃσι (Il. 1. 324), Pf. ἐρρίγ-ῃσι

(Il. 3. 353). The 2 Sing. sometimes takes -σθἄ; ἐθέλ-ησθα, εἴπ-ησθα, πίησθα, &c.

The Subj. in -ωμι had almost disappeared at one time from the text of Homer, having been generally corrupted into -οιμι, sometimes -ωμαι. It was restored by Wolf, chiefly on the authority of the ancient grammarians. Some of the best MSS. (especially Ven. A) have occasionally preserved it.

It is interesting to observe the agreement in form between the Thematic Indic. and the Non-Thematic Subj. ; e. g. Indic. ἄγω and Subj. γνώ-ω, in contrast to Subj. ἐθέλω-μι : just as ἄγο-μεν and γνώ-ομεν agree in contrast to ἄγω-μεν.

A few forms of the Aorist in -σἄ follow the analogy of the Thematic Stems, as ὄρσ-ωμεν (Il. 7. 38), ὄρσ-ητε (Il. 23. 210), δηλήσ-ηται (Il. 3. 107), μνησώμεθα (Il. 15. 477, &c.), παύσωμεν (Il. 7. 29), παυσώμεσθα (Il. 7. 290., 21. 467), πέμψωμεν (Od. 20. 383), ἐνιπλήξωμεν (Il. 12. 72), φθίσωμεν (Od. 16. 369), περάσητε (Od. 15. 453), ἀντιάσητον (Il. 12. 356), τρώσητε (Od. 16. 293., 19. 12), δείσητε (Il. 24. 779), βουλεύσωμεν (Od. 16. 234).

In most of these instances the original reading is probably either a Pres. Subj. or an Opt. Thus in Il. 21. 467 the best MSS. have παυώμεσθα, and in Od. 20. 383 there is good authority for πέμπωμεν (in Il. 15. 72 the MSS. are divided between παύω and παύσω). Similarly we may read παύωμεν and ἐνιπλήσσωμεν. Again φθίσωμεν follows a Past Tense (§ 298), περάσητε an Opt. (§ 308, 1, b) : read φθίσαιμεν, περάσαιτε. For ἀντιάσητον we may have either the Opt. ἀντιάσαιτον or a Pres. Subj. ἀντιάητον. For τρώσητε we should perhaps read τρώητε (cp. the Pres. Ind. τρώει), and for βουλεύσωμεν βουλεύωμεν.

There are no clear instances of Thematic Stems forming the Subjunctive with a short vowel (ε or ο).

The forms μίσγεαι, κατίσχεαι (Il. 2. 232, 233), for μίσγηαι, κατίσχηαι, are like βέβληαι (Il. 11. 380) in which the η forms a short syllable.

In Il. 14. 484 τῷ καί κέ τις εὔχεται ἀνήρ κτλ. Hermann's conjecture καί τέ τις is found in two of La Roche's MSS., and in any case the κε is unsuitable to the sense. The true reading is probably καί τίς τ' (§ 332).

In Od. 4. 672 ὡς ἂν ἐπισμυγερῶς ναυτίλλεται write ναυτίλεται, the Aor. Subj.

Three places remain to be mentioned :

Il. 1. 66 αἴ κέν πως ἀρνῶν κνίσης αἰγῶν τε τελείων
βούλεται ἀντιάσας ἡμῖν ἀπὸ λοιγὸν ἀμῦναι.

Curtius adopts the suggestion of Stier, βούλητ' ἀντιάσας (Curt. Stud. ii. 138).

Il. 10. 360 ὡς δ' ὅτε καρχαρόδοντε δύω κύνε, εἰδότε θήρης,
ἢ κεμάδ' ἠὲ λαγωὸν ἐπείγετον ἐμμενὲς αἰεὶ
χῶρον ἀν' ὑλήενθ', ὁ δέ τε προθέῃσι μεμηκώς.

Here ἐπείγετον is difficult because the Subj. προθέῃσι is used in the next clause. Possibly the author of book 10 used the archaic form in -ῃσι as an Indicative.

Il. 12. 42 ὡς δ' ὅτ' ἂν ἔν τε κύνεσσι καὶ ἀνδράσι θηρευτῇσι
κάπριος ἠὲ λέων στρέφεται.

The use of ὅτ' ἄν in a simile is doubtful in Homer (see § 289). Should we read ὡς δ' ὅτ' ἔναντα? Cp. Il. 20. 67.

The Optative.

83.] The Optative Stem is formed from the Tense Stem by the Suffix ιη or ι, as διδο-ίη-ν, τύχο-ι-το.

1. Non-Thematic Tenses (except the Aorist in -σᾰ) take ιη before Light Endings, ι before Heavy Endings; as εἴη-ν (for ἐσ-ιη-ν), θε-ίη-ν, δο-ίη, κιχε-ίη, τεθνα-ίη-s, δαμε-ίη; but Plur. φα-ῖ-μεν, δια-κοσμηθε-ῖ-μεν, ἐπι-θε-ῖ-τε. The 3 Plur. ends in -ιεν, as ἐ-ῖεν, δαμε-ῖεν, δο-ῖεν : once -ιη-σαν, viz. στα-ίησαν (Il. 17. 733). The ι is lost in δύη (Od. 9. 377., 18. 348., 20. 286, for δυ-ίη), ἐκ-δῦμεν, λελῦτο (Od. 18. 238 La Roche), δαινῦτο (Il. 24. 665), δαινύ-ατο (Od. 18. 248), φθῖτο, ἀπο-φθίμην (for φθι-ι-το, ἀπο-φθι-ι-μην).

2. In Thematic Tenses the scheme of Endings is :—

	Sing.		Dual.		Plur.	
1.	-οιμι	Mid. -οίμην	. . .	Mid.	-οιμεν	Mid. -οίμεθα
2.	-οιs	-οιο	-οιτον	-οισθον	-οιτε	-οισθε
3.	-οι	-οιτο	-οίτην	-οίσθην	-οιεν	-οίᾰτο.

3. The Aorist in -σᾰ forms the Optative in two ways—

    (1) In -σειᾰ the (so-called) Æolic Optative.

    (2) In -σαι-μι with Endings as in the Thematic Tenses, putting α for ο throughout.

The scheme of the Homeric forms is :—

1 Sing. -αιμι   Plur. -αιμεν

2 ,,   -ειᾰs, rarely -αιs   ,,   -αιτε

3 ,,   -ειε(ν), sometimes -αι   ,,   -ειᾰν (-αιεν Il. 24. 38).

The Mid. Endings are of the second kind, -αίμην, -αιο, -αιτο, &c.

The Perfect forms the Opt. from the weak Stem, as τετλα-ίη, τεθνα-ίη-s, ἑστα-ίη. The Opt. of οἶδα is formed (like the Plpf., see § 68, 2) from an Aor. ἐ-Ϝείδε-σα (εἰδείη-ν for Ϝειδεσ-ιη-ν).

The instances of the Pf. Opt. with Thematic -οι-μι, -οι-s, &c. are doubtful. βεβλήκοι is the reading of Aristarchus in Il. 8. 270, where the best MSS. have βεβλήκει. In Il. 21. 609 γνώμεναι ὅs τε πεφεύγοι ὅs τ' ἔθαν' κτλ., the reading πεφεύγει is given by one good MS. (D.), and evidently agrees better with ἔθανε. βεβρώθοιs (Il. 4. 35) points to a form βέβρωθα, of which however there is no other evidence. ἰλήκοι (H. Apoll. 165) may be Pf. or Pres.

Irregular forms :—

Thematic ἔοι-s, ἔοι (Il. 9. 142, 284), ἴοι (Il. 14. 21), δίοι-το (Od. 17. 317). Homer has also ἰε-ίη (Il. 19. 209), to be compared with εἰδείη, δεδιείη.

The so-called 'Æolic' Opt. of Contracted Verbs (-ῳη-ν, -οιη-ν) appears in φιλοίη (Od. 4. 692) and φοροίη (Od. 9. 320).

In Il. 14. 241 most authorities give ἐπισχοίης as an Opt. (τῷ κεν ἐπισχοίης λιπαροὺς πόδας εἰλαπινάζων. Three of the chief MSS. (A. B. C.) have ἐπίσχοιες, and this was quoted by Herodian, apparently as the only reading known to him (see Ludwich, A. H. T. i. 374). The Syr. palimpsest has ἐπίσχοιας. All three forms are anomalous; ἐπισχοίης finds a parallel in ἀγαγοίην (Sappho) and one or two other forms, but can hardly be Homeric.

The forms σόῳς (Il. 9. 681), σόῳ (Il. 9. 424) are so written by modern editors. Most MSS. have σόης, σόη. In the former place we learn that Ar. doubted between σαῷς and σοῷς (or σόῳς, for the accent here is conjectural). The ancient grammarians apparently took both forms as Opt. (which suits the sense, § 304, a). Some wrote σαῷs, σαῷ (or σοῷs, σοῷ), deriving them directly from σαόω : others σόῳs, σόῳ, from σώω or σόω. It is not difficult to restore the uncontracted σαόοις, σαόοι, or, if the Subj. is preferred, σαόῃς, σαόῃ (so Nauck).

For the 3 Plur. in -οιε-ν Bekker finds one instance of -οι-ν, viz. in Od. 20. 382, where the common text has—

    τοὺς ξείνους ἐν νηὶ πολυκλήϊδι βαλόντες
    ἐς Σικέλους πέμψωμεν ὅθεν κέ τοι ἄξιον ἄλφοι,

for which he would read ἄλφοιν. The 1 Sing. in -οι-ν (instead of the anomalous -οι-μι) was not unknown in Attic (Bekker, H. B. p. 111 ff) *.

παρα-φθα-ίη-σι (Il. 10. 346), with Primary instead of Secondary Ending, is perhaps a pseudo-archaic form, made on the analogy of the Subjunctives in -ησι.

The Verbal Nouns.

84.] **Infinitives and Participles** are not properly speaking Verbs—since they do not contain a Subject and Predicate—but Nouns : the Infinitive is a kind of Substantive and the Participle an Adjective. In certain respects however they belong to the scheme of the Verb :—

1. They answer in form and meaning to the Tense Stems; each Tense Stem has in general an Infinitive and a Participle formed from it.

2. They are distinguished as Active and Middle (or Passive) in sense.

3. They are construed with the same oblique cases of Nouns, and the same Adverbs and Adverbial phrases, as the corresponding Verbs.

---

* It must not be supposed, however, that the 1 Sing. and the 3 Plur. in -οιν are *primitive* forms. The termination -οιν was originally impossible in Greek (as -em and -om are in Sanscrit) ; we should expect -οιᾰ, -οιᾱν (Sanscr. -eyam, -eyus). Hence -οι-μι probably made its way into Greek in place of *-οιᾰ, as -σαι-μι in the Aor. in place of -σειᾰ (see Brugmann, in Curt. Stud. ix. 313). The 3 Plur. form ἀποτίνοιᾱν is found in the Eleian dialect.

85.] The Infinitive Active is formed—

(1) In Non-Thematic Tenses (except the Aor. in -σᾰ) by the Suffixes -μεναι, -μεν, -εναι, -ναι.

Of these -μεναι is the most usual, as θέ-μεναι, γνώ-μεναι, μιγή-μεναι, ἴδ-μεναι, τεθνά-μεναι, ζευγ-νύ-μεναι : -μεν occurs after short vowels, as ἴ-μεν, δό-μεν, τεθνά-μεν, ὀρ-νύ-μεν; also in ἔμμεν (five times, but always where we may write ἔμμεν'), ἴδ-μεν (Il. 11. 719), and ζευγ-νῦ-μεν (Il. 16. 145), in which the long υ is irregular.

The full Suffix -εναι only occurs in ἰ-έναι; but there are many other Infinitives in -ναι, all of them containing a long vowel or diphthong in which an ε may be supposed to have been absorbed; as δοῦναι (for δο-έναι, see Max Müller, *Chips*, iv. 56), θεῖναι, στῆναι, βῆναι, δῦναι, γνῶναι, ἁλῶναι, βιῶναι, ἀῆναι, φορῆ-ναι, διδοῦναι (Il. 24. 425). The original form of the Suffix seems to have been -ϝεναι.

From εἰμί (ἐσ-) are formed ἔμμεναι, ἔμμεν, ἔμεναι, ἔμεν, and εἶναι. Of these ἔμεναι, ἔμεν are irregular; they follow the analogy of θέμεναι, &c. Cp. the 1 Plur. ἐμέν (Soph. El. 21). From εἶ-μι are formed ἴ-μεναι, ἴ-μεν, and ἰ-έναι. In one place (Il. 20. 365) ἴμεναι is scanned with ῑ—perhaps in imitation of ἔμμεναι (Solmsen, *K. Z.* xxix. 72).

The common Attic Present Infinitives ἱστά-ναι, τιθέ-ναι, διδό-ναι, δεικ-νύ-ναι, &c., as well as the Perfect Infinitives in -έναι, are entirely unknown in Homer.

(2) In Thematic Tenses by -έ-μεναι, -έ-μεν, -ειν ; as εἰπ-έ-μεναι, εἰπ-έ-μεν, βάλλ-ειν.

The Ending -ε-ειν only occurs in the Thematic Aor., and is anomalous; compare βαλ-έ-ειν (Stem βαλε-) and βάλλ-ειν (Stem βαλλε-). The original ending was doubtless -έεν : thus—

$$\text{Stem } βαλε-, \quad \text{Inf. } βαλέ-εν, \quad \text{contr. } βαλεῖν.$$
$$βαλλε-, \quad \text{,,} \quad βάλλε-εν, \quad \text{,,} \quad βάλλειν.$$

In the Aor. the metre usually allows us to restore -έεν (see Renner, *Curt. Stud.* i. 2. p. 33).

It is possible that the forms βαλέ-ειν, &c., are genuine, since -εεν might pass into -εειν from the analogy of the Pres. Inf. in -ειν, just as in the Rhodian dialect -έμεν became -ίμειν. Leo Meyer (*Vergl. Gr.* ii. 284) proposed to read βαλέ-μεν, &c. But, as Renner points out (*l. c.*), the change from -εεν to -εειν is very much slighter, indeed is a mere matter of spelling. Original βαλέμεν, &c. would probably have been retained.

(3) The Aor. in -σᾰ forms -σαι, as στῆ-σαι.

(4) The Inf. Middle is formed by -σθαι : βλῆ-σθαι, πεφά-σθαι, ἵστα-σθαι, ἰδέ-σθαι, βάλλε-σθαι, στή-σα-σθαι.

The Infinitive is originally a Case-form of an abstract Noun (*nomen actionis*). Thus -μεναι consists of the Nominal Suffix -μεν (§ 114) with the Dative ending -αι : ἴδ-μεν-αι 'for knowing'

(Sanscr. *vid-mán-e*). Similarly δοῦναι is δο-Fεν-αι (*dā-ván-e*) 'for giving.' Probably the Infinitives in -σαι and -σθαι also are Datives (Max Müller, *l.c.*). Infinitives in -μεν and -εν appear to be Locatives formed without Case-ending (§ 99). If so, the Infinitives in -μεν and -εν (-ειν) originally differed in meaning from those in -μεναι, -εναι, &c. In Greek, however, the sense of the Inf. as a Case-form is lost, so that the different forms are all construed in exactly the same way.

86.] The Participle. The Aorist, the Present, and the Future Tense Stems form the Active Participle by the Suffix -ντ- : thus we have, Non-Thematic στα-ντ-, τιθε-ντ-; Thematic βαλο-ντ-, στη-σο-ντ-, &c.

The vowel before ντ is always short, as γνο-ντ-, μιγε-ντ-.

The Perfect Stem takes -οτ or -οσ (originally -Fοτ, -Fοσ), Fem. -υιᾰ (for -υσ-ιᾰ, the -υσ originally a weak form for -Fοσ). The Middle Participle is formed by -μενος, which in the Perfect is accented -μένος.

For the Verbal Adjectives in -το-s, see § 114. The Verbal in -τέος is post-Homeric.

CHAPTER IV.

ACCENTUATION OF THE VERB.

87.] The general rule is that the accent is thrown back as far as possible; and the chief departures from this rule are found in the Infinitives and Participles, which are in reality Nouns. In the forms of the Verb properly so called the following exceptions have to be noted:—

I. εἰμί and φημί. The 2 Sing. Imper. φα-θί is oxytone.

The disyllabic forms of the Pres. Indicative, εἰμί, ἐσσί, φημί, φησί, &c., are enclitic, and, when they do not lose the accent altogether, are oxytone; but ἔστι is accented in the ordinary way when it occurs at the beginning of a sentence, or after certain words (οὐκ, καί, ὡς).

Such was the commonly accepted account; but the ancient grammarians were not agreed as to the enclitic character of the Dual and Plural forms (on ἐστόν see Charax 1151 ; on φαμέν, φατέ, φασί, ibid. ; on ἐσμέν, ἐστέ, εἰσί, Eust. 1457, 48). Again, one grammarian denies that φημί was ever enclitic (Charax 1152) ; another holds that it should be written φῆμι, at least in such instances as φῆμι γὰρ οὖν κατανεῦσαι, κτλ. (Tyrannio ap. Eust. 1613, 18). In all likelihood the original forms were, Sing. ἔστι, φῆμι, Plur. ἐσμέν, φαμέν, and we may suppose that φημί and ἐστί are not properly oxytone, but are unaccented forms made oxytone as enclitics (ὠξύνθη διὰ τὴν ἐποῦσαν αὐτοῖς ἔγκλισιν Apoll. Synt.). The Sanscrit Verbs of the same kind follow the rule of accenting the Stem in the Sing., the Ending in the Dual and Plur.; and this must be connected with the difference of quantity between strong and weak Stems (§ 6). See Benfey, *Vedica und Linguistica*, pp. 90 ff.

The 2 Sing. εἰς is enclitic, though the corresponding Attic form εἶ is not; but see § 5. As to φής there is a contradiction; it is not enclitic according to Arc. 142, 8, but enclitic according to Schol. A. Il. 17. 147—both notices being supposed to rest on the authority of Herodian (ed. Lentz, i. 553, 4 and ii. 105, 5).

2. The 3 Plur. ἰστᾶσι, τιθεῖσι, διδοῦσι, δεικνῦσι, are properispomena (Herodian, i. 459, ed. Lentz).

This can hardly have been the original accentuation, since they are not contracted forms, but represent ἵστα-ντι, &c. Probably it comes from the Attic ἰστᾶσι (contracted from ἰστά-ασι, cp. τιθέ-ασι, &c.). The Doric forms are written τιθέντι, &c. by Eustath. Od. 1557, 45; but we do not know that this represents the usage of any living dialect.

3. Subjunctives such as φανῇ, δαῶμεν are circumflexed, as being contracted forms (for φανήῃ, δαήομεν). On εἰδέω, εἰδῇς, εἰδῇ, εἰδέωσι see § 80.

Optatives in which -ιη- becomes -ι- before Heavy Endings are accented on the ι throughout, as διακρινθεῖτε, δαμεῖεν.

But Middle forms to which there is no corresponding Active follow the general rule: δύνωμαι, δύνηαι (so Herodian, but Tyrannio wrote δυνῶμαι, δυνῆαι, Schol. Il. 6. 229), κέρωνται (Il. 4. 260), ἐπίστηται (§ 280); ἐπίσταιτο, ὄναιο, ὄνοιτο.

4. The Imperatives εἰπέ, ἐλθέ, are oxytone (and so in Attic εὑρέ, ἰδέ, λαβέ). Similarly Tyrannio wrote πιθέσθε, λαβέσθε (Schol. V. Il. 18. 266); cp. the Attic βαλοῦ, &c.

The rule in Sanscrit is that the Verb loses the accent, except in subordinate clauses, or when it begins the sentence. Hence the verbs εἰμί and φημί in fact retain the original accentuation, which was doubtless that of the Indo-European language. The Imperatives εἰπέ, ἐλθέ, &c., are evidently words that would often be used to begin a sentence.

The ordinary accent of a Greek verb, the so-called 'recessive' accent, represents the original enclitic condition. The Opt. φαιήν, for example, is originally oxytone. On the Sanscrit rules it loses its accent, and we should have (e. g.) ἐγώ-φαιην. But owing to the Greek rhythmical law this is impossible. Accordingly the accent goes back as far as the Greek rules will allow, and we have ἐγὼ-φαίην.

5. The final -αι of the Endings -μαι, -σαι, -ται, -νται, and of the Inf. is treated as short. These are all cases in which -αι represents the original *final* sound of the word. But the -αι of the Opt., which is for original -αιτ, counts as long.

88.] Accent in Composition. Unaugmented forms of Compound Verbs are accented as though the Verb were an enclitic

following the Preposition : hence σύν-εχον, πρό-ες, παρά-θες, περί-
κειται. ἀπό-σχωνται.   If the final syllable of the Preposition is
lost by elision or apocope the accent falls on the first syllable;
hence ὔφ-ελκε, κάτ-θανε.

But the accent falls if possible upon the Augment : hence
προσ-έβᾶν, ἐπ-έσχον, ἐπ-ῆλθε. In other words, the Augment is
treated in accentuation *as a Preposition.*

The form ἔσται keeps the accent (παρ-έσται, &c.); perhaps
because it is formed by syncope from ἔσεται.

The Subj. ξυμ-βλῆται (Od. 7. 204) ought to be properispo-
menon, if it is a contracted form; cp. βλήεται (Od. 17. 472).
The grammarians however wrote ἀπό-θωμαι (in spite of ἀπο-
θείομαι, Il. 18. 409) and διά-θωμαι (Herodian, i. 469, 7, ed. Lentz).
We have to recognise in such cases the encroachment of the
common Thematic type, though we may doubt whether the
change reaches back to the earliest form of the text of Homer.

According to Herodian, the 2 Sing. Imperative ἐνί-σπες is paroxytone, but
the other Imperative form ἔνι-σπε, and the Indic. forms ἔνι-σπε-s, ἔνισπε, are
proparoxytone ; see Schol. on Il. 24. 388. That is to say, the Imper.
ἐνί-σπε-s is regular, the others are accented as if compounds of ἴσπω.

The Imperative ἐπισχε in Hes. Scut. 446 may be divided ἔπ-ισχε or ἐπι-σχε,
and in the latter case we may write ἐπίσχε (with the MSS.), or ἔπισχε, like
the ἔνισπε of Herodian.

The MSS. vary between (Imper.) ἐνίσπες and ἔνισπε : in the two places of
the Iliad (11. 186., 14. 470) the Venetus has ἐνίσπες : on the other hand in the
only Homeric passage in which the metre gives any help (Od. 4. 642) it is
decisive for ἔνισπε. The accent in the MSS. nearly always follows Herodian's
rule.   .

89.] The Infinitive and Participle. Infinitives in -ειν and
-μεναι follow the general rule : those in -μεν have the same
accent as the corresponding forms in -μεναι, as φευγέ-μεν. On
the Aor. Inf. in -εῖν, see § 85, 2.

The forms in -ναι, -σαι accent the penultimate, as ἰέναι, ἀλῶναι,
ἐρύσαι. The Middle forms of the Thematic Aorist and Perfect
are also paroxytone, as πιθέσθαι, λελαθέσθαι, κεκλῆσθαι, τετύχθαι.
The ancient grammarians doubted between ἀκάχησθαι, ἀλάλησθαι
and ἀκαχῆσθαι, ἀλαλῆσθαι. The former were adopted in the
common texts, and were explained as Æolic forms of the Pres.
Infinitive (Herodian, ii. 111, 21, ed. Lentz).

It may be conjectured that the forms in -μεναι and -μεν were originally
accented on the suffix, like Sanscr. *vidmáne, dāváne.* If so, this is one of the
cases in which the accent of an *archaic* form in Homer has been lost.

Active Participles, except the Thematic Present and Future,
accent the Suffix, as διδούς, στρεφθείς, μεμαώς, λαβών, τεταγών.
So the Presents ἐών, ἰών.

The Part. of the Pf. Middle is paroxytone. But ἀκαχήμενος follows ἀκάχησθαι.

In Composition the Infinitive and Participle retain the accent of the simple word; in other words, they do not become enclitic. Hence we have Impf. σύν-εχον, but Neut. Part. συν-έχον.

CHAPTER V.

Nouns and Pronouns.

90.] The words to which we now proceed are incapable of forming Sentences except in combination with a Verb.

The relation of such words to the Verb is shown in general either by a *Case-Ending*—as in the words which are said to be 'declined,'—or by an *Adverbial Ending* (such as -ως, -θεν, &c.). The Ending in either case is suffixed to a *Stem* or *Theme.* Thus, λογο- is the Stem of the Case-forms, Nom. λόγο-s, Acc. λόγο-ν, Gen. λόγο-ιο, &c.: αὐτο- is the Stem of the Case-forms αὐτό-s, αὐτό-ν, αὐτο-ῖο, and also of the Adverbs αὐτό-θεν, αὐτό-θι, αὕτως, &c.

The Stems now in question belong to two great classes, those of *Nouns* and of *Pronouns*, called *Nominal* and *Pronominal* Stems respectively. The term 'Noun' includes Substantives and Adjectives. The other 'parts of speech'—Adverbs, Prepositions, Conjunctions—may ultimately be resolved into Case-forms or Adverbial forms either of Nouns or Pronouns.

The distinction between Nouns and Pronouns brings before us in a new form the fundamental antithesis involved in the division of a Verb into a Stem which 'predicates,' and a Person-Ending which marks the Subject. A Noun either denotes a single object or group of objects (*i. e.* when it is a 'proper name'), or denotes objects through their permanent attributes, as belonging to a class; whereas a Pronoun denotes an object by its local position, or momentary relation to something else, as 'this' or 'that,' 'here' or 'there,' 'same' or 'other.' This contrast is shortly expressed by saying that Nominal Stems are *Predicative*, and Pronominal Stems *Demonstrative;* the former name or describe, the latter only 'point out' what is intended. Accordingly, Nominal Stems are in general either identical with, or formed from, the Stems of Verbs: Pronouns are found to contain the same elements as those which furnish the Person-Endings of Verbs. The simplest forms obtained by analysis are thus of two kinds. They were first clearly distinguished by Bopp, and called by him *Verbal* and *Pronominal Roots* respectively (*Vergl.-Gr.* § 105).

The Cases.

91.] **Declensions.** The main distinction is that between the *Consonantal Declension* (including that of Stems in -ι and -υ),

which forms the Genitive in -ος, and the *Vowel Declensions*, of
which three may be distinguished:—

    (1) Stems in -ο (chiefly Masc. and Neut.): Gen. -οιο.
    (2)   ,,   -ᾱ, -η (chiefly Fem.): Gen. -ας, -ης. .
    (3)   ,,   -ε (Personal Pronouns): Gen. -ειο.

92.] Vocative. A Noun used in addressing a person by his
name or title has properly no Case-Ending. Accordingly the
Vocative Case consists in general of the simple Stem; e.g. Ζεῦ
βασιλεῦ, Αἶαν (for Αἰαντ-), διόγενες, ὦ ἄνα (for ἀνακτ-).
In Il. 1. 86 Κάλχαν (Voc. of Κάλχας) was read by Aristarchus,
Κάλχα by Zenodotus. On the other hand in Il. 12. 231 Ar.
read Πουλυδάμα, but Zen. Πουλυδάμαν. The form Λαοδάμα in
Od. 8. 141 probably has the authority of Aristarchus.

    Stems in -ο form the Voc. in -ε, as φίλε ἐκυρέ. Some Stems
in -ᾱ(η) shorten the final vowel, as νύμφᾰ, Voc. of νύμφη, and
the Masc. συβῶτᾰ, ἠπεροπευτᾰ, τοξότᾰ, κυνῶπᾰ, &c. But the
long vowel of the Stem is used in the Voc. Ἑρμεία, Ἀτρείδη,
ὑψαγόρη, αἰναρέτη (Il. 16. 31). Feminines in -ω or -ῳ form the
Voc. in -οι, as Λητοῖ (Il. 21. 498). Evidently -ῳ : -οι :: η : ᾰ.

    The words of address, πάππα, ἄττα, τέττα, μαῖα, may be ranked
as Vocatives. So ἠθεῖε, as to which see the note on § 96.

93.] Case-Endings. These are given in the following Table.
The Endings of the Consonantal Declension are in larger type:
the two Vowel Declensions of Nouns are numbered (1), (2), and
the Pronominal Declension (3).

	Sing.	*Dual.*	*Plur.*
Nom.	**-ς**	-ε	**-ες,** Neut. -ᾰ
	(1) -ο-ς, Neut. -ο-ν	-ω	-οι
	(2) -ᾱ(η), -ιᾰ ; -η-ς	-ᾱ	-αι
Acc.	**-ν, -ᾰ**	-ε	**-ᾰς,** Neut. -ᾰ
		(1) -ω	-ους (for -ο-νς)
		(2) -ᾱ	-ᾱς (-α-νς)
Gen.	**-ος**	**-οιιν**	**-ων**
	(1) -οιο, -οο, -ου	-οιιν	-ων
	(2) -ης ; -ᾱο, -εω		-ᾱων, -εων
	(3) -ειο, -εο, -εν	-ῐ(ν)	-ειων, -εων
Dat.	**-ι**	**-οιιν**	**-σι(ν),-εσσι(ν)**
	(1) -ῳ (Loc. -οι)	-οιιν	-οισι(ν), -οις
	(2) -η (Loc. -αι ?)	—	-ησι(ν), -ης
	(3) -οι	-ῐ(ν)	-ῑν, -ῐ(ν)
Instrum.	**-φι(ν)**		**-φι(ν)**

94.] Stems ending in ι, υ, and σ are liable to lose the final letter before the Case-Endings which begin with a vowel.

1. Stems in -ηυ, -ευ : e. g.—

νηῦ-s, Gen. νη-ός (for νηϝ-ός), rarely νε-ός. The ε arises by shortening from η ; so νέες, νεῶν, νέεσσι, νέας—all less common than the corresponding forms with η-, νῆες, νηῶν, νήεσσι, νῆας.

The forms νηῦ-s, νην-σί are irregular, since original *au* before a consonant would appear in Greek as ᾰν (cp. Ζεύς for original *dyēus*). Hence the true Greek form is preserved in the Instrum. ναῦ-φιν (§ 104) and the Compounds ναυσι-κλυτός, Ναυσι-κάα, &c. The η of νηῦ-s and νην-σί is taken by analogy from the other Cases.

βασιλεύ-s, Gen. βασιλῆ-os (but Dat. Plur. βασιλεῦ-σι).
Πηλεύ-s, Gen. Πηλῆ-os and Πηλέ-os. In oblique Cases of Stems in -ευ the ε seems to be nearly confined to proper names; cp. Τυδέος Τυδέϊ Τυδέα, Ἀτρέος Ἀτρέϊ, Θησέα, Νηλέα, &c. On Ζεύς, βοῦς see § 106, 2.

2. Stems in -ι and -υ form the same Cases in two ways :—

(1) Retaining the Stem-vowel, as κόνι-s κόνι-os, Πάρι-s Πάρι-os, ἰλύς ἰλῦos, ἰχθύ-s ἰχθύ-εs, σῦ-s συ-ός, συ-ί, σύ-εs. It is probable that this form of declension was originally confined to monosyllables.

(2) Inserting ε and dropping ι or υ : as πόσι-s, Dat. πόσε-ϊ, ἄστυ ἄστε-os, πῆχυ-s πήχε-os, πολύ-s πολέ-os. Here the Stem of the oblique Cases ends in -ει, -ευ : hence Gen. -εos for -ει-os, -εϝ-os, &c.

πόλις forms several of its Cases in three ways :

(1) Gen. πόλι-os, Dat. πόλῑ (for πόλι-ι, § 99), Plur. Nom. πόλι-εs, Gen. πολί-ων, Dat. πολί-εσσι, Acc. πόλι-as and πόλῑs (§ 100).

(2) Gen. πόλεος (so Bekk. reads in Il. 2. 811., 21. 567, with the scanning ∪ –; cp. πόλευς in Theognis), Dat. πόλει, πτόλεϊ (Il. 17. 152, perhaps should be πτόλιϊ, cp. the Cyprian form πτολιγι).

(3) Gen. πόλη-os, Dat. πόλη-ϊ, Plur. Nom. πόλη-εs, Acc. πόλη-as.

The stem πολη- which furnishes the last of these three forms of inflexion has been traced by Joh. Schmidt (*K. Z.* xxvii. p. 287) to a primitive Locative in -η (cp. Sanscr. *agni*, Loc. *agnā*), to which the ordinary Loc. -ῐ was suffixed. From this new Loc. πόλη-ϊ the other Cases were then formed by analogy.

The Nouns in -ᾰ (from -ιᾰ) answer to the original Stems in -ῑ, as ἰδυῖα, for ἰδυσ-ια, Sanscr. *vidush-ī*.

ἠΰ-s or ἐΰ-s *good* makes Gen. ἐῆ-os, perhaps by transference of quantity for ἠέ-os. Other Adjectives in -ύs form -έ-os, -έ-ι, &c.

3. Stems in -εσ, -ασ, -οσ drop the σ, as ἔπε-os, κέρα-os, αἰδό-os.

95.] **Original** ᾱ as the final vowel of the Stem becomes η; except (1) after ε, ει, ᾰ, as in θεά, and the proper names Ἑρμείας, Αἰνείας, Αὐγείας, Ναυσικάα, Ῥεία (Ar. on Il. 14. 203), Φειά (Il. 7. 135, Od. 15. 297), and (2) in the Gen. in -ᾱο and -ᾱων. Other exceptions to the scheme given above will be best treated under the separate Cases.

96.] **Nominative Singular.** The final -ς is retained after vowels and mutes, but lost with Stems ending in ρ, as πατήρ, μήστωρ. Stems ending in ν either (1) take final -ς (with loss of ν), as εἶς (for ἐν-ς), θίς Acc. θῖν-α, μέλας Gen. μέλαν-ος, or (2) do not take -ς, but lengthen a preceding vowel, as χθών Gen. χθον-ός, ποιμήν Gen. ποιμέν-ος. So with Stems in -ντ: δούς Gen. δόντ-ος, but ἰδών. Originally it seems that all monosyllables took -ς and all others -ν (J. Schmidt, K. Z. xxvii. 392). If so, χθών, φρήν, &c. are forms due to the -ν of the oblique Cases: and on the other hand διδούς, τιθείς, &c. have followed the analogy of corresponding monosyllabic words, δούς, θείς, &c.

There is a remarkable group of Masc. Stems in -ᾱ(η), with Nom. Sing. in -ᾰ, viz.—

Titles of gods : νεφεληγερέτα, στεροπηγερέτα, μητίετα, εὐρύοπα (Ζεύς); ἀκάκητα (Ἑρμείας ἀ.); κυανοχαῖτα (Ποσειδάων).

Titles of heroes : ἱππότα, ἱππηλάτα, αἰχμητά; ἠπύτα (κῆρυξ).

One proper name, Θυέστα (Il. 2. 107).

Except Θυέστα these words are only found as adjectives : thus we have αἰχμητὰ Λυκάων, κυανοχαῖτα Ποσειδάων, but αἰχμητής, κυανοχαίτης when the same words are substantives.

The accent generally follows the forms in -η-ς *where such forms exist;* thus ἱππότα, αἰχμητά, like ἱππότης, αἰχμητής. But it is thrown back in εὐρύοπα, μητίετα, ἀκάκητα,—ancient epithets only known from the traditional Homeric use.

These are in reality Vocatives which have been turned into Nominatives. That is to say, they belonged originally to certain established forms of address —μητίετα Ζεῦ, κυανοχαῖτα Ποσείδαον, ἱππότα Πηλεῦ, &c.—and were not inflected when the names to which they were attached came to be used in the Nom. In this way the *rhythm*, which doubtless had a traditional sacredness, remained unaltered, and the whole phrase retained something of its vocative character. The feeling which might lead to this is that expressed by Eumaeus in Od. 14. 145 ff.—

τὸν μὲν ἐγών, ὦ ξεῖνε, καὶ οὐ παρεόντ᾽ ὀνομάζειν
αἰδέομαι· περὶ γάρ μ᾽ ἐφίλει καὶ κήδετο θυμῷ·
ἀλλά μιν ἠθεῖον καλέω καὶ νόσφιν ἐόντα.

I call him by the title ἠθεῖος *even in his absence,*—the word ἠθεῖος being only used as a form of address. Cp. also § 111 (2). The Nominatives in -ᾰ are evidently part of the archaic and conventional style of Epic poetry. They are commoner in the Iliad than in the Odyssey in the proportion of 3 to 1. The ancient grammarians regarded them as Æolic, but without sufficient reason.

G

The form εὐρύοπα also appears as an Acc., and has accordingly been explained from a Nom. εὐρύ-οψ. It is improbable however that it is a different word from the Nom. Voc. εὐρύοπα. Probably the fact that it had the appearance of an Acc. of one of the numerous Compounds in -οψ led to an extension of use *.

97.] Accusative Sing. The Ending -ᾰ is found after consonants and the diphthongs ηυ, ευ; as νηῦ-s νῆα (for νηυα, νηϝα), βασιλεύ-s βασιλῆα, Τυδεύ-s Τυδέα†. Otherwise the Acc. takes -ν; e. g. πόλι-ν, ἰχθύ-ν, βοῦ-ν.

But εὐρύ-s makes εὐρέα in the phrases εὐρέα πόντον, εὐρέα κόλπον : the common form being εὐρύ-ν.

The original Ending is -m, which becomes -ν after a vowel and -ᾰ (for ṃ) after a consonant. The preference for ᾰ after ηυ, ευ is due to the semiconsonantal nature of the υ in these combinations. We may compare the Aorists ἔκηα (for ἐκηυ-α), ἔχευα (also ἔχεα), &c., and on the other hand ἔδυ-ν, ἔφυ-ν.

Several Stems form the Acc. in -ιν and also in -ιδα : ἔριδα and ἔριν (Od.), φυλόπιδα (Od. 11. 313) and φύλοπιν, γλαυκώπιδα (Il. 8. 373) and γλαυκῶπιν (Od. 1. 156), ἀνάλκιδα and ἄναλκιν (Od. 3. 375), ὅπιδα and ὅπιν, Κύπριδα and Κύπριν ; θοῦριν, Ἶριν, αὖλιν, Θέτιν. Cp. also χάρι-ν (for χάριτ-α), and κόρυ-ν (for κόρυθ-α), found in the line Il. 13. 131 (=16. 215),—

ἀσπὶς ἄρ᾽ ἀσπίδ᾽ ἔρειδε, κόρυς κόρυν, ἀνέρα δ᾽ ἀνήρ.

In Attic there are many more such forms; ὄρνιν, &c. Note that no oxytones form the Acc. in -ιν.

The Accusatives ζαῆν (Od. 12. 313), Ἄρην, Μέγην are probably formed directly from the Nom. ζαής, Ἄρης, Μέγης, on the analogy of Masc. Nouns in -η-s. On the other hand Ζῆν (Ζεύς), βῶν (βοῦς), are very ancient forms, answering to the Sanscr. dyâm, gâm (Joh. Schmidt in K. Z. xxv. 17) : see § 106, 2.

A final δ is lost in the Neut. Pronouns ὅ, τό, τοῦτο, ἐκεῖνο, ἄλλο (Lat. id, is-tud, illud, aliud), and in τί (Lat. quid) : perhaps also in the Personal Pronouns, Acc. Sing. ἐμέ (με), σέ, ἕ, Dual νώ, σφώ, σφῶε, Plur. ἄμμε, ὕμμε, σφέ (Curt. Stud. vi. 417 ff.; Max Müller, Chips, iv. 44).

---

* It will be shown hereafter (§ 116, 2) that the Masc. Nouns in -της are probably derived from Feminines in -τη, of abstract or collective meaning. Hence it is possible that the Homeric Nominatives in -τᾰ come directly from these Feminines : so that (e. g.) μητίετα meant literally Counsel rather than Counsellor. The abstract word may have been used as a title, like βίη Πριάμοιο and the like. According to Joh. Schmidt (Pluralb. p. 400) εὐρύοπα is originally a Neuter : see § 107, 2.

† The forms Τυδῆ (Il. 4. 348) and Μηκιστῆ (Il. 15. 339) are probably false : see Nauck, Mél. gr.-rom. iii. 222.

98.] Genitive Singular. The Stems in -o form the Gen. in -οιο, -οο, -ου. Of these forms only -οιο and -ου are read in the existing text of Homer; but there are sufficient traces of -οο, and indeed several places where it is called for by the metre. Thus we must read—

Il. 2. 518 υἱέες Ἰφίτοο μεγαθύμου.
　15. 66 (= 21. 104) Ἰλίοο προπάροιθεν.
　22. 313 ἀγρίοο, πρόσθεν δὲ κτλ.
Od. 10. 36 δῶρα παρ' Αἰόλοο μεγαλήτορος.
　60 βῆν εἰς Αἰόλοο κλυτὰ δώματα.
Il. 9. 440, &c. ὁμοίοο πτολέμοιο (for ὁμοίου πολέμοιο).
　2. 325 ὄο κλέος οὔποτ' ὀλεῖται ⎱ (for ὄου).
Od. 1. 70 ὄο κράτος ἔσκε μέγιστον ⎰
Il. 2. 731 Ἀσκληπίοο δύο παῖδε.
　15. 554 ἀνεψιόο κταμένοιο.
　5. 21 ἀδελφεόο κταμένοιο: so in—
　6. 61 (= 7. 120., 13. 788) ἀδελφεόο φρένας ἥρως.
Od. 14. 239 χαλεπὴ δ' ἔχε δήμοο φῆμις.

Also in the two lines—

Il. 6. 344 εἵνεκ' ἐμεῖο κυνὸς κακομηχάνου ὀκρυοέσσης,
　9. 723 ὃς πολέμου ἔραται ἐπιδημίου ὀκρυόεντος,

since ὀκρυόεις does not occur elsewhere, but κρυόεσσα (Il. 5. 740), κρηόεντος (Il. 9. 2), κρυερός &c., we should probably read—

　　. . . κακομηχάνοο κρυοέσσης.
　　. . . ἐπιδημίοο κρυόεντος.

A trace of -οο may also be found in the fact that Nouns in -αος sometimes form the Gen. in -εωο, which is for -αοο; e. g. Πετέ-ωο, Πηνελέ-ωο.

Masc. Stems in -ᾰ(η) form the Gen. in -ᾱο (original -ᾱσιο), less commonly -εω (by transference of quantity). This -εω is often scanned as one syllable; after another vowel it is written -ω, as Βορέ-ω (for Βορέ-εω), Ἑρμεί-ω, Αἰνεί-ω, ἐϋμμελί-ω. (So in Ionic, Curt. Stud. v. 294., viii. 172.)

The Pronominal Stems in -ε, viz. ἐμε (με), σε (for τϝε), and ἑ or ἑε, form the Gen. in -ε-ιο, -εο and (by contraction) -ευ. Thus we find ἐμεῖο, ἐμέο (Il. 10. 124), ἐμεῦ; σεῖο, σέο, σεῦ; εἶο, ἕο, εὖ. For σεῖο there is also a longer form τεοῖο (Il. 8. 37 = 468), and for ἕο in one place (Il. 19. 384) Zenodotus read ἑοῦ.

99.] Dative Singular. In Homer the ι of the Dat. is sometimes long (as in Latin), chiefly in forms which otherwise could not be easily brought into the verse; in the Iliad, Ἀχιλλῆϊ, ὑπερμενέϊ, κράτεϊ, σάκεϊ, πτόλεϊ, σθένεϊ, ἔριδι; in the Odyssey, Ὀδυσσῆϊ, ἔτεϊ, δέπαϊ, ὕδατι, But we find also Ζηνὶ μενεαίνομεν (Il. 15. 104), πὰρ νηΐ τε μένειν (Od.) See § 373.

The Dat. of Neuters in -ας was commonly written -ᾳ; but the long α is anomalous, and -αι is now read by La Roche from good MSS. (in σέλαι, κέραι). The forms in -ᾳ appear to have become established in later Greek (Hdn. II, 316, 10, ed. Lentz).

Stems in -ι, Gen. -ι-ος, form the Dat. in -ῑ, as κόνι, μῆτι, μάστι, κνήστι, Θέτι, νεμέσσι (with v. l. νεμέσσει Il. 6. 335). So Bekker restored the forms πόλι (Il. 5. 686, &c.), ἀγύρι (Il. 16. 661), ὄψι, ὕβρι, δυνάμι, πόσι, for which the common texts give forms in -ει.

Stems in -υ, Gen. -υ-ος, form the Dat. in -υι (a diphthong which in later Greek can only occur before a vowel), πληθυῖ (Il. 22. 458), νέκυι, ὀρχηστυῖ, ὀϊζυῖ, ἰξυῖ, θρήνυι. But δρῦ-ς, σῦ-ς form the disyllables δρυ-ί, συ-ί.

It is possible, however, that the Datives in -ῑ are Instrumental forms, and similarly that the Datives in -υι have taken the place of Instrumentals in -ῦ. For the Vedic and Zend Instrum. in -ῑ, -ῦ see Osthoff, *M. U.* ii. 139.

Sanscrit Nouns in -*an* and -*as* sometimes form the Locative from the Stem without any Case-ending (Whitney, 425, c). Traces of this are to be found in Greek in the form αἰέν (cp. αἰεί), and the Inf. in -μεν and -εν (§ 85).

Stems in -ο sometimes form a Locative in -οι, as well as the true Dat. in -ῳ, e. g. οἶκο-ι. So χαμα-ί and perhaps πάλα-ι. Cp. the adverbial ending -ει (§ 110).

Pronominal Stems in -ε form -οι; ἐμοί (enclitic μοι), σοί (encl. τοι), ἑοῖ and οἷ. For σοί there is another form τείν (Il. 11. 201): so in Doric we find ἐμίν and τείν, ἵν.

99*.] Plural. Several Stems in -ο which are Masc. (or Fem.) in the Sing. form a Neut. Plur.: κέλευθος, Plur. κέλευθοι and more commonly κέλευθα; μηρός, Plur. μηροί and μῆρα; κύκλος, Plur. κύκλοι and κύκλα; ἰός, Plur. ἰοί and ἰά: Τάρταρος, Plur. Τάρταρα (Hes.). There is probably a slight change of meaning, the Neuter expressing vague mass or quantity rather than plurality: cp. δρυμά *thicket*, and post-Homeric δεσμά, θεσμά, σῖτα, Lat. *loca, joca*. Thus κέλευθα means *a group of paths*, and could not be used (*e. g.*) in such a passage as Il. 10. 66 πολλαὶ γὰρ ἀνὰ στρατόν εἰσι κέλευθοι. So κύκλα of a set of wheels, Τάρταρα of *one* place so called, &c.

100.] Accusative Plural. Stems in -ι and -υ which admit an Acc. Sing. in -ν often form the Plur. in -ῑς, -ῦς (for -ινς, -υνς): thus ὄϊς (Il. 11. 245), ἀκοίτις (Od. 10. 7), βοῦς ἤνις (Il. 6. 94). So we should read πόλις (with Bekker) for πόλεις. Again we have δρῦς, γένυς, κλιτῦς, γραπτῦς, σῦς and σύ-ας, ἰχθῦς and ἰχθύ-ας (Od. 22. 384), ὀφρῦς (Il. 16. 740) and ὀφρύ-ας (Od. 9. 389), νέκυς (Od. 24. 417) and νέκυ-ας, βοῦς and βό-ας.

Stems in -υ, Gen. -εος, have only -εας in Homer: except πολύς, read by Zenodotus in Il. 2. 4, perhaps in other places (Il. 1. 559., 13. 734., 15. 66., 20. 313., 21. 59, 131, Od. 3. 262., 4. 170), where the MSS. have πολέας or πολεῖς.

The MS. of Schol. A in Il. 2. 4 gives πολεῖς as read by Zen., but the context shows that the true reading of the scholium is πολύς. But there is no trace of this form in any of the other places.

The Personal Pronouns have ἡμέας (once ἧμας), ὑμέας, σφέας (once σφᾶς encl., Il. 5. 567), as well as ἄμμε, ὔμμε, σφέ. The forms in -ᾰς are later, the result of adding the common ending of the Acc. Plur.: see on the Acc. Sing.

101.] Genitive Plural. Stems in -ᾱ(η) and -ᾰ form the Gen. Plur. in -ᾱων, less commonly -εων. The -εων is generally scanned -ε͡ων, and after a vowel is written -ῶν, as κλισι-ῶν, παρει-ῶν, τρυφαλει-ῶν, Σκαι-ῶν (cp. the Gen. Sing. in -ᾱο, -εω).

The Pronominal Stems ἡμε-, ὑμε-, σφε- form ἡμείων and ἡμέων, ὑμείων and ὑμέων, σφείων σφέων (encl.) and σφῶν.

These forms are plausibly explained by supposing that originally the Gen. was in -ειο, as in the Singular. Then *ἀμμεῖο, *ὑμμεῖο, were assimilated to the Gen. Plur. in -ων; and σφείων followed the same analogy later (Brugmann, *K. Z.* xxvii. 397).

102.] Dative Plural. The two Endings of the Dat. Plur. are -σι(ν) and -εσσι(ν). Many Nouns in Homer form the Case in both ways, e. g. βου-σί and βό-εσσι (for βού-εσσι), χερ-σί and χείρ-εσσι, ποσσί or ποσί (for ποδ-σί) and πόδ-εσσι, ἀνδρά-σι and ἄνδρ-εσσι, μνηστῆρ-σι and μνηστήρ-εσσι. The accent is often different, the forms in -εσσι being always proparoxytone. The ending -σι(ν) originally belongs to the Locative Plur. (Sanscr. -su).

A final dental or -σ with -σι forms -σσι, and this σσ may be reduced to σ, as in ποσσί and ποσί, ἔπεσ-σι and ἔπεσι, δέπασ-σι and δέπασι. But -εσι for the ending -εσσι is very rare: χείρ-εσι, ἴν-εσι, αἴγ-εσι, οἴ-εσι, ἀνάκτ-εσι occur once each.

An ending -σσι (instead of -σι) occurs in a few stems in -υ (Gen. -vos): γένυ-σσι (Il. 11. 416), νέκυ-σσι (Od.), πίτυ-σσι (Od.). This is an extension of the type ἔπεσ-σι, &c.: cp. ἴρισσι (Il. 13. 27) for ἴριδ-σι. Or possibly, as Brugmann suggests (*G. G.* p. 62), these are forms in -ῠσι, -ῑσι, the vowel retaining its original quantity (cp. § 116, 3 and 4).

Final ι or υ of the Stem becomes ε in ἐπάλξε-σι, πολέ-σι (πολύ-s), from the analogy of the other Cases, as ἐπάλξε-ος, πολέ-ος. Similarly on the analogy of forms with -εσσι (as in ἔπεσσι) we have the rare forms πολ-έσσι (πολ-ύς), πελέκ-εσσι (πέλεκ-υς).

The Ending -εσσι(ν) is itself the result of a similar analogy. In ἔπεσσι, βέλεσσι, &c. the -εσσι was felt as characteristic of the

Case, and then combined with other Stems; hence κύν-εσσι,
σύ-εσσι, &c. Thus forms like ἐπέ-εσσι (for ἐπεσ-εσσι) really
contain the Suffix εσ twice over. (Bopp, *Vergl. Gr.* § 292 of the
first edition; Meyer, *G. G.* p. 355.)

Stems in -ο and -ᾱ (η) form the Dat. Plur. in -οισι(ν) and -ῃσι(ν)
respectively, also in -οις and -αις or -ῃς. The latter forms are
common in the existing text of Homer, but (as was pointed out
by Gerland, *K. Z.* ix. 36, and again by Nauck, *Mél. gr.-rom.* iii.
244) in the great majority of instances the loss of ι may be
regarded as due to elision: *e.g.* for σοῖς ἑτάροισι we may write
σοῖσ᾽ ἑτάροισι. The Fem. -αις appears only in the forms θεαῖς
(Od. 5. 119), ἀκταῖς (Il. 12. 284), and πάσαις (Od. 22. 471).
Hence it is a question whether the forms in -οις, -αις are
Homeric.

The Endings -οισι, -ῃσι are those of the Locative (Sanscr.
-*ēshu*, -*āsu*). Originally -ῃσι was without ι (as in the adverbial
Ἀθήνῃσι, θύρᾱσι). The Endings -οις, -αις are probably not to be
derived from -οισι, -ῃσι, but from the original Instrumental of
Stems in -ο. This was in Sanscr. -*āis*, in Greek *-ωις, becoming
-οις: and from this again by an easy analogy the corresponding
Fem. -αις was formed.

The Pronouns of the First and Second Person use two forms,
viz. (1) -ῖν in ἡμῖν (encl. ἧμιν) and ὑμῖν (encl. ὗμιν), and (2) -ῐ(ν)
in ἄμμι(ν), ὔμμι(ν), also ἧμῐν, ὗμῐν. This is evidently the same
Suffix as in ἐμίν, τείν, ἑίν, and the form -ῖν is presumably the
older (for which -ῐν was perhaps adopted from the analogy of
the Dat. in -σῐν).

The 3 Plur. σφῐ(ν) is originally in all probability the Instrum.
Plur. of the Stem σϝε- (for σϝ-φιν): cp. Lat. *sibi*, for *s-bi*. If
so, the other Case-forms σφέ, σφείων, σφί-σι as well as the
corresponding Duals σφώ, &c. are the result of analogy.

103.] Dual. The Nom. Acc. in -ᾱ, from Stems in ᾱ, η is
only found as a Masc.: Ἀτρείδᾱ, κορυστά (Il. 18. 163), ὠκυπέτᾱ
(Il. 8. 42): but Fem. προφανέντε, πληγέντε (of two goddesses, Il.
8. 378, 455).

The Genitive and Dative Ending in all Nouns is -οιϊν, as
ποδ-οῖιν, ἱππ-οιϊν. The contracted form -οιν and the Fem. -αιν
do not occur. The Personal Pronouns have:—

1. Nom. Acc. νῶϊ, νώ (νῶϊν Il. 16. 99, σφῶϊν Od. 23. 52?);
Gen. Dat. νῶϊν.

2. Nom. Acc. σφῶϊ, σφώ; Gen. Dat. σφῶϊν (σφῷν Od. 4. 62).

3. Acc. σφωέ (encl.); Dat. σφωΐν (encl.).

104.] Instrumental. The Homeric poems have preserved
many instances of an Ending -φι(ν); *e.g.* ὄρεσ-φιν, στήθεσ-φι,

ναῦ-φιν, ζυγό-φι, βίη-φι, κοτυληδον-ό-φιν (Od.) : probably also the
Pronoun σ-φι(ν), Lat. *si-bi*. These are relics of an original
Instrumental Case.

105.] Contraction, &c. The loss of ι, υ and σ between vowels
(§ 94) does not generally lead to contraction in the Homeric
dialect : note that—

1. The Dat. Sing. of Stems in -εσ and -υ (Gen. -εος) often
forms ει (for -ε-ϊ), but nearly always before a vowel, so that the
ει is scanned as a short syllable (§ 380); e.g. τείχει ὕπο Τρώων, ἢ
ἔπει ἢ ἔργῳ, &c. No such rule will be found to hold for the Dat.
Sing. of Stems in -ι, as πόλει, ἀγύρει &c.—either because -ει from
-ει-ι became monosyllabic earlier than -ει from -εσ-ι or -εϝ-ι ; or
because, as has been suggested (§ 99), the true form of the Dat.
is πόλῑ, ἀγύρῑ, &c.
   Exceptions, real or apparent, to this rule are—
      Il. 6. 126 σῷ θάρσει (read θάρσεϊ σῷ, cp. Il. 7. 153 θάρσεϊ ᾧ).
         17. 647 ἐν δὲ φάει καὶ ὄλεσσον (read ἐν φάεϊ).
         23. 515 οὔ τι τάχει γε (read οὐ τάχεΐ γε).
         23. 639 πλήθει (read πληθυΐ).
   Also οὔδει, Dat. of οὖδας (Il. 5. 734., 8. 385., 14. 467., 17. 92.,
23. 719., 24. 527), for which read οὔδαι or οὔδᾳ (§ 99).

2. The combinations -εα, -εο, -εω are often scanned as one
syllable by 'Synizesis,' as θεοί (Il. 1. 18), σάκεᾱ (Il. 4. 113), τεύχεᾱ
(Il. 7. 207, &c.); so with the Pronouns ἡμέας, ὑμέας, σφέας.

   In Il. 1. 18 ὑμῖν μὲν θεοὶ δοῖεν Ὀλύμπια δώματ᾽ ἔχοντες the word θεοί is not
certain, since Ὀλύμπια δώματ᾽ ἔχοντες *the lords of Olympus* is used as a Substantive, and θεοί is therefore unnecessary (Fick, *Ilias* p. 75).

3. The Gen. Sing. has -ευς for -ε-ος in a few words ; Ἐρέβευς,
θάρσευς, θέρευς, θάμβευς—chiefly ἅπαξ εἰρημένα. It is probably
better to write -εος and admit Synizesis.
   On -ευ in ἐμεῦ, σεῦ, εὖ, τεῦ see § 378*.

4. Nouns with Stems in -εεσ (as κλέος, δέος) and some Nouns
in -ᾰς are liable to 'Hyphaeresis,' or dropping a vowel before
another vowel : as κλέα (for κλέε-α), and so δυσκλέα, ἀκλέα,
ἀκλέ-ες ; νηλής, νηλέϊ, νηλέα (Neut. Sing. νηλεές) ; θεουδής, θεουδέα
(for θεο-δϝής *god-fearing*), ὑπερδέα (Il. 17. 330) ; γέρᾰ, δέπα, κέρα,
κρέα, σφέλα (for γέρα-α, &c.), χρέα *debts* (Hes. Op. 647). Cp.
δαΐ (for δαϊ-ι), Dat. of δάϊ-ς ; also ἀποαίρεο for ἀποαιρέ-εο (§ 5).

   The forms κλέα (ἀκλέα, δυσκλέα), δέπα, κέρα, σφέλα are only found before
hiatus ; *e.g.* κλέα only occurs in the phrase κλέα ἀνδρῶν : so that we must
either suppose -ᾱ to be shortened by the hiatus, or (better) read κλέε᾽ ἀνδρῶν,
&c. But γέρα occurs before a consonant (Il. 2. 237 γέρα πεσσέμεν, and so

9. 334, Od. 4. 66). κρέα occurs in the phrase κρέα ἔδμεναι, and in one or two other places before a vowel ; but more frequently it is followed by a consonant, and is to be scanned κρέᾰ or κρέᾱ (necessarily so in Od. 9. 347, where it ends the line). Possibly the ᾱ is shortened by the analogy of the ordinary Neut. Plur. forms in -ᾰ (Meyer, *G. G.* p. 348). Or, as is now maintained by Joh. Schmidt (*Pluralb.* p. 321 ff.), κρέα, γέρα, &c. are stems in -ᾰ, originally distinct from the corresponding stems in -ᾰσ, and are therefore properly Singular, but capable of being used in a collective sense. On this view κρέᾰ meant *flesh*, κρέαα *pieces of flesh* : cp. μῆρα and μηροί (§ 99*). Schmidt does not admit hyphaeresis in most of these words, holding that it only occurred when *three* vowels came together in the oldest Greek : so that (*e. g.*) we may have δέα for δϜέεα (δϜεϳεσ-α), but not κλέα for κλέϜεα.

5. There are also several contracted forms from Stems in -εεσ which offer some difficulty : ἀκληεῖς (Il. 12. 316), ἀκλειῶς (Od. 1. 241., 14. 371), ἐϋκλειῶς (Il. 22. 110), ἐϋκλείας (Il. 10. 281, Od. 21. 331 ; al. ἐϋκλῆας), ἀγακλῆος (ἀγακλεῖος Hesych.), Πατροκλῆος, Πατροκλῆα, Ἡρακλῆος, Ἡρακλῆα, Ἡρακλῆϊ, Βαθυκλῆα, Διοκλῆος, Διοκλῆα ; ζαχρηεῖς, ζαχρειῶν (also ζαχρηῶν Hesych.) ; ἐϋρρεῖος ; δείους (Il. 10. 376., 15. 4) ; σπείους, σπῆϊ, σπέσσι and σπήεσσι.

But the η or ει always occurs where it can be resolved into εε, as Πατροκλεέ-ος, ἐϋρρεέ-ος, ἀκλεέ-ως, &c. ; moreover the long final syllable so lost (e. g. in writing ἀκλεέ-ες, δέε-ος, σπέε-ος) is never necessary to the metre. Hence we can hardly doubt that these are the true Homeric forms. So κρειῶν (Gen. Plur. of κρέας) should be κρεά-ων (as in H. Merc. 130), or perhaps κρεέων (see § 107, 3) ; and ζαχρηεῖς, ζαχρειῶν should be ζαχραέες, ζαχραέων. For σπέσσι we can read σπέεσι.

The Voc. of Πατροκλέης should be written in the uncontracted form Πατρόκλεες in the phrase Πατρόκλεες ἱππεῦ (which ends the line in Il. 16. 20, 744, 812, 843), and also whenever it comes before the Bucolic Diaeresis (§ 368). When it stands at the beginning of the line (Il. 16. 693, 859) we should perhaps read Πάτροκλος : see § 164.

6. The Case-forms of Nouns in -ως and -ω (Gen. -οος) ought generally to be written without contraction ; thus ἠώς, Dat. ἠόϊ, Acc. ἠόα (see § 368) ; αἰδώς, Dat. αἰδόϊ, Acc. αἰδόα : ἱδρώς, Acc. ἱδρόα (Il. 10. 574). But the Genitive in -οῦς (ἠοῦς, Λητοῦς, &c.) is required by the metre in several places. Naturally the contraction of οο was earlier than that of two *unlike* sounds, as οι, οα. See L. Meyer, *Decl.* 23.

106.] **Variation of the Stem.** The phonetic influence of the Ending on the form of the Stem, which plays so large a part in the inflexion of Non-Thematic Tenses, was originally no less important in the Nouns. In Sanscrit a Nominal Stem of the consonantal Declension appears in general in at least two forms,

a 'strong' and a 'weak' form; the strong form being used in
the Nom. and Acc. Sing. and Dual and the Nom. Plur., the
weak form in other Cases. The weak form, again, may have
two degrees, which are then called the 'weak' or 'middle' and
the 'weakest' form. A few traces of these variations remain
in the Greek Declension:—

1. In the words of relationship, πατήρ, μήτηρ, &c. and in ἀνήρ.
Thus we find Nom. πατήρ, Acc. πατέρ-α, but Gen. πατρ-ός (πατέρ-ος
only Od. 11. 500), Dat. πατρ-ί (sixty times in Homer, πατέρ-ι
thrice); μήτηρ, Acc. μητέρα (only), Gen. and Dat. μητρ-ός, μητρ-ί,
less commonly μητέρ-ος, μητέρ-ι. ἀνήρ uses ἀνερ- and ἀνδρ- (for
ἀνρ-) almost promiscuously; the latter is also seen in the Dat.
Pl. ἀνδρά-σι (for ἀνδρ-σι). The Gen. Plur. δαέρων (Il. 24. 769) is
scanned as a spondee: it should probably be written δαιϜ-ῶν,
the stem δαιϜρ- standing to δαήρ (for δαϜήρ) as ἀνδρ- to ἀνήρ
(Ebel, K. Z. i. 293).

2. Ζεύς, for δι̯ηύς (Sanscr. *dyáus*) forms the Gen. and Dat. from
the Stem διϜ. The original Acc. is Ζῆν, Sanscr. *dyám* (with loss
of *u*): Δία follows the analogy of Διός, Διί. Similarly βοῦς, for
*βωῦς (Sanscr. *gáus*), Gen. βοϜ-ός, Acc. in Hom. βῶν (Sanscr. *gám*).
κύων, Voc. κύον, forms the other Cases from the Stem κυν-.
Cp. Sanscr. *çvan*, Acc. *çván-am*, Gen. *çun-as*, &c. The Acc.
κύν-α (like Δία) follows the analogy of the Gen. and Dat.
Similarly, *Ϝρήν a lamb (surviving in πολύ-ρρην-ες) forms Gen.
ἀρν-ός (for Ϝρν-ός), &c.

3. Adjectives in -εις, Gen. -εντος (Stem -Ϝεντ-), form the Dat.
Plur. in -εσσι, -εσι. To explain this we must first suppose the
weak Stem in Ϝάτ- (with ἄ for εν, cp. § 31, 5 and § 37), which
would give a Dat. Plur. in -ασσι, -ᾶσι; this form then was assimilated to the other Cases by change of ἄ to ε. A form in -ασι
has survived in φρασί* for φρεσί (φρᾰ: φρεν=Ϝάτ: Ϝεντ). In the
same way δαίμοσι, ποιμέσι, &c. are not for δαίμον-σι, ποιμέν-σι, but
for *δαίμᾰ-σι, *ποιμᾰ-σι. The Adverb ἀγκάς has been explained
as ἀγκάσ(ι), the true Dat. Plur. of ἀγκών.

4. The primitive variation sometimes gives rise to parallel
forms of a word: e.g. πτώξ and πτάξ a hare (πτήσσω), which
originate in the declension πτώξ, Acc. πτῶκ-α, Gen. πτακ-ός. So
from πούς and Lat. *pēs, ped-is* we may infer original πούς (or
rather πώς), Acc. πόδα or πῶδα, Gen. πεδ-ός: and so in other
cases †.

---

* Found in Pindar, also in an Old Attic inscription given by Joh. Schmidt,
K. Z. xxv. p. 38.

† Much, however, remains uncertain in the attempts that have been made
to reconstruct the primitive declension of these and similar words. The
Sanscrit forms would furnish a fairly complete key, but for two defects: (1)

107.] Heteroclite Nouns. This term is applicable to Nouns that employ distinct Stems. The chief variations are—

1. Between the vowel Declension (Stems in -ο and -ᾱ, -η) and the corresponding consonantal forms :—

δίπτυχο-s; Acc. δίπτυχ-α.
ἐρίηρο-s; Plur. ἐρίηρ-ες, ἐρίηρ-ας.
(ἀνδράποδο-ν post-Hom.); Dat. Plur. ἀνδραπόδ-εσσι.
ἀλκή; Dat. ἀλκ-ί.
ὑσμίνη; Dat. ὑσμῖν-ι.
ἰωκή; Acc. ἰῶκ-α.
Ἀΐδη-s, Gen. Ἀΐδα-ο; also Ἄϊδ-ος, Dat. Ἄϊδ-ι.
φυλάκους (or φυλακούς, as Aristarchus accented the word); also φύλακ-ας, Dat. Plur. φυλάκ-εσσι.
ὄσσε, Dat. Plur. ὄσσοισι (Hes. Sc. 426).

πολλό-s and πολύ-s are both declined throughout: so δάκρυο-ν and δάκρυ.

2. With forms in -τ or -ᾰτ :—

γόνυ, Gen. γουνός (for γονϜ-ός), Plur. γοῦν-α, γούν-ων, γούν-εσσι; also γούνατ-ος, &c.
δόρυ, Gen. δουρός (for δορϜ-ος), &c.; δούρατ-ος, &c.
ὄνειρο-s; Plur. ὀνείρατ-α.
πρόσωπο-ν; Plur. προσώπατ-α, Dat. προσώπασι. Hence the form ὦπα (εἰς ὦπα ἰδέσθαι, κατ' ἔν-ωπα ἰδών) may be a Neut. Sing.: cp. Æolic ὄππατα *eyes** *.
οὖς; Gen. οὔατ-ος, Dat. Plur. οὔασι and ὠσί.
ἦμαρ (cp. ἡμέρ-α); ἦματ-ος, &c. (cp. ἠμάτ-ιος). So πεῖραρ (πείρατ-α), ἧπαρ, οὖθαρ, εἶδαρ, ὄνειαρ, φρεῖαρ, κτέαρ, ἄλειφαρ, στέαρ.
ὕδωρ, ὕδατ-ος. See § 114*, 8, d.
χάρις, Acc. χάρι-ν (cp. χαρί-εις); Plur. χάριτ-ες, &c.
μέλι (μείλι-νος, μελι-ηδέα); μέλιτ-ος, &c.
χρώς, χρο-ός, χρο-ί, χρό-α; also χρωτ-ός (Il. 10. 575) and χρῶτ-α (Od. 18. 172, 179).

We should add the whole class of Nouns in -μα, Gen. -ματ-ος: since the -μᾰ of the Nom. Acc. is not for -μᾰτ, but answers to the Latin -men, Gen. -min-is.

3. Between -ασ- and -εσ- :—

τέρας, τέραα, τερά-ων, τερά-εσσι; but τείρεα (in the sense of 'stars,' Il. 18. 485).

---

the Sanscr. *a* may represent either ε or ο, so that (e. g.) *padás* may be ποδός or πεδός, and similarly *ā* may be η or ω: and (2) Sanscr. *ā* often answers to Greek o, so that (e. g.) *pādam* may point to either πόδα or πῶδα. See Joh. Schmidt, *K. Z.* xxv. 23 ff., Brugmann, *Grundr.* i. § 311, p. 251.

* The old explanation of ὄππα from ὀπ-μα, by 'progressive assimilation,' seems to be groundless.

οὖδας, οὔδε-ος, &c. : so κῶας, κώε-α, κτέρας, κτέρε-α (and
New Ionic γέρεα, &c. ; Attic βρέτους, κνέφους).

This variation doubtless arose from the Ionic change of ᾰο, ᾱω into εο, εω.
Thus the ε first appeared in the Gen., giving (e. g.) τέρας, τέρεος, τέραι, Plur.
τέραα, τερέων, τέρασι or τερά-εσσι. Then ε was extended to other Cases, and on
the other hand α was sometimes restored, as in τεράων, κρεάων. See § 106, 4,
and Joh. Schmidt, *Pluralb.* p. 325.

4. Comparatives in -ων (Gen. -ον-ος) sometimes form Cases as
if by contraction with a Stem in -οσ ; ἀμείνω (for ἀμείνοσ-α,
ἀμείνο-α), πλείους (for πλείοσ-ες), ἀρείους (§ 114* 7 ; § 121).

5. Other variations are—

ἡνίοχο-ς ; Acc. ἡνιοχῆ-α, Nom. Plur. ἡνιοχῆ-ες.

Αἰθίοπ-ες, &c., but Acc. Αἰθιοπῆ-ας.

Ἀντιφάτη-ς, Acc. Ἀντιφατῆ-α.

Ἄρης, Voc. Ἄρες ; Gen. Ἄρη-ος and Ἄρε-ος, &c. ; Acc.
Ἄρηα and once Ἄρη-ν (Il. 5. 909).

ζαής, Acc. ζαῆ-ν (Od. 12. 313) : see § 97.

λᾶα-ς, Acc. λᾶα-ν ; Gen. λᾶ-ος, Dat. λᾶ-ϊ, Dual λᾶε, Plur.
λᾶ-ες, λά-ων, λά-εσσι. The latter forms are doubtless
by hyphaeresis (§ 105, 4) for λάα-ος, &c.

γρῆϋς, Dat. γρηΐ, as if from a monosyllabic γρηῦς.

μέγα (for μεγη̨, cp. *magn-us*), Masc. μέγα-ς, μέγα-ν ; the
other Cases from the derivative stem μεγα-λο-.

Three apparently distinct Stems are used in υἱός *son*, viz.—

(1) υἱό-ς, Voc. υἱέ ; the forms υἱοῦ, υἱῷ, υἱοῖσι are very
rare in Homer.

(2) (υἱυ-), Acc. υἱέ-α, Gen. υἱέ-ος, Dat. υἱέ-ϊ, Plur. υἱέ-ες,
υἱέ-ας : and from these by hyphaeresis—

(3) Acc. υἷ-α, Gen. υἷ-ος, Dat. υἷ-ι, Dual υἷ-ε, Plur. υἷ-ες,
υἷ-ας, υἱά-σι ; cp. γρηῦς, λᾶας.

The form υἱάσι (instead of υἱύ-σι) follows the type πατράσι, &c.

The Neut. κάρη *head* forms—

(1) Gen. καρήατ-ος, κάρητ-ος, Dat. καρήατ-ι, κάρητ-ι.

(2) Gen. κράατ-ος, Dat. κράατ-ι, Plur. κράατ-α(ᾶα).

(3) Acc. Sing. κρᾶτ-α (Od. 8. 92), Gen. κρᾱτ-ός, Dat.
κρᾱτ-ί, Plur. Gen. κρᾱτ-ων, Dat. κρᾱσί. The Dat. Sing.
form κράτεσφι (Il. 10. 156) is quite anomalous*.

---

* We might add the stem κρη-, in κατὰ κρῆθεν *down from the head*, cp. κρήδεμνον, κρή-νη. The relations of these forms have hardly yet been satisfactorily
cleared up: see especially Joh. Schmidt, *Pluralb.* p. 363 ff. It is highly
probable that κέρας is originally the same word, so that the original declension, answering to Sanscr. çiras, çîrshnás, &c., was κέρας, Gen. κρᾱ(σ)νός and
κρᾱ(σ)-ατος (like γόνυ, Gen. γονϝ-ός and γόνϝ-ατος, &c.). The form κάρη must

The declension of ἔρως, γέλως and ἰδρώς in Homer is open to some doubt ; it is clear however that the Stems in -τ are post-Homeric.

Nom. ἔρος occurs in Il. 14. 315, Acc. ἔρον in the phrase ἐξ ἔρον ἕντο *put away desire*, Dat. ἔρῳ in Od. 18. 212 ; Nom. ἔρως is read in Il. 3. 442., 14. 294, but the metre allows ἔρος in both places. ἔρωτ-α occurs first in H. Merc. 449.

Nom. γέλως occurs in Il. 1. 599, Od. 8. 326, 343, 344 : in the two last passages (in the Song of Demodocus) the metre is rather against γέλος. The Dat. γέλῳ occurs in Od. 18. 100 (most MSS. γέλω) ; the Acc. γέλον or γέλω in Od. 18. 350., 20. 346 (MSS. γέλων, γέλον, and γέλω). Thus the word may be either γέλο-s (Gen. -ου) or γέλως, Acc. γέλω (for γέλω-α or γέλο-α) : cp. αἰδῶ for αἰδόα. The Stem γελοσ- appears in γελοῖος, cp. αἰδοῖος, ἠοῖος.

From ἰδρώς we have Acc. ἰδρῶ ; but this must be read ἰδρόα in one place (Il. 10. 574 ἰδρῶ πολλόν at the end of the line), and always may be so read. The Dat. is ἰδρῷ (Il. 17. 385, 745), possibly to be written ἰδροῖ. Hence ἰδρώς is probably like χρώς.

Two other Case-forms of this type are ἰχῶ (Il. 5. 416), Acc. of ἰχώρ, and κυκειῶ (Il.) or κυκεῶ (Od.), Acc. of κυκεών. Cp. also αἰῶ (Aesch. fr. 413), Acc. of αἰών.

The history of all these instances is very similar. The original Stem ended with a spirant (commonly σ), the loss of which in the oblique Cases caused hiatus (-οος, -οϊ, -οα, &c.) : then these forms were replaced by adopting Stems in -τ and -ν. Cp. § 114*, 6–8.

108.] Heteroclite Pronouns. The following points remain to be noticed :—

1. The stems ἐμε (με) and ἐε, ἐ do not form a Nom. Sing.

It is evident that the original Nom. coalesced at a very early period with the Stem of the Verb, becoming the ending -μι ; just as the French *je* has ceased to be used except in a fixed place before the Verb, so that it is hardly a separate word.

In the Plural also the Nom. was not originally formed from the same Stems as the oblique Cases. Both ἄμμε-s, ὔμμε-s and ἡμέ-es, ὑμέ-es are comparatively late, and due to the analogy of the Nominal declension (Meyer, *G. G.* p. 388).

2. The Interrogative and Indefinite τίς is declined from three Stems, viz.

(1) τι-, giving Neut. τί (for τίδ), also the Plur. Neut. traceable in ἄσσα (for ἅ τια). The Indef. ἄσσα occurs in Od. 19. 218 ὁπποῖ’ ἄσσα, where it would be better to write ὁπποῖά ’σσα (for τια).

(2) τε-, giving Gen. τέο, τεῦ (cp. ἐμέο, &c.), Dat. τέῳ, τῷ (Il. 16. 227, H. Apoll. 170).

Gen. τέων (ἐω), Dat. in ὁ-τέοισι (ἐοι), Il. 15. 491.

(3) τιν-, giving Acc. τίν-α, Dat. (very rarely) τίν-ι, Plur. Nom. τίνες (only in the Od.).

---

have been originally a derivative, introduced to mean *head* when κέρας had come to be limited to the sense of *horn*. From it again καρή-ατος, &c. were obtained by analogy.

In the Compound ὅσ-τις the first part is sometimes declined as ὅς, ἥ, ὅ, sometimes undeclined, giving ὅ-τις, ὅ-τευ, &c. The Neut. Plur. is once ὅ-τιν-α (Il. 22. 450), usually ἅσσα.

In the forms with ττ, ππ (as ὅττι, ὅππως) we have to recognise the original Neuter ὅδ (Sanscr. *yad*). Thus ὅδ τι becomes ὅτ τι (not ὅστι, since τι is a distinct word, not a Suffix). In ὅττεο, which occurs in the Odyssey (1. 124., 17. 121., 22. 377), ὁδ- is indeclinable (cp. ὅ-τις), and so in ὅππως, ὅπποσος, ὁπποῖος, &c. For the assimilation we may compare κὰδ δέ, κὰπ πεδίον, &c. (for κὰτ δέ, κὰτ πεδίον).

3. The Article is declined from two Stems :—

ὁ-, Fem. ἁ-, which gives ὁ, ἡ, οἱ, αἱ : perhaps also ὥς *thus*, if it is distinct from the Relatival ὡς *as*.

το-, Fem. τᾱ-, which gives the other Cases, and second forms of the Nom. Plur. τοί, ταί : also the Adverb τώς *thus*.

The Compound ὅ-δε uses the Stem ὅ- for the forms ὅ-δε, ἥ-δε, οἵ-δε, αἵ-δε, and the Adverb ὧ-δε. The second part is sometimes declined in the Dat. Plur., τοίσ-δεσσιν or τοίσ-δεσιν (Il. 10. 462 and Od.). The -δε is enclitic : hence the accent, ἥ-δε, not ἥδε. Strictly, therefore, it should be written ὅ δε, ἥ δε, &c.

The forms ἐμαυτόν, σεαυτόν, &c. are post-Homeric. The earliest instance of a Compound of this kind is the word ἑαυτῇ, in Hes. Th. 216.

Adverbial Suffixes.

109.] The Suffixes employed in Homer to form Adverbs are as follows :—

-θι expresses the *place where:* the chief instances are—from Pronouns and Prepositions, τό-θι, ὅ-θι, πό-θι, αὖ-θι, αὐτό-θι, κεῖ-θι (ἐκεῖ-θι only Od. 17. 10), ἑτέρω-θι, ἑκάστο-θι, ἄλλο-θι, ἔκτο-θι, ἔνδο-θι, ἀπό-προ-θι, ὑψό-θι, ἐγγύ-θι ; from Nouns, νειό-θι, θήρη-θι (Od. 14. 352), οἴκο-θι, ἠῶ-θι, οὐρανό-θι, κηρό-θι ; Ἰλιό-θι, Κορινθό-θι, Ἀβυδό-θι. Note that ἐκεῖ is not found in Homer.

-θα *place* ; ἔν-θα, ἐνταῦ-θα, ὕπαι-θα (cp. also δηθά, μίνυνθα).

-θε(ν) *place*, from Prepositions ; πρόσ-θε(ν), ὄπισ-θε(ν) and ὄπι-θε(ν), ὕπερ-θε(ν), πάροι-θε(ν), ἔνερ-θε(ν).

-θεν *place whence*, used with nearly the same Stems as -θι ; ὅ-θεν, πό-θεν, ἔν-θεν, κεῖ-θεν, ἄλλο-θεν, ὑψό-θεν, πάντο-θεν, ἀμφο-τέρω-θεν, ἑτέρω-θεν. From Nouns, ἠῶ-θεν, Διό-θεν (Il.), οὐρανό-θεν, ἱππό-θεν, &c.

This Suffix is often used with the Prepositions ἐξ and ἀπό, as ἐκ Διό-θεν, ἀπ' οὐρανό-θεν, &c. With the Stems ἐμε, σε, ἑ, it forms a Genitive ; as Il. 1. 280 σέθεν δ' ἐγὼ οὐκ ἀλεγίζω. The form ἔθεν is only found in the Iliad.

-θοι, only in ἐνταυ-θοῖ *there* (Od.).

-τος *place ;* ἐν-τός, ἐκ-τός. Originally, perhaps, it expressed the *place whence,* as Lat. *caeli-tus, divini-tus.*

-τις, in αὖ-τις *back, again* (Attic αὖ-θις).

-σε *place whither ;* πό-σε, ὁππό-σε, κεῖ-σε, ἑτέρω-σε, ἀμφοτέρω-σε, ὁμό-σε. From Nouns, πάντο-σε, κυκλό-σε.

-φι(ν), -φις, in νόσ-φι(ν) *apart,* λικρι-φίς *sideways* (Il. 14. 463). This may be the Instrumental Ending -φι(ν).

-φα, in μέσ-φα *until,* lit. *meanwhile* (Il. 8. 508).

-χι, in ᾖ-χι *where* (lit. *which way,* Lat. *quā*).

-χα, with Numerals ; δί-χα *two ways,* τρί-χα, πέντα-χα, ἕπτα-χα.

-χθα, in the same sense, τρι-χθά, τετρα-χθά.

-κις, -κι ; with Numerals, in δεκά-κις, τετρά-κις, εἰνά-κις, εἰκοσά-κις ; and with similar meaning πολλάκις and πολλάκι, ὁσσάκι, τοσσάκι.

The original Suffix is -κις or -κι (not -ἄκις), but in consequence of its having been used at first with Stems ending in -ἄ (τετρᾰ-, ἑπτᾰ-, δεκᾰ-, εἰνᾰ-), the combination -α-κις came to be felt as the Suffix, and was extended to other words by analogy. A similar explanation applies to the ᾰ of πέντα-χα.

-κας expresses *manner ;* ἀνδρα-κάς = Lat. *viritim.*

-δε *place whither,* suffixed to the Accusative ; οἶκόν-δε, πόλε-μόνδε, ἅλαδε. This Suffix is peculiar in being an enclitic ; in strictness we should write οἶκόν δε, πόλεμόν δε, &c.

-δις expresses *direction* or *manner ;* χαμά-δις, ἄμυ-δις, ἄλλυ-δις, ἐπαμοιβα-δίς (Od. 5. 481).

110.] Case-forms as Adverbs. The Suffixes which follow have been explained, with more or less probability, as Case-Endings.

-α *manner ;* ἄρ-α (lit. *fittingly*), ἅμ-α, μάλ-α, θάμ-α, τάχ-α, σάφ-α, κάρτ-α, ῥεῖ-α or ῥέ-α, ὦκ-α, ἦκ-α, αἶψ-α, λίγ-α, σῖγ-α, ῥίμφ-α, πύκ-α, λίπ-α ; in Attic κρύφ-α, ἠρέμ-α.

The Adverbs in -ᾰ belong to an early stage of Greek, most of them being confined to Homer. They have generally been taken to be primitive Instrumental forms (so Brugmann, M. U. ii. 158, G. G. § 83). It is a question, however, whether the original Instr. ending was -ᾰ or -ε : see Joh. Schmidt, K. Z. xxvii. 292. Those which answer to adjectives in -ύ-s, viz. τάχα, ὦκα, λίγα, κάρτα, θάμα, are explained by Joh. Schmidt as older Neut. Plur. forms (ταχϝ-α, &c.), cp. αἰπά Neut. Plur. of αἰπύ-s, and πρέσβᾰ (for πρεσβϝ-ᾰ ?) Fem. of πρέσβυ-s. This will not apply to ἄρα, μάλα (since ἀρ-ϝα, μαλ-ϝα would give ἄρα, μᾶλα). Some may be stems in -ῃ, like μέγα : cp. λίγα and λιγαίνω (-ῃιω), λίπα and λιπαίνω, πύκα and πυκν-ός, also the stems κρεα-, γερα- (§ 105, 4).

-ῃ or -η *way, direction ;* ᾖ, τῇ, πῇ, ὅπῃ (or πῆ, ὅπη), πάντ-η, λάθρῃ. These forms represent the Instrumental of the *way by which* (Lat. *quā,* &c.).

It is a question whether they should be written with *iota subscr.* or not. The ancient grammarians prescribed *iota* (Apoll. de Adv. 625, 1), and this is confirmed by the forms ᾷ, ὁπᾷ, ἀλλᾷ, παντᾷ on Doric inscriptions (Ahrens, ii. 369). In Homer however the final vowel of πάντῃ (or -η) is frequently shortened before another vowel, which is rarely done in the case of final -ῃ (§ 380). It is not unlikely therefore that the original Instrum. Fem. -η took *iota subscr.* from the analogy of the Dat. Fem. in -ῃ. There were also Doric adverbs of *place* in -η or ῃ (πή ποκα, ἑκατερῇ, see Ahrens, ii. 362, Brugmann, *M. V.* ii. 244), in which η is of course pan-Hellenic ; but Ionic πῇ, &c. are connected by the meaning with the Doric forms in -ᾷ. Cp. also λάθρῃ (-η) with Attic λάθρᾱ (or -ᾳ). The form πάντ-η is an extension of the ending -η to the consonantal declension (as with the adverbs in -ως).

-ει, -ι *time, manner ;* αὐτο-νυχ-εί (or -ί) *that very night,* Il. 8. 197 ; τρι-στοιχ-ί *in three rows,* ἀναιμωτ-ί (ῑ) *bloodlessly,* ἀμογητ-ί, ἀμαχητί, ἀνουτητί, ἀνιδρωτί, ἀνωϊστί, ἐγρηγορτί : with ῐ, ἕκητι *with the will,* ἀέκητ-ι *without the will,* μελεϊστ-ί *limb by limb,* μεγαλωστί *in mighty fashion.*

Short -ῐ is certain in ἕκητι, ἀέκητι, μελεϊστί, μεγαλωστί, and is not excluded by the metre in ἀμογητί and ἀμαχητί. Where the syllable is long the MSS. are usually divided between -ει and -ι. The evidence of inscriptions is strongly in favour of -ει (H. W. Smyth, *The reduction of* ει *to* ι *in Homer,* p. 10) : but -ῑ can hardly be due to mere itacism, and we have further to explain the forms in -ῑ. The generally accepted view is that -ει is the original Locative ending of the ο- declension, which is preserved in the Doric adverbs εἰ, πεῖ, τουτεῖ, τηνεῖ, &c., also in οἴκει (Menander fr. 456). On this view short ῑ must be the corresponding ending of the consonantal declension, and the analogy of forms of that declension must have been extended so as to create a new adverbial ending -τῑ (cp. ἐγερτῑ́ in Soph.). The -ῑ of ἀναιμωτί, &c., if not a mere error, may be due to contamination between -ει and -ῑ.

αἰεί has been taken to be a Loc. from the stem αἰϝεσ- (of which the Doric αἰές is the Acc.). Mr. H. W. Smyth (*l. c.*) justly objects to this that the Homeric form would be αἰϝεῖ : and this form, we may add, would become αἰεῖ, not αἰεί. Hence he derives it from the stem αἰϝο-, Lat. *aevo-m.*

A different account of the Adverbs in -ει and -ι is given by Mahlow (*Die langen Vocale,* p. 121). Noticing that they are mainly compounds, especially with ἀ *priv.,* he compares the numerous Latin adjectives such as *ex-animi-s, in-ermi-s, im-belli-s,* and shows that change to an I-stem is found in similar words in other European languages. This I- stem in the Acc. Neut. gives the adverbs in -ῑ, in the Loc. those in -ει or -ῑ. On this view the doubt between -ει and -ῑ is the same that we meet with in the Dat. of Nouns in -ι-s (§ 98).

-ως *manner ;* a Suffix of which there are comparatively few examples in Homer : the commonest are from Stems in -ο, viz. τῶς, ὥς, πῶς, οὕτ-ως (also οὕτ-ω), ὁμ-ῶς, φίλ-ως, αἰνῶς, καρπαλίμως, ἀσπασίως, ῥηϊδίως, ἐκπάγλως, κρατερῶς, μεγάλως (rare) ; from other Stems, ἀφραδέ-ως, περιφραδέ-ως.

-ω, chiefly from Prepositions ; εἴσ-ω, ἔξ-ω, πρόσσ-ω, ὀπίσσ-ω, ἄν-ω, κάτ-ω, προτέρ-ω (*further on*), ἑκαστέρ-ω, ἑκαστάτ-ω (*farther, farthest*), ἀσσοτέρ-ω *nearer.*

Two others are Adverbs of *manner,* ὧ-δε, οὕτ-ω (for which οὕτως is only written when a vowel follows in the same sentence).

The ending -ως has long been considered to be the Greek form of the original Ablatival -ōt (Lat. -ōd) of o- stems In Greek, however, a final -d would disappear (as in ἄλλο, Lat. aliu-d, &c.) and consequently the theory applies only to the forms without -s, viz. ὧδε and οὕτω. The difficulty was met by Curtius (Curt. Stud. x. 219) with the suggestion that -τ would pass into -s before a dental or σ : e. g. οὕτως σοί, οὕτως τίθημι for οὕτωτ σοί, οὕτωτ τίθημι. When two forms οὕτω and οὕτως had thus come into existence as 'sentence-doublets' (like οὐ and οὐκ, ἐξ and ἐκ), it would be natural to use οὕτως when it served to prevent hiatus, and the more regular οὕτω in other cases. This explanation was rejected by later scholars (as Brugmann and G. Meyer), and is certainly not quite satisfactory. If Curtius is right we should expect ὧτ δέ to become ὧσδε rather than ὧδε. His view is however defended by Joh. Schmidt (Pluralb. p. 352).

The ending -ω in ἄν-ω, &c. may be either the Ablatival -ōt, or (more probably) an Instrumental ending -ō (Mahlow, Die langen Vocale, p. 86). In Latin, as Mahlow shows, it is probable that the Instrum. is represented by the adverbs in -ŏ, as modo, cito, the Abl. by archaic -ōd, later -ō. If -ως and -ω were alternative Ablative endings—sentence-doublets—it seems possible that the adoption of -ως rather than -ω in the Adverbs of manner was partly determined by the circumstance that -ω was already familiar in the In-strumental use.

The extension of -ως, -ω to the consonantal declension presents no difficulty. It may be observed, perhaps, that the proper Ablat. of that declension was unsuited for adverbial use, because it was the same in form as the Genitive : e. g. ταχέος was already = of a swift, and accordingly a new word ταχέως swiftly was coined on the model of φίλως, &c.*

-ου place ; ποῦ, ὁμοῦ, ἀγχοῦ, τηλοῦ, ὑψοῦ, αὐτοῦ,—all perispomena. They are the same in meaning as the corresponding Adverbs in -όθι.

-δον, -δην, -δα, forming Adverbs of manner, are evidently Accusatives from Stems in -δο-, -δη- (§ 114) ; e.g. σχε-δόν nearly, lit. holding-wise, ἀποστα-δόν aloof, ἐμβα-δόν on foot, ἀμφα-δόν openly, ἰλα-δόν in crowds ; so βοτρυ-δόν, πυργη-δόν, ῥυδόν, συνωχα-δόν, &c. ; βά-δην steppingly, τμή-δην, κρύβ-δην, κλή-δην, ἐπιγράβ-δην, &c. (all from Verbs), also a peculiar group in -ά-δην, as ἐπιστροφά-δην wheeling about, προτροπά-δην headlong, ἐπιτροχά-δην, μεταδρομά-δην, ἀμβολά-δην ; μίγ-δα, κρύβ-δα, ἀποσταδά, ἀμφα-δά, ἀναφαν-δά, αὐτοσχε-δά. It is evident that these are much more numerous than the Noun-Stems in -δο, -δη can ever have been. In such cases we have to explain, not the derivation of the indi-vidual forms, but the origin of the type.

Other Adverbs obtained from Accusatives are : ἄκην in silence,

---

* As adverbs of the -ōt Gen. Abl. form (ταχέος, &c.) must have existed at one time alongside of those in -ωτ from o- stems, the conjecture may be hazarded that this adverbial -ος was one of the influences which determined the choice of -ως rather than -ω for original -ōt. If so, such a form as πάντ-ως is a sort of contamination of the Gen. Abl. παντ-ός and the forms in -ω(s).

ἄντην (ἀντίον, ἐναντίον, &c.) *opposite*, πάλιν *backwards*, δηρόν *long*, σχεδίην *hand to hand*, ἀμφαδίην *openly*, ἀπριάτην *without purchase;* perhaps also ἄγχι *near*, ὕψι *aloft*, ἶφι *mightily*. The form ἶφι is generally taken as the Instrum. of ἴ-ς *force* (§ 104): but this does not explain how it comes to be used as a Stem in the Adj. ἶφι-α (μῆλα), as well as in Compounds, Ἰφι-άνασσα, &c. (Bekker, *H. B.* i. 160).

Many Adverbs are formed with a final -ς, which is liable to be lost before a word beginning with a consonant, as οὕτω(ς) and the Adverbs in -κι(ς) already mentioned; other Homeric instances are, ἄχρι(ς) and μέχρι(ς) *until*, ἰθύς(ς) *straight towards*, μεσσηγύ(ς) *between*, ἀτρέμα(ς) *quietly:* also the Prep. ἀμφί, Adv. ἀμφίς, and Homeric ἀντικρύ, later ἀντικρύς. Similar Adverbs in which -ς is not lost are, ἅλι-ς, μόγι-ς, χωρί-ς; ἀγκάς, ἑκά-ς, πέλα-ς, ἐντυπάς (Il. 24. 163); ἐγγύ-ς; χθέ-ς; and those in -δι-ς, as ἄλλυδις, ἀμοιβηδίς. Note also the group formed by -ς subjoined to a monosyllabic Verbal Stem; πύξ *with the fist*, ἐπί-μιξ *in confusion*, ἅ-παξ *once*, μάψ *idly*, ὀ-δάξ *with the teeth* (δάκ-νω). The nature of this -ς is obscure. Brugmann (*K. Z.* xxiv. 74) connects it with the -ς of the Prepositions ἐξ, ἄψ, ἀμφί-ς, holding that it is Ablatival. Joh. Schmidt (*Pluralb.* 357) supposes a group of Neuter stems, like the nouns in -ας, -ες, &c.

Accentuation of Case-forms.

111.] For the purpose of accentuation Nouns may be divided into those in which the accent remains on the Stem (and as far as possible on the same syllable of the Stem), and those in which it passes in the Gen. and Dat. to the Case-Ending.

Nouns of the Vowel-Declensions generally belong to the first of these groups. The last syllable if accented has the acute in the Nom. and Acc., the circumflex in the Gen. and Dat., and in the Adverbs in -ου and -ως: *e.g.* καλός, καλοῦ, καλῷ &c., Adv. καλῶς; but Acc. Plur. καλούς. On the Nouns in -ᾰ, see § 96.

One or two Feminines with Nom. Sing. in -ᾰ accent the Ending in those Cases in which the last syllable is long, as μία, Gen. μιῆς; ἴα, Dat. ἰῇ; ταρφύς *thick*, Fem. ταρφεῖα, but Plur. ταρφειαί, Acc. ταρφειάς; ἄγυια *street*, Gen. ἀγυιῆς, Plur. ἀγυιαί, ἀγυιάς. So θαμειαί and θαμειάς answer to a Nom. Sing. θαμεῖα, Masc. *θαμύς (cp. θαμέ-ες, θαμέας); and καυστειρῆς (Il. 4. 342, &c.) is Gen. of καύστειρα.

αὔτως *in the very way* (from αὐτός), is made barytone by the authorities. The word is only Homeric, and the original accentuation αὐτῶς had evidently been lost, perhaps by a confusion with οὕτως.

The oxytone Adverbs in -ει and -ι, as αὐτονυχεί, ἀσπουδί, μελεϊστί, may date from a time when the Loc. of the ο- declension was regularly oxytone—the accent determining the appearance of ε for ο.

H

The second group consists of—

(1) Nouns with monosyllabic Stem, as πούς, ποδ-ός, ποδ-ί, ποδ-οῖν, ποδ-ῶν, ποσσί; κύων, κυν-ός, κυν-ί, κυν-ῶν, κυσί; θήρ, θηρ-ός, θηρ-ί, θηρ-ῶν, θηρ-σί.

(2) The words πατήρ, μήτηρ, θυγάτηρ, ἀνήρ, γαστήρ; Gen. πατρ-ός, μητρ-ός, θυγατρ-ός, ἀνδρ-ός, γαστρ-ός &c.

The accent of μήτηρ and θυγάτηρ is anomalous: cp. the Accusatives μητέρ-α, θυγατέρ-α. Probably the Nom. Sing. was originally oxytone. The change of accentuation may be explained by supposing that the Nom. was influenced by the accent of the Vocative—that in fact the Voc. *pro tanto* took the place of the Nom. (cp. § 96). It is evident that the Voc. of these words would be especially familiar to the ear.

The Dat. ending -εσσι never takes the accent; hence πόδ-εσσι, νή-εσσι, ἄνδρ-εσσι, κύν-εσσι, &c. The reason doubtless is that these are forms that have followed the analogy of the Stems in -εσ, as ἔπεσ-σι, βέλεσ-σι, &c.

The Genitives παίδ-ων, δᾳδ-ῶν, Τρώ-ων, δμώ-ων, θώ-ων, are barytone; perhaps because the Stems are originally disyllabic.

It appears that in an earlier stage of the language the shifting of the accent to the Case-Ending was always accompanied by 'weakening' of the Stem (§ 106). The few instances of the type of κύων, Gen. κυν-ός, and πατήρ, Gen. πατρ-ός, are to be regarded as surviving examples of the older declension.

112.] The **Vocative** in the Consonantal Declension sometimes retracts the accent, as πατήρ, Voc. πάτερ; δαήρ, Voc. δᾶερ; διογενής, Voc. διόγενες.

Proper Names with a long vowel in the penultimate are often properispomena, as Σαρπηδών, Voc. Σαρπῆδον; 'Αντήνωρ, Voc. 'Αντῆνορ; Μαχάων, Voc. Μαχᾶον. Otherwise they are mostly proparoxytone, as 'Αγάμεμνον, "Απολλον.

Oxytones in -εύς form the Voc. in -εῦ, as Ζεῦ, 'Οδυσεῦ. This may be regarded as a retraction of the accent, since the circumflex stands for a double accent, viz. an acute followed by a grave in the same syllable (Ζεῦ = Ζέὺ).

Originally the Vocative, unless it stood at the beginning of a sentence, was enclitic. Hence the barytone accent is to be explained as in the case of the Verb (§ 87), viz. as the result of an original *loss* of accent.

CHAPTER VI.

FORMATION OF NOUNS.

113.] Nominal Stems. Some Nouns are formed with Stems identical with Verb-Stems; πτύχ-ες *folds* (πτύσσω for πτυχ-ι̯ω), στίχ-ες *ranks* (στείχω, ἔ-στιχ-ον), φλόξ *flame* (φλέγω), πτῶκ-α *cowering* (πτήσσω, ἔ-πτακ-ον), δῶ *house*, for δωμ, cp. δᾰ- (*dṃ*) in δᾰ-πεδον (lit. *house-floor*), ῥῶπ-ας *twigs* (ῥέπ-ω), ῥῶγ-ας *clefts*, *openings* (ῥήγ-νυμι), θώς *jackal* (θέω), ὄπ-α *voice* (ϝεπ-), φρίξ, θρίξ, Στύξ. In these Nouns the Stem is usually either in the weak form or in the O-form (§ 38).

Originally the Stem was long (and accented) in the Nom. and Acc., weak (with the accent on the Case-Ending) in the Gen. and Dat. Instances of this variation have been given in § 106; cp. § 114*.

Commonly however a Nominal Stem is formed from a Verb-Stem by means of one or more Suffixes, which we may call *Nominal Suffixes*. These are of two kinds :—

1. *Primary,* by which Nouns are formed from Verb-Stems; as -ο in ἀγ-ό-s *leader*, -τι in φά-τι-s *saying*. Nouns so formed are called *Primitive* (sometimes *Verbal:* but this term is better known in a more restricted sense, § 84).

2. *Secondary,* by which Nouns are formed from other Nouns; as -ιο in δίκα-ιο-s *just*, -ευ in ἱππ-εύ-s *horseman*. These Nouns are called *Denominative*.

The Suffixes' which mark the Feminine Gender might be classified as Secondary; thus the Stem καλη- might be said to be formed by a fresh suffix from καλο-, the Stem δμητειρᾱ- (for δμη-τερ-ι̯ᾰ) from δμη-τερ-, &c. But it is more convenient to treat the Feminine Endings as mere *inflexions,* along with the corresponding Masc. forms.

In the same way we might treat Suffixes like -τρο (in ἰη-τρό-s *healer*, ἄρο-τρο-ν *plough*) as compounded of -τηρ or -τερ (ἰη-τήρ *healer*, ἀρο-τήρ *ploughman*), and a secondary -ο. Practically, however, -τρο is a single Primary Suffix: and this applies also to -μνο (in βέλε-μνο-ν *dart*), which might be resolved into μο + εν + ο, and to many similar cases.

Primitive Nouns.

114.] Primary Suffixes. The form of the Verb-Stem in Primitive Nouns is liable to the same variations as in the Tenses (§ 38). It will be seen that these variations are connected with the accent; but this part of the subject will be best treated separately (§ 115).

The chief Primary Suffixes are as follows :—

-ο, Fem. -ᾱ, -η ; the Verb-Stem taking three forms—

(1) The weak form ; as ἀγ-ό-s *leader,* ζυγ-ό-ν *yoke,* φυγ-ή *flight:* with reduplication, ἰαχή (Ϝι-Ϝαχ-ή) *cry,* ἴ-στο-s (στα-) *web.*

(2) The O-form ; as τόκ-ο-s (τεκ-) *offspring,* ἀρωγ-ό-s (ἀρήγ-ω) *helper,* σπονδ-ή (σπένδ-ω) *libation,* ποτ-ή *flight,* ῥοή *flow.*

(3) Attic reduplication ; as ἀγ-ωγ-ή *leading,* ἀκωκή *point,* ἐδωδή *eating,* ὀπωπή *sight,* ὀδωδή *smell.* The radical vowel appears as ω.

-ι : as τρόφ-ι (τρέφ-ω) *thick,* τρόπ-ι-s *keel of a ship,* φρόν-ι-s *understanding* (with the Verb-Stem in the O-form).

-ιᾰ : seldom with Stems of clearly Verbal meaning, as in φύζα (φυγ-ια) *flight,* σχίζα (σχιδ-ια) *chip ;* more often with roots used as Nouns, as δῖα (διϜ-ια), πέζα (πεδ-), μυῖα (μυσ-), πίσσα (πῐκ-) ; and as a Fem. suffix in Adjectives (*infra*).

The Greek -ια takes the place of -ῑ, the original declension of which is lost in Greek: see Brugmann, *Grundr.* ii. § 109, p. 313 ; Joh. Schmidt, *Plurab.* p. 42.

-υ : with two forms of declension—

(1) Gen. **-ε-οs**, with the weak Stem ; chiefly in Masc. and Neut. Adjectives, as ταχ-ύ-s *swift,* ταρφ-ύ-s (τρέφ-ω) *thick ;* βαθ-ύ-s, λιγ-ύ-s, γλυκ-ύ-s, βαρύs, βραδύs, κρατύs, παχύs, εὐρύs (for ἐ-Ϝρυ-, root Ϝερ-). But ἡδύ-s has the strong Stem : and ὠκύ-s the O-form.

Fem. **-ειᾰ** (for -εϜ-ια), **-εᾰ**, as ἡδεῖα, ὠκέα.

(2) Gen. **-υ-οs** ; in Substantives (chiefly Fem.), as πληθ-ύ-s *multitude,* ἰθ-ύ-s *path, aim,* ἰλύs *mud,* νέκ-υ-s (Masc.) *corpse,* γενύ-s *chin,* γῆρυ-s *voice, cry.*

As to the declension of Nouns in -ις, Gen. -ιοs, and -υς, Gen. -υοs, see § 94.

-εσ, with the strong form of the Stem, as τεῖχ-οs *wall,* τεύχ-ε-α *arms,* ἔπ-οs *word,* πένθ-οs *suffering,* βένθ-οs *depth* (cp. βαθ-ύ-s), θέρ-οs *warmth, summer,* ἧδ-οs *pleasure.*

Fem. **-ειᾰ** (for -εσ-ια), as ἠριγένεια.

The O-form of the Stem is found in ὄχ-οs *chariot* (cp. the Pf. ὄκωχα, § 26, 5); the weak form in θάλ-οs *blossom* (but cp. νεο-θηλ-ήs), κάρτοs (also κράτοs), θάρσοs (cp. Θερσ-ίτηs, Ἁλι-θέρσ-ηs), ἄχ-οs *grief.* The forms πάθ-οs, βάθ-οs are not Homeric.

Note however that in Homer the Substantive is θάρσος (for which θράσος occurs only once, Il. 14. 416), the Adj. always θρασύς; so that a distinction of quantity is kept up in place of the original distinction between * θέρσος and θρασύς. On θέρσος as the original Greek form see Osthoff, *M. U.* ii. 49.

ῑ and ῡ appear in these Stems as in the Present tense (§ 29): e.g. ῥῑγ-os *cold*, ψῡχ-os *warmth*, κῦδ-os *glory*.

-ωσ, -οσ; in ἠώς (Sanscr. *ush-ás*) *dawn*, αἰδώς *shame*, and in the older declension of γέλως, ἵδρως, αἰών, ἰχώρ (§ 107 *ad fin.*). The Stem is probably in the weak form; see § 30.

-α.σ; as δέμ-ας '*build.*' The Stem is in the strong form; indeed the Stem-vowel is always ε, except in γῆρας *old age*, κῶας *fleece*, and οὖδας *floor*; cp. γέρας, δέπας, κέρας, κνέφας, κρέας, κτέρας, πέρας, σέβας, σέλας, σκέπας, σφέλας, τέρας: also *ἔρας (ἐραννός for ἐρασ-νός) and *γέλας (ἐ-γέλασ-σα).

-εν, -ᾰν, -ον, -ων: e.g. τέρ-ην, Gen. -εν-os (τείρω) *soft*, ἄρσ-ην *male*, αὐχ-ήν *neck*; πέπ-ον (Voc.) *tender one*, ἀρηγ-όν-ες *defenders*, τέκτων, περι-κτίονες; ἀγκ-ών, Gen. -ῶν-os *elbow*, ἀγών, αἴθων.

Fem. -αινα (-αν-ι̯α), in λέαινα: imitated by way of sarcasm in θέ-αινα (Il. 8. 5).

-ντ, -οντ, in Participles, and in a few Substantives, as δράκ-ων *a serpent*, lit. the '*staring*' animal (δέρκ-ομαι), τέν-ων, γέρων.

-ᾰτ, in oblique Cases of Neuter Nouns as (ὕδωρ), ὕδατ-os, &c. The ᾰ of this Suffix represents the weak form of a nasal syllable; see § 38, and § 114*, 8, c.

-αντ, notably in Compounds, as ἀκάμας, ἀδάμας, πολύτλας.

-ᾰν, in τάλας, μέλας: perhaps originally Stems in -αντ, which have followed the analogy of -εν, -ον (Meyer, *G. G.* p. 304).

-ερ, -ωρ, -ᾰρ; as ἀήρ (ἀϝ-ήρ) *air*, αἰθ-ήρ (αἴθ-ω) *bright sky*, δα-ήρ *husband's brother* (*levir*); ἔλ-ωρ *booty*, ὕδ-ωρ *water*; μάκ-αρ *great* (Il. 11. 68), ἔαρ *spring*.

-ορ in the Homeric ἄορ *sword*, ἦτορ *breast* is perhaps only the Æolic form of -αρ (-ῃ̣). As to the Nom. and Acc. Neut. forms in -ωρ see § 114*, 8, d.

-ιο, -ι̯ο is very rare in Greek as a Primary Suffix: Brugmann gives ἐρείπ-ια *ruins* and (post-Hom.) ἄγ-ιος, στύγ-ιος, σφάγ-ιον, πάγ-ιος. We may add ταμ-ίη *dispenser*, πεν-ίη *poverty*: also δῖος (διϝ-ι̯ο-s) *bright*, πεζός (πεδ-) *on foot*, κραδ-ίη (κῆρ for κηρ-δ) *heart*, in which the Stem is a Root-Noun.

The word ἀ-οσση-τήρ *helper* pre-supposes a Stem ὀσσο- for σοκ-ι̯ο-, answering to Latin *soc-iu-s* (*seq-*, Gr. ἐπ-).

In ἄλλος (*al-ius*), μέσσος (*medius*), δεξιός the Suffix appears to give the force of a Comparative: see Brugmann, *Grundr.* ii. § 63, p. 125.

-ιοσ, -ιοσ, -ισ: the Comparative Suffix, as πλέω (πλε-ιοσ-α) πλεῖστος (πλε-ισ-τος): see § 114*, 7.

-Fο: κεινός (κεν-Fός) *empty*, οὖλος (ὀλ-Fος) *whole*, λαι-ός *laerus*, ὀρθός *ard-uus*.

-Fεν, -Fον, -Fων, -Fν: πίων *fat*, αἰών *age, life* (Loc. αἰέν, see § 99), ἀ-πείρων (ἀ-περ-Fων, cp. πειραίνω for περ-Fυ-ιω): -Fεν appears in the Inf. in -εν-αι, as εἰδέναι for Fιδ-Fέν-αι (§ 84).

-Fωσ, -Fοτ, Fem. -υιᾰ; in the Pf. Part., and in the Nouns ὄργ-υια *fathom*, ἅρπ-υια *storm-wind*, ἄγ-υια *street*.

-Fᾰρ; as πῖαρ (for πῖ-Fαρ) *fatness*, ὄνειαρ (ὀνη-Fαρ?) *help*, εἶδαρ (ἐδ-Fαρ) *food*, εἶλαρ *shelter*, &c.; -Fερ in πίειρα, Fem. of πίων *fat*. The ancient grammarians noticed that the Stem before -ᾰρ is long (Herodian ii. 769 ed. Lentz).

-μο; with the O-form, as πότ-μο-s (πετ-) *fall*, κορ-μό-s (κείρω) *a trunk*, ὄλ-μο-s (Fελ-) *a rolling stone*, ῥωχ-μός (ῥηγ-) *gully*.

-μι; in φῆ-μι-s *report*, δύνα-μι-s *power*.

-μῖν in ῥηγ-μῖν *beach on which the waves break*, Dat. ὑσμῖν-ι *fight*: also Nom. ὑσμίνη.

-μεν, -μον, -μων; πυθ-μήν (Gen. -μέν-ος) *base*, ἀϋτ-μήν *breath*, λιμήν *haven*, ποιμήν *shepherd*, δεί-μων (-μον-ος) *fearing*, μνή-μων *mindful*, ἤ-μων *shooter*, τέρ-μων *end*, θη-μῶν-α (Acc.) *a heap*. Also the Infinitives in -μεν-αι (Dat.) and -μεν (Loc.): see § 84.

-μᾰτ; as δεῖ-μα, Gen. -ματ-ος, *fear*, ὄνομα *name*, &c. Of these Suffixes -μον and -μᾰτ go with the strong form of the Stem, -μεν with the weak form.

With -ο, -η are formed -μενο (in Participles), and -μνο, -μνη, as βέλε-μνο-ν *a dart*, λί-μνη *a marsh*; -μνᾰ (-μν-ιᾰ), in μέρι-μνα *care*.

-μαρ, -μωρ; as τέκ-μαρ and τέκ-μωρ *a device*; -μερο, in ἵ-μερο-s *desire*.

-νο, -ᾰνο; as δει-νό-s *fearful*, πτη-νός *flying*, τέχ-νη *art*, ποι-νή *atonement*; ὄχ-ανο-ν *handle*, δρεπάνη *sickle*, τρύπ-ανον *auger*, στέφ-ανος.

-νεσ; τέμε-νος *enclosure*, ἴχ-νος *imprint*, γλῆ-νος *jewel*.

-νυ; θρῆ-νυ-s *a foot-stool*.

-ρο, -λο; generally with the weak Stem; πικ-ρό-s *bitter*, ἄκ-ρο-s *point*, ἕδ-ρη *seat*: also with an auxiliary ᾰ, σθεν-αρό-s *strong*, ἁπαλός *tender*, στιβαρός, λιπαρός.

-ρι; in ἴδ-ρι-s *knowing*, ἄκ-ρι-s *mountain-top*.

-ρυ, -λυ: δάκ-ρυ *tear*, θῆ-λυ-s *female* (θῆ-σθαι).

-τ: θής θη-τ-ός, νύξ νυκ-τ-ός; but chiefly in Compounds, as προ-βλής, ἀ-γνώς.

-ετ, -ητ : Acc. ἀργ-έτ-α *white* (Il. 21. 127), also ἀργῆτα (Il. 8. 133), Dat. ἀργέτι and ἀργῆτι (Il. 11. 818), κέλ-ης, λέβ-ης.

-ΤΟ ; found with Stems—

(1) In the O-form, as κοῖ-το-s, κοί-τη (κεῖ-μαι) *lair*, φόρ-το-ν *burden*, νόσ-το-s *going, return* (νέομαι for νεσ-ο-μαι), οἶ-τος (εἶ-μι) *course, fortune*, βροντή (βρέμ-ω) *thunder.*

(2) In the weak form, as στα-τό-s *stalled*, δρα-τό-s *flayed ;* ἀκ-τή *beach ;* δέκ-τη-s *beggar*, παραι-βά-τη-s.

For the use of -το to form Superlatives and Ordinal Numerals see §§ 121 and 130.

-ΤΙ, -σι ; generally with the weak Stem, as φά-τι-s *saying*, πίσ-τι-s (for πιθ-τις) *trust*, τί-σι-s *vengeance*, δόσις, βόσις, βρῶσις, γένεσις, νέμεσις, ἄνυσις, ἄροσις.

-σιη, as κλισίη *a tent*, ὑπο-σχε-σίη *promise.*

-τινη in δω-τίνη (from δῶ-τις) *gift.*

-ΤΥ ; βρω-τύ-s *food*, κλῑ-τύ-s *a slope*, μνησ-τύ-s *wooing*, δαι-τύ-s *feasting*, ἐδη-τύ-s *eating.* This Suffix is especially common in Homer : ἀγορητύς, ἀλαωτύς, βοητύς, γραπτύς, ἐλεητύς, κιθαριστύς, ἀκοντιστύς, δαριστύς, ὀρχηστύς, ὀτρυντύς, ῥυστακτύς, ταινυστύς.

-ΤΕΡ, in πατήρ, μήτηρ, θυγάτηρ, εἰνά-τερ-ες, γαστήρ, ἀστήρ.

-τηρ, -τορ, -τωρ ; as δο-τῆρ-α and δώ-τορ-α (Acc.) *giver*, βοτῆρ-ες and βώτορες *herdsmen*, ἴστωρ *witness*, ἀφ-ήτωρ *shooter*, ἐπ-ακτήρ 'driver,' *huntsman*, δι-οπτήρ *spy*, ληϊστήρ *spoiler*, κοσμήτωρ *arrayer*, μήσ-τωρ-α (μήδ-ομαι) *adviser :* also of *things*, with a touch of personification, κρητήρ, ζωστήρ, λαμπτήρ. Fem. -τειρα (-τερ-ι̯ᾰ), as δμή-τειρα *subduer.*

-τρ-ο, as ἰη-τρός *healer*, ἄρο-τρο-ν *plough*, σκῆπ-τρον, λέκτρον.

-δ, -ῐδ, -ᾰδ ; as Acc. ἐλπ-ίδ-α *hope ;* λευκ-άδ-α *white.*

-δο, -δη : κέλα-δο-s *noise* (κέλ-ομαι), κομί-δη *tending*, κλά-δος *branch*, ὅμαδος, χρόμαδος, ῥάβδος.

This Suffix is chiefly seen in the Adverbs in -δον, -δην, as σχε-δό-ν *near*, βά-δη-ν *at a walk*, &c. : see § 110, and cp. the secondary forms στά-δ-ιος, &c. (§ 118).

The Suffixes -θ-ρο, -θ-λο, -θ-μο are produced by combining the Verbal suffix or Root-determinant -θ (§ 45) with -ρο, -λο, -μο : thus ὄλε-θ-ρος, γενέ-θ-λη, στα-θ-μός presuppose the Verbs *ὀλέ-θω, *γενέ-θω, *στά-θω (cp. ἐΰ-σταθ-ής, also στῆ-θος) formed like πλή-θω, φλεγέ-θω, μινύ-θω, &c. Practically, however, they are single Primary Suffixes : -θμο is especially common in Homer, cp. ἀρ-θμός, ἀρι-θμός, κηλη-θμός, ἑλκη-θμός, ὀρχη-θμός, κνυζη-θμός : λύ-θρον, ῥέε-θρα, μέλπη-θρα, μέλα-θρον, βέρε-θρον. Cp. also -θμα in ἴ-θμα-τα *going.*

Similarly from Verb-Stems with the suffix -τ we have λαῖ-τ-μα
gulf (cp. λαι-μός *throat*), ἀϋ-τ-μή *breath*, also ἀϋ-τ-μήν (root αυ-),
ἐρε-τ-μός *oar*, ἐφ-ε-τ-μή *injunction*.

114*. *Variation of Suffixes.*

1. Primary Suffixes were originally liable to variation of
the kind already noticed (§ 106). From the Sanscrit declension,
in which the variation is preserved with singular fidelity, it
appears that a Suffix in general has three different forms or
degrees of quantity, called by Sanscrit grammarians the *strong*,
the *middle*, and the *weakest* form. Just as in the declension of
dyaus, Gr. Ζεύς, we find (1) *dyāu-* in the Nom., (2) *dyău-* in the
Loc. *dyăv-i* (Lat. *Jŏvi* for *diĕv-i*), and (3) *dĭv-* or *diu-* in other
Cases, so in *dā-tā́* 'giver' we have (1) -tā́r- in the Acc. *dā-tár-am*,
(2) -*tar*- in the Loc. *dā-tár-i*, and (3) -*tr*- in the Dat. *dā-tr-é*,
Instrum. *dā-tr-ā́*.

Similarly we have the series -*ār*, -*ăr*, -*r* ; -*mān*, -*măn*, -*mn* ;
-*vān*, -*văn*, -*vn* ; -*ān*, -*ăn*, -*n*, &c.: the rule being that the first
or strong form contains a long vowel, which in the second is
short, and in the third disappears altogether.

In the combinations -*va*, -*ia* the *a* is lost and the semivowel
becomes a vowel, thus giving -*u*, -*i*.

2. In Greek we find the same Suffixes as in Sanscrit, with the
further distinction that the vowel may be η or ω, ε or ο. Thus
we may have -τωρ, -τορ, -τηρ, -τερ, -τρ ; -μων, -μον, -μην, -μεν, -μν
(-μᾰ, -μᾰν) ; -ωσ, -οσ, -εσ ; -ϝωσ, -ϝοσ, -ϝεσ, -υσ ; -ιωσ, -ιοσ, -ιεσ,
-ισ ; and so in other cases. Sometimes both sets of forms
occur with the same root; as δώ-τωρ, δώτορ-ος and δο-τήρ,
δοτῆρ-ος.

The interchange of ο and ε in the Suffix -ο (as φίλο-ς, Voc.
φίλε) belongs to this head.

The three forms of a Suffix are hardly ever to be seen in the
Greek declension; one of them being usually taken as the
Stem of all the oblique Cases. Thus the strong form is
generalised in μήσ-τωρ, -τωρ-ος, the second in δώ-τωρ, -τορ-ος,
to the exclusion of the original *μηστρ-ός, *δωτρ-ός, &c. The
'weakest' form, however, often appears in derivatives ; *e. g.*
ποιμήν, ποιμέν-ος, ποίμν-η : δείμων, δείμον-ος, δειμαίνω (for -μᾰν-ιω,
-μν-ιω) : θεράπων, Fem. θεράπν-η, also θεράπαινα (for -πν-ια) :
ἰη-τήρ, ἰατρ-ός : ὕδωρ, ὕδρ-ος : τέκ-μωρ, τεκμαίρομαι (for τεκμᾰρ-
ιο-μαι), &c. Cp. Lat. *car-ō(n)*, Gen. *car-n-is*.

3. The relation of the forms -ων (-μων, -ϝων), -ωρ (-τωρ), &c.
to -ην, -μην, -ϝην, -ηρ, -τηρ, &c. has been the subject of much
controversy. It is generally agreed that the difference is not
original, but arises in each case by differentiation from a single

form. Probably it is due to shifting of accent, the Suffixes with η being generally accented, while those with ω are found in barytone words. Thus we have the pairs δοτήρ and δώτωρ, ῥητήρ and ῥήτωρ, βοτῆρες and βώτορες, πατήρ but φράτωρ, also Lat. *sor-ōr* (Sanscr. *svásā*). In composition, too, the loss of accent is regularly accompanied by the change from η, ε to ω, ο : πατήρ, μητρο-πάτωρ; δμητήρ, παν-δαμάτωρ; ἀνήρ, εὐ-ήνωρ; φρήν, ἄφρων, &c. Many exceptions, however, remain unexplained.

4. The Nouns of Relationship (the group πατήρ &c.) with one or two similarly inflected words (ἀστήρ, γαστήρ) are distinguished from the Nouns of the Agent in -τηρ (-τωρ) by the use of the shorter form -τερ in the Accusative: πατέρ-α, Sanscr. *pitár-am*, but δοτῆρ-α, Sanscr. *dātár-am*. Similarly among Stems in -*n* ἄρσην, ἄρσεν-α answer to Sanscr. *vŕsh-a*, *vŕshan-am* (instead of -*ān-am*). This peculiarity has been explained as the result of an original difference of quantity. That is to say, the form *pitar* (Gr. πατερ-) has been taken to be the *strong* Stem, because it is the Stem of the Acc. If so, the η of the Nom. has to be explained as due to the analogy of the -ηρ of δοτήρ, &c. But this view cannot well be reconciled with the fact that the Stem *pitar-* occurs not only in the Acc. *pitáram* but also in the Loc. *pitár-i*. The Loc. is a Case which regularly takes the *middle* Stem; cp. *dātár-am*, Loc. *dātár-i*, *áçmān-am*, Loc. *áçman-i*. Hence we must recognise a group of Stems in -*r* and -*n forming the Acc. with the middle form*. Thus the original declension would be (*e. g.*), Strong form, Nom. πα-τήρ,—Middle form, Acc. πα-τέρ-α, Loc. πα-τέρ-ι, Voc. πά-τερ,—Weakest form, Gen. πα-τρ-ός. The cause of this difference in the treatment of the Accusative has still to be found *.

5. The Stems in -*ant*, -*mant*, -*vant*, (Gr. -οντ, &c.) interchange with shorter forms in -*at*, -*mat*, -*vat*, Gr. -ᾰτ, -μᾰτ, -Fᾰτ. In Greek the Suffix -οντ is used to form the Part. Pres., as φέροντ-α. The chief trace of -ᾰτ is the Doric ἔασσα (ἐσ-ᾰτ-ι̯α) for ἐοῦσα. The forms -μᾰτ, -Fᾰτ are found in the Neuters, such as δεί-ματ-ος, πείρατος, (περ-Fᾰτ-ος), &c. So in Latin *nōmen, nōminis*, for *nō-mn-is* (Sanscr. *nā-mn-as*). On the other hand some Stems in -*v* take -*vt* in the oblique Cases : λέων, λέοντ-ος, but Fem. λέαινα (for λε-Fν-ι̯α, cp. Lat. *leō, leōn-is*): θεράπων, -οντος, but θεράπ-ν-η : πρόφρων, Fem. πρόφρασσα for προφρα-τι̯ᾰ. Cp. § 107, 2.

6. The Suffix of the Pf. Part. Act. presents anomalies, both in Sanscrit and Greek, which are not yet satisfactorily explained. The Sanscr. -*vāms*, -*vas*, -*us* and Greek -Fως, -Fοτ, -ῠσ (in -υια for

---

* Collitz in *Bezz. Beitr.* x. 37 ff.

-ῠσ-ῐᾰ) seem to represent the original gradation; but the τ of the Masc. and Neut. oblique cases is peculiar to Greek, as the nasal to Sanscrit. If we suppose a primitive declension (*e. g.*) Ϝιδ-Ϝώς, Acc. Ϝιδ-Ϝῶσ-α, Gen. Ϝιδ-ύσος, &c. this might become Acc. Ϝιδ-Ϝόσ-α, Gen. Ϝιδ-Ϝόσ-ος, &c. (by the same levelling which we have in δώ-τωρ, Acc. δώ-τορ-α, Gen. δώ-τορ-ος), then Acc. Ϝιδ-Ϝό-α, Gen. Ϝιδ-Ϝό-ος &c. At this stage the endings -ότ-ος, -ότ-α &c. may have been introduced through analogy— perhaps of the Pres. Part. However this may be, this is one of several instances in Nominal Declension of τ creeping in to form a Stem for the oblique Cases.

7. A Suffix which originally was closely parallel to the -Ϝώς of the Pf. is to be seen in the -ίων or -ῐων of the Comparative; Sanscr. -*yāms*, -*yas*, (-*is*), Greek -ιων, -ιον, -ισ (in -ισ-τος). Here the ν, in spite of the Sanscr. nasal, is as difficult to explain as the τ of the Pf. However the older endings -ο-α, -ο-ες (for -οσ-α, -οσ-ες) are preserved in the Acc. Sing. Masc. and Nom. and Acc. Plur. Neut. (ἀμείνω for ἀμειν-οσ-α), and the Nom. Plur. (ἀμείνους, &c.). In the Latin -*iŏr*, -*iŏr-is*, &c. there is no trace of a nasal. We may compare the variation in αἰών, κυκεών (§ 107 *ad fin*)*.

8. Heteroclite forms occur when different Suffixes are brought into a single declension. In particular—

(*a*) Suffixes ending in -ν interchange with Suffixes in -ρ. Thus we find πίων, Gen. πίον-ος *fat*, but Fem. πίειρα (πῑ-Ϝερ-ῐᾰ) and the Neut. Substantive πῖαρ *fatness*. Also χειμών, but χειμέρ-ιος. (Cp. the Lat. *femur, femin-is*, and *jec-ur, jecin-or-is*, which is for an older *jecin-is*.)

(*b*) Similarly along with ἠώς we have ἠέρ-ιος *at dawn*, and the Adv. ἦρι (Sanscr. *ushás* and *ushár*).

(*c*) Final τ is introduced in the Suffix; as in ἥπα-τ-ος (for ἥπν-τ-ος, cp. the Sanscr. *yakṛt*, Gen. *yakn-as*, and the other

---

* Th᾿ uffixes of the Pf. Part. Act. and the Comparative have lately been the subject of much controversy: see Brugmann, *K. Z.* xxiv. 79 ff., *Grundr.* §§ 135, 136, pp. 403, 417; Joh. Schmidt, *K. Z.* xxvi. 341 ff., 378 ff., *Pluralb.* p. 157; Collitz, *Bezz. Beitr.* x. 25, 63. The chief difficulty lies in the nasal of the Sanscrit strong Cases. Such a gradation as -*vōns* (or -*vēns*), -*ves*, -*us*, or -*iōns*, -*ios* (or -*ies*), -*is*, is unexampled. Joh. Schmidt takes the nasalised forms (Sanscr. -*vāms*-, -*iāms*) as his point of departure, but has been unable to explain -*vas*, -*ias*, -*us*, -*is* to the satisfaction of other scholars. Those who assume a primitive -*vŏs*, -*iŏs* have hitherto been equally unsuccessful in accounting for Sanscr. -*vāms*, -*iāms* and Greek -ῐων. The explanation of the τ of -οτ-ες, &c. is also difficult, but there it is at least certain that it is of secondary origin. It is to be noted that the traces of -ῐσ in the Comparative are confined to *strong* Cases, as Acc. Sing. -οσ-α, Nom. Plur. -οσ-ες. Hence the Gen. -ῐον-ος, Dat. -ῐον-ι, &c. perhaps did not take the place of *middle* forms -ιοσ-ος, -ιοσ-ι, but of the primitive weak forms (-ισ-ος, -ισ-ι ?).

Neuters in -ᾰρ, -ωρ, Gen. -ᾰτ-ος, as πεῖραρ, -ᾰτος (for περ-Ϝᾰρ, -Ϝν-τ-ος): also in Neuters in -μᾰ, Gen. -μᾰτ-ος (for -μν-τ-ος).

(*d*) It is probable that the Neuters in -ωρ—viz. ὕδωρ, ἔλωρ, πέλωρ, ἐέλδωρ, τέκμωρ, νύκτωρ (Acc. used adverbially)—were originally Collective or Abstract nouns (Joh. Schmidt, *Pluralb.* p. 193). On this view ὕδωρ *waters* (Germ. *gewässer*) is properly a different word from the stem *ύδα or *ύδαρ which we infer from the oblique Cases: τέκμωρ is originally a Collective or Abstract from τέκμαρ: and similarly ἔλωρ, ἐέλδωρ, πέλωρ, νύκτωρ (cp. νυκτερ-ίς), which only occur in the Nom. Acc., are nouns formed like χειμών (χεῖμα), αἰδώς (αἰδεσ- in αἰδέομαι, ἀν-αιδής), γέλως (γελασ- in γελάω), &c. When ὕδωρ, &c. were brought into use as Nominatives answering to Neuter oblique Cases, they naturally followed these in respect of gender. Cp. § 110 (*ad fin.*).

115.] Accentuation. The accent is often connected with the form of the Suffix, and sometimes varies with the meaning. But the rules that can be given on this subject are only partial.

1. Stems in -ο are generally oxytone when they denote an agent, barytone when they denote the thing done; e. g. φορό-ς *bearer*, but φόρο-ς *that which is brought*; ἀγό-ς *leader*, ἀρωγό-ς *helper*, σκοπ-ός *watcher*, τροφό-ς *nurse*, τόκο-ς *offspring.* But νομό-ς *pasture*, λοιγό-ς *pestilence* (perhaps thought of as an agent, 'destroyer').

2. Stems in -η are generally oxytone, but there are many exceptions (as δίκ-η, μάχ-η).

3. Most stems in -ιδ, and all in -ᾰδ, are oxytone. But those which admit an Acc. in -ιν are all barytone.

4. Adjectives in -υ-ς are oxytone; except θῆλ-υ-ς and the isolated Fem. θάλεια. Substantives in -υ-ς are mostly oxytone; but see § 116, 4.

5. Neuters with Stems in -εσ (Nom. Acc. -ος) are barytone, but Adjectives in -ης, and Fem. Nouns in -ως, Gen. -οος, are oxytone.

6. Nouns in -ηρ and -ην are oxytone, except μήτηρ, θυγάτηρ (but see § 111, 2), ἄρσην, τέρην.

Nouns in -ωρ and -ων are mostly barytone, but there are many exceptions, esp. the Abstract Nouns in -δων, the Substantives in -μων, as δαιτυμών, ἡγεμών, κηδεμών, and most Nouns in -ων, Gen. -ωνος, as ἀγών, ἀγκών, χειμών, τελαμών.

7. Stems in -το with the O-form are barytone, with the weak form oxytone; e. g. κοῖ-το-ς, νόσ-το-ς, but στα-τό-ς, &c.

8. Stems in -τη are mostly oxytone. Accordingly the Prim-

itive Masculines in -τη-s, which are Nouns of the Agent, can generally be distinguished from the Denominatives in -της (§ 117): *e. g.* ἀγορητής *a speaker,* but ναύτης *a ship-man.*

9. Abstract Nouns in -τι, -σι are barytone; in -τῡ oxytone.

It will be seen that, roughly speaking, when the Verbal Stem is in the weak form, the Suffix is accented, and *vice versâ:* also that words with an active meaning (applicable to a personal *agent*) are oxytone, those with a passive meaning (expressing the *thing done*) are barytone.

116.] Gender. The Gender of Nouns is determined in most cases by the Suffix. The following rules do not apply to Compounds, as to which see § 125.

1. Stems in -o are Masc. or Neut., with some exceptions, as ὁδός, ἀταρπός, κέλευθος, νῆσος, φηγός, ἄμπελος, νάσος, ταφρός, ψῆφος, σποδός, ψάμαθος, ῥάβδος, δοκός, ῥινός, πρό-χοος. In these the change of gender seems to be due to the meaning. κλυτός is used as a Fem. in Il. 2. 742 κλυτὸς Ἱπποδάμεια. In Od. 4. 406 πικρὸν ἀποπνείουσαι . . ὀδμήν it is best to take πικρόν as an adverb, not with ὀδμήν: cp. Il. 6. 182. Πύλος has the two epithets ἠμαθόεις and ἠγαθέη, and is probably therefore of both Genders.

2. Stems in -η (for -ā) are mainly Fem.; but—

Stems in -τη denoting an agent are Masc., as δέκ-τη-s *a beggar,* αἰχμη-τή-s *a warrior.* Also, πόρκη-s *the ring of a spear,* ἔτη-s *comrade,* ταμίη-s *dispenser,* νεηνίη-s *a youth,* perhaps ἀγγελ-ίη-s *a messenger;* also the proper names Βορέα-s, Ἑρμεία-s, Αἰνεία-s, Αὐγεία-s, Τειρεσία-s, Ἀγχίση-s, Ἀΐδη-s.

The Masc. Nouns in -ās, -ηs are probably formed originally from Feminine abstract or collective Nouns in -ā, -η. The first step is the use of the word as a concrete: cp. Od. 22. 209 ὁμηλικίη δέ μοί ἐσσι *thou art one of the same age* (ὁμῆλιξ) *with me;* Il. 12. 213 δῆμον ἐόντα *being one of the common people.* So in Latin *magistratus, potestas* (Juv. 10. 100), *optio:* English *a relation* (= a relative). The next step is the change to the Masc., which leads to the use of the Endings -ηs, Gen. -αο on the analogy of the Masc. -os, Gen. -οιο. We may compare Fr. *un trompette bearer of a trumpet,* Italian *il podestà the magistrate,* where the change of meaning is marked by the gender only. So ἔτη-s is probably from a word σϝέ-τη *kindred,* νεηνίη-s from a Fem. νεηνίη *youth,* ἀγγελίη-s (if the word exists, see Buttmann, *Lexil.* s. v.) from ἀγγελίη. The Masc. ταμίη-s may be formed from the concrete Fem. ταμίη, the office of household manager being generally filled by a woman (γύνη ταμίη Od.). And so the Nouns in -τηs owe their origin to the older abstract or collective Nouns in -τη, as ἀκ-τή, βροντή, ἀρε-τή, γενε-τή, πινυ-τή, &c. See Delbrück, *Synt. Forsch.* iv. pp. 7–13.

3. Stems in -ιἄ, -ῑδ, -ἄδ are Fem. ; also most Stems in -ι. But μάν-τι-ς is Masc., and some Adjectives— ῑδ-ρι-ς, τρόφ-ι-ς, εὖνι-ς—are of all genders.

Masc. Nouns in -ο sometimes form a Fem. in -ι, -ιδ, -ἄδ : as θοῦρο-ς, Fem. θοῦρι-ς (Acc. θοῦρι-ν, Gen. θούριδ-ος); φόρ-το-ς *burden*, φόρ-τι-ς (Gen. φόρτιδ-ος) *a ship of burden* ; τόκ-ος, Fem. τοκάδ-ες ; λευκό-ς, Fem. λευκάδ-α (πέτρην).

Originally (as in Sanscrit) the chief Feminine Suffix was -ῑ. The metre shows that the long ι should be restored in ἦνι-ς (βοῦν ἦνιν εὐρυμέτωπον Il. 10. 292, Od. 3. 382), βλοσυρῶπις (Il. 11. 36), and βοῶπις (Il. 18. 357, where Ven. A has βοῶπι πότνια"Ηρη). The ῑ appears also in ἀψῖδ-ος, κνημῖδ-ας, ἐϋπλοκαμῖδ-ες.

4. Adjectives in -ŭ generally form the Fem. in -εια or -εᾰ (for -εϜ-ιᾰ), as ἡδεῖα, ὠκέα. But θῆλυ-ς as a Fem. is commoner than θήλεια; and we also find ἡδὺς ἀϋτμή (Od. 12. 369), πουλὺν ἐφ᾽ ὑγρήν (Il. 10. 27).

On the other hand most Substantives in -υ-ς are Fem. (and oxytone), and this υ is frequently long, as in ἰθύ-ς *aim* (whereas the Adj. ἰθύ-ς *straight* has ŭ), πληθύ-ς *multitude*, ἰλύ-ς *mud*, ’Ερινύ-ς, and the Abstract Nouns in -τῡ-ς, as βρω-τύ-ς, ὀρχησ-τύ-ς, κλι-τύ-ς. But there are a few Masc. Substantives in -υ-ς, viz. θρῆνυ-ς, στάχυ-ς, βότρυ-ς, νέκυ-ς, ἰχθύ-ς.

5. The Suffix -εσ is almost confined in Homer to Neut. Substantives of abstract meaning : the only clear example of an Adjective is ὑγιής (Il. 8. 524). For ἐλεγχέ-ες (Il. 4. 242., 24. 239) we should probably read ἐλέγχεα. In Il. 4. 235 (οὐ γὰρ ἐπὶ ψευδέσσι πατὴρ Ζεὺς ἔσσετ᾽ ἀρωγός) we may equally well read ψεύδεσσι (*Zeus will not help falsehood*). The Gen. φραδέ-ος (Il. 24. 354) may come from φραδής or φραδύς.

It seems very probable that these words are to be accounted for in much the same way as the Masculines in -της, viz. as abstract turned into concrete Nouns by a simple change of gender. The transition to a concrete meaning may be observed in ψεῦδος in such uses as Il. 9. 115 οὐ γὰρ ψεῦδος ἐμὰς ἀτὰς κατέλεξας *not falsely* (lit. *not falsehood*) *hast thou related my folly.* So ἐλέγχεα *reproaches!*

6. Suffixes which are used to express an *abstract* or a *collective* meaning are generally Feminine ; e. g. κακό-ς *coward*, κάκη *cowardice* ; ὁσίη *piety* ; φύζα, φυγ-ή *flight* ; βουλή *counsel*, also *the body of counsellors, a council* ; φρόν-ι-ς *understanding* ; νιφ-άς (-άδ-ος) *a snow-storm* ; πληθ-ύ-ς *multitude* (collective and abstract) ; and the Nouns in -τις (-σις), -τυς, -ως, -δων.

It is probable that all the Collective Nouns in -ων, -ως, -ωρ (§ 114, 8, *d*) were originally Feminine. The change of gender may be traced in αἰών (Fem. in Homer), and ἱδρώς (Fem. in Æolic). In the case of ἔρως, γέλως it may be connected with the confusion between -ωσ-stems and -ο-stems (§ 107 *ad fin.*). It is to be noted that no nouns in -μων form the Fem. with -ιᾰ.

Denominative Nouns.

117.] **Secondary Suffixes.** The following are the chief
Secondary or 'Denominative' Suffixes. (Note that -ο and -η of
the Primitive Stem disappear before Secondary Suffixes beginning
with a vowel*.)

-ιο, -ιη ; as δίκα-ιο-s *just,* ἀρμον-ίη a *joining,* ἄρθμ-ιο-s *friendly,*
αἰδοῖο-s (for αἰδοσ-ιο-s) *reverenced,* γελοῖιο-s (probably to be
written γελώ-ϊο-s) *laughable,* ὥρ-ιο-s *in season,* σοφ-ίη *skill,*
σκοπ-ιή *watch,* ἀναγκα-ίη *necessity.*

-ειο, -εο (chiefly used to denote *material,* especially the
animal which furnishes the material of a thing) ; e. g. ἵππ-ειο-s,
ταύρ-ειο-s, αἴγ-ειο-s, βό-ειο-s and βό-εο-s, κυν-έη, χάλκ-ειο-s and
χάλκ-εο-s, κυάν-εο-s, δουράτ-εο-s, φλόγ-εο-s, ἠγάθ-εο-s (from
ἀγαθό-s), δαιδάλ-εο-s, &c.   These must be distinguished from the
Adjectives in which ειο stands for εσ-ιο, as τέλειο-s (for τελεσ-
ιο-s), ὀνείδειο-s, Ἀργεῖο-s.

-ευ ; ἱππ-εύ-s *horseman,* ἀριστ-εύ-s *one who does best,* χαλκ-εύ-s,
ἱερ-εύ-s, νομ-εύ-s, Σμινθ-εύ-s, &c.—all from Nouns in -ο.

-ίδη, -ιαδη ; in patronymics, as Ἀτρε-ίδη-s, Πηλη-ϊάδη-s,
Ἀσκληπι-άδη-s.   Cp. the compound -ιδ-ιος (§ 118).

-ρο, -ερο ; as λιγυ-ρό-s *shrill,* δνοφ-ερός *dark ;* μέγα-ρο-ν.

-ιμο ; ἀοίδ-ιμο-s *matter of song,* μόρ-ιμο-s *fated,* &c.

-νο, -ινο ; as φαεινός (φαεσ-) *shining,* ἐρεβεννός (ἐρεβεσ-) *dark,*
ἐραννός *lovely ;* φήγ-ινο-s *oaken,* εἰαρ-ινό-s *of spring,* &c.

-ῖνο ; ὀπωρ-ῖνός *of autumn,* ἀγχιστ-ῖνος.

-ηνο ; πετε-ηνός *flying* (πετ-εσ-).

-σῦνο, -σύνη ; γηθό-συνο-s *joyful ;* ἱππο-σύνη *horsemanship,* &c.

-εντ (for -Fεντ), Fem. -εσσᾰ ; ὑλή-εντ-α, Fem. ὑλή-εσσ-α
wooded, δινή-εντ-α *full of eddies,* λειριό-εντ-α *like the lily,* &c.

-ικο ; only found in ὀρφαν-ικό-s *orphan,* παρθεν-ική *virgin,* and
a few Adjectives from proper names, as Τρω-ϊκό-s, Ἀχαι-ϊκό-s,
Πελασγ-ικό-s.   In these words it is evident that there is no
approach to the later meaning of the Suffix.

---

* This is probably not the result of an 'elision,' but analogous to the weakening of a Suffix (cp. § 114, 1).   Thus the Stem of σοφό-s, Voc. σοφέ, is related
to the form σοφ- (in σοφ-ίη) as πάτερ to πατρ- in πατρ-ύς, πάτρ-ιος (Brugmann,
Grundr. ii. § 59, p. 102).

-τη ; ναύ-τη-s, ἱππό-τα, τοξό-τα (Voc.), ἀγρό-ται, αἰχμη-τή-s, κορυνή-τη-s, ὑπηνή-τη-s, πολιή-τη-s and πολί-τη-s, ὁδί-τη-s. Some of these are perhaps Primitive : e. g. αἰχμη-τή-s may come from an obsolete *αἰχμάω *to wield the spear* : see § 120.

-τητ ; φιλό-τητ-α *love*, δηϊο-τῆτ-α *battle*.

-ιγγ ; φόρμιγξ *a lyre*, σύριγξ *a reed-pipe*, σάλπιγξ *a trumpet*, λάϊγγ-ες *pebbles*, στροφάλιγξ *eddy*, ῥαθάμιγγ-ες *drops*.

The ῐ of -ιδη, -ιμο, -ινο, -ικο was probably not part of the original Suffix, but was the final vowel of the Stem. We may either suppose (*e. g.*) that μόρ-ι-μος was formed directly from a Stem μορ-ι (cp. μοῖρα for μορ-ῐᾰ), or that it followed the analogy of ἄλκι-μος, φύξι-μος, &c. Cp. the account given in § 109 of the ᾰ of -ακις. It is remarkable that o, which is regular as a ' connecting vowel ' of Compounds, is extremely rare before Suffixes (except -τη, -τητ, -συνο). Note that the -εϊ- of the Patronymics Ἀτρε-ΐδης, Πηλε-ΐδης, &c. does not become a diphthong in Homer.

Of the use of Secondary Suffixes to form *Diminutives* there is no trace in Homer. It may be noted here as another difference between Homeric and later Greek that the Verbals in -τέος are entirely post-Homeric.

118.] Compound Suffixes. There are some remarkable instances in Homer of a Secondary amalgamating with a Primary Suffix. E. g.—

-ᾰλ-εο ; ἀζ-αλέο-s *dry*, ἀργ-αλέο-s (for ἀλγ-αλέο-s) *painful*, θαρσ-αλέο-s, καρφ-αλέο-s, κερδ-αλέο-s, λευγ-αλέο-s, μυδ-αλέο-s, ῥωγ-αλέο-s, σμερδ-αλέο-s. It is used as a Secondary Suffix in λεπτ-αλέο-s *thin*, ὀπτ-αλέο-s *roast*.

-ᾰλ-ιμο ; κῦδ-άλιμο-s *glorious*, καρπ-άλιμο-s *swift*, πευκ-άλιμο-s *shrewd*.

-εινο (for -εσ-ινο or -εσ-νο) ; φα-εινό-s *shining*, αἰπ-εινό-s *lofty*, ἀλεγ-εινό-s *painful*; Secondary in ἐρατ-εινό-s, κελαδ-εινό-s, ποθ-εινό-s. This Suffix takes the form -εννο in ἀργ-εννό-s *shining* and ἐρεβ-εννό-s *murky*.

-δ-ιο, -ιδ-ιο, -αδ-ιο : στά-διο-s, ἀμφά-διος, σχε-δίη (σχε-δό-ν), παυ-συ-δίη ; also as a Secondary Suffix in κουρίδιος, μαψ-ιδίως, ῥη-ΐδιος, ἐπινεφρ-ίδιον : κρυπτ-άδιος, διχθ-άδιος, μινυνθ-άδιος.

-δ-ον, in τηκε-δόν-ι (Dat.) *wasting*, ἀηδών *nightingale* : -δωνη in μελε-δῶναι *cares*.

-δ-ᾰνο, in ῥιγε-δανός *horrible*, ἠπεδανός, πευκεδανός, οὐτιδανός.

118*.] Suffixes of different Periods. In the great variety of Suffixes discovered by the analysis of the Greek Noun it is important to distinguish those which are ' living ' in the period of

the language with which we are concerned, and those which only
survive in words handed from an earlier period. Thus in Homer
the oldest and simplest Suffixes, as -o, -ι, -υ, -εσ, -ασ, -εν, -ερ, -Ϝo,
evidently belong to the latter class. They are no longer capable
of being used to form new words, because they are no longer
separable in meaning from the Stems to which they are attached.
On the other hand the Nouns in -μο-ς, -μων, -μα, -τηρ, -τρο-ν, -σι-ς,
-τυ-ς, and the Denominatives in -ιο-ς, -ερο-ς, -ινο-ς, -τη-ς, &c. are
felt as derivatives, and consequently their number can be in-
definitely increased by new coinage. Again the use of a Suffix
may be restricted to some purpose which represents only part of
its original usage. Thus -τη ceased, as we have seen, to form
abstract Nouns, but was largely used to form Masculine Nouns
of the Agent. So too the Suffix -δο, -δη survived in two isolated
uses, (1) in Adverbs in -δο-ν, -δη-ν and (2) in Patronymics.
Compare in Latin the older use of -tus in the adjectives cautus,
certus, &c. with the living use in amā-tus, &c. Sometimes too a
Suffix dies out in its original form, but enters into some combination which remains in vigour. Thus -νο survives in the form
-ινο, and in -εινο (-εσ-νο).

The distinction of Primary and Secondary Suffixes is evidently
one which grew up by degrees, as the several forms came to be
limited to different uses. In this limitation and assignment of
functions it is probable that the original meaning of the Suffix
seldom had any direct influence*. The difference between the
Suffixes of the two great classes is mainly one of *period*. The
elements which go to form them are ultimately much the same,
but the Primary Suffixes represent on the whole earlier *strata* of
formation.

119.] Gender. The rules previously given (§ 116) apply to
Denominative Nouns; the exceptions are few. Note Il. 18.
222 ὅπα χάλκεον (χαλκέην Zenod.), 19. 88 ἄγριον ἄτην (the
passage is probably corrupt, since it appears that the Homeric
form of ἄτη is the uncontracted ἀάτη, ἀϜάτη), 20. 299 (= Od. 5.
410) ἁλὸς πολιοῖο, Od. 3. 82 πρῆξις . . δήμιος, 4. 442 ὀλοώτατος
ὀδμή, 23. 233 ἀσπάσιος γῆ (al. ἀσπασίως).

The origin of the Masc. patronymics in -δη-ς may be explained in the same way as the Nouns of the Agent in -τη-ς
(§ 116, 2). We may suppose them to be derived from a group
of Collective Nouns in -δη : e. g. Ἀτρείδη meaning the *family of
Atreus*, Ἀτρείδη-ς would mean one of the Ἀτρείδη †.

---

* On this point see Brugmann (*Grundr.* ii. § 57, p. 99). It will be seen
that he gives no countenance to the view (which has been put forward in
Germany and elsewhere) that the Suffixes were originally without meaning.

† It may be conjectured that the epithets in -ιων, such as Κρονίων, Ὑπερίων,

120.] Denominative Verbs. Some apparent anomalies in the Denominative Verbs may be explained by the loss of an intermediate step of formation. Thus, there are many Verbs in -ευω not formed from Nouns in -ευ-ς, as βουλεύω (βουλ-ή), ἀγορεύω (ἀγορή), θηρεύω (θήρ); so that, instead of the three stages—

νομό-ς, Denom. Noun νομ-εύ-ς, Denom. Verb νομ-εύ-ω
ἄριστο-ς,   „   „   ἀριστ-εύ-ς   „   „   ἀριστ-εύ-ω

the language goes directly from any Noun to a Verb in -ευω.

Again, the Verbs in -ιαω (§ 60) presuppose Nouns in -ιη, which are seldom found in use: δηριάο-μαι (cp. δῆρι-ς from which an intermediate δηρί-η might be formed), μητιάω (cp. μῆτι-ς), κυδιόων, ἀοιδιάουσα, ἐδριόωντο, μειδιόων, θαλπιόων, φυσιόωντες, φαληριόωντα, ἐψιάασθαι (Od. 21. 429), δειελιήσας.

Similarly, a Primitive Noun may appear to be Denominative because the Verb from which it is formed is wanting. *E. g.* if in the series—

ἀνί-η *vexation,* ἀνι-άω, ἀνι-η-ρό-ς
ὀϊζύ-ς *grief,* ὀϊζύ-ω, ὀϊζυ-ρό-ς

the Verb were passed over, we should appear to have a Denominative Noun in -ρο-ς. Again, if the Primitive Noun in -η and the Verb in -αω were both wanting, we should practically have the Compound Suffix -η-ρο : and this accordingly is the case (*e. g.*) in αἰψ-ηρό-ς (αἶψα) *swift,* θυ-ηλή (θύ-ω), ὑψ-ηλό-ς (ὕψι), φύξ-ηλι-ς.

In this way are formed the peculiar Homeric -ωρη, -ωλη, which are used virtually as Primary Suffixes (forming abstract Nouns); ἐλπ-ωρή *hope,* θαλπ-ωρή *comfort,* ἀλεωρή (ἀλεϝ-) *escape,* τερπ-ωλή *delight,* φειδ-ωλή *sparing,* παυσ-ωλή *ceasing.* Note that the difference between -ωρη and -ωλη is euphonic; -ωρη is found only when there is a preceding λ in the Stem.

The Verb-Stem in Denominative Verbs is not always the same as that of the Noun from which it is formed: in particular—

1. Verbs in -εω, -οω lengthen the final -ο of the Noun-Stem to -η and -ω; as φόβο-ς, ἐ-φόβη-σα; χόλο-ς, ἐ-χόλω-σα.

The ground of this peculiarity must be sought in the fact that the Denominative Verbs were originally confined (like the Tenth Class of Sanscrit) to the Present Tense and its Moods. Consequently the other Tenses, the Fut., the Aor., and the Pf., were formed not directly from the Noun, but from the Stem as it appeared in the Present Tense. Hence such forms as

Οὐρανίωνες, are derived from Collectives in -ων (§ 116, 6). Thus from οὐρανίων (Sing. Fem.) *the heavenly powers* we might have οὐρανίωνες *heavenly ones,* and finally οὐρανίων as a Sing. Masc. Cp. φυγάς originally 'a body of exiles,' then φυγάδες 'exiles,' then φυγάς 'an exile.' So in French, first *la gent* 'people,' then *les gens,* finally *un gens-d'armes.*

I

φοβή-σω, ἐ-φόβη-σα, πε-φόβη-μαι go back to a period when the Pres. was either φόβη-μι or φοβή-ω.

2. Verbs in -ζω form Tenses and derivative Nouns as if from a Verb-Stem in -δ ; as ὕβρι-s, ὑβρί-ζω, ὑβριστής (as if ὑβριδ-τη-s, although there is no δ in the declension of ὕβρι-s).

3. Verbs in -ιω from Nominal Stems in -ρο, -λο, -νο often suppress the final -ο, as καθαρό-s, καθαίρω (for καθαρ-ιω) ; ποι-κίλο-s, ποικίλλω (for ποικιλ-ιω), ποικίλ-ματα. So perhaps ἀπι-νύσσω from ἀπίνυτο-s, and even ἐρέσσω from ἐρέτ-η-s. We may compare the loss of -ο, -η before a Suffix such as -ιο : see § 117 (*foot-note*).

Comparatives and Superlatives.

121.] The Suffixes which express comparison—either between two sets of objects (Comparative) or between one and several others (Superlative)—are partly Primary, partly Secondary. Hence it is convenient to treat them apart from the Suffixes of which an account has been already given.

The Comparative Suffix -ιον is Primary : the Positive (where there is one) being a parallel formation from the same (Verbal) Root. The Homeric Comparatives of this class are :—

γλυκ-ίων (γλυκ-ύ-s), αἴσχ-ιον (αἰσχ-ρό-s), πάσσων (for παχ-ίων, παχ-ύ-s), βράσσων (βραχ-ύ-s), θάσσων (ταχ-ύ-s), κρείσσων (for κρετ-ίων, κρατ-ύ-s), κακ-ίων, ὑπ-ολίζον-es better written ὑπολεί-ζονes, ὀλίγ-ο-s), μείζων (μέγ-α-s), μᾶλλον (μάλ-α), ᾶσσον (ἄγχ-ι), ἐλάσσων (ἐλαχ-ύs), ἥσσων (ἧκα), χείρων and χερε-ίων, ἀρε-ίων (ἀρε-τή), κέρδ-ιον (κέρδ-οs), ῥίγ-ιον (ῥῖγ-οs), κάλλ-ιον (κάλλ-οs), ἄλγ-ιον (ἄλγ-οs), πλε-ίων, μείων, φιλ-ίων, ἀμείνων, βέλτ-ιον, λώ-ϊον, βραδίων (Hes.).

The Stem is properly in the strong form, as in κρείσσων (but κρατ-ύs, κάρτ-ιστοs) ; but it is assimilated to the Positive in πάσσων, βράσσων, γλυκίων. In θάσσων, ἐλάσσων the ā points to forms *θαγχ-ιων, *ἐλαγχ-ιων, in which the nasal of the original *θεγχ-ιων, *ἐλεγχ-ιων was retained, but the ε changed into ᾰ.

The Superlative -ιστο is used in the same way ; we have :—

ἤδ-ιστο-s (ἡδ-ύ-s), ὤκ-ιστο-s (ὠκ-ύ-s), βάρδ-ιστο-s (βραδ-ύ-s), κύδ-ιστο-s (κῦδ-οs), κήδ-ιστο-s (κῆδ-οs), ἔχθ-ιστο-s (ἐχθ-ρό-s), ἐλέγχ-ιστο-s (ἔλεγχ-οs), οἴκτ-ιστο-s (οἶκτ-ο-s), μήκ-ιστα (μῆκ-οs), βάθ-ιστο-s (βαθ-ύ-s), ῥή-ϊστο-s (ῥεῖα, for ῥήϊ-α), φέρ-ιστο-s (φέρ-ω); also, answering to Comparatives given above, αἴσχ-ιστο-s, πάχ-ιστο-s, τάχ-ιστα, κάρτ-ιστο-s, κάκ-ιστο-s, μέγ-ιστο-s, μάλ-ιστα, ἄγχ-ιστα, ἥκ-ιστο-s, ἄρ-ιστο-s, κέρδ-ιστο-s, ῥίγ-ιστα, κάλλ-ιστο-s, ἄλγ-ιστο-s, πλε-ῖστο-s : finally the anomalous πρώτ-ιστο-s.

The Suffix -ιον has taken the place of -ιοσ (§ 107, 7) ; the ' weakest ' form may be traced in -ισ-τοs. The middle form -ιεσ perhaps appears in the two Comparatives πλέες *more* (Il. 11. 395, Acc. πλέας Il. 2. 129) and χέρεια *worse* (Acc. Sing. and Neut. Plur., also Dat. Sing. χέρηϊ, Nom. Plur. χέρηες). Original πλέεες (for πλε-ιεσ-ες) became πλέες by Hyphaeresis (§ 105, 4): and so χέρεια is for χερε-ιεσ-α *. The weakest form of -ιον would be -ιν, which may be found in πρίν (cp. Lat. *pris-cus*), and the Attic πλε-ῖν. Evidently πλεοσ- : πλεισ- : πλε-ῖν = *prios* : *pris-* : πρῖν.

Traces of a Comparative Suffix -ερο appear in ἔν-εροι *those beneath* (Lat. *inf-eru-s, sup-eru-s*).

The Suffix -το or -ἄτο is found in the Ordinals τρί-το-s, &c., and with the Superlative meaning in ὕπ-ατο-s, νέ-ατο-s, πύμ-ατο-s. μέσσ-ατος, ἔσχ-ατο-s, and πρῶτος (for πρό-ατο-s); also combined with Ordinal Suffixes in the Homeric τρί-τ-ατο-s, ἑβδόμ-ατο-s, ὀγδό-ατο-s. The form -ἄτο is probably due to the analogy of the Ordinals τέτρα-το-s, ἕνα-το-s, δέκα-το-s, in which the ἄ is part of the Stem †.

A Suffix -μο may be recognised in πρό-μο-s *foremost man* (Lat. *infi-mu-s, sum-mu-s, pri-mu-s, ulti-mu-s, mini-mus*).

The common Suffixes -τερο, -τᾰτο appear with a Verb-Stem in φέρ-τερο-s, φέρ-τατο-s (cp. φέρ-ιστο-s), βέλ-τερο-s (βόλ-ομαι), φίλ-τερο-s, φίλ-τατο-s (cp. ἐ-φίλα-το *loved*), δεύ-τερο-s, δεύ-τατο-s (δεύ-ω *to fail, to come short of* ‡). So φαάν-τατος, for φαέν-τατος (φαείνω). Otherwise they are used with Nominal Stems : as πρεσβύ-τερο-s, βασιλεύ-τερο-s, μελάν-τερο-s, κύν-τατο-ν, μακάρ-τατο-s, ἀχαρίστερος (ἀ-χαριτ-τερος) : and Pronouns, as ἡμέ-τερος, ὑμέ-τερος, πό-τερος, ἀμφό-τερος, ἑκά-τερος, ἕτερος (for ἅ-τερος, *ἁ- one*, with assimilation to ἑν-). Final o of the Stem becomes ω when a long syllable is needed to give dactylic rhythm ; as κακώ-τερο-s, κακοξεινώ-τερο-s §. In ἀνιηρέσ-τερος (Od. 2. 190) the Stem follows the analogy of θυμ-ῆρες, &c. In χαριέσ-τερος (for χαριϜᾰτ-τερος) there is the same assimilation as in the Dat. Pl. χαρίεσσι (§ 106, 3). In μυχοί-τατο-s *innermost* the Stem appears to be a Locative case-form ; cp. παροί-τεροι *more forward*, and

---

* So G. Mahlow and J. Schmidt, *K. Z.* xxvi. 381. A different analysis is given by Collitz in *Bezz. Beitr.* ix. 66 and Brugmann (*Grundr.* ii. § 135, p. 402), who explain πλέες as *plē-is-es, i. e.* from the weakest form of the Stem. This view does not apply so well to χέρει-α, since it leaves unexplained the divergence between it and the Superl. χείρισ-τος. It may be noticed as an argument for the supposition of Hyphaeresis that we do not find the Gen. πλέος, χέρειος, just as we do not find Hyphaeresis in the Gen. of Nouns in -εος, -ηης (§ 105, 4). Cp. however, the absence of trace of a Gen. ἀμείνο-ος (§ 114, 7, *foot-note*).

† Ascoli in *Curt. Stud.* ix. p. 339 ff.

‡ This very probable etymology is given by Brugmann, *K. Z.* xxv. p. 298.

§ According to Brugmann the ω of σοφώτερος, &c. is not a metrical lengthening, but comes from the adverbs * σοφῶ, &c. (related to σοφῶς as οὕτω to οὕτως, § 110), like the later κατώ-τερος from κάτω, &c.

later forms like κατώ-τερο-s, ἀνώ-τατο-s, &c. ; so probably in παλαίτερος and ὑπέρ-τερος. On the analogy of ὑπέρ-τερος we can
explain ἐνέρ-τερος (cp. ὕπερ-θε : ἔνερ-θε, &c.). The form γεραί-
τερος, again, may be suggested by παλαίτερος, through the
relation γεραιός : παλαιός and the likeness of meaning (Meyer,
G. G. p. 372). The words δεξι-τερός, ἀριστερός are formed like
Comparatives, but are distinguished by their accent.

The Suffix -τερο is combined with the Suffix -ιον in ἀσσο-
τέρω (Adv.) *nearer*, ἐπ-ασσύτεροι *drawing on*, χειρό-τερο-s and
χερειό-τερο-s *worse*.

-τερο, -τᾰτο are combinations of -το (in τρί-το-s, &c.) with the Suffixes -ερο
and -ᾰτο respectively. The tendency to accumulate Suffixes of comparison is
seen in ἐν-έρ-τερος (-τατος), ὑπ-έρ-τερος (-τατος), ἀσσο-τέρω, χειρό-τερος and χερειό-
τερος ; τρί-τ-ατος, ἑβδό-μ-ατος, πρῶτ-ιστος ; Lat. -issimu-s (for -is-ti-mu-s),
mag-is-ter, min-is-ter.

122.] Comparative and Superlative Meaning. The Stem is
often that of a Substantive, as κύν-τερο-s *more like a dog*, βασιλεύ-
τατο-s *most kingly ;* so that the Adjectival character is given by
the Suffix.

The meaning is often, not that an object has more of a
quality than some other object or set of objects, but that it has
the quality *in contradistinction to objects which are without it.*
Thus in πρό-τερο-s the meaning is not *more forward*, but *forward*,
opposed to ὕσ-τερο-s *behind*. So ὑπέρ-τερο-s and ἐνέρ-τερο-s,
δεξι-τερό-s, and ἀρισ-τερό-s, δεύ-τερο-s, &c. The same thing
appears in the Pronouns ἡμέ-τερο-s, ὑμέ-τερο-s, ἕ-τερο-s, πό-τερο-s,
ἑκά-τερο-s, ἀμφό-τερο-s, &c. ; ἡμέ-τερο-s is not *more belonging
to us*, but *belonging to us (not you)*. So in the Homeric Comparatives :—

ἀγρό-τερο-s *of the country* (opp. to the town).
ὀρέσ-τερο-s *of the mountains* (opp. to the valley).
θεώ-τεραι, opp. to καταιβαταὶ ἀνθρώποισιν (Od. 13. 111).
θηλύ-τεραι *female* (opp. to male).
κουρό-τεροι ⎫
ὁπλό-τεροι ⎬ *the class of youths.*

Cp. Il. 19. 63 Τρωσὶ τὸ κέρδιον *that is a gain to the Trojans (rather
than to us).* Hence the Comparative is sometimes used as a softened
way of expressing the notion of the Positive : as Il. 19. 56 ἄρειον
'good rather than ill '; Il. 1. 32 σαώτερος *safe* (as we speak
of being ' on the safe side ') : so θᾶσσον with an Imper. Hence
too the idiomatic use of the double Comparative, Od. 1. 164
ἐλαφρότεροι πόδας εἶναι ἢ ἀφνειότεροι *to be light of foot rather than
wealthy.*

Composition.

123.] It is a general law of Greek and the kindred languages that while a Verb cannot be compounded with any prefix except a Preposition, a Nominal Stem may be compounded with any other Nominal Stem, the first or prefixed Stem serving to limit or qualify the notion expressed by the other.

The Homeric language contains very many Compounds formed by the simple placing together of two Nominal Stems : as πτολί-πορθο-s *sacker of cities,* ῥοδο-δάκτυλο-s *rose-fingered,* τελεσ-φόρο-s *bringing to an end,* βουλη-φόρο-s *bringing counsel,* ὑψ-αγόρη-s *talking loftily,* πρωθ-ήβη-s (for πρωτο-ήβη-s) *in the prime of youth,* &c.

124.] Form of the Prefixed Stem. The instances which call for notice fall under the following heads :—

a. Stems in -ο, -η :—

The great number of Nominal Stems in -ο created a tendency (which was aided by the convenience of pronunciation) to put -ο in place of other Suffixes. Thus we have—

-ο for -η, as ὑλο-τόμο-s *wood-cutter,* &c.*

-ο for -εσ, in εἰρο-κόμο-s *wool-dresser,* μενο-εικής *pleasing to the spirit ;* and for -ᾰσ, as γηρο-κόμο-s *tending old age.*

-μο for -μον, as ἀκμό-θετο-ν *anvil-block ;* and for -μᾰ, as αἱμο-φόρυκτο-s *dabbled with blood,* Κυμο-δόκη, &c.

-ρο for -ρᾰ, in πατρο-κασίγνητος, μητρο-πάτωρ, ἀνδρο-φόνος, and the like. In ἀνδρά-ποδον the short Stem (as in ἀνδρά-σι) is retained, but probably this form is due to the analogy of τετράποδον : slaves and cattle being thought of together as the two main kinds of property in early times (Brugm.).

-ο inserted after a consonant ; παιδ-ο-φόνο-s *child-slayer,* ἁρ-ματ-ο-πηγό-s *chariot-builder,* ὑδατ-ο-τρεφής *water-fed,* ἐλε-ύ-θρεπ-το-s (ἐλεσ-ο-) *grown in a marsh,* ἠερ-ο-φοῖτι-s *flying in air,* δουρο-δόκη (δορϝ-ο-) *spear-holder,* κεραο-ξόο-s (κερασ-) *worker in horn.* Sometimes the -ο is a real Suffix ; *e. g.* in δι-ο-γενής (διϝ-ι̯ο) Zeus-*sprung* (= δῖον γένος ἔχων).

Stems in -η instead of -ο appear in θαλαμη-πόλο-s *attendant of a chamber,* πυρη-φόρο-s *bearing wheat,* ἐλαφη-βόλο-s, ἑκατη-βόλο-s, κραναή-πεδο-s, ὑπερή-φανο-s. We may suppose that there was a collateral Stem in -η (*e. g.* θαλάμη is found, but in a different sense from θάλαμο-s Od. 5. 432), or that the Compound follows the analogy of βουλη-φόρο-s, &c.

Fem. -ᾰ becomes either -ο, as ἀελλό-πος *storm-foot ;* or -η, as γαιή-οχο-s *earth-holder,* μοιρη-γενής *born by fate.*

---

* It is possible however that Feminine Nouns in -η were regarded as formed from Stems in -ο, the long vowel being of the nature of a Case-ending (§ 113). This is especially applicable to Adjectives : e. g. ἀκρό-πολις comes directly from Masc. ἄκρο-s (Brugm.).

The result of these changes is to make o the 'connecting vowel' in the great majority of Compounds. In later Greek this form prevails almost exclusively.

b. Stems in -ῐ :—

The Compounds which contain these stems are mostly of an archaic stamp : ἀργί-ποδ-ες *with swift* (or *white*) *feet*, ἀργι-όδοντ-ες *white-toothed*, ἀργι-κέραυνο-s *with bright lightning*, τερπι-κέραυνο-s *hurling thunderbolts* (τέρπω = τρέπω, Lat. *torqueo*), εἰλί-ποδ-ες *trailing* (?) *the feet* (of oxen), ἁλί-πλοο-s *washed by the sea*, also ἁλι-αής, ἁλι-πόρφυρος, Ἁλί-αρτος, Ἁλί-ζωνοι, Ἁλι-θέρσης (cp. ἁλι-εύς *fisherman*), αἰγί-βοτο-s *fed on by goats*, αἰγί-λιψ *deserted by goats*, χαλί-φρων *of light mind*, δαΐ-φρων *warlike* (or *prudent*), ἀλεξί-κακο-s *defender against ill*, λαθι-κηδής *forgetting care*, πυκι-μηδής *with shrewd counsel*, καλλι-γύναικ-α *with beautiful women* (cp. κάλλι-μος), κυδι-άνειρα *glorifying men* (cp. κυδι-όων); with the Proper Names, Αἰθί-οπ-ες, Πειρί-θοο-s, Ἀλκί-νοο-s, Ἀλκι-μέδων (cp. ἄν-αλκι-s), and the words beginning with ἀρι- and ἐρι-.

The meaning of several of these words is very uncertain, owing to the merely ornamental and conventional way in which they are used in Homeric poetry. It seems to follow that they are survivals from an earlier period, one in which the number of Stems in -ι was probably greater than in Homeric times.

Loss of o may be recognised in ἀρτί-πος (= ἄρτιος τοὺς πόδας), ζεί-δωρος *grain giving* (ζειά), κραται-γύαλος *of strong pieces*, Δηΐ-φοβος, perhaps also μιαι-φόνος, Ἀλθαι-μένης, ταλαί-πωρος : cp. γεραί-τερος from γεραιό-s.

c. Stems in -σῐ :—

This group is mainly Homeric : ἐρυσί-πτολι (Voc.) *deliverer of the city* (with v. l. ῥυσί-πτολι Il. 6. 305), ἀερσί-ποδ-ες *lifting the feet* (i. e. with high action), πλήξ-ιππο-s *smiter of horses*, λυσι-μελής *loosening the limbs* (of sleep), τανυσί-πτερο-s, ταλασί-φρων, ἀεσί-φρων, ταμεσί-χρως, φαεσί-μβροτο-s, φυσί-ζοος, φθισί-μβροτο-s, τερψί-μβροτο-s, Τερψι-χόρη (Hes.), ἐνοσί-χθων (ἐννοσί-γαιος, εἰνοσί-φυλλος, &c.), πηγεσί-μαλλο-s, ὠλεσί-καρπο-s, ἀλφεσί-βοιος, ἑλκεσί-πεπλο-s, φθισ-ήνωρ, πλησ-ίστιο-s, ἐρυσ-άρματ-ες, ῥηξ-ήνωρ, γαμψ-ῶνυξ; and Proper Names, Πρωτεσί-λαο-s, Ἀρσί-νοο-s, Δεισ-ήνωρ, Λύσ-ανδρος, Πεισ-ήνωρ, Πεισί-στρατο-s, Ὀρσί-λοχο-s, Ἀναβησί-νεως, Ἡσί-οδος (Hes.), &c.

There are a few Stems in -τῐ ; βωτι-άνειρα *feeding men*, Καστι-άνειρα (cp. κε-κασ-μένος).

We may add the Hesiodic φερέσ-βιος *life-bearing*, and φερεσ-σακής *shield-bearing* with φερεσ- apparently for φερεσι-.

These Stems were originally the same as those of the abstract Nouns in -τι-s, -σι-s : cp. Τέρψι-χόρη, τερψί-μβροτος, &c. with τέρψι-s, πλήξ-ιππος with πλῆξι-s.　But in many cases new Stems have been formed under the influence of the sigmatic Aorist, with a difference of quantity, as in φυσί-ζοο-s *life-giving* (φῠσι-s), λῡσι-μελής, φθῑσί-μβροτο-s.　Compare also ταμεσί-χρως with τμῆσι-s, Πεισί-στρατο-s with πίστι-s, &c.

The group of Compounds is also to be noticed for the distinctly *Verbal* or *participial* meaning given by the first part of the word; cp. the next group, and § 126.

d. Stems in -ε :—

These are nearly all Verbal, both in form and meaning : ἑλκε-χίτων-ες *trailing the chiton*, μενε-δήϊο-s *withstanding foemen* (so μενε-χάρμη-s, μενε-πτόλεμο-s, Μενέ-λαο-s, Μενε-σθεύς, &c.) : ἐχέ-θυμο-s *restraining passion*, ἐχέ-φρων *possessing judgment*, ἐχε-πευκές *carrying sharpness*, ’Εχέ-πωλο-s, ’Εχέ-νηος, ’Εχε-κλῆς ; ἀγε-λείη *driving spoil*, ἀρχέ-κακο-s *beginning mischief*, ἀγχέ-μαχο-s *fighting close*, λεχε-ποίη *with beds of grass* : ’Αρχέ-λοχο-s, Φέρε-κλος, Μελέ-αγρο-s ; φερέ-οικος *carrying his house* (of the snail in Hes.), ἐγρε-κύδοιμος *stirring tumult :* also (if ε is elided) ψευδ-άγγελο-s *bringing false news*, αἴθ-οψ *fiery*, μισγ-άγκεια *the meeting-place of glens*, ἀλεξάνεμος *keeping off wind*, ’Αλέξ-ανδρος.

Stems in -σε ; ἀκερσε-κόμη-s *with unshorn hair*, Περσε-φόνεια.

With the Stems in -ε may evidently be placed ταλα-, in ταλά-φρων *with enduring mind*, ταλα-εργό-s *enduring in work*, ταλαύρινος (for ταλα-Ϝρινο-s) *bearing a shield of hide*, ταλα-πενθής *bearing sorrow*, ταλα-πείριος *bearing trial ;* and τλη- in Τλη-πόλεμος &c. : also τανυ-, in τανύ-γλωσσος *with outstretched tongue, long-tongued*, τανύ-φυλλος *long-leaved*, τανυ-γλώχινες *long-notched* (arrows), and ἐρυ- in ’Ερύ-λαος, *defender of the host*.

e. Stems in -ν :—

ᾰ for η appears in ὀνομά-κλυτος *of famous name*, κυνά-μυια for κυα-μυια on the analogy of κύν-α.

f. Case-forms :—

Nom. Acc. in Numerals, as ἕν-δεκα, δυώ-δεκα.

The Dative is probably to be recognised in ἀρηΐ-φατο-s *slain in war* (and so ’Αρηΐ-θοο-s, ’Αρηΐ-λυκο-s), πυρι-ηκής *sharpened by fire* (πυρί-καυστο-s, Πυρι-φλεγέθων), διϊ-πετής *falling in the sky ;* the Dat. Plur. in κηρεσσι-φόρητο-s *brought by the fates*, ὀρεσί-τροφο-s *nursed in mountains*, ἐγχεσί-μωρο-s *great with spears*, ἐντεσι-εργό-s *working in harness*, τειχεσι-πλῆτα (Voc.) *drawing near to* (*assailing*) *walls*, Ναυσι-κάα, Μηδεσι-κάστη, Πασι-θέη, Χερσι-δάμας ; a Locative form in χαμαι-εύνης *sleeping on the ground*, ὁδοι-πόρο-s *a wayfarer*, χοροι-τυπίη *figuring in the dance*, Πυλοι-γενής *born at Pylus*, παλαί-φατο-s *of ancient fame*, and perhaps (to express *manner*) in ἰθαι-γενής *duly born*, ὀλοοί-τροχο-s *rolling.* Cp. ἐμ-πυρι-βήτης *made to stand over the fire*, i. e. *a kettle.*

This use of the Dative may have been suggested by the Stems in -ι and -σι. Compounds such as ἐλκεσί-πεπλος, ὠλεσί-καρπος, ἀλφεσί-βοιος, containing forms which sounded like the Dat. Plur. of Stems in -εσ, may have served as types for the group ἐγχεσί-μωρος, τειχεσι-πλήτης, ὀρεσί-τροφος, &c. in which the Dat. Plur. takes the place of the Stem. Cp. Πρωτεσί-λαος.

Conversely, φερέσ-βιο-s *life-bearing*, and φερεσ-σακής (Hes.) ought to be * φερεσί-βιο-s, but have followed the type of ὀρέσ-βιο-s, τελεσ-φόρο-s, &c.

The forms διΐ-φιλο-s, ἀρηΐ-φιλο-s, ἀρηϊ-κτάμενο-s, δαϊ-κτάμενο-s, δουρι-κλυτό-s, δουρι-κλειτό-s, ναυσι-κλυτό-s, should probably be written as separate words, Διὶ φίλος, Ἄρηϊ κτάμενος, &c. As to -κτάμενος see § 125, 6 : as to -κλυτός, -κλειτός, cp. § 128.

The Genitive is very rare : οὐδενόσ-ωρο-s *not worth caring for*, Ἑλλήσ-ποντος.

The Accusative may be recognised in δικασ-πόλο-s *busied about suits* (δίκαι), ἀταλά-φρων *with childish thought* (=ἀταλὰ φρονέων, which is also used in Homer), ἀκαλα-ρρείτης *gently flowing*, Ἀλκά-θοος (cp. Dat. ἀλκ-ί), ποδά-νιπτρον, also πᾶν- (*altogether*) in πάμ-παν, παν-αίολος, παν-άποτμος, πάμ-πρωτος, &c.

An ending -η (for -ᾱ) may be seen in νεή-φατος *new-slain*, ὀλιγη-πελέων. This is perhaps an Instrum., as πάντη (§ 110).

125.] Form of the second Stem. 1. The use of a Root-Noun, *i. e.* a Verbal Stem without a distinct Nominal Suffix (§ 113), is more common in Composition than in simple Nouns : as, δί-ζυγ-ες *yoked in a pair*, δί-πλακ-α *two-fold*, χέρ-νιβ-α *hand-washing*, οἶν-οπ-α *wine-like*, νήϊδα (νή-Fιδ-α) *ignorant*, αἰγί-λιπ-ος (Gen.) *left by goats*, πολυ-αῖξ *much starting*, βου-πλήξ *an ox-whip*. The Stem, it will be seen, is in the Weak form.

2. Nouns in -ώς (Gen. -ο-ος) and in -ος (Gen. -ε-ος) form the Compound in -ης, Neut. -ες, as ἀν-αιδής *without shame* (αἰδώς), θυμ-αλγής *grieving the spirit* (ἄλγος).

The Stem in these Compounds is often weak, though in the simple Neuters in -ος it is strong (§ 114) : *e. g.* αἰνο-παθής (as well as ταλα-πενθής, νη-πενθής, from πένθος), ἀγχι-βαθής (βένθος, πολυ-βενθής), οἰνο-βαρής, πρωτο-παγής, ἀ-σινής, θυμο-δακής, ἀρι-φραδής, ἑτερ-αλκής, τηλε-φανής, &c. So we find ἀϊκῶς (Il. 22. 336) as Adv. to ἀεικής, and ἀλλο-ϊδέα (Od. 13. 194) alongside of θεο-ειδής, μυλο-ειδής, &c.

This weakening of the Stem, accompanied by shifting of the accent to the suffix, apparently represents the original rule—words like ταλα-πενθής being formed afresh from the Simple Noun. Conversely, the analogy of the Compounds has given rise to the forms **πάθος, βάθος, βάρος,** &c. and also to the simple Adjectives such as **ψευδής, σαφής.**

3. Stems in ην (εν-) usually take ων (ον-) in Composition : as φρήν (Gen. φρεν-ός) forms πρό-φρων, Gen. πρό-φρον-ος : and

Neuters in -μᾰ form Compounds in -μων, Gen. -μον-ος, as ἀν-αίμον-ες (αἷμα) *bloodless.* Cp. ἀπείρων *boundless* (πεῖραρ, περαίνω). So too πατήρ, μήτηρ, ἀνήρ, &c. form -ωρ (Gen. -ορ-ος), as μητρο-πάτωρ, εὐ-ήνωρ.

4. Some Stems take a final -τ, as ἀ-βλῆ-τ-α (Acc. Sing.) *un-thrown,* ἀ-κμῆ-τ-ες *unwearied;* so ἐπι-βλής, ἀ-δμής, ἀ-γνώς.

5. In Adjectives the Suffix is often replaced by one ending in -ο; as ὅ-πατρο-s *of one father,* βαρβαρό-φωνο-s *with strange voice* (from φώνη), χρυσ-ηλάκατο-s *with golden distaff* (ἠλακάτη), δυσ-ώνυμο-s *of evil name* (ὄνομα), ἀ-σπερμο-s *without seed* (σπέρμα), &c. In other cases the Suffix is retained, and thus we find in Compounds (contrary to the general rules of Noun-formation)—

Masc. Stems in -η, as ἀργυρο-δίνη-s,
and -ιδ, as λευκ-άσπιδ-ες.

Masc. and Fem. Stems in -εσ, as μελι-ηδής *honey-sweet,* ἠρι-γένεια (for -εσ-ιᾰ) *early born.*

Fem. Stems in -ο, as χρυσό-θρονο-s (Ἥρη), ῥοδο-δάκτυλο-s (Ἠώς), and many other adjectives ' of two terminations.'

A Masc. Stem in -μᾰτ, viz. ἐρυσ-άρματ-ες (ἵπποι).

6. The use of a Participle in the second part is rare : it is found in some Proper Names, as Οὐκ-αλέγων, Πυρι-φλεγέθων, Θεο-κλύμενος : also where it is a mere Adjective without any *Tense*-meaning, as πολύ-τλας, cp. ἀ-δάμας. In other cases we can write the words separately, as πάλιν πλαγχθέντας, δάκρυ χέων, πᾶσι μέλουσα, κάρη κομόωντες, εὖ ναιετάων, εὐρὺ ῥέων, ἐὺ κτίμενος, πάλιν ὄρμενος, Ἄρηϊ κτάμενος, δαὶ κτάμενος, &c.

7. Abstract Primitive Nouns are not used in the second part : thus we do not find ἐπεσ-βολή, but ἐπεσ-βολίη (through a con-crete ἐπεσ-βόλο-s) : and so βο-ηλασίη (not βο-ήλασι-s), ἀνδρο-κτασί-η, εὐ-δικ-ίη, ἁμα-τροχιή, ἀλαο-σκοπιή. Except after Prepo-sitions ; as ἀμφί-βασι-s, ἐπί-κλησι-s, προ-χοή, προ-δοκή.

Note however παλίωξις (for παλι-ίωξι-s), βου-λυτό-s *the time of unyoking,* βού-βρωστι-s.

8. When the latter part of a Compound is derived from a disyllabic Verbal Stem beginning with a vowel, its initial vowel is often lengthened : as—

ἐλα- *drive,* ἱππ-ηλάτα, ἐξ-ήλα-τος, βο-ηλα-σίη.
ἐρα- *love,* ἐπ-ήρα-τος, πολυ-ήρα-τος.
ἀμελγ- *milk,* ἀν-ήμελκτος, Ἱππ-ημολγοί.
ἀρό-ω *plough,* ἀν-ήρο-τος.
ἀλέγ-ω *care,* δυσ-ηλεγ-έος (Gen.), ἀπ-ηλεγ-έως.
ἐρέφ-ω *cover,* κατ-ηρεφ-ής, ἀμφ-ηρεφ-ής, ὑπ-ωρόφ-ιος.
ἀμείβ-ω *change,* ἐξ-ημοιβ-ός.
ἐρετ- *row,* φιλ-ήρετ-μος, δολιχ-ήρετμος.
ἐνεκ- *carry,* δι-ηνεκ-ής, ποδ-ηνεκ-ής, δουρ-ηνεκ-ής.

ἐλυ(θ)- *come*, νε-ήλυθ-ες.

ἀγερ- *assemble*, ὀμ-ηγερ-έες, θυμ-ηγερ-έων (= θυμὸν ἀγείρων).

ἐριδ- *strive*, ἀμφ-ήριστος *striven about*.

So ποδ-ήνεμος, εὐ-ώνυμος (πολυ-ώνυμος, &c.), εὐ-ήνωρ (ἀνερ-), εὐ-ηφενής (from ἄφενος *wealth*), γαμψ-ῶνυξ, πεμπ-ώβολον, ἀν-ήκεστος, ἀν-ώϊστος, ἐρι-ούνης (ὀνα- *help*), ὑπ-ώρεια (ὄρος), δι-ηκόσιοι and τρι-ηκόσιοι (ἑκατόν).

Similar lengthening is found, but less frequently, in the first part of the Compound; ὠλεσί-καρπος, ἠλιτό-μηνος, 'Ωρεί-θυια. Also in other derivatives, as ἠνεμό-εις, ἠνορ-έη, τηλεθόωσα (θἄλέθω), ἠγερέθονται (ἀγερ-).

126.] Meaning of Compounds. The general rule is that the prefixed Stem limits or qualifies the meaning of the other : as ὠμο-γέρων *hale old man*, δημο-γέρων *elder of the people*, τρι-γέρων (Aesch.) *thrice aged*; ἱππό-δαμο-s *tamer of horses*, ἱππό-βοτο-s *pastured by horses*, ἱππό-κομος *with plume of horse-hair*, ἱππο-κέλευθος *making way with horses*; βαθυ-δινήεις *deep-eddying*.

The prefixed Stem may evidently express very different relations—that of an Adjective, as ὠμο-γέρων, βαθυ-δίνης, or a Genitive, as δημο-γέρων, ἱππό-κομος, or an Object, as ἱππό-δαμος, or an Adverb of manner or place or instrument, as ὀμ-ηγερέες, ἠερο-φοῖτις, &c.—and various attempts have been made to classify Compounds according to these relations. Such attempts are usually unsatisfactory unless the differences of meaning upon which they are based are accompanied by differences of grammatical *form*.

In respect of form an important distinction is made by the fact that in the second part of many Compounds a Substantive acquires the meaning of an Adjective without the use of a new Suffix; *e. g.* ῥοδο-δάκτυλο-s, literally *rose-finger*, means not *a rosy finger*, but *having rosy fingers*; so ἱππό-κομος *with a horse-plume*, ἱππιο-χαίτη-s *with horse's mane (as a plume)*, βαθυ-δίνη-s (= βαθυ-δινή-εις), &c. Such Compounds are called by Curtius *Attributive*. The formation is analogous to the turning of abstract into concrete Nouns by a mere change of Gender (instead of a Suffix), § 116. Thus διο-γενής (= δῖον γένος ἔχων) is to δῖον γένος as ψευδής *false* to ψεῦδος *falsehood*.

Among the meanings which may be conveyed by a Stem in a Compound, note the poetical use to express *comparison* : as ἀελλό-πος *storm-foot*, i. e. *with feet (swift) as the storm*, μελί-γηρυ-s *honey-voiced*, ῥοδο-δάκτυλο-s, κυν-ῶπι-s, &c. So too ποδ-ήνεμο-s *like the wind in feet*, θυμο-λέων *like a lion in spirit*.

The order of the two Stems may be almost indifferent; *i. e.* it may be indifferent which of the two notions is treated as qualifying the other; *e. g.* ποδ-ώκης *swift of foot* (= ὠκὺς τοὺς πόδας) is the same in practical effect as ὠκύ-πους *swift-foot, with swift feet* (ὠκεῖς πόδας ἔχων).

In the Compounds called by Curtius *Objective, i. e.* where the relation between the two parts is that of governing and governed word, the general rule requires that the governed word should come first, as in ἱππό-δαμο-s *horse-taming*. This order appears to be reversed in certain cases in which the first Stem has the force of a Verb. The Stems so used are—

1. Stems in -ε (§ 124, *d*), as ἑλκε-χίτωνες, ἐχέ-φρων, &c.

2. Stems in -σι (§ 124, *c*), as ἑλκε-σί-πεπλος, φθι-σ-ήνωρ, &c.

3. Some of the Stems in -ι, as εἰλί-ποδες, κυδι-άνειρα, ἁμαρτί-νοος (Hes.), λαθι-κηδής, λαθί-φρων, τερπι-κέραυνος (§ 124, *b*) ; and in -ο, as φιλο-πτόλεμος *loving war*, φιλο-κέρτομος, φιλο-κτέανος, φυγο-πτόλεμος *flying from war*, ἁμαρτο-επής *blundering in speech*, ἠλιτό-μηνος *astray as to the month :* also the Compounds of ταλα-, τλη-, as ταλα-πενθής *enduring sorrow*, Τλη-πόλεμος, &c., and τανυ-, as τανύ-πτερος (Hes.), which is=the Homeric τανυσί-πτερος.

In most of these cases the inversion is only apparent. For instance, ἑλκεσί-πεπλος means *trailing* the robe as distinguished from other ways of wearing it ; the notion of trailing is therefore the limiting one. So τανυσί-πτερος means *long-winged ;* μενε-πτόλεμος, φυγο-πτόλεμος, Τλη-πόλεμος, Νεο-πτόλεμος describe varieties of the genus ' warrior.'

Nevertheless we must recognise a considerable number of Compounds in which the Prefixed Stem is Verbal in form as well as in meaning. A similar group has been formed in English (e. g. *catch-penny, make-shift, do-nothing,* &c.), and in the Romance languages (French *vau-rien, croque-mitaine,* Italian *fa-tutto,* &c.). These groups are of relatively late formation, and confined for the most part to colloquial language. The corresponding Greek forms represent a new departure of the same kind.

The process by which the second part of a Compound passes into a *Suffix* cannot often be traced in Greek. An example may be found in -απο-s (ποδ-απός, ἡμεδ-απός, ἀλλοδ-απός),= Sanscr. -añc, Lat. -inquu-s (*long-inquus, prop-inquus*). In the adjectives in -οψ, as οἶνοψ, αἶθοψ, ἦνοψ, νῶροψ, μέροψ, the original sense of the Stem -οπ is evidently very faint. In the proper names Αἰθίοπες, Δόλοπες, Ἕλλοπες, Πέλοψ, &c. it becomes a mere Suffix.

127.] **Stems compounded with Prepositions.** These are of two readily distinguishable kinds :—

1. The Preposition qualifies ; as ἐπι-μάρτυρος *witness to (some-thing),* περι-κτίον-ες *dwellers around,* ἀμφί-φαλο-s *with crest on both sides,* πρό-φρων *with forward mind.* Forms of this kind are

sometimes obtained directly from Compound Verbs : *e.g.* ἔξοχος from ἐξ-έχω, not from ἐξ and ὄχος.

2. The Preposition governs, *i.e.* the Compound is equivalent to a Preposition governing a Noun ; ἐν-νύχ-ιο-s *in the night*, κατα-χθόν-ιο-s *under-ground*, ἀπο-θύμ-ιο-s *displeasing* (lit. *away from the mind*), &c. ; also (but less commonly) without a Secondary Suffix, as ἐγ-κέφαλο-s *brain* (lit. *within the head*), ἐπ-άρουρο-s *attached to the soil.*

The placing of the Preposition before the *governed* Stem is a departure from the general rule stated above. It may be held, however, that the Preposition serves (in some of these Compounds at least) as the limiting or qualifying member of the word. Compare *ι*νύχ-ιο-s *by night*, ἐν-νύχ-ιο-s *within the night :* it is evident that the ἐν limits the sense of νύχιος in essentially the same way as παν- in παν-νύχ-ιο-s *all the night.* So κατα-χθόν-ιο-s is nearly equivalent to χθόν-ιο-s ; the Preposition merely makes it clear in what sense the Suffix -ιο is to be understood—' belonging to the earth ' by being *under* it.

128.] Accentuation. The Accent generally falls on the last syllable of the prefixed Stem, or if that is impossible, then as far back as possible ; χρυσό-θρονος, ἀελλό-πος, ἐπ-ήρατο-s (ἐρατό-s), αἰν-αρέτη-s (ἀρετή), &c. The chief exceptions are the following : —

1. When the second Stem ends in -ο and has the force of an Active Participle, it is oxytone, or, if the penult is short, paroxytone ; as ὑ-φορβό-s, δημιο-εργό-s, τοξο-φόρο-s. Except Compounds with Prepositions, as ἐπί-κλοπο-s, πρό-μαχο-s, ὑπό-τροπο-s ; also those in -οχο-s, and one or two more, πτολί-πορθο-s, ἀγχί-μολο-ν, ἱππό-δαμος.

2. Adjectives in -ης (Stems in -εσ), Nouns in -ευ-s, Nouns of the agent in -τηρ and -τη-s, and Abstract Nouns in -η and -ιη retain their accent ; οἰνο-βαρής, ἡνι-οχεύ-s, μηλο-βυτῆρ-as, ἱππο-κορυστή-s, ἐπ-ιωγή, ἀρμα-τροχιή, ἀλαοσκοπιή.

But a few Adjectives in -ης are barytone, as ὑψι-πέτης, ποδ-ώκης, χαλκ-ήρης, τανυ-ήκης ; also the Fem. forms ἠρι-γένεια, ληϊ-βότειρα, δυσ-αριστο-τόκεια, μισγ-άγκεια.

3. When the second Stem is a long monosyllable, it is accented : βου-πλήξ, ἀπο-ρρώξ, παρα-βλῶπ-ες, παρα-πλῆγ-ας, ἀ-βλής, &c. (§ 125, 2). Hence the Fem. forms βο-ῶπ-ι-s, γλαυκ-ῶπ-ι-s, &c. (as if from βο-ώψ, γλαυκ-ώψ, &c.).

129.] Proper Names in Greek are generally Compounds ; the exceptions are chiefly names of gods, as Ζεύς, Ἥρη, Ἀθήνη, &c., and of certain heroes, as Πάρις, Πρίαμος, Αἴας, Τεῦκρος, &c.

Note that the gods whose names are Compound, as Διό-νυσος, Δη-μήτηρ, Περσε-φόνεια, are less prominent in Homer.

The second part of a Proper Name is liable to a peculiar shortening; Πάτρο-κλο-s, Φέρε-κλος, for Πατρο-κλέης, Φερε-κλέης, Σθένε-λος for Σθενέ-λαο-s, Αἴγι-σθος for Αἰγι-σθένης, Μενεσθεύς for Μενε-σθένης; cp. Εὐρυμίδης (Od. 9. 509), patronymic of Εὐρυμέδων. In these names the shorter form has (or had originally) the character of a 'nick-name,' or pet name.

In general, however, the 'pet' name is formed by dropping one of the two Stems altogether: the other Stem taking a Suffix in its place *. Thus we have in Homer the names—

in -το-s, as Ἕκα-τος (for ἑκατη-βόλος), Εὔρυ-τος (Εὐρυ-βάτης, Εὐρύ-αλος, &c.), Ἴφι-τος, Ἔχε-τος, Λήι-τος.

in -τωρ, as Ἄκ-τωρ (for Ἀγέ-λαος or some other name beginning Ἀγε-), Ἕκ-τωρ (Ἐχε-), Μέν-τωρ (Μενε-), Καλή-τωρ, Ἀμύν-τωρ, &c.

in -τη-s, as Θερσί-της (cp. Θερσί-λοχος, &c.), Πολί-της, Ὀρέσ-της, Θυέσ-της, Μέν-της (cp. Μέν-τωρ).

in -ων, as Δόλ-ων, Ἀγάθ-ων (cp. Λάκων = Λακεδαιμόνιος).

in -ευ-s, as Περσ-εύς (from Περσε-φόνος), Οἰν-εύς (cp. Οἰνό-μαος, &c.), Πρωτ-εύς, Λεοντ-εύς, &c.

in -ιο-s; Δολ-ίος (Δόλ-οψ, &c.) Ὀδ-ίος, Τυχ-ίος, Φήμ-ιος, Καλήσ-ιος, and many more.

in -ια-s, -εια-s; Πελ-ίης, Τειρεσ-ίας; Ἑρμείας, Αἰνείας, Αὐγείας.

In these names the Suffix is not used with its proper force, but merely in imitation of the corresponding groups of Common Nouns. This is evident from the fact that so many of these words are inexplicable as Simple Nouns. Note especially the names in -το-s and -ων from Adjectives, as Εὔρυ-το-s, Ἴφι-το-s, Ἀγάθ-ων; and those in -ευ-s from Nouns of the consonantal declension (§ 118), as Λεοντ-εύ-s, Αἰγ-εύ-s, and even from Verbs, as Περσ-εύ-s *.

The first part of the Compound has probably been dropped in Κλυμένη (cp. Περι-κλύμενος), Θόων (cp. Ἱππο-θόων), &c.

130.] Numerals. Although the Numerals are not properly to be counted as 'Nouns,' it will be convenient to notice here the chief peculiarities of formation which they exhibit.

1. There are two Fem. forms for εἷς, viz. μία and ἴα; also a Neut. Dat. ἰῷ (Il. 6. 422). The Stem ἁ- (for sm-) in ἅ-παξ, ἅ-πλοος, &c. is to be regarded as a weak form of the Stem ἑν- (sam). The weak form sm- is to be traced in μία, for σμ-ιά.

2. The forms δύο and δύω are equally common in Homer.

---

* Aug. Fick, *Die griechischen Personennamen nach ihrer Bildung erklärt*, Göttingen, 1874.

For the number 12 we find the three forms δυώδεκα, δώδεκα, and δυοκαίδεκα; also the Ordinals δυωδέκατος and (rarely) δωδέκατος.

3. Besides τέσσαρ-ες there is a form πίσυρ-ες, applied to horses in Il. 15. 680 and 23. 171, to other objects in Il. 24. 233 and three times in the Odyssey (5. 70., 16. 249., 22. 111).

The Stem τετρᾰ- appears in the Dat. τέτρα-σι, also in the Ordinal (τέτρα-τος and τέταρ-τος), and most derivatives, as τετρά-κις, τετρα-χθά, τετρά-φαλος *four-crested*, &c. (but cp. τεσσαρά-βοιος *worth four oxen*): also with loss of the first syllable in τρά-πεζα.

The variation in the Stem of this Numeral has been fully discussed by Joh. Schmidt (*K. Z.* xxv. p. 47 ff.). He shows that the Stem had three forms (§ 114*). The strong form is seen in Sanscr. *catváras*, which would lead us to expect Greek *τετϝῶρες (hence perhaps Dor. τέτορες); the weakest in the Sanscr. Ordinal *turîya*, for *ktur-iya*, in which the shortening affects both syllables, and the first is consequently lost. This weakest Stem appears in τρυ-φάλεια *a four-ridged helmet*, and is not derived from the form τετρᾰ-. It probably fell into disuse owing to its unlikeness to τέσσαρες; accordingly it has only survived in words in which the meaning 'four' had ceased to be felt.

The form πίσυρες may be akin to Lesbian πέσσυρες or πέσυρες, but there is no decisive ground for regarding it as Æolic.

4. ὀκτώ, like δύω, is a Dual in form. The primitive ending -ωυ (Sanscr. *ashtâu*) may be traced in ὄγδοος (ὄγδωϝ-ος, ὄγδωος, Lat. *octâvus*).

5. Under ἐννέα note the varieties ἔνα-τος and εἴνα-τος *ninth*, probably for ἐνϝα-τος; so εἰνά-κις, εἰνά-νυχες, εἰνά-ετες; also ἐνν-ῆμαρ (for ἐννέ-ημαρ), ἐννέ-ωρος *of nine seasons*, ἐννήκοντα (for ἐννε-ήκοντα, cp. τρι-ήκοντα, &c.) and ἐνενήκοντα—the last a form difficult to explain.

The numbers above ten are generally denoted by Compounds of the kind called *Copulative* (Sanscr. *dvandva*): δυώ-δεκα *two and ten*.

The analogy of the Numerals ending in -ᾰ (ἑπτά, δέκα, with the Stems τετρᾰ-, εἰνᾰ-) has led to the use of ᾰ as a connecting vowel in Numerals generally; hence πεντά-ετες and ἑξά-ετες (Od. 3. 115), ὀκτά-κνημος, τεσσαρά-βοιος, ἐεικοσά-βοιος. But inversely ο is found for ᾰ in πεντηκοντό-γυος (Il. 9. 579); cp. § 124, *a*.

CHAPTER VII.

USE OF THE CASES.

Introductory.

131.] The Case-Endings and Adverbial Endings serve (as has been said in § 90) to show the relation in which the words to which they are suffixed (Nouns, Pronouns, Adverbs, &c.) stand to the Verb of the Sentence.

This relation may be of three kinds :—

1. The Noun or Pronoun may express the Subject of the Verb : or rather (since a Subject is already given by the Person-Ending) it may *qualify* or *define* the Subject so given. *E. g.* in the sentence βασιλεὺς δίδω-σι *the-king he-gives* βασιλεύς explains the Subject given by the Ending -σι.

2. The Noun &c. may qualify the Predicate given by the Stem of the Verb. *E. g.* in ταῦτα δίδω-σι, ἐμοὶ δίδω-σι, καλῶς δίδω-σι, ἀπο-δίδω-σι the Noun (Pronoun, Adverb, Preposition) qualifies the meaning expressed in the Stem δίδω-.

Constructions of these two kinds are found in Sentences which involve the addition of one word only to the Verb. Those of the second kind might be called ' Adverbial '—using the term in the widest sense, for a word construed with a Verb-Stem.

Note that a Nominative may be used 'adverbially' : *e. g.* βασιλεύς ἐσ-τι may mean *he-is king* (as well as *the king he-is*). See § 162.

3. The Noun &c. may be connected with, and serve to qualify, another Noun or Adverbial word. *E. g.* in the sentences βασιλέως υἱὸς δίδωσι, Κύρου βασιλέως περιγίγνεται, the word βασιλέως is not connected with the Verb, but with a Noun.

If the former constructions are ' Adverbial,' these might be called ' Adnominal' or 'Adjectival.' The Sentences in which they are found must contain at least *two* words besides the Verb ; they are therefore of a higher order of structure than the two former kinds.

From these relations, again, more complex forms of structure are derived in several ways, which it will be enough to indicate in the briefest manner.

A Verb compounded with a Preposition becomes for the purposes of construction a new Verb, with a syntax of its own.

Similarly, the phrase formed by a Verb and a Noun (Case-form or Adverb) may be equivalent in the construction to a single Verb, and may take a further Adverb, or govern Cases of Nouns accordingly. *E. g.* in κακὰ ῥέξει τινά *he does evil to some one* the Acc. τινά is governed by the phrase κακὰ ῥέζει : in τίεν ἶσα τέκεσσι *honoured like his children* the Dat. τέκεσσι is governed by τίεν ἶσα.

Again, the new Case-form or Adverb so 'governed' by a Verb and Noun may belong in sense to the Noun. Thus in the sentence μέγ' ἔξοχος ἔπλετο *he is greatly eminent*, since ἔξοχος expresses the meaning which μέγα is intended to qualify, we may consider that practically μέγα is construed with ἔξοχος alone. Evidently a qualification of this kind will generally apply only to an Adjective * (just as the degrees of comparison are essentially adjectival). In this way it comes about that an Adverb may in general be used to qualify an Adjective ; and that very many Adjectives and Adverbs 'govern' the same Cases as the Verbs which correspond to them in meaning. *E. g.* in σοὶ εἴκελος ἀλκήν the Adj. εἴκελος takes the construction of a Verb meaning *to be like*.

In a strictly scientific treatment of the Cases the various constructions with the Verb should come before the constructions with Nouns and Prepositions. Such a treatment, however, would have the inconvenience of frequently separating uses of the same Case which are intimately connected. *E. g.* the construction ἀλγεῖ τὴν κεφαλήν (2) cannot well be separated from the extension of the same construction in μέγας ἐστὶ τὸ σῶμα (3). The Nominative, too, is used not only as the Subject, but also as the Predicate, or part of it. It will be best therefore to take the several Cases in succession, and to begin with the ' oblique' Cases.

The Accusative.

132.] **Internal and External Object.** The uses of the Accusative have been divided into those in which the Acc. repeats, with more or less modification, the meaning given by the Verb, and those in which the action of the Verb is limited or directed by an 'Object' wholly distinct from it. *E. g.* in the sentence ἕλκος ὅ με οὔτασε, lit. *the wound which he wounded me*, ὅ (ἕλκος) qualifies οὔτασε by a word which expresses to some extent the same *thing* as the Verb οὔτασε : whereas με qualifies it in a different way. As the latter kind of Acc. had been known as the Acc. of the EXTERNAL OBJECT, so the former has more recently been termed the Acc. of the INTERNAL OBJECT. We shall take first the different uses which fall under the description of the ' Acc. of the Internal Object.'

The foundation of this division (as Delbrück observes, *Synt. Forsch.* iv. p. 29) is the circumstance that all Accusatives which

---

* In later Greek Adverbs are constantly used to qualify substantives : as ὁ ἀεὶ βασιλεύς, ὁ πρὶν χρόνος, &c. But this use only becomes possible when we have the Article to show how the Adverb is to be understood.

do not express the external Object of an action may be explained in nearly the same way. The real difficulty arises when we try to find a principle which will explain these different Accusatives and at the same time exclude the relations expressed by other Cases or Adverbial forms. No such principle can be laid down. The fact seems to be that the Accusative originally had a very wide ' Adverbial ' use, which was encroached upon by the more specific uses of other Cases. The different constructions included under the ' Internal Object' have all the appearance of fragments of an earlier more elastic usage.

133.] **Neuter Pronouns** may be used in the Accusative ' adverbially,' *i. e.* to define the action of the Verb: as Il. 1. 289 ἅ τιν' οὐ πείσεσθαι ὀίω *in which I think that some one will not obey;* Il. 14. 249 ἄλλο ἐπίνυσσεν *gave another lesson;* Od. 23. 24 τοῦτο ὀνήσει *will do this benefit;* Od. 10. 75 τόδ' ἱκάνεις *comest as thou dost;* Il. 5. 827 μήτε σύ γ' Ἄρηα τό γε δείδιθι *fear not Ares as to this;* τόδε χώεο *be angry at this;* τάδε μαίνεται *does these mad things* (=is mad with these acts).

This use includes the Adverbial τί *why?* (*e.g.* τί ἦλθες *in regard to what have you come?* = what means your coming?): τό *therefore* (§ 262, 3), ὅ, ὅτι *because, that* (§ 269): τὶ *in any way,* οὐδέν *not at all,* ἀμφότερον *for both reasons* (Il. 7. 418), δοιά *in two ways* (Od. 2. 46), πάντα *altogether,* &c.; also the combination of Pronoun and Adverb in τὸ πρίν, τὸ πάρος, &c. *the time before* (see § 260, *b*).

134.] **Neuter Adjectives** are often used in this way; as εὐρὺ ῥέει *flows in a broad stream,* ὀξέα κεκληγώς *uttering shrill cries;* so πρῶτον, πρῶτα *in the first place,* πολύ, πολλόν, πολλά *much,* μέγα *greatly,* ὀλίγον, τυτθόν *little,* ἶσον, ἶσα *equally;* ὅσον, τόσον, τοῖον; ἀντίον, ἐναντίον; ὕστερον, ὕστατα, μᾶλλον, μάλιστα, ἆσσον, ἄγχιστα; εὖ (Neut. of ἠΰς or ἐΰς), ἠδύ, δεινόν, δεινά, αἰνά, καλόν, καλά, πυκνά, μακρά, ἀδινά, βαρύ, βαρέα, ὀξύ, ταρφέα, ὑπέρμορα, ἐνδέξια, ὄχα, ἔξοχα; and many more.

In general there is no difference perceptible between the Neut. Sing. and Neut. Plur. But compare τυτθόν *for a little space,* and τυτθὰ κεάσαι *split into little pieces* (Od. 12. 388).

Note the combination of Pronoun and Adjective in τὸ πρῶτον, τὰ πρῶτα, τὸ τρίτον, τὸ τέταρτον: also in τὰ ἄλλα *in other respects.*

This construction is very common in Homer, and may almost be said to be the usual Homeric mode of forming an Adverb. It has been already observed that Adverbs in -ως are comparatively rare in Homer (§ 110).

135.] **Cognate Accusative.** This term denotes that the Verb

K

is construed with a Substantive in the Acc. of 'cognate' form, or at least of equivalent meaning.

A Cognate Acc. is generally used to introduce the Adjective or Pronoun which really qualifies or defines the predication contained in the Verb : *e.g.* ἄπρηκτον πόλεμον πολεμίζειν *to wage a war without result* (cp. the adverbial use of a Neut. Adj. in ἄλληκτον πολεμίζειν *to war without ceasing*) ; ὅς κεν ἀρίστην βουλὴν βουλεύσῃ *who shall give the best counsel* (= ἄριστα βουλεύσῃ); ἐφίλει παντοίην φιλότητα *treated with all manner of love; ἰέναι τὴν αὐτὴν ὁδόν *to go the same way*. So ἐπί-κλησιν καλέουσι *call by way of surname :* and with a Noun in the Plural, βουλὰς βουλεύειν *to give counsel* (*from time to time*); δάσσαντο μοίρας *divided into the several shares ;* αἰχμὰς αἰχμάσσουσι νεώτεροι (with repetition for the sake of emphasis), &c.

With a Pronoun referring to a cognate Noun ; λώβης .. ἣν ἐμὲ λωβήσασθε, ἕλκος ὅ με βροτὸς οὔτασεν, ὑπόσχεσις ἥν περ ὑπέστην, &c.

136.] Other Adverbial Accusatives. The following uses may be placed here as more or less analogous to the Cognate Accusative :

(1) Substantives expressing a particular *sphere* or *kind* of the action denoted by the Verb : as—

Il. 6. 292 ἤγαγε Σιδονίηθεν .. τὴν ὁδὸν ἣν Ἑλένην περ ἀνήγαγε *the voyage on which he brought back Helen:* (cp. Od. 6. 164 ἦλθον γὰρ καὶ κεῖσε .. τὴν ὁδὸν ᾗ δὴ κτλ.); so ὁδὸν οἴχεσθαι, ὁδὸν ἡγήσασθαι *to lead on the way ;* and again ἐξεσίην ἐλθεῖν *to go on an expedition* (and in Od. 21. 20 ἐξεσίην πολλὴν ὁδὸν ἦλθεν *went a long way on an expedition*), ἀγγελίην ἐλθόντα *going on a message ;* βουλὰς ἐξάρχων ἀγαθάς *taking the lead in good counsels ;*   Od. 8. 23 ἀέθλους .. τοὺς .. ἐπειρήσαντ' Ὀδυσῆος; Od. 19. 393 οὐλὴν τήν ποτέ μιν σῦς ἤλασε. So δαινύντα γάμον *holding a wedding-feast,* δαίνυ τάφον *gave a funeral feast* (whereas the cognate δαίτην δαινυμένους means *holding an ordinary feast*); ξυνάγωμεν Ἄρηα *let us join battle,* ἔριδα ῥήγνυντο βαρεῖαν *broke in grievous strife.*

So probably we should explain Il. 1. 31 ἐμὸν λέχος ἀντιόωσαν, like Il. 15. 33 φιλότης τε καὶ εὐνὴ ἣν ἐμίγης (cp. Pind. N. 1. 67 ὅταν θεοὶ .. γιγάντεσσιν μάχαν ἀντιάζωσι). Also Od. 6. 259 ὄφρ' ἂν μέν κ' ἀγροὺς ἴομεν καὶ ἔργ' ἀνθρώπων *so long as our way is through fields and tillage of men,*—ἀγρούς = ὁδὸν ἐν ἀγροῖς.

Note that this construction is chiefly applied to the *familiar* spheres of action—battle, council, feasting, &c.

(2) Abstract Nouns expressing an *attribute* of the action. Il. 9. 115 οὔ τι ψεῦδος ἐμὰς ἄτας κατέλεξας *with no falsehood*

hast thou recounted my folly : Od. 7. 297 ταῦτά τοι . . ἀληθείην
κατέλεξα.

So δέμας (in phrases like δέμας πυρός *like fire*), and the Adverbs
ἄκην, ἄδην, λίην, with many others (see § 110), are originally the
Accusatives of Abstract Nouns.

Add the poetical expressions such as πῦρ ὀφθαλμοῖσι δεδορκώς
with look of fire, μένεα πνείοντες *breathing martial fury.*

The phrase πῦρ δεδορκώς is a boldness of language (compared *e. g.* with δεινὸν
δερκόμενοι) analogous to that which we observed in Compounds such as ἀελλό-
πος *with storm-(like) feet,* as compared with ὠκύ-ποδες, &c. ; see § 126.

(3) The words ἔργον, ἔπος, μῦθος, with Pronouns, are used
nearly as the Neuter of the same Pronouns : as—

Il. 1. 294 πᾶν ἔργον ὑπείξομαι *I shall yield in every matter* (πᾶν
ἔργον = πάντα) : 5. 757 οὐ νεμεσίζῃ Ἄρει τάδε καρτερὰ ἔργα (constr.
like τόδε χώεο); cp. 9. 374.

Od. 3. 243 ἔπος ἄλλο μεταλλῆσαι *to ask another question.*

Il. 5. 715 ἦ ῥ' ἅλιον τὸν μῦθον ὑπέστημεν *our promise was idle.*

(4) Words expressing the *sum* or *result* of an action are put
in the Acc.; as Il. 4. 207 ἔβαλεν . . τῷ μὲν κλέος ἄμμι δὲ πένθος ;
24. 735 ῥίψει χειρὸς ἑλὼν ἀπὸ πύργου λυγρὸν ὄλεθρον : Od. 6. 184.
So ποινήν *in compensation,* πρόφασιν *on the pretence,* ἐπίκλησιν
nominally, χάριν *as a favour* (only in Il. 15. 744).

The use of Substantives to qualify a Verb evidently bears the
same relation to the use of Neut. Adjectives as Nouns in Apposition bear to ordinary Adjectives qualifying Nouns.

Note. Many of these constructions have been treated as varieties or extensions of the ' Cognate Accusative.' *E.g.* from ὁδὸν ἐλθεῖν have been
explained, on the one hand, ὁδὸν ἡγήσασθαι, ὁδὸν ἀνήγαγε, &c., on the other,
ἀγγελίην ἐλθεῖν, &c. ; so δαίνυντο γάμον, δαίνυ τάφον, have been regarded as
modelled on δαίτην δαίνυσθαι ; μῦθον ὑπέστημεν as justified because a promise is
a μῦθος, ψεῦδος κατέλεξας because ψεῦδος = *a false tale,* and so on. It must not
be supposed, however, that these analogies *explain* any of the uses in question,
or that the ' Cognate ' Acc. is *prior* to the others, either in simplicity or in the
order of development. If we compare the Cognate Acc. with the use of
Neuter Adjectives and Pronouns, we see that (*e. g.*) ἄριστα βουλεύειν is simpler,
and doubtless earlier in type, than ἀρίστην βουλὴν βουλεύειν, ἅ περ ὑπέστην than
ὑπόσχεσιν ἥν περ ὑπέστην, τὰ ὑπέστημεν than τὸν μῦθον ὑπέστημεν. Again,
δαίνυσθαι γάμον is probably an earlier phrase than the tautologous δαίνυσθαι
δαίτην, τὸν μῦθον ὑποστῆναι than ὑπόσχεσιν ὑποστῆναι, &c. The repetition in
the Noun of the Stem already given in the Verb is a feature of complexity
which itself needs explaining. The Cognate Acc., in short, is only a special
form of the use of the Acc. *as a defining or qualifying word.* Grammarians have
explained other constructions by its help because it is familiar ; but in so
doing they have fallen into the error of deriving the simple from the complex.

137.] Accusatives of the ' part affected.' Many verbs that
are Intransitive or Reflexive in sense take an Acc. restricting

K 2

the force of the Verb to a *part* or *attribute* of the subject : as κάμνει χεῖρα *his hand is weary*, πυρὶ χεῖρας ἔοικε *his hands are as fire*, βλῆτο κνήμην *was wounded in the shin*, ἀλλάων περίειμι νόον *I am beyond others in understanding;* φρένα τέρπετ᾽ ἀκούων *was pleased at heart listening;* οὐ λῆγε μένος *ceased not in his fury;* γένος δ᾽ ἦν ἐκ ποταμοῖο *in descent he was from the river,* γενεὴν ἐῴκει (Il. 14. 474) *was like in descent,* i. e. bore 'a family likeness' ; ἀθανάτῃσι δέμας καὶ εἶδος ἐρίζειν *to rival the immortals in form and feature.* See § 141.

These uses differ from other Accusatives of the *sphere* of an action in the distinctly *concrete* nature of the words employed. The Acc. does not express the notion of the Verb, or an attribute of it, but merely denotes a *thing* by reference to which it is limited or characterised. Thus in κάμνει χεῖρα the Acc. limits the action κάμνει—'feels hand-weariness.' The relation is local or instrumental, though not so expressed. The meaning 'in or with the hand' is conveyed, because it is the only one possible— the only way in which the notion *hand* can qualify the notion *weariness*.

The 'Acc. of the part affected,' or 'Acc. of reference,' is characteristic of Greek : hence it is called *Accusativus Graecus* by the Latin grammarians. It is unknown, or nearly so, in Sanscrit. We cannot infer, however, that it originated with the Greeks, especially as it is found in Zend (Delbrück, *Synt. Forsch.* iv. 33) : but it may have been extended in Greek. The alternative Case is generally the Instrumental : cp. Il. 3. 194 εὐρύτερος ὤμοισιν ἰδὲ στέρνοισιν ἰδέσθαι, but 2. 478 ὄμματα καὶ κεφαλὴν ἴκελος Διΐ. Or the sense may be further defined by a Preposition : πρὸς στῆθος, κατὰ φρένα, &c.

138.] Accusative of Time and Space. The word expressing *duration* of time is put in the Acc., as ἕνα μῆνα μένων *waiting a month*, χεῖμα εὕδει *sleeps through the winter*, τρὶς ἀνάξασθαι γένε᾽ ἀνδρῶν *to reign for three generations of men.*

The Accusative of Space expresses the *extent* of an action, as Il. 23. 529 λείπετο δουρὸς ἐρωήν *was a spear's throw behind.*

These Accusatives are to be compared with the Neuter Adjectives of quantity, as πολύ, ὀλίγον, τυτθόν, τόσον, &c.

139.] Accusative with Nouns. The chief uses are :—

(1) Neut. Adjectives, as μέγ᾽ ἔξοχος *greatly surpassing.*

(2) Cognate Accusative, as Il. 15. 641 ἀμείνων παντοίας ἀρετάς *better in every kind of excellence.* This is rare in Homer.

(3) Acc. of the 'part affected' ; ὄμματα καὶ κεφαλὴν ἴκελος *like in eyes and head,* (cp. χεῖρας ἔοικε), βοὴν ἀγαθός *good in shouting,*

γένος κακὸς καὶ ἄναλκις *a coward by right of descent.* With a Substantive: χεῖράς τ᾽ αἰχμητὴν ἔμεναι.

140.] Accusative of the External Object. Under this head it is unnecessary to do more than notice one or two points :—

(1) The ceremonial words ἀπάρχω, κατάρχομαι, &c. are construed according to the acquired meaning : as τρίχας ἀπάρχειν *to cut off hair as a preliminary,* cp. Od. 3. 445 (with the note in Riddell and Merry's edition). So Il. 24. 710 τὸν . . τιλλέσθην *mourned him by tearing their hair :* and ὅρκια τέμνειν *to make a treaty* (by slaying a victim).

(2) The Verbs εἶπον, αὐδάω, &c. may take an Acc. of the person spoken to : Il. 5. 170 ἔπος τέ μιν ἀντίον ηὔδα : Il. 13. 725 Πουλυδάμας θρασὺν Ἕκτορα εἶπε. Cp. Il. 9. 59., 17. 651, Od. 4. 155. But this construction is rare with the simple Verbs : it is found *passim* with Compounds (προσηύδα, προσέειπε, &c.).

(3) An Acc. may be used of the person *about* whom something is *told, known, thought,* &c.—

(*a*) If a person or a thing is treated as the *thing said, known,* &c. (not merely spoken or known *about*) : as Il. 1. 90 οὐδ᾽ ἦν Ἀγαμέμνονα εἴπῃς *not even if you say Agamemnon* (cp. οὔνομα εἰπεῖν) ; 3. 192 εἴπ᾽ ἄγε μοι καὶ τόνδε *tell me this man too.* So with οἶδα when it means only to know *what a thing is :* as Il. 6. 150 ὄφρ᾽ ἐῢ εἰδῇς ἡμετέρην γενεήν, πολλοὶ δέ μιν ἄνδρες ἴσασιν : and with μέμνημαι, as Il. 9. 527 μέμνημαι τόδε ἔργον ; Il. 23. 361 ὡς μεμνέῳτο δρόμους *that he might remember the courses* (*i.e.* remember how many there were) ; Il. 6. 222 Τυδέα δ᾽ οὐ μέμνημαι (of remembering his existence). The Acc. implies that the person is the whole *fact* remembered. But with a Gen. μέμνημαι means *I remember something about, I bethink myself of* (§ 151, *d*).

(*b*) If the real Object of the Verb is a *fact* expressed by a limiting word or clause : as Il. 2. 81 ψεῦδός κεν φαῖμεν *we should call it false ;* Il. 6. 50 αἴ κεν ἐμὲ ζωὸν πεπύθοιτο *if he heard of me alive* (of my being alive) ; Il. 5. 702 ἐπύθοντο μετὰ Τρώεσσιν Ἄρηα *heard of Ares* (as) *among the Trojans.* Especially with a Participle, as Od. 17. 549 εἴ κ᾽ αὐτὸν γνώω νημερτέα πάντ᾽ ἐνέποντα *if I find him telling* (that he is telling) *nothing but truth* (§ 245, 2). And with a subordinate clause, as Il. 2. 409 ᾔδεε γὰρ κατὰ θυμὸν ἀδελφεὸν ὡς ἐπονεῖτο ; Il. 8. 535 αὔριον ἦν ἀρετὴν διαείσεται εἴ κ᾽ ἐμὸν ἔγχος μείνῃ ἐπερχόμενον *he will know about his valour, whether he will withstand my spear* (*i.e.* whether his valour is such that &c.) ; cp. 13. 275., 18. 601., 20. 311.

(4) The Acc. of the object to which motion is directed (*terminus ad quem*) is common with ἱκνέομαι, ἵκω, ἱκάνω (which always

imply *reaching* a point), but is comparatively rare with other simple Verbs, such as εἶμι, ἔρχομαι, νέομαι, ἄγω, ἡγέομαι. The words so used with these Verbs are mostly Nouns denoting *house* (δῶ, Il. 7. 363, &c.; δόμον, Od. 7. 22, Il. 22. 482; οἶκον, Od. 14. 167), *city* (Od. 6. 114., 15. 82), *native land* (Il. 7. 335., 15. 706): cp. also Il. 1. 322 ἔρχεσθον κλισίην; 6. 37 ξυνάγουσα γεραιὰς νηόν; 21. 40 Λῆμνον ἐπέρασσεν; Od. 4. 478 Αἰγύπτοιο ὕδωρ ἔλθῃς.

Compound Verbs—esp. with the Prepositions εἰς, ἐπί, πρός, ὑπό, παρά—usually take an Acc. of this kind.

There is no reason to infer from these and similar instances that the Accusative is originally the Case of ͺthe *terminus ad quem*. It is natural that a Verb of motion should be defined or qualified by a Noun expressing *place*, and that such a Noun should generally denote the place *to which* the motion is directed. But this is not necessary. The Acc. is used with Verbs denoting *motion from*, as φεύγω, νοσφίζομαι, ὑποείκω (Il. 15. 228); and even with other Verbs of motion it may express the *terminus a quo* if the context suggests it, as ἀνεδύσετο κῦμα *rose from the wave*, ὑπερώϊα κατέβαινε *came down from the upper chambers*.

The uses with Prepositions are treated of in the sections dealing with the several Prepositions (181–218).

141.] Double Accusatives. It is needless to enumerate the different circumstances in which a Verb may be construed with two Accusatives. Many examples will be found among the passages already quoted; and it will be seen that the combination of an Acc. of the External Object with one of the various ' Accusatives of the Internal Object ' is especially frequent. Thus with Verbs of *saying* the Acc. of the *thing* said may be combined with an Acc. of the *person* spoken to: as Il. 5. 170 ἔπος τέ μιν ἀντίον ηὔδα (so 9. 58., 16. 207, Od. 23. 91). Again, with Verbs of *taking away* there may be an Acc. of the *thing* taken and the *person* from whom it is taken: as Il. 8. 108 οὕς ποτ' ἀπ' Αἰνείαν ἑλόμην, Il. 6. 70 ἔπειτα δὲ καὶ τὰ ἔκηλοι νεκροὺς ἀμ πεδίον συλήσετε (cp. 16. 58., 17. 187). So with Verbs of *cleansing*; Il. 16. 667 κελαινεφὲς αἷμα κάθηρον ἐλθὼν ἐκ βελέων Σαρπηδόνα (cp. 18. 345); also Od. 6. 224 χρόα νίζετο δῖος Ὀδυσσεὺς ἅλμην, and (with three Accusatives) Il. 21. 122 οἵ σ' ὠτειλὴν αἷμ' ἀπολιχμήσονται. In such cases the Verb almost seems to be used in different senses—*cleanse* Sarpedon, *cleanse away* the blood, &c.

In some cases the two Accusatives are not to be explained independently, but one is construed with the phrase formed by the Verb in combination with the other. Thus we cannot say ῥέζειν τινά *to do to a person*, but we may have κακὸν ῥέζειν τινά *to do evil to a person* or *thing*: e.g.—

Il. 9. 540 ὃς κακὰ πόλλ' ἔρδεσκεν ἔθων Οἰνῆος ἀλωήν.

647 ὥς μ' ἀσύφηλον ἐν Ἀργείοισιν ἔρεξεν.

The notion 'doing' given by ῥέζω is so vague that an Acc. of
the person would be ambiguous : but the more definite notions
of doing evil, &c. become susceptible of the construction. So
with εἰπεῖν, as Od. 1. 302 ἵνα τίς σε ἐῢ εἴπῃ *may speak well of thee*:
cp. Il. 6. 479.

A similar account is to be given of the 'Accusative of the
Whole and Part,' which is very common in Homer; *e. g.* τὸν
βάλε κνήμην *him he smote on the shin*, σὲ φύγεν ἕρκος ὀδόντων *has
escaped you over the fence of teeth*. The second Acc. has been
sometimes explained as parallel in construction to the first, the
part being added 'epexegetically' or in 'Apposition' to the
whole. But it is impossible to separate τὸν βάλε κνήμην from
βλῆτο κνήμην : in both the Acc. of the part is a *limiting* Accusative. The difference between this and a double Acc. arising from
Apposition appears if we consider that

    Τρῶας δὲ τρόμος αἰνὸς ὑπήλυθε γυῖα ἕκαστον

is equivalent to Τρῶες ἔτρεμον τὰ γυῖα ἕκαστος, where ἕκαστος is
(as before) epexegetic of Τρῶες, but γυῖα is an Acc. qualifying
the Verb.

The Dative.

142.] Comparison of the Case-system of Greek with that of
Sanscrit shows that the Greek Dative does the work of three
Sanscrit Cases, the Dative, the Instrumental, and the Locative.
There is also reason to think that distinct forms for these three
Cases survived down to a comparatively late period in Greek
itself. This is made probable (1) by the traces in Homeric
Greek of Instrumental and Locative Case-*forms*, and (2) by the
readiness with which the *uses* of the Greek Dative (especially
in Homer) can be re-apportioned between the three Cases—the
original or true Dative, and the two others.

143.] **The true Dative** expresses the person *to* or *for* whom
something is done, or who is regarded as chiefly affected or
interested : *e. g.*—

Il. 1. 283 Ἀχιλλῆϊ μεθέμεν χόλον *to put away his anger for* (*in
favour of*) *Achilles ;* cp. Od. 11. 553.

Od. 1. 9 τοῖσιν ἀφείλετο *took away for* (i. e. *from*) *them.*

Il. 21. 360 τί μοι ἔριδος καὶ ἀρωγῆς ; *what is there for me* (*that
concerns me*) *in strife and help ?*

Od. 7. 303 μή μοι τοὔνεκ' ἀμύμονα νείκεε κούρην *chide not for me
on that account the blameless maiden ;* cp. Il. 14. 501.

Od. 9. 42 ὡς μή τίς μοι ἀτεμβόμενος κίοι ἴσης *that for me no one
should go away wronged* (i. e. *that I might see that no one* &c.).

Il. 1. 250 τῷ δύο γενεαὶ ἐφθίατο *he had seen two generations pass.*

Il. 12. 374 ἐπειγομένοισι δ' ἵκοντο *they came for them when hard pressed*, i. e. their coming was (what such a thing is) to hard pressed men. So Il. 14. 108 ἐμοὶ δέ κεν ἀσμένῳ εἴη *it would be for me when welcoming it*, i. e. would be what I welcome : Od. 21. 115 οὔ κέ μοι ἀχνυμένῳ κτλ.

The Dat. with Verbs of *giving, showing, telling* (*a fact*), *praying, helping, pleasing, favouring, being angry*, &c., and the corresponding Adjectives (φίλος, ἐχθρός, &c.), is evidently of this kind.

The so-called *Dativus commodi*, 'Ethical Dative,' &c. need not be separated from the general usage. Note however that—

1. The Dative of the Personal Pronouns is very often used where we should have a Possessive agreeing with a Noun in the Clause; as Il. 1. 104 ὄσσε δέ οἱ πυρὶ ἐΐκτην *his eyes were like fire;* Od. 2. 50 μητέρι μοι μνηστῆρες ἐπέχραον *the suitors have assailed my mother;* so Il. 1. 55, 150, 188, 200, &c.

2. δέχομαι with the Dat. means *to take as a favour:* Il. 15. 87 Θέμιστι δέκτο δέπας *accepted the cup from Themis* (as a compliment); or *to take as an attendant does*, Il. 2. 186., 13. 710., 17. 207, Od. 15. 282. For the Gen. see § 152.

3. ἀκούω with the Dat. means *to hear favourably;* Il. 16. 515 ἀκούειν ἀνέρι κηδομένῳ; and so κλῦθί μοι in prayers (Il. 5. 115, Od. 2. 262). See § 151, *d.*

4. The Dat. with Verbs meaning *to give commands* (κελεύω, σημαίνω, &c.), and *to lead the way* (ἄρχω, ἡγέομαι, ἡγεμονεύω) is apparently the true Dat. But this does not apply to Verbs meaning *to have power, to be king* (as κρατέω, ἀνάσσω): e.g. ἀνασσέμεν Ἀργείοισι probably means *to be king among the Argives* (Loc.). See § 145 (7, *a*).

5. The ' Dat. of the Agent' with Passive Verbs seems to be a special application of the true Dat.; cp. Il. 13. 168 ὅ οἱ κλισίηφι λέλειπτο *which for 'him was* (=*which he had*) *left in the tent*, ἔχεθ' Ἕκτορι *was had as wife by Hector*. So Τρωσὶν δαμναμένους, Πηλείωνι δαμείς, &c. because the victory is *gained* by the victor ; and so in Attic, ἠθροίσθη Κύρῳ τὸ Ἑλληνικόν ' *Cyrus got his Greek force collected*.' The restriction to Past Tenses is intelligible, because the *past fact* is thought of as a kind of *possession* or advantage (cp. the English auxiliary *have* of past events). This view is strongly supported by the Latin Dat. of the Agent, which is not common except with Verbals and Past Participles (Roby, § 1146). Evidently *nobis facienda*=' things *for* us to do,' *nobis facta*=' things we *have got* done.'

The true Dat. of Nouns denoting *things* is rare in Greek (perhaps only used when the thing is regarded as an agent, or stands for a person, as Πριάμοιο βίη for Πρίαμος).

In this respect Latin offers a marked contrast ; cp. the various uses, especially of abstract Substantives, explained by Mr. Roby under the headings 'indirect object' (1143, *n.* 11), 'work contemplated' (1156), 'predicative dative' (1158 ff.). The source of the difference evidently is that the Dat. is not liable, as in Greek, to be confounded with the Loc. and Instrum. It will be seen however that the Greek Infinitive is in fact the Dat. of an abstract Substantive.

144.] The Instrumental Dative. The so-called Instrumental Case appears to have been employed to express whatever accompanies or shares in an action :—not only the instrument or cause, but any attendant object or circumstance. Hence it covers the ground of the Datives of 'circumstance,' 'manner,' &c.

The Dat. of *circumstance* &c. is common with abstract or semiabstract words : as ἠχῇ *with noise* (κλαγγῇ, ἀλαλητῷ, ἐνοπῇ, &c.) ; σιγῇ, σιωπῇ ; αἰδοῖ *with reverence* (Od. 8. 172) ; ἀνάγκη, βίῃ, σπουδῇ : κακῇ αἴσῃ *with evil fortune ; φυγῇ* (ἵκοντο) *in flight ;* κερδοσύνη *in his cunning ; γενεῇ by descent.*

In Homer it often expresses the *reason* or *occasion* (for which διά with the Acc. is regular in later Greek) : Od. 3. 363 φιλότητι ἕπονται *accompany out of friendship* (*propter amorem*) ; Od. 9. 19 ὃς πᾶσι δόλοισιν ἀνθρώποισι μέλω *who am regarded by men for my craft* (cp. 13. 299) ; Il. 16. 628 ὀνειδείοις ἐπέεσσι χωρήσουσι *will give way for reviling words ;* Od. 14. 206 τίετο . . ὄλβῳ τε πλούτῳ τε καὶ υἱάσι ; Od. 17. 423 οἷσίν τ' εὖ ζώουσι καὶ ἀφνειοὶ καλέονται *things because of which men live well and are called opulent.* So of an almost personal agent, Od. 14. 299 ἡ δ' ἔθεεν Βορέῃ ἀνέμῳ *the ship coursed on with* (driven by) *the North wind.*

The 'comitative' or 'sociative' sense is chiefly found in the Plural, which denotes *attendants, surroundings, adjuncts,* &c.; Il. 18. 506 τοῖσιν ἔπειτ' ἤϊσσον *with these* (the sceptres) *they started up ;* Od. 4. 8 ἵπποισι καὶ ἅρμασι πέμπε *sent with horses and chariots* (cp. 4. 533) ; Od. 11. 161 νηΐ τε καὶ ἑτάροισι *with a ship and comrades ;* Il. 12. 28 κύμασι πέμπε *let go with the waves ;* Il. 2. 818 μεμαότες ἐγχείῃσι *ardent with their spears ;* Il. 6. 243 ξεστῆς αἰθούσῃσι τετυγμένον *built with smooth porticoes* (cp. Od. 9. 185, &c.) : Il. 2. 148 ἐπί τ' ἠμύει ἀσταχύεσσι *bends forward with the ears* (of a field of corn) : Il. 6. 513 τεύχεσι παμφαίνων *glittering with his armour ;* similarly 11. 100 στήθεσι παμφαίνοντας *shining with* (*naked*) *breasts.* For the corresponding Sing. cp. Od. 10. 140 νηΐ κατηγαγόμεσθα ; Od. 9. 68 ἐπῶρσ' ἄνεμον Βορέην λαίλαπι θεσπεσίῃ ; Od. 12. 241 ὑπένερθε δὲ γαῖα φάνεσκε ψάμμῳ κυανέη *the ground showed beneath with its dark sand ;* Il. 15. 282 ἐπιστάμενος ἄκοντι.

This Dative is idiomatically used with αὐτός : as Il. 8. 24 αὐτῇ κεν γαίῃ ἐρύσαιμ' αὐτῇ δὲ θαλάσσῃ *with the earth and sea as well* (without their losing hold) : Od. 14. 77 θέρμ' αὐτοῖς ὀβελοῖσι *hot with the spits as they were* *.

The Dative with Verbs meaning *to be with, to follow, to join, to agree with, to be like*, &c., and again with the Prepositions σύν and ἅμα, and the various Pronouns and Adjectives meaning *the same, equal, like*, &c., is generally Instrumental.

The Dat. with Verbs meaning to *fight, strive*, &c. may be the Instrumental or (more probably) the true Dat. Words meaning *to trust* &c. probably take an Instrumental Dat. of the *ground* of trust, a true Dat. of the *person* trusted or obeyed : cp. the Lat. construction of *confidere* with a Dat. or Abl.

With Verbs meaning *to be pleased* the Dat. is doubtless Instrumental : as Il. 21. 45 ἐτέρπετο οἷσι φίλοισι *had pleasure with his friends* (so Od. 14. 245). This is still more clear in Il. 5. 682 χάρη δ' ἄρα οἱ προσιόντι and Il. 23. 556 χαίρων 'Αντιλόχῳ ὅτι κτλ. ' rejoiced at the *fact* (of his coming, &c.).'

The Instrum. is used in Sanscrit of the space *over which* action extends. The nearest approach to this in Greek is the Dat. of the *way by which :* cp. the Adverbs ᾗ, τῇ, τῇδε, πῇ, ὅπῃ, πάντῃ. But see § 158, *note*.

The Dat. is probably Instrumental (not Locative) in Od. 1. 197 κατερύκεται εὐρέϊ πόντῳ (*by*, not *on*, the sea). Also with δέχομαι, &c., as Il. 6. 136 ὑπεδέξατο κόλπῳ, Od. 16. 70 ὑποδέξομαι οἴκῳ. In later Greek δέχομαι is construed with οἴκῳ, πόλει, &c. without a Preposition.

Note the occasional use of the Instrumental Dat. with Verbs of *buying*, as Il. 7. 475 οἰνίζοντο ἄλλοι μὲν χαλκῷ κτλ., Od. 15. 483 πρίατο κτεάτεσσιν ἑοῖσιν (cp. Il. 4. 161 σύν τε μεγάλῳ ἀπέτισαν) : with Verbs of *abounding*, Il. 17. 56 βρύει ἄνθεϊ λευκῷ (§ 151, *e*) :

---

* Delbrück (*Synt. Forsch.* iv. p. 58) notices the difficulty of finding a special explanation of the ' sociative ' use of the Dat. in combination with αὐτός. It may help towards such an explanation to observe that the use of a Case-form in a particular sense not unfrequently depends upon the presence of a qualifying word in agreement with it. *E. g.*—

ἐμοὶ βουλομένῳ ἐστί it is *for me what I desire.*
τοίχου τοῦ ἑτέρου *by the wall on the other side.*
μέσσου δουρὸς ἑλών *taking the spear by the middle.*
εἰ τεθνεῶτος ἀκούσαι *if he were to hear of his being dead.*
ἤχθετο Τρωσὶν δαμναμένους *he was vexed at their being subdued by Trojans.*

In each of these instances the qualifying word indicates the sense in which the Case is used, and so makes the use possible. The 'ethical Dat.' is suggested by βουλομένῳ, the Gen. of *place* by ἑτέρου, the Gen. of *part* by μέσσου, the *fact about* the person by τεθνεῶτος, the *cause* of feeling by δαμναμένους. Now, in such a phrase as αὐτοῖς ὀβελοῖσι *spits and all*, the force of αὐτός is ' without change,' ' as before,' and so the phrase means *with the meat sticking to the spits as before* (cp. αὔτως, αὐτοῦ, αὖθι). Thus the sociative sense is emphasised by the addition of αὐτοῖς. Without such an addition there would generally be nothing to decide between the different possible meanings of the Dative, and consequently a Preposition (σύν or ἅμα) would be needed.

also with a Verb of 'cognate' meaning, as θάνον οἰκτίστῳ θανάτῳ (Od. 11. 412), ῥέον ὕδατι (Od. 5. 70).

145.] The Locatival Dative. The Dative without a Preposition denoting the *place* of an action is much commoner in Homer than in later Greek, though already restricted to a comparatively narrow range. It is used—

(1) Of towns and countries: Ἰλίῳ εἰσί are in *Ilios*, Φρυγίῃ ναίεσκε dwelt in *Phrygia*: so Οὐλύμπῳ, Λακεδαίμονι, Δήλῳ. Σχερίῃ, Κυθήροισι, Θήβῃ, Κρήτῃ, Ἄργεϊ, Ἑλλάδι, &c. So too Ἄϊδι.

(2) Of the great divisions of the world, the chief spheres of action, &c., as αἰθέρι, οὐρανῷ, οὔρεσι, ἀγρῷ *afield*, δόμῳ *in the house*, νομῷ *at pasture*, πόντῳ *out at sea*, αἰγιαλῷ *on the shore*, χέρσῳ *on dry land* (Il. 4. 424–5), οὔδει *on the ground*, πεδίῳ, χθονί; χορῷ *at the dance*, μάχῃ, βουλῇ, ἀγορῇ, τραπέζῃ *at table* (Od. 21. 35), σέλαι πυρός *in the fire light*.

But the Dat. in ἔριδι ξυνέηκε μάχεσθαι (Il. 1. 8), ὑσμῖνι μάχεσθαι (Il. 2. 863), &c. is one of *manner* (Instr.), rather than of place.

(3) Of the *parts* of a thing, especially of the body; ὤμῳ and ὤμοισι, κεφαλῇ, χροΐ; καρδίῃ, φρεσί, θυμῷ; ἀκροτάτῃ κορυφῇ, ἐσχατίῃ πολέμοιο, μύχῳ Ἄργεος (θαλάμοιο, &c.), μέσῳ ἕρκεϊ, πρώτῃσι πύλῃσι, γουνῷ ἀλωῆς, βένθεσι λίμνης, τάρφεσιν ὕλης, &c.

The Dat. of the part *with* which a person does something may be Instrumental; as χερσὶ μαχήσομαι, κεφαλῇ κατανεύσομαι, ἑκὼν ἀέκοντί γε θυμῷ. But the Locative mode of expression is the prevailing one; cp. ἐν χείρεσσι λάβ' ἡνία, ἐν ὀφθαλμοῖσιν ἰδέσθαι, ἔγνω ᾗσιν ἐνὶ φρεσί, ἐν θυμῷ μεμαῶτες, &c. Hence the common use of χειρί, χερσί, &c. with ἔχω, αἱρέω, λαμβάνω, and the use of θυμῷ, φρεσί, &c. with Verbs of *knowing, thinking, feeling*, are doubtless Locatival.

(4) With some Verbs that imply locality, ναίω, τίθημι, κεῖμαι, ἧμαι (Od. 20. 22 πτυχὶ Οὐλύμποιο ἥμενος); esp. κλίνω, as Il. 11. 371 στήλῃ κεκλιμένος, and (in the derived sense) Il. 5. 709 λίμνῃ κεκλιμένος.

(5) Of *time*: ἤματι τῷ ὅτε κτλ. *on the day when &c.*, θέρεϊ *in summer*, ὥρῃ χειμερίνῃ *in the season of winter*, &c.

(6) After a Verb of motion (where we expect εἰς or πρός with the Acc.): as Il. 5. 82 πεδίῳ πέσε *fell on the plain;* Il. 7. 187 κυνέῃ βάλε *threw into the helmet;* Il. 3. 10 εὖτ' ὄρεος κορυφῇσι Νότος κατέχευεν ὀμίχλην *has spread a mist over the tops of the mountains;* προκαλέσσατο χάρμῃ *called out (to meet) in combat*. This idiom helps to show that the use of the Accusative for the *terminus ad quem* of motion does not represent the original force of that Case.

The Dat. after the Prepositions ἐν, ἐπί, παρά, μετά, ὑπό, ἀνά, περί, ἀμφί, and the Verbs compounded with them, is generally Locatival. It is used (like the simple Dat.) after Verbs of motion: see §§ 194, 198, 202, 206.

The sense may admit or require a true Dat.: cp. Il. 1. 174 πάρ' ἐμοί γε καὶ ἄλλοι *others are at hand with me* (Loc.), or *I have others at my command* (true Dat.). So Il. 7. 73 ὑμῖν ἐν γὰρ ἔασι may mean *there are among you* (Loc.), or *you have* (true Dat.) *among you*. Cp. Lat. *inesse alicui* or *in aliquo*.

(7) The Locatival Dat. of *persons* is chiefly found in the Plural :—

(*a*) with **κρατέω, ἀνάσσω, βασιλεύω**: Il. 2. 669 θεοῖσι καὶ ἀνθρώ-ποισιν ἀνάσσει *is king among gods and men;* Od. 1. 71 ὅου κράτος ἐστὶ μέγιστον πᾶσιν Κυκλώπεσσι; Il. 13. 217 ὃς πάσῃ Πλευρῶνι καὶ αἰπεινῇ Καλυδῶνι Αἰτωλοῖσιν ἄνασσε. Cp. the equivalent constructions with Prepositions, as Il. 1. 252 μετὰ δὲ τριτάτοισιν ἄνασσε, Od. 7. 62 ὃς ἐν Φαίηξιν ἄνασσε, and the compound ἐμβασιλεύω. This group of uses is almost confined to Homer.

(*b*) in phrases introducing a speech, as τοῖσι δ' ἀνέστη, τοῖσι δὲ μύθων ἦρχε, and the like; cp. Il. 19. 175 ἐν Ἀργείοισιν ἀναστάς, 9. 528 ἐν δ' ὑμῖν ἐρέω, Od. 10. 188 μετὰ πᾶσιν ἔειπον, 16. 378 ἐρέει δ' ἐν πᾶσιν ἀναστάς.

(*c*) meaning 'in the sight of,' 'in the opinion of,' &c. as Il. 2. 285 πᾶσιν ἐλέγχιστον θέμεναι μερόπεσσι βροτοῖσι: 11. 58 ὃς Τρωσὶ θεὸς ὣς τίετο δήμῳ. Cp. Il. 23. 703 ἐνὶ σφίσι τῖον. So in Sanscrit the Loc. is used of the person *with* or *before* whom conduct is judged : ' may we be guiltless before Varuṇa ' (Delbrück, *A. S.* p. 118).

(*d*) occasionally with Adjectives implying eminence &c., as Il. 6. 477 ἀριπρεπέα Τρώεσσι *distinguished among the Trojans*, Od. 15. 227 Πυλίοισι μέγ' ἔξοχα δώματα ναίων.

The Genitive.

146.] The Greek Genitive, as appears at once by comparison with Latin or Sanscrit, stands for the original or ' true ' Genitive, and also for the Ablative. The uses of the Gen. may therefore be divided (theoretically at least) between these two Cases. The distinction however is more difficult than in the case of the Dative; partly, perhaps, because the Case-forms of the Ablative were earlier lost than those of the Locative and Instrumental, but also from the peculiar syntactical character of the Genitive.

The Ablative (like the cases already treated of) belongs originally to the second group of constructions distinguished in § 131, *i. e.* it is construed with the predicate given by a *Verb*. The Genitive is originally of the third group ; and properly qualifies a *Noun*. Hence the Ablative and Genitive uses are generally distinguished partly in meaning, partly in grammatical structure. But they are not always distinguished by the structure, since (1) the Ablative (like the Acc. and Dat.) *may* be construed with an Adjective, and (2) the true Gen. may be predicative (like an Adj.), and thus apparently construed with a Verb.   To give a single example : θεῶν γόνος ἐστί might be (theoretically) = *he is offspring from-gods* (Abl.), and on the other hand θεῶν γέγονε may be = *he is offspring of-gods* (Gen., see § 148).

147.] The Genitive with Nouns.   The manner in which a Genitive serves to define or qualify the 'governing' Noun may be very various.   *E. g.* Τρώων χόλος may mean *anger of* (i. e. *felt by*) *the Trojans*, or (as in Il. 6. 335) *anger at the Trojans*, or *anger on account of the Trojans* (as in Il. 15. 138 χόλον υἱὸς ἑῆος means *anger about the death of his son*).   Compare also—

ἕρκος πολέμοιο *a bulwark in* (or *against*) *war.*
ἕρκος ὀδόντων *the fence (made) of teeth.*
τέρας μερόπων ἀνθρώπων *a sign to men.*
λάθρῃ Λαομέδοντος *with secrecy from Laomedon.*
βίῃ ἀέκοντος *with force used to one unwilling.*
κύματα παντοίων ἀνέμων *the waves raised by all winds.*
ὄμφαλοι κασσιτεροῖο *bosses made of tin.*
Ἰλίου πτολίεθρον *the town of Ilios.*
Ὀϊλῆος ταχὺς Αἴας *swift Ajax son of Oileus.*
δαιμόνιε ξείνων *unaccountable stranger !*
νομὸς ὕλης *pasture ground in the wood.*
νόστος γαίης Φαιήκων *return to the land of the Phaeacians.*
ὑπόψιος ἄλλων *suspected by others.*
ἐπίστροφος ἀνθρώπων *going about among men.*
ἀφνειὸς βιότοιο *rich in substance.*
ἰθὺς Διομήδεος *straight for Diomede.*

The different uses of the Genitive often answer to the different meanings given by the Suffixes which serve to form Adjectives from Nouns (§ 117).   Compare, for instance, Il. 2. 54 Νεστορέῃ παρὰ νηὶ Πυλοιγενέος βασιλῆος *by the ship of Nestor the Pylian king ;* Il. 6. 180 θεῖον γένος οὐδ' ἀνθρώπων *the offspring of gods, not of men ;* τόξον αἰγός (Il. 4. 105) *a bow of goat's horn,* but ἀσκὸς αἴγειος *a bag of goatskin ;* Ὀϊλῆος ταχὺς Αἴας and Αἴας Ὀϊλιάδης ; Τελαμώνιος υἱός *the son of Telamon ;* and so in the Pronouns, ἐμεῖο ποθή (Il. 6. 362), but σῇ ποθῇ (Il. 19. 321).

These uses have been classified as Objective and Subjective, Possessive, Partitive, Material, &c.   In many cases however the variety of relations expressed by the Gen. eludes this kind of analysis.   Such classifications, moreover, are apt to lead us into the fallacy of thinking that relations which are distinct to us, because expressed by different language, were distinctly conceived by those who expressed them all in the same way ;—the fallacy, in short, of supposing the distinctions of thought to be prior to the language which embodies them.

The relation of the Genitive to the governing Noun is in many ways analogous to the relation of the Accusative to the Verb, and also to that which subsists between the first part of a Compound Noun and the second. In each of these cases the relation is that of a defining or qualifying word to the notion defined or qualified, and it is one which may be of various kinds, as may be suggested by particular combinations of meaning.

Notice, as especially frequent in Homer—

(1) the use of a Gen. after Nouns meaning *grief, anger*, &c., to express the *object* or *cause* of the feeling : as ἄχος ἡνιόχοιο *grief for the chariot-driver* (Il. 8. 124, 316, &c.), ἄχος σέθεν (Il. 4. 169); ὀδύνη Ἡρακλῆος (Il. 15. 25); πένθος παιδὸς ἀποφθιμένοιο (Il. 18. 88); κήδε᾽ ἐμῶν ἑτάρων (Il. 22. 272, Od. 11. 382); and so in the much-disputed phrase Ἑλένης ὁρμήματά τε στοναχάς τε (Il. 2. 356, 590), which can only mean *efforts and groans about Helen.*

(2) the 'partitive' use after τίς (Interrog.) and τις (Indef.), often with several words interposed : as Il. 1. 8 τίς τ᾽ ἄρ σφωε θεῶν κτλ.; Il. 1. 88 οὔ τις ἐμεῦ ζῶντος . . χεῖρας ἐποίσει συμπάντων Δαναῶν *no one shall . . . of all the Greeks.*

The partitive Gen. is also seen in the Homeric phrases δῖα θεάων *bright one among goddesses*, δῖα γυναικῶν, δαιμόνιε ξείνων, πάντων ἀριδείκετον ἀνδρῶν (Il. 14. 320): where the governing word implies some kind of distinction or eminence. So when there is a contrast, as—

Il. 11. 761 πάντες δ᾽ εὐχετόωντο θεῶν Διὶ Νέστορί τ᾽ ἀνδρῶν.

148.] **Genitive in the Predicate.** Among the various uses of the Gen. in construction with a Verb the first to be noticed are those in which the Case evidently retains its attributive or adjectival character. This use is rare in Homer : examples are,— αἵματός εἰς ἀγαθοῖο *thou art of good blood*, ἐποίησεν σάκος αἰόλον ἑπταβόειον ταύρων ζατρεφέων *made a shield seven hides thick, of* (*hides of*) *goodly bulls.* In classifying the Greek uses of the Gen. the chief object is to separate constructions of this kind (in which the Case is ultimately the adjectival or 'true' Gen.) from those in which it represents an Ablative, and therefore is essentially akin to the Adverbs.

---

* Prof. Max Müller (*Lectures*, I, p. 103) shows how the Genitive Ending -οιο (for -ο-σιο) may be explained as a Suffix of the same kind as those which form Adjectives from Nouns. If his hypothesis is admitted, the Genitive is simply 'an Adjective without Gender,' in respect of *form* as well as *use*. And even if the identification on which he chiefly relies (of the Case-ending -*sya* and Suffix -*tya* with the Pronoun *syas, syâ, tyad*) should be thought open to question, there can be little doubt that the Case is originally 'adnominal' or adjectival in character.

This use of the Gen. is singularly common in Latin : see Roby, § 1282. The reason for this difference between Greek and Latin evidently is that in Latin the Gen. is not confounded with the Abl. The same explanation has been given of the free use which Latin makes of the predicative Dative (§ 143, *note*).

149.] Genitive of Place. A Gen. expresses a vague local relation (*within, in the sphere of*, &c.), in the following uses :—

(1) After a negative—
Il. 17. 372 νέφος δ᾽ οὐ φαίνετο πάσης γαίης οὔτ᾽ ὀρέων.
Od. 3. 251 ἢ οὐκ Ἄργεος ἦεν Ἀχαιϊκοῦ. Cp. 14. 98., 21. 109.

(2) When two *sides* or *alternative* places are contrasted—
Il. 9. 219 αὐτὸς δ᾽ ἀντίον ἷζεν Ὀδυσσῆος θείοιο
τοίχου τοῦ ἑτέροιο. Cp. 24. 598.
Od. 1. 23 Αἰθίοπας, τοὶ διχθὰ δεδαίαται, ἔσχατοι ἀνδρῶν,
οἱ μὲν δυσομένου Ὑπερίονος, οἱ δ᾽ ἀνιόντος,
and so perhaps Od. 12. 27 ἢ ἁλὸς ἢ ἐπὶ γῆς, and Od. 4. 678 αὐλῆς
ἐκτὸς ἐών *in the court outside* (cp. 9. 239).

(3) With Verbs of motion, to express the space *within* which the motion takes place, as Il. 2. 785 διέπρησσον πεδίοιο *made their way over the plain* : so ἰὼν πολέος πεδίοιο, ἵππω ἀτυζομένω πεδίοιο, πεδίοιο διώκειν, κονίοντες πεδίοιο, &c. ; 10. 353 ἑλκέμεναι νειοῖο βαθείης πηκτὸν ἄροτρον : 24. 264 ἵνα πρήσσωμεν ὁδοῖο, cp. Od. 2. 404., 3. 476. This use of the Gen. is almost confined to *set phrases ;* accordingly it is only found with the Gen. in -οιο (the archaic form).

The difference of meaning between this Genitive and the Accusative of Space (§ 138) seems to be that the Acc. *measures* the action of the Verb, whereas the Gen. only gives a local relation in which the action stands. When an Acc. of quantity and a Gen. are both used, the Acc. often seems to govern the Gen. ; e. g. ὁμίλου πολλὸν ἐπελθών *advancing far in the throng,* παρεξελθεῖν πεδίοιο τυτθόν *to go a short space of plain beyond.* So with Adverbs : ἔνθα καὶ ἔνθ᾽ ἴθυσε μάχη πεδίοιο : ἄδην ἐλάσαι πολέμοιο ; and with a negative : οὐκ Ἄργεος ἦεν=*he was nowhere in Argos.* Thus the Gen. has a partitive character.

150.] Genitive of Time. This Gen. expresses a period of time to which the action belongs, without implying anything as to its duration ; e. g.—
Od. 14. 161 τοῦδ᾽ αὐτοῦ λυκάβαντος ἐλεύσεται *he will come* (*sometime in*) *this very year.* So Il. 5. 523 νηνεμίης *in calm weather ;* 8. 470 ἠοῦς *in the morning ;* 11. 691 τῶν προτέρων ἐτέων *in former years ;* 22. 27 ὀπώρης εἶσι *goes in autumn.*

It appears from the corresponding construction in Sanscr. and

Zend that this is the true Genitive (Delbrück, *Synt. Forsch.* iv. p. 45).

For the ' Gen. Absolute '—which is akin to the Gen. of *time*— see § 246.

151.] The quasi-partitive Genitive. Under this term we may include a number of constructions in which the Gen. is used (in preference to some other Case) because the action of the Verb does not affect the person or thing in a sufficiently direct and unqualified way : *e.g.* in λωτοῖο φαγών *eating of the lotus* (not *eating up the lotus*) ; πτέρυγος λάβε *took by the wing* (not *took the wing*) ; λούεσθαι ποταμοῖο *to bathe in a river* (but λούειν ὕδατι *to bathe with water*).*

The chief uses to which this view may be applied are :—

(*a*) With Verbs that imply *fastening to, holding by*, &c. : Il. 1. 197 ξανθῆς δὲ κόμης ἕλε Πηλείωνα *took Achilles by the hair.*

So χειρὸς ἑλών *taking by the hand* (but δεξιτερὴν ἕλε χεῖρα *took the right hand*), ποδὸς ἕλκε *dragged by the foot*, δῆσεν ποδός *fastened by the foot*, κόνιος δεδραγμένος *clutching the dust*, λισσέσκετο γούνων *entreated by seizing the knees*, ἐρείσατο γαίης *propped himself against the earth* (*i. e.* his hand touching it), μέσσου δουρὸς ἑλών *taking his spear by the middle ;* and with a metaphorical sense, περίσχεο παιδός *take charge of thy child*, σέο ἕξεται *will depend upon thee.*

---

* Delbrück (*Synt. Forsch.* iv. p. 39) aptly quotes from J. Grimm the saying that ' the Accusative shows the fullest, most decided mastering of an object by the notion contained in the Verb of the sentence. Less " objectifying" is contained in the Gen. ; the active force is tried and brought into play by it, not exhausted.' The contrast, however, is to be traced not merely between the Gen. and the Acc., but generally between the Gen. and all the Cases which are used primarily with Verbs. Thus the Gen. of Space and Time may be compared with the Locative, the Gen. of Material with the Instrumental ; and perhaps other Genitives with the Abl. (§ 151, *e, note*, § 153, *note*).

It is important to observe here (especially since we have adopted the term ' quasi-Partitive ' for these uses) that the partitive relation is not the only one which may lie at the root of the construction. The Gen. expresses any relation, however indefinite, in which one Noun may stand to another.

1. The Gen. of Place noticed in § 149 (2) is not partitive ; for δυσομένου Ὑπερίονος (*e. g.*) does not mean *within sunset*, but *on the side of, belonging to*, sunset. The Gen. is like the Latin ' novarum rerum esse ' *to be on the side of change ;* cp. Liv. 22. 50 ad Cannas fugientem consulem vix septuaginta secuti sunt, alterius morientis prope totus exercitus fuit.

2. The Gen. of Time is similar. Such a Gen. as ἠοῦς *in the morning* is to be compared with the use of the Adj. in ἑσπέριοι ἀφίκοντο *they came in the evening*, lit. *belonging to the evening, as men of the evening.* It differs from the Dat. of Time negatively, in the want of a distinct Locative meaning.

3. The Gen. of the *person* with Verbs of *hearing*, &c. (§ 151, *d*) is clearly not partitive. The *thing* heard is not *part* of, but something *belonging to*, the person. But the Gen. of the *sound* heard may be partitive ; and so is doubtless the Gen. of *material*, § 151, *e*.

As to the Gen. of *price*, see § 153. If a true Gen., it is not partitive.

The Gen. in this group of uses is probably akin to the Gen. of the *space within which* action takes place, § 149. Compare, for example, ἐρείσατο γαίης with ἷζε τοίχου τοῦ ἐτέρου,—passages given under the same head by Kühner (§ 418, 8, *a*). Or it may be Ablatival: cp. πρύμνηθεν λάβε, § 159.

(*b*) With Verbs meaning *to touch, to hit* (an object aimed at), *to reach* (a person), *to put in* or *on* (a chariot, ship, wall, &c.), with the derivative meanings, *to attain to, get a place or share in*, &c.; as ἀλλήλων ἐφίκοντο *got at each other* ; τύχε γάρ ῥ' ἀμάθοιο βαθείης *he happened to fall in deep sand* ; so νεκροὺς πυρκαϊῆς ἐπενήνεον *heaped the corpses on the funeral pile*; so metaphorically, κακῶν ἐπιβασκέμεν *to bring into mischief*; ἀντίααν πολέμοιο *to join in war*, ἀντιόων ἐκατόμβης (but Il. 1. 31 ἐμὸν λέχος ἀντιόωσαν because λέχος is the *whole* object, cp. § 136, 1).

(*c*) With Verbs meaning *to aim at, strive after, desire, care for, complain of, grieve for, be angry about*, &c.; as Αἴαντος ἀκόντισε *threw a dart at Ajax*, οὗ παιδὸς ὀρέξατο *held out his arms for his child*, σκοπέλων ἐπιμαίεο *feel for the rocks* (but ἐπεμαίετο ἵππους *touched up the horses*), ἐπειγόμενος Ἄρηος *hasting to* (*eager for*) *battle*, τῶν οὔ τι μετατρέπῃ οὐδ' ἀλεγίζεις *these you do not regard or heed*, Κύκλωπος κεχόλωται *is enraged on behalf of the Cyclops* ; and many similar instances.

Kühner (§ 416, *Anm.* 9) quotes Il. 5. 582 χερμαδίῳ ἀγκῶνα τυχὼν μέσον as a use of τυγχάνω with the Acc. But it is possible to construe ἀγκῶνα with βάλε in the earlier part of the sentence.

(*d*) With Verbs meaning *to hear, perceive, know of, remember*, and the like; the Gen. expressing—

(1) the *person from* whom sound comes ;

(2) the *person about* whom something is heard, known, &c.

(3) the *sound* heard (but the Acc. is more usual).

The particular thing heard or known is often indicated by a Participle agreeing with the Genitive : *e.g.*—

Il. 1. 257 εἰ σφῶϊν τάδε πάντα πυθοίατο μαρναμένοιϊν (= *if they heard of all this fighting on your part*).

Il. 4. 357 ὡς γνῶ χωομένοιο (= ὡς ἔγνω αὐτοῦ ὅτι ἐχώετο).

Od. 2. 220 εἰ δέ κε τεθνηῶτος ἀκούσω : so 4. 728, &c.

The Verb οἶδα, when it means *to know about, to be skilled in*, takes a Gen., as Il. 11. 657 οὐδέ τι οἶδε πένθεος *knows nothing of the sorrow*. So Od. 21. 506 φόρμιγγος ἐπιστάμενος καὶ ἀοιδῆς : Il. 16. 811 διδασκόμενος πολέμοιο.

So μέμνημαι takes a Gen. when it means *I bethink myself of, am affected by the memory* (Il. 2. 686, Od. 15. 23): see § 140, 4, *a*. Cp. Lat. *memini* with the Gen. or Acc., perhaps with a similar difference of meaning (Roby, § 1332).

L

(e) The Gen. of *material,* &c. The construction so termed is found with Verbs that imply the use of a material (especially one of indefinite quantity), a stock drawn upon, &c. *E. g.*—

Il. 1. 470 κοῦροι μὲν κρητῆρας ἐπεστέψαντο ποτοῖο *filled up the cups to the brim with liquor ;* 9. 214 πάσσε δ' ἁλός *sprinkled with salt.* So πυρός in the phrases πρῆσαι πυρός *to burn with fire,* πυρὸς μειλισσέμεν *to propitiate (the dead) with fire.*

Il. 18. 574 χρυσοῖο τετεύχατο *were made of gold.*

Od. 3. 408 ἀποστίλβοντες ἀλείφατος *shining with fat.*

And with a distinctly *partitive* force :—

Od. 1. 140 χαριζομένη παρεόντων *favouring him (with good things) from her store ;* 9. 102 λωτοῖο φαγών *eating of the lotus ;* and so with γεύω *to give a taste of.*

Il. 5. 268 τῆς γενεῆς ἔκλεψε *stole (a strain) from the brood.*

9. 580 πεδίοιο ταμέσθαι *to cut off (a τέμενος) from the plain.*

14. 121 Ἀδρήστοιο δ' ἔγημε θυγατρῶν *married (one) from the daughters of Adrastus* (so Od. 9. 225., 12. 64., 15. 98).

The Gen. with Verbs meaning *to stint, grudge, spare* is probably of the same nature *(to stint* being=*to give little).*

The Genitives in λούεσθαι ποταμοῖο *to bathe in a river,* χεῖρας νιψάμενος πολιῆς ἁλός *washing his hands in the sea,* &c. are intermediate between this group and the Genitives of Space (§ 149).

A Gen. of the *person* may be used with Verbs meaning *to gain profit from ; e. g.* Il. 1. 410 ἵνα πάντες ἐπαύρωνται βασιλῆος : 16. 31 τί σευ ἄλλος ὀνήσεται ; Od. 11. 452 υἷος ἐνιπλησθῆναι (υἷος=*the company of his son*): also with πειράομαι *to try* (Od. 8. 23); cp. the Gen. with γεύω.

Note also the elliptical expression, Il. 21. 360 τί μοι ἔριδος καὶ ἀρωγῆς *what (share) have I in combat and aid ?*

Most of these Genitives are clearly 'partitive,' and all of them can be explained as 'true' Genitives. There is a similar use of the Gen. in Sanscrit with Verbs meaning *to enjoy,* &c. (Delbrück, *A. S.* § 109). Some however may be Ablatives. In particular, the Gen. of *material* with τεύχω, ποιέω, &c. is so regarded by Delbrück *(Synt. Forsch.* iv. p. 48) on the ground of the Sanscrit use. It may be that in certain cases the original usage allowed either Gen. or Abl., according to the shade of meaning to be expressed; just as with Verbs of *filling* Latin employs the Gen. or the Abl.

(ƒ) With Verbs meaning *to rule, be master ;* viz.—

ἀνάσσω, Gen. of the *place* or *thing,* as Il. 1. 38 Τενέδοιό τε ἶφι ἀνάσσεις : Od. 24. 30 τιμῆς ἧς περ ἄνασσες : of the *people,* only Il. 10. 32, Od. 11. 376. The Gen. of the *thing* and Dat. of the *people* combined, Il. 20. 180 Τρώεσσιν ἀνάξειν τιμῆς τῆς Πριάμου.

βασιλεύω : Od. 1. 401., 11. 285.

κρατέω : Il. 1. 79 Ἀργείων κρατέει *has power over the Argives.*

σημαίνω : Il. 14. 85 στρατοῦ ἄλλου σημαίνειν : so ἡγοῦμαι, &c.
θεμιστεύω : Od. 9. 114 θεμιστεύει δὲ ἕκαστος παίδων ἠδ' ἀλόχων.
It is probable, from the analogy of Sanscrit, that this is the
true Gen.; but the original force of the Case is obscure.

152.] The Ablatival Genitive. The Ablative expressed the
object (person, place, or thing) from which separation takes
place, and is represented by the Gen. in various uses : as—

> ἀνέδυ πολιῆς ἁλός *rose from the grey sea.*
> χάζοντο κελεύθου *gave way from the path.*
> ἔσχοντο μάχης *were stayed from the fight.*
> παιδὸς ἐέργει μυῖαν *keeps off a fly from her child.*
> διώκετο οἷο δόμοιο *was chased from his house.*
> κακότητος ἔλυσαν *delivered from ill.*
> ἀτεμβόμενος ἴσης *defrauded of a share.*
> παιδὸς ἐδέξατο *received from her son.*
> πίθων ἠφύσσετο οἶνος *wine was drawn from casks.*
> Ἀντιλόχοιο λείπετο *was left behind Antilochus.*
> γόνυ γουνὸς ἀμείβων *exchanging knee past knee* (=*putting them
>   in front by turns*).
> ἄρχομαι *I begin from* (*a point*), Il. 9. 97, Od. 21. 142.
> ἁμαρτάνω *I miss, lose, fail in.*
> Τρῶας ἄμυνε νεῶν *keep off the Trojans from the ships :* so with
>   ἀλαλκεῖν.
> ἀκούω, πυνθάνομαι, ἔκλυον *hear from :* see § 151, *d.*
> τεύχω, ποιέω *I make of* (*material*): see § 151, *e.*

For the Gen. with Verbs of *buying, selling,* &c., see § 153.
Adjectives implying separation (want, freedom, &c.) may take
an Ablatival Gen. by virtue of their equivalence to Verbs of
similar meaning ; or they may be construed as Nouns, that is
to say, with a true Gen. *E.g.* λεῖος πετράων might be *smooth*
(i. e. *cleared*) *from rocks,* or *smooth as to rocks.* Cp. the similar
Latin Adjectives which take either Abl. or Gen.

The Gen. with Adjectives of *comparison* represents the Ablative (cp. the Latin construction). It expresses the point *from
which the higher degree of a quality is separated :* cp. the Gen.
with Verbs of *excelling* and *falling behind,* and with Adjectives
of similar meaning, as Od. 21. 254 βίης ἐπιδευέες εἰμὲν Ὀδυσῆος
we are wanting in strength behind (*compared with*) *Ulysses.*

In Sanscrit the Abl. is used with numerals to express the point *from* which
we count. A trace of this may be seen in the elliptical form δωδεκάτη ὅτε κτλ.
the twelfth day (*from the day*) *when* &c. (Il. 21. 81, cp. Od. 3. 180).

The Gen. with ἐξ, ἀπό, παρά, πρός, πρό, ὑπέρ, περί (*beyond*), ὑπό
(*from under*), κατά (*down from*), and the Verbs compounded with
them, is Ablatival ; with some of the 'improper Prepositions,' as

χωρίς, ἄνευ, τῆλε, ἄτερ, νόσφι, ἀμφίς, ἑκάς, ἐκτός, ἄψ, πάλιν, it may
be either the Ablative or the true Genitive. When *motion from*
is not implied, the Case is probably the true Gen.; see § 228.

It should be observed that the use of the Ablatival Gen. with
simple Verbs is comparatively restricted in Homer. It is not
used, as it is in Sanscrit, with simple Verbs of *going, coming,
bringing* (*e. g.* we could not substitute the Gen. for the form in
-θεν in such phrases as κλισίηθεν ἰοῦσα, ἀγρόθεν ἐρχομένη, οἴκοθεν
ἦγε, ᾽Ιλιόθεν με φέρων, &c.), but only with Verbs which imply
separation or *distance from* a point, or which are compounded with
Prepositions such as ἐξ, ἀπό, &c.

Later poets seem to be more free in this respect (probably because they
treated the usage as an archaism, adopted as being poetical): *e.g.* Soph. O. T.
142 βάρρων ἵστασθε, Ant. 418 χθονὸς ἀείρας, Phil. 630 νεὼς ἄγοντα, &c. Further
extensions are,—the use for the place from which something is *seen*, as Soph.
El. 78, 324, and for the *agent*, Eur. Or. 497, El. 123.

153.] Gen. of Price. Verbs meaning *to change places with*
take an Ablatival Gen., as γόνυ γουνὸς ἀμείβων (quoted in the
last section): hence the constructions—

Il. 6. 235 τεύχε᾽ ἄμειβε χρύσεα χαλκείων *exchanged armour,
golden* (*passing in exchange*) *for bronze.*

Il. 1. 111 Χρυσηΐδος ἀγλά᾽ ἄποινα .. δέξασθαι *to accept a splen-
did ransom for Chryseïs;* so Od. 11. 327 ἢ χρῦσον φίλου ἀνδρὸς
ἐδέξατο *who took gold for* (*to betray*) *her husband.*

Il. 11. 106 ἔλυσεν ἀποίνων *released for a ransom.*

Hence we may explain the construction with Verbs meaning
to value at, set off against (*a price*); as Il. 23. 649 τιμῆς ἧς τέ μ᾽
ἔοικε τετιμῆσθαι; so with the Adjectives ἀντάξιος, &c.

It is possible however that a word expressing value or price may be construed as a Gen. with a Noun. As we can say τεύχεα ἑκατόμβοια *armour worth
a hundred oxen*, we might have τεύχεα ἑκατὸν βοῶν (as in Attic prose, *e. g.* δέκα
μνῶν χωρίον *a plot worth ten minae*) ; cp. the Latin *magni emere, magni facere,* &c.

Case-forms in -φι(ν).

154.] The Case-Ending -φι(ν) is found in a number of
Homeric forms which appear to be construed indifferently as
Datives or Genitives. It will be shown, however, that there is
ground for believing these forms to have been used for the Dat.
only in the instrumental and locatival senses (the latter being
comparatively rare), and for the Gen. only in the ablatival
sense. They formed, therefore, a 'mixed Case,' composed of the
same elements as the Latin Ablative, viz. the original Instr.
Abl. and Loc.

In respect of usage these forms are archaic: that is to say,
they are confined for the most part to lines and phrases of a

fixed conventional type. In several instances the survival is evidently due to the influence of the metre: thus δακρυόφι, στή-θεσφι take the place of δακρύων, στηθέων; ὀστεόφιν and ἰκριόφιν, of ὀστέων, ὀστέοισι, and ἰκρίων, ἰκρίοισι—forms impossible in a hexameter. So δι' ὄρεσφι, κατ' ὄρεσφι, ὑπ' ὄχεσφι, for δι' ὀρέων, κατ' ὀρέων, ὑπ' ὀχέων.

155.] Instrumental. The forms in -φι(ν) appear to have been forms of the Instrumental (Sing. and Plur.), and the majority of the Homeric examples may be referred to that Case: ἑτέρηφι *with the other hand* (Il. 16. 734, &c.), δεξιτερῆφι (Od. 19. 480); βίηφι *by force* (Il. 16. 826, Od. 1. 403, &c., and in the phrase κρατερῆφι βίηφι), also *in strength* (βίηφι φέρτερος, Od. 6. 6, &c.); ἀναγκαίηφι δαμέντας (Il. 20. 143); γενεῆφι νεώτατος (Il. 14. 112, &c.): δακρυόφι πλῆσθεν *were filled with tears* (Il. 17. 696, &c.).

In the 'comitative' use, αὐτοῖσιν ὄχεσφιν *chariot and all*, ἵπποισιν καὶ ὄχεσφιν *with horses and chariot* (Il. 12. 114, Od. 4. 533); with Prepositions, ἅμ' ἠοῖ φαινομένηφιν, σὺν ἵπποισιν καὶ ὄχεσφιν (often in the Iliad), also παρ' ὄχεσφιν (construed with Verbs of *rest*, Il. 5. 28, 794., 8. 565., 12. 91., 15. 3)—unless ὄχεσφιν is a Loc. (§ 157); with words expressing *agreement*, *likeness*, &c., as παλάμηφιν ἀρήρει *fitted his hand*, θεόφιν μήστωρ ἀτάλαντος (Il. 7. 366, &c.).

With Verbs of *trusting*; Il. 4. 303 ἱπποσύνῃ τε καὶ ἠνορέηφι πεποιθώς; so ἀγλαΐηφι (Il. 6. 510), βίηφι (several times).

156.] Ablative. Forms used as Ablatival Genitives are—

Il. 2. 794 ναῦφιν ἀφορμηθεῖεν *start from the ships*.

13. 700 ναῦφιν ἀμυνόμενοι *defending the ships* (§ 152).

3. 368 ἐκ δέ μοι ἔγχος ἠΐχθη παλάμηφιν.

10. 458 ἀπὸ μὲν .. κυνέην κεφαλῆφιν ἕλοντο.

Od. 5. 152 δακρυόφιν τέρσοντο *were dried from tears*.

8. 279 καθύπερθε μελαθρόφιν ἐξεκέχυντο.

With the Prepositions—

ἐξ: as ἐξ εὐνῆφι, ἐκ θεόφιν, ἐκ πασσαλόφι, ἐκ ποντόφιν, ἐκ στή-θεσφιν, ἐξ Ἐρέβεσφιν, &c.

ἀπό: as ἀπὸ νευρῆφιν, αὐτόφιν, χαλκόφι, στήθεσφιν, ναῦφι, &c.

παρά when it means *from*: Il. 12. 225 παρὰ ναῦφιν ἐλευσόμεθ' αὐτὰ κέλευθα, Od. 14. 498 παρὰ ναῦφιν ἐποτρύνειε νέεσθαι. So—

18. 305 παρὰ ναῦφιν ἀνέστη δῖος Ἀχιλλεύς.

8. 474 πρὶν ὄρθαι παρὰ ναῦφι ποδώκεα Πηλεΐωνα.

16. 281 ἐλπόμενοι παρὰ ναῦφι ποδώκεα Πηλεΐωνα
μηνιθμὸν μὲν ἀπορρῖψαι, φιλότητα δ' ἑλέσθαι.

In these three places the notion of *leaving* the ships is implied, so παρὰ ναῦφι has the meaning of παρὰ νεῶν.

κατά *down from* : κατ' ὄρεσφι (Il. 4. 452., 11. 493).
ὑπό *from under* : ὑπ' ὄχεσφι (Il. 23. 7), ὑπὸ ζυγόφιν (Il. 24. 576).

With this use of -φι we may compare the use of the *Dative* with ἐξ and ἀπό, which is one of the peculiarities of the Arcadian and Cyprian dialects (Meister, ii. 119, 296). The parallel of the Latin Abl. has been noticed.

157.] Locative. This use is found in several clear instances, as well as others of an indecisive kind :—

Il. 19. 323 Φθίηφι *in Phthia* ; Il. 13. 168 κλισίηφι λέλειπτο *was left in the tent* ; θύρηφιν *out of doors, foris* (Od. 9. 238., 22. 220); κεφαλῆφιν ἔθηκε *put on the head* (Il. 10. 30, 257, 261 ; cp. 496, Od. 20. 94) ; Il. 11. 474 ὡς εἴ τε δαφοινοὶ θῆρες ὄρεσφιν : 19. 376 τὸ δὲ καίεται ὑψόθ' ὄρεσφιν : 22. 139 ἠΰτε κίρκος ὄρεσφιν κτλ. ; 22. 189 ὡς δ' ὅτε νεβρὸν ὄρεσφι κυὼν κτλ.; Il. 2. 480 ἠΰτε βοῦς ἀγέληφι μέγ' ἔξοχος ἔπλετο πάντων : 16. 487 ἀγέληφι μετελθών *coming into the herd.*

With the Prepositions :—ἐν, as Il. 24. 284 ἐν χειρὶ . . δεξιτερῆφιν (= Od. 15. 148): πρός, in Od. 5. 432 πρὸς κοτυληδονόφιν (*sticking*) *to the suckers*: ἀμφί, in Od. 16. 145 φθινύθει δ' ἀμφ' ὀστεόφι χρώς: ὑπό, in ὑπ' ὄχεσφι, ὑπὸ ζυγόφι (Il. 19. 404, unless the meaning is *from under*).

With ἐπί *on, at*, in the combinations ἐπὶ ἰκριόφιν, ἐπ' ἐσχαρόφιν, ἐπὶ νευρῆφιν (all in the Od.) the Case may be Loc. or Gen.

παρ' αὐτόφι occurs four times in the Iliad (12. 302., 13. 42., 20. 140., 23. 640). In three of these places there is a v. l. παρ' αὐτόθι (or παραυτόθι), which generally gives a better sense, and which is required by the grammar in 13. 42 ἕλποντο δὲ νῆας Ἀχαιῶν αἱρήσειν κτενέειν τε παρ' αὐτόφι (= παρὰ νηυσί). So 19. 255 ἐπ' αὐτόφιν ἧατο σιγῇ where αὐτόθι (Nauck) is probably right. It seems that the Endings -θι and -φι were confused, possibly at a very early period.

158.] The true Dat. and Gen. There is only one example of the true Dat., viz. Il. 2. 363 ὡς φρήτρη φρήτρηφιν ἀρήγῃ, φῦλα δὲ φύλοις *that phratria may bear aid to phratria, and tribe to tribe.*

The instances of the true Gen. are—

(1) Il. 21. 295 κατὰ Ἰλιόφι κλυτὰ τείχεα λαὸν ἐέλσαι *to coop up the army within the famous walls of Ilios.*

(2) Il. 21. 367 τεῖρε δ' αὐτμὴ Ἡφαίστοιο βίηφι πολύφρονος *the breath of Hephaestus* (Ἡφαίστοιο βίη) *wore him out.*

(3) Od. 12. 45 πολὺς δ' ἀμφ' ὀστεόφιν θὶς ἀνδρῶν πυθομένων *there is around a great heap of bones, of men rotting.* But this may be an Instr. of *material*, = ' a heap (is made) of bones.'

(4) Il. 16. 762 κεφαλῆφιν ἐπεὶ λάβεν οὐχὶ μεθίει (Gen., § 151, a); and 11. 350 οὐδ' ἀφάμαρτε τιτυσκόμενος κεφαλῆφιν (but the Gen. might be construed with ἀφάμαρτε, as an Abl.).

(5) Certain uses with Prepositions; viz. ἐπί in Il. 13. 308 ἢ ἐπὶ δεξιόφιν .. ἢ ἐπ' ἀριστερόφιν *towards right or left;* πρόσθε in Il. 5. 107 πρόσθ' ἵπποιϊν καὶ ὄχεσφιν : διά *through,* in διὰ δὲ στήθεσφιν ἔλασσεν (Il. 5. 41, &c.), also 10. 185 ἔρχηται δι' ὄρεσφι.

The first four of these references evidently do not prove much. The first would be a clear instance of the true Gen. if we could be sure of the text : but there is some probability in favour of Ἰλίοο (§ 98), proposed by Leo Meyer (*Decl.* p. 35). In Il. 21. 367 we may perhaps take βίηφι as an Instr.: *hot breath vexed him through (by reason of) the might of Hephaestus.*

Again, the use with ἐπί may be locatival, with πρόσθε ablatival (as with πρό). The uses with διά are more important, because they are not isolated, but form a distinct group. It is improbable that διά *through* should take an ablatival Gen. or a Locative. The Sanscrit Instr. is used of the space or time *over which* an action extends (Delbrück, *A. S.* § 88) : and so the Abl. in Latin (Roby, §§ 1176, 1189). This use appears in Greek as the Dat. of the *way by which,* and perhaps in the phrases περιϊόντι τῷ θέρει, &c. It may be thought possible that δι' ὄρεσφι and διὰ στήθεσφι are fragments of this use. If so, one or two other uses assigned above to the Loc. may be really Instr.; especially ὄρεσφι, Il. 11. 474., 22. 139, 189.

On the other hand, if the forms in -φι(ν) constitute a 'mixed Case' (Locative, Instrumental, and Ablative), there must have been a tendency to extend its sphere from the Loc. and Instr. to the Dat., and from the Abl. to the Gen. Thus the few instances of forms in -φι(ν) standing for the true Dat. and Gen. may be first steps towards an amalgamation of five Cases (such as we have in the Greek Dual). One or two are probably among the 'false archaisms' which doubtless exist in Homer, though not to the extent supposed by some commentators : see § 216.

Forms in -θεν and -ως.

159.] The Ending -θεν expresses the point *from which motion* takes place; hence it is common in construction with Verbs of motion, and after the Prepositions ἐξ and ἀπό. Cp. also—

Il. 3. 276 Ζεῦ πάτερ Ἴδηθεν μεδέων *ruling from Ida.*

8. 397 Ἴδηθεν ἐπεὶ ἴδε *when he saw, looking from Ida.*

15. 716 Ἕκτωρ δὲ πρύμνηθεν ἐπεὶ λάβε *when he had got hold from* (i. e. *in the direction from, beginning with*) *the stern ;* so ἑτέρωθεν *on the other side,* ἀμφοτέρωθεν *on both sides.*

Of *time ;* ἠῶθεν *from (beginning with) dawn.*

In a metaphorical sense ; of an *agent* (regarded as the source of action), as Il. 15. 489 Διόθεν βλαφθέντα βέλεμνα : Od. 16. 447 οὐδέ τί μιν θάνατον τρομέεσθαι ἄνωγα ἔκ γε μνηστήρων· θεόθεν δ' οὐκ ἔστ' ἀλέασθαι. Also, Il. 10. 68 πατρόθεν ἐκ γενεῆς ὀνομάζων *naming from (on the side of) the father.* And in two phrases, Il. 7. 39, 226 οἰόθεν οἶος *quite alone,* and Il. 7. 97 αἰνόθεν αἰνῶς *quite terribly,—* where the force of the Ending is indistinct.

It is to be observed that (except in the Personal Pronouns) this form is not found with Verbs meaning to *deprive of, free from*, *defend*, *surpass*, or with the corresponding Adjectives and Adverbs. Hence it cannot be held to be equivalent to an Ablative (§ 152), and probably differed from the Abl. in expressing *motion from* rather than *separation*.

On the other hand, the Pronominal forms ἐμέθεν, σέθεν, ἔθεν are freely construed—

(1) as Ablatives : πρὸ ἔθεν, ὑπὲρ σέθεν, ἄνευ ἐμέθεν ; and with a Comparative, Il. 1. 114 οὔ ἑθέν ἐστι χερείων, &c. Cp. also Il. 9. 419 μάλα γάρ ἔθεν . . χεῖρα ἑὴν ὑπερέσχε.

(2) as true Genitives : Il. 4. 169 ἀλλά μοι αἰνὸν ἄχος σέθεν ἔσσεται *I shall have terrible grief for thee ;* with Verbs of *hearing* (Il. 2. 26, &c.), *remembering* (Od. 4. 592), *caring* (Il. 1. 180 σέθεν δ' ἐγὼ οὐκ ἀλεγίζω), *reaching* or *touching* (ἀντιάζω, πειράζω, &c.) : and with ἆσσον, πρόσθε, ἄντα, ἀντίον, ἕνεκα, ἕκητι.

160.] **The Ending -ως** is generally derived from the Ablative of Stems in -ο (§ 110), although -ōt would not regularly become -ως, and the transition of meaning is not a very easy one. The chief examples in common use in Homer are—

From Pronominal Stems : ὥς, τῶς, πῶς, ὁμῶς, αὔτως, ἄλλως.

From Stems in -ο : αἰνῶς, ἀσπασίως, ἐκπάγλως, ἐπισταμένως, θαρσαλέως, κακῶς, καρπαλίμως, κραιπνῶς, κρατερῶς, ὀτραλέως, πυκινῶς, ῥηϊδίως, στερεῶς, στυγερῶς, χαλεπῶς, μεγάλως, καλῶς, αἰσχρῶς, φίλως.

From other Stems : πάντως, λιγέως, ἀτρεκέως, ἀσφαλέως, ἀφραδέως, περιφραδέως, διηνεκέως, ἐνδυκέως, νωλεμέως, προφρονέως, ἐπικρατέως, ταχέως.

It will be seen that comparatively few of these Adverbs come from the *short familiar* Adjectives. Thus καλῶς, αἰσχρῶς, μεγάλως, ταχέως, φίλως are very rare in Homer ; and there is no Adverb of the kind from δεινός, ἴσος, ὀρθός, βαρύς, ὠκύς, ὀξύς.

The Nominative.

161.] **Impersonal Verbs.** It is evident that in a language which distinguishes the Person and Number of the Verb by the Ending, it is not essential that there should be a distinct word as Nominative. ἐσ-τί (*e.g.*) stands for *he is, she is, it is ;* the person or thing meant by the Ending may be left to be gathered from the context. In certain cases, however, the Subject meant by an Ending of the Third Person is too indefinite to be expressed by a particular Noun, such as the context could supply to the mind. For instance, in the sentence οὕτως ἐσ-τί *it is so*, the real Subject given by the Ending -τι (in English by the word *it*) is not a particular thing already mentioned or implied, but a vague notion—'the case,' 'the course of things,' &c.* Verbs used with a vague unexpressed Subject of this kind are called IMPERSONAL.

The vague Subject may be a Plural, as Il. 16. 128 οὐκέτι φυκτὰ πέλονται *the case no longer allows of flight,* Od. 2. 203 ἶσα ἔσσεται *things will be even.*

A Neuter Pronoun used as the Subject sometimes gives a vague meaning, not far removed from that of an Impersonal Verb; *e.g.* Il. 1. 564 εἰ δ' οὕτω τοῦτ' ἐστί *if this is so* (cp. οὕτως ἐστί *it is so*); ἐσθλὸν καὶ τὸ τέτυκται *it is a good thing too.*

An Impersonal Verb is often followed by an Infinitive, or dependent Clause, which supplies the want of a Subject. See § 234, 2.

162.] Nominative in the Predicate. In certain cases the Predicate of a sentence may be limited or modified by a Nominative in agreement with the Subject. This is especially found—

1. With Adjectives of *time;* as ἑσπέριοι ἀφίκοντο *they came in the evening,* ἐννύχιος προμολών *coming forth by night,* εὗδον παννύχιοι *slept all night,* χθιζὸς ἔβη *went yesterday.*

Such Adjectives seem to answer most nearly to the Gen. of time *within* which, but may also express *duration,* as πανημέριος and παννύχιος.

2. In describing the *attitude, manner, position,* &c. in which an action is done: as παλίνορσος ἀπέστη *stood off with a start backwards,* ὕπτιος οὔδει ἐρείσθη *was dashed face upwards on the ground;* so πεζὸς εἰλήλουθα, λαβρὸς ἐπαιγίζων, πρόφρων τέτληκας (cp. προφρονέως), ἀμετροεπὴς ἐκολῴα, &c.

3. The Pronouns ὅδε and κεῖνος are sometimes used instead of Adverbs of place: Il. 5. 604 καὶ νῦν οἱ πάρα κεῖνος Ἄρης *now too yonder is Ares at his side;* 10. 434 Θρήϊκες οἵδ' ἀπάνευθε *here are the Thracians apart;* Od. 6. 276 τίς δ' ὅδε Ναυσικάᾳ ἕπεται; So οὗτος in Il. 10. 82 τίς δ' οὗτος κτλ.

4. With Verbs meaning *to be, to become, to appear, to be made, called, thought,* &c.; as κάρτιστοι τράφεν *they were nurtured the mightiest,* (i. e. *to be the mightiest*); εἰσωποὶ ἐγένοντο νεῶν *they came to be in front of the ships:* ἥδε ἀρίστη φαίνετο βουλή *this appeared the best counsel.*

In all such cases the Nominative which goes with the Verb not only qualifies the notion given by the Verb-Stem, but also becomes itself a Predicate (i. e. the assertion of an attribute). *E.g.* κάρτιστοι τράφεν implies that they *were* κάρτιστοι. A Noun so used is called a SECONDARY Predicate.

The use of εἰμί as the 'logical copula' is merely a special or 'singular' case

---

* See Riddell's *Digest,* §§ 95–100: Sigwart, *Impersonalien.*

of this type of sentence. The Verb has then little or no meaning of its own, but serves to mark the following Noun as a Predicate. The final stage of the development is reached when the Verb is omitted as being superfluous.

5. With Impersonal or half-Impersonal Verbs meaning *to be*, &c.; the Predicate being—

(*a*) a Neuter Adjective; as μόρσιμόν ἐστι *it is fated*; νεμεσσητὸν δέ κεν εἴη *it would be worthy of indignation*; οὔ τοι ἀεικές *it is not unmeet for thee*: with a Pronominal Subject, ἐσθλὸν γὰρ τὸ τέτυκται *it is a good thing*.

In the Plural, οὐκέτι φυκτὰ πέλονται *there is no more escaping*; cp. λοίγια ἔργα τάδ' ἔσσεται *this will be a pestilent business*.

In one or two instances the Adverbial form in -ως is used in phrases of this kind: Il. 11. 762 ὡς ἔον εἴ ποτ' ἔον γε *such I was if I was*; Il. 9. 551 Κουρήτεσσι κακῶς ἦν *things went ill for the Curetes*; Il. 7. 424 διαγνῶναι χαλεπῶς ἦν *it was hard to distinguish*; Il. 11. 838 πῶς τ' ἄρ' ἔοι τάδε ἔργα; Od. 11. 336 πῶς ὕμμιν ἀνὴρ ὅδε φαίνεται εἶναι. This may be regarded as older than the Neut. Nominative, since it indicates that the Verb is not a mere 'copula,' but has a meaning which the Adverb qualifies. Cp. Il. 6. 131 δὴν ἦν *lived long* (=δηναιὸς ἦν): also the Adverbial Neut. Plur., as Thuc. 1. 25. 4 ὄντες . . ὅμοια, 3. 14. 1 ἴσα καὶ ἱκέται ἐσμέν.

(*b*) an abstract Noun; as Il. 17. 556 σοὶ μὲν δὴ Μενέλαε κατηφείη καὶ ὄνειδος ἔσσεται εἰ κτλ. *to thee it will be a humbling and reproach if &c.*; οὐ νέμεσις *it is no wrong*; οὐκ ἄρα τις χάρις ἦεν *it was no matter of thanks*; εἰ δέ μοι αἶσα *but if it is my fate*: with a Pronominal Subject, λώβη τάδε γ' ἔσσεται *this will be a shame*.

The use of an abstract Noun instead of an Adjective is a license or boldness of language of which we have already had examples; see § 116 and § 126.

It is worth while to notice the tendency to import the ideas of *obligation, necessity*, &c. into these phrases: *e.g.* οὐ νέμεσις *it is not* (*worthy of, a matter of*) *indignation*, ὄνειδος ἔσσεται *it will be* (*ground of*) *reproach*. So in Latin *vestra existimatio est = it is matter for your judgment*.

The Latin idiom called the Predicative Dative (Roby, Pt. II. pp. xxv-lvi) may be regarded as a less violent mode of expression than this Nom., since the Dat. is a case which is originally 'adverbial,' *i. e.* construed with the Predicate given by the Verb-Stem. In other words, *dedecori est* is a less bold and probably more primitive way of saying *it is disgraceful* than *dedecus est*: just as κακῶς ἦν is more primitive than κακὸν ἦν.

6. The ordinary use of the Participle belongs to this head: as διαστήτην ἐρίσαντε *parted after having quarrelled*. In this use the Participle qualifies the Verb-Stem, and at the same time makes a distinct assertion: see Chapter X.

163.] Interjectional Nominative. The Nom. is not unfrequently used in Homer without any regular construction, as a kind of exclamation : e.g.—

Il. 5. 405 σοὶ δ' ἐπὶ τοῦτον ἀνῆκε θεὰ γλαυκῶπις 'Αθήνη,
νήπιος, οὐδὲ τὸ οἶδε κτλ. *fool! he knows not &c.*
Similarly σχέτλιος *cruel!* δύσμορος *the unhappy one!* (Od. 20. 194) : and so Il. 1. 231 δημοβόρος βασιλεύς! Cp. the interjectional use of αἰδώς *shame!* (Il. 5. 787., 13. 95., 16. 422).

A similar account may be given of one or two passages in which commentators generally suppose ' anacoluthon ' : viz.—

Il. 10. 436 τοῦ δὴ καλλίστους ἵππους ἴδον ἠδὲ μεγίστους·
λευκότεροι χιόνος, θείειν δ' ἀνέμοισιν ὁμοῖοι
whiter than snow they are! &c. ; and so in the equally abrupt—

Il. 10. 547 αἰνῶς ἀκτίνεσσιν ἐοικότες ἠελίοιο.

2. 353 ἀστράπτων ἐπιδέξι' ἐναίσιμα σήματα φαίνων (*he did so I tell you*) *by lightning on the right &c.*

Od. 1. 51 νῆσος δενδρήεσσα, θεὰ δ' ἐνὶ δώματα ναίει *an island (it is) well wooded, and a goddess has her dwelling there!*

These forms of expression, when we seek to bring them under the general laws of the grammatical Sentence, resolve themselves into *Predicates with an unexpressed Subject.* On the logical Propositions of this kind see Sigwart (*Logik,* I. p. 55). The Predicate, he shows, is always expressed in a word (or words); but the Subject, when it is of the kind which would be expressed by a Pronoun (*it, this,* &c.) may be indicated by a gesture. The simplest examples of the type are the imperfect sentences used by children, such as *horse!* for *this is a horse.* When such sentences are introduced into literary language, they give it an abrupt and interjectional character, as in the examples quoted. We might add the phrases such as οὐ νέμεσις *it is no wrong* (§ 162), in which the want of a Verb makes the expression somewhat interjectional. Compare, for instance, οὐ νέμεσις with αἰδώς, 'Αργεῖοι *shame on you, Greeks!* also the so-called ellipse in commands, as ἀλλ' ἄνα *but up!*

The Vocative.

164.] Regarding the use of the Vocative in Homer the chief point to be noticed is the curious one (common to Greek and Sanscrit) that when two persons are addressed, connected by τε, the second name is put in the Nominative.* For instance—

Il. 3. 277 Ζεῦ πάτερ Ἴδηθεν μεδέων κύδιστε μέγιστε,
'Ηέλιος θ' ὃς κτλ.
Similarly, the Vocative is not followed by δέ or any similar Conjunction, but the Pronoun σύ is interposed ; as Il. 1. 282 'Ατρείδη σὺ δὲ παῦε κτλ. *but, son of Atreus, cease &c.*

---

* Delbrück, *Synt. Forsch.* iv. p. 28.

The Nominative is often used for the Voc., especially, it would seem, in order to avoid the repetition of the Voc.; *e.g.* Il. 4. 189 φίλος ὦ Μενέλαε. On this point however it is not always possible to trust to the accuracy of the text. Cobet (*Misc. Crit.* p. 333) has good grounds in the metre for proposing to change a great many Vocatives into Nominatives : *e.g.*—

Il. 23. 493 Αἶαν Ἰδομενεῦ τε (read Αἴας Ἰδομενεύς τε).

Il. 2. 8 οὖλε ὄνειρε (read οὖλος).

Od. 8. 408 χαῖρε πάτερ ὦ ξεῖνε.(read πατήρ).

Il. 18. 385 τίπτε Θέτι τανύπεπλε ἱκάνεις (Θέτις Zenod.).

Adjectival Use of the Noun.

165.] **Substantive and Adjective.** This seems a convenient place for one or two remarks on the distinction expressed by these terms.

It will be seen from §§ 114 and 117 that there is no general difference in the mode of forming Substantives and Adjectives. Certain Suffixes, however, are chiefly or wholly employed in the formation of *abstract* and *collective* Nouns : as in the Feminine Nouns in -τι-s, -τυ-s, -δων, the Neuters in -μα(τ), the Denominatives in -της (Gen. -τητ-ος).

In respect of meaning and use the distinction between the *concrete* Substantives and Adjectives is practical rather than logical. Certain Nouns are mainly used as qualifying words in agreement with other Nouns ; these are classed as Adjectives. In such combinations as βοῦς ταῦρος, ἀνέρες ἀλφησταί, χαλκῆες ἄνδρες, βασιλεὺς Κῦρος, Ἀγαμέμνων Ἀτρείδης, where the qualifying word is one that is not generally used as an Adjective, we speak of the ' adjectival use ' of a Substantive. Conversely, when an Adjective stands by itself to denote an individual or group of objects, the use is called ' substantival ' : *e.g.* κακός *a base fellow*, κακά *evils*, τυκτὸν κακόν *a made mischief.* This is a use which arises when the objects to which an Adjective applies are such as *naturally* form a distinct class. Thus the Suffixes which form Nouns in -τη-s, -τηρ, -τωρ and -ευς are practically confined to Substantives.

Abstract and Collective Nouns, it is evident, are essentially Substantives. Thus there is a clear distinction, both in form and meaning, between Abstract and Concrete Nouns; but not between Substantives and Adjectives.

The common definition of an Adjective as a word that expresses ' quality ' (' Adjectives express the notion of QUALITY,' Jelf, ii. p. 7) is open to the objections (1) that an abstract Substantive may be said to express quality, and (2) that every concrete Noun of which the etymological meaning is clear expresses quality in the same way as an Adjective. *E. g.* the definition does not enable us to distinguish μαχητής from μαχήμων.

It is evident that the use of a Nominative in the Predicate—as βασιλεύς ἐστι *he is king*—is strictly speaking an adjectival use.

The corresponding distinction in the Pronouns does not need much explanation. The Personal Pronouns are essentially Substantives (being incapable of serving as limiting or descriptive words); the Possessive Pronouns are essentially Adjectives. The others admit of both uses; *e.g.* οὗτος *this one*, and ἀνὴρ οὗτος (in Attic ὁ ἀνὴρ οὗτος) *this man*.

166.] Gender of Adjectives. In a few cases the Gender of the Adjective is independent of the Substantive with which it is construed.

1. When a *person* is described by a word which properly denotes a *thing* (viz. a Neuter, as τέκνον, τέκος, &c., or an abstract Noun, βίη Πριάμοιο, &c.), the concord of Gender is not always observed. Thus we have φίλε τέκνον (but φίλον τέκος, φίλη κεφαλή); again—

Il. 11. 690 ἐλθὼν γάρ ῥ᾽ ἐκάκωσε βίη Ἡρακληείη (= Heracles).

Od. 11. 90 ἦλθε δ᾽ ἐπὶ ψυχὴ Θηβαίου Τειρεσίαο
         χρύσεον σκῆπτρον ἔχων.

In such cases grammarians speak of a 'construction according to the meaning' (κατὰ σύνεσιν). The term is unobjectionable, provided that we remember that constructions according to the meaning are generally older than those in which meaning is overridden by idiom or grammatical analogy.

2. Where an Adjective refers to more than one Noun, it follows the most prominent : or (if this is at all doubtful) the Masc. is used of *persons*, the Neut. of *things*: *e.g.*—

Il. 2. 136 αἱ δέ που ἡμέτεραί τ᾽ ἄλοχοι καὶ νήπια τέκνα
         ἥατ᾽ ἐνὶ μεγάροις ποτιδέγμεναι

because the wives are chiefly thought of : but—

Il. 18. 514 τεῖχος μέν ῥ᾽ ἄλοχοί τε φίλαι καὶ νήπια τέκνα
         ῥύατ᾽ ἐφεσταότες, μετὰ δ᾽ ἀνέρες οὓς ἔχε γῆρας

because the boys and old men are also in the speaker's mind.

Od. 13. 435 ἀμφὶ δέ μιν ῥάκος ἄλλο κακὸν βάλεν ἠδὲ χιτῶνα,
         ῥωγαλέα ῥυπόωντα.

The Neut. Plur. is especially used of sheep and cattle : Il. 11. 244 πρῶθ᾽ ἑκατὸν βοῦς δῶκεν, ἔπειτα δὲ χίλι᾽ ὑπέστη, αἶγας ὁμοῦ καὶ ὄϊς ; Il. 11. 696 ἐκ δ᾽ ὁ γέρων ἀγέλην τε βοῶν καὶ πῶϋ μέγ᾽ οἰῶν εἵλετο, κρινάμενος τριηκόσι᾽ ἠδὲ νομῆας (*three hundred head*) : cp. also Il. 5. 140, Od. 12. 332.

3. A Noun standing as Predicate may be Neuter, although the Subject is Masc. or Fem. : as οὐκ ἀγαθὸν πολυκοιρανίη. This is a kind of substantival use.

167.] Gender of Pronouns. A substantival Pronoun denoting a *person* may retain its proper Gender although the antecedent is a Neuter, or an abstract word ; as Il. 22. 87 φίλον θάλος, ὃν τέκον αὐτή.

Conversely a Neuter Pronoun may be used substantivally of a *thing* which has been denoted by a Masc. or Fem. word :

Il. 2. 873 ὃς καὶ χρῦσον ἔχων πόλεμόνδ' ἴεν ἠΰτε κούρη,
νήπιος, οὐδέ τί οἱ τό γ' ἐπήρκεσε λυγρὸν ὄλεθρον.

Cp. Il. 11. 238., 18. 460, Od. 12. 74 (with the note in Merry and Riddell's edition).

On the other hand, a Pronominal Subject sometimes follows the Gender of a Noun standing as Predicate, as αὕτη δίκη ἐστί *this is the manner*, ἣ θέμις ἐστί *which is right*. But the Neuter is preferred if a distinct object is meant by the Pronoun ; as Od. 1. 226 οὐκ ἔρανος τάδε γ' ἐστί *what I see is not a club-feast*.

168.] Implied Predication. An Adjective (or Substantive in an adjectival use) construed with a Noun in an oblique Case may be so used as to convey a distinct predication ; as οὐκέτ' ἐμοὶ φίλα ταῦτ' ἀγορεύεις = *this (that you now speak) is not pleasing to me*.

So after Verbs meaning *to make, cause to be, call, think,* &c. ; λαοὺς δὲ λίθους ποίησε Κρονίων *Zeus made the people (to be) stones*.

This use is parallel to that of the Nominative in the Predicate (§ 162) : cp. the forms of sentence λαοὶ ἐγένοντο λίθοι, λαοὺς ἐποίησε λίθους. In the latter the predicative Noun (λίθους) is construed with an oblique Case, instead of with the Subject. A Noun so used is called a TERTIARY PREDICATE : cp. § 162, 3.

CHAPTER VIII.

Use of the Numbers.

169.] Collective Nouns. The Subject of a Plural Verb may be expressed by means of a Collective Noun ; as ὡς φάσαν ἡ πληθύς *thus they said, the multitude* (cp. Il. 15. 305., 23. 157).

Conversely, a Participle construed with a Collective Noun and Singular Verb may be Plural : as Il. 18. 604 περίσταθ' ὅμιλος τερπόμενοι. Cp. Il. 16. 281 ἐκίνηθεν δὲ φάλαγγες ἐλπόμενοι, also Od. 11. 15.

In these instances, again, the construction is said to be 'according to the meaning' (§ 166). The principle is evidently that an abstract or collective word may be used in 'apposition' to a concrete word. It may be noticed however that the com-

binations such as ὅμιλος - τερπόμενοι are only found when there is
some pause between the words ; otherwise the Genitive would be
used (construed as in Τρώων κατεδύσεθ᾽ ὅμιλον, &c.).

170.] Distributive use of the Singular. The word ἕκαστος
is often used in the Sing. with a Plural Verb, as ἔβαν οἰκόνδε
ἕκαστος *they went home, each one,* δεδμήμεσθα ἕκαστος *we are each
one obedient.* Other words in a clause may follow ἕκαστος in
respect of Number : as Il. 2. 775 ἵπποι δὲ παρ᾽ ἅρμασιν οἷσιν
ἕκαστος *the horses each beside his chariot ;* Il. 9. 656 οἱ δὲ ἕκαστος
ἑλὼν δέπας ἀμφικύπελλον σπείσαντες παρὰ νῆας ἴσαν πάλιν. Even
the Verb is made Sing. in Il. 16. 264 οἱ δ᾽ ἄλκιμον ἦτορ ἔχοντες
πρόσσω πᾶς πέτεται καὶ ἀμύνει οἷσι τέκεσσι : but this is a slight
boldness of expression.

On the same principle we may explain the Sing. in Od. 4. 300
αἱ δ᾽ ἴσαν ἐκ μεγάροιο δάος μετὰ χερσὶν ἔχουσαι (= *each with a torch
in her hands*); Il. 13. 783 τετυμμένω κατὰ χεῖρα (*each of the two*)
wounded in the hand ; Il. 3. 235 οὕς κεν ἐὺ γνοίην καί τ᾽ οὔνομα
μυθησαίμην. So in Il. 17. 260 τῶν δ᾽ ἄλλων τίς κεν . . οὐνόματ᾽
εἴποι we should doubtless read οὔνομα (Ϝείποι).

Similarly the Dual is used of a group of *pairs :* —

Il. 16. 370 πολλοὶ δ᾽ ἐν τάφρῳ ἐρυσάρματες ὠκέες ἵπποι
　　　　ἄξαντ᾽ ἐν πρώτῳ ῥυμῷ λίπον ἅρματ᾽ ἀνάκτων
where the Dual ἄξαντε (like the Sing. ῥυμῷ) refers to *one* chariot.
Probably, too, we should read ἅρμα ἀνάκτων (*i. e.* Ϝανάκτων). So
Il. 23. 362 οἱ δ᾽ ἅμα πάντες ἐφ᾽ ἵπποιιν μάστιγας ἄειραν, Od. 20.
348 ὄσσε δ᾽ ἄρα σφέων δακρυόφιν πίμπλαντο, also Il. 9. 503,
Od. 19. 444.

The Dual is often used in this way in Aristophanes : cp. Av. 622 ἀνατείνοντες
τὼ χεῖρε, and other instances given by Bieber (*De duali numero,* p. 44).

In Il. 5. 487 μή πως ὡς ἀψῖσι λίνου ἁλόντε πανάγρου, the Dual ἁλόντε is explained by Schol. B ὑμεῖς καὶ αἱ γυναῖκες. If so, it is a distributive use : ʻsee
that ye be not taken, man and wife in one net.ʼ But more probably it refers
to Hector and Paris.

In speaking of the characteristics of a group or class it is
common to pass from the Plural to the Singular, or *vice versâ ;*
e. g. Od. 4. 691 ἥ τ᾽ ἐστὶ δίκη θείων βασιλήων, ἄλλον κ᾽ ἐχθαίρῃσι
βροτῶν κτλ. *it is the way of kings, (a king) will hate one &c. ;* and
in the same clause, Il. 10. 259 ῥύεται δὲ κάρη θαλερῶν αἰζηῶν (of
a kind of helmet); Il. 2. 355 πρίν τινα πὰρ Τρώων ἀλόχῳ κατα-
κοιμηθῆναι *beside the wife of some Trojan ;* Il. 19. 70 ἀλλά τιν᾽ οἴω
. . ὑπ᾽ ἔγχεος ἡμετέροιο *before the spear of one of us.* The distributive τις is equivalent to a Plural.

Hence a peculiar *vague* use of the Plural, as Il. 3. 49 νυὸν
ἀνδρῶν αἰχμητάων *the bride of some warrior's son* (lit. *daughter-in-*

law of warriors, i.e. of this or that warrior); 4. 142 παρήϊον
ἔμμεναι ἵππων (v. l. ἵππῳ); 21. 499 πληκτίζεσθ᾽ ἀλόχοισι Διός
(less directly personal than ἀλόχῳ).

171.] Plural of Things. The Plural form is not confined in
Greek (or indeed in any language) to the expression of 'plurality'
in the strict sense, *i.e.* to denote a group composed of distinct
individuals, but is often used (esp. in Homer) of objects which
it is more logical to think of in the Singular. Many words,
too, are used both in the Sing. and the Plur., with little or no
difference of meaning.

Notice especially the uses of the Plural in the case of—

(1) Objects consisting of parts : τόξον and τόξα *bow and arrows:*
ὄχος and ὄχεα, ἅρμα and ἅρματα *a chariot:* δῶμα, μέγαρον *a hall or
room,* δώματα, μέγαρα *a house:* λέκτρον and λέκτρα *a bed.*

πύλαι *a gate* is only used in the Plur.; θύρη is used as well as
θύραι, but only of the door of a *room* (θάλαμος).

(2) Natural objects of undefined extent : ψάμαθος and ψάμαθοι
(as we say *sands*), ἅλες (once ἅλς) *salt,* κονίη and κονίαι *dust,* πυρός
and πυροί *wheat,* ῥέεθρον and ῥέεθρα, κῦμα (in a collective sense)
and κύματα, δάκρυ and δάκρυα, κρέα (seldom κρέας) *meat,* σάρκες
(once Sing.) *flesh.*

(3) Parts of the body : νῶτον (or νῶτος—the Nom. Sing. does
not occur in Homer) and νῶτα, στῆθος and (more commonly)
στήθεα, πρόσωπον and πρόσωπα *the countenance,* φρήν and φρένες.

(4) Abstract words : λελασμένος ἱπποσυνάων *forgetting horsemanship,* ποδωκείῃσι πεποιθώς *trusting to speed of foot,* ἀναλκείῃσι
δαμέντες *overcome by want of prowess,* πολυϊδρείῃσι νόοιο *through
cunning of understanding:* so ἀτασθαλίαι, ἀφραδίαι, ἀγηνορίαι, ἀεσι-
φροσύναι, τεκτοσύναι, μεθημοσύναι, &c.; note also προδοκαί *ambush,*
προχοαί *mouth of a river,* δῶρα *gift* (Il. 20. 268 χρῦσος γὰρ ἐρύκακε,
δῶρα θεοῖο), κυνῶν μέλπηθρα *the sport of dogs,* φυκτά *escaping,* ἶσα
fairness (§ 161).

The Plural in such cases is a kind of imperfect abstraction ; the particular
manifestations of a quality are thought of as units in a *group* or mass,—not
yet as forming a single *thing.*

(5) Collective words : μῆλα *flocks;* so πρόβατα is only Plur. in
Homer (cp. πρόβασις Od. 2. 75).

(6) Pronouns and Adjectives; see the examples of adverbial
uses, §§ 133, 134; cp. also § 161.

172.] Neuter Plural. The construction of the Neut. Plur.
with a Singular Verb is the commoner one in Homer, in the proportion of about three to one. When the Plural is used, it will

generally be found that the word is really Plural in meaning (*i. e.* that it calls up the notion of distinct units). Thus it is used with—

Nouns denoting agents; as ἔθνεα applied to the men of the Greek army (Il. 2. 91, 464), to birds (Il. 2. 459), to swine (Od. 14. 73); so with φῦλ᾽ ἀνθρώπων (Od. 15. 409).

Distinctly plural parts of the body: πτερά, χείλεα, οὔατα, μέλεα: so πέδιλα (of the shoes of Hermes).

Numerals: δέκα στόματα (Il. 2. 489), οὔατα τέσσαρα (Il. 11. 634), τέσσαρα δέρματα (Od. 4. 437), αἰπόλια ἕνδεκα πάντα (Od. 14. 103); so with πάντα and πολλά (Il. 11. 574., 15. 714., 17. 760, Od. 4. 437, 794., 9. 222., 12. 411), and when the context shows that distinct things are meant: as Il. 5. 656 τῶν μὲν δούρατα (the spears of *two* warriors), 13. 135 ἔγχεα . . ἀπὸ χειρῶν.

A few instances occur in fixed phrases, which may represent an earlier syntax; λύντο δὲ γυῖα (but also λύτο γούνατα), ἀμήχανα ἔργα γένοντο, &c. Note especially the lines ending with πέλονται (τά τε πτερὰ νηυσὶ πέλονται, ὅτε τ᾽ ἤματα μακρὰ πέλονται, φυκτὰ πέλονται, &c.).

The exceptions to the use of the Sing. are fewest with Pronouns and Adjectives: doubtless on account of their want of a distinct Plural meaning (see the end of last section).

173.] The **Dual** is chiefly used (1) of two objects thought of as a distinct pair, and (2) when the Numeral δύω is used.

1. Thus we have the natural pairs χεῖρε, πήχεε, τένοντε, ὤμω, μηρώ, ὄσσε, ὀφθαλμώ, and (in the Gen. Dat.) ποδοῖιν, βλεφάροιιν: σταθμώ door-posts; ἵππω *the horses of a chariot*, βόε *a yoke of oxen*, ἄρνε *a pair of lambs* (for sacrifice); δοῦρε (in Il. 13. 241., 16. 139 of the two spears usually carried, but δύο δοῦρε is more common); ποταμώ (Il. 5. 773) of the two rivers of the Troad, and so κρουνώ (Il. 22. 147). So of the two warriors in a chariot (Il. 5. 244, 272, 568), two wrestlers (Il. 23. 707), two dancers (Od. 8. 378), the Sirens (Od. 12. 52, &c.); the Ἀτρείδα and Αἴαντε.

The Numeral is generally added in speaking of two wild animals (θῆρε δύω, λέοντε δύω, &c.): κάπρω (Il. 11. 324) and λέοντε (Il. 16. 756) are hardly exceptions, since the context shows that two are meant. Also αἰετώ (Od. 2. 146) of two eagles sent as an omen, and γῦπε (Od. 11. 578) of the vultures that devoured Tityos.

The Dual in Il. 8. 185–191 (where Hector calls to *four* horses by name) might be defended, because two is the regular number; but probably v. 185 is spurious. In Il. 23. 413, again,—αἴ κ᾽ ἀποκηδήσαντε φερώμεθα χεῖρον ἄεθλον—the Dual is used because

M

it is the horses that are chiefly in the driver's mind, although he associates himself with them. In Il. 9. 182–195 the Dual refers to the two envoys, Phoenix being overlooked.

Again, when two agents have been mentioned together, or are represented as acting together in any way, the Dual may be used: as Il. 1. 531 τώ γ' ὣς βουλεύσαντε (of Thetis and Achilles), 16. 823 (of a lion and boar fighting), Od. 3. 128., 13. 372, &c. Similarly, of the meeting of two rivers, Il. 4. 453 ἐς μισγάγκειαν συμβάλλετον ὄβριμον ὕδωρ (cp. 5. 774).

The Dual Pronouns νῶϊ and σφῶϊ are used with comparative regularity : see Il. 1. 257, 336, 574., 5. 34, 287, 718, &c. This usage may be a matter of traditional courtesy. Hence perhaps the scrupulous use where the First Person Dual is meant; Il. 4. 407 ἀγαγόνθ' ('Diomede and I'); 8. 109 θεράποντε *our attendants;* 11. 313 τί παθόντε λελάσμεθα κτλ.; 12. 323 ὦ πέπον εἰ . . φυγόντε; Od. 3. 128 ἕνα θυμὸν ἔχοντε ('Ulysses and I'). In Od. 2. 78 for ἀπαιτίζοντες ἕως should be read ἀπαιτίζονθ' ἦος, since Telemachus there is speaking of his mother and himself. So with the Second Person, Il. 1. 216 (Athene and Here), 322 (the heralds), 3. 279., 7. 279.

In Il. 3. 278 καὶ οἳ ὑπένερθε καμόντας ἀνθρώπους τίνυσθον, ὅτις κ' ἐπίορκον ὀμόσσῃ the two gods indicated by the Dual are doubtless Hades and Persephone, as appears from Il. 9. 456 θεοὶ δ' ἐτέλειον ἐπαράς, Ζεύς τε καταχθόνιος καὶ ἐπαινὴ Περσεφόνεια, and 9. 569, where Althaea beats upon the earth κικλήσκουσ' Ἀΐδην καὶ ἐπαινὴν Περσεφόνειαν. And since these were the gods especially called upon as witnesses and avengers of wrong, it is probable that they are meant in Od. 1. 273 θεοὶ δ' ἐπιμάρτυροι ἔστων. The omission of the names may be a mark of reverence. If this view is correct, it removes the difficulty as to ἔστων (Meyer, *G. G.* § 577, 1).

2. Of the use with the Numeral the most significant examples are Od. 8. 35, 48 κούρω δὲ κρινθέντε δύω καὶ πεντήκοντα βήτην : where the Dual is used by a kind of attraction to the word δύω.

The Dual is never obligatory in Homer, since the Plural may always be used instead of it. Hence we often have a Dual Noun or Pronoun with a Plural Verb or Adjective, and *vice versâ.*

The Neut. Dual (like the Neut. Plur.) may go with a Sing. Verb : thus we have ὄσσε with all three Numbers.

Certain of the ancient grammarians—Zenodotus among them—supposed that Homer sometimes used the Dual for the Plural. But Aristarchus showed that in all the passages on which this belief was founded the Dual either had its proper force, or was a false reading.

The use of the Dual in Attic is nearly the same as in Homer : in other dialects it appears to have become obsolete. This was one of the reasons that led some grammarians to maintain that Homer was an Athenian.

CHAPTER IX.

THE PREPOSITIONS.

Introductory.

174.] **Prepositions** are words expressing some local relation, and capable of being used as prefixes in forming Compound Verbs. The Prepositions are also used in construction with oblique Cases of Nouns and Pronouns.

The Adverbs that are construed with oblique Cases, but do not enter into composition with Verbs, are called *Improper Prepositions.*

The list of Homeric Prepositions is the same (with perhaps one exception, see § 226) as that of later classical Greek. In the use of Prepositions, however, there are some marked differences between the two periods (§ 229).

There are no 'Inseparable' Prepositions in Greek: see however § 221.

175.] **Adverbial use.** In post-Homeric Greek it is a rule (subject to a few exceptions only) that a Preposition must either (1) enter into Composition with a Verb or (2) be followed immediately by and 'govern' a Noun or Pronoun in an oblique Case. But in the Homeric language the limitation of the Prepositions to these two uses is still far from being established. A Preposition may not only be separated from the Case-form which it governs (a licence sometimes found in later writers), but may stand as a distinct word without governing any Case. In other words, it may be placed in the sentence with the freedom of an Adverb: *e.g.* ἀμφί may mean either *on both sides* (of an object expressed by an oblique Case) or simply *on both sides;* ἐν may mean *in* (taking a Dat.), or simply *inside;* and so of the others, *e.g.*—

γέλασσε δὲ πᾶσα περὶ χθών *all the earth smiled round about.*
ὑπαὶ δέ τε κόμπος ὀδόντων γίγνετο *beneath arose rattling of teeth.*

These uses, in which the Preposition is treated as an ordinary 'Adverb of place,' may be called in general the *adverbial uses.*

176.] **Tmesis.** The term TMESIS is sometimes applied generally to denote that a Preposition is 'separated' from the Verb which it qualifies, thus including all 'adverbial' uses, but is more properly restricted to a particular group of these uses, viz. those in which the meaning is the same as the Preposition and Verb have in Composition : *e. g.*—

οἱ κατὰ βοῦς Ὑπερίονος Ἠελίοιο ἤσθιον *who ate up* (κατήσθιον) *the oxen of the sun.*

οὕς ποτ' ἀπ' Αἰνείαν ἑλόμην *which I took from* (ἀφειλόμην) *Aeneas.*

ὑπὸ δ' ἔσχετο μισθόν *and promised* (ὑπέσχετο) *hire.*

μετὰ νῶτα βαλών *turning his back.*

χεῖρας ἀπὸ ξίφεϊ τμήξας *cutting off his hands by a sword.*

This is the sense in which the word τμῆσις was employed by the Greek grammarians, who looked at the peculiarities of Homer as deviations from the later established usage, and accordingly regarded the independent place of the Preposition as the result of a 'severance' of the Compound Verb. We may retain the term, provided that we understand it to mean no more than the fact that the two elements which formed a single word in later Greek were still separable in the language of Homer.

The distinction between Tmesis (in the strict sense) and other 'adverbial' uses cannot be drawn with any certainty. The clearest cases are those in which the compound Verb is necessary for the construction of other words in the sentence; *e. g.* in ἀπ' Αἰνείαν ἑλόμην or ὑπὸ δ' ἔσχετο μισθόν. On the other hand, the use is simply adverbial in—

περὶ φρένας ἵμερος αἱρεῖ *desire seizes his heart all round* (because the Compound περιαιρέω means *to strip off*, *to take away from round* a thing).

ὡς τοὺς ἡγεμόνες διεκόσμεον . . μετὰ δὲ κρείων Ἀγαμέμνων *and in the midst the king Agamemnon.*

ὡς Τρῶες πρὸ μὲν ἄλλοι ἀρηρότες, αὐτὰρ ἐπ' ἄλλοι *the Trojans, arrayed some in front, others behind.*

177.] Ellipse of the Verb. In certain cases, viz. when the Verb is understood, a Preposition may represent the whole Predicate of a clause :—

οἰωνοὶ δὲ πέρι πλέες ἠὲ γυναῖκες *about* (*him*) *are more &c.*

ἔνθ' ἔνι μὲν φιλότης *therein is love.*

οὔ τοι ἔπι δέος *there is no fear for thee.*

ἀλλ' ἄνα *but up !*

πάρα δ' ἀνήρ *the man is at hand.*

πάρ' ἔμοιγε καὶ ἄλλοι *others are at my command* (not *are beside me*, but=πάρεισι in its derived sense).

So when a Verb is to be repeated from a preceding clause ; as Il. 24. 229–233 ἔνθεν δώδεκα μὲν περικαλλέας ἔξελε πέπλους . . ἐκ δὲ δύ' αἴθωνας τρίποδας : Il. 3. 267 ὥρνυτο δ' αὐτίκ' ἔπειτα ἄναξ ἀνδρῶν Ἀγαμέμνων, ἀν δ' Ὀδυσεύς (sc. ὥρνυτο).

178.] Use with oblique Cases. Prepositions are frequently used in Greek with the Accusative, the locatival and instrumental Dative, and the ablatival Genitive; much less commonly (if at all) with the true Genitive.

It may be shown (chiefly by comparison with Sanscrit) that the government of Cases by Prepositions belongs to a later stage of the language than the use of Prepositions with Verbs. In the first instance the Case was construed directly with the Verb, and the Preposition did no more than qualify the Verbal meaning. *E. g.* in such a sentence as εἰς Τροίην ἦλθε the Acc. Τροίην originally went with ἦλθε. If however the construction Τροίην ἦλθε ceased to be usual except with εἰς, the Preposition would be felt to be necessary for the Acc., *i. e.* would 'govern' it.

In Homer we find many instances of a transitional character, in which a Case-form which appears to be governed by a Preposition may equally well be construed directly with the Verb,— modified, it may be, in meaning by the Preposition.

Thus we have ἀμφί with the Dat. in the recurring form—

ἀμφὶ δ᾽ ἄρ᾽ ὤμοισιν βάλετο ξίφος,

but the Preposition is not necessary for the Case, as we see from its absence in τόξ᾽ ὤμοισιν ἔχων, &c., and again from forms such as—

ἀμφὶ δὲ χαῖται | ὤμοις ἀίσσονται,
περὶ μὲν ξίφος ἀργυρόηλον | ὤμοιϊν βαλόμην

where the Preposition is best taken in the adverbial use. Cp. Il. 17. 523 ἐν δέ οἱ ἔγχος | νηδυίοισι μάλ᾽ ὀξὺ κραδαινόμενον λύε γυῖα, where ἐν is adverbial.

Again, we seem to have ἀμφί governing the Accusative in—

Il. 11. 482 ὥς ῥα τότ᾽ ἀμφ᾽ Ὀδυσῆα . . Τρῶες ἕπον.

But ἀμφί must be taken with ἕπον, as in Il. 11. 776 σφῶϊ μὲν ἀμφὶ βοὸς ἕπετον κρέα. So in ὑπὸ ζυγὸν ἤγαγε *brought under the yoke* the supposition of Tmesis is borne out by the form ὕπαγε ζυγὸν ὠκέας ἵππους. And in the line—

Il. 1. 53 ἐννῆμαρ μὲν ἀνὰ στρατὸν ᾤχετο κῆλα θεοῖο

the rhythm is against taking ἀνὰ στρατόν together (§ 367, 1), and points therefore to ἀνᾤχετο.

Again, the ablatival Genitive in—

ἦλθ᾽ ἐξ ἁλός *came out from the sea*

may be explained like τείχεος ἐξελθεῖν, &c.; and in νηὸς ἀπὸ πρύμνης χαμάδις πέσε like νηὸς ἀποθρῴσκων, and numerous similar constructions.

Thus the history of the usage of Prepositions confirms the general principle laid down in a previous chapter (§ 131), that the oblique Cases, with the exception of the true Genitive, are primarily construed with Verbs, and that consequently the construction of these Cases with Nouns and (we may now add) Prepositions is always of a derivative kind.

179.] Use with the Genitive. Where the Genitive with a Preposition is not ablatival, it may usually be explained in two ways, between which it is not always easy to choose :—

(1) It may be derived from one of the uses with Verbs discussed in §§ 149–151. *E. g.* the Genitive in—

ὅς τ' εἰσὶν διὰ δουρός *which goes through the wood*

is probably the Genitive of the space *within which* motion takes place. For εἰσὶν διὰ δουρός has the same relation to πεδίοιο διώκειν and πεδίοιο διαπρήσσειν, that ἦλθεν εἰς Τροίην has to Τροίην ἦλθεν and Τροίην εἰσῆλθεν.

(2) It may be of the same kind as the Genitive with a Noun : *e. g.* the construction with ἀντί may be the same as with the Adverbs ἄντα, ἀντίον, ἀντία, &c., and the Adjectives ἀντίος, ἐναντίος, &c., and this is evidently not akin to any of the constructions with Verbs, but falls under the general rule that a Noun or Pronoun qualifying a Noun is put in the Genitive (§ 147).

It is held by Curtius (*Elucidations,* c. 17) that the Genitive with ἀντί, πρό, διά, ὑπέρ, ὑπό, when they do not necessarily imply *motion from,* is of the same kind as the ordinary Genitive with Adjectives and Adverbs, *i. e.* the true Genitive. This view is supported by the Improper Prepositions, which nearly all govern the Genitive, whatever their meaning : *e. g.* ἐγγύς and ἑκάς, ἐντός and ἐκτός, ἄντα, μέχρι, ἕνεκα, &c. For in these cases the construction evidently does not depend upon the local relation involved, but is of the same kind as in δέμας πυρός, χάριν Τρώων, &c.

On the other hand, it is pointed out by Delbrück (*Synt. Forsch.* iv. p. 134) that such a construction of the Genitive is unknown in Sanscrit, and this argument, which applies to πρό, ὑπό, ὑπέρ (Sanscr. *prá, úpa, upári*), is confirmed by the Latin construction of *pro, sub, super* with the Abl. He would allow the supposition however in the case of ἀντί (the Sanscrit *ánti* being an Adverb), and perhaps διά ; regarding these words as having become Prepositions more recently than the others.

180.] Accentuation. The rules for the accentuation of Compound Verbs have been already given in § 88. They proceed on the general principle that (except in the augmented forms) the accent falls if possible on the Preposition ; either on the last syllable (as ἀπό-δος), or, if that is elided, then on the first (as ὕπ-αγε).

In regard to the other uses, and in particular the use with

Cases, the general assumption made by the Greek grammarians is that all Prepositions are oxytone. They do not recognise the modern distinction according to which ἐν, εἰς, and ἐξ are unaccented. This distinction rests entirely on the practice of the manuscripts (Chandler, p. 254), and apparently arises from the accident of the smooth breathing and accent falling on the same letter (Wackernagel, *K. Z.* xxix. 137).

Disyllabic Prepositions, however, are liable in certain cases to become barytone. The exact determination of these cases was a matter of much difficulty with the ancients, and unfortunately we cannot now determine how far their *dicta* rest upon observation of usage, and how far upon analogy and other theoretical considerations. The chief points of the accepted doctrine are :—

(1) The disyllabic Prepositions, except ἀμφί, ἀντί, ἀνά, and διά (except also the dialectical forms καταί, ὑπαί, παραί, ἀπαί, ὑπείρ, προτί), are liable to ' Anastrophe ;' that is to say, when placed *immediately after* the Verb or the Case-form to which they belong, they throw back the accent; as λούσῃ ἄπο (= ἀπο-λούσῃ), ἔχεν κάτα, ᾧ ἔπι, μάχῃ ἔνι, Ζεφύρου ὕπο, &c. Some held that the insertion of δέ before the Preposition did not prevent Anastrophe, and accordingly wrote ὦσε δ' ἄπο, &c.

(2) Also, according to some, if the Prep. stands at the end of a verse, or before a full stop (Schol. A on Il. 5. 283).

(3) Also, when it is equivalent to a Compound Verb (§ 177) ; as ἔνι, ἔπι, πέρι, πάρα (for ἔν-εστι, &c.). So ἄνα (for ἀνάστηθι) ; although ἀνά according to most authorities was not liable to Anastrophe. Some wrote πάρα γὰρ θεοί εἰσι καὶ ἡμῖν (Il. 3. 440), on the ground that in πάρ-εισι the accent is on the syllable παρ-.

(4) Two Prepositions are barytone in the adverbial use,—
ἄπο when it is = ἄποθεν *at a distance*, and
πέρι when it is = περισσῶς *exceedingly*.
To which some added ὕπο (as τρομέει δ' ὕπο γυῖα, &c.).

(5) Monosyllabic Prepositions when placed after the governed word take the acute accent (as an equivalent for Anastrophe) ; but only when they come at the end of the line. Some however accented Od. 3. 137—

κ ̓αλεσσαμένω ἀγορὴν ἐς πάντας Ἀχαιούς.

Most Prepositions, as appears from the Sanscrit accent, are originally barytone, and the so-called Anastrophe is really the *retention* of the accent in certain cases in which the Preposition is emphatic, or has a comparatively independent place in the sentence. Just as there is an orthotone ἔστι and an enclitic ἐστι (§ 87, 1), so there is an orthotone πέρι and a 'proclitic' περι, written περὶ before a governed Noun, but in reality unaccented.

This view will serve to explain one or two minor peculiarities of Greek usage. Thus (1) it is the rule that when the last syllable of a Preposition is elided before a Case-form, the accent is not thrown back. This is intelligible on the ground that the Preposition is in fact without accent ; and the same account will apply to the same peculiarity in the case of ἀλλά and τινά. On the other hand, (2) in the case of elision before a Verb (as ὕπ-αγε) the accent is retracted, because the Preposition is then the accented word.* Again, (3) the general rule of the Æolic dialect, that all oxytones become barytone, does not extend to Prepositions, because they are not real oxytones.

The word ἔτι (Sanscr. *áti*) is a Preposition which happens to have survived (with the original accent) in the adverbial use only : cp. πρός = *besides*.

One or two suggestions may be added in reference to the Prepositions which are generally said to be incapable of Anastrophe :—

ἀνά was thought by some to be capable of Anastrophe, and this view is supported by the adverbial use ἄνα *up !*

ἀμφί is probably a real oxytone, like the Adverb ἀμφίς. The corresponding Sanscrit Preposition *abhi* is oxytone, contrary to the general rule.

The assertion that ὑπαί, παραί, προτί, &c. are not liable to Anastrophe is difficult of interpretation. It may mean only that these words are not Attic, and by consequence that later usage furnished the grammarians with no examples.

If this is the true account of Anastrophe, it is probable that the Prepositions retained their accent in all quasi-adverbial uses, including Tmesis—not only when they followed the Verb or governed Noun. The doctrine of the grammarians is unintelligible unless it admits of this extension. For if we write πάρ' ἐμοί γε καὶ ἄλλοι because πάρα = πάρεισι, we must also write πάρα γὰρ θεοί εἰσι, where πάρα is equally emphatic. In Sanscrit too the Preposition when separated from its Verb is accented.

It is not so clear how far the later rules for Prepositions in Composition are to be applied to Homer. In Sanscrit there is an important difference between Principal and Subordinate Clauses. In a Principal Clause the Verb loses its accent, unless it begins the sentence (§ 87); the Preposition (which usually precedes the Verb, but is not always immediately before it) is accented. Thus we should have, on Sanscrit rules, such forms

---

* See Wackernagel, *K. Z.* xxiii. 457 ff. On this view, however, the original accent would be ἀπο-δος, ἐνι-σπες, πάρα-σχες, &c. It may perhaps be preserved in the Indic. ἐνι-σπες and Imper. ἐνι-σπε (see § 88, where a different explanation of these forms was suggested).

as πέρι δείδια, πέρι πάντων οἶδε, &c. But in Subordinate Clauses the accent is on the Verb, and the Preposition commonly forms one word with it, as in περιδείδια. If the Preposition is separated from the Verb, both are accented. In classical Greek two changes have taken place: (1) the Preposition and Verb are inseparable, and (2) the accent is placed almost uniformly according to the 'law of three syllables' (§ 88):—if it falls on the Preposition, as in σύμ-φημι, κάτ-εχεν, or on the Verb, as in συμ-φήσει, κατ-έχει, the reason is purely rhythmical. The first of these changes had not taken place in the time of Homer. As to the second we are practically without evidence. We do not even know when the law of three syllables obtained in Greek. It may be observed however that—

(1) When a word of three syllables could not be unaccented, the form πέρι δείδια became impossible; but it does not follow that πέρι lost its accent at the same time. An intermediate πέρι δείδια is quite admissible as a hypothesis.

(2) In many places in Homer it is uncertain whether a Preposition is part of a Compound or retains its character as a separate word. Thus we find—

Il. 4. 538 πολλοὶ δὲ περὶ κτείνοντο καὶ ἄλλοι (Wolf, from Ven. A.).

16. 497 ἐμεῦ πέρι μάρναο χαλκῷ (πέρι sic Ven. A.).

18. 191 στεῦτο γὰρ Ἡφαίστοιο πάρ᾽ οἰσέμεν ἔντεα καλά (so Ar.).

1. 269 καὶ μὲν τοῖσιν ἐγὼ μέθ᾽ ὁμίλεον (Ar.).

with the variants περικτείνοντο, περιμάρναο, παροισέμεν, μεθομίλεον. And the existing texts contain a good many Compounds which we might write divisim without loss to the sense; as Il. 18. 7 νηυσὶν ἐπικλονέονται, Od. 8. 14 πόντον ἐπιπλαγχθείς, Od. 16. 466 ἄστυ καταβλώσκοντα, Il. 2. 150, 384., 3. 12., 4. 230., 5. 332, 763, 772., 6. 100, &c.

In reference to such forms we may fairly argue that the tendency of grammarians and copyists, unfamiliar with the free adverbial use of the Prepositions, would be always towards forming Compounds; hence that modern critics ought to lean rather to the side of writing the words separately, and giving the Prepositions the accent which belonged to them as Adverbs.

With regard to the accent of Prepositions in the ordinary use with Case-forms it is still more difficult to decide. A Sanscrit Preposition generally follows the Noun which it governs : hence it does not furnish us with grounds for any conclusion about the Greek accent.

180*.] Apocope. Most Prepositions appear in Homer under several different forms, due to loss of the final vowel combined (in most cases) with assimilation to a following consonant.

Thus we find—

παρά and πάρ :
ἀνά, ἄν, ἄμ (βωμοῖσι, φόνον) :
κατά, κὰδ (δέ), κάβ-(βαλε), κάτ-(θανε), κὰρ (ῥόον), καμ-(μονίη),
    κὰγ (γόνυ), κὰκ (κεφαλῆς), κάλ-(λιπε), κὰπ (πεδίον) :
ὑπό, ὑβ-(βάλλειν) :
προτί, πρός (for προτ-), cp. ποτί, πός :
ὑπείρ (for ὑπέρι), ὑπέρ :
ἐνί, εἰν (εἰνί), ἐν :
ἀπό, ἀπ-(πέμψει).

This phenomenon appears to be connected with the loss of
accent which the Preposition suffers when closely connected with
a Verb or Case-form. That is to say, from the adverbial forms
πάρα, πρότι, κάτα, ἔνι, ἄνα (or ἀνά), &c. were formed in the first
instance the unaccented παρ, προς, κατ or κα, ἐν, ἀν. Then the
pairs πάρα and παρ, &c. were used promiscuously. Finally one
form was adopted as normal.

ἀμφί.

181.] The Preposition ἀμφί means *on both sides*, or (if the
notion of two sides is not prominent) *all round*. It is doubtless
connected with ἄμφω *both*.

The adverbial use is common ; *e.g.* with a Verb understood,
Od. 6. 292 ἐν δὲ κρήνη νάει, ἀμφὶ δὲ λειμών *and around is a
meadow*.

It is especially used in reference to the two sides of the body :
Il. 5. 310 ἀμφὶ δὲ ὄσσε κελαινὴ νὺξ ἐκάλυψε *black night covered
his eyes on both sides* (*i.e.* both eyes); Il. 10. 535 ἀμφὶ κτύπος
οὔατα βάλλει : Il. 18. 414 σπόγγῳ δ' ἀμφὶ πρόσωπα καὶ ἄμφω
χεῖρ' ἀπομόργνυ : Od. 2. 153 παρειὰς ἀμφί τε δειράς : Od. 9. 389
πάντα δέ οἱ βλέφαρ' ἀμφὶ καὶ ὀφρύας κτλ.

So Il. 6. 117 ἀμφὶ δέ μιν σφυρὰ τύπτε καὶ αὐχένα δέρμα κελαινόν
the shield smote him on the ankles on both sides and on the neck.
Here ἀμφί is generally taken to mean *above and beneath ;* wrongly,
as the passages quoted above show.

This use of ἀμφί is extended to the *internal* organs, esp. the
midriff (φρένες) regarded as the seat of feeling : as—

Il. 3. 442 οὐ γάρ πώ ποτέ μ' ὧδε ἔρως φρένας ἀμφεκάλυψε.
  6. 355 ἐπεὶ σὲ μάλιστα πόνος φρένας ἀμφιβέβηκε.
 16. 481 ἔνθ' ἄρα τε φρένες ἔρχαται ἀμφ' ἀδινὸν κῆρ.
Od. 8. 541 μάλα πού μιν ἄχος φρένας ἀμφιβέβηκεν.

So Hesiod, Theog. 554 χώσατο δὲ φρένας ἀμφί : Hom. H. Apoll.

273, H. Ven. 243; Mimnerm. 1. 7 φρένας ἀμφὶ κακαὶ τείρουσι
μέριμναι. Hence read—

Il. 1. 103 μένεος δὲ μέγα φρένες ἀμφὶ μέλαιναι πίμπλαντ',
and similarly in Il. 17. 83, 499, 573.

182.] The Dative with ἀμφί is a natural extension of the
ordinary locatival Dative—the Preposition being adverbial, and
not always *needed* to govern the Case. Compare (*e. g.*)—

Il. 1. 45 τόξ' ὤμοισιν ἔχων (Loc. Dat., § 145, 3).
20. 150 ἀμφὶ δ' ἄρ' ἄρρηκτον νεφέλην ὤμοισιν ἕσαντο.
11. 527 ἀμφ' ὤμοισιν ἔχει σάκος *has a shield on both sides on
his shoulders, i.e.* across his shoulders.

In a metaphorical sense ἀμφί is applied to the object *about*
which two parties contend : as Il. 3. 70 ἀμφ' Ἑλένῃ καὶ κτήμασι
πᾶσι μάχεσθαι : so of a negotiation, Il. 13. 382 συνώμεθα ἀμφὶ
γάμῳ *we shall agree about the marriage* ; Il. 7. 408 ἀμφὶ δὲ νεκροῖ-
σιν *as to the question of the dead* ; Il. 16. 647 ἀμφὶ φόνῳ
Πατρόκλου μερμηρίζων. Cp. the use with περί (§ 186). So too
in Sanscrit the Loc. is used with Verbs of *fighting* to express the
object *over* which the fighting is.

It is a further extension of this use when ἀμφί with the Dat.
is construed with Verbs meaning *to speak, think*, &c., as Od. 4.
151 ἀμφ' Ὀδυσῆϊ μυθεόμην. This last variety (in which the
notion of *two sides* disappears) is confined to the Odyssey: cp. 5.
287., 14. 338, 364.

A **true Dative** may follow ἀμφί, but cannot be said to be
governed by it; *e.g.* in Il. 14. 420 ἀμφὶ δέ οἱ βράχε τεύχεα *his
arms rattled about him* the Dat. is 'ethical,' as in Il. 13. 439
ῥῆξεν δέ οἱ ἀμφὶ χιτῶνα. So in Il. 4. 431 ἀμφὶ δὲ πᾶσι τεύχεα
ποικίλ' ἔλαμπε, the Dat. is not locatival, but the true Dat. The
two kinds of Dat. may be combined, as Il. 18. 205 ἀμφὶ δέ οἱ
κεφαλῇ νέφος ἔστεφε.

The construction of ἀμφί with the Dat. is not found in Attic
prose. It survives in the poetical style, and in Herodotus.

183.] The Accusative with ἀμφί is used when the Verb expresses *motion*, as—

Il. 5. 314 ἀμφὶ δ' ἐὸν φίλον υἱὸν ἐχεύατο πηχέε λευκώ.

Also to express *extent*, diffusion over a space, &c. (ideas naturally
conveyed by terms denoting motion) :—

Od. 11. 419 ὡς ἀμφὶ κρητῆρα τραπέζας τε πληθούσας κείμεθα
as we lay (scattered) about &c.

Accordingly it is especially used in Homer—
(1) of dwellers *about* a place, as Il. 2. 499, 751, &c.

(2) of attendants or followers; as Il. 2. 445 οἱ δ' ἀμφ' 'Ατρεΐωνα
. . θῦνον *they bustled about Agamemnon.*

The description *about* (*a person*) does not exclude the person
who is the centre of the group; *e.g.* in Il. 4. 294 (Agamemnon
found Nestor) οὓς ἑτάρους στέλλοντα . . ἀμφὶ μέγαν Πελάγοντα
'Αλάστορά τε Χρομίον τε, where Pelagon &c. are included under
the word ἕταροι. This is an approach to the later idiom, οἱ ἀμφὶ
Πλάτωνα = *Plato and his school.*

It should be observed that the motion expressed by the Verb
when ἀμφί takes an Acc. is not motion *to a point,* but motion
over a space. Hence this Acc. is not to be classed with Accusatives of the *terminus ad quem,* but with the Accusatives of Space
(§ 138). This remark will be confirmed by similar uses of other
Prepositions.

184.] The Genitive with ἀμφί is found in two instances,—

Il. 16. 825 μάχεσθον πίδακος ἀμφ' ὀλίγης *fight over a small
spring of water.*

Od. 8. 267 ἀείδειν ἀμφ' 'Αρεος φιλότητος κτλ.

Another example may perhaps lurk in—

Il. 2. 384 εὖ δέ τις ἅρματος ἀμφὶς ἰδὼν κτλ.

if we read ἀμφὶ Ϝιδὼν (*having looked over, seen to his chariot*).
With this meaning compare Il. 18. 254 ἀμφὶ μάλα φράζεσθε:
and for the construction the Attic use of περιορῶμαι with a Gen.
= *to look round after, take thought about* (Thuc. 4. 124): also the
Gen. with ἀμφιμάχεσθαι Il. 16. 496., 18. 20., 15. 391.

περί.

185.] The Preposition περί (or πέρι, § 180) has in Homer the
two meanings *around* and *beyond.*

Both these meanings are common in the adverbial use; the
second often yields the derivative meaning *beyond measure, exceedingly,* as—

Il. 16. 186 πέρι μὲν θείειν ταχύν *exceeding swift to run.*

18. 549 πέρι θαῦμα τέτυκτο *was an exceeding wonder.*

Od. 4. 722 πέρι γάρ μοι 'Ολύμπιος ἄλγε' ἔδωκε *for Zeus has
given to me griefs beyond measure.*

The meaning *beyond* is found in Tmesis, Il. 12. 322 πόλεμον
περὶ τόνδε φυγόντες *escaping this war:* Il. 19. 230 πολέμοιο περὶ
στυγεροῖο λίπωνται *shall remain over from war:* and in Composition, περίειμι *I excel,* περιγίγνομαι *I get beyond, surpass,* περίοιδα *I
know exceeding well* (Il. 13. 728 βουλῇ περιίδμεναι ἄλλων *to be
knowing in counsel beyond others;* cp. Od. 3. 244., 17. 317). The
Gen. in such constructions is ablatival (§ 152).

186.]　The Dative with περί (as with ἀμφί) is Locatival;
as Il. 1. 303 ἐρωήσει περὶ δουρί *will gush over* (lit. *round upon*) *the
spear ;* 2. 389 περὶ δ' ἔγχεϊ χεῖρα καμεῖται *his hand will be weary
with holding the spear ;* 2. 416 χιτῶνα περὶ στήθεσσι δαΐξαι *to tear
the chiton about* (*round on*) *the breast.* Also of an object of con-
tention, *over ;* as Il. 16. 568 περὶ παιδί . . πόνος εἴη the toil (*of
battle*) *might be over his son,* cp. Il. 17. 4, 133, Od. 5. 310 : and
in a derivative sense, Od. 2. 245 μαχήσασθαι περὶ δαιτί *to fight
about a feast.*

1. It is a question which meaning is to be given to περί in—

　　Il. 5. 566 περὶ γὰρ δίε ποιμένι λαῶν (so 9. 433., 11. 556).
　　　10. 240 ἔδεισεν δὲ περὶ ξανθῷ Μενελάῳ.
　　　17. 242 ὅσσον ἐμῇ κεφαλῇ πέρι δείδια (or περιδείδια).

and in the Compound (Il. 11. 508 τῷ ῥα περίδεισαν, 15. 123 περιδείσασα θεοῖσι, 21.
328., 23. 822). Most commentators here take **περί** = *exceedingly* and the Dat. of
the person as a *Dativus ethicus :* περὶ γὰρ δίε ποιμένι *for he feared exceedingly
for the shepherd,* &c. But it is difficult to find Homeric analogies for such a use
of the Dative, and the meaning *over, on behalf of* is supported by later writers :
H. Merc. 236 χωόμενον περὶ βουσί, H. Cer. 77 ἀχνυμένην περὶ παιδί, Hdt. 3. 35 περὶ
ἑωυτῷ δειμαίνοντα, Thuc. 1. 60 δεδιότες περὶ κτλ. ; also by the use of ἀμφί with
the Dat. (§ 182) in nearly the same meaning.

2. Much difficulty has been felt about the use of **περί** in a group of phrases
of which the following are the chief instances :—

　　Il. 4. 53 τὰς διαπέρσαι, ὅτ' ἄν τοι ἀπέχθωνται περὶ κῆρι (cp. 4. 46, &c.).
　　Od. 6. 158 κεῖνος δ' αὖ περὶ κῆρι μακάρτατος ἔξοχον ἄλλων.
　　Il. 21. 65 περὶ δ' ἤθελε θυμῷ (so 24. 236).
　　　22. 70 ἀλύσσοντες περὶ θυμῷ.
　　Od. 14. 146 περὶ γάρ μ' ἐφίλει καὶ κήδετο θυμῷ.
　　Il. 16. 157 τοῖσίν τε περὶ φρεσὶν ἄσπετος ἀλκή.
　　Od. 14. 433 περὶ γὰρ φρεσὶν αἴσιμα ᾔδη.

In all these places the Dative may be construed as a Locative (although
κῆρι without περί is only found in Il. 9. 117) : the only question is whether
the Preposition is to be taken in the literal local sense *round, all over,* or in the
derivative sense *exceedingly.* In favour of the latter it may be said that the
same combinations of Preposition and Verb are found without a Dat. such as
κῆρι or θυμῷ, where accordingly **περί** must mean *exceedingly ;* compare—

　　Il. 13. 430 τὴν περὶ κῆρι φίλησε πατὴρ　⎫
　　Od. 8. 63 τὸν περὶ Μοῦσ' ἐφίλησε　　　⎭
　　Od. 14. 433 περὶ γὰρ φρεσὶν αἴσιμα ᾔδη　⎫
　　　2. 88 περὶ κέρδεα οἶδε　　　　　　　　⎭
　　Il. 16. 157 τοῖσίν τε περὶ φρεσὶν ἄσπετος ἀλκή　⎫
　　Od. 12. 279 πέρι τοι μένος　　　　　　　　　⎭
　　Od. 5. 36 περὶ κῆρι θεὸν ὡς τιμήσουσι　⎫
　　Il. 8. 161 περὶ μέν σε τίον Δαναοί.　　　⎭

Again, in Il. 4. 46 τάων μοι περὶ κῆρι τιέσκετο the meaning *beyond* is required
by the Gen. τάων ; cp. 4. 257 περὶ μέν σε τίω Δαναῶν ταχυπώλων, 7. 289 περὶ δ'
ἔγχει Ἀχαιῶν φέρτατός ἐσσι, 17. 22 περὶ σθένεϊ βλεμεαίνει. So with the Acc. in
Il. 13. 631 περὶ φρένας ἔμμεναι ἄλλων.

On the other side, the representation of a feeling as something *surrounding* or *covering* the heart, midriff, &c. is common in Homer. Thus we have—

Il. 11. 89 σίτου τε γλυκεροῖο περὶ φρένας ἵμερος αἱρεῖ.
Od. 9. 362 ἐπεὶ Κύκλωπα περὶ φρένας ἦλθεν οἶνος.

So of a sound, Il. 10. 139 περὶ φρένας ἦλθ' ἰωή (cp. Od. 17. 261). And more frequently with ἀμφί; cp. Od. 19. 516 πυκιναὶ δέ μοι ἀμφ' ἀδινὸν κῆρ ὀξεῖαι μελεδῶνες ὀδυρομένην ἐρέθουσι; and the other passages quoted at the end of § 181. Similarly περὶ κῆρι, περὶ φρεσί, may have been meant in the literal sense,—the feeling (fear, anger, &c.) being thought of as *filling* or *covering* the heart. On the whole, however, the evidence is against this view;—unless indeed we explain περὶ κῆρι as a traditional phrase, used without a distinct sense of its original meaning.

The occasional use of the Dat. with περί in Attic is probably due to familiarity with Homer.

187.] The Accusative with περί is used (as with ἀμφί) when *motion* or *extent in space* is expressed: as Il. 1. 448 ἑκατόμβην ἔστησαν περὶ βωμόν *placed the hecatomb round the altar*; 2. 750 περὶ Δωδώνην οἴκι' ἔθεντο *made their dwellings round Dodona.* Generally speaking the Accusative implies surrounding in a less exact or complete way than the Dative. It makes us think of the *space about* an object rather than of its actual circumference. Occasionally, of course, the circumference *is* the space over which motion takes place, or extent is measured: as Il. 12. 297 ῥάψε ῥάβδοισι διηνεκέσιν περὶ κύκλον *round in a circle*; Il. 18. 274 ἑστάμεναι περὶ τοῖχον *to stand along the wall all round it.*

188.] The Genitive with περί is used in three distinct ways:—

1. With περί meaning *beyond* (in the figurative sense, = excelling) it expresses the object of comparison: Il. 1. 287 περὶ πάντων ἔμμεναι *to surpass all*, Od. 1. 235 ἄϊστον ἐποίησαν περὶ πάντων *have made him unseen more than all men*, 4. 231 ἐπιστάμενος περὶ πάντων. This use is distinctively Homeric. The Gen. is ablatival, as with Adjectives of comparison (§ 152).

2. With περί = *round, over* (in the local sense) the Gen. is very rare; the instances are—

Od. 5. 68 ἠδ' αὐτοῦ τετάνυστο περὶ σπείους γλαφυροῖο
ἡμερὶς ἡβώωσα.
130 τὸν μὲν ἐγὼν ἐσάωσα περὶ τρόπιος βεβαῶτα.

The Gen. may be akin to the (partitive) Gen. of place (§ 149): the vine *e. g.* grew *round in* or *over* (but not *covering*) the cave.

3. With περί = *over* (the object of a contest), as Il. 16. 1 ὡς οἱ μὲν περὶ νηὸς ἐϋσσέλμοιο μάχοντο, 12. 142 ἀμύνεσθαι περὶ νηῶν *to defend the ships*; sometimes also in the figurative sense, *about*, Il. 11. 700 περὶ τρίποδος γὰρ ἔμελλον θεύσεσθαι, Od. 9. 423 ὥς τε

περὶ ψυχῆς *as when life is at stake;* and of *doubt,* Il. 20. 17 ἤ τι περὶ Τρώων καὶ ᾿Αχαιῶν μερμηρίζεις. The use with Verbs of *anger* and *fear* is closely akin; Il. 9. 449 παλλακίδος πέρι χώσατο; 17. 240 νέκυος πέρι δείδια (unless we read περιχώσατο, περιδείδια). The *weapons* of the contest are said to be fought *over* in Od. 8. 225 ἐρίζεσκον περὶ τόξων; so Il. 15. 284 ὁππότε κοῦροι ἐρίσσειαν περὶ μύθων. And this is also applied to the quarrel itself, Il. 16. 476 συνίτην ἔριδος πέρι θυμοβόροιο (cp. 20. 253).

Under this head will come the Gen. in Il. 23. 485 τρίποδος περιδώμεθον *let us wager a tripod,* Od. 23. 78 ἐμέθεν περιδώσομαι αὐτῆς *I will stake myself.* Whatever may be the original meaning of περιδόσθαι, it is construed as if = *to join issue, contend* (Lat. *pignore certare*): cp. the Attic use περιδίδομαί τινι περί (Gen. of the thing staked).

By a not unnatural extension, περί with the Gen. follows Verbs meaning to *speak, know,* &c., but only in the Odyssey; viz. 1. 135 (= 3. 77) ἵνα μιν περὶ πατρὸς ἀποιχομένοιο ἔροιτο; 15. 347 εἴπ᾽ ἄγε μοι περὶ μητρὸς κτλ.; 17. 563 οἶδα γὰρ εὖ περὶ κείνου; also 1. 405., 7. 191., 16. 234., 17. 371., 19. 270. Note that the corresponding use of ἀμφί with the Dat. is similarly peculiar to the Odyssey (§ 182).

The origin of this group of constructions is not quite clear. It may be noted, however, that they answer for the most part to constructions of the Gen. without a Preposition; cp. ἀμύνεσθαι περὶ νηῶν and ἀμύνεσθαι νηῶν; and again εἰπὲ περὶ μητρός, οἶδα περὶ κείνου, &c. with the examples given in § 151, *d.*

παρά.

189.] The Preposition παρά (παραί, by Apocope **πάρ)** means *alongside.* It is common in the adverbial use (see § 177), and also in Tmesis and Composition. Note the derivative meanings—

(1) *at hand,* hence *at command;* as Il. 9. 43 πάρ τοι ὁδός *the way is open to you;* Od. 9. 125 οὐ γὰρ Κυκλώπεσσι νέες πάρα.

(2) *aside;* as Il. 11. 233 παραὶ δέ οἱ ἐτράπετ᾽ ἔγχος *the spear was turned to his side* (instead of striking him).

(3) hence figuratively, παρά μ᾽ ἤπαφε *cozened me ' aside,'* away from my aim : and so παρπεπιθών *changing the mind by persuasion,* παρειπών *talking over,* &c.; also, with a different metaphor, *wrongly.*

(4) *past,* with Verbs of motion, as ἔρχομαι, ἐλαύνω, &c.

190.] With the Dative παρά means *beside, in the company of, near.* It is applied in Homer to both persons and things (whereas in later Greek the Dat. with παρά is almost wholly confined to persons); thus we have παρὰ νηί, παρὰ νηυσί (very frequently), παρ' ἅρμασι, παρὰ βωμῷ, πὰρ ποσί, παρὰ σταθμῷ, &c. This Dat. is either locatival or instrumental: see § 144. It may be used after a Verb of motion (*e.g.* Il. 13. 617), see § 145, 4.

191.] The Accusative with παρά is commonly used—

(1) when *motion* ends *beside* or near a person or thing: as Il. 3. 406 ἧσο παρ' αὐτὸν ἰοῦσα *go and sit by him;* Il. 7. 190 τὸν μὲν πὰρ πόδ' ἑὸν χαμάδις βάλε. Hence the use of the Acc. often *implies* motion: as Il. 11. 314 παρ' ἔμ' ἵστασο *place yourself beside me;* Od. 1. 333 στῆ ῥα παρὰ σταθμόν *came and stood beside the pillar;* Il. 6. 433 λαὸν δὲ στῆσον παρ' ἐρινεόν. Similarly of the *place near which* a weapon has struck, as Il. 5. 146 κληῖδα παρ' ὦμον πλῆξε *struck the collar-bone by the shoulder.*

(2) of *motion* or *extent alongside* of a thing (esp. a coast, a river, a wall, &c.); Il. 1. 34 βῆ δ' ἀκέων παρὰ θῖνα *went along the shore;* Od. 9. 46 πολλὰ δὲ μῆλα ἔσφαζον παρὰ θῖνα *sacrificed many sheep along the shore;* Il. 2. 522 πὰρ ποταμὸν ἔναιον *dwelt by the side of the river;* Il. 3. 272 πὰρ ξίφεος κουλεὸν ἄωρτο *hung beside the sword-scabbard.*

(3) of *motion past* a place; as Il. 11. 166, 167 οἱ δὲ παρ' Ἴλου σῆμα .. παρ' ἐρινεὸν ἐσσεύοντο *they sped past the tomb of Ilus, past the fig-tree;* Il. 6. 42 παρὰ τρόχον ἐξεκυλίσθη *rolled out past the wheel;* Il. 16. 312 οὖτα Θόαντα στέρνον γυμνωθέντα παρ' ἀσπίδα *passing the shield* (implied motion, οὖτα=*thrust at and struck*). The derivative meaning *beyond* (=*in excess of*) is only found in Homer in the phrases πὰρ δύναμιν (Il. 13. 787) and παρὰ μοῖραν (Od. 14. 509): but cp. the Adj. παραίσιος *against fate.*

192.] With a Genitive παρά properly means *sideways from, aside from.* As with the Dative, it is used of *things* as well as *persons* (whereas in later Greek it is practically restricted to *persons*). On the other hand it is confined in Homer to the local sense; thus it is found with Verbs meaning to *go, bring, take,* &c. not (as afterwards) with ἀκούω, μανθάνω, οἶδα, or the like. An apparent exception is —

Il. 11. 794 εἰ δέ τινα φρεσὶν ᾗσι θεοπροπίην ἀλεείνει,

καί τινά οἱ πὰρ Ζηνὸς ἐπέφραδε πότνια μήτηρ,

where however the notion of *bringing* a message is sufficiently prominent to explain the use. So Il. 11. 603 φθεγξάμενος παρὰ νηός *sending his voice from the ship;* and Hes. Op. 769 αἵδε γὰρ ἡμέραι εἰσὶ Διὸς πάρα, i. e. *coming from Zeus.* The later use is to be seen in Emped. 144 θεοῦ πάρα μῦθον ἀκούσας, Xenophanes 3. 1 ἀβροσύνας δὲ μαθόντες ἀνωφελέας παρὰ Λυδῶν.

The original meaning *sideways* or *at the side from* is visible in some of the uses with a Gen. denoting a *thing*: as Il. 4. 468 παρ' ἀσπίδος ἐξεφαάνθη *appeared beyond (outside the shelter of)* the *shield*: so probably Il. 4. 500 υἱὸν Πριάμοιο νόθον βάλε .. παρ' ἵππων ὠκειάων *struck him* (aiming) *past the chariot.* So too a sword is drawn παρὰ μηροῦ *sideways from the thigh.* The same meaning lies at the root of the frequent use of παρά in reference to the act of passing from one person to another (as in παραδίδωμι and παραδέχομαι), hence of gifts, messages, &c.

It is usual to regard παρά with the Gen. as meaning *from the side of, from beside, de chez.* But this is contrary to the nature of a prepositional phrase. The Case-ending and the Stem must form a single notion, which the Preposition then modifies ; hence (*e. g.*) παρὰ μηροῦ means *beside from-the-thigh*, not *from beside-the-thigh.* This is especially clear where the Preposition is joined to a Verb ; Od. 19. 187 παραπλάγξασα Μαλειῶν *driving-aside from-Maleae:* and in—

Il. 4. 97 τοῦ κεν δὴ πάμπρωτα παρ' ἀγλαὰ δῶρα φέροιο the rhythm connects παρά with φέροιο rather than with τοῦ—*thou wilt bring-aside* (= *trans-fer*) *from-him.* So with other Prepositions : ἀπὸ Τροίης *off from-Troy*, not *from off-Troy* : κατ' οὐρανοῦ *down from-heaven*, not *from under-heaven.* As to ὑπό with the Gen. =*from under*, see § 204.

μετά.

193.] The Preposition μετά in the adverbial use means *midway, in the middle ; e. g.* with a Verb understood, Il. 2. 446 μετὰ δὲ κτλ. *and among them &c.* Hence *alternately,* as Od. 15. 460 χρύσεον ὅρμον ἔχων, μετὰ δ' ἠλέκτροισιν ἕερτο *strung with electrum between (the gold)*; so in *succession, afterwards,* as Od. 21. 231 πρῶτος ἐγώ, μετὰ δ' ὔμμες *I first and you in turn ;* Od. 15. 400 μετὰ γάρ τε καὶ ἄλγεσι τέρπεται ἀνήρ = *a man has his turn of being pleased even in the course of his sufferings.*

The notion of *alternation* appears in Compounds with μετά, as μεταβάλλω, μεταστρέφω : in Tmesis, Od. 12. 312 μετὰ δ' ἄστρα βέβηκε *the stars have changed their place.* So μεταπαυόμενοι (Il. 17. 373) means *with turns* or *intervals of rest.*

194.] With the Dative μετά means *between* or (less exactly) *among.* The meaning *between* is found in phrases such as μετὰ χερσί, μετὰ ποσσί, μετὰ φρεσί (on the double character of the φρένες cp. § 181); also, of two *parties,* μετ' ἀμφοτέροισι.

The use in reference to several objects (*among*) is mostly restricted to *persons,* since it conveys the idea of *association* of units forming a group, &c. (whereas ἐν is more *local*). Hence μετ' ἀστράσι (Il. 22. 28, 317) is said of a star *among other stars* (with a touch of personification): and in Il. 21. 122 κεῖσο μετ'

N

ἰχθύσι there is a sarcastic force—*lie there with the fish for company*. Cp. also the phrase Od. 5. 224 μετὰ καὶ τόδε τοῖσι γενέσθω *let this be as one among them*. The expression in Il. 15. 118 μεθ' αἵματι καὶ κονίῃσι is equivalent to a Collective Noun, = 'the crowd of wounded and fallen.' So Il. 21. 503 μετὰ στροφάλιγγι κονίης. a somewhat bolder phrase of the same kind.

The Dat. with μετά is locatival (whereas with σύν and ἅμα it is comitative). This appears in the restriction to Plurals or Collectives, also in the use with Verbs of *motion*, as Il. 4. 16 φιλότητα μετ' ἀμφοτέροισι βάλωμεν (§ 145, 6).

The construction of μετά with the Dative is in the main Homeric. It is occasionally imitated in later poetry.

195.] With the Accusative μετά has the two meanings *among* and *after*.

The meaning *among* is found after Verbs of motion with Plurals, and also with Collective Nouns, as μεθ' ὁμήγυριν, μεθ' ὅμιλον; so μετὰ δεῖπνον to (*join the company at*) *a feast*, μετά τ' ἤθεα καὶ νομὸν ἵππων = *to the pasture ground where other horses are.* It occurs without a Verb of motion in Il. 2. 143 πᾶσι μετὰ πληθύν *to all among the multitude;* Il. 9. 54 μετὰ πάντας ὁμήλικας ἔπλεν ἄριστος (so Od. 16. 419). And with a Singular in Il. 18. 552 δράγματα μετ' ὄγμον πίπτον *the handfuls of corn fell in the middle of the furrow* (between the ridges).

Of the other meaning we may distinguish the varieties—

(1) *after, following;* Il. 13. 513 ἐπαΐξαι μεθ' ἑὸν βέλος *following his weapon*, Od. 2. 406 μετ' ἴχνια βαῖνε θεοῖο.

(2) *after, in order to find* (with a Verb of motion), as μετ' ἔμ' ἤλυθες *has come in search of me*, Od. 1. 184 ἐς Τεμέσην μετὰ χαλκόν.

(3) *in succession to, next to;* τὸν δὲ μετὰ κτλ. *and after him &c.;* Il. 8. 289 πρώτῳ τοι μετ' ἐμὲ πρεσβήϊον ἐν χερὶ θήσω *to thee after myself;* of rank, Il. 7. 228 οἷοι .. μετέασι καὶ μετ' Ἀχιλλῆα *even (in the second rank) after Achilles.*

196.] With the Genitive μετά occurs in five places (with a Plural Noun), in the meaning *among* or *with*—

Il. 13. 700 μετὰ Βοιωτῶν ἐμάχοντο.
21. 458 οὐδὲ μεθ' ἡμέων πειρᾷ κτλ.
24. 400 τῶν μέτα παλλόμενος κλήρῳ λάχον.
Od. 10. 320 μετ' ἄλλων λέξο ἑταίρων.
16. 140 μετὰ δμώων τ' ἐνὶ οἴκῳ πῖνε κτλ.

Of these instances the first is in a passage probably inserted afterwards to glorify the Athenians; the second is in the θεῶν μάχη, and therefore doubtful; in the third we should perhaps write μεταπαλλόμενος and construe *of them casting lots in turn I was chosen*. But the last two indicate that the use had crept into colloquial language as early as the Odyssey, taking the place of σύν or ἅμα with the Dative. See § 221.

ἐπί.

197.] The Preposition ἐπί means *over, upon*; sometimes *after* (as we speak of following *upon*); *with, at* (i. e. close *upon*); *in addition, besides*, esp. of an addition made to *correspond with* or *complete* something else; also, *attached to*, as an inseparable *incident* or *condition* of a person or thing; and conversely, *on the condition, in the circumstances*, &c.

Examples of these meanings in the adverbial use are—

Il. 1. 462 ἐπὶ δ' αἴθοπα οἶνον λεῖβε *poured wine over* (the meat).

13. 799 πρὸ μέν τ' ἄλλ', αὐτὰρ ἐπ' ἄλλα *in front—behind*.

Od. 1. 273 θεοὶ δ' ἐπὶ μάρτυροι ἔστων *the gods be witnesses thereto*.

5. 443 ἐπὶ σκέπας ἦν ἀνέμοιο *there was thereto* (the place was *furnished* with) *a shelter from the wind*.

Il. 18. 529 κτεῖνον δ' ἐπὶ μηλοβοτῆρας *killed the shepherds with the sheep*.

1. 233 ἐπὶ μέγαν ὅρκον ὀμοῦμαι *I will swear in confirmation*. With a Verb understood, ἔπι = *is present, is in the case*, as Od. 2. 58 οὐ γὰρ ἔπ' ἀνήρ *there is no man* (*for the purpose*); Il. 1. 515 οὔ τοι ἔπι δέος *there is no fear with* or *for you* (as part of your circumstances); Il. 21. 110 ἔπι τοι καὶ ἐμοὶ θάνατος *death is my lot too* (cp. 6. 357 οἷσιν ἐπὶ Ζεὺς θῆκε κακὸν μόρον).

It is very much used in Composition. Note the meaning *over* in ἐπι-πλέω *to sail over*, also ἐπ-οίχομαι *to go over, review*, ἐπι-πωλέομαι, ἐπ-αλάομαι (Il. 17. 650 μάχη δ' ἐπὶ πᾶσα φαάνθη *the fight was lighted up all over*); *besides*, in ἐπι-δίδωμι, &c.; *to* (of bringing aid, joining, &c.) in ἐπ-αρήγω, ἐπ-αλέξω, ἐπ-αραρίσκω, ἐπ-αλλάσσω, &c.; *for*, in ἐπι-κλώθω *to spin for* (so as to *attach to*); hence of assent, ἐπι-νεύω, ἐπι-τλῆναι, ἐπι-είκω (with a general affirmative meaning, *on* as opposed to *off*, *for* as opposed to *against*).

198.] With the Dative ἐπί has the same group of meanings; note especially—

(1) ἐπὶ νηυσί *by the ships*, ἐπ' ὄεσσι *with the sheep* (of a shepherd), ἐπὶ κτεάτεσσι *with* (in charge of) *the possessions*; Il. 4. 235 ἐπὶ ψεύδεσσιν ἔσσετ' ἀρωγός *will be a helper with* (*on the side of*) *falsehood* (or *false men*, reading ψευδέσσι).

(2) Il. 4. 258 ἀλλοίῳ ἐπὶ ἔργῳ *in* (engaged *upon*) *other work*, so ἀτελευτήτῳ ἐπὶ ἔργῳ *with a work unfinished*: so Il. 4. 178 ἐπὶ πᾶσι *in all cases dealt with*.

(3) Od. 17. 454 οὐκ ἄρα σοί γ' ἐπὶ εἴδεϊ καὶ φρένες ἦσαν *with form thou hast not understanding too*; Il. 13. 485 τῷδ' ἐπὶ θυμῷ *with this spirit (too)*; Hes. Theog. 153 ἰσχὺς .. μεγάλῳ ἐπὶ εἴδει.

(4) Od. 11. 548 τοιῷδ' ἐπ' ἀέθλῳ *with such a prize* (when such a thing is prize); μισθῷ ἔπι ῥητῷ *for fixed hire* (*given* the hire, hence *in view* of it).

(5) ἐπ' ἤματι *for the day*, i. e. *as the day's work, in a single day.* Note also that ἐπί meaning *upon* very often takes the Dat. after Verbs of motion, as κατέχευεν ἐπ' οὔδει *poured on to the ground*: hence with the meaning *against*, as ἐπ' ἀλλήλοισιν ἰόντες, μάρνασθαι ἐπ' ἀνδράσι, &c.

199.] With the Accusative ἐπί implies (1) motion *directed to* a place, seldom (2) to a *person*; or (3) motion or (4) diffusion, extent, &c. *over* a space or (5) time.

1. After Verbs of motion the Acc. does not (like the Dat.) distinctly express that the motion *terminates on* the place : *e.g.* ἐπὶ χθόνα is merely *to* or *towards the ground*, but ἐπὶ χθονί implies *alighting on it*. Cp. Il. 18. 565 ἀταρπιτὸς ἦεν ἐπ' αὐτήν *there was a path leading to it*; Il. 2. 218 ἐπὶ στῆθος συνοχωκότε *bent in over the chest.*

Hence the phrases expressing *attitude*, as ἐπὶ στόμα, ἐπὶ γοῦνα, &c. Two forms, ἐπὶ δεξιά and ἐπ' ἀριστερά, are used even when motion is not expressed ; as Il. 5. 355 εὖρεν ἔπειτα μάχης ἐπ' ἀριστερὰ θοῦρον Ἄρηα ἥμενον. Note however that ἐπ' ἀριστεροῖς and ἐπ' ἀριστερῶν are metrically impossible.

2. The use with *persons* in the meaning *towards, in quest of*, is rare, and almost confined to the Iliad : as 2. 18 βῆ δ' ἄρ' ἐπ' Ἀτρείδην Ἀγαμέμνονα, τὸν δ' ἐκίχανεν: also 5. 590., 10. 18, 54, 85, 150., 11. 343, 805., 12. 342., 13. 91, 459., 14. 24., 16. 535., 21. 348, Od. 5. 149.

3. The meaning *over*, with Verbs of motion, is very common ; ἐπὶ πόντον (ἰών, πλέων, φεύγων, &c.), ἐπὶ γαῖαν, ἐπὶ χθόνα, ἐπὶ κύματα, &c. Also with Verbs of *looking*, as Il. 1. 350 ὁρόων ἐπ' ἀπείρονα πόντον.

Hence such phrases as ἐπὶ στίχας, of troops &c. moving *in ranks*, i. e. *over* or *along* certain lines: as Il. 3. 113 ἵππους ἔρυξαν ἐπὶ στίχας: and so Od. 5. 245 ἐπὶ στάθμην ἴθυνε *straightened along* (hence *by*) *the rule*.

So with Plural Nouns, Il. 14. 381 οἰχόμενοι ἐπὶ πάντας *going over them all*, Od. 15. 492 πολλὰ βροτῶν ἐπὶ ἄστε' ἀλώμενος ; and of a distribution, Od. 16. 385 δασσάμενοι κατὰ μοῖραν ἐφ' ἡμέας i. e. equally, so as to go *round.*

4. The instances in which *extent* (without *motion*) is implied are chiefly found in the Odyssey (2. 370, &c.). Examples from the Iliad are : 9. 506 φθάνει δέ τε πᾶσαν ἐπ' αἶαν *she is beforehand all the world over* (so 23. 742) : 10. 213 κλέος εἴη πάντας ἐπ' ἀνθρώπους, 24. 202, 535. It will be seen that they are from books 9, 10, 23, 24.

Notice also the use with Neuters expressing *quantity;* as Il. 5. 772 τόσσον ἔπι θρῴσκουσι *to such a distance they bound ;* also ἐπὶ πολλόν *a long way,* ἐπὶ ἶσα *to an equal extent;* and esp. the common phrase ὅσον τ' ἐπί, see Il. 2. 616, &c.

5. Of *time:* Il. 2. 299 μείνατ' ἐπὶ χρόνον *wait for* (lit. *over*) *a time ;* Od. 7. 288 εὗδον παννύχιοι καὶ ἐπ' ἠῶ καὶ μέσον ἦμαρ *slept all night and on through morning and midday.*

200.] The Genitive with ἐπί is used in nearly the same sense as the Dative, but usually with less definitely local force; in particular—

(1) with words expressing the great divisions of space, esp. when a contrast is involved (land and sea, &c.); as ἐπὶ χέρσου, ἐπ' ἠπείρου, ἐπ' ἀγροῦ; Od. 12. 27 ἢ ἁλὸς ἢ ἐπὶ γῆς ἀλγήσετε (cp. Il. 13. 565). This is evidently a Gen. of place, § 149. For the difference of Gen. and Dat. cp. Il. 1. 485 ἐπ' ἠπείροιο ἔρυσσαν ὑψοῦ ἐπὶ ψαμάθοις.

(2) where the local relation is a familiar one; as ἐπὶ νηός, ἐπ' ἀπήνης, ἐφ' ἵππων, ἐπὶ θρόνου, ἐπ' οὐδοῦ, ἐπὶ πύργου, ἐπ' ἀγκῶνος, ἐπὶ μελίης (ἐρεισθείς). Thus ἐπὶ νηυσί means *on* or *beside* ships, ἐπὶ νηῶν *on board* ships.

(3) with Verbs of motion, *upon* (of the *terminus ad quem*), as Il. 3. 293 κατέθηκεν ἐπὶ χθονός; so *bearing down on,* as Il. 3. 6 πέτονται ἐπ' Ὠκεανοῖο ῥοάων : Il. 5. 700 προτρέποντο μελαινάων ἐπὶ νηῶν : Od. 3. 171 νεοίμεθα νήσου ἔπι Ψυρίης *taking the course by the island Psyria.* So perhaps Il. 7. 195 (εὔχεσθε) σιγῇ ἐφ' ὑμείων (*keeping the words*) *to yourselves.*

(4) of *time;* ἐπ' εἰρήνης (Il. 2. 797, &c.); ἐπὶ προτέρων ἀνθρώπων (Il. 5. 637, &c.). Cp. the Gen. of Time, § 150.

In later prose the Gen. is very common, and the uses become indistinguishable from those of the Dat.

ὑπό.

201.] The Preposition ὑπό (also ὑπαί) usually means *beneath,* as in Il. 2. 95 ὑπὸ δὲ στεναχίζετο γαῖα *the earth groaned beneath* (*their tread*). The original sense, however, seems to have been *upwards,* as in the Superlative ὕπ-ατος *uppermost* (cp. ὕψι *aloft,* ὕπ-τιος *facing upwards*). On this view we can understand why

ὑπό is not applied (like κατά) to express *downward* motion.
Hence, too, it is especially used of *supporting* a thing, as Il. 1.
486 ὑπὸ δ' ἕρματα μακρὰ τάνυσσαν: and on the same principle it
expresses resistance to a motion (whereas κατά implies *yielding*,
going *with the stream* &c.); as Il. 5. 505 ὑπὸ δ' ἔστρεφον ἡνιοχῆες
the drivers wheeled them up, i. e. *to face* (the Trojans) : and so
ὑπ-αντιάσας *meeting face to face*, ὑπο-μένω *to stand against* (as we
say, *up to*); and with the derived notion of *answering*, ὑπ-αείδω
I sing in correspondence, ὑπο-κρίνομαι (= Att. ἀποκρίνομαι), ὑπο-
βάλλω *I take up* (a speaker), ὑπ-ακούω *I hear in reply*, i. e. *show
that I hear* (by answering or obeying).

So too the Compounds ὑφ-ορῶ, ὑπ-όψιος, ὑπό-δρα, &c. do not
express looking *down*, but looking *upwards from under;* even in
Il. 3. 217 στάσκεν ὑπαὶ δὲ ἴδεσκε κατὰ χθονὸς ὄμματα πήξας it is
the *face* that is bent downwards : cp. Il. 19. 17.

From the notion of being *immediately under* is derived that of
being moved *by*, i. e. of *agency* or *cause*. The transition may be
seen in ὑπο-είκω *I give way (before)*, ὑπο-τρέω &c.; so Il. 16. 333
ὑπεθερμάνθη *was warmed by (the blood)*.

202.] **With the Dative** ὑπό is very common in the simple local
meaning, *under*. It is sometimes found with Verbs of motion,
as Od. 4. 297 δέμνι' ὑπ' αἰθούσῃ θέμεναι; and even when motion
from is intended, in Il. 18. 244 ἔλυσαν ὑφ' ἅρμασιν ὠκέας ἵππους.
In this case however we have to consider that ἁρμάτων is metrically impossible.

The derived sense *under the charge* or *power* is found in such
uses as Il. 5. 231 ὑφ' ἡνιόχῳ (of horses), 6. 139 Ζεὺς γάρ οἱ ὑπὸ
σκήπτρῳ ἐδάμασσε, 6. 171 θεῶν ὑπ' ἀμύμονι πομπῇ : also, with the
notion of an effect produced (where the Gen. would therefore be
rather more natural), ὑπὸ χερσί (δαμῆναι, θανέειν, &c.), ὑπὸ δουρί
(τυπείς, &c.); Il. 13. 667 νούσῳ ὕπ' ἀργαλέῃ φθίσθαι, Od. 4. 295
ὕπνῳ ὕπο γλυκερῷ ταρπώμεθα : and often of *persons*, as Il. 5. 93
ὑπὸ Τυδείδῃ πυκιναὶ κλονέοντο φάλαγγες.

203.] **The Accusative** is used with ὑπό (1) of motion *to a
point under*, as—

Il. 2. 216 ὑπὸ Ἴλιον ἦλθε *came under (the walls of) Troy*.

17. 309 τὸν βάλ' ὑπὸ κληῖδα μέσην (so often with Verbs *of
striking*, &c.).

Also (2) of motion *passing under*, and hence of *extent under*: Od.
15. 349 εἴ που ἔτι ζώουσιν ὑπ' αὐγὰς ἠελίοιο i. e. *anywhere that the
sun shines* (cp. ὑπ' ἠῶ τ' ἠέλιόν τε—an equivalent phrase).

Il. 2. 603 οἳ δ' ἔχον Ἀρκαδίην ὑπὸ Κυλλήνης ὄρος.

3. 371 ἄγχε δέ μιν πολύκεστος ἱμὰς ἁπαλὴν ὑπὸ δειρήν (i. e.
passing under the throat).

In one or two places it is applied to *time* : Il. 16. 202 πάνθ' ὑπὸ
μηνιθμόν *all the time that my anger lasted* ; so perhaps Il. 22. 102
νύχθ' ὕπο τήνδ' ὀλοήν (but night is often regarded as a *space* of
darkness).

204.] The Genitive with ὑπό is found in two or three distinct
uses :—

(1) with the force of *separation from* : as Il. 17. 235 νεκρὸν ὑπ'
Αἴαντος ἐρύειν *from under Ajax* ; Od. 9. 463 ὑπ' ἀρνειοῦ
λυόμην : so Il. 19. 17 ὄσσε δεινὸν ὑπὸ βλεφάρων ὡς εἰ σέλας
ἐξεφάανθεν.

In this use the Gen. is ablatival, cp. § 152. Originally ὑπό
with an Abl. probably meant *upwards from* : see § 192.

(2) of *place under*, with *contact* (especially *of a surface*) ; as—

Il. 8. 14 ὑπὸ χθονός ἐστι βέρεθρον.

Od. 5. 346 τόδε κρήδεμνον ὑπὸ στέρνοιο τανύσσαι.

Il. 1. 501 δεξιτερῇ δ' ἄρ' ὑπ' ἀνθερεῶνος ἐλοῦσα *taking hold of
him under the chin.*

4. 106 ὑπὸ στέρνοιο τυχήσας.

16. 375 ὕψι δ' ἄελλα σκίδναθ' ὑπὸ νεφέων, i. e. *seeming to
reach the clouds* (cp. 15. 625., 23. 874).

These uses of the Gen. are evidently parallel to some of those
discussed in § 149 and § 151 ; compare (*e.g.*) ὑπὸ νεφέων with
the Gen. of *space within* which (πεδίοιο διώκειν, &c.), and ὑπ'
ἀνθερεῶνος ἐλοῦσα with κόμης ἕλε (§ 151 a) *took by the hair.*
They are doubtless to be regarded (like the Gen. with ἐπί, § 200)
as varieties or developments of the Genitive of Place.

As with the Dative, the notion *under* passes into—

(3) the metaphorical (or half metaphorical) meaning *under the
influence of, by the power of* ; as Il. 3. 61 ὅς τ' εἶσιν διὰ δουρὸς
ὑπ' ἀνέρος *under the man's hand* ; Od. 19. 114 ἀρετῶσι δὲ λαοὶ
ὑπ' αὐτοῦ *under his rule ;* and many similar uses.

Cases may be noted in which the agency intended is *indirect*
(where later writers would rather use διά with an Acc.) :—

Il. 16. 590 ἥν ῥά τ' ἀνὴρ ἀφέῃ πειρώμενος ἢ ἐν ἀέθλῳ
ἠὲ καὶ ἐν πολέμῳ δηΐων ὕπο θυμοραϊστέων,
= *under the stress of an enemy* (so 18. 220);

Il. 23. 86 εὖτέ με .. ἤγαγεν ὑμέτερόνδ' ἀνδροκτασίης ὑπὸ λυγρῆς
by reason of a homicide (committed by me).

As a sound is said to be *over* or *about* (περί, ἀμφί) the person
hearing, so he is *under* the sound : hence (*e.g.*) with a half metaphorical meaning Il. 15. 275 τῶν δέ θ' ὑπὸ ἰαχῆς ἐφάνη λίς. So
of other accompaniments, as Il. 18. 492 δαΐδων ὕπο λαμπομενάων
by the light of blazing torches.

προτί.

205.] The Preposition προτί (πρός, ποτί) expresses attitude or direction *towards* an object. It is found in the adverbial use; Od. 5. 255 πρὸς δ' ἄρα πηδάλιον ποιήσατο *he made a rudder to be put to (the raft)*; hence commonly *in addition, besides*—a use which remained in later Greek.

It is a question whether προτί and ποτί are originally the same word. The present text of Homer does not indicate any difference of usage.

206.] With the **Dative** προτί means *resting on, against, beside* a thing: as Il. 4. 112 ποτὶ γαίῃ ἀγκλίνας *resting (the bow) against the ground*: Od. 5. 329 πρὸς ἀλλήλῃσιν ἔχονται *hold on to one another*. With Verbs of motion it implies that the motion *ends on* or *beside* the object; Od. 9. 459 θεινομένου πρὸς οὔδεϊ. The later meaning *besides, in addition*, is only found in Od. 10. 68 ἄασάν μ' ἕταροί τε κακοὶ πρὸς τοῖσί τε ὕπνος.

207.] With the **Accusative** προτί is very common, meaning *towards:* as πρὸς πόλιν *towards the city* (not necessarily reaching it), Il. 8. 364 κλαίεσκε πρὸς οὐρανόν *cried out to heaven;* hence *to, on to* (mostly with Verbs of motion), as Od. 4. 42 ἔκλιναν πρὸς ἐνώπια *leaned against the walls: against* (persons), as πρὸς δαίμονα φωτὶ μάχεσθαι *to fight with a man in opposition to a god;* also *addressing* (persons), with Verbs of speaking, &c.; in one place of *time*, Od. 17. 191 ποτὶ ἕσπερα *towards evening*.

Note that the literal local sense appears in all the Homeric uses of προτί with the Acc.: the metaphorical uses, viz. *in respect of, for the purpose of, in proportion to, according to,* &c., are later.

208.] With the **Genitive** προτί expresses *direction* without the idea of motion *towards* or rest *on* the object: as Od. 13. 110 αἱ μὲν πρὸς βορέαο .. αἱ δ' αὖ πρὸς νότου *i. e.* not *at* or *facing* the north and south, but more generally, *in the direction fixed by* north and south; Il. 10. 428–430 πρὸς μὲν ἁλός .. πρὸς Θύμβρης: Il. 22. 198 ποτὶ πτόλιος *in the direction of Troy;* Od. 8. 29 ἠὲ πρὸς ἠοίων ἢ ἑσπερίων ἀνθρώπων (=*from east or west*).

Among derived senses we may distinguish—

(1) *at the hand of, from* (persons), as Il. 1. 160 τιμὴν ἀρνύμενοι πρὸς Τρώων, 11. 831 τά σε προτί φασιν Ἀχιλλῆος δεδιδάχθαι.

(2) *on the part of, by the will of,* as Il. 1. 239 οἵ τε θέμιστας πρὸς Διὸς εἰρύαται *who uphold judgments on behalf of Zeus;* Il. 6. 456 πρὸς ἄλλης ἱστὸν ὑφαίνοις *at another's bidding:* and, perhaps in a metaphorical sense, Od. 6. 207 πρὸς γὰρ Διός εἰσιν ἅπαντες ξεῖνοί τε πτωχοί τε.

(3) *before, by* (in oaths and entreaties); as Il. 13. 324 πρὸς
πατρὸς γουνάζομαι *I entreat in the name of thy father.* The
Preposition here implies that the god or person sworn by is
made a party to the act; cp. Od. 11. 66 νῦν δέ σε τῶν ὄπιθεν
γουνάζομαι οὐ παρεόντων, πρός τ' ἀλόχου καὶ πατρός κτλ. *on the
part of the absent ones I entreat &c.*

It will be seen that προτί with a Gen. is seldom used in the
strictly local sense except when there is a *contrast between two
directions.* Hence the use approaches closely to that of the Gen.
of Place given in § 149 (2); compare (*e.g.*) πρὸς βορέαο—πρὸς
νότου with Od. 1. 24 οἱ μὲν δυσομένου Ὑπερίονος οἱ δ' ἀνιόντος.
The Case is accordingly 'quasi-partitive' (*i.e.* true) Genitive,
and has no ablatival character.

ἀνά.

209.] The Preposition ἀνά (ἄν) means *up, upwards, up through.*
It is rarely used as a pure Adverb (the form ἄνω being preferred)
except in the elliptical ἄνα *up!* But it has a derivative adverbial
sense in Il. 18. 562 μέλανες δ' ἀνὰ βότρυες ἦσαν *there were dark
grapes throughout.* Tmesis may be seen in Il. 2. 278 ἀνὰ δ' ὁ
πτολίπορθος Ὀδυσσεὺς ἔστη, and in ἀνὰ δ' ἔσχετο (ἀνέσχετο), &c.
In Tmesis and Composition it sometimes expresses *reverse* action,
as ἀνα-λύω. So ἀνα-βάλλω *to put off.*

ἀνά is seldom used with the **Dative**; the meaning is *up on* (a
height of some kind), as Il. 1. 15 χρυσέῳ ἀνὰ σκήπτρῳ *raised on a
golden staff;* 15. 152 ἀνὰ Γαργάρῳ; so 8. 441., 14. 352., 18. 177.,
Od. 11. 128., 23. 275., 24. 8. This use is occasionally found in
Pindar (Ol. 8. 67, Pyth. 1. 10), and lyric parts of tragedy, but is
not Attic.

With the **Genitive** ἀνά is only used in three places in the
Odyssey (2. 416., 9. 177., 15. 284), and only of going on board
a ship (ἀνὰ νηὸς βαίνω). The meaning *up from* is only found in
Composition : ἀνέδυ πολιῆς ἁλός, &c.

210.] With the Accusative ἀνά means *up along, up through,*
of motion or extent : ἀνὰ ἄστυ, ἂμ πεδίον, ἀνὰ δώματα, ἀν' ὁδόν, ἀν'
Ἑλλάδα, &c. ; Il. 5. 74 ἀν' ὀδόντας ὑπὸ γλῶσσαν τάμε χαλκός *the
spear cut its way up through the teeth and under the tongue ;* so
ἀνὰ στόμα, used literally (Il. 16. 349., 22. 452, &c.), and also of
words uttered, Il. 2. 250 βασιλῆας ἀνὰ στόμ' ἔχων *having the kings
passing through your mouth* (*i.e.* talking freely of them); similarly
ἀνὰ θυμόν of thoughts *rising in the mind.* Note also the application to *mixing,* as Od. 4. 41 πὰρ δ' ἔβαλον ζειάς, ἀνὰ δὲ κρῖ λευκὸν
ἔμιξαν ; cp. Od. 9. 209 (with the note in Merry and Riddell's
edition). The Accusative is evidently one of Space (§ 138).

The use with collective Nouns, as ἀν' ὅμιλον *through the press*, μάχην ἀνά, ἄμ φόνον ἀν νέκυας, &c. seems to be peculiar to the Iliad.

The use in Il. 14. 80 ἀνὰ νύκτα may be explained either of *time* or of *space:* cp. ὑπὸ νύκτα (§ 203), διὰ νύκτα (§ 215).

The meaning *up on, up to* (of motion) may be traced in Il. 10. 466 θῆκεν ἀνὰ μυρίκην : Od. 22. 176 κίον' ἀν' ὑψηλὴν ἐρύσαι *draw* (*the cord*) *up to a high pillar;* perhaps in the phrase ἀνά θ' ἅρματα ποικίλ' ἔβαινον (Od. 3. 492, &c.).

κατά.

211.] The Preposition κατά (by Apocope κάδ, &c.) means *down*, and is parallel in most uses to ἀνά. It is never purely adverbial (κάτω being used instead, cp. ἄνω), but is common in Tmesis, as Il. 1. 436 κατὰ δὲ πρυμνήσι' ἔδησαν, 19. 334 κατὰ πάμπαν τεθνάμεν, &c., and in Composition. Besides the primary sense (seen in κατ-άγω *I bring down*, κατα-νεύω *I nod downwards*, i. e. *in assent*, &c.) it often has the meaning *all over*, as κατα-εινύω *I clothe*, καταχέω *I pour over;* hence *completely*, as κατὰ πάντα φαγεῖν *to eat all up*, κατα-κτείνω *I kill outright:* also *in the place, as before*, as καταλείπω *I leave where it was*, &c.

κατά is not used with the **Dative**. If such a use ever existed it was superseded by ὑπό (just as ἀνά with the Dat. gave way to ἐπί). The possibility of the combination may be seen from the phrases κατ' αὐτόθι, κατ' αὖθι.

212.] With the Accusative κατά means *down along, down through*, as κατὰ ῥόον *down stream;* cp. Il. 16. 349 ἀνὰ στόμα καὶ κατὰ ῥῖνας (of blood). But it is very often used (like ἀνά) of motion that is not upward or downward, except from some arbitrary point of view; as καθ' ὁδόν *along the way*, κατὰ πτόλιν *through the city*, &c.: again, κατὰ φρένα καὶ κατὰ θυμόν *in mind and spirit*.

Other varieties of use are :—

(1) with collective Nouns (chiefly in the Iliad), as κατὰ στρατόν *through the camp*, πόλεμον κάτα, κατὰ κλόνον, &c.

(2) with Plurals (less common), as κατ' αὐτούς *going among them*, κατ' ἀνθρώπους ἀλάλησθαι.

(3) of the character or general description of an action, as κατὰ πρῆξιν (ἀλάλησθε) *on a piece of business*, ἦλθον κατὰ χρέος, πλαζόμενοι κατὰ ληΐδα (all in the Odyssey).

(4) to express place ; esp. of wounds, e.g. κατ' ὦμον *about* (*some-where on*) *the shoulder.* Cp. Il. 1. 484 ἵκοντο κατὰ στρατόν *arrived opposite* (within the space adjoining) *the camp ;* Od. 5. 441 ποταμοῖο κατὰ στόμα ἵξε νέων.

(5) to express *agreement* (from the notion of *falling in with*), in the phrases κατὰ θυμόν, κατὰ κόσμον, κατὰ μοῖραν, κατ᾽ αἶσαν.

(6) distributively: as Il. 2. 99 ἐρήτυθεν δὲ καθ᾽ ἕδρας *in their several seats;* and so in 2. 362 κρῖν᾽ ἄνδρας κατὰ φῦλα κατὰ φρήτρας.

(7) κατὰ σφέας (μάχεσθαι) *by themselves* (to the extent constituted by themselves): so Il. 1. 271 κατ᾽ ἔμ᾽ αὐτόν.

These uses may generally be identified in principle with some of the Accusatives mentioned in §§ 136-138. Thus the Acc. in ἦλθον κατὰ χρέος is like ἀγγελίην ἐλθεῖν: in κατὰ κόσμον it is like the adverbial δέμας, ἄκην, &c. : κρῖνε κατὰ φῦλα = μοίρας δάσασθαι ; and κατ᾽ ὦμον like the Acc. of the 'part affected.'

213.] With the Genitive κατά has two chief meanings :—

(1) *down from;* as κατ᾽ οὐρανοῦ *down from heaven,* καθ᾽ ἵππων ἆλτο *leaped from the chariot.* This Genitive is clearly ablatival in origin.

(2) *down on (in, over,* &c.): as Il. 3. 217 κατὰ χθονὸς ὄμματα πήξας *fixing his eyes on the ground;* κατὰ δ᾽ ὀφθαλμῶν κέχυτ᾽ ἀχλύς *a mist was shed over his eyes;* κατὰ γαίης *down in the earth.*

Comparing the similar uses of ἐπί (§ 200), ὑπό (§ 204, 2), and προτί (§ 208), we can hardly doubt that the Gen. in this latter group is originally akin to the Genitives of Place (§ 149).

διά.

214.] The Preposition διά seems to mean properly *apart, in twain.* It is not used freely as an Adverb; but the original sense appears in the combinations διαπρό, διαμπερές, and in Tmesis and Composition, as δια-στῆναι *to stand apart;* δια-τάμνω *I cut asunder;* διὰ κτῆσιν δατέοντο *divided the possession.* From the notion of *going through* it means *thoroughly,* as in δια-πέρθω *I sack utterly.*

In several Compounds, as δια-τάμνω, δι-αιρέω, δια-δάπτω, the notion of division is given by the Preposition to the Verb; *e.g.* δια-τάμνω *I separate by cutting,* &c.

215.] The Accusative with διά is often used to denote the *space through* which motion takes place: as—

Il. 1. 600 διὰ δώματα ποιπνύοντα *bustling through the palace* (so διὰ σπέος, διὰ βήσσας, διὰ ῥωπήϊα, &c.).

14. 91 μῦθον ὃν οὔ κεν ἀνήρ γε διὰ στόμα πάμπαν ἄγοιτο (=*with which a man would not sully his mouth:* cp. ἀνὰ στόμα, § 210).

Od. 9. 400 ᾤκεον ἐν σπήεσσι δι᾽ ἄκριας *dwelt in caves about* (*scattered through*) *the headlands.*

So Il. 2. 40 διὰ κρατερὰς ὑσμίνας *lasting through hard fights*: and διὰ νύκτα (chiefly in the Odyssey, and books 10 and 24 of the Iliad).

This use is distinctively Homeric. Sometimes also διά with the Acc. is used in Homer to express *cause* or *agency*; as Il. 1. 73 ἦν διὰ μαντοσύνην (Calchas led the army) *by virtue of his soothsaying*; Od. 8. 520 διὰ μεγάθυμον Ἀθήνην (to conquer) *by the help of Athene*; so Il. 10. 497., 15. 41, 71, Od. 8. 82., 11. 276, 282, 437., 13. 121., 19. 154, 523. These places do not show the later distinction between *by means of* and *by reason of*.

216.] The Genitive with διά implies passing *through* something in order to get *beyond* it; esp. getting through some *obstacle*: as—

Il. 4. 135 διὰ μὲν ἂρ ζωστῆρος ἐλήλατο.

So of a gate, Il. 3. 263 διὰ Σκαιῶν ἔχον ἵππους : and of lower and upper air, &c. δι' ἠέρος αἰθέρ' ἵκανεν, δι' αἰθέρος οὐρανὸν ἷκε, πεδίονδε διὰ νεφέων. So again διὰ προμάχων, δι' ὁμίλου &c. of making way through the press.

The Acc. is used where we expect this Gen. in Il. 7. 247 ἐξ δὲ διὰ πτύχας ἦλθε *went through six folds*: but this may be partly due to the metrical impossibility of πτυχῶν. Conversely, in Il. 10. 185 ὅς τε καθ' ὕλην ἔρχηται δι' ὄρεσφι the Acc. would be right, and ὄρεσφι is perhaps a false archaism: but cp. § 158.

ὑπέρ.

217.] The Preposition ὑπέρ (or ὑπείρ) means *higher*, hence *over, beyond*. It is not found in the adverbial use, or in Tmesis, or with a Dative.

In Composition ὑπέρ expresses going *across* or *beyond*, hence *excess*, violation of limits, &c.

218.] With the Accusative ὑπέρ is used—

(1) of motion or extent *over* a space, as Il. 23. 227 ὑπεὶρ ἅλα κίδναται ἠώς. This use is not common; Il. 12. 289., 24. 13, Od. 3. 68., 4. 172., 9. 254, 260.

(2) of motion *passing over* an object: as Il. 5. 16 ὑπὲρ ὦμον, ἀριστερὸν ἤλυθ' ἀκωκή; Od. 7. 135 ὑπὲρ οὐδὸν ἐβήσετο.

(3) metaphorically, *in excess of*, *in violation of*: ὑπὲρ αἶσαν, ὑπὲρ μοῖραν, ὑπὲρ ὅρκια: also, somewhat differently, Il. 17. 327 ὑπὲρ θεόν *in spite of God*.

219.] With the Genitive ὑπέρ is used both of position and of motion *over* an object, esp. at some distance from it; as στῆ δ' ἄρ' ὑπὲρ κεφαλῆς; Il. 15. 382 νηὸς ὑπὲρ τοίχων (of a wave coming) *over the sides of a ship:* Il. 23. 327 ὅσον τ᾽ ὄργυι᾽ ὑπὲρ αἴης *a fathom's length above ground.*

Metaphorically it means *over* so as to protect, hence *in defence of, on behalf of;* as Il. 7. 449 τεῖχος ἐτειχίσσαντο νεῶν ὕπερ ; Il. 1. 444 ἑκατόμβην ῥέξαι ὑπὲρ Δαναῶν. So Il. 6. 524 ὅθ᾽ ὑπὲρ σέθεν αἴσχε᾽ ἀκούω *when I listen to reproaches on your account* (of which I bear the brunt). But Hes. Op. 217 δίκη δ᾽ ὑπὲρ ὕβριος ἴσχει *justice rises* (prevails) *over insolence.*

In respect of form ὑπέρ (for ὑπέρι, Sanscr. *upári*) is a Comparative of ὑπό ; cp. the Superlative ὕπατος, and the Lat. *superus, summus.* Hence the Gen. is ablatival, like the Gen. with words of comparison ; see § 152.

ἐνί.

220.] The Preposition ἐνί (also εἰνί, εἰν, ἐν) means *within, in ;* it is used adverbially (as Il. 5. 740 ἐν δ᾽ ἔρις, ἐν δ᾽ ἀλκή &c.), in Tmesis (as ἔν τ᾽ ἄρα οἱ φῦ χειρί), and with a (locatival) Dative.

Notice, as departures from the strict local sense, the uses—

(1) with Plurals denoting persons (= μετά *among*), as ἐν ὑμῖν (Il. 9. 121, 528., 10. 445), ἐν πᾶσι (Od. 2. 194., 16. 378), ἐνὶ σφίσι (Il. 23. 703).

(2) with abstract words (rare in the Iliad) ; ἐν πάντεσσι πόνοισι (Il. 10. 245, 279), ἐν πάντεσσ᾽ ἔργοισι (Il. 23. 671), ἐν ἄλγεσι (Il. 24. 568) ; θαλίῃ ἔνι (Il. 9. 143, 285), ἐν νηπιέῃ (Il. 9. 491) ; ἐν φιλότητι ; ἐν μοίρῃ *aright* (Il. 19. 186), αἴσῃ ἐν ἀργαλέῃ (Il. 22. 61), ἐν Καρὸς αἴσῃ (Il. 9. 378) ; ἐν δὲ ἰῇ τιμῇ (Il. 9. 319).

These two uses are nearly confined in the Iliad to books 9, 10, 23, 24.

σύν.

221.] The Preposition σύν (or ξύν) means *in company with.* It is not used as a pure Adverb, but is found in Tmesis, as Il. 1. 579 σὺν δ᾽ ἡμῖν δαῖτα ταράξῃ *and disturb* (συνταράσσω) *our feast.* It is used with an Instrumental Dative (§ 144).

To express *equally with,* or *at the same time as,* Homer uses ἅμα with a Dat. ; while σύν commonly means *attended by, with the help of,* &c. Hence σὺν ἔντεσι *with armour on,* σὺν νηυσί *in ships,* σὺν ὅρκῳ *on oath,* σὺν Ἀθήνῃ *aided by Athene:* so Il. 4. 161 σύν τε μεγάλῳ ἀπέτισαν *they pay with a great price.*

The use of σύν with the Dative has been recently shown by Tycho Mommsen to be confined, generally speaking, to poetry. The Attic prose writers (with the singular exception of Xenophon) use μετά with the Gen. ; the practice of the poets varies, from Homer, who hardly ever uses μετά with the Gen., down to Euripides, who uses it about half as often as σύν. It is evident that in post-Homeric times μετά with the Gen. became established in the ordinary colloquial language, while σύν with the dat. was retained as a piece of poetical style, but gradually gave way to living usage. See Tycho Mommsen's dissertation Μετά, σύν und ἅμα bei den Epikern (Frankfurt am Main, 1874).

εἰς.

222.] The Preposition εἰς (or ἐς) expresses motion *to* or *into*. It is not used adverbially (the Adverb being εἴσω), and seldom in Tmesis : Il. 8. 115 τὼ δ' εἰς ἀμφοτέρω Διομήδεος ἅρματα βήτην. The motion is sometimes *implied*: as Il. 15. 275 ἐφάνη λῖς ἠϋγένειος εἰς ὁδόν : 16. 574 ἐς Πηλῆ' ἱκέτευσε (*came as suppliant*). Of *time*; ἐς ἠέλιον καταδύντα *to sun-set*; so ἐς τί *how long*? εἰς ὅ *until*: Od. 14. 384 ἐς θέρος ἢ ἐς ὀπώρην *as late as summer or autumn*.

Metaphorical uses : Il. 2. 379 εἰ δέ ποτ' ἔς γε μίαν βουλεύσομεν *if we take counsel to one purpose*; Il. 9. 102 εἰπεῖν εἰς ἀγαθόν *to speak to good effect* (so 11. 789., 23. 305).

ἐξ.

223.] The Preposition ἐξ (or ἐκ) usually expresses motion *out from* an object. It is not used purely adverbially, but there are many examples of Tmesis : as ἐξ ἔρον ἔντο, ἐκ δέ οἱ ἡνίοχος πλήγη φρένας *his charioteer lost* (lit. *was struck out of*) *his wits*, ἔκ τε καὶ ὀψὲ τελεῖ (Il. 4. 161) *he brings it to pass* (ἐκτελεῖ) *late*.

With a Gen. (ablatival) ἐξ is used of motion *from* or *out of*. Sometimes the idea of motion is *implied*:—

> Il. 13. 301 ἐκ Θρῄκης Ἐφύρους μέτα θωρήσσεσθον *armed themselves to come from Thrace after the Ephyri*.
> 14. 129 ἔνθα δ' ἔπειτ' αὐτοὶ μὲν ἐχώμεθα δηϊοτῆτος ἐκ βελέων *hold back from fighting (going) out of range*: cp. 16. 122, 678., 18. 152.

So of *direction*: Il. 14. 153 Ἥρη δ' εἰσεῖδε .. στᾶσ' ἐξ Οὐλύμποιο *stood and looked from Olympus*; Od. 21. 420 (drew the bow) αὐτόθεν ἐκ δίφροιο καθήμενος *from the chair as he sat*; Il. 19. 375 ὅτ' ἂν ἐκ πόντοιο σέλας ναύτῃσι φανήῃ *when a meteor appears to sailors at sea* (seeing it from the sea): of *choosing* out of, Il. 15. 680 ἐκ πολέων πίσυρας συναείρεται ἵππους, and similarly, Il. 18. 431 ὅσσ' ἐμοὶ ἐκ πασέων Κρονίδης Ζεὺς ἄλγε' ἔδωκε *to me* (taken *from*, hence) *more than all*.

ἐξ is also used of an *agent* as the *source* of action ; as Il. 5. 384 τλῆμεν .. ἐξ ἀνδρῶν *have endured at the hands of men*; cp. Il. 22. 280, Od. 7. 70., 9. 512: also Il. 24. 617 θεῶν ἐκ κήδεα πέσσει *endures heaven-sent troubles*, and Hes. Theog. 94 ἐκ γὰρ Μουσάων καὶ ἑκηβόλου Ἀπόλλωνος ἄνδρες ἀοιδοὶ ἔασιν. The meaning *in*

consequence of (a *thing*) occurs in Il. 9. 566 ἐξ ἀρέων μητρὸς κεχολωμένος, and in the Odyssey (3. 135., 5. 468, &c.).

Of *time:* ἐκ τοῖο *from that time,* ἐξ ἀρχῆς *from the first* (Od. 1.
188, &c.), ἐκ νεότητος (Il. 14. 86).

With an abstract word, Il. 10. 107 ἐκ χόλου ἀργαλέοιο μετα-
στρέψῃ φίλον ἦτορ. Note also : Il. 10. 68 πατρόθεν ἐκ γενεῆς
ὀνομάζων *calling them by the father's name according to family;* Il.
9. 343 (486) ἐκ θυμοῦ *from the heart, heartily* (but Il. 23. 595 ἐκ
θυμοῦ πεσέειν *to fall away from a person's favour*).

ἀπό.

224.] The Preposition **ἀπό** means *off, away, at a distance from.*
It is not used adverbially, but is common in Tmesis; as Il. 8.
108 οὕς ποτ᾽ ἀπ᾽ Αἰνείαν ἑλόμην *which I took from Aeneas.* In
Composition it generally gives the Verb the notion of *separating;*
e.g. ἀπο-κόπτω is not *I hew at a distance,* but *I separate by hew-
ing:* so ἀπεκόσμεον *cleared away* (Od. 7. 232), and similarly ἀπο-
δύω, ἀποβάλλω, ἀπολούω, ἀπορρήγνυμι, ἀποκαπύω (all used in
Tmesis). Hence we must explain Il. 19. 254 ἀπὸ τρίχας ἀρξά-
μενος *cutting hair as an* ἀπαρχή, or first offering ; cp. Od. 3. 446.,
14. 422.

Sometimes ἀπό has the force of *restoration* or *return,* as in ἀπο-
δίδωμι, ἀπο-νοστέω (cp. ἄψ *backwards*). So ἀπο-ειπεῖν means
either *to speak out* or *to forbid, refuse.* In a few cases it has an intensive force, as in ἀπομηνίω, ἀπήχθετο, ἀποθαυμάζω.

With the Genitive ἀπό generally expresses motion *away from,*
not implying previous place within the object (whereas ἐξ means
proceeding from). It is also used of position, as Il. 8. 16 ὅσον
οὐρανός ἐστ᾽ ἀπὸ γαίης *as far as heaven is from earth;* Od. 1. 49
φίλων ἄπο πήματα πάσχει *suffers woes far from his friends;* metaphorically, Il. 1. 562 ἀπὸ θυμοῦ μᾶλλον ἐμοὶ ἔσεαι *you will be the
more out of favour with me;* ἀπὸ δόξης *away from expectation.*
This Gen. is clearly ablatival.

πρό.

225.] The Preposition **πρό** means *forward, in front.* It is
seldom used as an Adverb; Il. 13. 799 πρὸ μέν τ᾽ ἄλλ᾽, κτλ.; Il. 16.
188 ἐξάγαγε πρὸ φόωσδε *brought forth to the light:* and of time,
Il. 1. 70 πρό τ᾽ ἐόντα *the past.* In one or two other instances we
may recognise either the free adverbial use or Tmesis : Il. 1. 195
πρὸ γὰρ ἧκε, 1. 442 πρό μ᾽ ἔπεμψε, Od. 1. 37 πρό οἱ εἴπομεν.

Traces of a use of πρό with the Locative may be seen in the
phrases οὐρανόθι πρό *in the face of heaven,* ᾽Ιλιόθι πρό *in front of
Troy,* and (perhaps in the temporal sense) ἠῶθι πρό *before dawn.*
In these cases the meaning is *to the front in,* hence *immediately
before.*

With a Genitive, on the other hand, πρό means *in front with respect to, in advance of;* hence, in a more or less metaphorical sense, *in defence of,* as Il. 8. 57 πρό τε παίδων καὶ πρὸ γυναικῶν. The Case is here the ablatival Gen. (as with ὑπέρ and words of comparison).

But in Il. 4. 382 πρὸ ὁδοῦ ἐγένοντο the Gen. is partitive, *got forward on the way;* and so perhaps Il. 16. 667 πρὸ φόβοιο *forward in the flight,* i. e. *having betaken themselves to flight* (so Düntzer *a. l.*).

The temporal sense is rare in Homer; Od. 15. 524., 17. 476 πρὸ γάμοιο *before marriage;* Il. 10. 224 καί τε πρὸ ὃ τοῦ ἐνόησε *one thinks of a thing before another.*

ἀντί.

226.] The only certain Compound with ἀντί in Homer appears to be ἀντι-φέρεσθαι *to oppose* (Il. 1. 589., 5. 701., 22. 482, Od. 16. 238): for the Verbs ἀντιβολέω *meet* and ἀντιτορέω *pierce* may be derived from the Nouns ἀντί-βολος, ἀντί-τορος : also in Il. 8. 163 we may read γυναικὸς ἄρ' ἀντὶ τέτυξο, not ἀντετέτυξο (cp. Od. 8. 546 ἀντὶ κασιγνήτου ξεῖνός θ' ἱκέτης τε τέτυκται), and in Od. 22. 74 for ἀντίσχεσθε (*hold up against*) ἄντ' ἴσχεσθε (*i. e.* ἄντα ἴσχεσθε, cp. Od. 1. 334 ἄντα παρειάων σχομένη λιπαρὰ κρήδεμνα).

ἀντί also resembles the Improper Prepositions (esp. the Adverbs ἄντα, ἀντίον, &c.) in being used with the Gen., but not with the Dat. or Acc. It means *in place of,* hence *in the character of, equivalent to:* as Il. 21. 75 ἀντί τοί εἰμ' ἱκέταο.

Double Prepositions.

227.] It is characteristic of Homer to form a species of compound by combining two Prepositions. We have—

ἀμφὶ περί, like our *round about:* also περί τ' ἀμφί τε *round and about:* used adverbially, as Il. 22. 10 ὄχθαι δ' ἀμφὶ περὶ μεγάλ' ἴαχον; in Composition, ἀμφιπεριστρώφα (Il. 8. 348), &c.

παρέξ *out besides, out along, out past:* adverbial in Od. 14. 168 ἄλλα παρὲξ μεμνώμεθα: with the Acc., παρὲξ ἅλα *alongside the sea,* παρὲξ τὴν νῆσον *past the island;* παρὲκ νόον *beyond* (=*contrary to*) *reason:* with the Gen., παρὲξ ὁδοῦ *aside from the way.*

ὑπέξ, with a Gen. *away from under,* as Il. 13. 89 φεύξεσθαι ὑπὲκ κακοῦ.

διέξ, with a Gen. *right through,* as διὲκ προθύρου, διὲκ μεγάροιο.

ἀποπρό *quite away,* used adverbially and with a Gen.

διαπρό *right through,* adverbially and with a Gen.

περιπρό *round about;* Il. 11. 180 περιπρὸ γὰρ ἔγχεϊ θῦε.

In all these instances the meaning and construction are mainly determined by the first of the two Prepositions (so that *e. g.* παρέξ is used nearly as παρά, διέξ and διαπρό as διά, &c.). The second does little more than add some emphasis.

The treble Preposition ὑπεκπρό is found in Composition : ὑπεκπροθέω, ὑπεκπρορέω, &c. The sense is represented by dividing the words ὑπεκ-προθέω, &c.

A curious variety is found in the Compound προ-προκυλινδόμενος *rolling forward before*, where a second πρό is added to give emphasis to the first.

Improper Prepositions.

228.] The term 'Improper Preposition' may be applied to any Adverb used to govern a Case. The following are some of the most important words of the kind :—

Used with a Genitive : ἄγχι *near, close to,* ἐγγύθι, ἐγγύς *near,* ἄντα, ἀντίον, &c. *facing,* πρόσθε(ν) *before,* πάροιθε(ν) *in front of,* ὄπισθε(ν) *behind,* μεσσηγύς *between,* ἐντός, ἔντοσθε, ἔνδοθεν *within,* ἔξω *out,* ἐκτός, ἔκτοθι, ἔκτοσθε(ν) *outside,* ἔνερθε *beneath,* ἄνευ, ἄνευθε(ν) *apart from, without,* ἄτερ *without,* νόσφι *away from,* ἑκάς, ἑκάτερθε(ν) *apart from,* μέσφα *until,* πέρην *beyond,* πάλιν *back from,* ἀντικρύ *straight to,* ἰθύς *straight towards,* τῆλε, τηλόθι *far off,* ὕπαιθα *under,* εἵνεκα (ἕνεκα) *on account of,* ἕκητι *by the favour of.* The Gen. with some of these words may be ablatival (§ 152). In general, however, it appears to be used with little or no reference to the meaning of the governing Adverb, and merely in order to connect the two words. Hence these constructions are best brought under the general rule that a Noun governs the Genitive (§ 147).

With a Dative : ἅμα *together with,* μίγδα *in company with,* ὁμῶς *in like manner.*

ἀμφίς takes a Gen. in the meaning *aside from* (Il. 8. 444., 23. 393, Od. 14. 352). It is also found with the Acc. in the same sense as ἀμφί, in the phrase θεοὶ Κρόνον ἀμφὶς ἐόντες, Il. 14. 274., 15. 225 (see also Il. 11. 634, 748, Od. 6. 266); and once with a Dat., viz. in Il. 5. 723 σιδηρέῳ ἄξονι ἀμφίς. Also as an Adv. =*around* in Il. 9. 464., 24. 488.

εἴσω generally takes an Accusative, as Ἴλιον εἴσω *to Ilium :* but a Gen. in Od. 8. 290 ὁ δ' εἴσω δώματος ᾔει *went inside the house* (not merely *to* the house).

The word ὡς was supposed to govern an Accusative in one place in Homer, viz. Od. 17. 218 ὡς αἰεὶ τὸν ὁμοῖον ἄγει θεὸς ὡς τὸν ὁμοῖον. But the true construction is (as Mr. Ridgeway has pointed out) ὡς—ὡς *as God brings like as he brings like, i. e.* deals with a man as he dealt with his like (see *Journal of Philology,* vol. xvii. p. 113).

Note the frequency of Compounds formed by one of these words following a Preposition : ἔν-αντα, εἴσ-αντα, ἄν-αντα, κάτ-αντα, πάρ-αντα, ἐν-αντίον, κατ-εναντίον : ἐμ-προσθεν, προ-πάροιθε, μετ-όπισθεν, ἀπ-άνευθεν, ἀπ-άτερθεν, ἀπό-νοσφι, ὑπ-ένερθε, κατ-αντικρύ. Cp. ἄν-διχα, δι-αμπέρες, κατ-αντύθι, &c. These are not true Compounds (σύνθετα), but are formed by παράθεσις, or mere juxta-position : *i. e.* they do not consist of two members, of which the first is wholly employed in limiting or qualifying the second, but of two adverbial words qualifying the same Verb. Thus they are essentially akin to the combinations formed by a Preposition and its Case : see § 178.

Homeric and Attic uses of Prepositions.

229.] The development of the language between the Homeric and the Attic period is especially shown in the uses of Preposi-tions. It may be convenient here to bring together some of the chief points.

1. Most of the Prepositions,—but esp. ἀμφί, περί, παρά, ἐπί, ὑπό, προτί, ἐνί—are used in Homer adverbially, *i. e.* as distinct words Afterwards they become mere unaccented words or prefixes.

2. A variety of the same process shows itself in the disuse of Tmesis. Besides the Prepositions already mentioned, this applies to μετά, ἀνά, κατά, διά, ἐξ, ἀπό, εἰς.

In these processes of development we have seen that the loss of independent meaning is accompanied by a change (which is in all probability simply a *loss*) of accent.

3. The construction with the Dative (which is mostly loca-tival) is the one in which the Preposition retains most nearly its own 'adverbial' meaning—so much so that it is often doubtful whether the Preposition can be said to 'govern' the Case at all. Accordingly we find that this construction is comparatively rare in Attic. It is virtually lost (except as a poetical survival) with ἀμφί, περί, μετά, ἀνά, and σύν.

4. On the other hand the Genitive is more frequent in Attic, and not confined (as it generally is in Homer) to uses in which it has either an ablatival or a quasi-partitive sense. Thus it is used with ἀμφί, περί, and μετά : also with διά of motion *through*. In such uses as these the Case ceases to have a distinct meaning : it merely serves (as with the Improper Prepositions) to show that the Noun is governed by the Preposition.

5. The development of meaning is chiefly seen in the exten-sion from the literal sense of *place* to various derivative or metaphorical senses. Some of these senses are beginning to be used in the Homeric language : *e.g.* ἀμφί with the Dat. = *about, concerning ;* περί with the Gen. (probably also the Dat.) in the same meaning ; παρά with the Acc. = *in excess of, in violation of ;* μετά with the Acc. = *after ;* ἐπί with the Acc. = *towards* (a person) : διά with the Acc. = *owing to :* ἐξ = *in consequence of.* Others may safely be counted as post-Homeric ; note in particular—

περί with the Acc. = *about, nearly* (of time and number); also = *concerning, in relation to*:

παρά with the Dat. = *in the opinion of;* with the Acc. = *during the continuance of;* also *compared with:*

κατά with the Acc. = *answering to;* also *during the time of:* with the Gen. = *about, against:*

ἐπί with the Dat. = *in the power of:*

with many phrases in which the force of the Preposition is vague, such as δι' ὀργῆς, ἀνὰ κράτος, πρὸς βίαν, ἐκ τοῦ ἐμφανοῦς, &c.

6. There are slight but perceptible differences between the usage of the Iliad and that of the Odyssey (§§ 182, 188, 196, 199, 215). Some uses, again, are peculiar to one or two books of the Iliad, esp. 9, 10, 23, 24 : see §§ 199 (4), 220, 223 (*fin.*).

CHAPTER X.

The Verbal Nouns.

Introductory.

230.] The preceding chapters deal with the Simple Sentence : that is to say, the Sentence which consists of a single Verb, and the subordinate or qualifying words (Case-forms, Adverbs, Prepositions) construed with it (§ 131). We have now to consider how this type is enlarged by means of the Verbal Nouns.

The Infinitive and Participle, as has been explained (§ 84), are in fact Nouns : the Infinitive is an abstract Noun denoting the action of the Verb, the Participle a concrete Noun expressing that action as an attribute. They are termed ' Verbal ' because they suggest or imply a predication, such as a finite Verb expresses (*e. g.* ἔρχεται ἄγων αὐτούς *implies* the assertion ἄγει αὐτούς), and because the words which depend upon or qualify them are construed with them as with Verbs (ἄγων αὐτούς, not ἄγων αὐτῶν *bringer of them*). Thus they have the character of subordinate Verbs, ' governed ' by the finite Verb of the sentence, and serving at the same time as centres of dependent Clauses.

The distinction between Infinitives and other abstract Substantives, and again between Participles and other primitive Adjectives, was probably not always so clearly drawn as it is in Greek. The Infinitives of the oldest Sanscrit hardly form a distinct group of words ; they are abstract Nouns of various formation, used in several different Cases, and would hardly have

been classed apart from other Case-forms if they had not been recognised as
the precursors of the later more developed Infinitive. The Participles, too,
are variously formed in Sanscrit, and moreover they are not the only Nouns
with which the construction is ‘adverbial’ instead of being ‘adnominal.’

The peculiarity of the Verbal Nouns in point of meaning may be said to
consist in the *temporary* and *accidental* character of the actions or attributes
which they express. Thus πράττειν and πρᾶξαι suggest a *particular* doing,
momentary or progressive, at or during a time fixed by the context; whereas
πρᾶξις means *doing*, irrespective of time; πράκτωρ *one who does*, generally or
permanently, a *doer;* and so in other cases. The distinction is especially
important for Homer. In the later language there are uses of the Infinitive
and Participle in which they lose the Verbal element, and have the character
of ordinary Nouns; *e. g.* τὸ πράττειν is nearly equivalent to πρᾶξις, οἱ πράττοντες
to πράκτορες, &c.

The Infinitive.

231.] **Form and original meaning.** The Greek Infinitive
is a Case-form—usually the Dative—of an abstract Verbal
Noun (*nomen actionis*). As a Dative it expresses an action *to*
which that of the governing Verb is *directed*, or *for* which it
takes place,—viz. a purpose, effect, bearing, &c. of the main
action. Thus δόμεν-αι *to give*, being the Dative of a Stem δο-μεν
giving, means ‘*to* or *for* giving,’ hence *in order to give, so as to
give*, &c. But owing to the loss of all other uses of the Dative
in Greek (§ 143), and the consequent isolation of the Infinitive,
its meaning has been somewhat extended. For the same reason
the Infinitives derived from other Cases (§ 85) are no longer used
with different meaning, but are retained merely as alternative
forms.

The Dative meaning evidently accounts for the common constructions of the Infinitive with Verbs expressing *wish, command,
power, expectation, beginning*, and the like: as ἐθέλω δόμεναι lit.
I am willing for giving, δύναμαι ἰδέειν *I have power for seeing*, &c.
In Homer it may be said to be the usual meaning of the Infinitive. It is found in a great many simple phrases, such as
ξυνέηκε μάχεσθαι *urged together to fight* (*so that they fought*),
δὸς ἄγειν *give for leading away* (*to be led away*), οἶδε νοῆσαι *knows*
(*has sense*) *to perceive*, βῆ δ᾽ ἰέναι *stepped to go* (= *took his way*,
cp. γούνατ᾽ ἐνώμα φευγέμεναι); προέηκε πυθέσθαι, πέμπε νέεσθαι,
ὦρτο πέτεσθαι, &c. Cp. also—

Il. 1. 22 ἐπευφήμησαν Ἀχαιοί, αἰδεῖσθαι κτλ. *the Greeks uttered
approving cries for* (*to the effect of*) *respecting, &c.;* so 2. 290
ὀδύρονται οἶκόνδε νέεσθαι.

2. 107 Ἀγαμέμνονι λεῖπε φορῆναι, πολλῇσιν νήσοισι καὶ Ἀργεϊ
παντὶ ἀνάσσειν *left* (*the sceptre*) *to Agamemnon to bear, there-
with to rule over many islands and Argos.*

Od. 4. 634 ἐμὲ δὲ χρεὼ γίγνεται αὐτῆς Ἦλιδ' ἐς εὐρύχορον διαβή-
μεναι *I have need of it for crossing over to Elis.*

The notion of *purpose* often passes into that of adaptation,
possibility, necessity, &c.; *e.g.*—

Il. 6. 227 πολλοὶ μὲν γὰρ ἐμοὶ Τρῶες . . κτείνειν *there are many
Trojans for me to kill (whom I may kill);* cp. 9. 688 εἰσὶ καὶ
οἶδε τάδ' εἰπέμεν *these too are here to tell this,* 11. 342 ἐγγὺς
ἔσαν προφυγεῖν *were near for escaping, to escape with.*

13. 98 εἴδεται ἦμαρ ὑπὸ Τρώεσσι δαμῆναι *the day is come for
being subdued (when we must be subdued) by the Trojans;* cp.
Od. 2. 284.

Again, from the notion of direction or effect the Infinitive
shades off into that of *reference*, sphere of action, &c.; as Il. 5.
601 οἷον δὴ θαυμάζομεν Ἕκτορα δῖον αἰχμητήν τ' ἔμεναι κτλ. *for
being a warrior;* Od. 7. 148 θεοὶ ὄλβια δοῖεν ζωέμεναι *may the
gods grant blessings for living,* i. e. *in life;* ἀριστεύεσκε μάχεσθαι
was best for (and so *in*) *fighting,* εὔχεται εἶναι *boasts for (of) being.*

In the passages quoted the Infinitive is so far an *abstract Noun*
that the action which it denotes is not predicated of an *agent*.
The agent, if there is one in the speaker's mind, is not given by
the form of the sentence; *e.g.* ἐγγὺς ἔσαν προφυγεῖν (*were near
for escaping*) might mean *were near so as to escape* or (as the
context of Il. 11. 342 requires) *were near so that he could escape;*
δῦναι ἐπειγόμενος would usually mean *eager to set,* but in Od. 13.
30 it means *eager for (the sun's) setting.* Hence the apparently
harsh change of subject in such a case as—

Od. 2. 226 καί οἱ ἰὼν ἐν νηυσὶν ἐπέτρεπεν οἶκον ἅπαντα
             πείθεσθαί τε γέροντι καὶ ἔμπεδα πάντα φυλάσσειν

*to the intent that it should obey the old man and he should guard
all surely* (lit. *for obeying—for guarding*). And so in Il. 9. 230 ἐν
δοιῇ δὲ σαωσέμεν ἢ ἀπολέσθαι νῆας, where νῆας is first Object,
then Subject. The harshness disappears when we understand
that the abstract use is the prevailing one in Homer.

It may also be noticed here that—

(1) With Verbs of privative meaning, the Infinitive may be
used as with the corresponding affirmative words: as ἔρριγ' ἀντι-
βολῆσαι *shudders as to (from) meeting;* Od. 9. 468 ἀνὰ δ' ὀφρύσι
νεῦον ἑκάστῳ κλαίειν *I nodded backwards to each for weeping (=for-
bidding him to weep),* Il. 22. 474 εἶχον ἀπολέσθαι. But the proper
use also appears, as in Il. 22. 5 αὐτοῦ μεῖναι ἐπέδησε *fettered so
that he remained.* Here the context must determine the meaning.

(2) With φρονέω, ὀίω, &c. the Infinitive may express the
effect or conclusion: *I think to the effect—,* hence *I think fit;* as
Il. 13. 263 οὐ γὰρ ὀίω . . πολεμίζειν *I have no mind to &c.* So

εἰπεῖν *to speak to the intent that, to bid*, as Od. 3. 427 εἴπατε δ'
εἴσω δμωῆσιν . . πένεσθαι. Other examples are given in § 238.

In this use, as was observed by Mr. Riddell (*Dig.* § 83), the 'dictative
force'—the notion of thinking right, advising, &c.—comes through the
Infinitive to the governing Verb, not vice versa. The same remark holds of
the use with ἔστι *it is possible*, lit. *it is* (a case) *for* (something to happen).

232.] **Infinitive with Nouns, &c.** It will be useful to bring
together instances in which the Infinitive depends upon some
qualifying word—Preposition, Adverb, Adjective, &c.—construed
with the Verb :—

Il. 1. 258 οἳ περὶ μὲν βουλὴν Δαναῶν περὶ δ' ἐστὲ μάχεσθαι *excel
them in fighting.*

1. 589 ἀργαλέος γὰρ Ὀλύμπιος ἀντιφέρεσθαι *the Olympian is hard
to set oneself against ;* cp. 20. 131.

4. 510 ἐπεὶ οὔ σφι λίθος χρὼς οὐδὲ σίδηρος χαλκὸν ἀνασχέσθαι
*since their flesh is not stone or iron for withstanding (so as to
be able to withstand) bronze.*

8. 223 ἥ ῥ' ἐν μεσσάτῳ ἔσκε γεγωνέμεν ἀμφοτέρωσε *for shouting
(* = *so that one could shout) both ways.*

13. 775 ἐπεί τοι θυμὸς ἀναίτιον αἰτιάασθαι *since your mind is for
blaming (is such that you must blame) the innocent.*

Od. 17. 20 οὐ γὰρ ἐπὶ σταθμοῖσι μένειν ἔτι τηλίκος εἰμί *I am not
yet of the age to remain.*

17. 347 αἰδὼς δ' οὐκ ἀγαθὴ κεχρημένῳ ἀνδρὶ παρεῖναι *shame is not
good to be beside a needy man* (is not a good 'backer' for).

21. 195 ποῖοί κ' εἶτ' Ὀδυσῆι ἀμυνέμεν εἴ ποθεν ἔλθοι; = *how would
you behave in regard to fighting for Ulysses ?*

Od. 2. 60 ἡμεῖς δ' οὔ νύ τι τοῖοι ἀμυνέμεν may be either *we are not like him,
so as to defend,* or simply *we are not fit to defend.* The construction of the Inf.
is the same in either case : the difference is whether τοῖοι means 'of the kind'
with reference to οἷος Ὀδυσσεὺς ἔσκε or to the Inf. ἀμυνέμεν. The latter may
be defended by Od. 17. 20 (quoted above).

This construction is extended to some Nouns even when they
are not used as predicates; as θείειν ταχύς *swift to run*, θαῦμα
ἰδέσθαι *a wonder to behold* (cp. the use of the Accusative with
Adjectives, § 131 *fin.*).

233.] **Impersonal Verbs.** The Infinitive is used with ἔστι
there is (*means, room, occasion, &c.*), ἔοικε *it is fit*, πέπρωται *it is
determined*, εἴμαρτο *it was fated.* For ἔστι cp.—

Il. 14. 313 κεῖσε μὲν ἔστι καὶ ὕστερον ὁρμηθῆναι.

Od. 15. 392 αἵδε δὲ νύκτες ἀθέσφατοι· ἔστι μὲν εὕδειν,
ἔστι δὲ τερπομένοισιν ἀκούειν *there is* (enough) *for
sleeping and for listening.*

It is very common with a negative : οὐκ ἔστι, οὔ πως ἔστι, &c. meaning *there is no way, it may not be that, &c.*

The Impersonal use is also found in phrases of the two kinds noticed in § 162, 4 ; viz.—

(*a*) With a Neuter Adjective ; as ἀργαλέον δέ μοί ἐστι θέσθαι κτλ. *it is difficult for me to make &c.* ; μόριμον δέ οἵ ἐστ' ἀλέασθαι *it is fated for him to escape ;* so with αἰσχρόν, νεμεσσητόν, αἴσιμον, ἄρκιον, βέλτερον, and the like.

(*b*) With an abstract Noun : as—

Il. 14. 80 οὐ γάρ τις νέμεσις φυγέειν κακόν *there is no wrong in escaping ill.*

Od. 5. 345 ὅθι τοι μοῖρ' ἐστὶν ἀλύξαι *where it is thy fate to &c.*

11. 330 ἀλλὰ καὶ ὥρη εὕδειν *there is a time for &c.*

So with αἶσα, μόρος, θέμις, χρεώ, ἀνάγκη, αἰδώς, δέος, ἐλπωρή, &c. followed by an Infinitive to express what the *fate, need, shame,* &c. brings about, or in what it consists.

These examples throw light on two much-debated passages :

Il. 2. 291 ἦ μὴν καὶ πόνος ἐστὶν ἀνιηθέντα νέεσθαι

verily there is toil for a man to return in vexation, i. e. 'I admit that the toil is enough to provoke any one to return.' Thus understood, the expression is a slightly bold use of the form of sentence that we have in ὥρη ἐστὶν εὕδειν, μοῖρα ἐστὶν ἀλύξαι, θυμός ἐστιν ἀναίτιον αἰτιάασθαι, &c. The other interpretation, ' it is toil to return vexed,' though apparently easier, is not really more Homeric ; and it certainly does not fit the context so well.

Il. 7. 238 οἶδ' ἐπὶ δεξιά, οἶδ' ἐπ' ἀριστερὰ νωμῆσαι βῶν
                   ἀζαλέην, τό μοι ἔστι ταλαύρινον πολεμίζειν

I know how to turn my shield of seasoned ox-hide to the right and to the left, wherefore I have that wherewith to war in stout-shielded fashion (= I have a good claim to the title of ταλαύρινος πολεμιστής, elsewhere an epithet of Ares). Here ἔστι is used as in ἔστιν εὕδειν, &c.

In Il. 13. 99–101 ἦ μέγα θαῦμα τόδ' ὀφθαλμοῖσιν ὁρῶμαι, Τρῶας ἐφ' ἡμετέρας ἱέναι νέας the Inf. follows θαῦμα, or rather the whole phrase θαῦμα τόδε ὁρῶμαι (= θαῦμά ἐστι) : ὁράω does not take an Inf. (§ 245).

234.] Infinitive as apparent Subject, &c. In the Impersonal uses the Infinitive appears to stand as Subject to the Verb ; ἀργαλέον ἐστὶ θέσθαι = *making is hard ;* οὐ μὲν γάρ τι κακὸν βασιλευέμεν *to be a king is not a bad thing.* This construction however is not consistent with the original character of the Infinitive. It is plain that ἔστιν εὕδειν can never have meant 'sleeping is,' but ' there is (room &c.) *for* sleeping' : and so ἀργαλέον ἐστὶ θέσθαι is originally, and in Homer, *it (the case, state of things, &c.) is hard in view of making.* It is only in later Greek that we have the form ἀργαλέον ἐστὶ τὸ θέσθαι, in which θέσθαι is an indeclinable Neuter Noun.

The process by which the Infinitive, from being a mere word

of *limitation,* comes to be in sense the Subject or Object of the
principal Clause, can be traced in sentences of various forms:—

(1) With a personal Subject; *e. g.* in—

Il. 5. 750 τῆς ἐπιτέτραπται μέγας οὐρανὸς Οὔλυμπός τε
　　　ἠμὲν ἀνακλῖναι πυκινὸν νέφος ἠδ᾽ ἐπιθεῖναι

the meaning 'to them is entrusted the opening and shutting of
the thick cloud of heaven,' is expressed by saying 'to them
heaven is entrusted for opening and shutting the cloud.' So—

Il. 1. 107 αἰεί τοι τὰ κάκ᾽ ἐστὶ φίλα φρεσὶ μαντεύεσθαι.

4. 345 ἔνθα φίλ᾽ ὀπταλέα κρέα ἔδμεναι.

Meaning *you love to prophesy evils (to eat roast flesh, &c.).*

(2) The Impersonal form (ἀργαλέον ἐστί) only differs from the
other in the vagueness of the Subject, which makes it easier for
the Infinitive to become the Subject in sense, while it is still
grammatically a word limiting the vague unexpressed Subject.

The use of a Neuter Pronoun as Subject (*e. g.* τό γε καλὸν
ἀκουέμεν *the thing is good, to listen*) may be regarded as a link
between the personal and impersonal forms of expression: cp. §
161 (*note*), also § 258.

(3) Similarly an Infinitive following the *Object* of a Verb may
become the logical Object; as—

Il. 4. 247 ἦ μένετε Τρῶας σχεδὸν ἐλθέμεν; *do ye wait for the
Trojans for their coming on? i. e.* for the coming on of the
Trojans.

14. 342 Ἥρη, μήτε θεῶν τό γε δείδιθι μήτε τιν᾽ ἀνδρῶν ὄψεσθαι
*do not fear any one of gods or of men for their being about to
see, i. e.* that any one will see: cp. Od. 22. 39, 40.

A further development of this use leads, as we shall see, to the
'Accusative with the Infinitive.'

(4) Again, the Infinitive sometimes takes the place of a vague
unexpressed Object. Thus οἶδε νοῆσαι means *knows (enough) to
perceive:* the full construction being such as we have in Il. 2. 213
ὅς ῥ᾽ ἔπεα φρεσὶν ᾗσιν ἄκοσμά τε πολλά τε ᾔδει .. ἐριζέμεναι *who
knew (had a store of) words wherewith to wrangle.* So too δίδωμι
with an Infinitive is originally construed as Od. 8. 44 τῷ γάρ ῥα
θεὸς πέρι δῶκεν ἀοιδὴν τέρπειν: Il. 11. 20 τόν ποτέ οἱ Κινύρης δῶκε
ξεινήϊον εἶναι; thence it comes to mean 'to give (such a state of
things) that some event shall happen,' *i. e. to grant the happening;*
as δὸς τίσασθαι *grant that I may punish.* In such a passage as Il.
3. 322 τὸν δὸς ἀποφθίμενον δῦναι κτλ. we may take τόν with δός
or as an Acc. with the Inf. δῦναι.

A Neuter Pronoun, too, may serve as a vague Object, explained by an Infinitive; *e. g.* Il. 5. 665–6 τὸ μὲν οὔ τις ἐπεφρά-
σατ᾽ .. ἐξερύσαι: cp. Od. 21. 278 καὶ τοῦτο ἔπος κατὰ μοῖραν ἔειπε,
νῦν μὲν παῦσαι τόξον κτλ.

(5) The Infinitive may also be equivalent in sense to the Genitive depending on a Noun; as—

Il. 7. 409 οὐ γάρ τις φειδὼ νεκύων κατατεθνηώτων
γίγνετ’ ἐπεί κε θάνωσι πυρὸς μειλισσέμεν ὦκα

i.e. there is no grudging about the appeasing of the dead. Hence is developed an idiomatic use of the Genitive parallel to that of the *Accusativus de quo:* see Shilleto on Thuc. 1. 61, 1.

235.] With Relatives. It is remarkable that the use of the Infinitive with ὡς, ὥς τε, οἶος, ὅσος, &c. is rare in Homer. The familiar construction of ὥς τε only occurs twice : Il. 9. 42 ἐπέσσυται ὥς τε νέεσθαι *is eager to return,* and Od. 17. 20 οὐ γὰρ ἐπὶ σταθμοῖσι μένειν ἔτι τηλίκος εἰμί, ὥς τ’ ἐπιτειλαμένῳ . . πιθέσθαι. The other instances are : Od. 21. 173 τοῖον—οἶόν τε ἔμεναι *such a one as to be ;* Od. 5. 484 ὅσσον τε . . ἔρυσθαι *so far as to shelter ;* Od. 19. 160 ἀνὴρ οἶός τε μάλιστα οἴκου κήδεσθαι, 21. 117 οἶός τ’ . . ἀνελέσθαι.

236.] With πρίν and πάρος. This use is common in Homer : as Il. 1. 98 πρίν γ’ ἀπὸ πατρὶ φίλῳ δόμεναι *before they give back to her father ;* 11. 573 πάρος χρόα λευκὸν ἐπαυρεῖν *before touching the white flesh.*

The tense is nearly always the Aorist : the exceptions are, Od. 19. 475 πρὶν ἀμφαφάασθαι (a verb which has no Aorist), and Il. 18. 245 πάρος δόρποιο μέδεσθαι. Perhaps however μέδεσθαι is an Aorist: see § 31, 2.

πρίν with the Indicative first appears in H. Apoll. 357 πρίν γέ οἱ ἰὸν ἐφῆκεν. For the use with the Subj. see § 297.

The origin of this singularly isolated construction must evidently be sought in the period when the Infinitive was an abstract Noun ; so that (*e.g.*) πρὶν δόμεναι meant *before the giving.* The difficulty is that a word like πρίν would be construed with the Ablative, not the Dative : as in fact we find Ablatives used as Infinitives in Sanscrit with *purâ* 'before' (Whitney, § 983). It may be conjectured that the Dative Infinitive in Greek was substituted in this construction for an Ablative. Such a substitution might take place when the character of the Infinitive as a Case-form had become obscured.

It is held by Sturm (*Geschichtliche Entwickelung der Constructionen mit πρίν,* p. 15) that the Inf. has the force of *limitation :* e.g. πρὶν οὐτάσαι 'before in respect to wounding,' before the time of wounding. But on this view the sense would rather be 'too soon to wound.' It is better to say, with Mr. Goodwin (§ 623), that πρίν is 'quasi-prepositional' : and if so the Infinitive had ceased to be felt as a Dative when the use arose.

The restriction to the Aor. Inf. may date from the time when Infinitives— or Case-forms on the way to become Infinitives (§ 242)—were chiefly formed from the same Stem as the Aorist. Cp. the Aor. Participles which are without Tense-meaning (§ 243, 1).

237.] Accusative with the Infinitive. Along with the use of the Infinitive as an abstract Noun, we find in Homer the later use by which it is in sense the Verb of a dependent Clause, the Subject of the Clause being in the Accusative.

In the examples of the Acc. with the Infinitive we may distinguish the following varieties or stages of the idiom :—

1. The Acc. has a grammatical construction with the governing Verb : *e. g.*—

Il. 1. 313 λαοὺς δ' Ἀτρείδης ἀπολυμαίνεσθαι ἄνωγε *Agamemnon ordered the people to purify themselves* (= that they should purify).

5. 601 οἷον δὴ θαυμάζομεν Ἕκτορα δῖον αἰχμητήν τ' ἔμεναι κτλ. (*for being a warrior, how he was a warrior*).

This might be called the *natural* Acc. with the Infinitive.

2. The Acc. has not a sufficient construction with the Verb alone, but may be used if it is accompanied by an Infinitive of the *thing* or *fact : e.g.*—

βούλομ' ἐγὼ λαὸν σῶν ἔμμεναι *I wish the people to be safe* (the safety of the people).

οὕνεκ' ἄκουσε τείρεσθαι Τρῶας *because he heard of the Trojans being hard pressed.*

τῷ οὐ νεμεσίζομ' Ἀχαιοὺς ἀσχαλάαν *wherefore I do not think it a shame in the Greeks to chafe.*

In this construction the logical Object is the fact or *action* given by the Infinitive, to which the Acc. furnishes a Subject or *agent*, and thus turns it from an abstract Noun to a predication (so that *e.g.* τείρεσθαι Τρῶας is virtually = ὅτι ἐτείροντο Τρῶες). It is found with Verbs that usually take only a ' Cognate Acc.' (Neuter Pronoun, &c.), as φημί, εἶπον, ἀκούω, πυνθάνομαι. οἶδα, δίω, φρονέω, ἐθέλω, βούλομαι, ἔλπομαι, νεμεσίζομαι, φθονέω, &c. Thus it is in principle a particular form of the *Accusativus de quo* (see § 140, 3, *b*, also § 234, 3).

3. The Acc. has no construction except as the Subject of the Infinitive. This Acc. is chiefly found in Homer—

(*a*) after Impersonal Verbs (§ 162, 4) : as—

Il. 18. 329 ἄμφω γὰρ πέπρωται ὁμοίην γαῖαν ἐρεῦσαι *it is fated for both to &c.*

19. 182 οὐ μὲν γάρ τι νεμεσσητὸν βασιλῆα ἄνδρ' ἀπαρέσσασθαι *it is no shame that a king should &c.*

(*b*) after πρίν and πάρος ; as πρὶν ἐλθεῖν υἷας Ἀχαιῶν *before the Greeks came,* πάρος τάδε ἔργα γενέσθαι *before these things came to pass.*

The other examples are from the Odyssey, viz.—

Od. 4. 210 ὡς νῦν Νέστορι δῶκε διαμπερὲς ἤματα πάντα αὐτὸν μὲν λιπαρῶς γηρασκέμεν (10. 533., 14. 193).

This may be called the purely *idiomatic* Acc. with the Infinitive. It has evidently been formed on the analogy of the older varieties.

238.] Tenses of the Infinitive. So long as the Infinitive is merely a Verbal Noun, it does not express anything about the *time* of the action as past, present, or future. But when it is virtually a predication, the idea of time comes in ; *e.g.*—

Il. 5. 659 ἀλλ' οἷόν τινά φασι βίην Ἡρακληείην
ἔμμεναι (' what they say he *was* '): cp. Od. 8. 181.

14. 454 οὐ μὰν αὖτ' ὀΐω . . ἅλιον πηδῆσαι ἄκοντα,
ἀλλά τις Ἀργείων κόμισε χροΐ.

The Future Infinitive is used with φημί, ὀΐω, ἔλπομαι, ὑπισχνέομαι, ὄμνυμι and other Verbs implying *expectation* or *promise ;* also with μέλλω when it means *to be about to.*

When the Inf. expresses, not simple expectation as to the future, but *fitness, obligation, necessity,* or the like (§ 231, 2), the Aorist or Present is used. Thus Il. 13. 262 οὐ γὰρ ὀΐω πολεμίζειν means, not ' I do not think I shall fight,' but *I do not think fit, I have no mind, to fight ;* so Il. 3. 98 φρονέω διακρινθήμεναι *my mind is* (= δοκεῖ μοι) *that they should be parted :* 9. 608 φρονέω τετιμῆσθαι *I claim to be honoured :* 22. 235 νοέω φρεσὶ τιμήσασθαι *I see* (*understand*) *that I should honour thee* (= I purpose to honour thee) : 24. 560 νοέω δὲ καὶ αὐτὸς Ἕκτορά τοι λῦσαι : and so in a prophecy, Od. 2. 171 φημὶ τελευτηθῆναι ἅπαντα *I say that all must be accomplished :* and—

Il. 13. 665 ὅς ῥ' εὖ εἰδὼς κῆρ' ὀλοὴν ἐπὶ νηὸς ἔβαινε,
πολλάκι γάρ οἱ ἔειπε γέρων ἀγαθὸς Πολύιδος
νούσῳ ὑπ' ἀργαλέῃ φθίσθαι οἷς ἐν μεγάροισιν
that he must perish (according to his *fate*).

So with μοῖρα and θέσφατόν ἐστι : also with μέλλω when it means *to be likely :* Il. 11. 364 ᾧ μέλλεις εὔχεσθαι *to whom it is like that you pray ;* Od. 9. 475 οὐκ ἄρ' ἔμελλες ἀνάλκιδος ἀνδρὸς ἑταίρους ἔδμεναι *he proves to be no helpless man whose comrades you ate ;* Il. 21. 83 μέλλω που ἀπέχθεσθαι *it must be that I am become hateful ;* Il. 18. 362 μέλλει βροτὸς τελέσσαι *a man is likely to accomplish* (*i. e.* it may be expected of him).

The instances in which a Pres. or Aor. Inf. appears to be used of future time may be variously accounted for. The Inf. ἰέναι has a future sense in Il. 17. 709 οὐδέ μιν οἴω νῦν ἰέναι κτλ. ; so Il. 20. 365., Od. 15. 214. Again in Od. 9. 496 καὶ δὴ φάμεν αὐτόθ' ὀλέσθαι the Aor. is used for the sake of vividness—*we thought ' we are lost ' :* cp. Il. 9. 413 ὤλετο μέν μοι νόστος (§ 78). Similarly Il. 3. 112 ἐλπόμενοι παύσασθαι may be *hoping that they had ceased* (by the fact of the proposed duel); cp. Il. 7. 199., 16.

281.　So Od. 13. 173 ὃς ἔφασκε Ποσειδάων' ἀγάσασθαι *who said
that Poseidon was moved to indignation* (= ὅτι ἠγάσατο).

In several places the reading is uncertain, the Fut. being of the same
metrical value as the Aor. or the Pres. (-εσθαι and -ασθαι, -ιξειν and -ιξειν,
&c.). In such cases the evidence of the ancient grammarians and the MSS. is
usually indecisive, and we are justified in writing the Fut. throughout, according to the general rule. Thus—

Il. 3. 28 φάτο γὰρ τίσεσθαι (so Ven. A.: most MSS. τίσασθαι). Hence we
may read φάτο γὰρ τίσεσθαι in Od. 20. 121.

22. 118 (ἀλλ' ἀποδάσσεσθαι (so Aristarchus: most MSS. -ασθαι).

22. 120 μή τι κατακρύψειν, ἀλλ' ἄνδιχα πάντα δάσεσθαι (MSS. -ασθαι).

23. 773 ἔμελλον ἐπαίξεσθαι (the best MSS. have -ασθαι).

20. 85 (ὑπίσχεο) ἐναντίβιον πτολεμίξειν (so A. D.: other MSS. πολεμίζειν).

16. 830 ἦ που ἔφησθα πόλιν κεραϊξέμεν (MSS. -ιξέμεν).

Od. 2. 373 ὄμοσον μή .. τάδε μυθήσεσθαι (so Ar.: MSS. -ασθαι).

Two exceptions remain: Od. 2. 280 ἐλπωρή τοι ἔπειτα τελευτῆσαι τάδε ἔργα (τε-
λευτήσειν in one of Ludwich's MSS.): Il. 12. 407 ἐπεί οἱ θυμὸς ἐέλπετο κῦδος
ἀρέσθαι (some good authorities give ἐέλδετο).*

The only example of an Inf. representing an Optative is—

Il. 9. 684 καὶ δ' ἂν τοῖς ἄλλοισιν ἔφη παραμυθήσασθαι
which is the report of the speech (v. 417) καὶ δ' ἂν .. παραμυθησαίμην. But cp. Od. 3. 125 οὐδέ κε φαίης .. μυθήσασθαι *you
would not think that .. would speak.*

239.] Dative with the Infinitive. An idiomatic use of the
Dative arises when the Noun which stands as logical subject to
an Inf. of *purpose* is put in the same Case with it, *i. e.* in the
Dative. Thus the construction in—

αἰσχρὸν γὰρ τόδε γ' ἐστὶ καὶ ἐσσομένοισι πυθέσθαι

is idiomatic (as compared with σφῶϊν δὸς ἄγειν, &c.), because the
meaning is, not ' is shameful for future men,' but ' is shameful
for (with a view to) the hearing of future men.' The principle
is evidently the same as has been pointed out in the case of the
Nominative and the Accusative (§ 234). Because the *action* of
the Infinitive stands in a Dative relation to the governing Verb,
the *agent* or Subject of the action is put in the Dative.

This construction is found in the ' double Dative' of Latin (e. g. ἐσσομένοισι
πυθέσθαι would be in Latin *posteris auditui*), and of Sanscrit (Delbrück, *A. S.*
p. 149). It is usually classified as ' Attraction '—the Dat. of the *person* being
regarded as following the Dat. of the *thing* or action. In Greek it evidently
goes back to the time when the Inf. was still felt as a Dative.

240.] Predicative Nouns—' Attraction.' Corresponding to
the Nominative in the Predicate (§ 162), an Infinitival Clause

---

* See Madvig, *Bemerkungen über einige Punkte der griech. Wortfügungslehre*, p. 34 :
Cobet, *Misc. Crit.* p. 328.

may have a Predicative *Accusative*, in agreement with its (expressed or understood) Subject: as Il. 4. 341 σφῶϊν μέν τ᾽ ἐπέοικε μετὰ πρώτοισιν ἐόντας ἑστάμεν *it becomes you that you should stand among the foremost;* Il. 8. 192 τῆς νῦν κλέος οὐρανὸν ἵκει πᾶσαν χρυσείην ἔμεναι *whose fame reaches heaven that it is all gold.*

Or the words which enter in this way into an Infinitival Clause may follow the construction of the principal Clause, and thus be put in the Nom. or Dat.; as—

> Il. 1. 76 καί μοι ὄμοσσον, ἦ μέν μοι πρόφρων . . ἀρήξειν
> 12. 337 οὔ πώς οἱ ἔην βώσαντι γεγωνεῖν.

Here πρόφρων is said to be 'attracted' into the Nom. (agreeing with the subject of ὄμοσσον), and βώσαντι into the Dat. (agreeing with οἱ).

The difference of meaning given by the two constructions is generally to be observed in Homer, at least in the case of the Dative. A Noun or Participle is put in the Acc. if it is closely connected with the Inf., so as to become an essential *part* of the predication: whereas a Dat. construed with the principal Clause expresses something *prior to* the Inf. (either a *condition* or a *reason*). Thus—

> Il. 1. 541 αἰεί τοι φίλον ἐστὶν ἐμεῦ ἀπὸ νόσφιν ἐόντα
> κρυπτάδια φρονέοντα δικαζέμεν,

means 'you like to decide apart from me,' *i.e.* 'you like, when you decide, to be apart from me': whereas with ἐόντι the sense would be '*when you are apart from me* you like to decide.' So Il. 15. 57 εἴπῃσι Ποσειδάωνι ἄνακτι παυσάμενον πολέμοιο ἱκέσθαι 'shall bid Poseidon to cease from war *and* come'—not '*when* he has ceased, to come.'

But with a Dat.—

> Il. 6. 410 ἐμοὶ δέ κε κέρδιον εἴη σεῦ ἀφαμαρτούσῃ χθόνα δύμεναι

it were better for me, if (or *when*) *I lose thee, to &c.*

> Il. 8. 218 εἰ μὴ ἐπὶ φρεσὶ θῆκ᾽ Ἀγαμέμνονι πότνια Ἥρη
> αὐτῷ ποιπνύσαντι θοῶς ὀτρῦναι Ἀχαιούς

'who had of himself made hot haste,' αὐτῷ as in the phrase μεμαῶτε καὶ αὐτώ (13. 46., 15. 604).*

> Il. 15. 496 οὔ οἱ ἀεικὲς ἀμυνομένῳ περὶ πάτρης τεθνάμεν

to die when fighting for his country.

So Il. 5. 253., 13. 96., 20. 356., 21. 185., 22. 72.

There are some exceptions, however, if our texts are to be trusted; *i. e.* there are places where a word which belongs to the predication is put in the Dat. owing to a preceding Dat.: *e. g.*—

> Il. 15. 117 εἴ πέρ μοι καὶ μοῖρα Διὸς πληγέντι κεραυνῷ
> κεῖσθαι ὁμοῦ νεκύεσσι (cp. Od. 19. 139, 284).

---

* This is pointed out by Dingeldein, *De participio Homerico*, p. 8.

This seems to be always the case when there are two successive
Participles, the first of which is properly in the Dat. : as—

Il. 12. 410 ἀργαλέον δέ μοί ἐστι καὶ ἰφθίμῳ περ ἐόντι
μούνῳ ῥηξαμένῳ θέσθαι παρὰ νηυσὶ κέλευθον.

Here the meaning is, 'to break through and make' &c.,—and
therefore ῥηξάμενον would be correct; but after ἐόντι the change
from the Dat. to the Acc. would be very harsh. So Il. 13. 317–
319, Od. 10. 494–5. In other places the text may be at fault.
As attraction became the rule in later Greek, and the two
Case-forms are generally of the same metrical form, it would be
easy for a Dat. to take the place of an Acc.: e.g. in Il. 9. 398–
400 ἔνθα δέ μοι . . ἐπέσσυτο θυμὸς ἀγήνωρ γήμαντι . . κτήμασι τέρ-
πεσθαι, where for γήμαντι, the reading of Aristarchus, others gave
γήμαντα, which conforms to the principle laid down.

When the Subject of the Infinitive is also Subject of the
governing Verb the Nominative is generally used : as Il. 1. 76
(quoted above), 1. 415., 4. 101–3., 8. 498, &c. An exception is—

Od. 9. 224 ἔνθ' ἐμὲ μὲν πρώτισθ' ἕταροι λίσσοντ' ἐπέεσσι,
τυρῶν αἰνυμένους ἰέναι πάλιν.

that they might take of the cheeses and so go back.

241.] **Infinitive as an Imperative.** This use is often found
in Homer, but chiefly after an Imperative, so that the Infinitive
serves to carry on the command already given :—

Il. 1. 322 ἔρχεσθον κλισίην 'Αγαμέμνονος 'Ατρεΐδαο,
χειρὸς ἑλόντ' ἀγέμεν Βρισηΐδα.

2. 8–10 βάσκ' ἴθι . . ἀγορευέμεν ὡς ἐπιτέλλω.

3. 459 ἔκδοτε, καὶ τιμὴν ἀποτινέμεν.

Od. 4. 415 καὶ τότ' ἔπειθ' ὑμῖν μελέτω κάρτος τε βίη τε,
αὖθι δ' ἔχειν κτλ. (cp. v. 419, 422 ff.).

Or after a Future, to express what the person addressed is to do
as *his* part in a set of acts :—

Il. 22. 259 νεκρὸν 'Αχαιοῖσιν δώσω πάλιν, ὡς δὲ σὺ ῥέζειν.

Od. 4. 408 εὐνάσω ἐξείης· σὺ δ' εὖ κρίνασθαι ἑταίρους.

So after a clause which leads up to a command; Il. 11. 788
ἀλλ' εὖ οἱ φάσθαι (Achilles is the mightier) *but do you advise him
well:* 17. 691., 20. 335. Cp. also, Il. 10. 65 αὖθι μένειν (answer
to the question *am I to remain here?*): 5. 124 θαρσέων νῦν . .
μάχεσθαι (in answer to a prayer) *without fear now you may fight.*

The use for the Third Person is rare: in a *command*, Il. 6.
86–92 εἰπὲ δ' ἔπειτα μητέρι σῇ καὶ ἐμῇ· ἡ δὲ . . θεῖναι κτλ.; 7. 79
ᶜῶμα δὲ οἴκαδ' ἐμὸν δόμεναι πάλιν (let him take my arms) *but give
back my body;* so 17. 155., 23. 247, Od. 11. 443 : in a *prayer,*
with a Subject in the Accusative,—

Il. 2. 412 Ζεῦ κύδιστε, μέγιστε, κελαινεφές, αἰθέρι ναίων,
       μὴ πρὶν ἐπ' ἠέλιον δῦναι κτλ. (cp. 3. 285., 7. 179).
Od. 17. 354 Ζεῦ ἄνα, Τηλέμαχόν μοι ἐν ἀνδράσιν ὄλβιον εἶναι.
An Infinitive of wish is used with the Subject in the Nom.,
once of the Second Person, and once of the First Person :—

Od. 7. 311 αἲ γὰρ Ζεῦ τε πάτερ καὶ 'Αθηναίη καὶ "Απολλον
        τοῖος ἐὼν οἷός ἐσσι, τά τε φρονέων ἅ τ' ἐγώ περ,
        παῖδά τ' ἐμὴν ἐχέμεν καὶ ἐμὸς γαμβρὸς καλέεσθαι.
   24. 376 αἲ γὰρ . . οἷος Νήρικον εἷλον . . τοῖος ἐὼν . . ἐφεστά-
μεναι καὶ ἀμύνειν.

The force of the Infinitive in all these uses seems to be that of
an *indirect* Imperative. The command is given as something
following on an expressed or implied state of things. Thus we
may connect the idiom with the use of the Infinitive to imply
fitness, obligation, &c. (§ 231); compare εἰσὶ καὶ οἵδε τάδ' εἰπέμεν
these are here to say this with καὶ δὲ σὺ εἰπέμεναι *it is your part to
say*. There is a similar use of the Infinitive in Sanscrit, with
ellipse of the verb *to be* (Delbrück, *A. S.* p. 15 : Whitney, § 982,
c, d).

It should be noticed, however, that other languages have developed a use of
the Infinitive in commands, to which this explanation does not apply : as
Germ. *schritt fahren !* In these cases we may recognise a general tendency
towards the impersonal form. It is very probable that the ordinary 2 Sing.
Imper. λέγε represents an original use of the Tense-stem without any Person-
ending (Paul, *Principien*, p. 108).

242.] Origin and history of the Infinitive. That the Greek
Infinitive was originally the Dative of an abstract Noun is
proved by comparison with Sanscrit. ' In the Veda and Brāh-
maṇa a number of verbal nouns, *nomina actionis*, in various of
their cases, are used in constructions which assimilate them to
the infinitive of other languages—although, were it not for these
other later and more developed and pronounced infinitives, the
constructions in question might pass as ordinary case-construc-
tions of a somewhat peculiar kind' (Whitney, § 969). In the
Veda these Infinitives, or Case-forms on the way to become
Infinitives (*werdende Infinitive*, Delbr.), are mostly Datives, expressing *end* or *purpose*, and several of them are identical in
formation with Greek Infinitives ; as *dávane* δοῦναι (δοϜεναι),
vidmane Ϝἴδμεναι, *-dhyai* -σθαι,* *-ase* -σαι. In Greek, however, the
Dative Ending -αι is not otherwise preserved, and the ' true
Dative ' construction is not applied to *things* (§ 143): conse-

* So Delbrück and others ; but see Max Müller's *Chips*, Vol. IV. p. 58.

quently these forms stand quite apart from the Case-system, and have ceased to be felt as real Case-forms. Thus the Greek Infinitive is a *survival*, both in form and in construction, from a period when the Dative of purpose or consequence was one of the ordinary idioms of the language. In Latin, again, this Dative is common enough, and often answers in meaning to the Greek Infinitive; compare (*e.g.*) ὥρη ἐστὶν εὕδειν with *munitioni tempus relinquere* (Roby, § 1156), ἀμύνειν εἰσὶ καὶ ἄλλοι with *auxilio esse*, &c. The retention of the construction in Latin is connected, on the one hand with the fact that the Latin Dative is a 'true Dative,' on the other hand with the comparatively small use that is made in Latin of the Infinitive of purpose. Similarly in classical Sanscrit the Dative of purpose &c. is extremely common, but the Dative Infinitives have gone entirely out of use (Whitney, § 287 and § 986)—a result of the 'struggle for existence' which precisely reverses the state of things in Greek.

The growth of the Dative of purpose into a distinct subordinate Clause was favoured by the habit of placing it at the end of the sentence, after the Verb, so that it had the appearance of an addition or afterthought. This was the rule in Vedic Sanscrit (see Delbrück, *A. S.* p. 25). It may be traced in Greek, not merely in collocations like ἔριδι ξυνέηκε μάχεσθαι, &c., but even in such forms as—

Il. 5. 639 ἀλλ' οἷόν τινά φασι βίην Ἡρακληείην
ἔμμεναι (*what they call him as to being*),

where the Inf. appears to be added epexegetically after a slight pause: cp. Il. 2. 249., 17. 27., 21. 463, 570, Od. 1. 233, 377., 6. 43., 17. 416.

The development of the Infinitival Clause which we find in Greek and Latin may be traced chiefly under two heads; (1) the construction of the 'Accusative with the Infinitive,' by which the predication of the Infinitive was provided with an expressed Subject (§ 237): and (2) the system of Tenses of the Infinitive, which was gradually completed by the creation of new *forms*,— esp. the Future Infinitive, peculiar to Greek,—and by the use of the Present Infinitive as equivalent in meaning to the Present and Imperfect Indicative. In the post-Homeric language the Infinitive came to be used as an equivalent, not only for the Indicative, but also for other Moods.

The use of the Infinitive as an indeclinable Noun is subsequent to Homer; it became possible with the later use of the Article. Some of the conditions, however, out of which it grew may be traced in Homeric language. The first of these was the complete separation of the Infinitive from the Case-system; so that it

ceased to be felt as a Case-form, and could be used in parallel
construction to the Nom. or Acc.: as—

Il. 2. 453 τοῖσι δ' ἄφαρ πόλεμος γλυκίων γένετ' ἠὲ νέεσθαι.

7. 203 δὸς νίκην Αἴαντι καὶ ἀγλαὸν εὖχος ἀρέσθαι.

Again, an Infinitive following a Neuter Pronoun, and expressing
the logical Subject or Object, easily came to be regarded as in
'Apposition' to the Pronoun: as—

Od. 1. 370 ἐπεὶ τό γε καλὸν ἀκουέμεν ἐστὶν ἀοιδοῦ.

11. 358 καί κε τὸ βουλοίμην, καί κεν πολὺ κέρδιον εἴη,
　　　πλειοτέρῃ σὺν χειρὶ φίλην ἐς πατρίδ' ἱκέσθαι.

The only instance which really comes near the later 'Articular
Infinitive' is Od. 20. 52 ἀνίη καὶ τὸ φυλάσσειν (§ 259). The use
of the Infinitive with an Article in the Gen. or Dat. is wholly
post-Homeric.

The Participle.

243.] **Uses of the Participle.** Following out the view of the
Participle as a Verbal Adjective, we may distinguish the following uses :—

1. The Participle is often used as an ordinary Adjective qualifying a Noun ; as θεοὶ αἰὲν ἐόντες, βροτοὶ σῖτον ἔδοντες, πίθοι ποτὶ
τοῖχον ἀρηρότες, σάκος τετυγμένον, and the like. In one or two
cases it is Substantival : as τὸ γὰρ γέρας ἐστὶ θανόντων, ψυχαὶ
εἴδωλα καμόντων, Ὀλύμπια δώματ' ἔχοντες.

A few Participles have lost their Verbal character altogether :
esp. οὐλόμενος *miserable*, ὀνήμενος *happy*, ἵκμενος *secundus*, ἄσμενος
glad, ἑκών *willing*, ἔθων (better ἐθών, since it is an Aor. in form,
§ 31, 1) *according to wont*, περιπλόμενος (in the phrase περιπλο-
μένων ἐνιαυτῶν *the revolving years*) ; also the Substantival μέδοντες
rulers, τένοντες *muscles*, ἀμείβοντες *rafters*, αἴθουσα *a portico*, δράκων
a serpent, γέρων, μοῦσα. The word κρείων *ruler* retains a trace of
the Verb in εὐρὺ κρείων *widely ruling*. Cp. also the compounds
πολύ-τλας, ἀ-κάμας, ἀ-δάμας, λυκά-βας.

2. Much more frequently, the Participle qualifies or forms
part of the predication (§ 162): *e.g.* in such combinations as—

　　　διαστήτην ἐρίσαντε *parted having quarrelled*
　　　ἐϋφρονέων ἀγορήσατο *spoke with good thought*

the Participle has the same construction as the Adjective in
παλίνορσος ἀπέστη, or πρόφρων τέτληκας (§ 162, 2). Thus it
serves to express a predication which the speaker wishes to subordinate in some way to that of the governing Verb.

The Participle may express different relations : attendant *cir-*

P

cumstance or *manner* (as in the examples quoted); *cause*, as Il. 11. 313 τί παθόντε λελάσμεθα θούριδος ἀλκῆς; *opposition*, as often with καί and περ, &c. (Goodwin, §§ 832–846).

3. Finally, a Participle construed in 'Apposition' to a Noun in an oblique Case may imply a predication (§ 168); as καπνὸν ἀποθρῴσκοντα νοῆσαι *to descry the smoke rising* (i. e. *when it rises*, or *that it rises*, &c.). Note that—

(*a*) A Participle of this kind often has the character of a distinct Clause, coming at the end of a sentence, and after a metrical pause : as—

Il. 4. 420 δεινὸν δ' ἔβραχε χαλκὸς ἐπὶ στήθεσσιν ἄνακτος ὀρνυμένου (*as he roused himself*).

Od. 23. 205 ὡς φάτο, τῆς δ' αὐτοῦ λύτο γούνατα καὶ φίλον ἦτορ σήματ' ἀναγνούσης (*when she recognised the token*).

(*b*) Not unfrequently the word with which the Participle should be construed is understood : especially when it is a Partitive or quasi-Partitive Gen. (§§ 147, 151) :—

Il. 2. 153 ἀϋτὴ δ' οὐρανὸν ἷκεν οἴκαδε ἱεμένων *a cry rose to heaven* (*of men*) *eager to return home :* so Il. 12. 339., 13. 291, 498., 15. 689.

5. 162 πόρτιος ἠὲ βοὸς ξύλοχον κάτα βοσκομενάων *a heifer or cow* (*of those*) *that are feeding in a thicket.*

5. 665 τὸ μὲν οὔ τις ἐπεφράσατ' οὐδ' ἐνόησε μηροῦ ἐξερύσαι δόρυ μείλινον, ὄφρ' ἐπιβαίη, σπευδόντων *no one* . . . (*of them*) *in their haste :* cp. 15. 450 τό οἱ οὔ τις ἐρύκακεν ἱεμένων περ.

18. 246 ὀρθῶν δ' ἑσταότων ἀγορὴ γένετ' *an assembly was held upstanding* (*of them standing up*).

Od. 17. 489 Τηλέμαχος δ' ἐν μὲν κραδίῃ μέγα πένθος ἄεξε βλημένου (*for his having been wounded*).

So with the Dative ; Il. 12. 374 ἐπειγομένοισι δ' ἵκοντο *came as a relief* (*to them*) *when they were hard pressed;* Od. 5. 152 κατείβετο δὲ γλυκὺς αἰὼν νόστον ὀδυρομένῳ.

(*c*) The Subject thus understood may be indefinite :—

Il. 2. 291 πόνος ἐστὶν ἀνιηθέντα νέεσθαι (see § 233).

6. 267 οὐδέ πῃ ἔστι κελαινεφέϊ Κρονίωνι αἵματι καὶ λύθρῳ πεπαλαγμένον εὐχετάασθαι *for one who is bespattered* . . *to pray.*

13. 787 πὰρ δύναμιν δ' οὐκ ἔστι καὶ ἐσσύμενον πολεμίζειν.

So Il. 2. 234., 14. 63, Od. 2. 311 : cp. the phrase ὅσον τε γέγωνε βοήσας *as far as a man makes himself heard by shouting.*

(*d*) The Participle is sometimes found in a different Case from

a preceding Pronoun with which it might have been construed.
Thus we have—

Il. 14. 25 λάκε δέ σφι περὶ χροΐ χαλκὸς ἀτείρης
νυσσομένων (construed with χροΐ instead of σφι).

16. 531 ὅττι οἱ ὦκ' ἤκουσε μέγας θεὸς εὐξαμένοιο
(with ἤκουσε instead of οἱ).

Od. 9. 256 ὡς ἔφαθ', ἡμῖν δ' αὖτε κατεκλάσθη φίλον ἦτορ
δεισάντων (so Il. 3. 301, Od. 6. 157., 9. 458).

Il. 20. 413 τὸν βάλε . . . νῶτα παραΐσσοντος *wounded him* . . .
in the back as he darted past.

Od. 4. 646 ἤ σε βίη ἀέκοντος ἀπηύρα.

Il. 10. 187 ὡς τῶν νήδυμος ὕπνος ἀπὸ βλεφάροιϊν ὀλώλει
νύκτα φυλασσομένοισι κακήν : so Il. 14. 141-3.

Od. 17. 555 μεταλλῆσαί τί ἑ θυμὸς
ἀμφὶ πόσει κέλεται καὶ κήδεά περ πεπαθυίῃ.

We need not consider these as instances of 'Anacoluthon' or
change of the construction. The Participle, as we saw, does not
need a preceding Pronoun : it may therefore have a construction
independent of such a Pronoun. And it is characteristic of
Homer not to employ concord as a means of connecting distant
words when other constructions are admissible.

244.] **Tenses of the Participle.** The distinction between the
Present and Aorist Participle has already been touched upon in
§§ 76-77, and the meaning of the Perfect Participle in § 28.

It may be remarked here, as a point of difference between the two kinds of
Verbal Noun, that the Aorist Participle almost always represents an action
as past at the time given by the Verb (*e. g.* ὡς εἰπὼν κατ' ἄρ' ἕζετο *having thus
spoken he sat down*), whereas the Aor. Inf. generally conveys no notion of time.
This however is not from the Participle itself conveying any notion of past
time. Indeed it is worth notice that the Participles which are without
Tense-meaning are chiefly Aorists in form (§ 243, 1).

The Future Participle is used predicatively with Verbs of
motion : ἦλθε λυσόμενος *came to ransom,* καλέουσ' ἴε *went to call,*
ἦγ' ἐπικουρήσοντα, ἐπέδραμε τεύχεα συλήσων, &c. The exceptions
to this rule are—

(1) ἐσσόμενος *future,* in Il. 1. 70 τά τ' ἐσσόμενα πρό τ' ἐόντα
things future and past ; 2. 119 καὶ ἐσσομένοισι πυθέσθαι.

(2) ἐπιβησόμενος, in Il. 5. 46 (16. 343) νύξ' ἵππων ἐπιβησόμενον,
23. 379 αἰεὶ γὰρ δίφρου ἐπιβησομένοισιν ἐΐκτην. But see § 41.

(3) Il. 18. 309 καί τε κτανέοντα κατέκτα, see § 63.

(4) Od. 11. 608 αἰεὶ βαλέοντι ἐοικώς *like one about to cast.*

245.] Implied Predication. Where the Participle is predicative, we often find the Noun or Pronoun taking the place in the construction of the whole Participial Clause : as Il. 17. 1 οὐδ' ἔλαθ' Ἀτρέος υἱὸν Πάτροκλος Τρώεσσι δαμείς *that Patroclus had fallen :* Od. 5. 6 μέλε γάρ οἱ ἐὼν ἐν δώμασι νύμφης *it troubled her that he was &c.:* Il. 6. 191 γίγνωσκε θεοῦ γόνον ἠῢν ἐόντα *knew him for the offspring of a god :* Od. 10. 419 σοὶ μὲν νοστήσαντι ἐχάρημεν *we were gladdened by thy return :* Il. 13. 417 ἄχος γένετ' εὐξαμένοιο *there was vexation at his boasting :* Il. 5. 682., 14. 504., 17. 538, 564., 18. 337, &c.

We have here the idiom already observed in the use of the Infinitive (§ 237) by which the weight of the meaning is shifted from the grammatical Subject, Object, &c. to a limiting or qualifying word. Note especially that—

1. The Aor. Participle may be used in this way to express a fact which *coincides* in time with the Verb of the sentence : as Il. 6. 284 εἰ κεῖνόν γε ἴδοιμι κατελθόντ' Ἄϊδος εἴσω. So especially when the *time* of the fact is the important point, as ἐς ἠέλιον καταδύντα *till sun-set :* Il. 13. 38 μένοιεν νοστήσαντα ἄνακτα *should await the master's return :* 13. 545 Θόωνα μεταστρεφθέντα δοκεύσας.

2. With Verbs of *saying, hearing, knowing,* &c., also of *rejoicing* and *grieving,* the Acc. with a Participle is used like the Acc. with the Inf. (both being evidently applications of the *Accusativus de quo,* § 140, 3, *b*) : *e.g.*—

Il. 7. 129 τοὺς νῦν εἰ πτώσσοντας ὑφ' Ἕκτορι πάντας ἀκούσαι *if he were to hear of their shrinking.*

Od. 4. 732 εἰ γὰρ ἐγὼ πυθόμην ταύτην ὁδὸν ὁρμαίνοντα.

23. 2 δέσποινη ἐρέουσα φίλον πόσιν ἐνδὸν ἐόντα.

Il. 1. 124 οὐδέ τί που ἴδμεν ξυνήϊα κείμενα πολλά.

Od. 7. 211 οὕς τινας ὑμεῖς ἴστε μάλιστ' ὀχέοντας ὀϊζύν.

Il. 8. 378 ἢ νῶϊ . . γηθήσει προφανεῖσα *will rejoice at our appearing.*

13. 353 ἤχθετο γάρ ῥα Τρωσὶν δαμναμένους *he was vexed at their being subdued by the Trojans.*

A further extension, analogous to the Acc. with the Inf. after Impersonal Verbs, may perhaps be seen in Od. 6. 193 ὧν ἐπέοιχ' ἱκέτην ταλαπείριον ἀντιάσαντα *which it is fit that a suppliant should meet with.*

246.] Genitive Absolute. This is a form of implied predication, in which the Noun or Pronoun has no regular construction with the governing Verb. The Participial Clause expresses the *time* or *circumstances* in which the action of the Verb takes place :—

Il. 1. 88 οὔ τις ἐμεῦ ζῶντος κτλ. *no one, while I am living shall &c.*

2. 551 περιτελλομένων ἐνιαυτῶν *as years go round.*

5. 203 ἀνδρῶν εἰλομένων *where men are crowded ;* so ἀνδρῶν λικμώντων, ἀνδρῶν τρεσσάντων, πολλῶν ἑλκόντων, &c.

Od. 1. 390 καί κεν τοῦτ᾽ ἐθέλοιμι Διός γε διδόντος ἀρέσθαι *that too I would be willing to obtain if Zeus gave it.*

The Subject is understood in Od. 4. 19 μολπῆς ἐξάρχοντος *when the singer began the music.*

The Aorist Participle is less common in Homer than the Present, especially in the Odyssey : the instances are, Il. 8. 164, 468., 9. 426., 10. 246, 356., 11. 509., 13. 409., 14. 522., 16. 306., 19. 62, 75., 21. 290, 437., 22. 47, 288, 383, Od. 14. 475., 24. 88, 535 (Classen, *Beob.* p. 180 ff.).

The ' Genitive Absolute ' must have begun as an extension of one of the ordinary uses of the Gen. ; most probably of the Gen. of *Time* (§ 150). For, ἠελίου ἀνιόντος *within the time of the sun's rising* is a Gen. like ἠοῦς *in the morning*, νυκτός *by night*, &c., and answers, as a phrase denoting time, to ἅμ᾽ ἠελίῳ καταδύντι *at sunset*, ἐς ἠέλιον καταδύντα *up to sun-set*, &c. So we may compare τοῦδ᾽ αὐτοῦ λυκάβαντος ἐλεύσεται *he will come within this year* with ἦ σέθεν ἐνθάδ᾽ ἐόντος ἐλεύσεται *he will come within your being here ;* and again περιτελλομένων ἐνιαυτῶν *in the years as they go round*, with τῶν προτέρων ἐτέων *in the former years.* The transition may be seen in ἔαρος νέον ἱσταμένοιο *in the spring when it is beginning.* Compare also the phrases ἐπειγομένων ἀνέμων, Βορέαο πεσόντος, &c. with νηνεμίης *in calm weather*, &c.

The circumstance that the Ablative is the ' Absolute ' Case in Latin is far from proving that the Greek Gen. in this use is Ablatival. In Sanscrit the Case used in this way is the Locative, occasionally the Genitive : and the Latin Abl. Absolute may represent a Locative of *time at which*, or an Instrumental of *circumstance* (§ 144). The hypothesis that such Participial Clauses in Greek expressed *space* of time *within which* (rather than *point* of time, or *circumstance*) is borne out by the interesting fact, noticed above, that in Homer this construction is chiefly found with the Participle which implies continuance, viz. the Present : whereas in Latin the Abl. Abs. is commonest with the Perfect Participle.

An approach to a ' Dative Absolute ' may be seen in such uses as—

Il. 8. 487 Τρωσὶν μέν ῥ᾽ ἀέκουσιν ἔδυ φάος.

12. 374 ἐπειγομένοισι δ᾽ ἵκοντο.

Od. 21. 115 οὔ κέ μοι ἀχνυμένῳ τάδε δώματα πότνια μήτηρ λείποι (= *it would be no distress to me if &c.*)

which are extensions or free applications, by the help of the Participle, of the true Dat. (*Dativus ethicus*).

246.*] The Verbal Adjectives. The formations to which this
term is applied resemble the Participles in some of their
characteristics.

Several groups of Nouns are used as Participles or ' Gerun-
dives' in the cognate languages, such as the Latin forms in
-*tu-s*, the Sanscr. in -*ta-s*, -*na-s*, -*ya-s*, -*tavya-s*, &c. Of the corresponding Greek forms the Verbal in -το-ς is the most important,
and approaches most nearly to the character of a Participle.* It
is used mainly in two senses :—

(1) To express the *state* corresponding to or brought about by
the action of a Verb : τυκ-τός *made*, κρυπτός *secret*, κλυ-τός *heard
about, famed*, στα-τός *standing* (*in a stall*), τλη-τός *enduring* (Il. 24.
49), ἀγαπη-τός *object of love*, ἑρπε-τόν *creeping thing*, φυ-τόν *growth,
plant*, πινυ-τός *wise*. So with ἀ- *priv.*, ἄ-κλαυτος *unweeping*, ἄ-
παστος *fasting*, ἄ-πυστος *not having news*, also *of whom there is no
news*, ἄ-πιστος *faithless*, &c. The force of the Verb in these
words is intransitive rather than passive, and they have no
reference to *time* as past or present. Compare the Latin *aptus,
cautus, certus, catus, falsus, scītus*, &c. We may note that there
is a similar (but more complete) divergence of use between the
Sanscr. Participles in -*na-s* and the Greek Adjectives in -νο-ς, as
στυγ-νός.

(2) To express *possibility*, as κτη-τός *that can be acquired*,
ληϊστός *that can be taken as plunder* (Il. 9. 406), ῥηκτός *vulnerable*
(Il. 13. 323), ἀμ-βα-τός *approachable*. This meaning is chiefly
found in Compounds with ἀ- *priv.*: as ἄ-λυ-τος *that cannot be
loosed*, ἄρρηκτος, ἄ-φυκτος, ἄ-λαστος, ἀ-κίχητος, ἄ-σβεστος, ἄ-τλητος,
ἄ-φθι-τος, &c.: and in other negative expressions, as οὐκ ὀνό-
μαστος, οὐκέτ' ὀνοστά, οὐκέτ' ἀνεκτῶς, οὔ τι νεμεσσητόν. Hence,
as Brugmann observes, it is probable that this use of the Verbal
in -τος began in the use with the negative.

It is evident that in respect of meaning the Verbals in -τος are closely
akin to the Perfect Participle. Compare (*e. g.*) τυκτός and τετυγμένος, στατός and
ἑστηώς, πινυτός and πεπνυμένος. Hence the readiness with which in Latin
they have taken the place of the Pf. Part. Passive. The extension by which
they came to convey the notion of *past time* took place in the Perfect tense
itself, in Latin and Sanscrit.

The Verbals in -τέο-ς (for -τεϝ-ιο-ς) are post-Homeric. The
earliest instance seems to be φα-τειό-ς, in Hesiod, Th. 310
δεύτερον αὖτις ἔτικτεν ἀμήχανον, οὔ τι φατειόν, Κέρβερον κτλ.

---

* See the fine observations of Brugmann, *Grundr.* ii. § 79, p. 207.

CHAPTER XI.

Uses of the Pronouns.

Introductory.

247.] The preceding chapter has dealt with the two grammatical forms under which a Noun, by acquiring a verbal or
predicative character, is developed into a kind of subordinate
Clause. We have now to consider the Subordinate Clause properly so called : that is to say, the Clause which contains a true
(finite) Verb, but stands to another Clause in the relation of a
dependent word. *E. g.* in the Sentence λεύσσετε γὰρ τό γε πάντες
ὅ μοι γέρας ἔρχεται ἄλλη *ye see that my prize goes elsewhere,* the
Clause ὅ μοι γέρας ἔρχεται ἄλλη stands in the relation of *Object*
to the Verb of the principal Clause.

As the grammatical structure of Subordinate Clauses is shown
in general by means of Pronouns, or Conjunctions formed from
Pronominal Stems, it will be proper to begin with an account
of the meaning and use of the different words of this class.

The Greek Grammarians divided the Pronouns (ἀντωνυμίαι)
into δεικτικαί 'pointing,' and ἀναφορικαί 'referring' or 'repeating.'
These words have given us, through the Roman grammarians,
the modern terms Demonstrative and Relative ; but the meaning,
as often happens in such cases, has undergone a considerable
change. A *Deictic* Pronoun—it will be convenient to adopt
the Greek words—is one that marks an object by its position in
respect to the speaker : *I, thou, this* (here), *yonder,* &c. ; an *Anaphoric* Pronoun is one that denotes an object already mentioned
or otherwise known,—the term thus including many ' Demonstratives ' (*that* same man, *the* man, &c.), as well as the ' Relative.'
In all, therefore, we may distinguish three kinds of Pronouns :—

1. DEICTIC, in the original sense.
2. ANAPHORIC, *i. e.* referring to a Noun, but Demonstrative (in
   the modern sense).
3. RELATIVE, in the modern sense.

This however, it should be observed, is a classification of the *uses* of Pronouns, not of the words or Stems themselves : for the same Pronoun may be
Deictic or Anaphoric, Demonstrative or Relative, according to the context. It
is probable, indeed, that all Pronouns are originally Deictic, and become
Anaphoric in the course of usage.

248.] **Interrogative Pronouns.** The Interrogatives used in
Homer are τίς (§ 108), πότερος, πόστος, ποῖος, πῇ, πῶς, ποῦ, πόθι,

πόθεν, πότε, πόσε. The form πόσος only occurs in the compound ποσσῆμαρ (Il. 24. 657).

The Pronoun τίς is used both as a Substantive and as an Adjective. The adjectival use is chiefly found in the Odyssey (e.g. 1. 225 τίς δαίς, τίς δὲ ὅμιλος ὅδ' ἔπλετο; 13. 233 τίς γῆ, τίς δῆμος, τίνες ἀνέρες ἐγγεγάασι;) and in the 24th book of the Iliad (ll. 367, 387). The only clear instance in the rest of the Iliad is 5. 633 τίς τοι ἀνάγκη; for in Il. 1. 362., 18. 73, 80 τί is probably adverbial.

Notice also as peculiar to the Odyssey the combination of τίς with ὅδε, as Od. 6. 276 τίς δ' ὅδε Ναυσικάᾳ ἕπεται; 20. 351 τί κακὸν τόδε πάσχετε; The corresponding use with οὗτος is only found in Il. 10. 82 τίς δ' οὗτος .. ἔρχεαι; cp. H. Merc. 261 τίνα τοῦτον ἀπηνέα μῦθον ἔειπας;

The use of the Interrogative in Dependent Questions is rare :—

Il. 5. 85 Τυδείδην δ' οὐκ ἂν γνοίης ποτέροισι μετείη.

Od. 15. 423 εἰρώτα δὴ ἔπειτα τίς εἴη καὶ πόθεν ἔλθοι.

17. 368 ἀλλήλους τ' εἴροντο τίς εἴη καὶ πόθεν ἔλθοι.

17. 373 αὐτὸν δ' οὐ σάφα οἶδα πόθεν γένος εὔχεται εἶναι.

With these it is usual to reckon the anomalous—

Il. 18. 192 ἄλλου δ' οὔ τευ οἶδα τεῦ ἂν κλυτὰ τεύχεα δύω.

But in this case we have the further difficulty that the form of the Principal clause leads us to expect a Relative, not an Interrogative—the Indefinite ἄλλου τευ standing as Antecedent: cp. Od. 2. 42 (§ 282). Hence there is probably some corruption in the text.

The use of the Interrogative in a Dependent Question doubtless grew out of the habit of announcing that a question is going to be asked. A formula, such as ἀλλ' ἄγε μοι τόδε εἰπὲ καὶ ἀτρεκέως κατάλεξον, or καί μοι τοῦτ' ἀγόρευσον ἐτήτυμον ὄφρ' ἐὺ εἰδῶ, though grammatically a distinct sentence, may be regarded as on the way to become a governing clause. It is a step to this when there is no Pronoun as object—not 'tell me this,' but simply 'tell me': as Od. 4. 642 νημερτές μοι ἔνισπε, πότ' ᾤχετο καὶ τίνες αὐτῷ κοῦροι ἕποντ' κτλ.; 11. 144 εἰπέ, ἄναξ, πῶς κτλ.; 24. 474 εἰπέ μοι εἰρομένῃ, τί νύ τοι νόος ἔνδοθι κεύθει; It is to be observed that nearly all the passages of this kind are to be found in the Odyssey and in the 10th and 24th books of the Iliad. The only instance in the rest of the Iliad is 6. 377 εἴ δ' ἄγε μοι, δμωαί, νημερτέα μυθήσασθε· πῇ ἔβη κτλ.

ὅδε, κεῖνος, οὗτος.

249.] The Pronoun ὅδε is almost purely Deictic. It marks an object as near the speaker,—*this here, this on my side,* &c.; as ναὶ μὰ τόδε σκῆπτρον *by this sceptre* (*in my hand*); Ἕκτορος ἥδε γυνή *this*

is the wife of Hector; Od. 1. 76 ἡμεῖς οἵδε περιφραζώμεθα *let us
here consider* (§ 162, 2): 1. 226 οὐκ ἔρανος τάδε γ᾽ ἐστί *what I see
here is not a club-feast.* It is especially applied to a person or
thing to which the speaker turns for the first time, as—

Il. 3. 192 εἴπ᾽ ἄγε μοι καὶ τόνδε, φίλον τέκος, ὅς τις ὅδ᾽ ἐστί.
Hence the use to denote what is *about to be* mentioned—the new
as opposed to the known. This is an approach to an Anaphoric
use, in so far as it expresses not *local* nearness, but the place of
an object in the speaker's thought. So in—

Il. 7. 358 οἶσθα καὶ ἄλλον μῦθον ἀμείνονα τοῦδε νοῆσαι
the speech is the *present* one, opposed to a better one which
should have been made.

The derivatives τοσόσδε, τοιόσδε, ὧδε, ἐνθάδε, are similarly
Deictic: as Il. 6. 463 χήτεϊ τοιοῦδ᾽ ἀνδρός *from want of a man
such as I am now.*

250.] The Pronoun κεῖνος is sometimes used in the Deictic
sense, pointing to an object as distant:—

Il. 3. 391 κεῖνος ὅ γ᾽ ἐν θαλάμῳ *yonder he is in the chamber.*

5. 604 καὶ νῦν οἱ πάρα κεῖνος Ἄρης *there is Ares at his side.*
So of an absent object: as Od. 2. 351 κεῖνον ὀϊομένη τὸν κάμμορον
thinking of that (absent) one, the unhappy.

Hence in an Anaphoric use, κεῖνος distinguishes what is *past* or
done with, in contrast to a new object or state of things:—

Il. 2. 330 κεῖνος τὼς ἀγόρευε *he (on that former occasion),* &c.

3. 440 νῦν μὲν γὰρ Μενέλαος ἐνίκησεν σὺν Ἀθήνῃ,
κεῖνον δ᾽ αὖτις ἐγώ.

Od. 1. 46 καὶ λίην κεῖνός γε ἐοικότι κεῖται ὀλέθρῳ·
ἀλλά μοι ἀμφ᾽ Ὀδυσῆϊ κτλ.

Here κεῖνος marks the contrast with which the speaker turns to
a new case. The literal sense of local distance is transferred to
remoteness in *time,* or in the *order of thought.*

251.] The Pronoun οὗτος is not unfrequently Deictic in
Homer, expressing an object that is present to the speaker, but
not near him, or connected with him. Hence it is chiefly used
(like *iste* in Latin) of what belongs to or concerns the person
spoken to, or else in a hostile or contemptuous tone. Instances
of the former use are:—

Il. 7. 110 ἀφραίνεις, Μενέλαε διοτρεφές, οὐδέ τί σε χρὴ
ταύτης ἀφροσύνης.

10. 82 τίς δ᾽ οὗτος κατὰ νῆας ἀνὰ στρατὸν ἔρχεαι οἶος;

Od. 2. 40 οὐχ ἑκὰς οὗτος ἀνήρ *the man you want is not far off.*

6. 218 στῆθ᾽ οὕτω ἀποπρόθεν (*as you are*).

Again, οὗτος is regularly used of one of the enemy; as—

Il. 5. 257 τούτω δ' οὐ πάλιν αὖτις ἀποίσετον ὠκέες ἵπποι.

22. 38 μή μοι μίμνε, φίλον τέκος, ἀνέρα τοῦτον.

Similarly, with a tone of contempt,—

Il. 5. 761 ἄφρονα τοῦτον ἀνέντες (cp. 831, 879).

Od. 1. 159 τούτοισιν μὲν ταῦτα μέλει (of the Suitors).

More commonly, however, **οὗτος** is Anaphoric, denoting an object already mentioned or known. In later Greek it is often employed where Homer (as we shall see) would use the Article.

αὐτός.

252.] The Pronoun **αὐτός** is purely Anaphoric: its proper use seems to be to emphasise an object as the one that has been mentioned or implied,—the *very* one, *that and no other*. It conveys no local sense, and is used of the speaker, or the person addressed, as well as of a third person. Specific uses are—

(1) To distinguish a person from his surroundings, adjuncts, company, &c. : as—

Il. 3. 195 τεύχεα μέν οἱ κεῖται ἐπὶ χθονὶ πουλυβοτείρῃ, αὐτὸς δὲ κτλ.

9. 301 αὐτὸς καὶ τοῦ δῶρα *he and his gifts.*

14. 47 πρὶν πυρὶ νῆας ἐνιπρῆσαι, κτεῖναι δὲ καὶ αὐτούς.

17. 152 ὅς τοι πόλλ' ὄφελος γένετο πτόλεΐ τε καὶ αὐτῷ *to thy city and thyself.*

So of the *body*, as the actual person, in contradistinction to the soul or life (ψυχή), Il. 1. 4, Od. 11. 602, &c.

Hence, too, **αὐτός** = *by himself* (without the usual adjuncts) :—

Il. 8. 99 Τυδείδης δ' αὐτός περ ἐὼν προμάχοισιν ἐμίχθη.

So Achilles in his complaint of Agamemnon, Il. 1. 356 ἑλὼν γὰρ ἔχει γέρας αὐτὸς ἀπούρας, i. e. *at his own will*, without the usual sanction: cp. 17. 254., 23. 591.

This meaning appears also in αὔτως = *merely*, as—

Od. 14. 151 ἀλλ' ἐγὼ οὐκ αὔτως μυθήσομαι ἀλλὰ σὺν ὅρκῳ.

Cp. Il. 1. 520 ἦ δὲ καὶ αὔτως . . νεικεῖ *as it is* (without such provocation) *she reproaches me.*

The Gen. αὐτοῦ, &c. is used to strengthen the Possessives : as Od. 2. 45 ἐμὸν αὐτοῦ χρεῖος : Il. 6. 490 τὰ σ' αὐτῆς ἔργα : Il. 10. 204 ᾧ αὐτοῦ θυμῷ (*suo ipsius animo*): Od. 16. 197 ᾧ αὐτοῦ γε νόῳ.

Hence in Il. 9. 342 τὴν αὐτοῦ φιλέει—where the use of the Art. is not Homeric—we should probably read ἣν αὐτοῦ.

(2) To express *without change, the same as before*:—

Il. 12. 225 οὐ κόσμῳ παρὰ ναῦφιν ἐλευσόμεθ᾽ αὐτὰ κέλευθα.

Od. 8. 107 ἦρχε δὲ τῷ αὐτὴν ὁδὸν ἥν περ οἱ ἄλλοι κτλ.

Hence the use with a Dat., noticed in § 144; as Od. 8. 186 αὐτῷ φάρεϊ *with his cloak as it was* (without putting it off); and so αὐτόθι, αὐτοῦ *in the place, without moving;* and αὔτως *without doing more,* hence *without effect, idly*: as—

Il. 2. 342 αὔτως γάρ ῥ᾽ ἐπέεσσ᾽ ἐριδαίνομεν.

(3) The unemphatic use, as it may be called, in which it is an ordinary Anaphoric Pronoun of the Third Person (Eng. *he, she, it*). In this use the Pronoun cannot stand at the beginning of a Clause (the emphatic position), or in the Nominative—an unemphasised *Subject* being sufficiently expressed by the Person-Ending of the Verb. The use is derived from that of the emphatic αὐτός in the same way that in old-fashioned English 'the same' often denotes merely the person or thing just mentioned: and as in German *derselbe* and *der nämliche* are used without any emphasis on the idea of sameness.

(4) The Reflexive use of αὐτός is very rare: Od. 4. 247 ἄλλῳ δ᾽ αὐτὸν φωτὶ κατακρύπτων ἤϊσκε, and perhaps Il. 20. 55 ἐν δ᾽ αὐτοῖς ἔριδα ῥήγνυντο βαρεῖαν (among them *there*, in heaven *itself*). On Il. 9. 342 τὴν αὐτοῦ φιλέει see above (1). In Il. 12. 204 κόψε γὰρ αὐτὸν ἔχοντα it is best to take αὐτόν in agreement with ἔχοντα (of the eagle). In Il. 19. 255 read αὐτόθι (§ 157).

The Reflexive Pronoun.

253.] The Pronoun ἕο (*i. e.* the Personal Pronoun declined from the Stems ἑε- or ἑ- and σφε-) is sometimes Reflexive (*i. e.* denotes the Subject of the Sentence or Clause), sometimes a simple Anaphoric Pronoun. In the latter use it is always unemphatic.

(1) The Reflexive sense is chiefly found either (*a*) after a Preposition, as ἀμφὶ ἓ παπτήνας *looking round him*, and so ἀπὸ ἕο, ἐπὶ οἷ, προτὶ οἷ, μετὰ σφίσι, κατὰ σφέας, &c.; or (*b*) when it is reinforced by αὐτός, as Il. 20. 171 ἑὲ δ᾽ αὐτὸν ἐποτρύνει μαχέσασθαι *stirs himself up to fight*. Other examples are few in number:—

Il. 2. 239 ὃς καὶ νῦν Ἀχιλῆα, ἕο μέγ᾽ ἀμείνονα φῶτα κτλ.

5. 800 ἦ ὀλίγον οἷ παῖδα ἐοικότα γείνατο Τυδεύς.

So Il. 4. 400., 5. 56., 24. 134, Od. 11. 433., 19. 446, 481. We should add however such Infinitival Clauses as—

Il. 9. 305 ἐπεὶ οὔ τινά φησιν ὁμοῖον οἷ ἔμεναι κτλ.

where the reference is to the Subject of the governing Verb: so

Il. 17. 407, Od. 7. 217, &c. Compare also the similar use in Subordinate Clauses, as—

Il. 11. 439 γνῶ δ' 'Οδυσεὺς ὅ οἱ οὔ τι τέλος κατακαίριον ἦλθεν.

The strictly Reflexive use is commoner in the Iliad than in the Odyssey. Excluding Infinitival and Subordinate Clauses, there are 43 examples in the Iliad, against 18 in the Odyssey. Note that the use is mainly preserved in fixed combinations (ἀπὸ ἕο, προτὶ οἷ, &c.).

(2) The Anaphoric (non-Reflexive) use is very much commoner. In this use—which is doubtless derived from the other by loss of the original emphasis—the Pronoun is enclitic: whereas in the Reflexive use it is orthotone.

Accentuation. According to the ancient grammarians this Pronoun is orthotone (1) when used in a reflexive sense, (2) when preceded by a Preposition, and (3) when followed by a Case-form of αὐτός in agreement with it. The first and second rules, as we have seen, practically coincide: and the third is not borne out by the usage of Homer. In such places as Od. 2. 33 εἴθε οἱ αὐτῷ Ζεὺς ἀγαθὸν τελέσειε, Il. 6. 91 καί οἱ πολὺ φίλτατος αὐτῇ, Od. 8. 396 Εὐρύαλος δέ ἑ αὐτὸν ('Οδυσσέα) ἀρεσσάσθω,—add Il. 24. 292, Od. 4. 66, 667., 6. 277— the Pronoun is evidently unemphatic, and is accordingly allowed to be enclitic by good ancient authorities. This is amply confirmed by the instances of μιν αὐτόν (Il. 21. 245, 318, Od. 3. 19, 237, &c.), and the parallel use of αὐτός with the enclitic μοι, τοι, &c.

In one instance, viz.—

Od. 4. 244 αὐτόν μιν πληγῇσιν ἀεικελίῃσι δαμάσσας

it would seem that μιν has a reflexive sense. The reading, however, is not certain, some ancient authorities giving αὐτὸν μέν or αὐτὸν μέν.

254.] The Possessive ἑός, ὅς is nearly always Reflexive. Occasionally it refers to a prominent word in the same Sentence which is not grammatically the Subject: as—

Il. 6. 500 αἱ μὲν ἔτι ζωὸν γόον "Εκτορα ᾧ ἐνὶ οἴκῳ.

Od. 9. 369 Οὖτιν ἐγὼ πύματον ἔδομαι μετὰ οἷς ἑτάροισι.

Cp. Il. 16. 800., 22. 404, Od. 4. 643., 11. 282., 23. 153. And it is occasionally used in a Subordinate Clause to refer to the Subject, or a prominent word, of the Principal Clause:—

Od. 4. 618　　　πόρεν δέ ἑ Φαίδιμος ἥρως
　　　　　Σιδονίων βασιλεύς, ὅθ' ἑὸς δόμος ἀμφεκάλυψε
　　　　　κεῖσέ με νοστήσαντα (cp. 4. 741).

Il. 10. 256 Τυδείδῃ μὲν δῶκε μενεπτόλεμος Θρασυμήδης
　　　　　φάσγανον ἄμφηκες, τὸ δ' ἑὸν παρὰ νηὶ λέλειπτο.

16. 753 ἔβλητο πρὸς στῆθος, ἑή τέ μιν ὤλεσεν ἀλκή.

It will be seen that where ἑός does not refer to the grammatical Subject it is generally emphatic: e.g. in the line last quoted, ἑὴ ἀλκή *his own prowess*, not that of an enemy. This indicates the

original force of the Pronoun, which was to confine the reference
emphatically to a person or thing just mentioned.

255.] Use of ἑός, ὅς as a general Reflexive Pronoun. It has
been a matter of dispute with Homeric scholars, both ancient and
modern, whether ἑός (ὅς) was confined to the Third Person
Singular (*his own*) or could be used as a Reflexive of any Number
and Person (*own* in general—*my own, thy own, their own,* &c.).*
The question is principally one of textual criticism, and depends
in the last resort on the comparative weight to be assigned to the
authority of the two great Alexandrian grammarians, Zenodotus
and Aristarchus. It is connected with another question, of less
importance for Homer, viz. whether the forms ἕο, οἷ, ἕ are confined to the Singular, and those beginning with σφ- to the Plural.

(1) In regard to the latter of these questions there is no room
for doubt. The only instance in dispute is Il. 2. 197, 198, where
Zenodotus read—

> θυμὸς δὲ μέγας ἐστὶ διοτρεφέων βασιλήων
> τιμὴ δ᾽ ἐκ Διός ἐστι, φιλεῖ δέ ἑ μητίετα Ζεύς,

and so the first line is quoted by Aristotle (Rhet. 2. 2). Aristarchus read διοτρεφέος βασιλῆος. However, admitting Zenodotus
to be right, ἑ need not be a Plural. The change from Plural to
Singular is not unusual in passages of a gnomic character, *e.g.*—

> Od. 4. 691   ἥ τ᾽ ἐστὶ δίκη θείων βασιλήων·
> ἄλλον κ᾽ ἐχθαίρῃσι βροτῶν, ἄλλον κε φιλοίη.

(2) Again, the 'general' Reflexive use, if it exists in Homer,
is confined to the Adjective ἑός, ὅς. The only contrary instance
is Il. 10. 398 (Dolon tells Ulysses that he has been sent by
Hector to find out)—

> ἠὲ φυλάσσονται νῆες θοαὶ ὡς τὸ πάρος περ,
> ἦ ἤδη χείρεσσιν ὑφ᾽ ἡμετέρῃσι δαμέντες
> φύξιν βουλεύοιτε μετὰ σφίσιν, οὐδ᾽ ἐθέλοιτε κτλ.

So the MSS., but Ar. read βουλεύουσι, ἐθέλουσι, making Dolon
repeat the exact words of Hector (ll. 309-311); and this reading,
which gives σφίσι its usual sense, is clearly right. The Optative
is not defensible (esp. after the Indic. φυλάσσονται), and was
probably introduced by some one who thought that Dolon, speaking of the Greeks to Ulysses, must use the Second Person Plural.
But the Third Person is more correct; for Ulysses is not one of

---

* The question was first scientifically discussed by Miklosich, in a paper
read to the Vienna Academy (I, 1848, p. 119 ff.). He was followed on the
same side by Brugmann (*Ein Problem der homerischen Textkritik und der vergleichenden Sprachwissenschaft,* Leipzig, 1876).

the Greeks who can be supposed to be 'consulting among themselves.'

The form ἓ is found as a Plural in Hom. H. Ven. 267. In later Epic poets the Substantival εἷο, &c. are used as Reflexives of any Person or Number: see Theocritus 27. 44, Apollonius Rhodius 1. 893., 2. 635, 1278., 3. 99 (Brugmann, *Probl.* p. 80). But the use is exclusively post-Homeric.

(3) The case is different with the Adjective. We find forms of ἑός (ὅς) read by Zenodotus in a number of places in which our MSS. and editions—following the authority of Aristarchus—have substituted other words. Thus in—

Il. 3. 244 ὣς φάτο, τοὺς δ' ἤδη κάτεχεν φυσίζοος αἶα,
   ἐν Λακεδαίμονι αὖθι, φίλῃ ἐν πατρίδι γαίῃ·

for φίλῃ Zenodotus read ἑῇ (*their own*). So, again, in—

Il. 1. 393 ἀλλὰ σύ, εἰ δύνασαί γε, περίσχεο παιδὸς ἑῆος,

and in similar passages (Il. 15. 138., 19. 342., 24. 550), it is known from the Scholia that Aristarchus read ἑῆος, Zenodotus ἑοῖο (= *thine own*). Again, in—

Il. 11. 142 νῦν μὲν δὴ τοῦ πατρὸς ἀεικέα τίσετε λώβην

Zenodotus read οὗ πατρὸς (*your own father*). It is probable that he read οὗ in the similar places Il. 19. 322, Od. 16. 149, &c.

Besides the instances of undoubtedly ancient difference of reading, there are several places where one or more MSS. offer forms of ἑός in place of ἐμός and σός. Thus—

Il. 14. 221 ὅ τι φρεσὶ σῇσι μενοινᾷς (ᾗσι D).

19. 174 σὺ δὲ φρεσὶ σῇσιν ἰανθῇς (ᾗσιν in several MSS.). Similar variations (with φρεσί) are found in Od. 5. 206., 6. 180., 13. 362., 15. 111., 24. 357. Again—

Od. 1. 402 δώμασι σοῖσιν ἀνάσσοις (οἷσιν ten MSS.). Similarly in Od. 8. 242., 15. 89 (ἑοῖσι for ἐμοῖσι): also—

Od. 7. 77 καὶ σὴν ἐς πατρίδα γαῖαν (ἣν ἐς in one MS.).

13. 61 σὺ δὲ τέρπεο τῷδ' ἐνὶ οἴκῳ (ᾧ ἐνὶ one MS.).

Another instance of variation is detected by Brugmann in—

Il. 9. 414 εἰ δέ κεν οἴκαδ' ἵκωμι φίλην ἐς πατρίδα γαῖαν,

where the MSS. (except A) have ἵκωμαι, pointing to ἑὴν (*my own*).*

The existing text of the Odyssey contains three passages which Brugmann claims as instances of a general Reflexive sense, viz. Od. 4. 192 (as to which see Merry and Riddell's note),

---

* Brugmann carries his theory into other passages where he supposes Aristarchus to have corrected the text in order to get rid of the use of ἑός for the First or Second Person: but the examples quoted above will suffice to give an idea of the strength of his argument.

Od. 13. 320 (where there is some reason to suspect an interpolation), and—

Od. 9. 28   οὔ τοι ἐγώ γε
   ἧς γαίης δύναμαι γλυκερώτερον ἄλλο ἰδέσθαι.

But there is no reason to take ἧς otherwise than in v. 34 ὡς οὐδὲν γλύκιον ἧς πατρίδος οὐδὲ τοκήων γίγνεται *nothing is sweeter than a man's own country, &c.* The reference of the Pronoun is to a typical or imaginary person, as in Od. 1. 392 αἶψά τε οἱ δῶ ἀφνειὸν πέλεται *a man's house* (when he is a king) *quickly grows rich.*

We have seen that post-Homeric poets use the substantival ἕο, &c. in the sense in question. The corresponding use of the adjective ἑός, ὅς is still more common, as Brugmann shows. It is found in Hesiod for the Third Person Plur. (Op. 58, Theog. 71), and in Callimachus, Apollonius Rhodius, and Quintus Smyrnaeus (*Probl.* pp. 28, 78–83).

(4) In attempting to arrive at a conclusion on this matter we must begin by understanding that the issue does not lie between supposing on the one hand that Aristarchus was entirely right, and on the other hand that he introduced a strange form like ἑῆος on his own authority, and merely to satisfy a theory. The latter is improbable, not only from the respect for manuscript authority which is expressly attributed to him, but also because the various readings are not all capable of being explained on this supposition. Thus, (1) the word ἑῆος is proved to exist by Od. 14. 505., 15. 450, and in the latter place ἑοῖο, though excluded by the sense, is found as a variant. Also (2) ἑῆος is found for ἑοῖο meaning *his own* in Il. 14. 9., 18. 71, 138. It cannot therefore be regarded as certain that ἑῆος was systematically introduced merely to get rid of ἑοῖο = *my own, thy own.* Again, (3) the use of the Article in τοῦ πατρός, τῆς μητρός, τοῦ παιδός, is not clearly un-Homeric (see § 258). And if in Il. 11. 763 οἷος τῆς ἀρετῆς ἀπονήσεται Bentley was right in reading ἧς (cp. 17. 25), it follows that the Article might creep in for οὗ, ἧς, &c. apart from the intention of carrying out a grammatical theory.

On the other side it must be conceded that the generalised Reflexive use of ἑός, ὅς,—if not of the substantival ἕο, &c.—is of high antiquity, so that sporadic instances of it may have occurred in the genuine text of Homer. If so, the error of Aristarchus will consist in a somewhat undue purism.

Brugmann holds that the general Reflexive sense is the primary one, belonging to the Stem *sva* in the original Indo-European language, and surviving in the Homeric use of ἑός, ὅς. But even if the readings of Zenodotus which give this sense are right, it does not follow that they represent the oldest use of the Pronoun.

Brugmann has himself given excellent instances of the extension
to the First and Second Person of a Reflexive Pronoun originally
confined to the Third (*Probl.* pp. 119 ff.).   In the present case it
is significant that the generalised use of the substantival forms
ἕο, &c. is clearly post-Homeric.   If ἑός (ὅς) is sometimes used in
Homer, as well as afterwards, of the First and Second Persons,
it is natural to see in this the result of an extension of usage.
The case is different with the use of the Stem *sva* for the Plural.
That use, as we see from the Latin *se* and *suus*, was the original
one.   It is noteworthy that this undoubtedly primitive use is precisely the one of which there is least trace in Homer.

ὁ ἡ τό.

256.]   The Article ὁ ἡ τό may be defined as a purely Anaphoric Pronoun, conveying some degree of emphasis.   It differs
from ὅδε οὗτος and ἐκεῖνος in the absence of Deictic meaning :
for while it usually marks some contrast between objects, it does
not distinguish them as *near* or *far*, *present* or *absent*, &c.   On
the other hand it is distinguished from the non-Reflexive use of
αὐτός and ἕο by greater emphasis.

Three chief uses of ὁ ἡ τό may be distinguished :—

1. The use as an independent Pronoun; ὁ ἡ τό=*he she it*.
    This may be called the SUBSTANTIVAL use : it embraces
    the great majority of the instances in Homer.

2. The use as an ' Article ' in the later sense of the term, *i. e.*
    with a Noun following.   This may be called the ATTRI-
    BUTIVE use.

3. The use as a Relative.

257.]   The Substantival Article.   This use of the Article is
very much the commonest in Homer, and it is also the use from
which the others may be easily derived.

The Substantival Article either (1) is simply ' resumptive,'
recalling a person or thing already mentioned, as ὁ γάρ *for he*,
τόν ῥα *him I say*, αὐτὸς καὶ τοῦ δῶρα *the man and his gifts:* or
(2) marks a contrast, as ὁ δέ *but the other*.

The following points of usage are to be noticed :—

1. The most frequent—we may almost say the regular—place
    of the Article is at the beginning of a Clause, followed
    by μέν, δέ, γάρ, ἄρα, or preceded by αὐτάρ, ἀλλά, ἦ τοι, or
    an equivalent Particle.   Hence the familiar combinations
    ὁ μέν, ὁ δέ, ὁ γάρ, καὶ γὰρ ὁ, αὐτὰρ ὁ, ἦ τοι ὁ, τόν ῥα, ἀλλὰ
    τόν, &c. of which it is needless to give instances.

The later Substantival use with μέν and δέ is a surviving fragment of this group of uses. A few others are found in Attic poets, as ὁ γάρ (Aesch. Sept. 17, Soph. El. 45, O. T. 1082).

The use to contrast *indefinite* persons or things (ὁ μὲν—ὁ δὲ = *one—another*, οἱ μὲν—οἱ δὲ = *some—others*) is not very common in Homer.

The use of the Article with an adversative Particle (δέ, αὐτάρ, ἀλλά) generally marks a change of Subject : ὁ δέ *but the other*, &c. But this is not always the case : *e.g.* Il. 4. 491 τοῦ μὲν ἅμαρθ᾿, ὁ δὲ Λεῦκον . . . βεβλήκει *him he missed, but smote Leucus* (so Il. 8. 119, 126, 302., 11. 80, &c.); Il. 1. 496 Θέτις δ᾿ οὐ λήθετ᾿ ἐφετμέων παιδὸς ἑοῦ, ἀλλ᾿ ἥ γ᾿ ἀνεδύσετο κτλ. : cp. Il. 5. 321., 6. 168, Od. 1. 4, &c. The Article in all such cases evidently expresses a contrast : not however between two persons, but between two characters in which the same person is thought of.

This last use—in which the Article is pleonastic, according to Attic notions—occurs in Herodotus, as 5. 120 τὰ μὲν πρότερον οἱ Κᾶρες ἐβουλεύοντο μετῆκαν, οἱ δὲ αὖτις πολεμεῖν ἐξ ἀρχῆς ἀρτέοντο. We may compare it with the pleonastic use of the Pronoun in—

Il. 11. 131 ζώγρει ᾿Ατρέος υἱέ, σὺ δ᾿ ἄξια δέξαι ἄποινα,

where the effect of inserting σύ is to oppose the two acts denoted by ζώγρει and δέξαι ἄποινα.

2. The Article is frequent in Disjunctive sentences :—

Il. 12. 240 εἴ τ᾿ ἐπὶ δεξί᾿ ἴωσι πρὸς ἠῶ τ᾿ ἠέλιόν τε,
εἴ τ᾿ ἐπ᾿ ἀριστερὰ τοί γε κτλ. (*or else to left*).

Od. 2. 132 ζώει ὅ γ᾿ ἢ τέθνηκεν.

Here also it serves to contrast the alternative things said about the same Subject.

3. The principle of contrast often leads to the placing of two Articles together : Il. 21. 602 ἧος ὁ τὸν πεδίοιο διώκετο, 10. 224 καί τε πρὸ ὁ τοῦ ἐνόησεν. So an Article and a Personal Pronoun, ἐν δὲ σὺ τοῖσι (Il. 13. 829, &c.); cp.—

Il. 8. 532 εἴσομαι εἴ κέ μ᾿ ὁ Τυδείδης κρατερὸς Διομήδης
πὰρ νηῶν πρὸς τεῖχος ἀπώσεται, ἦ κεν ἐγὼ τόν.

Note that when the second of the two is in the Nom., it usually takes γε : hence τοῦ ὅ γε, τῇ ῥ᾿ οἵ γε, &c.

4. The Article often stands for the object to be defined by a following Relative Clause, *e.g.*—

Il. 9. 615 καλόν τοι σὺν ἐμοὶ τὸν κήδειν ὅς κ᾿ ἐμὲ κήδῃ.

1. 272 τῶν οἳ νῦν βροτοί εἰσι &c.

The use is to be classed as Anaphoric ; the intention of saying something about the object is equivalent to a previous mention. So in Latin the Anaphoric *is* is used to introduce *qui*.

The Neuter Article is similarly used to introduce Clauses beginning with ὅτε, ὡς, and the like :—

Il. 15. 207 ἐσθλὸν καὶ τὸ τέτυκται ὅτ' ἄγγελος αἴσιμα εἰδῇ.

Od. 9. 442 τὸ δὲ νήπιος οὐκ ἐνόησεν ὥς οἱ κτλ.

Il. 3. 308 Ζεὺς μέν που τό γε οἶδε . . . ὁπποτέρῳ κτλ.

So Il. 14. 191., 20. 466., 23. 545. It may even introduce an independent sentence, as—

Od. 4. 655 ἀλλὰ τὸ θαυμάζω· ἴδον ἐνθάδε Μέντορα δῖον.

5. The uses in which the Article is least emphatic (*i. e.* does not begin the Clause, or express a contrast) appear to be—

(*a*) after Prepositions : esp. in the Dat. Plur. after μετά, παρά, προτί, σύν, ἐν, ἅμα : as Il. 1. 348 ἡ δ' ἀέκουσ' ἅμα τοῖσι γυνὴ κίεν. This is to be connected with the fact that the forms ἕο, οἷ, σφίσι, &c. are not used with Prepositions in the simple Anaphoric sense (§ 253), and thus the Art. is used instead of them.

(*b*) when the Neuter Article is used for a fact or set of facts ; as Il. 4. 353 ὄψεαι ἢν ἐθέλησθα καὶ αἴ κέν τοι τὰ μεμήλῃ. Here again the want of a corresponding form of ἕο makes itself felt. This use is chiefly found in the Nom. and Acc.; but also in τοὔνεκα *therefore*, ἐκ τοῖο *from that time*, &c.

258.] **The Attributive Article.** The Attributive Article is found in Homer in a limited range of cases, and has evidently grown out of the use of the Substantival Article followed by a Noun in 'Apposition;' *e.g.* Il. 4. 20 ὡς ἔφαθ', αἱ δ' ἐπέμυξαν Ἀθηναίη τε καὶ Ἥρη *thus he spoke, but they murmured, Athene and Here:* Il. 1. 348 ἡ δ' ἀέκουσ' ἅμα τοῖσι γυνὴ κίεν. So with μιν, Il. 21. 249 ἵνα μιν παύσειε πόνοιο | δῖον Ἀχιλλῆα, cp. Od. 11. 570. In such cases the Pronoun is still substantival, the Noun being added by way of afterthought.

It is a step towards an Attributive use when the Article *needs* the addition of the Noun to explain it ; *e.g.*—

Il. 4. 501 τόν ῥ' Ὀδυσεὺς ἑτάροιο χολωσάμενος βάλε δουρὶ
κόρσην· ἡ δ' ἑτέροιο διὰ κροτάφοιο πέρησεν
αἰχμὴ χαλκείη.

Here ἡ δέ would not be clear without αἰχμή. So in—

Il. 1. 408 αἴ κέν πως ἐθέλησιν ἐπὶ Τρώεσσιν ἀρῆξαι,
τοὺς δὲ κατὰ πρύμνας τε καὶ ἀμφ' ἅλα ἔλσαι Ἀχαιούς.

Od. 15. 54 τοῦ γάρ τε ξεῖνος μιμνήσκεται ἤματα πάντα
ἀνδρὸς ξεινοδόκου.

So too with Proper Names,—when a *new* person is about to be mentioned the Art. *anticipates* the Noun : *e.g.*—

Il. 2. 402 αὐτὰρ ὁ βοῦν ἱέρευσεν ἄναξ ἀνδρῶν Ἀγαμέμνων.

And where the Neut. τό is followed by an epexegetic Infinitive:—
Od. 1. 370 ἐπεὶ τό γε καλὸν ἀκουέμεν ἐστὶν ἀοιδοῦ.
Il. 17. 406   ἐπεὶ οὐδὲ τὸ ἔλπετο πάμπαν,
          ἐκπέρσειν πτολίεθρον ἄνευ ἔθεν.
In all these cases the combination of Article and Noun is not
sufficiently close to constitute an Attributive use; but they serve
to show how such a use is developed.

The Attributive uses in Homer may be classified as follows:—

1. Uses with *connecting Particles*, where some contrast is made
   in passing to the new sentence or clause.
2. Uses with certain *Adjectives* that imply contrast.
3. Uses to mark a person or thing as *definite*.

259.] Article of Contrast—with connecting Particles. The
uses that fall under this head, though not very numerous, are
characteristic of Homer. The following are the chief:—

(*a*) The Article with an adversative δέ, αὐτάρ, &c. is not unfrequently used to bring out the contrast in which the Noun
stands to something already mentioned: *e.g.*—

Il. 2. 217 φολκὸς ἔην, χωλὸς δ' ἕτερον πόδα, τὼ δέ οἱ ὤμω κτλ.
but then his shoulders; so τὼ δέ οἱ ὄσσε (Il. 13. 616), &c.

Il. 22. 405 ὡς τοῦ μὲν κεκόνιτο κάρη ἅπαν, ἡ δέ νυ μήτηρ κτλ.
but on the other hand his mother &c.

Il. 1. 382 ἧκε δ' ἐπ' Ἀργείοισι κακὸν βέλος, οἱ δέ νυ λαοὶ
          θνῆσκον ἐπασσύτεροι, τὰ δ' ἐπῴχετο κῆλα θεοῖο.

4. 399 τοῖος ἔην Τυδεὺς Αἰτώλιος· ἀλλὰ τὸν υἱὸν κτλ.
So we should explain the Article in Il. 1. 20 παῖδα δέ μοι λύσαιτε φίλην, τὰ δ' ἄποινα δέχεσθαι *release my daughter, and on the
other side accept ransom.* The usage is common in the Iliad, but
perceptibly rarer in the Odyssey.

(*b*) The use of the Art. with μέν—in contrast with something
that follows—is rare: Il. 11. 267 αὐτὰρ ἐπεὶ τὸ μὲν ἕλκος ἐτέρσετο:
cp. 8. 73., 9. 1., 13. 640., 19. 21., 20. 75, Od. 3. 270 (seemingly
the only instance in the Odyssey). There is a similar use with
the Art. following the Noun in Od. 1. 116 μνηστήρων τῶν μὲν
σκέδασιν κατὰ δώματα θείη, κτλ.

(*c*) The corresponding use with copulative and illative Particles, καί, τε, ἠδέ, καὶ γάρ, is much less common: cp.—

Il. 1. 339 πρός τε θεῶν μακάρων πρός τε θνητῶν ἀνθρώπων
          καὶ πρὸς τοῦ βασιλῆος ἀπηνέος.

15. 36 ἴστω νῦν τόδε γαῖα καὶ οὐρανὸς εὐρὺς ὕπερθεν,
          καὶ τὸ κατειβόμενον Στυγὸς ὕδωρ (cp. 18. 486).

Od. 22. 103 δώσω δὲ συβώτῃ | καὶ τῷ βουκόλῳ ἄλλα.

Il. 14. 503 οὐδὲ γὰρ ἡ Προμάχοιο δάμαρ κτλ.

The Article singles out its Noun as the special object intended, or turns to it with fresh emphasis. So with an Infinitive, Od. 20. 52 ἀνίη καὶ τὸ φυλάσσειν, where we need not take τὸ φυλάσσειν closely together. So Hes. fr. 192 ἡδὺ δὲ καὶ τὸ πυθέσθαι κτλ. also Op. 314 τὸ ἐργάζεσθαι ἄμεινον.

These uses should be carefully distinguished from the later Definite Article. For instance, in Il. 1. 20 τὰ ἄποινα does not mean *this* or *the ransom*, in contradistinction to other ransoms. It means *the other*, *the ransom*, in contrast to the person ransomed. Again, the 4th book of the Iliad begins οἱ δὲ θεοί, which we naturally take to mean simply *but the gods*. But, taking in the last line of the 3rd book, we have—

> ὣς ἔφατ' Ἀτρείδης, ἐπὶ δ' ἥνεον ἄλλοι Ἀχαιοί·
> οἱ δὲ θεοὶ πὰρ Ζηνὶ καθήμενοι ἠγορόωντο.

Clearly the Article marks the turning from the one scene to the other,—from the battlefield to Olympus. Thus the Attic οἱ (θεοί) distinguishes the gods from other beings: the Homeric οἱ (δὲ θεοί) marks, not this permanent distinction, but the contrast arising out of the particular context.

The difference appears also in the use with Proper Names. In Attic the Article shows that a particular known person is spoken of; in Homer it marks the turning of attention to a person—ushers in the name, as it were. In short, the Homeric Article *contrasts*, the Attic Article *defines*.

260.] With Adjectives. The Article is used before adjectival words that imply a contrast or distinction, especially between definite or well-known alternatives: in particular—

(*a*) ἄλλος and ἕτερος, *passim:* also αὐτός = *same*.

(*b*) Comparatives and Superlatives; οἱ πλέονες, οἱ ἄριστοι, &c. So in the adverbial expressions τὸ πρίν, τὸ πάρος, τὰ πρῶτα, and the like, in which the Neut. Article is used adverbially (τὸ πάρος = *then formerly*). It is quite different when a Masc. or Fem. Article is used with an Adverb, as οἱ ἔνερθε θεοί (Il. 14. 274), ἀνδρῶν τῶν τότε (Il. 9. 559), τά τ' ἐνδόθι καὶ τὰ θύρηφιν (Od. 22. 220),—a use which is extremely rare in Homer.

(*c*) Ordinal Numerals: as τῇ δεκάτῃ: so τὸ ἥμισυ. Also Cardinal Numerals, when a *division* is made; as Il. 5. 271 τοὺς μὲν τέσσαρας αὐτὸς ἔχων ἀτίταλλ' ἐπὶ φάτνῃ, τὼ δὲ δύ' Αἰνείᾳ δῶκεν *four he kept, and the (other) two he gave to Aeneas:* Il. 11. 174 πάσας· τῇ δέ τ' ἰῇ κτλ. (*the lion chases*) *all, but to one &c.*

(*d*) Possessives; τὸν ἐμὸν χόλον, τὰ σὰ κῆλα, &c.

(*e*) A few words expressing the standing contrasts of great and small, many and few, good and evil, &c., esp. when the contrast is brought out by the context:—

Il. 1. 106 μάντι κακῶν, οὔ πώ ποτέ μοι τὸ κρήγυον εἶπας·
αἰεί τοι τὰ κάκ' ἐστὶ φίλα φρεσὶ μαντεύεσθαι.

3. 138 τῷ δέ κε νικήσαντι φίλη κεκλήσῃ ἄκοιτις
(*the conqueror* being one of two definite persons).

So ἡ πληθύς (Il. 2. 278., 15. 305) *the many* (in contrast to a
single man, or to the few): τὸ χθιζόν (Il. 13. 745); τὸν δεξιὸν
ἵππον (Il. 23. 336); Αἴας ὁ μέγας *the greater Ajax: θεοὺς* . . *τοὺς*
ὑποταρταρίους (Il. 14. 279) *the gods of the lower world: ἄνακτες οἱ*
νέοι (Od. 14. 61) *masters of the younger generation: ἰχθύσι τοῖς*
ὀλίγοισι (Od. 12. 252) *the smaller kinds of fish.* So—
Il. 1. 70 ὃς ᾔδη τά τ' ἐόντα τά τ' ἐσσόμενα πρό τ' ἐόντα.

The use to contrast *indefinite* individuals (*one—another*) is rare
in Homer: Il. 23. 325 τὸν προὔχοντα δοκεύει *waits on the one in*
advance: Il. 16. 53 ὁππότε δὴ τὸν ὁμοῖον ἀνὴρ ἐθέλησιν ἀμέρσαι:
Il. 9. 320 κάτθαν' ὁμῶς ὅ τ' ἄεργος ἀνὴρ ὅ τε πολλὰ ἐοργώς: Od.
17. 218 ὡς αἰεὶ τὸν ὁμοῖον ἄγει θεὸς ὡς τὸν ὁμοῖον.

(*f*) Patronymics and geographical epithets: *e.g.* Il. 11. 613
Μαχάονι πάντα ἔοικε τῷ Ἀσκληπιάδῃ (cp. 13. 698., 14. 460., 23.
295, 303, 525): Il. 2. 595 Θάμυριν τὸν Θρήϊκα: Il. 6. 201 πεδίον
τὸ Ἀλήϊον, cp. 2. 681., 10. 11: and so perhaps Il. 21. 252 αἰετοῦ
. . τοῦ θηρητῆρος *an eagle, the hunting kind.* This use is rare.

(*g*) In a very few places, a Genitive: Il. 20. 181 τιμῆς τῆς
Πριάμου: Od. 24. 497 υἱεῖς οἱ Δολίοιο: Il. 9. 342., 10. 408., 23.
348, 376, Od. 3. 145.

261.] The defining Article. The few and somewhat isolated
uses which fall under this description may be grouped as follows:

1. The use before a Relative is combined with 'Apposition'
to a preceding Noun: as—
Il. 5. 319 οὐδ' υἱὸς Καπανῆος ἐλήθετο συνθεσιάων
τάων ἃς ἐπέτελλε κτλ. (cp. 5. 331 θεάων τάων αἳ—).
This is the primitive order, the Article being 'resumptive'—*the*
injunctions, those namely which, &c. So ἤματι τῷ ὅτε—, and commonly in the Iliad. The later order—that in which the Noun
follows the Article—appears in a few places of the Iliad:—
5. 265 τῆς γάρ τοι γενεῆς ἧς Τρωΐ περ κτλ. (cp. v. 268),
also 6. 292., 8. 186., 19. 105. It is commoner in the Odyssey.

2. Occasionally the Article conveys a hostile or contemptuous
tone: Il. 2. 275 τὸν λωβητῆρα: 13. 53 ὁ λυσσώδης: 21. 421
ἡ κυνάμυια: 22. 59 τὸν δύστηνον: Od. 2. 351 τὸν κάμμορον: 12.
113 τὴν ὀλοήν: 14. 235 τήν γε στυγερὴν ὁδόν: 18. 26 ὁ μολοβρός:
18. 333 τὸν ἀλήτην: 19. 372 αἱ κύνες αἵδε. So in Il. 3. 55 ἥ τε
κόμη τό τε εἶδος.
In Od. 18. 114 τοῦτον τὸν ἄναλτον does not mean (as it would
in Attic) '*this ἄναλτος*,' but '*this man—ἄναλτος that he is.*' Cp.

Il. 13. 53 ἦ ῥ' ὅ γ' ὁ λυσσώδης κτλ., where ὁ λυσσώδης—*the mad-man*—is used as a single term, in Apposition to ὅ γε. This use —which is characteristic of Homer—may be regarded as a relic of the Deictic force of ὁ ἡ τό. It answers to the later use of οὗτος, Latin *iste*.

3. The use of the Article to show that the Noun denotes a *known* person or thing—the defining Article of later Greek—is rare in Homer. It is found in the Iliad—

(*a*) with γέρων, γεραιός, ἄναξ, ἥρως : where however the Pronoun is the important word, the Noun being subjoined as a kind of title : τοῖο ἄνακτος = 'of his lordship' (cp. the German *allerhöchst derselbe*). Accordingly, when the name is added the Art. is generally not used ; as γέρων ἱππηλάτα Πηλεύς (not ὁ γέρων).

(*b*) with ἔπος and μῦθος, in certain phrases, as ποῖον τὸν μῦθον ἔειπες ; In these cases the Noun is of vague meaning, adding little to the Article : cp. ἐπεὶ τὸν μῦθον ἄκουσε with ἐπεὶ τό γ' ἄκουσε. So in the formula ὄμοσέν τε τελεύτησέν τε τὸν ὅρκον, perhaps with a touch of ceremonial verbiage.

In the Odyssey it occurs with several other Nouns : ὁ ξεῖνος (*passim*) ; ἡ νῆσος Od. 5. 55., 9. 146., 12. 201, 276, 403, &c. ; τὰ μῆλα Od. 9. 464., 11. 4, 20 : ὁ μόχλος Od. 9. 375, 378 : τὸ τόξον Od. 21. 113, 305. The other examples in the Iliad are chiefly found in books x, xxiii, xxiv : see Il. 10. 97, 277, 321, 322, 330, 408, 497., 23. 75, 257, 465., 24. 388, 801, also 2. 80., 7. 412., 20. 147.

We may perhaps add a few uses with words of relationship :—

Il. 11. 142 νῦν μὲν δὴ τοῦ πατρὸς ἀεικέα τίσετε λώβην.

But here the Art. is resumptive with emphasis : (if ye are sons of Antimachus) *ye shall now pay for his, your father's, outrage.*

Il. 19. 322 οὐδ' εἴ κεν τοῦ πατρὸς ἀποφθιμένοιο πυθοίμην

not even if I heard of such a one as my father being dead : Od. 2. 134 ἐκ γὰρ τοῦ πατρὸς κακὰ πείσομαι *for from my father* (*for one*) *I shall suffer* (cp. Il. 15. 641 τοῦ γένετ' ἐκ πατρὸς κτλ.) : Od. 16. 149, Il. 21. 412. See however § 255.

It has been a question whether the Article is ever equivalent to a Possessive Pronoun. If so it would be a kind of *defining* Article—defining a thing as belonging to a known person. In most of the instances, however, the reference to a person is given by a distinct Pronoun : Il. 19. 331 ὡς ἄν μοι τὸν παῖδα κτλ. : Od. 11. 492 ἀλλ' ἄγε μοι τοῦ παιδὸς κτλ. : Od. 8. 195 καί κ' ἀλαός τοι .. τὸ σῆμα : Od. 18. 380 οὐδ' ἄν μοι τὴν γαστέρ' κτλ. : Od. 19. 535 ἀλλ' ἄγε μοι τὸν ὄνειρον κτλ. : Il. 1. 167 σοὶ τὸ γέρας πολὺ μεῖζον. Hence the Art. in these places has much the same function as with a Possessive (μοι τὸν παῖδα = τὸν ἐμὸν παῖδα); it reinforces the Pronoun which conveys the idea of possession. This account does not apply to τῆς εὐνῆς (Il. 9. 133, 275., 19. 176), and τῆς ἀρετῆς (Od. 2. 206). But here the Art. is probably substantival: τῆς εὐνή *her couch*, τῆς ἀρετή *her perfection*. In 23. 75 καί μοι δὸς τὴν χεῖρα the Art. is quite anomalous.

262.] The Article as a Relative. The Article at the beginning of a clause may often be translated either as a Demonstrative or as a Relative. It has the character of a Relative when the clause which it introduces is distinctly subordinate or parenthetical: as—

Il. 1. 36 Ἀπόλλωνι ἄνακτι, τὸν ἠΰκομος τέκε Λητώ
Apollo—son of the fair-haired Leto.

The use of ὁ ἡ τό as a Relative is less common in Homer than that of ὅς ἥ ὅ, and is restricted in general to clauses which refer to a *definite* antecedent. Thus in the line just quoted the clause τὸν ἠΰκομος τέκε Λητώ does not *define* Apollo, *i. e.* does not show who is meant by the name; it assumes that a definite person is meant, and adds something further about him.

From this principle it evidently follows that—

(1) The Art. when used as a Relative must *follow* the Noun or Pronoun to which it refers; whereas a Relative Clause often precedes. The only exceptions are—

Il. 1. 125 ἀλλὰ τὰ μὲν πολίων ἐξεπράθομεν, τὰ δέδασται.
Od. 4. 349 (= 17. 140) ἀλλὰ τὰ μέν μοι ἔειπε . . τῶν κτλ.
We may perhaps read ἀλλά θ' ἃ μὲν (§ 332).

(2) The Art. cannot stand as correlative to a Demonstrative (*i.e.* we must have τό—ὅ *that which*, not τό—τό). Hence in—

Il. 7. 452 τοῦ δ' ἐπιλήσονται, τὸ ἐγὼ καὶ Φοῖβος Ἀπόλλων κτλ.
τοῦ—τό are not meant as correlatives: the sense is *and will forget the other—(a wall) which &c.* But some MSS. have ὅ τ' ἐγώ. So Od. 13. 263 (τῆς ληΐδος) τῆς εἵνεκ' ἐγὼ πάθον ἄλγεα θυμῷ *my share of the spoil—(spoil) for which I had suffered &c.* Exceptions are, Od. 14. 227 αὐτὰρ ἐμοὶ τὰ φίλ' ἔσκε τά που θεὸς ἐν φρεσὶ θῆκεν, 19. 573 τοὺς πελέκεας τοὺς κτλ. (perhaps also Od. 9. 334).

(3) The Art. is not used in *epexegetic* clauses, as Il. 2. 338 νηπιάχοις, οἷς οὔ τι μέλει κτλ., Il. 5. 63 ἀρχεκάκους, αἳ πᾶσι κακὸν κτλ., Il. 15. 526 Λαμπετίδης, ὃν Λάμπος ἐγείνατο.

Instances at variance with the general principle are to be found in Il. 5. 747 ἡρώων τοῖσίν τε κοτέσσεται (οἷσίν τε in some MSS.), Il. 9. 592 κήδε' ὅσ' ἀνθρώποισι πέλει τῶν ἄστυ ἀλώῃ, also Il. 17. 145., 18. 208, Od. 1. 17., 6. 153., 11. 545., 16. 257., 23.

355, &c. It is probable however that the text is sometimes at fault, the Art. having been substituted for ὅς, especially in order to avoid hiatus : e.g.—

Il. 17. 145 οἷος σὺν λαοῖσι τοὶ Ἰλίῳ (λαοῖς οἳ Ϝιλίῳ).

Od. 16. 263 ἐσθλώ τοι τούτω γ' ἐπαμύντορε τοὺς ἀγορεύεις, (where οὕς is not excluded by the hiatus, § 382).

As the Art. usually adds some new circumstance about a known antecedent, it sometimes has the effect of representing a fact as *unexpected :* as Il. 1. 392 τήν μοι δόσαν υἷες Ἀχαιῶν (*Briseis*)—*whom the Greeks gave me* (=although the Greeks had given her to me): Od. 16. 19 μοῦνον τηλύγετον, τῷ ἐπ' ἄλγεα πολλὰ μογήσῃ *his only son, after he has endured many sorrows about him* (cp. 19. 266., 23. 6): Il. 1. 160 πρὸς Τρώων, τῶν οὔ τι μετατρέπει *the Trojans—while you pay no heed to them.* So in—

Il. 1. 319 λῆγ' ἔριδος τὴν πρῶτον ἐπηπείλησ' Ἀχιλῆϊ, the meaning is not *the same quarrel which he had declared,* but *his quarrel—now that he had declared it.* And so—

Od. 19. 393 οὐλήν, τήν ποτέ μιν σῦς ἤλασε *a wound—one that once a boar gave him.* Similarly τῇ =*at a place where* (Il. 14. 404., 21. 554., 23. 775).

The Acc. Neut. τό used adverbially means *wherefore* (§ 133), as—

Il. 3. 176 ἀλλὰ τά γ' οὐκ ἐγένοντο· τὸ καὶ κλαίουσα τέτηκα. So Il. 7. 239., 12. 9., 17. 404., 19. 213., 23. 547. There is one instance in the Odyssey, in the song of Demodocus (8. 332).

The Relatival use does not extend to the Adverbs τώς, τότε, τέως (τῆος), or to the derivative adjectives τοῖος, τόσος, &c.

263.] The Article with τε serves as a Relative. In accordance with the use of τε in Homer (§ 332) ὅ τε expresses a constant or *general* characteristic, but only of a *definite* Antecedent : as—

Il. 6. 112 Ἕκτορι Πριαμίδῃ, τόν τε στυγέουσι καὶ ἄλλοι.

15. 621 κύματά τε τροφόεντα, τά τε προσερεύγεται αὐτήν.

Od. 18. 273 οὐλομένης ἐμέθεν, τῆς τε Ζεὺς ὄλβον ἀπηύρα.

It is especially used in similes (where a *typical* case is described), as Il. 13. 390 πίτυς βλωθρὴ τήν τ' οὔρεσι κτλ.: Il. 5. 783., 11. 554., 12. 146., 13. 571., 15. 581., 23. 712, &c.

264.] **Homeric and Attic Article.** After the account given in the preceding §§ of the Homeric uses of the Article it is hardly necessary to show in detail where they differ from the corresponding uses in Attic Greek. What we have chiefly to observe is that the difference is often greater in reality than it appears to be at first sight. Familiar as we are with the defining Article of modern languages, and of Attic Greek, we naturally import it into Homer whenever it is not made impossible by the context. But even when a Homeric use falls under the general head of the 'defining Article' (§ 261), the effect is perceptibly different from that of the 'Definite Article' properly so called. In Homer the Article indicates, not that a person or thing is a known or definite one, but *that it is presented to us in an antithesis or contrast*. Objects so contrasted are usually definite, in the sense that they are already known or suggested by the context: and hence the readiness with which the later defining sense can be applied to passages in Homer. Thus αὐτὰρ ὅ γ' ἥρως can usually be translated *but the hero* (*before mentioned*), as though ὁ distinguished him from other heroes. But when we find that αὐτὰρ ὁ in Homer constantly means *but he*, or *but the other*, and that it may be followed by an epexegetic Noun (as αὐτὰρ ὁ βοῦν ἱέρευσεν ἄναξ ἀνδρῶν Ἀγαμέμνων), we see that ὁ is more important than a mere Article, is in fact a Substantival Pronoun, to which ἥρως is added as a kind of epithet—*but he the hero*.

This point has been explained in connexion with the use of the Attributive Article, § 259, a. It may be further illustrated from instances in which the Article marks contrast, *but not definition*, and consequently cannot be translated by *the*. Such are :—

Il. 15. 66   πολέας ὀλέσαντ' αἰζηοὺς
τοὺς ἄλλους, μετὰ δ' υἱὸν ἐμὸν Σαρπηδόνα δῖον

not *the others*, but *others as well, certain others*.

Il. 5. 672 ἦ προτέρω Διὸς υἱὸν ἐριγδούποιο διώκοι,
ἦ ὅ γε τῶν πλεόνων Λυκίων ἀπὸ θυμὸν ἕλοιτο

or *should take the lives of more Lycians instead*. Here οἱ πλέονες does not mean 'the greater number,' but '*a greater number*,' in contrast to the one person mentioned.

Il. 22. 162 ὡς δ' ὅτ' ἀεθλοφόροι περὶ τέρματα μώνυχες ἵπποι
ῥίμφα μάλα τρωχῶσι· τὸ δὲ μέγα κεῖται ἄεθλον

and there a great prize lies ready. So Od. 20. 242 αὐτὰρ ὁ . . ὄρνις *but a bird*. The same thing is shown by μνηστήρων τῶν μὲν κτλ. (§ 259, b). It is evident that τῶν is used, not because the suitors are definite persons, but because a contrast is made by μέν.

The same remark applies to the use with Adjectives (§ 260), especially to the use by which they are turned into Substantives, as τὸ κρήγυον, τὰ κακά. In Homer τὰ κακά is said because in the particular context κακά *evils* are opposed to *good*. In Attic τὰ κακά or τὸ κακόν implies that evils form a *class* of things, distinguished from all other things. This again is a difference,

which does not come out in translating Homer, and is therefore
apt to be overlooked.

The use with Cardinal Numerals (§ 260, c) is to be similarly
explained. It is not peculiar to Homer, but is regular in Attic
also, where it may be regarded as a survival of the Homeric use
of the Article.

The use of the Art. in Hesiod shows some advance. Thus the use to form
a *class* is no longer confined to the case of a particular contrast given in the
context: Op. 280 τὰ δίκαι' ἀγορεῦσαι, Op. 353 τὸν φιλέοντα φιλεῖν καὶ τῷ
προσιόντι προσεῖναι. The use with Adverbs is commoner, Op. 365 τὸ θύρηφιν,
Op. 457 τῶν πρόσθεν. The Prepositional phrase in Op. 364 τὸ ἐν οἴκῳ κατακεί-
μενον is quite post-Homeric. The same may be said of the 'articular' Inf. in
Op. 314 τὸ ἐργάζεσθαι ἄμεινον (§ 259, 3). It will be found that the Art.
occurs nearly twice as often in Hesiod as in Homer.

It is a further question, and one that cannot be fully discussed here,
whether any uses of the Article found in our text of the Iliad and Odyssey
are post-Homeric, and evidence of a later origin of the books or passages
where they occur. It will be seen that in the case of the uses which have
been noticed as rare or exceptional most of the examples come from books ix,
x, xxiii, and xxiv. See especially the uses treated of in § 260,*f*,*g*, and § 261, 3.
Others again seem to belong to the Odyssey; see § 261, 3, and cp. § 259, *a*.
The use of the Article in the 10th book of the Iliad seems clearly later than
in any other part of Homer : *e. g.*—

Il. 10. 97 δεῦρ' ἐς τοὺς φύλακας καταβήομεν.

277 χαῖρε δὲ τῷ ὄρνιθ' 'Οδυσεύς.

322 ἦ μὲν τοὺς ἵππους τε καὶ ἅρματα κτλ. (so 330).

408 πῶς δ' αἱ τῶν ἄλλων Τρώων φυλακαί κτλ.

Also πεδίον τὸ Τρωϊκόν (v. 11), ὁ τλήμων 'Οδυσεύς (v. 231, 498), τὴν νύκτα (v. 497).
So in the Catalogue of the Ships we have Θάμυριν τὸν Θρήϊκα (Il. 2. 595), and
τὸ Πελασγικὸν Ἄργος (2. 681).

ὅς ἥ ὅ.

265.] The Pronoun ὅς ἥ ὅ, and the Adverbs formed from the
same Stem, esp. ὡς, ὅτε, ἕως, are occasionally used in a Demonstrative or quasi-Demonstrative sense; viz.—

(1) After καί, οὐδέ, μηδέ : as Il. 21. 198 ἀλλὰ καὶ ὃς δείδοικε
even he fears : Il. 6. 59 μηδ' ὃς φύγοι *may not even he escape :* and
often in the combinations καὶ ὥς *even so,* οὐδ' ὥς *not even so.* So
οὐδ' ἔνθα *not even there* (Od. 1. 18).

(2) With μέν and δέ, to express a contrast between indefinite
objects : as—

Il. 11. 64 ὡς Ἕκτωρ ὀτὲ μέν τε μετὰ πρώτοισι φάνεσκεν,
ἄλλοτε δ' ἐν πυμάτοισι κτλ. (so 18. 599., 20. 49).

12. 141 οἳ δ' ἦ τοι ἧος μὲν κτλ. *up to a certain time.*

17. 178 ὀτὲ δ' αὐτὸς ἐποτρύνει *but sometimes &c.*

(3) In the Adverb ὥς *so* ; especially as the second member of

the Correlation ὡς—ὡς *as—so*. A single ὡς is often used where
it may be either a Relative or a Demonstrative, as in the formula
ὡς φάτο, ὡς εἰπών, &c. : cp. the Latin *quae quum dixisset,* &c. The
other instances in which we have to translate ὡς as a Demonstrative are rare : *e. g.* Il. 3. 339 ὡς δ' αὔτως *and in like manner.*

Among Demonstrative uses of ὅς it is usual to count the use
with γάρ, as ὃς γάρ, ὡς γάρ, ἵνα γάρ. This however is an error,
arising from the occasional use of γάρ where it cannot be translated *for:* see § 348, 3.

Some commentators find a Demonstrative ὅς in—

Od. 4. 388 τόν γ' εἴ πως σὺ δύναιο λοχησάμενος λελαβέσθαι,
ὅς κέν τοι εἴπῃσιν ὁδόν κτλ.

Here however the clause ὅς κέν τοι κτλ. is not the Apodosis, but a Relative
Clause expressing *purpose.* The peculiarity of the passage is merely that the
Apodosis is left to be understood : *if you can seize him,* (do so), *that he may tell
you &c.:* cp. Od. 5. 17., 10. 539.

These idioms are usually regarded as the remains of an earlier
use of ὅς in the simple Anaphoric sense. The growth of a
Relative out of a Demonstrative has been already exemplified in
the Article (§ 262). But the Relatival use of ὅς is so ancient
that any attempt to trace its growth from an earlier syntax must
be of very uncertain value.

266.] ὅς τε, ὅς τις. The simple ὅς may be used in any kind of
Relative Clause, although in certain cases (§ 262) the Article is
preferred. Thus we have—

Il. 4. 196 ὅν τις ὀϊστεύσας ἔβαλεν (a particular fact).

1. 403 ὃν Βριάρεων καλέουσι (a constant, characteristic fact).

In these two places the Art. might be put in place of ὅς : but
not in—

Il. 2. 205 εἷς βασιλεύς, ᾧ ἔδωκε (a characteristic fact, defining).

1. 218 ὅς κε θεοῖς ἐπιπείθηται (definition of a class).

So ὅς is used to convey a *reason* (which implies a *general* cause
or tendency): as Od. 1. 348 Ζεὺς αἴτιος ὅς τε δίδωσιν κτλ. ; cp.
Il. 2. 275., 5. 650., 8. 34.

If the Relative is meant to refer to an indefinite number of
individuals falling under a common description, ὅς τις is generally used, = *who being any one, whoever.*

If, again, the Relative Clause generalises by making us think,
not so much of all possible *individuals* in a class, as of different
times and circumstances,—in other words if it lays stress on the
general and permanent element in facts—ὅς τε is used : *e. g.*—

Il. 1. 279 σκηπτοῦχος βασιλεύς, ᾧ τε Ζεὺς κῦδος ἔδωκε *to whom
as king, to whom in every such case.*

Il. 4. 361 τὰ γὰρ φρονέεις ἅ τ' ἐγώ περ (such things as &c.).

5. 545 Ἀλφειοῦ ὅς τ' εὐρὺ ῥέει (cp. 5. 876).

9. 117 ἀνὴρ ὅν τε Ζεὺς κῆρι φιλήσῃ.

Od. 7. 74 οἷσίν τ' εὖ φρονέῃσι they to whom she is well inclined.

Thus ὅς τε is constantly used in *comparisons*: as Il. 3. 61 (πέλεκυς)
ὅς τ' εἶσιν διὰ δουρὸς ὑπ' ἀνέρος ὅς ῥά τε τέχνῃ νήϊον ἐκτάμνῃσι.

So ὥς τε, ὅθι τε, ὅθεν τε, ὅτε τε : ἔνθα τε, ἵνα τε : ὅσος τε, οἷός τε.

Od. 12. 22 δισθανέες, ὅτε τ' ἄλλοι ἅπαξ θνήσκουσ' ἄνθρωποι.

19. 179 Κνωσός, μεγάλη πόλις, ἔνθα τε Μίνως κτλ.

Thus Homer has *five* Relatives, viz. ὅς, ὅς τε, ὅς τις, ὁ, ὅ τε, each
with a distinct use : Attic retains only ὅς and ὅς τις.*

267.] Correlative Clauses. 1. We have first to distinguish
between the simple structure in which the Relative Clause only
qualifies a Noun or Pronoun in the Principal Clause, as—

>   τῶν οἱ νῦν βροτοί εἰσι *of those who are now living.*
>   ἐν πεδίῳ ὅθι περ κτλ. *in the plain where &c.*

and the *parallel* structure, in which the Relative is an Adverb of
the same form as the Antecedent; as—

>   τὼς δέ σ' ἀπεχθήρω ὡς νῦν ἔκπαγλ' ἐφίλησα.
>   τόφρα δ' ἐπὶ Τρώεσσι τίθει κράτος, ὄφρ' ἂν Ἀχαιοὶ κτλ.
>   τῇ ἴμεν ᾗ κεν δὴ σύ, κελαινεφές, ἡγεμονεύῃς.

Here the notion given by the adverbial ending—*manner, time,
way*, &c.—is the point of comparison, and must be understood to
qualify both clauses.

In both these kinds of compound sentence the Demonstrative
Antecedent may often be omitted, but this is especially the case
with the second, in which a Relatival Adverb implies a *corresponding* Demonstrative. Thus ὡς ἐφίλησα implies τὼς—ὡς ἐφίλησα : ὄφρ' ἂν is equivalent to τόφρα—ὄφρ' ἂν, &c.

In this way, then, it came about that ὡς (lit. *in which manner*)
means *in the manner in which*: and so ὄφρα *to the time up to
which*, ᾗ *by the way by which*, ὅθι *at the place where*, ὅτε *at the
time when*, and so on.† The whole Relative Clause in fact serves
as an Adverb (of *manner, time, way*, &c. as the ending may
determine), construed with the Verb of the Principal Clause.
Such clauses accordingly are called *adverbial*: while clauses
which merely qualify a Noun or Pronoun are *adjectival*.

---

* It is worth notice that ὅς τις in Attic has some of the uses of ὅς τε : see
Jowett, *Thucyd.* ii. p. 372, Stein. *Hdt.* 4. 8.

† In the corresponding sentences in English it is often the Relative that is
wanting : thus τῇ ἴμεν ᾗ κεν ἡγεμονεύῃς *to go by the way* [by which] *you lead*. This
forms a characteristic difference between Greek and English Syntax.

2. The omission of the antecedent from the governing clause leads to various idiomatic uses :—

(a) The Relative Clause comes to be equivalent to a Noun or Pronoun in any Case which the governing clause may require : thus—

Il. 5. 481 τά τ᾽ ἐέλδεται ὅς κ᾽ ἐπιδευής *which (he) desires who is in need.*

1. 230 δῶρ᾽ ἀποαιρεῖσθαι ὅς τις σέθεν ἀντίον εἴπῃ *to take away gifts (from him, from any one) who &c.*

7. 401 γνωτὸν δὲ καὶ ὃς μάλα νήπιός ἐστιν.

Od. 15. 281 αὐτὰρ κεῖθι φιλήσεαι οἷά κ᾽ ἔχωμεν *you will be entertained (with such things) as we have.*

Il. 14. 81 βέλτερον ὃς φεύγων προφύγῃ κακόν *it is better (for one) who by flying escapes evil,* i.e. *it is better when a man &c.*: cp. Od. 15. 72, Il. 3. 109.

(b) The omission is especially characteristic of clauses with ὅτε *when* (for τὸ—ὅτε *the time when*): Il. 15. 18 ἦ οὐ μέμνῃ ὅτε *do you not remember (the time) when:* Il. 8. 229 πῇ ἔβαν εὐχωλαί, ὅτε δὴ κτλ. *where are gone the boastings (of the time) when &c.:* Il. 19. 337 λυγρὴν ἀγγελίην ὅτ᾽ ἀποφθιμένοιο πύθηται : and with Numerals, Il. 21. 80 ἠὼς δέ μοί ἐστιν ἥδε δυωδεκάτη ὅτε κτλ. *this is the twelfth morn (from the time) when &c.* So in Il. 2. 303 χθιζά τε καὶ πρωΐζ᾽ ὅτε means *a day or two (from the time) that.* Hence too the forms εἰς ὅτε *to the time that,* πρίν γ᾽ ὅτε *before the time when.*

Similarly with ὅθι *where,* as ἵκανον ὅθι *they came (to the place) where.*

(c) With a Verb of *saying* or *knowing* the Relative Clause has apparently the force of a dependent question :—

Il. 2. 365 γνώσῃ ἔπειθ᾽ ὅς θ᾽ ἡγεμόνων κακός, ὅς τέ νυ λαῶν,
ἠδ᾽ ὅς κ᾽ ἐσθλὸς ἔῃσι

you will recognise (γιγνώσκω, not οἶδα) of the leaders him who is a weakling, and who of the people, and again him who shall be (found to be) brave.

So Il. 13. 278., 21. 609, Od. 3. 185., 17. 363 : compare the form with the antecedent expressed—

Il. 23. 498　　τότε δὲ γνώσεσθε ἕκαστος
ἵππους Ἀργείων, οἳ δεύτεροι οἵ τε πάροιθεν.

The construction is the same with a Verb which *implies* knowing, finding out, or the like : e.g.—

κλήρῳ νῦν πεπάλασθε διαμπερὲς ὅς κε λάχῃσι

cast lots (to find him) whose portion it shall be.

3. The suppressed antecedent, again, may have no clear or grammatical construction :—

(*a*) This is especially found when the Relative Clause expresses a *reason*, as—

Od. 4. 611 αἵματός εἰς ἀγαθοῖο, φίλον τέκος, οἷ᾽ ἀγορεύεις

lit. *you are of good blood (seeing the things) such as you speak*, i.e. as I see by the manner of things that you speak.

Il. 14. 95 νῦν δέ σευ ὠνοσάμην πάγχυ φρένας οἷον ἔειπες

I blame your thought, because of the kind of thing you have said.

Od. 2. 239 νῦν δ᾽ ἄλλῳ δήμῳ νεμεσίζομαι, οἷον ἅπαντες
      ἧσθ᾽ ἄνεῳ *at the way that ye all sit silent.*

Il. 17. 586 Ἕκτωρ, τίς κέ σ᾽ ἔτ᾽ ἄλλος Ἀχαιῶν ταρβήσειεν,
      οἷον δὴ Μενέλαον ὑπέτρεσας ;

who would fear you any more, seeing the way you shrank before Menelaus ?

Od. 15. 212 οἷος ἐκείνου θυμὸς ὑπέρβιος, οὔ σε μεθήσει.

Il. 16. 17 ἦε σύ γ᾽ Ἀργείων ὀλοφύρεαι ὡς ὀλέκονται.

Od. 10. 326 θαῦμά μ᾽ ἔχει ὡς κτλ. *I wonder at the way that &c.*

This is the idiom generally described by saying that **οἷος** is put for ὅτι τοιοῦτος, **ὡς** for ὅτι οὕτως, and so on. So when **ὅς** introduces a reason (§ 266) we might say that it is for ὅτι οὗτος (*e.g.* Ζεὺς αἴτιος ὅς τε δίδωσι = ὅτι οὗτος δίδωσι). The peculiarity, however, of the clauses now in question is that the Relative can have no grammatical Antecedent, that is to say, that the Correlative which it implies as an Antecedent has no regular construction in the Principal Clause.

(*b*) This is also found after Verbs of *knowing*, &c.—the Relative Clause expressing the Object or *thing* known : as—

Il. 2. 409 ἤδεε γὰρ κατὰ θυμὸν ἀδελφέον ὡς ἐπονεῖτο

he knew of his brother (as to the manner) in which he laboured.

24. 419 θηοῖό κεν . . οἷον ἐερσήεις κεῖται.

Od. 7. 327 εἰδήσεις . . ὅσσον ἄρισται νῆες ἐμαί.

This is evidently an extension of the form γνώσῃ ὃς κακός (*supra*, 2 *c*), with the difference that the suppressed Correlative in the Principal Clause is without a regular construction.

(*c*) Sometimes the Relative Clause is used without any Principal Clause, as an exclamation : *e.g.*—

Il. 7. 455 ὦ πόποι, Ἐννοσίγαι᾽ εὐρυσθενές, οἷον ἔειπες.

Od. 1. 32 ὦ πόποι, οἷον δή νυ θεοὺς βροτοὶ αἰτιόωνται.

Il. 5. 601 ὦ φίλοι, οἷον δὴ θαυμάζομεν Ἕκτορα.

The ellipse gives an expression of surprise : (*to think*) *what a thing you have said !* (*to see*) *how men blame the gods !* (*to remember*) *how we wondered at Hector!* The want of a construction has much the same effect as with the exclamatory use of the Nominative (§ 163). Similarly—

Od. 4. 240 πάντα μὲν οὐκ ἂν ἐγὼ μυθήσομαι οὐδ' ὀνομήνω,
        ὅσσοι Ὀδυσσῆος ταλασίφρονός εἰσιν ἄεθλοι·
        ἀλλ' οἷον τόδ' ἔρεξε κτλ.

I will not tell of all his feats: but (just to mention) what a feat this was that he did &c. So Od. 4. 269., 11. 517 ; cp. also Il. 5. 638 ἀλλ' οἷόν τινά φασι κτλ. (*just to instance) the kind of man that they tell &c.*

If the explanation now given of these Relative Clauses is right, it is evidently incorrect to accent and punctuate as is done by editors (*e.g.*) in—

Il. 6. 108 φὰν δέ τιν' ἀθανάτων ἐξ οὐρανοῦ ἀστερόεντος
        Τρωσὶν ἀλεξήσοντα κατελθέμεν· ὣς [or ὣς] ἐλέλιχθεν

taking it as an Independent Clause—'so they wheeled.' The same editors do not hesitate to write in Il. 16. 17 ὀλοφύρεαι, ὡς ὀλέκονται, where the construction is precisely the same.

It is sometimes maintained that in all such cases we have a survival of the primitive 'parataxis'—that (*e. g.*) ὀλοφύρεαι ὡς ὀλέκονται was originally ὀλοφύρεαι, ὣς ὀλέκονται *you lament, they so perish,* hence *you lament how they perish,* or *that they thus perish.* On the same view the exclamatory οἷον ἔειπες is not elliptical, but represents the original independent *what a thing you have said!* (See Mr. Leaf on Il. 2. 320 θαυμάζομεν οἷον ἐτύχθη). This hypothesis, however, is not borne out by the facts of language. In the first place, it is strange that the traces of parataxis should be found with the Relatives ὡς, οἷος, ὅσος, &c. rather than with the corresponding Demonstrative forms. Again, if the Relative retained an original Demonstrative use, we should expect to find this, like other survivals, in some *isolated* group of uses: whereas the clauses now in question are very various in character. Again, the passages which favour the notion of parataxis are indistinguishable in structure from others to which it cannot be applied, such as most of the examples given under 2. Yet we cannot separate τά τ' ἐέλδεται ὅς κ' ἐπιδευής from φιλήσεαι οἷά κ' ἔχωμεν, or that again from ὠνοσάμην οἷον ἔειπες. In particular it will be found that the theory does not apply to clauses which are *conditional* so well as to those which give a *reason.* The exclamatory use—οἷον ἔειπες and the like—does not furnish a good argument, because the pronoun used in a simple exclamation would not be Demonstrative, but Interrogative (ποῖον ἔειπες, &c.). The most decisive consideration, however, is that the Relatival use of ὅς and its derivatives is common to Greek and Sanscrit, and may be regarded therefore as Indo-European. Consequently there is a strong presumption against any hypothesis which explains the Homeric use of the Relative from a still earlier or pre-Indo-European stage of language.

4. Sometimes an Antecedent is not construed with the Governing Clause, but follows the Case of the Relative. This is allowed if the Antecedent is separated from its own clause, as—

Il. 14. 75 νῆες ὅσαι πρῶται εἰρύαται ἄγχι θαλάσσης
        ἔλκωμεν (so Il. 6. 396., 10. 416., 14. 371).

This ' Inverse Attraction ' may be placed with the forms in which the Antecedent is wanting, because it can only arise when the original construction of the Antecedent (ἕλκωμεν νῆας ὅσαι—) has been forgotten.

5. Again, the Correlative structure is liable to an extension, the characteristic of which is that the Relatival Adverb *has no proper construction in its own clause*.

This may be most clearly seen in the use of οὕνεκα (*i.e.* οὗ ἕνεκα) *for which reason : e.g.*—

Il. 1. 110 ὡς δὴ τοῦδ' ἕνεκά σφιν ἐκηβόλος ἄλγεα τεύχει,
οὕνεκ' ἐγὼ . . οὐκ ἔθελον κτλ.

Apollo causes sorrow for this reason, that I would not &c. Here we cannot translate οὕνεκα *for which reason :* the reason does not precede, but is given by the Relative Clause. That is, the first ἕνεκα is rational ; the second is logically unmeaning. Hence the οὕνεκα can only be due to the correlation : as it is usually expressed, οὕνεκα is *attracted* to the antecedent τοὕνεκα. Then— since οὕνεκα comes to imply a correlative τοὕνεκα—the antecedent τοὕνεκα is omitted, and the relatival οὕνεκα by itself comes to mean *for the reason that, because.*

The process may be traced more or less distinctly in all the Relatival Adverbs. Thus ὡς (*in which manner*) comes to mean *in such manner that :* and so ὄφρα *for so long that,* ἵνα (lit. *where*) to *the end that.* Also, as will be shown presently, ὅ, ὅτι and ὅ τε are Adverbial Accusatives, meaning literally *in which respect,* hence *in respect that, because :* cp. εἰπεῖν ὅ τι ἐχώσατο *to say for what he was angered* with χώσατο ὅτι *he was angered for (the reason) that.* The qualifying force of the Adverb is transferred from its own clause to the Verb of the Governing Clause.

On the same principle ἐκ τοῦ ὅτε *from the time when* becomes ἐξ οὗ (for ἐκ τοῦ οὗ—) : and εἰς τὸ ὅτε becomes εἰς ὅ *to the time that.*

268.] οὕνεκα. This Conjunction (which may be treated as a single word) is used in two ways :—

(*a*) to assign a *cause* or *reason :*

(*b*) to connect the fact expressed in the Relative Clause with a Verb of *saying, knowing,* &c.

The second of these uses is evidently derived from the first by a kind of degeneration, or loss of meaning. The *fact* told or known is originally given as the *ground* of the saying or knowing. The transition may be seen in—

Od. 7. 299 ξεῖν', ἦ τοι μὲν τοῦτό γ' ἐναίσιμον οὐκ ἐνόησε
παῖς ἐμή, οὕνεκά σ' οὔ τι μετ' ἀμφιπόλοισι γυναῖξιν
ἦγεν ἐς ἡμέτερον

my daughter did not judge aright in this, because she did not &c., more simply, *in this, that she did not &c.* Again—

Od. 5. 215 οἶδα καὶ αὐτὸς
πάντα μάλ᾽, οὕνεκα σεῖο περίφρων Πηνελόπεια κτλ.

I know all, inasmuch as Penelope is &c.; i. e. *I know that she is.* This use is found with Verbs of *saying* in Od. 13. 309., 15. 42., 16. 330, 379. In the Iliad it occurs only once, viz. Il. 11. 21 πεύθετο . . μέγα κλέος, οὕνεκ᾽ Ἀχαιοί κτλ.

Note that (except in Od. 13. 309., 16. 379) the Verb is followed by an Acc. of the *thing;* so that the Relative Clause does not directly take the place of the Object. Thus (*e. g.*) πεύθετο κλέος οὕνεκα is literally *heard a rumour the ground of which was that* &c.

A peculiar use to state a *consequence* which is made the *ground* of inference may be seen in Il. 9. 505 ἡ δ᾽ Ἄτη σθεναρή τε καὶ ἀρτίπος, οὕνεκα πάσας πολλὸν ὑπεκπροθέει *Ate is strong and sound of foot, (as we know) because she &c.*

269.] ὅ, ὅτι, ὅ τε. The Acc. Neut. of the Relative, when used adverbially (§ 133), yields the three ' Conjunctions' ὅ, ὅτι, ὅ τε, which mean properly *in respect that,* hence usually (*a*) *because,* or (*b*) *that* (after a Verb of *saying, knowing,* &c.). The antecedent τό is generally wanting, but is found in a few instances: as Il. 19. 421 τὸ οἶδα καὶ αὐτός, ὅ τοι κτλ.: Il. 5. 406 οὐδὲ τὸ οἶδε . . ὅττι μάλ᾽ οὐ δηναιός κτλ.: Il. 1. 120 λεύσσετε τό γε πάντες, ὅ μοι κτλ.; also Il. 15. 217., 19. 57., 20. 466, and Od. 13. 314 (seemingly the only instance in the Odyssey). These places, however, serve to show the origin of the idiom. We have here the phenomenon already noticed in § 267, 5. viz. the Relative has no construction in its own Clause, but reflects the construction of the Demonstrative in the principal Clause. *E.g.* Il. 20. 283 ταρβήσας ὅ οἱ ἄγχι πάγη βέλος *dreading because the dart stuck near him* represents an older ταρβήσας (τὸ) ὃ πάγη βέλος. The adverbial Accusative with ταρβήσας would express the *nature* or *ground* of dread (as in τό γε δείδιθι, τόδε χώεο, &c.); hence the meaning *dreading in respect of* (or *because of*) *this, that the dart stuck.* Accordingly we find ὅ=*because* chiefly with Verbs of *feeling,* which regularly take a Neuter Pronoun of the *ground* of feeling.*

---

* The Clauses of this type are the subject of Dr. Peter Schmitt's monograph, *Ueber den Ursprung des Substantivsatzes mit Relativpartikeln im Griechischen* (Würzburg, 1889). He rightly takes ὅ (ὅτι, &c.) to be an Acc. of the ' inner object' (§ 133), but he seems to have overlooked the real difficulty ; which is that ὅ supplies an object to the Verb of the principal Clause, not to the Verb of its own Clause. Thus he says ' ὁρῶ ὃ νοσεῖς war ursprünglich : ich weiss, was du krankst ; οἶδ᾽ ὅ σε ἐπήνεσε ich weiss, was er dich gelobt hat' (p. 21). But the

(1) ὅ *in respect that, because* may be exemplified by—

Il. 16. 835 Τρωσὶ φιλοπτολέμοισι μεταπρέπω, ὅ σφιν ἀμύνω
       ἦμαρ ἀναγκαῖον (*for that I keep off*).

Od. 1. 382 Τηλέμαχον θαύμαζον ὅ θαρσαλέως ἀγόρευε.

So Il. 9. 534 (χωσαμένη), Od. 19. 543., 21. 289 (οὐκ ἀγαπᾷς ὅ).

The use to state a *consequence* as a *ground* of inference (like
that of οὕνεκα in Il. 9. 505, § 268) occurs in—

Od. 4. 206 τοίου γὰρ καὶ πατρός, ὅ καὶ πεπνυμένα βάζεις

for you are of a wise father, (*as I know*) *because you speak wisely :*
so Od. 18. 392, and probably also—

Il. 21. 150 τίς πόθεν εἰς ἀνδρῶν, ὅ μευ ἔτλης ἀντίος ἐλθεῖν ;

who are you that you dare &c.

The transition to the use of ὅ = *that* may be seen in—

Od. 2. 44 οὔτε τι δήμιον ἄλλο πιφαύσκομαι οὐδ' ἀγορεύω
       ἀλλ' ἐμὸν αὐτοῦ χρεῖος, ὅ μοι κακὸν ἔμπεσεν οἴκῳ

what I tell is my own case (*which consists in the fact*) *that evil has
fallen on my house.* It is common with οἶδα, γιγνώσκω (Il. 5. 433,
&c.), ἀΐω (Il. 15. 248): and is found with Verbs of *seeing*, as Il. 1.
120 λεύσσετε γὰρ τό γε πάντες ὅ μοι γέρας ἔρχεται ἄλλῃ *ye see this,
that my prize goes elsewhere* (Il. 19. 144., 22. 445, Od. 17. 545).

(2) ὅτι *because* is common after the Verbs of *feeling*. We need
only stop to notice some instances (parallel to those of ὅ just
quoted) in which ὅτι is = *as I know because :*—

Il. 16. 33 νηλεές, οὐκ ἄρα σοί γε πατὴρ ἦν ἱππότα Πηλεύς,
       οὐδὲ Θέτις μήτηρ, γλαυκὴ δέ σε τίκτε θάλασσα,
       πέτραι τ' ἠλίβατοι, ὅτι τοι νόος ἐστὶν ἀπηνής

meaning *now I know that you are no child of Peleus &c., because
your mind is relentless.* So—

Il. 21. 410 νηπύτι', οὐδέ νύ πώ περ ἐπεφράσω ὅσσον ἀρείων
       εὔχομ' ἐγὼν ἔμεναι, ὅτι μοι μένος ἀντιφερίζεις.

Od. 5. 339 κάμμορε, τίπτε τοι ὧδε Ποσειδάων ἐνοσίχθων
       ὠδύσατ' ἐκπάγλως, ὅτι τοι κακὰ πολλὰ φυτεύει

why is Poseidon so enraged against you (*as he seems to be*) *since he*

---

two meanings, *I know in what respect you are sick* and *I know that you are sick* are
quite distinct, and are given by essentially different constructions of the
Relative. Let us take as example a Clause which follows a Verb of *feeling* :
ἐχώσατο ὅτι οἱ βέλος ἔκφυγε χειρός. The construction with ἐχώσατο is the Acc.
of the 'inner object' (as τόδε χώεο, τό γε δείδιθι, &c.). But ὅτι is in a different
Clause from ἐχώσατο : the full construction would be ἐχώσατο (τὸ) ὅτι.
Schmitt would say that ὅ τι ἔκφυγε also is an Acc. of the 'inner object,'—
that the sentence meant originally *was angered in respect of this in respect of which
it flew out.* It is surely more probable that ἐχώσατο ὅ τι was like ἐξ οὗ *from the
time that*, εἰς ὅ *to the time that*, οὕνεκα *for the reason that*, &c. (§ 267, 5), so that ὅ τι
was an Acc. by Attraction, and had no real construction with its own Verb.

causes you many evils? So Il. 10. 142., 21. 488., 24. 240, Od. 14. 367., 22. 36.

The transition to the meaning *that* may be seen in—

Il. 2. 255 ἦσαι ὀνειδίζων ὅτι οἱ μάλα πολλὰ διδοῦσι *reproaching him in respect that, with the fact that, &c.* 24. 538. It is the regular meaning with Verbs of *knowing:* Il. 8. 175 γιγνώσκω δ᾽ ὅτι μοι πρόφρων κατένευσε Κρονίων *I know that &c.* Cp. Il. 1. 536 οὐδέ μιν Ἥρη ἠγνοίησεν ἰδοῦσ᾽ ὅτι οἱ κτλ.: 24. 563 καὶ δέ σε γιγνώσκω .. ὅττι θεῶν τίς σ᾽ ἦγε.

The use of ὅτι = *that* is commoner in the Iliad than in the Odyssey (where ὡς and οὕνεκα partly supply the place, see § 268).

(3) The form ὅ τε (so written by Bekker to distinguish it from ὅτε *when*) is found in Homer with the same varieties of meaning as ὅ and ὅτι. Thus we have ὅ τε = *because* in—

Il. 1. 244 χωόμενος ὅ τ᾽ ἄριστον Ἀχαιῶν οὐδὲν ἔτισας *angry because &c.*; Il. 6. 126., 16. 509, Od. 8. 78. So—

Od. 5. 356 ὤ μοι ἐγώ, μή τίς μοι ὑφαίνῃσιν δόλον αὖτε ἀθανάτων, ὅ τέ με σχεδίης ἀποβῆναι ἀνώγει

i. e. there is a snare in this bidding me to get off the raft. So probably Il. 1. 518 ἦ δὴ λοίγια ἔργ᾽ ὅ τέ μ᾽ κτλ. *it is a pestilent thing that you &c.*; Il. 19. 57 ἦ ἄρ τι τόδ᾽ ἀμφοτέροισιν ἄρειον ἔπλετο ὅ τε κτλ.: and the exclamatory use (§ 267, 3, c) in Il. 16. 433 ὤ μοι ἐγών, ὅ τε κτλ. *alas for me that &c.*

Again, ὅ τε is = *as I know because,* in—

Il. 4. 31 δαιμονίη, τί νύ σε Πρίαμος Πριάμοιό τε παῖδες τόσσα κακὰ ῥέζουσιν, ὅ τ᾽ ἀσπερχὲς μενεαίνεις

how do Priam and his sons do you such evil, (as they must do) since you are furiously enraged?

Il. 15. 467 ὦ πόποι, ἦ δὴ πάγχυ μάχης ἐπὶ μήδεα κείρει δαίμων ἡμετέρης, ὅ τέ μοι βιὸν ἔκβαλε χειρός

(as I judge from this) that he has thrown the bow from my hands. So Od. 13. 129 ὅ τέ με βροτοὶ οὔ τι τίουσι *for that mortals honour me not:* Od. 14. 89 οἴδε δέ τοι ἴσασι .. ὅ τ᾽ οὐκ ἐθέλουσι *they know something (as is plain) because they are not willing:* Od. 21. 254 τοσσόνδε βίης ἐπιδευέες εἰμὲν .. ὅ τ᾽ οὐ δυνάμεσθα *we are so wanting in strength, as appears by the fact that we are not able.*

With Verbs of *knowing,* again, ὅ τε has the meaning *that* —

Il. 1. 411 γνῷ δὲ καὶ Ἀτρείδης εὐρυκρείων Ἀγαμέμνων ἣν ἄτην, ὅ τ᾽ ἄριστον Ἀχαιῶν οὐδὲν ἔτισεν

may know his folly, in that he failed to honour &c.

Od. 14. 365 ἐγὼ δ᾽ εὖ οἶδα καὶ αὐτὸς νόστον ἐμεῖο ἄνακτος, ὅ τ᾽ ἤχθετο πᾶσι θεοῖσι

I know of the return of my lord, that (as it showed) he was hated

by all the gods. So Il. 8. 251 εἴδονθ᾽ ὅ τ᾽ ἄρ᾽ κτλ. *saw that &c.*;
and with γιγνώσκω, Il. 5. 231, &c.

The existence of a distinct ὅ τε with the meaning *because* or
that depends upon its being shown that in places such as those
now quoted the word cannot be either ὅτι *that* or ὅτε *when*. The
latter explanation of the reading ὅτε (or ὅτ᾽) is often admissible,
e.g. in Il. 14. 71 ἤδεα μὲν γὰρ ὅτε—, οἶδα δὲ νῦν ὅτε—; cp. Il. 15.
207 ἐσθλὸν καὶ τὸ τέτυκται ὅτ᾽ .. εἰδῇ, and instances in Attic, as
Soph. O. T. 1133 κάτοιδεν ἦμος κτλ. *he knows well of the time
when &c.*, Eur. Troad. 70 οἶδ᾽ ἡνίκ᾽ Αἴας εἷλκε. But the supposition of a distinct ὅ τε is supported by a sufficient number of examples in Homer,—*e.g.* Il. 5. 331 γιγνώσκων ὅ τ᾽ ἄναλκις ἔην θεός,
—and generally by the complete correspondence of meaning thus
obtained between ὅ, ὅτι, and ὅ τε. On the other hand it is extremely improbable that the ι of ὅτι was ever capable of elision.
In this respect ὅτι *that* stands on the same footing as τί and ὅτι.
Moreover, the adverbial use of these words, which gives them the
character of Conjunctions, is only a slight extension of the ordinary
Acc. of the Internal Object (§ 133). Hence if the Neut. of ὅς
and ὅς τις is used in this way, it is difficult to see any reason why
the Neut. of the equally familiar ὅς τε should be excluded. The
ancient authorities and the MSS. vary in some places between
ὅτε and ὅτι (as in Il. 14. 71, 72., 16. 35, Od. 13. 129), and on
such a point we have no good external authority.

270.] ὅ, ὅτι, ὅ τε **as Conjunctions.** In a few instances it is
impossible to explain these Relatives by supplying an Accusative
τό in the principal Clause. Thus in—

Od. 20. 333 νῦν δ᾽ ἤδη τόδε δῆλον, ὅ τ᾽ οὐκέτι νόστιμός ἐστι
the Antecedent is a Pronoun in the Nom. Similarly in—

Il. 5. 349 ἦ οὐχ ἅλις ὅττι γυναῖκας ἀνάλκιδας ἠπεροπεύεις;
the principal Clause is Impersonal, and the Antecedent might be
a Nom. (*is it not enough*) or Gen. (*is there not enough in this*), but
hardly an Accusative. Again in—

Il. 8. 362 οὐδέ τι τῶν μέμνηται, ὅ οἱ μάλα πολλάκις κτλ.

17. 207 τῶν ποινήν, ὅ τοι κτλ. (*as amends for the fact that*)
the Relative Clause serves as a Genitive: cp. Od. 11. 540 γηθο-
σύνη ὅ οἱ κτλ., 12. 374 ἄγγελος ἦλθεν .. ὅ οἱ κτλ.

Add Il. 9. 493 τὰ φρονέων ὅ μοι κτλ., 23. 545 τὰ φρονέων ὅτι οἱ
κτλ.: and also Od. 2. 116 τὰ φρονέουσ᾽ ἀνὰ θυμὸν ἅ οἱ κτλ., where
the *v. l.* ὅ for ἅ has good MS. authority.

In these instances, then, the forms ὅ, &c. have ceased to be felt
as Case-forms, and may properly be termed Conjunctions.

The Mood in all Clauses of this kind is the Indic.—not the
Opt., as in some Attic uses (Goodwin, § 714).

It may be worth while pointing out the parallel between this extension of the Relative Clause and the development which has been observed in the use of the Infinitive (§ 234). In the first instance the Clause serves as epexegesis of an Acc. with a Verb of *saying, knowing, feeling,* &c. (§ 237, 2): μὴ δείδιθί τινα ὄψεσθαι *fear not any one, for being likely to see;* ταρβήσας (τὸ) ὅ ἄγχι πάγη βέλος *fearing (this), that the spear stuck near him.* Then the Acc. is used without reference to the construction of the principal Verb and consequently the dependent Clause may stand to it as logical Subject : οὔ τι νεμεσσητὸν βασιλῆα ἀπαρέσσασθαι *for a king to make his peace is no shame;* οὐχ ἅλις ὅτι ἠπεροπεύεις is *(the fact) that you deceive not enough;*—where the Clause in both cases serves as a Nom. Finally the Clause is used as an indeclinable Noun of any Case : τῶν μέμνηται ὅ κτλ. *remembers this, that* &c. ; to which corresponds the so-called 'articular Infinitive,' or Inf. with the Article as a Substantive.

The three forms ὅ, ὅ τε, ὅτι do not differ perceptibly in meaning. Hence the reduction in Attic to the single ὅτι is no real loss.

270*.] Indirect Discourse. Clauses introduced by ὅ (ὅ τε, ὅτι), ὡς, οὕνεκα after Verbs of *saying* and *knowing* are evidently of the nature of *oratio obliqua,* or indirect quotation of the words of another person.

The Homeric language has no forms of Syntax peculiar to Indirect Discourse (such as the use of the Opt. or Pres. Indic. after a Secondary Tense). Every assertion is made from the speaker's own point of view: consequently what was present to the person quoted must be treated as now past. Accordingly the Present Tense of the *oratio directa* becomes the Impf., the Pf. becomes the Plpf. The Future is thrown into past time by the help of μέλλω, as in οὐδὲ τὸ ἤδη ὅ οὐ πείσεσθαι ἔμελλεν *he knew not that he would not be persuaded.* The only exception to this is Od. 13. 340 ἤδε ὅ νοστήσεις *I knew that you will* (i. e. *would*) *return.* For an instance of the Opt. with ὡς after a Verb of *saying* see § 306, 2 : and cp. the Dependent Question, § 248.

The Clauses now in question are commoner after Verbs of *knowing, hearing, remembering,* &c. than after Verbs of *saying.* Of the former kind there are about 70 in Homer ; of the latter, which may be counted as examples of true Indirect Discourse, there are 16. Of these, again, only three are in the Iliad (16. 131., 17. 654., 22. 439). This confirms the view that these Clauses are originally causal, the meaning *that* being derived from the meaning *because* (§ 268). If we confine ourselves to ὅ (ὅ τε) and ὅτι the proportion is still more striking, since out of more than 50 instances there are only four with a Verb of *saying* *.

271.] Form of the Relative Clause. It is characteristic of the Relative Clause that the Verb *to be* is often omitted: as—

Il. 8. 524 μῦθος δ' ὃς μὲν νῦν ὑγιής, εἰρημένος ἔστω,

---

* The figures are taken from Schmitt (*Ursprung des Substantivsatzes*), but in-clude instances of ὅ τε which he refers to ὅτε *when.*

and so ὅσσοι Ἀχαιοί, οἵ περ ἄριστοι, ἥ τις ἀρίστη, ὅς τ᾽ αἴτιος ὅς τε καὶ οὐκί, &c. Hence we should write in Il. 11. 535., 20. 500 ἄντυγες αἱ περὶ δίφρον, in Il. 21. 353 ἰχθύες οἳ κατὰ·δίνας. So with the Adverbs; as Od. 10. 176 ὄφρ᾽ ἐν νηὶ θοῇ βρῶσίς τε πόσις τε so long as there is food and drink in the ship.

1. This ellipse leads to a peculiar ' Attraction ' into the Case of the Antecedent, found chiefly with ὅσος τε, as—

Od. 10. 113 τὴν δὲ γυναῖκα | εὗρον ὅσην τ᾽ ὄρεος κορυφήν,

which is equivalent to τόσην ὅση ἐστὶ κορυφή; and so ὅσον τε, Od. 9. 322, 325., 10. 167, 517., 11. 25 ; also οἷόν τε, Od. 19. 233. The only instance in the Iliad is somewhat different :—

Il. 1. 262 οὐ γάρ πω τοίους ἴδον . . οἷον Πειρίθοον κτλ.

The later Attraction of the Relative into the Case of the Antecedent is not found in Homer. Kühner gives as an example Il. 5. 265 τῆς γάρ τοι γενεῆς ἧς Τρωῒ περ εὐρύοπα Ζεὺς δῶκε. But there the Gen. is partitive: 'the brood *from* which Zeus gave' (§ 151 e). So Il. 23. 649 (§ 153).

2. Another effect of this omission may be found in the use of double Relatival forms, especially ὡς ὅτε *as (it is) when;* which again may be used without any Verb following: *e.g.*—

Il. 13. 471 ἀλλ᾽ ἔμεν᾽ ὡς ὅτε τις σῦς οὔρεσιν ἀλκὶ πεποιθώς, ὅς τε μένει κτλ.

So ὡς εἰ and ὡς εἴ τε *as (it would be) if,* as in Il. 5. 373 τίς νύ σε τοιάδ᾽ ἔρεξε . . ὡς εἴ τι κακὸν ῥέζουσαν.

A similar account is probably to be given of the peculiar double Relative—

Il. 8. 229 πῇ ἔβαν εὐχωλαί, ὅτε δὴ φάμεν εἶναι ἄριστοι, ἃς ὁπότ᾽ ἐν Λήμνῳ κενεαυχέες ἠγοράασθε

when once (whenever it was) you made boast in Lemnos.

3. The want of a finite Verb also leads to the construction of οἷος, ὡς, &c. with the Infinitive. This is only beginning in Homer: see § 235. It arises by a kind of mixture or 'contamination' of two simple constructions, viz.—

(1) the ordinary Inf. with the Demonstratives τοῖος, τηλίκος, &c. (§ 232); as τοῖοι ἀμυνέμεν *of the kind to defend* (Od. 2. 60), μένειν ἔτι τηλίκος *of the age for remaining* (Od. 17. 20);

(2) the Correlative form, such as Il. 5. 483 τοῖον οἷόν κ᾽ ἠὲ φέροιεν Ἀχαιοὶ ἤ κεν ἄγοιεν: Il. 7. 231 ἡμεῖς δ᾽ εἰμὲν τοῖοι οἳ ἂν σέθεν ἀντιάσαιμεν.

Thus (*e.g.*) Od. 21. 172 τοῖον . . οἷόν τε ῥυτῆρα βιοῦ τ᾽ ἔμεναι καὶ ὀϊστῶν combines the forms τοῖον ἔμεναι *of the kind to be* and τοῖον οἷός τε (ἐστί) *of the kind that (is).* In other words, the construction of τοῖος is transferred to the Correlatives τοῖος—οἷος. Then τοῖος is omitted, and we get οἷος with the Inf. The same may be said of ὥς τε with the Inf., which is post-Homeric.

272.] Double Relative Clauses. When a Relative introduces two or more Clauses connected by καί or δέ, it need not be construed with any Clause after the first: *e. g.*—

Il. 1. 162 ᾧ ἔπι πόλλ' ἐμόγησα, δόσαν δέ μοι υἷες Ἀχαιῶν

for which I toiled, and which the sons of the Greeks gave me.

Od. 2. 114 τῷ ὅτεῴ τε πατὴρ κέλεται καὶ ἀνδάνει αὐτῇ

and who is pleasing to herself. The Relative is not repeated in any Clause of this form; but its place is often taken by another Pronoun (usually an enclitic, or an unemphatic αὐτός) :—

Il. 1. 78 ἦ γὰρ ὀίομαι ἄνδρα χολωσέμεν, ὃς μέγα πάντων
    Ἀργείων κρατέει καί οἱ πείθονται Ἀχαιοί.

Od. 9. 19 εἴμ' Ὀδυσεὺς Λαερτιάδης, ὃς πᾶσι δόλοισιν
    ἀνθρώποισι μέλω, καί μευ κλέος οὐρανὸν ἵκει.

This idiom, it should be observed, is not peculiar to Homer, but prevails in all periods of Greek (Kühner, II. p. 936).

On the same principle, when a succession of Clauses is introduced by a Relatival Adverb, the first Verb may be in the Subj. or Opt., while the rest are in the Indic. This is especially noticeable in similes, as—

Il. 2. 147 ὡς δ' ὅτε κινήσῃ Ζέφυρος βαθὺ λήιον ἐλθών,
    λαβρὸς ἐπαιγίζων, ἐπί τ' ἠμύει ἀσταχύεσσι.

4. 483 ἥ ῥά τ' ἐν εἰαμενῇ ἕλεος μεγάλοιο πεφύκῃ
    λείη, ἀτάρ τέ οἱ ὄζοι ἐπ' ἀκροτάτῃ πεφύασι.

Successive Relative Clauses not connected by a Conjunction are frequent in Homer. The Relative may be repeated for the sake of emphasis: Od. 2. 130 δόμων ἀέκουσαν ἀπῶσαι ἥ μ' ἔτεχ' ἥ μ' ἔθρεψε. Or the second Clause is epexegetic of the first: as—

Il. 5. 403 σχέτλιος, ὀβριμοεργός, ὃς οὐκ ὄθετ' αἴσυλα ῥέζων,
    ὃς τόξοισιν ἔκηδε θεούς (so 6. 131., 17. 674, &c.).

Or it marks the return to the main thread of the narrative: as—

Od. 14. 288 δὴ τότε Φοῖνιξ ἦλθεν ἀνήρ, ἀπατήλια εἰδώς,
    τρώκτης, ὃς δὴ πολλὰ κάκ' ἀνθρώποισιν ἐώργει,
    ὅς μ' ἄγε παρπεπιθὼν κτλ. (cp. Il. 15. 461–3).

Where different Pronouns are used as Relatives in successive Clauses, the reason of the variety may often be traced. Thus in Il. 16. 157 οἱ δὲ λύκοι ὡς ὠμοφάγοι, τοῖσίν τε περὶ φρεσὶν ἄσπετος ἀλκή, οἵ τ' ἔλαφον .. δάπτουσιν, the Art. τοῖσι gives a characteristic of *all* wolves, the Rel. οἵ passes to *the* wolves of the particular simile. In both the meaning is general, accordingly τε is used. Again, we find ὅς τε introducing a general assertion, while ὅς relates to a particular fact: as Il. 4. 442 ἥ τ᾽ ὀλίγη μὲν πρῶτα κορύσσεται . . ἥ σφιν καὶ τότε κτλ. ; 5. 545 Ἀλφειοῦ, ὅς τ᾽ εὐρὺ ῥέει Πυλίων διὰ γαίης, ὃς τέκετ᾽ Ὀρσίλοχον: and in the reverse order, Il. 18. 520 οἱ δ᾽ ὅτε δή ῥ᾽ ἵκανον ὅθι σφίσιν εἶκε λοχῆσαι ἐν ποταμῷ, ὅθι τ᾽ ἀρδμὸς ἔην.

The difference between ὅς τις and ὅς τε appears in Od. 6. 286 καὶ δ᾽ ἄλλῃ νεμεσῶ ἥ τις τοιαῦτά γε ῥέζοι, ἥ τ᾽ ἀέκητι φίλων πατρὸς καὶ μητρὸς ἐόντων ἀνδράσι μίσγηται. Here ἥ τις insists on the inclusion of all members of the class (*any one who*—), ἥ τε prepares us for the class characteristics (*one of the kind that*—).

CHAPTER XII.

Uses of the Moods.

Introductory.

273.] **Classification of Sentences.** Before entering upon an examination of the Homeric uses of the Moods, it will be convenient to give some account of the different kinds of Sentences and Clauses with which we shall have to deal.

A **Simple Sentence**—or the principal Clause in a Complex Sentence—may be purely *Affirmative.* Or, the affirmation may be turned (either by the use of a suitable Pronoun or Particle, or by the tone and manner in which it is uttered) into a question: *i. e.* the Sentence may be *Interrogative.* Or, a predication may be framed in order to be denied: in which case a Particle is added to make the Sentence *Negative.* Or, the Sentence may express *Wish, Purpose,* or *Command;* and any of these may again be combined with a Negative, so as to express some variety of *Prohibition.* Or, once more, the Sentence may be *Conditional, i. e.* may assert, deny, command, &c. subject to a hypothesis; and this hypothesis or condition may be expressed by a subordinate Clause, or by an Adverb or adverbial phrase (*then, in that case,* or the like): or the condition need not be expressed at all, but conveyed by the drift of the context.

A **subordinate Clause** may be so loosely connected with the principal Clause as to be virtually an independent sentence. We have seen that this is generally the case (for example) with Clauses introduced by the Article (§ 262). The Clauses which chiefly concern us now are—

1. Dependent Interrogative Clauses.

2. Prohibitive Clauses (μή = *lest*).

3. Relative Clauses proper (introduced by ὅς).

4. Clauses introduced by a Relatival Adverb (ὡς, ὅθι, ὅθεν, ὅτε, ἕως, ὄφρα, &c. ; also ἔνθα, ἵνα, and ἐπεί).

5. Clauses introduced by εἰ *if.*

This classification is based upon the grammatical *form* of the Clause. If we look to the relation in point of *meaning* between the two Clauses of a Complex Sentence, we find that subordinate Clauses fall into a wholly different set of groups. Thus there are—

(1) Clauses expressing *cause* or *reason:* as—

Il. 2. 274 νῦν δὲ τόδε μέγ' ἄριστον ἐν 'Αργείοισιν ἔρεξεν,
ὃς τὸν λωβητῆρα ἐπεσβόλον ἔσχ' ἀγοράων.

And clauses like Il. 4. 157 ὥς σ' ἔβαλον Τρῶες *since the Trojans have thus shot at you;* 6. 166 οἷον ἄκουσε *at hearing such a thing* (§ 267, 3): as well as in the regular Causal use of ὅ, ὅτι, ὅ τε (§ 269), and οὕνεκα.

(2) Clauses expressing the *Object* of Verbs of *saying, knowing, thinking,* &c. (*i. e.* the *fact* or *thing* said, &c.): as—

Il. 2. 365 γνώσῃ ἔπειθ' ὅς θ' ἡγεμόνων κακός, ὅς τέ νυ λαῶν.

Od. 6. 141 ὁ δὲ μερμήριξεν 'Οδυσσεὺς | ἦ . . ἦ κτλ.

Il. 18. 125 γνοίεν δ' ὡς δὴ δηρὸν ἐγὼ πολέμοιο πέπαυμαι.
601 πειρήσεται αἴ κε θέῃσιν (*tries if it will run*).

(3) Clauses expressing *condition* or *limitation;* which may be introduced—

By ὅς: as τῶν οἳ νῦν βροτοί εἰσι *of the mortals now living:* ὅς κ' ἐπιδευής *he who is in want:* ὅς κε θεοῖς ἐπιπείθηται *he who shall obey the gods:* ὅ τι οἱ εἴσαιτο *whatever seemed to him.*

By a Relatival Adverb: of *manner,* as ὡς ἐπιτέλλω *as I bid,* ὡς ἂν ἐγὼν εἴπω *as I shall speak;* of *time,* ἐπεί, ὅτε, &c., also ἕως and ὄφρα when they mean *so long as;* of *place,* as ὁππόθι πιότατον πεδίον *where is the richest of the plain.*

By εἰ—the common form of Conditional protasis.

It will be convenient to term all these Clauses 'Conditional'—the word being taken in a wide sense, so as to include every Clause of the nature of a *definition* or *limitation,* as well as those in which actual *priority* in time is implied.

(4) Final Clauses, expressing *end* or *purpose:* introduced—

By ὅς; as Il. 4. 190 ἐπιθήσει φάρμαχ' ἅ κεν παύσῃσι *will apply drugs which shall stay:* Il. 14. 107 νῦν δ' εἴη ὅς . . ἐνίσποι *may there be one who may tell.*

By ὡς, ὅπως, ἵνα—the ordinary forms expressing purpose.

By ἕως (better written ἧος in Homer *) and ὄφρα, when they mean *till such time that*. To these we may add εἰς ὅ *until*, which (like οὕνεκα) is practically a single word.

By εἰ or αἴ: as Il. 1. 420 εἶμ᾽ αὐτὴ .. αἴ κε πίθηται *I go in the hope that he will listen*.

By μή *lest* (= ἵνα μή).

It is important to observe that the several groups of Clauses now pointed out are generally indistinguishable in respect of grammatical form ; so that Clauses of the same form (introduced by the same Pronoun or Particle, and with a Verb of the same Tense and Mood) often bear entirely different meanings. This will be shown in detail in the course of the present chapter ; meanwhile a few instances may be noted as illustrations.

1. Final Clauses introduced by ὅς are in the same form as the Conditional or limiting Clauses such as ὅς κε τύχῃ, ὅττι κεν εἴπῃς, &c.

2. The regular Final Clauses with ὡς and ὅπως are in the same form as the limiting ὡς ἂν ἐγὼν εἴπω *as I shall speak*, ὅπως ἐθέλησιν *as he pleases*, &c.

3. Clauses with ἕως and ὄφρα may either be Conditional (when the Conjunction means *so long as*), or Final (when it means *until*).

4. The Final Clause with εἰ is indistinguishable in form from the ordinary Conditional Protasis : compare αἴ κε πίθηται *to see if he will listen* with Il. 24. 592 μή μοι Πάτροκλε σκυδμαινέμεν αἴ κε πύθηαι *be not angry in case you hear*.

5. Clauses with μή may either be Final (when μή = ἵνα μή), or Object-Clauses after a Verb of *fearing* (δείδω μή).

From these examples it is evident that in this as in so many parts of Greek grammar the most important differences of meaning are not expressed by corresponding distinctions of form. The Pronoun or Conjunction which connects the subordinate with the principal Clause generally leaves the real relation between the two Clauses to be gathered from the context.

These different kinds of Sentence are distinguished to some extent by means of Particles, of which it will be enough to say here that—

(1) Strong *Affirmation* is expressed by ἦ, and the same Particle is employed in *Interrogation* (especially with ironical force).

(2) *Negation* is expressed by οὐκί (οὐκ, οὐ), *Prohibition* by μή.

(3) The Particle εἰ, in its ordinary use, marks a *Conditional Protasis*, *i.e.* a Clause stating a condition or supposition.

(4) The Particles κε(ν) and ἄν mark a predication as being *Conditional*, or made in view of some *limitation* to particular conditions or circumstances.

---

* It is often convenient to use the Attic form ἕως as the name of the Particle, but this cannot be the true Homeric form. The metre shows that it must be a trochee ; and the Doric ἇς (Ahrens, *Dial. Dor.* p. 200) represents contraction of ἇος : cp. the Cretan τάως for τέως (Hesych.). Hence we should have in Homer either ἧος (the older Ionic form, cp. νηός) or ἆος, which would properly be Doric or Æolic, like λᾱός &c. Of these ἧος is evidently the more probable.

The Subjunctive—in Principal Clauses.

274.] The Subjunctive in a Simple Sentence, or in the Principal Clause of a Complex Sentence, may be said in general to express either the *will* of the speaker or his sense of the *necessity* of a future event. Like the English *must* and *shall*, by which it may usually be rendered, it is intermediate in meaning between an Imperative and a Future. Sometimes (as in ἴομεν *let us go*, or in Prohibitions with μή) it is virtually Imperative; sometimes it is an emphatic or passionate Future. These varieties of use will be best understood if treated with reference to the different kinds of sentence—Affirmative, Interrogative, Negative, Prohibitive, &c.—in which they occur.

275.] In *Affirmative* sentences the force of the Subj. depends in great measure on the Person used.

(*a*) In the First Person the Subj. supplies the place of an Imperative, so far as such a thing is conceivable : that is, it expresses what the speaker *resolves* or *insists* upon doing ; *e. g.*—

Il. 9. 121 ὑμῖν δ᾽ ἐν πάντεσσι περικλυτὰ δῶρ᾽ ὀνομήνω
(where the list of gifts immediately follows).

Od. 2. 222 σῆμά τέ οἱ χεύω καὶ ἐπὶ κτέρεα κτερεΐξω
πολλὰ μάλ᾽ ὅσσα ἔοικε, καὶ ἀνέρι μητέρα δώσω
(the Subj. expresses the decisive action to be taken by Telemachus, viz. to acknowledge his father's death : the Fut. δώσω expresses what would follow as a matter of course).

12. 383 δύσομαι εἰς Ἀίδαο καὶ ἐν νεκύεσσι φαείνω
(said by way of a threat).

Hence after a Clause containing an Imperative the Subj. is used to show what the speaker will do *as his part* of what he desires to be done : as—

Il. 6. 340 ἀλλ᾽ ἄγε νῦν ἐπίμεινον, ἀρήια τεύχεα δύω
do you wait, and I will put on my armour.

22. 416 σχέσθε, φίλοι, καί μ᾽ οἶον ἐάσατε κηδόμενοί περ
ἐξελθόντα πόληος ἱκέσθ᾽ ἐπὶ νῆας Ἀχαιῶν,
λίσσωμ᾽ ἀνέρα τοῦτον κτλ.

450 δεῦτε, δύω μοι ἕπεσθον, ἴδωμ᾽ ὅτιν᾽ ἔργα τέτυκται.

So after the phrases ἀλλ᾽ ἄγε, εἰ δ᾽ ἄγε, as Od. 6. 126 ἀλλ᾽ ἄγ᾽ ἐγὼν αὐτὸς πειρήσομαι ἠδὲ ἴδωμαι : 9. 37 εἰ δ᾽ ἄγε τοι καὶ νόστον ἐμὸν πολυκηδέ᾽ ἐνίσπω. On the phrase εἰ δ᾽ ἄγε see § 321.

To show that a purpose is *conditional* upon something else being done, the Subj. may be qualified by the Particle κε(ν) :

Il. 1. 137 εἰ δέ κε μὴ δώωσιν, ἐγὼ δέ κεν αὐτὸς ἕλωμαι
if they do not give her, I will (in that case) &c.

Il. 14. 235 πείθευ, ἐγὼ δέ κέ τοι εἰδέω χάριν
obey, and I will feel thankfulness.

16. 129 δύσεο τεύχεα θᾶσσον, ἐγὼ δέ κε λαὸν ἀγείρω.

Od. 17. 417 τῷ σε χρὴ δόμεναι καὶ λώϊον ἠέ περ ἄλλοι
σῖτον· ἐγὼ δέ κέ σε κλείω κτλ.

So too Il. 1. 183 τὴν μὲν . . πέμψω, ἐγὼ δέ κ' ἄγω Βρισηΐδα *I will
send her* (as required), *and then I will take Briseis*—the Subj. expressing the speaker's own threatened action, and κεν marking
that it is the counterpart to what is imposed upon him. It will
be found that κεν is used when the Clause with the Subj. is
introduced by δέ, but not when it follows without a connecting
Particle. *I. e.* it is when the two Clauses are set *against* one
another by δέ that it becomes necessary to express also the *conditional* nature of the second Clause.

This use of κεν with the Subj. is not found except in Homer.

The First Person Plural is similarly used, as Od. 3. 17 ἀλλ' ἄγε
νῦν ἰθὺς κίε Νέστορος ἱπποδάμοιο· εἴδομεν κτλ. And so in the
common Hortatory Subj., as φεύγωμεν *let us fly.*

(*b*) A Subj. of the Second and Third Person in an Affirmative
sentence is usually an emphatic Future, sometimes approaching
the force of an Imperative. The only example of a *pure* Subj.
(*i. e.* without κεν or ἄν) in this use appears to be the phrase καί
ποτέ τις εἴπῃσι *and men shall say* (Il. 6. 459, 479., 7. 87).

With ἄν we find—

Il. 1. 205 ἧς ὑπεροπλίῃσι τάχ' ἄν ποτε θυμὸν ὀλήται
(in effect a threat of what the speaker will do).

22. 505 νῦν δ' ἄν πολλὰ πάθῃσι φίλου ἀπὸ πατρὸς ἁμαρτών
but now he must suffer much &c.

With κεν the examples are rather more numerous:—

Od. 1. 396 τῶν κέν τις τόδ' ἔχῃσιν, ἐπεὶ θάνε δῖος Ὀδυσσεύς
let one of them have this (emphatic assent).

4. 80 ἀνδρῶν δ' ἤ κέν τίς μοι ἐρίσσεται ἠὲ καὶ οὐκί.

4. 391 καὶ δέ κέ τοι εἴπῃσι κτλ.

10. 507 ἧσθαι, τὴν δέ κέ τοι πνοιὴ Βορέαο φέρῃσι
*sit still, and her the breath of Boreas shall bear
along* (solemn prophetic assurance).

Il. 9. 701 ἀλλ' ἤ τοι κεῖνον μὲν ἐάσομεν, ἤ κεν ἴῃσιν
ἤ κε μένῃ (*let him go or let him stay*): cp. Od. 14. 183.

Note that where two alternatives are not expressed by the same
Mood, the Subj. gives the alternative on which the stress is laid:

Il. 11. 431 σήμερον ἢ δοιοῖσιν ἐπεύξεαι . .
ἤ κεν ἐμῷ ὑπὸ δουρὶ τυπεὶς ἀπὸ θυμὸν ὀλέσσῃς.

Il. 18. 308 στήσομαι, ἤ κε φέρῃσι μέγα κράτος ἤ κε φεροίμην
I shall stand firm, let him gain the victory (=*though
he shall gain*) *or I may gain it.*

Od. 4. 692 ἄλλον κ' ἐχθαίρῃσι βροτῶν, ἄλλον κε φιλοίη
a king will (*is sure to*) *hate one, he may love another.*

A curious combination of Opt. and Subj. is found in—

Il. 24. 654 αὐτίκ' ἂν ἐξείποι 'Αγαμέμνονι, ποιμένι λαῶν,
καί κεν ἀνάβλησις λύσιος νεκροῖο γένηται

*he would straightway tell Agamemnon, and then there must be a
delay in the ransoming of the dead.* The Subj. appears to express
the certainty of the further consequence, as though the hypo-
thetical case (αὐτίκ' ἂν ἐξείποι) had actually occurred.

276.] In *Negative* Clauses properly so called (*i. e.* distinguished
from Prohibitions) the Subj. is an emphatic Future. We find—

(*a*) The pure Subj. (expressing a general denial):—

Il. 1. 262 οὐ γάρ πω τοίους ἴδον ἀνέρας οὐδὲ ἴδωμαι
I have not seen—I never shall see.

7. 197 οὐ γάρ τίς με βίῃ γε ἐκὼν ἀέκοντα δίηται
no man shall chase me against my will.

15. 349   οὐδέ νυ τόν γε
γνωτοί τε γνωταί τε πυρὸς λελάχωσι θανόντα.

Od. 16. 437 οὐκ ἔσθ' οὗτος ἀνὴρ οὐδ' ἔσσεται οὐδὲ γένηται
*there is not, there never will or can be, the man
who,* &c. (so 6. 201).

24. 29 μοῖρ' ὀλοή, τὴν οὔ τις ἀλεύεται (cp. 14. 400).

(*b*) The Subj. with ἄν:—

Il. 3. 54 οὐκ ἄν τοι χραίσμῃ κίθαρις κτλ.
be sure that then your lyre will not avail you.

11. 386 εἰ μὲν δὴ ἀντίβιον σὺν τεύχεσι πειρηθείης,
οὐκ ἄν τοι χραίσμῃσι βιὸς κτλ.

The reason for ἄν in these places is obvious: in the following
instances it seems to be used because there is a *contrast:*—

Il. 2. 488 πληθὺν δ' οὐκ ἂν ἐγὼ μυθήσομαι οὐδ' ὀνομήνω
but the multitude I cannot declare or tell by name.

Od. 6. 221 ἄντην δ' οὐκ ἂν ἔγωγε λοέσσομαι (ἄντην is emphatic :
cp. Od. 4. 240., 11. 328, 517).

277.] In *Interrogative* sentences the Subj. generally expresses
necessity, submission to some command or power; as Il. 10. 62
αὖθι μένω . . ἦε θέω κτλ. *am I to remain here, or am I to run &c. ;*
Od. 15. 509 πῇ γὰρ ἐγώ, φίλε τέκνον, ἴω ; τεῦ δώμαθ' ἵκωμαι κτλ.
where am I to go? to whose house &c.: Od. 5. 465 ὤ μοι ἐγώ, τί

πάθω; τί νύ μοι μήκιστα γένηται; *what am I to suffer? what is to become of me?* And rhetorically, with an implied negation —

Il. 18. 188 πῶς τ’ ἄρ’ ἴω μετὰ μῶλον; ἔχουσι δὲ τεύχε’ ἐκεῖνοι *how can I go into the battle? They have my arms.*

Il. 1. 150 πῶς τίς τοι πρόφρων ἔπεσιν πείθηται Ἀχαιῶν;

One or two passages given by Delbrück under this head should perhaps be classed as Subordinate Clauses. A transitional instance may be seen in Od. 22. 166 σὺ δέ μοι νημερτὲς ἐνίσπες, ἦ μιν ἀποκτείνω . . ἦε σοὶ ἐνθάδ’ ἄγω κτλ. *tell me, am I to kill him, or bring him here?* Here the Clause may be a distinct sentence; but not so Il. 9. 618 ἅμα δ’ ἠοῖ φαινομένηφιν φρασσόμεθ’ ἢ κε νεώμεθ’ κτλ., because this does not express an actual but an intended future deliberation. So in Od. 16. 73 μητρὶ δ’ ἐμῇ δίχα θυμὸς ἐνὶ φρεσὶ μερμηρίζει ἢ αὐτοῦ παρ’ ἐμοί τε μένῃ κτλ. the form of expression is changed from the First to the Third Person, as in *oratio obliqua* (§ 280).

278.] With the *Prohibitive* Particle μή the Subj. has the character of an Imperative. We may distinguish however—

(*a*) Direct forbidding, usually with the First Person Plural (answering to the Hortatory Subj.), and the Second Person Sing.; sometimes also with the Third Person, as—

Il. 4. 37 ἔρξον ὅπως ἐθέλεις· μὴ τοῦτό γε νεῖκος ὀπίσσω
σοὶ καὶ ἐμοὶ μέγ’ ἔρισμα μετ’ ἀμφοτέροισι γένηται
I do not want this to become a quarrel.

Od. 22. 213 Μέντορ, μή σ’ ἐπέεσσι παραιπεπίθῃσιν Ὀδυσσεύς
see that Ulysses does not persuade you.

And with the First Person Sing., as Il. 1. 26 μή σε κιχείω *let me not catch you;* Il. 21. 475 μή σευ ἀκούσω.

(*b*) Fear, warning, suggestion of danger, &c.; *e.g.*—

Il. 2. 195 μή τι χολωσάμενος ῥέξῃ (*I fear he will &c.*).

5. 487 μή πως ὡς ἀψῖσι λίνου ἁλόντε πανάγρου
ἀνδράσι δυσμενέεσσιν ἕλωρ καὶ κύρμα γένησθε
see that you do not become a prey &c.

22. 123 μή μιν ἐγὼ μὲν ἵκωμαι ἰών, ὁ δέ μ’ οὐκ ἐλεήσει.

Od. 5. 356 ὤ μοι ἐγώ, μή τίς μοι ὑφαίνῃσιν δόλον αὖτε
ἀθανάτων (*I hope some god is not weaving &c.*).

18. 334 μή τίς τοι τάχα Ἴρου ἀμείνων ἄλλος ἀναστῇ
see that a better than Irus does not rise up.

The construction is the same in principle when a Clause of this kind follows a Verb of *fearing;* and it is sometimes a question whether the Clause is subordinate or not. Thus the older editors (including Wolf) punctuated Il. 11. 470 δείδω, μή τι πάθῃσι—as though δείδω were parenthetical. It is probable, however, that in such cases the Clause with μή has acquired a subordinate character, serving as Object to the Verb (*thing* feared) ; see § 281.

On the other hand, the Clauses now in question are often explained by supposing an ellipse of a Verb of *fearing* : μὴ ῥέξῃ for δείδω μὴ ῥέξῃ. This is open to the objection that it separates Clauses which are essentially similar. For μὴ ῥέξῃ *I will not have him do* (hence *I fear he may do*) is identical in form with μὴ ῥέξῃs *I will not have you do*. In this case, then, we have the simple Sentence μὴ ῥέξῃ, as well as the Compound δείδω μὴ ῥέξῃ, into which it entered.

Similar questions may arise regarding Final Clauses with μή. Thus in Il. I. 586–7 τέτλαθι, μῆτερ ἐμή, . . μή σε . . ἴδωμαι we may translate *endure, mother ; let me not see you &c.*, or (bringing the two Clauses more closely together) *endure, lest I see you &c.* So in Il. 8. 522, Od. 13. 208. No clear line can be drawn between independent and subordinate Clauses : for the complex Sentence has been formed gradually, by the agglutination of the simple Clauses.

The combination μὴ οὐ—prohibition of a negative—is extremely rare in Homer. In Il. 5. 233 μὴ τὼ μὲν δείσαντε ματήσετον οὐδ' ἐθέλητον, and Il. 16. 128 μὴ δὴ νῆας ἕλωσι καὶ οὐκέτι φυκτὰ πέλωνται, the Particles are in distinct Clauses. It occurs in a Final Clause, Il. 1. 28 μή νύ τοι οὐ χραίσμῃ κτλ., Il. 24. 569 : and after δείδω in Il. 10. 39 δείδω μὴ οὔ τίς τοι κτλ.

The Subj. in this use does not take κεν or ἄν, the prohibition being always regarded as unconditional.

It is well known that the *Present* Subj. is not used as an Imperative of Prohibition (with μή). The rule is absolute in Homer for the Second Person. The Third Person is occasionally used when *fear* (not *command*) is expressed ; the instances are,— Od. 5. 356 (quoted above) ; 15. 19 μή νύ τι . . φέρηται ; 16. 87 μή μιν κερτομέωσιν. The restriction does not apply to the First Person Plur., as Il. 13. 292 μηκέτι ταῦτα λεγώμεθα. We shall see that a corresponding rule forbids or restricts the use of μή with the Aorist Imperative (§ 327).

279.] Homeric and Attic uses. In Attic the use of the Subj. in independent Clauses is either Hortatory, or Deliberative, or Prohibitive. Thus the use with ἄν (§ 275, *a*), the use in *Affirmation* (§ 275, *b*), and the *Negative* uses (§ 276) do not survive.

The Subjunctive in Subordinate Clauses.

280.] Clauses with ἠέ—ἠέ. Doubt or deliberation between alternative courses of action is expressed by Clauses of the form ἠέ (ἤ)—ἠέ (ἤ) with the Subj., dependent on a Verb such as φράζομαι, μερμηρίζω, &c., or an equivalent phrase : *e. g.*—

Il. 4. 14. ἡμεῖς δὲ φραζώμεθ' ὅπως ἔσται τάδε ἔργα,
　　ἤ ῥ' αὖτις πόλεμόν τε κακὸν καὶ φύλοπιν αἰνὴν
　　ὄρσομεν, ἢ φιλότητα μετ' ἀμφοτέροισι βάλωμεν.

Od. 19. 524 ὡς καὶ ἐμοὶ δίχα θυμὸς ὀρώρεται ἔνθα καὶ ἔνθα,
　　ἠὲ μένω . . ἢ ἤδη ἅμ' ἔπωμαι κτλ. (cp. 22. 167).

This form is also found (but rarely) expressing, not the speaker's own deliberation, but that of a third person:—

Od. 16. 73 μητρὶ δ' ἐμῇ δίχα θυμὸς ἐνὶ φρεσὶ μερμηρίζει,
  ἦ αὐτοῦ παρ' ἐμοί τε μένῃ καὶ δῶμα κομίζῃ, κτλ.

The speaker (Telemachus) here expresses himself from his mother's point of view, only putting the Third Person for the First.

So of doubt as to which of two possible results of the speaker's action will be realised:—

Il. 13. 327 εἴδομεν, ἠέ τῳ εὖχος ὀρέξομεν, ἠέ τις ἡμῖν.

  16. 243 εἴσεται ἦ ῥα καὶ οἷος ἐπίστηται πολεμίζειν
    ἡμέτερος θεράπων, ἦ οἱ κτλ.

where ἐπίστηται (is to know, = will prove to know) is used nearly as the Latin Subj. in Indirect Questions.* An example after a Past Tense is found in Il. 16. 646 ff.; see § 298 fin.

281.] Clauses with μή. These are mainly of two kinds —

(1) Final Clauses: the Verb of the principal Clause being—

  (a) an Imperative, or equivalent form: as—

Il. 3. 414 μή μ' ἔρεθε, σχετλίη, μὴ χωσαμένη σε μεθείω.

  (b) a Present or Future in the First Person: as—

Od. 6. 273 τῶν ἀλεείνω φῆμιν ἀδευκέα, μή τις ὀπίσσω
    μωμεύῃ.

In these places the governing Verb shows that the purpose expressed is the speaker's own. The only instance of a different kind is—

Il. 13. 648 ἂψ δ' ἑτάρων εἰς ἔθνος ἐχάζετο κῆρ' ἀλεείνων,
    πάντοσε παπταίνων, μή τις χρόα χαλκῷ ἐπαύρῃ.

Here (if the reading ἐπαύρῃ is right) the poet describes the fear as though it were present to himself (see however § 298 fin.).

The two groups of Clauses under discussion agree in using only the *pure* Subj. (not the Subj with κεν or ἄν). In this respect they adhere to the form of the Simple Prohibitive Clause (§ 278).

(2) Clauses following a Verb that expresses the *fear* of the speaker, as δείδω μή τι πάθῃσι *I fear that he will suffer*. Here the Clause with μή, although of the same form as the independent Clauses given in § 278, is practically subordinate, and serves as *Object* to the Verb. The Verb, it is to be observed, is always in a Present Tense, and in the First Person: *i.e.* it is the speaker's *own present* fear that is expressed.

---

* It is impossible to agree with the scholars who explain ἐπίστηται here as an Indicative; see G. Meyer, *G. G.* § 485.

Such a Clause may be Object to a Verb of *knowing, &c.*, as—

Il. 10. 100 δυσμενέες δ' ἄνδρες σχεδὸν ἥαται, οὐδέ τι ἴδμεν
μή πως καὶ διὰ νύκτα μενοινήσωσι μάχεσθαι.

The fear expressed by μή πως κτλ. is subordinated (or on the way
to be subordinated) to ἴδμεν : *we do not know* (said apprehensively)
whether they will not be eager &c. So Od. 24. 491 ἐξελθών τις
ἴδοι μὴ δὴ σχεδὸν ὦσι κιόντες *some one go out and look whether they
are not near.* And in the Prohibitive use—

Il. 5. 411 φραζέσθω μή τίς οἱ ἀμείνων σεῖο μάχηται,
μὴ δὴν κτλ. *let him see to it that no one &c., lest &c.*

Od. 22. 367 εἰπὲ δὲ πατρὶ μή με περισθενέων δηλήσεται.

So with a Verb of *swearing*, Od. 12. 298 ὀμόσσατε μή πού τις . .
ἀποκτάνῃ *swear that no one shall slay :* Od. 18. 55.

282.] Relative Clauses. These fall into the two groups of
Final Clauses and Conditional or limiting Clauses.

The **Relative Clauses** called Final in the strict sense of the
word are those which follow a Clause expressive of *will ;* and the
reference to the future is shown in most cases by κεν : *e.g.*—

Il. 9. 165 ἀλλ' ἄγετε κλητοὺς ὀτρύνομεν, οἵ κε τάχιστα
ἔλθωσ' ἐς κλισίην.

24. 119 δῶρα δ' Ἀχιλῆϊ φερέμεν τά κε θυμὸν ἰήνῃ.

Od. 13. 399   ἀμφὶ δὲ λαῖφος
ἔσσω, ὅ κε στυγέῃσιν ἰδὼν ἄνθρωπος ἔχοντα.

19. 403 ὄνομ' εὕρεο ὅττι κε θῆαι.

With ellipse of the antecedent, so that the Clause supplies an
Object to the governing Verb—

Il. 7. 171 κλήρῳ νῦν πεπάλασθε διαμπερὲς ὅς κε λάχῃσι.

In other instances the notion of *End* is less distinctly conveyed, so that the Subj. need only have the emphatic Future
meaning (§ 275, *b*) : as—

Il. 21. 126   μέλαιναν φρῖχ' ὑπαίξει
ἰχθύς, ὅς κε φάγῃσι Λυκάονος ἀργέτα δημόν.

Od. 10. 538 ἔνθα τοι αὐτίκα μάντις ἐλεύσεται, ὄρχαμε λαῶν,
ὅς κέν τοι εἴπῃσι κτλ. (so 4. 389, 756., 11. 135).

The prophetic tone prevails in these places : cp. Il. 8. 33 ἀλλ'
ἔμπης Δαναῶν ὀλοφυρόμεθ' αἰχμητάων, οἵ κεν δὴ . . ὄλωνται, where
the Subj. is used as in an independent sentence.

The chief examples of a *pure* Subj. in a Final Clause are—

Il. 3. 286 τιμὴν δ' Ἀργείοις ἀποτινέμεν ἥν τιν' ἔοικεν,
ἥ τε καὶ ἐσσομένοισι μετ' ἀνθρώποισι πέληται.

Od. 18. 334 μή τίς τοι τάχα Ἶρος ἀμείνων ἄλλος ἀναστῇ,
ὅς τίς σ' . . δώματος ἐκπέμψῃσι.

So Il. 18. 467 παρέσσεται οἷά τις . . θαυμάσσεται (unless this is Fut.) : also the *Object* Clause Il. 5. 33 μάρνασθ', ὁπποτέροισι πατὴρ Ζεὺς κῦδος ὀρέξῃ *to fight* (*out the issue*) *to which of the two Zeus shall give victory* (*i. e.* till one or other wins). The want of κεν or ἄν is owing to the *vagueness* of the future event contemplated, *i. e.* the wish to exclude reference to a particular occasion.

The Relative is sometimes used with the Subj. after a Negative principal Clause—where there is necessarily no *actual* purpose :—

Od. 6. 201 οὐκ ἔσθ' οὗτος ἀνὴρ . . ὅς κεν . . ἵκηται (*v. l.* ἵκοιτο).

Il. 23. 345 οὐκ ἔσθ' ὅς κέ σ' ἔλῃσι κτλ.

and without κεν, Il. 21. 103 νῦν δ' οὐκ ἔσθ' ὅς τις θάνατον φύγῃ (*v. l.* φύγοι). In these places the construction evidently follows that of οὐ and οὐκ ἄν with the Subj. in Simple sentences (οὐκ ἔσθ' ὃς φύγῃ = οὔ τις φύγῃ). Otherwise we should have the Opt. (§ 304, *b*).

The Subj. is quite anomalous in—

Od. 2. 42 οὔτε τιν' ἀγγελίην στρατοῦ ἔκλυον ἐρχομένοιο,

ἥν χ' ὑμῖν σάφα εἴπω, ὅτε πρότερός γε πυθοίμην.

But here the speaker is repeating what has been said in the Third Person (30, 31), and with the regular Opt. (εἴποι, πύθοιτο). He evidently uses εἴπω because εἴποιμι does not fit the metre.

It is worth notice that the Relative of purpose with the Subj. is much commoner in the Odyssey than in the Iliad. Of the group which Delbrück describes as Subjunctives of Will with κεν, eleven are from the Odyssey, two (Il. 9. 166., 24. 119) are from the Iliad (*Synt. Forsch.* I. pp. 130–132). In Attic the idiom survives in a few phrases, as ἔχει ὅ τι εἴπῃ (Goodwin, § 65, *n.* 3).

283.] Conditional Relative Clauses. The numerous Clauses which fall under this heading may be divided again into two classes distinguished by the presence or absence of κεν or ἄν.

(*a*) The *pure* Subj. is used when the speaker wishes to avoid reference to particular cases, especially to any *future* occasion or state of things. Hence the governing Verb is generally a Present or Perfect Indicative : examples are—

Il. 1. 554 τὰ φράζεαι, ἅσσ' ἐθέλῃσθα (*whatever you choose*).

14. 81 βέλτερον ὃς φεύγων προφύγῃ κακὸν ἠὲ ἀλώῃ.

Od. 8. 546 ἀντὶ κασιγνήτου ξεῖνός θ' ἱκέτης τε τέτυκται

ἀνέρι ὅς τ' ὀλίγον περ ἐπιψαύῃ πραπίδεσσι.

In *Similes* this usage is extremely common ; as—

Il. 5. 5 ἀστέρ' ὀπωρινῷ ἐναλίγκιον, ὅς τε μάλιστα

λαμπρὸν παμφαίνῃσι (3. 62., 5. 138., 10. 185, &c.).

Od. 13. 31 ὡς δ' ὅτ' ἀνὴρ δόρποιο λιλαίεται, ᾧ τε πανῆμαρ

νειὸν ἀν' ἕλκητον βόε οἴνοπε πηκτὸν ἄροτρον.

Where the principal Verb refers to the future, and κεν or ἄν is not used, the intention is to make the reference quite general and sweeping ; *e.g.*—

Od. 20. 334 ἀλλ' ἄγε σῇ τάδε μητρὶ παρεζόμενος κατάλεξον
γήμασθ' ὅς τις ἄριστος ἀνὴρ καὶ πλεῖστα πόρῃσι.

Forms of the 3 Sing. Plqpf. are sometimes given by the MSS. and older editions in Clauses of this kind : as πεφύκει (Il. 4. 483), ἑστήκει (Il. 17. 435), &c. These were corrected by Hermann (*Opusc.* ii. 44), reading πεφύκῃ, ἑστήκῃ, &c. : see La Roche on Il. 4. 483.

(*b*) The Subj. with **κεν** indicates *limitation* to particular circumstances in the future. Hence it is used (with few exceptions) when the govering Verb is a Future, or implies futurity (an Imperative, Subjunctive or Optative): as—

Il. 1. 139 ὁ δέ κεν κεχολώσεται ὅν κεν ἵκωμαι.

Od. 2. 25 κέκλυτε δὴ νῦν μευ, Ἰθακήσιοι, ὅττι κεν εἴπω.

Il. 21. 103 νῦν δ' οὐκ ἔσθ' ὅς τις θάνατον φύγῃ, ὅν κε θεός γε κτλ.

Od. 1. 316 δῶρον δ' ὅττι κέ μοι δοῦναι φίλον ἦτορ ἀνώγῃ,
αὖτις ἀνερχομένῳ δόμεναι (cp. Od. 6. 28).

And after a Verbal in -τος expressive of necessity :—

Il. 1. 527 οὐδ' ἀτελεύτητον ὅ τι κεν κτλ.

3. 65 οὔ τοι ἀπόβλητ' ἐστὶ .. ὅσσα κεν κτλ.

The reference to a particular future occasion may be evident from the context : as :—

Od. 6. 158 κεῖνος δ' αὖ περὶ κῆρι μακάρτατος ἔξοχον ἄλλων,
ὅς κέ σ' ἐέδνοισι βρίσας οἶκόνδ' ἀγάγηται.

In the following places this rule appears to be violated by κέ(ν) being used where the reference is *general*; Il. 1. 218., 3. 279., 6. 228, 229., 9. 313, 510, 615., 11. 409., 14. 416., 16. 621., 17. 99., 19. 167, 228, 260., 21. 24, 484., 23. 322., 24. 335, Od. 4. 196., 7. 33., 8. 32, 586., 10. 22, 74, 328., 14. 126., 15. 21, 55, 70, 345, 422., 19. 564., 20. 295., 21. 313, 345. There is strong reason, however, to believe that in most of these instances the appearance of the Particle is due to alteration of the original text. Of the three forms κεν, κε, κ', the first is on the whole the most frequent in Homer. But out of the 35 places now in question the form κεν only occurs in six (not counting Il. 14. 416 ὅς κεν ἴδηται, where κεν is more than doubtful on account of the ϝ) ; and these six are all in the Odyssey (8. 586., 15. 21, 55, 345., 20. 295., 21. 313). This can hardly be mere accident, and the obvious explanation is that in most of these places, at least in the Iliad, ὅς κε and ὅς κ' have been substituted for ὅς τε and ὅς τ'. Thus we should probably read (*e. g.*)—

Il. 1. 218 ὅς τε θεοῖς ἐπιπείθηται, μάλα τ' ἔκλυον αὐτοῦ.

9. 508 ὃς μέν τ' αἰδέσεται κούρας Διὸς ..

510 ὃς δέ κ' ἀνήνηται καί τε κτλ. (cp. 23. 322).

(instead of the strange correlation μέν τε—δέ κε).

The real exceptions are most commonly passages in which a Singular is used after a Plural antecedent : as—

Od. 20. 294　　　οὐ γὰρ καλὸν ἀτέμβειν οὐδὲ δίκαιον
ξείνους Τηλεμάχου, ὅς κεν τάδε δώμαθ᾽ ἵκηται.

With the change of Number we seem to pass from a general description to a particular instance. So in Od. 15. 345, 422, and perhaps in Il. 3. 279., 6. 228., 16. 621, Od. 7. 33 : see § 362, 6.

(c) The use of ἄν in the Clauses of this kind is very rare. In the two places Il. 8. 10 and 19. 230 the reference to the future is plain. The remaining instance is Od. 21. 293 ὅς τε καὶ ἄλλους βλάπτει, ὃς ἄν κτλ., where there is the change from the Plural to the Singular just noticed.

284.] The Relatival Adverbs. The most important are : the Adverbs of *manner*, ὡς and ὅπως ; ἵνα, originally an Adverb of *place* (=*where*) ; and the Adverbs of *time*, ὄφρα, ἕως (ἧος), εἰς ὅ, ὅτε and ὁπότε, εὖτε, ἦμος. It will be best to take these words separately.

285.] ὡς, ὅπως :

(1) Final Clauses with ὡς or ὅπως and the Subj. generally depend upon an Imperative, or some equivalent phrase, *i.e.* they express the aim or purpose of something which the speaker himself does, or wills to be done : as—

Il. 1. 32　ἀλλ᾽ ἴθι μή μ᾽ ἐρέθιζε, σαώτερος ὥς κε νέηαι.

7. 293　　　　　　ἀγαθὸν καὶ νυκτὶ πιθέσθαι,
ὡς σύ τ᾽ ἐϋφρήνῃς πάντας κτλ.

The only instance in which the purpose expressed is not *the speaker's own* is—

Od. 14. 181　　　　　τὸν δὲ μνηστῆρες ἀγαυοὶ
οἴκαδ᾽ ἰόντα λοχῶσιν, ὅπως ἀπὸ φῦλον ὄληται.

(2) With Verbs that by their own meaning imply aim or purpose a Clause of this kind becomes an *Object Clause* : thus—

Il. 4. 66 πειρᾶν δ᾽ ὥς κε Τρῶες .. ἄρξωσι κτλ. (so Od. 2. 316).

9. 112 φραζώμεσθ᾽ ὥς κέν μιν ἀρεσσάμενοι πεπίθωμεν.

Od. 1. 76　　　ἡμεῖς δ᾽ οἵδε περιφραζώμεθα πάντες
νόστον, ὅπως ἔλθῃσι (*how he is to come*).

3. 19 λίσσεσθαι δέ μιν αὐτὸς ὅπως νημερτέα εἴπῃ
entreat him so that he shall speak (i. e. *to speak*).

Here the Clause expresses the *thing* to be tried, thought about, &c., rather than a consequence of such action.

The purpose is sometimes that of some other person, *e. g.*—

Od. 1. 205 φράσσεται ὥς κε νέηται *he will devise how he is to return* (cp. 2. 368., 14. 329).

Il. 1. 558 τῇ σ᾽ ὀΐω κατανεῦσαι ἐτήτυμον ὡς Ἀχιλῆα
τιμήσῃς, ὀλέσῃς δὲ κτλ. (*hast nodded to the effect &c.*).

Regarding κεν and ἄν observe that in Final and Object Clauses after ὡς the Subj. with κεν is the commonest, occurring 32 times, while the Subj. with ἄν and the pure Subj. occur each 8 times. After ὅπως, which has a more indefinite meaning (*in some such manner that*), the pure Subj. occurs 7 times, the Subj. with κεν twice (Od. 1. 296., 4. 545,—both Object clauses).

(3) In Conditional or limiting Clauses :—

(*a*) After a Present the Subj. is pure in the phrase ὅπως ἐθέλῃσι as *he pleases* (Od. 1. 349., 6. 189). In Il. 16. 83 πείθεο δ᾽ ὥς τοι ἐγὼ μύθου τέλος ἐν φρεσὶ θείω the pure Subj. indicates that θείω is really an unconditional expression of *will*: 'listen to me—I will tell you': cp. the independent sentences such as Il. 6. 340 ἐπίμεινον, ἀρήϊα τεύχεα δύω (§ 275, *a*).

The use of ὡς and ὥς τε in *similes* belongs to this head : e. g.—

Il. 5. 161 ὡς δὲ λέων ἐν βουσὶ θορὼν ἐξ αὐχένα ἄξῃ κτλ.

11. 67 οἱ δ᾽ ὥς τ᾽ ἀμητῆρες ἐναντίοι ἀλλήλοισιν
ὄγμον ἐλαύνωσιν κτλ.

In this use, as in the corresponding use of the Relative (§ 283), the Subj. is pure, the case supposed being not a particular one actually expected, but a typical or recurring one.

Delbrück (*Synt. Forsch.* I. p. 161) makes the curious observation that if the simile begins (as in the second instance quoted) with a Demonstrative denoting the subject of the comparison, then the Adverb used is always ὥς τε. This rule appears to be without exception.

(*b*) The Subj. with ἄν occurs in the formula ὡς ἂν ἐγὼν εἴπω πειθώμεθα, which refers to a speech about to follow.

The use of κεν in—

Il. 20. 242 Ζεὺς δ᾽ ἀρετὴν ἄνδρεσσιν ὀφέλλει τε μινύθει τε
ὅππως κεν ἐθέλῃσιν

is perhaps due to the *contrast* between opposite cases : so with ὅτε, § 289, 2, *b*.

286.] ἵνα is used in Final Clauses only. With a Subj. it usually expresses the speaker's own purpose ; even in—

Od. 2. 306 ταῦτα δέ τοι μάλα πάντα τελευτήσουσιν Ἀχαιοί,
νῆα καὶ ἐξαίτους ἐρέτας, ἵνα θᾶσσον ἵκηαι

the meaning is ' I undertake that the Achaeans will do this for you.' Exceptions (out of about 80 instances) are : Il. 1. 203 ἦ ἵνα ὕβριν ἴδῃ *is it that you may see &c.* : Il. 9. 99., 12. 435., 24. 43, Od. 8. 580., 10. 24., 13. 327.

An Object Clause with ἵνα is perhaps to be recognised in—

Od. 3. 327 λίσσεσθαι δέ μιν αὐτὸς ἵνα νημερτὲς ἐνίσπῃ

if the reading is right.   The line may be an incorrect repetition
of 3. 19.

The pure Subj. only is used with ἵνα, except in Od. 12. 156 ἵνα
εἰδότες ἤ κε θάνωμεν ἤ κεν ἀλευάμενοι θάνατον καὶ κῆρα φύγοιμεν,
where two alternatives are given by the correlative ἤ κεν—ἤ κεν :
cp. § 275, *b*.   But some MSS. have ἠὲ θάνωμεν.

As Mr. Gildersleeve points out (*Am. Jour. of Phil.* iv. 425) ἵνα is the only
purely final Particle, *i. e.* the only one which does not limit the *purpose* by the
notion of *time* (ὄφρα, ἕως) or *manner* (ὡς, ὅπως).   Hence Clauses with ἵνα do not
take κεν or ἄν, because the purpose as such is unconditional.

287.] ὄφρα is sometimes Final, sometimes Conditional.

(1) In Final Clauses ὄφρα either retains a distinctly *temporal*
force—meaning *so long till, till the time when,*—or passes into the
general meaning *to the end that.*   Thus we have—

(*a*) ὄφρα = *until* (*as shall be*), used with κεν or ἄν, as—

> Il. 1. 509 τόφρα δ' ἐπὶ Τρώεσσι τίθει κράτος, ὄφρ' ἂν Ἀχαιοὶ
> υἱὸν ἐμὸν τίσωσιν, ὀφέλλωσίν τέ ἑ τιμῇ.

> 22. 192 ἀνιχνεύων θέει ἔμπεδον, ὄφρα κεν εὕρῃ.

With this meaning the pure Subj. is found in Il. 1. 82 ἔχει κότον
ὄφρα τελέσσῃ *he keeps his anger until he accomplishes it*—a general
reflexion : also in Il. 12. 281 (in a simile).

(*b*) ὄφρα = *to the end that,* used with the pure Subj., rarely with
κεν or ἄν.   The transition to this meaning may be seen in—

> Il. 6. 258 ἀλλὰ μέν', ὄφρα κέ τοι μελιηδέα οἶνον ἐνείκω
> *stay till I bring* (=*giving me time to bring*).

(2) Clauses with ὄφρα may be classed as Conditional when it
means *so long as* ; *e. g.*—

> Il. 4. 345 ἔνθα φίλ' ὀπταλέα κρέα ἔδμεναι .. ὄφρ' ἐθέλητον.

> Od. 2. 123 τόφρα γὰρ οὖν βίοτόν τε τεὸν καὶ κτήματ' ἔδονται,
> ὄφρα κε κείνη τοῦτον ἔχῃ νόον.

The use of κεν or ἄν in these Clauses is governed by the same
rule as with ὅς, viz. it is used when the reference is to the future,
and is not expressly meant to be general (as Il. 23. 47 ὄφρα
ζωοῖσι μετείω).   As to the form ὄφρ' ἂν μέν κεν, see § 363, 4.

In Il. 6. 112 ἀνέρες ἔστε, φίλοι, μνήσασθε δὲ θούριδος ἀλκῆς,
ὄφρ' ἂν ἐγὼ βήω (cp. 8. 375., 17. 186, Od. 13. 412., 19. 17) the
Clause seems to mean *until I go,* i. e. *long enough for me to go.*
Delbrück however counts the uses of ὄφρα in Il. 6. 112, &c. as
Conditional (*Synt. Forsch.* i. p. 170).

288.] ἕως (ἧος) and εἰς ὅ, used with the Subj., always take κεν.
The meaning *until,* with implied purpose, is the usual one : as—

Il. 3. 290 αὐτὰρ ἐγὼ καὶ ἔπειτα μαχήσομαι εἵνεκα κούρης
         αὖθι μένων, ἦός κε τέλος πολέμοιο κιχείω.
9. 48 νῶϊ δ' ἐγὼ Σθένελός τε μαχησόμεθ' εἰς ὅ κε τέκμωρ
      Ἰλίου εὕρωμεν.

The Conditional meaning is only found in the recurring expression εἰς ὅ κ' αὐτμὴ ἐν στήθεσσι μένῃ καί μοι φίλα γούνατ' ὀρώρῃ (Il. 9. 609., 10. 89)=*so long as I have life.*

289.] ὅτε, ὁπότε :

(1) Clauses with ὅτε and ὁπότε may be counted as Final in a few instances in which the governing Clause contains an expression of *time :*

(*a*) with the pure Subj.—

Il. 21. 111 ἔσσεται ἢ ἠὼς ἢ δείλη ἢ μέσον ἦμαρ,
            ὁππότε τις καὶ ἐμεῖο Ἄρει ἐκ θυμὸν ἔληται.

So Il. 19. 336 ἐμὴν ποτιδέγμενον αἰεὶ λυγρὴν ἀγγελίην, ὅτ' ἀποφθι-μένοιο πύθηται *waiting for the message when he shall hear &c.*, i. e. 'waiting for the time when the news shall come that &c.' Here the clause with ὅτε becomes a kind of Object Clause.

(*b*) with κεν or ἄν :—

Il. 4. 164 ἔσσεται ἦμαρ ὅτ' ἄν ποτ' ὀλώλῃ κτλ. (6. 448).
The use of ἄν gives definiteness to the expectation, as though a particular time were contemplated. Cp. also Il. 6. 454 ὅσσον σεῦ (μέλει), ὅτε κέν τις . . δακρυόεσσαν ἄγηται *as I am concerned for you (in respect of the time) when &c.*, and 8. 373 ἔσται μὰν ὅτ' ἄν κτλ.

It is obvious that in these places the Clause is not strictly Final, since the Subj. expresses *emphatic prediction* (§ 275, *b*) rather than purpose. But they have the essential characteristic of Final Clauses, viz. that the time of the Clause is fixed by that of the governing Verb.

(2) Clauses with ὅτε or ὁπότε which define the time of the principal Clause may be regarded as Conditional. In regard to the use of κεν and ἄν they follow the rules which hold in the case of Conditional Relative Clauses (§ 283) : viz.—

(*a*) The pure Subj. indicates that the speaker is supposing a case which may occur *repeatedly*, or *at any time*: as—

Od. 7. 71   οἵ μίν ῥα θεὸν ὡς εἰσορόωντες
         δειδέχαται μύθοισιν, ὅτε στείχησ' ἀνὰ ἄστυ
who look on him as a god, and salute him when he walks &c.

Il. 1. 163 οὐ μὲν σοί ποτε ἶσον ἔχω γέρας, ὁππότ' Ἀχαιοὶ
         Τρώων ἐκπέρσωσ' εὖ ναιόμενον πτολίεθρον
whenever the Greeks sack a Trojan town. So in maxims, &c. :—

Il. 1. 80 κρείσσων γὰρ βασιλεὺς ὅτε χώσεται ἀνδρὶ χέρηϊ.

Il. 15. 207 ἐσθλὸν καὶ τὸ τέτυκται ὅτ' ἄγγελος αἴσιμα εἰδῇ.
And in similes, as Il. 2. 395 ὅτε κινήσῃ Νότος ἐλθών. So with the
regular ὡς ὅτε *as when,* ὡς ὁπότε *as in any case when.*

In a few instances ὡς δ' ὅτ' ἄν is found instead of ὡς δ' ὅτε : viz.—

    Il. 15. 170 ὡς δ' ὅτ' ἄν ἐκ νεφέων πτῆται κτλ.
        19. 375 ὡς δ' ὅτ' ἄν ἐκ πόντοιο σέλας ναύτῃσι φανήῃ
    Od. 5. 394 ὡς δ' ὅτ' ἄν ἀσπάσιος βίοτος παίδεσσι φανήῃ
        23. 233 ὡς δ' ὅτ' ἄν ἀσπάσιος γῆ νηχομένοισι φανήῃ
    Il. 11. 269 ὡς δ' ὅτ' ἄν ὠδίνουσαν ἔχῃ βέλος ὀξὺ γυναῖκα
        17. 520 ὡς δ' ὅτ' ἄν ὀξὺν ἔχων πέλεκυν κτλ.

Also Il. 10. 5., 24. 480, Od. 22. 468. The resemblance that runs through these
instances would seem to indicate some common source of the peculiar ἄν.

In the one or two places where the pure Subj. occurs after a
Future there is an evident intention to speak quite generally : as
Il. 21. 322 οὐδέ τί μιν χρεὼ ἔσται τυμβοχόης ὅτε μιν θάπτωσιν
Ἀχαιοί: so Od. 16. 268., 23. 257. But κεν is used in the similar
passage Il. 10. 130 οὔ τις νεμεσήσεται . . ὅτε κέν τιν' ἐποτρύνῃ.

(*b*) κεν or ἄν connects a supposition with a *particular* event or
state of things : hence it is usually found after a Future,
Subjunctive, or Imperative, as—

    Il. 4. 53 τὰς διαπέρσαι ὅτ' ἄν τοι ἀπέχθωνται.
    Od. 1. 40 ἐκ γὰρ Ὀρέσταο τίσις ἔσσεται Ἀτρεΐδαο
        ὁππότ' ἄν ἡβήσῃ τε καὶ ἧς ἱμείρεται αἴης.
    Il. 20. 130 δείσετ' ἔπειθ', ὅτε κέν τις κτλ.
    Od. 2. 357 ἑσπέριος γὰρ ἐγὼν αἱρήσομαι ὁππότε κεν δὴ κτλ.
So after μοῖρα (Od. 4. 475), followed by an Inf.

In other places it is not so clear why an event is treated as
particular. Perhaps κεν or ἄν may be used with ὅτε, ὁπότε—

    (1) When a *contrast* is made between supposed cases, as—

    Il. 6. 224 τῷ νῦν σοὶ μὲν ἐγὼ ξεῖνος φίλος Ἄργεϊ μέσσῳ
        εἰμί, σὺ δ' ἐν Λυκίῃ, ὅτε κεν τῶν δῆμον ἵκωμαι.
        20. 166 πρῶτον μὲν . . ἀλλ' ὅτε κέν τις κτλ.
    Od. 20. 83 ἀλλὰ τὸ μὲν καὶ ἀνεκτὸν ἔχει κακόν, ὁππότε κέν τις
        κτλ.
        11. 17 οὔθ' ὁπότ' ἄν στείχῃσι . . οὔθ' ὅτ' ἄν ἄψ κτλ.
        (Here we should read ὁπότε στείχῃσι, § 363, 4).

So perhaps Il. 2. 397 παντοίων ἀνέμων, ὅτ' ἄν ἔνθ' ἢ ἔνθα γένωνται :
9. 101 κρηῆναι δὲ καὶ ἄλλῳ, ὅτ' ἄν τινα κτλ. and Od. 13. 100 ἔν-
τοσθεν δέ τ' ἄνευ δεσμοῖο μένουσι νῆες ἐΰσσελμοι, ὅτ' ἄν ὅρμου
μέτρον ἵκωνται (in contrast to those outside). But cp. the remark
as to ὅτ' ἄν in the last note.

    (2) When there is a change from Plural to Singular :—

    Il. 9. 501 λισσόμενοι, ὅτε κέν τις ὑπερβήῃ καὶ ἁμάρτῃ.

Od. 11. 218 ἀλλ' αὕτη δίκη ἐστὶ βροτῶν, ὅτε τίς κε θάνῃσι.
This last instance is doubtful, since the order ὅτε τίς κε is not
Homeric (§ 365). We should probably read ὅτε τίς τε.

290.] εὖτε, ἦμος. The word εὖτε is only once found with a
pure Subj., viz. Od. 7. 202 (in a general assertion): εὖτ' ἄν occurs
after a Future (Il. 1. 242., 19. 158), and an Imperative (Il. 2. 34);
also in one or two places where the use of ἄν is more difficult to
explain, viz. Il. 2. 227 (read εὖτε πτολίεθρον ἕλωμεν), Od. 1. 192.,
17. 320, 323., 18. 194. The combination εὖτε κέν is not found.
The pure Subj. with ἦμος occurs in one place—

　Od. 4. 400 ἦμος δ' ἠέλιος μέσον οὐρανὸν ἀμφιβεβήκῃ

where the reference is general, 'each midday.'

The Subjunctive with εἰ, *&c.*

291.] Clauses with εἰ. The use of the Particle εἰ (or αἴ), in
the Clauses with which we have now to do, is to make an *assumption* or *supposition*. In most cases (1) this assumption is made
in order to assert a consequence (εἰ = *if*) : in other words, it is a
condition. But (2) an assumption may also be made in order to
express *end* : εἶμι .. αἴ κε πίθηται *I go—suppose he shall listen* =
'I go in order that if he will listen (he may do so) : ' accordingly
the Clause may be virtually a Final Clause. Again (3) with
certain Verbs an assumption may be the Object : *e. g.* τίς οἶδ' εἴ
κεν .. ὀρίνω *who knows—suppose I shall rouse* = who knows whether
I shall rouse. We shall take these three groups of Clauses in
order.

292.] Conditional Protasis with εἰ. The chief point of interest under this head is the use of κεν or ἄν. The rules will be
found to be essentially the same as those already laid down for
the corresponding Clauses with the Relative (§ 283, *b*) and the
Relatival Adverbs (see esp. § 289, *b*), and to be even more uniform in their application.

(*a*) The pure Subj. is used in general sayings, and in similes :

　Il. 1. 80 κρείσσων γὰρ βασιλεὺς ὅτε χώσεται ἀνδρὶ χέρηϊ·
　　　　εἴ περ γάρ τε χόλον γε καὶ αὐτῆμαρ καταπέψῃ,
　　　　ἀλλά τε καὶ μετόπισθεν ἔχει κότον.

　12. 238　　　τῶν οὔ τι μετατρέπομ' οὐδ' ἀλεγίζω,
　　　　εἴ τ' ἐπὶ δεξί' ἴωσι πρὸς ἠῶ τ' ἠέλιόν τε,
　　　　εἴ τ' ἐπ' ἀριστερὰ τοί γε κτλ.

　Od. 16. 97　　　κασιγνήτοις .. οἷσί περ ἀνὴρ
　　　　μαρναμένοισι πέποιθε καὶ εἰ μέγα νεῖκος ὄρηται.

Il. 11. 116 ἢ δ' εἴ πέρ τε τύχῃσι κτλ. (so Il. 4. 261., 9. 481.,
10. 225., 16. 263., 21. 576., 22. 191, Od. 1. 188.,
7. 204., 12. 96., 14. 373.

If the principal Verb is a Future (or implies reference to the
future), the pure Subj. with εἰ indicates that the supposed occasion is *indefinite*,—one that happens repeatedly, or at any time,
or may not happen at all; so Il. 1. 340 εἴ ποτε δὴ αὖτε χρειὼ ἐμεῖο
γένηται κτλ.; 12. 245 εἴ πέρ γάρ τ' ἄλλοι γε περικτεινώμεθα πάντες
κτλ.; Od. 1. 204 οὐδ' εἴ πέρ τε σιδήρεα δέσματ' ἔχῃσι. This form
is naturally employed by a speaker who does not wish to imply
that the occasion will actually arise: thus in—

Il. 12. 223 ὡς ἡμεῖς εἴ πέρ τε πύλας καὶ τεῖχος Ἀχαιῶν
ῥηξόμεθα σθένεϊ μεγάλῳ, εἴξωσι δ' Ἀχαιοί,
οὐ κόσμῳ παρὰ ναῦφιν ἐλευσόμεθ' αὐτὰ κέλευθα

Polydamas is interpreting an omen which he wishes to remain
unfulfilled. Similarly Il. 5. 248 εἴ γ' οὖν ἕτερός γε φύγῃσι: Il. 22.
86 εἴ πέρ γάρ σε κατακτάνῃ, οὔ σ' ἔτ' ἔγωγε κλαύσομαι ἐν λεχέεσσι:
Od. 5. 221 εἰ δ' αὖ τις ῥαίῃσι θεῶν κτλ.: Od. 12. 348 εἰ δὲ χολω-
σάμενός τι . . νῆ' ἐθέλῃ ὀλέσαι κτλ. The object of the speaker in
these examples is to treat the supposed case as imaginary or un-
practical.

(*b*) The Subj. with κεν or ἄν indicates that a particular future
occasion is contemplated: hence—

Il. 4. 353 ὄψεαι ἢν ἐθέλῃσθα καὶ αἴ κέν τοι τὰ μεμήλῃ.

11. 404 μέγα μὲν κακὸν (sc. ἔσται) αἴ κε φέβωμαι.

24. 592 μή μοι . . σκυδμαινέμεν, αἴ κε πύθηαι κτλ.

Od. 2. 218 εἰ μέν κεν πατρὸς βίοτον καὶ νόστον ἀκούσω,
ἦ τ' ἂν τρυχόμενός περ ἔτι τλαίην ἐνιαυτόν.

11. 112 εἰ δέ κε σίνηαι, τότε τοι τεκμαίρομ' ὄλεθρον
(*I prophesy your destruction*).

So, though the Verb of the governing Clause is a Present—

Il. 6. 442 αἰδέομαι Τρῶας καὶ Τρωάδας ἑλκεσιπέπλους,
αἴ κε κτλ. (=*I fear what they will think if &c.*).

8. 477 σέθεν δ' ἐγὼ οὐκ ἀλεγίζω
χωομένης, οὐδ' εἴ κε τὰ νείατα πείραθ' ἵκηαι
=*I do not care for you, (and shall not) even if &c.*

Instances of κεν or ἄν in a sentence of *general* meaning are—

Il. 3. 25 μάλα γάρ τε κατεσθίει, εἴ περ ἂν αὐτὸν
σεύωνται κτλ. (*even in the case when—*, § 363, 1, *b*).

11. 391 ἦ τ' ἄλλως ὑπ' ἐμεῖο, καὶ εἴ κ' ὀλίγον περ ἐπαύρῃ,
ὀξὺ βέλος πέλεται.

12. 302 εἴ περ γάρ χ' εὕρῃσι παρ' αὐτόφι κτλ.

Od. 11. 158   τὸν οὔ πως ἔστι περῆσαι
       πεζὸν ἐόντ', ἣν μή τις ἔχῃ εὐεργέα νῆα.

But with εἴ κε there is the same doubt as with ὅς κε (§ 283), and ἐπεί κε (§ 296). As to ἤν, which occurs in a general saying in Il. 1. 166 and Od. 11. 159, see § 362.

293.] Final Clauses with εἰ. After a principal Verb expressive of the speaker's *will* (an Imperative, or First Person), a Final Clause may be introduced by εἴ κεν or ἤν : as—

Il. 8. 282 βάλλ' οὕτως εἴ κέν τι φόως Δαναοῖσι γένηαι.

   11. 791 ταῦτ' εἴποις Ἀχιλῆϊ δαΐφρονι εἴ κε πίθηται.

Od. 4. 34 δεῦρ' ἱκόμεθ' αἴ κέ ποθι Ζεὺς . . παύσῃ κτλ.

The effect of using εἰ (instead of ὡς or ἵνα) is to express some degree of uncertainty. The end aimed at is represented as a *supposition*, instead of being a direct *purpose*.

In the existing text the pure Subj. occurs only in Il. 14. 165 ἀρίστη φαίνετο βουλὴ ἐλθεῖν . . εἴ πως ἱμείραιτο . . τῷ δ' . . χεύῃ (where we should perhaps read χεύαι ; or change χεύῃ ἐπὶ to χεύειε); and in Od. 5. 471 εἰ δέ κεν . . καταδράθω, εἴ με μεθήῃ ῥῖγος καὶ κάματος, γλυκερὸς δέ μοι ὕπνος ἐπέλθῃ, where the MSS. have the Opt. μεθείη, ἐπέλθοι. But if ἤν has sometimes crept in instead of εἰ, as is probable (§ 362) there may be other examples : as—

Il. 22. 418 λίσσωμ' ἀνέρα τοῦτον . . ἤν πως κτλ.

Od. 1. 281 ἔρχεο πευσόμενος πατρὸς δὴν οἰχομένοιο,
       ἤν τίς τοι εἴπῃσι κτλ.

294.] Object Clauses with εἰ. This term will serve to describe the form of Clause in which the supposition made by εἰ takes the place of an Acc. of the thing. It may be regarded as a special form of the Final Clause (cp. § 285, 2): thus Il. 18. 600 ὡς ὅτε τις τροχὸν . . πειρήσεται εἴ κε θέῃσι 'tries in respect to the supposition that it will run,' hence *tries whether it will run:* so—

Il. 4. 249 ὄφρα ἴδητ' εἴ κ' ὔμμιν ὑπερσχῇ χεῖρα Κρονίων.

   15. 32 ὄφρα ἴδῃ ἤν τοι χραίσμῃ κτλ.

that you may see whether it will avail. Note that the Subj. here has a distinctly *future* meaning, as in Final Clauses; the same words taken as a Conditional Protasis would mean *if it has availed.* So after εἰπεῖν, Il. 7. 375 καὶ δὲ τόδ' [leg. τὸ] εἰπέμεναι πυκινὸν ἔπος, αἴ κ' ἐθέλωσι *say the word supposing that they shall be willing* (=ask if they will agree), Il. 17. 692 εἰπεῖν, αἴ κε τάχιστα νέκυν ἐπὶ νῆα σαώσῃ : and οἶδα in the phrase τίς οἶδ' εἴ κεν *who knows but* (Il. 15. 403., 16. 860, Od. 2. 332), and οὐ μὰν οἶδ' εἰ (Il. 15. 16).

The use of the *Accusativus de quo* (§ 140, 3) should be noticed; especially after οἶδα, anticipating the Clause with εἰ: as—

Il. 8. 535 αὔριον ἦν ἀρετὴν διαείσεται εἴ κ' ἐμὸν ἔγχος
　　　　μείνῃ ἐπερχόμενον

meaning 'he will know as to his prowess whether it will enable him to withstand my spear.' So Od. 22. 6 σκοπὸν ἄλλον . . εἴσομαι αἴ κε τύχωμι (cp. § 140, 3, *b*).

In one place the Clause with εἰ serves as explanation of a Neuter Pronoun in the *Nominative*:

Il. 20. 435 ἀλλ' ἦ τοι μὲν ταῦτα θεῶν ἐν γούνασι κεῖται,
　　　　εἴ κέ σε χειρότερός περ ἐὼν ἀπὸ θυμὸν ἕλωμαι.

295.] The Subj. with ὡς εἰ occurs in a single place only, viz.—

Il. 9. 481 καί με φίλησ' ὡς εἴ τε πατὴρ ὃν παῖδα φιλήσῃ.

Here the assumption εἰ . . φιλήσῃ is made for the purpose of comparison. Thus the meaning is nearly the same as with ὡς ὅτε (§ 289, 2), and the Clause is essentially Conditional.

296.] ἐπεί with the Subj. The use of ἐπεί implies that the action is prior in time to the action of the principal Clause; hence Clauses with ἐπεί properly fall under the definition of the Conditional Clause.

A pure Subj. after ἐπεί is found in four places, one a gnomic passage, Od. 20. 86 ἐπεὶ ἂρ βλέφαρ' ἀμφικαλύψῃ (*sleep makes men forget everything*) *when it has spread over their eyelids;* the other three in similes, viz. Il. 11. 478., 15. 363, 680. In Il. 16. 453 the best MSS. give αὐτὰρ ἐπεὶ δὴ τόν γε λίπῃ ψυχή τε καὶ αἰών, πέμπειν μιν κτλ., others ἐπὴν δή. The pure Subj. implies that the command is meant to be *general* in form: cp. § 292, *a.*

κεν or ἄν is invariably used when the principal Verb is future. It is also found after a Present, and even in similes: *e.g.*—

Il. 2. 474 τοὺς δ' ὥς τ' αἰπόλια πλατέ' αἰγῶν αἰπόλοι ἄνδρες
　　　　ῥεῖα διακρίνωσιν, ἐπεί κε νομῷ μιγέωσιν.

So ἐπεί κε(ν), Il. 7. 410., 9. 324., 21. 575, Od. 8. 554., 11. 221., 24. 7: and ἐπήν, Il. 6. 489., 19. 223, Od. 8. 553., 10. 411., 11. 192., 14. 130., 19. 206, 515. In Il. 1. 168 should perhaps be read ἐπεὶ κεκάμω (instead of ἐπεί κε κάμω), and so Il. 7. 5 ἐπεὶ κεκάμωσι, and Il. 17. 657 ἐπεὶ ἂρ κεκάμῃσι.

Regarding ἐπεί κε(ν) in this use there is the same question as with ὅς κε (§ 283). Out of 10 instances there is only one in which the form κεν appears, viz. Il. 21. 575 ἐπεί κεν ὑλαγμὸν ἀκούσῃ, and there Zenodotus read κυννλαγμὸν, which is strongly supported by the metre (§ 367, 2). Thus there is the same reason as before for supposing that κε is often merely a corruption of τε. The use of ἐπεί τε is sufficiently established in Homer (§ 332).

The form ἐπήν is open to doubt on other grounds, which it will be better to discuss in connexion with other uses of the Particle ἄν (§ 362).

297.] πρίν with the Subj. In general, as we have seen (§ 236), πρίν is construed with an Infinitive. If, however, the event is insisted upon as a *condition*,—the principal Verb being an Imperative or emphatic Future,—the Subj. may be used ; as—

Il. 18. 134 ἀλλὰ σὺ μὲν μή πω καταδύσεο μῶλον ˝Αρηος
    πρίν γ᾽ ἐμὲ δεῦρ᾽ ἐλθοῦσαν ἐν ὀφθαλμοῖσιν ἴδηαι

do not enter the battle before you see me coming hither.

Od. 10. 174 ὦ φίλοι, οὐ γὰρ πρὶν καταδυσόμεθ᾽ ἀχνύμενοί περ
    εἰς ᾽Αΐδαο δόμους πρὶν μόρσιμον ἦμαρ ἐπέλθῃ.

So Il. 18. 190., 24. 551, 781, Od. 13. 336., 17. 9. The Subj. is used in these examples without κεν or ἄν, because it is not meant to lay stress on a particular occasion when the condition will be fulfilled. When such an occasion is contemplated Homer sometimes uses πρίν γ᾽ ὅτ᾽ ἄν *before the time when* (Od. 2. 374., 4. 477): cp. Il. 16. 62 οὐ πρὶν μηνιθμὸν καταπαυσέμεν, ἀλλ᾽ ὁπότ᾽ ἂν κτλ. The use of πρὶν ἄν with the Subj. is post-Homeric.

It is evident that a conditional Clause of this kind can only occur after a *negative* principal Clause. ‘ Do not do this before I come ’ makes my coming into a condition, and a condition which may or may not be realised : but ‘ do this before I come ’ is merely a way of fixing the time of doing.

This construction is usually explained from Parataxis : thus it is held that in Il. 24. 551 οὐδέ μιν ἀνστήσεις πρὶν καὶ κακὸν ἄλλο πάθῃσθα stands for—

    οὐδέ μιν ἀνστήσεις· πρὶν καὶ κακὸν ἄλλο πάθῃσθα,

you will not raise him, sooner shall you suffer passing into ‘you will not raise him *before* you suffer.’ So Sturm (p. 26), and Goodwin (§ 624). But (1) this use of the Subj. in a Principal clause without κεν or ἄν, whether as a Future (§ 275, *b*) or as an Imperative, is not Homeric, and therefore cannot be used to explain a use which is only beginning in Homer. And (2) the change from *you will not raise, you will suffer before you do* to *you will not raise before you suffer* is not an easy one : it involves shifting πρίν as an Adverb from one clause to another. Above all (3) it is probable that the new construction of πρίν with the Subj. was directly modelled on the existing use with the Inf. : that is to say, πρὶν πάθῃσθα simply took the place of πρὶν παθεῖν when a more definite *conditional* force was wanted. This is confirmed by the analogy of the later change into the Indic. : thus in Aesch. P. V. 479 πρίν γ᾽ ἐγώ σφισιν ἔδειξα is used instead of πρὶν ἐμὲ δεῖξαι because the poet wishes to make the *assertion* ἔδειξα. So with the transition from the Inf. to the Indic. after ὥστε (Goodwin, § 585): the finite mood is not a survival of parataxis, but is used when the Infinitive is not sufficiently positive.

298.] **Subjunctive after a Secondary Tense.** The rule in Homer is that the Subj. is not used in a Subordinate Clause to express a *past* purpose, condition, &c. It may be used however (1) when the governing Verb is a ' gnomic ' Aorist :—

Il. 1. 218 ὅς κε θεοῖς ἐπιπείθηται μάλα τ᾽ ἔκλυον αὐτοῦ.

Od. 20. 85   ὁ γάρ τ᾽ ἐπέλησεν ἁπάντων
ἐσθλῶν ἠδὲ κακῶν, ἐπεὶ ἄρ βλέφαρ᾽ ἀμφικαλύψῃ.

Or an Aor. used to express a *general* denial, as—

Od. 10. 327 οὐδὲ γὰρ οὐδέ τις ἄλλος ἀνὴρ τάδε φάρμακ᾽ ἀνέτλη,
ὅς κε πίῃ κτλ. (cp. Od. 12. 66).

Or in a simile, as Il. 4. 486 ἐξέταμ᾽, ὄφρα ἴτυν κάμψῃ κτλ.

Further (2) if the action expressed by the Subordinate Clause is still future at the time of speaking ; as—

Il. 5. 127 ἀχλὺν δ᾽ αὖ τοι ἀπ᾽ ὀφθαλμῶν ἕλον ἣ πρὶν ἐπῆεν,
ὄφρ᾽ εὖ γιγνώσκῃς ἠμὲν θεὸν ἠδὲ καὶ ἄνδρα
I have taken away the mist—that you may know &c.

7. 394 καὶ δὲ τόδ᾽ ἠνώγει εἰπεῖν ἔπος, αἴ κ᾽ ἐθέλητε κτλ.

18. 189 μήτηρ δ᾽ οὔ με φίλη πρίν γ᾽ εἴα θωρήσσεσθαι
πρίν γ᾽ αὐτὴν . . ἴδωμαι (*before I shall see her &c.*).

Od. 11. 434 οἵ τε κατ᾽ αἶσχος ἔχευε καὶ ἐσσομένῃσιν ὀπίσσω
θηλυτέρῃσι γυναιξί, καὶ ἥ κ᾽ εὐεργὸς ἔῃσι.

So Il. 9. 99., 20. 126., 24. 781. In these places the governing Verb is generally to be translated by the English Perfect with *have* (cp. § 73).

The real exceptions to this rule are not numerous, and may be due in several cases to alteration of the text through the influence of the later usage. The reading is uncertain (*e. g.*) in—

Od. 14. 327 τὸν δ᾽ ἐς Δωδώνην φάτο βήμεναι ὄφρα θεοῖο
(= 19. 296) ἐκ δρυὸς ὑψικόμοιο Διὸς βουλὴν ἐπακούσῃ,

where the Subj. was read by Aristarchus, the Opt. ἐπακοῦσαι by Aristophanes and Herodian. Again in—

Od. 10. 65 ἦ μέν σ᾽ ἐνδυκέως ἀπεπέμπομεν, ὄφρ᾽ ἂν ἵκηαι

the best MSS. have ἵκηαι, but others have ὄφρ᾽ ἂν ἵκοιο and ὄφρ᾽ ἀφίκοιο. See also Il. 15. 23, Od. 15. 300., 22. 98 : and cp.—

Il. 5. 567 μή τι πάθοι, μέγα δέ σφας ἀποσφήλειε

15. 598 ἐμβάλοι . . Θέτιδος δ᾽ ἐξαίσιον ἀρὴν
πᾶσαν ἐπικρήνειε.

In these places the MSS. generally have πάθῃ, ἐμβάλῃ : but the Opt. in the clause following has led the editors to adopt πάθοι, ἐμβάλοι.

Other places where the Subj. is contrary to the rule now laid down are Il. 13. 649., 14. 165., 16. 650 (see La R.)., 19. 354., 24. 586, Od. 9. 102., 10. 24., 16. 369., 17. 60., 22. 467. In all

the Opt. may be substituted without affecting the metre ; and
when we consider the number of places where the MSS. vary
between Subj. and Opt. forms, we can hardly doubt that it would
generally be right to make the change.

The Homeric rule is observed by Plato (see Riddell, *Dig.* §§
90, 91), but not by Attic writers in general.

The Optative in Simple Sentences.

299.] The uses of the Optative in Simple Sentences range
from the expression of a wish on the part of the speaker to the
expression of mere supposition, or admission of possibility.

Without κεν or ἄν the Optative may express—

(*a*) Simple *wish* or *prayer:* as—

Il. 1. 42 τίσειαν Δαναοὶ ἐμὰ δάκρυα σοῖσι βέλεσσι.

Od. 1. 403 μὴ γὰρ ὅ γ' ἔλθοι κτλ. *never may he come &c.*

Regarding the Opt. of wish with εἰ or αἰ, εἴθε, αἴθε, &c. see § 311.

(*b*) A gentle or deferential Imperative, conveying *advice, suggestion*, or the like : as—

Il. 4. 17 εἰ δ' αὖ πως τόδε πᾶσι φίλον καὶ ἡδὺ γένοιτο,
          ἦ τοι μὲν οἰκέοιτο πόλις Πριάμοιο κτλ.
          (=*I presume the city is to remain inhabited*).

Od. 4. 735 ἀλλά τις ὀτρηρῶς Δολίον καλέσειε γέροντα
          (as we say, *would some one call &c.*).

18. 141 τῷ μή τίς ποτε πάμπαν ἀνὴρ ἀθεμίστιος εἴη,
          ἀλλ' ὅ γε σιγῇ δῶρα θεῶν ἔχοι
          I would have a man not be lawless, but &c.

Note especially this use of the Second Person, as in—

Od. 4. 193 πίθοιό μοι *pray listen to me :* so in the formal
          phrase ἦ ῥά νύ μοί τι πίθοιο (Il. 4. 93, &c.).

Il. 11. 791 ταῦτ' εἴποις Ἀχιλῆϊ *suppose you say this to Achilles.*

Od. 15. 24 ἀλλὰ σύ γ' ἐλθὼν αὐτὸς ἐπιτρέψειας ἕκαστα.

Il. 3. 406 ἧσο παρ' αὐτὸν ἰοῦσα, θεῶν δ' ἀπόεικε κελεύθου,
          μηδ' ἔτι σοῖσι πόδεσσιν ὑποστρέψειας Ὄλυμπον.

Hence in Il. 1. 20 we should read (with the best MSS.) παῖδα
δ' ἐμοὶ λύσαιτε (not λῦσαί τε, Wolf's conjecture).

(*c*) Rhetorical wish, implying *willingness*, or *indifference* to the
happening of some evil : as in imprecations—

Il. 2. 340 ἐν πυρὶ δὴ βουλαί τε γενοίατο μήδεα δ' ἀνδρῶν.

6. 164 τεθναίης, ὦ Προῖτ', ἢ κάκτανε Βελλεροφόντην
          (=*I care not if you were dead, unless you &c.*).

Od. 7. 224 ἰδόντα με καὶ λίποι αἰὼν κτῆσιν ἐμὴν κτλ.
          (=*I am content to die when I have seen &c.*).

(*d*) *Concession* or acquiescence:—

Il. 21. 359 λῆγ' ἔριδος, Τρῶας δὲ καὶ αὐτίκα δῖος Ἀχιλλεὺς
　　ἄστεος ἐξελάσειε (*cease strife, and I consent that &c.*).

Od. 1. 402 κτήματα δ' αὐτὸς ἔχοις καὶ δώμασι σοῖσιν ἀνάσσοις.

　2. 232 ἀλλ' αἰεὶ χαλεπός τ' εἴη καὶ αἴσυλα ῥέζοι
　　　(i. e. *he may as well be unjust as just*).

Hes. Op. 270 νῦν δὴ ἐγὼ μήτ' αὐτὸς ἐν ἀνθρώποισι δίκαιος
　　εἴην μήτ' ἐμὸς υἱός.

The following are instances of the First Person used in this way:

Il. 15. 45 αὐτάρ τοι καὶ κείνῳ ἐγὼ παραμυθησαίμην
　　　I am willing to advise him (a concession).

So Il. 4. 318 μάλα μέν τοι ἐγὼν ἐθέλοιμι κτλ., but some MSS.
have μέν κεν.

Il. 23. 150 νῦν δ' ἐπεὶ οὐ νέομαί γε φίλην ἐς πατρίδα γαῖαν,
　　Πατρόκλῳ ἥρωι κόμην ὀπάσαιμι φέρεσθαι
　　　since I am not to return, I may as well &c.

Od. 16. 383 ἀλλὰ φθέωμεν ἑλόντες ἐπ' ἀγροῦ νόσφι πόληος
　　ἢ ἐν ὁδῷ, βίοτον δ' αὐτοὶ καὶ κτήματ' ἔχωμεν
　　δασσάμενοι κατὰ μοῖραν ἐφ' ἡμέας, οἰκία δ' αὖτε
　　κείνου μητέρι δοῖμεν ἔχειν ἠδ' ὅς τις ὀπυίοι.

Here what the Suitors are to do for themselves is put in the
Subj., what they do or allow to be done for Penelope in the Opt.

Compare Hdt. 7. 5. 4 τὸ μὲν νῦν ταῦτα πρήσσοις τά περ ἐν χερσὶ ἔχεις, ἡμερώσας
δὲ Αἴγυπτον τὴν ἐξυβρίσασαν στρατηλάτεε ἐπὶ τὰς Ἀθήνας, i. e. ' I *consent* to your
doing what you have in hand, but when it is done, march against Athens.'

(*e*) Strong *denial* is sometimes implied, under the form of *de-
precation*, by the Opt. with μή : as—

Od. 7. 316 μὴ τοῦτο φίλον Διὶ πατρὶ γένοιτο *let us not admit
　　　that this is the will of father Zeus.*

　22. 462 μὴ μὲν δὴ καθαρῷ θανάτῳ ἀπὸ θυμὸν ἑλοίμην.

(*f*) *Admission of possibility*, i.e. willingness to *suppose* or
believe that the thing will happen. This use is rarely found
without κεν or ἄν : an instance is—

Od. 3. 231 ῥεῖα θεός γ' ἐθέλων καὶ τηλόθεν ἄνδρα σαώσαι.

This is said as a concession : ' we men must allow that a god can
save even from afar.' So perhaps Il. 10. 247, 557 : also—

Il. 15. 197 θυγατέρεσσιν γάρ τε καὶ υἱάσι βέλτερον εἴη κτλ.

Here the Opt. is in contrast to the preceding Imper. μή τί με
δειδισσέσθω : ' let him not threaten me : for his own children it
may be well enough that he should scold.' Other instances are
negative, viz.—

Il. 19. 321 οὐ μὲν γάρ τι κακώτερον ἄλλο πάθοιμι.

Od. 14. 122 ὦ γέρον, οὔ τις κεῖνον ἀνὴρ ἀλαλήμενος ἐλθὼν
                ἀγγέλλων πείσειε γυναῖκά τε καὶ φίλον υἱόν.
So in the Relative clauses, Il. 5. 303 (= 20. 286) ὃ οὐ δύο γ᾽
ἄνδρε φέροιεν, Od. 3. 319 ὅθεν οὐκ ἔλποιτό γε θυμῷ ἐλθέμεν. And
in one or two *interrogative* clauses, with implied negation : Il.
11. 838 πῶς τ᾽ ἄρ᾽ ἔοι τάδε ἔργα ; Od. 5. 100 τίς δ᾽ ἂν ἑκὼν διαδράμοι (since we should probably read τίς δὲ Ϝεκὼν). In such
case the absence of κεν or ἄν marks the negation as sweeping
and unconditional. We should compare the corresponding
Homeric use of οὐ with the pure Subj., which differs in the
degree of confidence expressed : οὐδὲ ἴδωμαι *I am sure I shall
never see*, οὐ πάθοιμι *I suppose I shall never suffer*.

300.] With κεν or ἄν the Optative does not express *wish* (which
is essentially unconditional), or even direct *willingness* on the part
of the speaker, but only *willingness to admit a consequence :* hence
expectation in view of *particular* circumstances : *e. g.*—

Il. 1. 100 τότε κέν μιν ἰλασσάμενοι πεπίθοιμεν
                then we may expect to appease him and gain grace.

The character of a Clause of this kind depends chiefly on the
manner in which the *condition* is indicated. The following are
the main points to be observed :—

(*a*) An Opt. with κεν or ἄν often follows an independent Clause
with a Future, Imperative, &c. :—

Il. 22. 108 ὥς ἐρέουσιν, ἐμοὶ δὲ τότ᾽ ἂν πολὺ κέρδιον εἴη κτλ.
Od. 10. 269 φεύγωμεν· ἔτι γάρ κεν ἀλύξαιμεν κακὸν ἦμαρ.
Il. 3. 410 κεῖσε δ᾽ ἐγὼν οὐκ εἶμι, νεμεσσητὸν δέ κεν εἴη.

(*b*) Or the preceding Clause may contain a *wish :*—

Il. 7. 157 εἴθ᾽ ὣς ἡβώοιμι, βίη δέ μοι ἔμπεδος εἴη·
                τῷ κε τάχ᾽ ἀντήσειε κτλ.

Cp. Il. 4. 93 (where the preceding Opt. is a gentle Imper.).

(*c*) The case supposed may be in past time, so that the Optative expresses what *would have* followed on an event which
did not occur : *e. g.*—

Il. 5. 311 καί νύ κεν ἔνθ᾽ ἀπόλοιτο ἄναξ ἀνδρῶν Αἰνείας,
                εἰ μὴ ἄρ᾽ ὀξὺ νόησε κτλ.

Od. 5. 73   ἔνθα κ᾽ ἔπειτα καὶ ἀθάνατός περ ἐπελθὼν
                θηήσαιτο ἰδών.

So Il. 2. 81., 3. 220., 4. 223, 429, 539., 5. 85, 311, 388., 12. 58.,
13. 127, 343., 15. 697., 17. 70, 366, 398, Od. 7. 293., 13. 86.
This use of the Optative is confined to Homer, and is chiefly
found in the Iliad.

A somewhat similar idiom occurs in Herodotus ; *e. g.* Hdt. 1. 2 εἴησαν δ᾽ ἂν
οὗτοι Κρῆτες 'these may have been Cretans' (= probably were), 7. 180 τάχα δ᾽

T

ἄν τι καὶ τοῦ οὐνόματος ἐπαύροιτο. But there the meaning is different—not *would have happened* (=*did not*), but *would be found to have happened* (if we knew more).

(*d*) The case supposed may be vague or imaginary :—

Il. 8. 143 ἀνὴρ δέ κεν οὔ τι Διὸς νόον εἰρύσσαιτο,

where the emphatic ἀνήρ suggests a condition: *if a man, he cannot &c.*; cp. Od. 4. 78., 23. 125, also—

Od. 12. 102 πλησίον ἀλλήλων· καί κεν διοϊστεύσειας
    one may (on occasion arising) shoot an arrow across.

9. 131 οὐ μὲν γάρ τι κακή γε, φέροι δέ κεν ὥρια πάντα.

It is natural that an *admission* that something *may* happen should generally be made more or less in view of circumstances, given or supposed. Hence the use of κεν or ἄν with an Opt. of this force became the prevailing use, and exceptions are rare, even in Homer.

The principal clause or Apodosis of an ordinary Complex Conditional Sentence belongs to this head. It is erroneous, however, to regard the varieties now explained as complex sentences with the Protasis understood. In this, as in some other cases, the complex is to be explained from the simple, not *vice versâ*.

In some instances the Opt. with κεν appears to be *concessive* (expressing *willingness*). Delbrück (*Synt. Forsch.* I. p. 200) gives as examples—

Il. 22. 252   νῦν αὐτέ με θυμὸς ἀνῆκε
    στήμεναι ἀντία σεῖο· ἕλοιμί κεν ἤ κεν ἁλοίην.

Od. 8. 570   τὰ δέ κεν θεὸς ἢ τελέσειεν
    ἤ κ᾽ ἀτέλεστ᾽ εἴη, ὥς οἱ φίλον ἔπλετο θυμῷ.

To which may be added Od. 14. 183 ἤ κεν ἁλοίη ἤ κε φύγοι κτλ. (but Il. 13. 486 is different). Possibly the use of κεν in these places is due to the opposition made between the two alternatives : cp. § 285, 3, *b*, § 286, and § 289, 2, *b*.

Il. 24. 618 ἀλλ᾽ ἄγε δὴ καὶ νῶϊ μεδώμεθα, δῖε γεραιέ,
    σίτου· ἔπειτά κεν αὖτε φίλον παῖδα κλαίοισθα.

Hes. Op. 33 τοῦ κε κορεσσάμενος νείκεα καὶ δῆριν ὀφέλλοις.

Also Od. 16. 391., 21. 161. But these instances need not be separated from others in which expectation rather than concession is recognised. We may notice as on the border between the two meanings—

(*a*) Uses of the First Person (esp. in the Odyssey): *e. g.*—

Od. 15. 506 ἠῶθεν δέ κεν ὕμμιν ὁδοιπόριον παραθείμην.

22. 262 ὦ φίλοι, ἤδη μέν κεν ἐγὼν εἴποιμι καὶ ἄμμιν κτλ.

16. 304 ἀλλ᾽ οἶοι σύ τ᾽ ἐγώ τε γυναικῶν γνώομεν ἰθύν,
    καί κέ τεο δμώων ἀνδρῶν ἔτι πειρηθεῖμεν.

14. 155 πρὶν δέ κε, καὶ μάλα περ κεχρημένος, οὔ τι δεχοίμην.

So Od. 2. 219., 4. 347., 12. 387., 15. 313, 449., 18. 166., 19. 579.,
20. 326., 21. 113, 193, Il. 9. 417., 24. 664.

(β) Negative Clauses, with the Second Person :—

Il. 14. 126 τῷ οὐκ ἄν με .. φάντες | μῦθον ἀτιμήσαιτε
                I do not think you will (*I expect you not to*) *&c.*

Od. 20. 135 οὐκ ἄν μιν νῦν, τέκνον, ἀναίτιον αἰτιόῳο.

So Il. 2. 250 τῷ οὐκ ἂν βασιλῆας ἀνὰ στόμ' ἔχων ἀγορεύοις is to be
understood as ironical courtesy (*you will not if you are advised by
me*).   This, again, when turned into a question yields another
form of polite Imperative; as Il. 3. 52 οὐκ ἂν δὴ μείνειας *will you
not await?*   So Il. 5. 32, 456., 10. 204, Od. 6. 57., 7. 22.

The fact that οὐ is the negative Particle in all these instances
shows that the Optative is grammatically more akin to a Future
than to an expression of *wish*.   So far as wish is intended, the
use is a *rhetorical* one, implying what it does not directly express,
like the similar use of the Future Indicative in Attic.

It will be seen that, except in one or two rare Homeric uses
of the pure Opt., the usage of the Opt. in independent Sentences is nearly the same in Homer as in later Greek.

Optative in Subordinate Clauses.

301.] The classification which has been followed in discussing
the Subordinate Clauses with the Subjunctive will also be the
most convenient in the case of the Optative.   Indeed there is so
close a parallelism between the uses of these two Moods that
little is now left to do except to take clauses of the several types
already analysed, and show in each case the difference which
determines the use of one Mood rather than the other.

The reason for using an Optative will generally be found in
the circumstance that the governing Verb is incompatible with
a subordinate clause expressing either the *will* or the *assured
expectation* of the speaker.   If the occasion to which the whole
sentence refers is *past*, or is a mere *possibility*, or an *imaginary*
case, these two meanings of the Subjunctive are generally out of
place—and we can only have the Mood which expresses a wish,
or an admission of possibility.   Hence it is a general rule—to
which however we have found important exceptions (§ 298)—
that the Optative must be used when the principal Verb is an
Optative, or one of the Secondary Tenses.

302.] **Clauses with ἠέ—ἦε.**   The Optative in the Homeric
examples is generally to be explained as the translation of the
Subjunctive into *oratio obliqua;* that is to say, it expresses a
doubt or deliberation thrown back into the past.

Thus (*a*) we have past *deliberation* in—

Il. 16. 713 δίζε γὰρ ἠὲ μάχοιτο κατὰ κλόνον αὖτις ἐλάσσας,
      ἢ λαοὺς ἐς τεῖχος ὁμοκλήσειεν ἀλῆναι

he debated—should he fight &c., or should he call to the people &c.:
so Il. 1. 189., 5. 671, Od. 4. 117., 6. 141., 10. 50, &c.

(*b*) Past *doubt* is less common : the examples are—

Od. 4. 789 ὁρμαίνουσ᾽ ἤ οἱ θάνατον φύγοι υἱὸς ἀμύμων
      ἦ ὅ γ᾽ ὑπὸ μνηστῆρσιν ὑπερφιάλοισι δαμείη.

15. 304   σὺβώτεω πειρητίζων
      ἤ μιν ἔτ᾽ ἐνδυκέως φιλέοι μεῖναί τε κελεύοι
      αὐτοῦ ἐνὶ σταθμῷ, ἦ ὀτρύνειε πόλινδε

*Ulysses tried the swineherd—whether would he still be hospitable
and bid him stay, or &c.*

In this use we once find κεν—κεν, viz. Od. 15. 300 ὁρμαίνων ἤ
κεν θάνατον φύγοι ἦ κεν ἀλοίη (La Roche reads ἀλώῃ).

303.] **Clauses with μή.** These are of two kinds, answering
to the similar Clauses with the Subj. (§ 281):—

(1) Final Clauses : a single example will suffice :—

Il. 5. 845 δῦν᾽ Ἄϊδος κυνέην μή μιν ἴδοι ὄβριμος Ἄρης
      (*so that*) *Ares should not see her.*

(2) Object Clauses, with Verbs of *thinking*, &c. :—

Il. 21. 516 μέμβλετο γάρ οἱ τεῖχος ἐϋδμήτοιο πόληος,
      μὴ Δαναοὶ πέρσειαν (his care was that) *the Greeks
      should not &c.:* so Od. 16. 179., 19. 390.

Od. 21. 394   πειρώμενος ἔνθα καὶ ἔνθα
      μὴ κέρα ἶπες ἔδοιεν ἀποιχομένοιο ἄνακτος
      to see that worms should not have eaten it.

So in the common use with Verbs of *fearing:* as Il. 18. 34
δείδιε γὰρ μὴ λαιμὸν ἐπαμήσειε *he feared lest &c.* But in—

Il. 9. 244 ταῦτ᾽ αἰνῶς δείδοικα κατὰ φρένα μή οἱ ἀπειλὰς
      ἐκτελέσωσι θεοί, ἡμῖν δὲ δὴ αἴσιμον εἴη κτλ.

the Subj. is used for the immediate object of the fear (the governing Verb being a Perfect), and the Opt. for the more remote
event : see § 304, *a*. The true reading however may be εἴῃ, a
Subj. like μετ-είω (Il. 23. 47).

These Object Clauses may be regarded as the *negative* forms
answering to the Clauses expressing *past deliberation.* As in the
corresponding uses of μή with the Subj. and Opt. in principal
Clauses (§ 278), the Mood is never qualified by κεν or ἄν.

304.] **Relative Clauses—Final and Object.** Sometimes the
Opt. in a Relative Clause is used precisely as in an independent
sentence ; the wish or supposition being expressed from the

speaker's present point of view, not subordinated to the point of view fixed by the governing Verb. Thus in—

Od. 4. 698 ἀλλὰ πολὺ μεῖζόν τε καὶ ἀργαλεώτερον ἄλλο
μνηστῆρες φράζονται, ὃ μὴ τελέσειε Κρονίων

we have an independent *parenthetical wish :* and in—

Il. 3. 234 νῦν δ' ἄλλους μὲν πάντας ὁρῶ . . οὕς κεν ἐΰ γνοίην κτλ.

5. 303 (= 20. 286) μέγα ἔργον, ὃ οὐ δύο γ' ἄνδρε φέροιεν

a parenthetical *expectation* (§ 299, *f*). In other places the Relative Clause is connected, by implication at least, with the action of the principal Clause, and expresses *an intended* or *expected consequence.* We may distinguish the following cases :—

(1) In Final Clauses—

(*a*) The choice of the Opt. shows *want of confident expectation* of the result intended :—

Il. 1. 62 ἀλλ' ἄγε δή τινα μάντιν ἐρείομεν ἢ ἱερῆα, . .
ὅς κ' εἴποι κτλ. (*with the view that he may tell :* cp.
7. 342., 21. 336, Od. 5. 166).

7. 231 ἡμεῖς δ' εἰμὲν τοῖοι οἳ ἂν σέθεν ἀντιάσαιμεν
καὶ πολέες (= *many of us are ready to meet thee*).

Od. 10. 431   τί κακῶν ἱμείρετε τούτων,
Κίρκης ἐς μέγαρον καταβήμεναι, ἥ κεν ἅπαντας
ἢ σῦς ἠὲ λύκους ποιήσεται ἠὲ λέοντας,
οἵ κέν οἱ μέγα δῶμα φυλάσσοιμεν καὶ ἀνάγκῃ.

Here ποιήσεται (Subj.) expresses the immediate result, φυλάσσοιμεν the *further* and therefore (in the nature of things) *less confidently* asserted consequence.

In this group of Clauses the Opt. always takes κεν or ἄν (cp. the corresponding Subj., § 282).

(*b*) The Opt. with κεν is especially common after a principal Clause of *negative* meaning (in which case the consequence is necessarily matter of mere *supposition*) : as—

Il. 5. 192 ἵπποι δ' οὐ παρέασι καὶ ἅρματα τῶν κ' ἐπιβαίην.

Od. 1. 253   ἦ δὴ πολλὸν ἀποιχομένου Ὀδυσῆος
δεύῃ, ὅ κε μνηστῆρσιν ἀναιδέσι χεῖρας ἐφείη.

5. 16 οὐ γάρ οἱ πάρα νῆες ἐπήρετμοι καὶ ἑταῖροι,
οἵ κέν μιν πέμποιεν.

The pure Opt. occurs in Il. 22. 348 οὐκ ἔσθ' ὃς . . ἀπαλάλκοι.

(*c*) The Opt. is used if the governing Verb is an Optative, or a Secondary Tense : *e. g.*—

Il. 14. 107 νῦν δ' εἴη ὃς τῆσδέ γ' ἀμείνονα μῆτιν ἐνίσποι.

Od. 6. 113 ὡς Ὀδυσεὺς ἔγροιτο, ἴδοι τ' εὐώπιδα κούρην,
ἥ οἱ Φαιήκων ἀνδρῶν πόλιν ἡγήσαιτο.

Od. 5. 240 αὖα πάλαι, περίκηλα, τά οἱ πλώοιεν ἐλαφρῶς
    dry, such as would float.

(2) After Verbs that express *asking* or *finding out* the Clause
acquires the force of a dependent Interrogative, and so of an
Object Clause :—

Od. 9. 331 αὐτὰρ τοὺς ἄλλους κλήρῳ πεπαλάσθαι ἄνωγον
        ὅς τις τολμήσειεν κτλ. (*for the man*) *who should &c.*

Il. 3. 316 κλήρους πάλλον . . ὁππότερος ἀφείη
        they cast lots for which of the two should throw.

14. 507 (=16. 283) πάπτηνεν δὲ ἕκαστος ὅπῃ φύγοι.

So Il. 6. 177., 10. 503, Od. 9. 88., 10. 101, 110., 19. 464. As
to the form of the Relative Clause see § 267, 2, c.

The Dependent Interrogative properly so called is rare in
Homer :—

Il. 5. 85 Τυδεΐδην δ᾽ οὐκ ἂν γνοίης ποτέροισι μετείη.

Od. 15. 423 εἰρώτα δὴ ἔπειτα τίς εἴη καὶ πόθεν ἔλθοι.

17. 368 ἀλλήλους τ᾽ ἐρέοντο τίς εἴη καὶ πόθεν ἔλθοι.

It is evidently akin to the Optatives with ἤ—ἤ which express
past *doubt* (§ 302, *b*): τίς εἴη *who he should be* comes to mean *who
he should prove to be.* Cp. the Subj. in the corresponding Clauses
relating to present time (§ 280).

305.] Relative Clauses—Conditional. When the event to
which the condition attaches is matter of *wish* or mere *expectation*, or is in *past* time, the condition is generally expressed by
the Optative. Hence we find the Optative—

(*a*) With an Optative of *wish* in the principal Clause :—

Il. 3. 299 ὁππότεροι πρότεροι ὑπὲρ ὅρκια πημήνειαν,
        ὧδέ σφ᾽ ἐγκέφαλος χαμάδις ῥέοι ὡς ὅδε οἶνος.

Od. 1. 47 ὡς ἀπόλοιτο καὶ ἄλλος ὅτις τοιαῦτά γε ῥέζοι.

(*b*) With an Optative of *expectation* :—

Il. 9. 125 οὔ κεν ἀλήϊος εἴη ἀνὴρ ᾧ τόσσα γένοιτο
        he will not be poor to whom such things come.

12. 228 ὧδέ χ᾽ ὑποκρίναιτο θεοπρόπος ὃς σάφα θυμῷ
        εἰδείη τεράων καί οἱ πειθοίατο λαοί
        so will a diviner answer, who knows &c.

Od. 4. 222 ὃς τὸ καταβρόξειεν . .
        οὔ κεν ἐφημέριός γε βάλοι κατὰ δάκρυ παρειῶν.

The Opt. of the governing Clause may be itself subordinate :—

Od. 2. 53   ὥς κ᾽ αὐτὸς ἐεδνώσαιτο θύγατρα,
        δοίη δ᾽ ᾧ κ᾽ ἐθέλοι καί οἱ κεχαρισμένος ἔλθοι.

(c) After a Present or Future, in one or two places where the time is purposely vague : —

Od. 6. 286 καὶ δ᾽ ἄλλη νεμεσῶ, ἥ τις τοιαῦτά γε ῥέζοι
= I am ready to be angry with any other who &c.

19. 510 καὶ γὰρ δὴ κοίτοιο τάχ᾽ ἔσσεται ἡδέος ὥρη,
ὅν τινά γ᾽ ὕπνος ἕλοι κτλ. (ἕλῃ La R.)

The Opt. avoids assuming that the case will ever occur.

The reading is very doubtful in Il. 5. 407 ὅττι μάλ᾽ οὐ δηναιὸς ὃς ἀθανάτοισι μάχοιτο, the Ambrosian and some others having μάχηται.

(d) When the principal Verb is in a past Tense; the Relative Clause generally expressing *indefinite frequency*, iteration, &c.: as—

Il. 2. 188 ὅν τινα μὲν βασιλῆα καὶ ἔξοχον ἄνδρα κιχείη,
τὸν δ᾽ ἀγανοῖς ἐπέεσσιν ἐρητύσασκε.

15. 22 ὃν δὲ λάβοιμι ῥίπτασκον τεταγὼν κτλ.

Od. 22. 315 παύεσκον μνηστῆρας ὅτις τοιαῦτά γε ῥέζοι.

In these uses, and generally, the Opt. is pure.   Exceptions are—

Od. 4. 600 δῶρον δ᾽ ὅττι κέ μοι δοίης κειμήλιον ἔστω

(where the Opt. may be substituted for the Subj. for the sake of courtesy, to avoid assuming the certainty of the gift),—

Od. 21. 161   ἦ δέ κ᾽ ἔπειτα
γήμαιθ᾽ ὅς κε πλεῖστα πόροι καὶ μόρσιμος ἔλθοι.

Clauses formed by a Relative and the *pure* Optative are strictly parallel to the Conditional Clauses formed by a Relative and the *pure* Subjunctive, such as χαίρει δέ μιν ὅς τις ἐθείρῃ, or βέλτερον ὃς φεύγων προφύγῃ (§ 283, a). In both groups of Clauses the reference is *indefinite;* but with the Subj. the instances must be thought of as *future* instances, and consequently the governing Verb must not imply that they are *past* or *imaginary.*

It may happen that the condition is expressed by the Subj. (because regarded as certain to be fulfilled), while the main action is uncertain, and therefore put in the Opt. : as—

Il. 14. 126 τῷ οὐκ ἄν με γένος γε κακὸν καὶ ἀνάλκιδα φάντες
μῦθον ἀτιμήσαιτε πεφασμένον, ὅν κ᾽ ἐὺ εἴπω.

20. 250 ὁπποῖόν κ᾽ εἴπησθα ἔπος, τοῖόν κ᾽ ἐπακούσαις.

So with εἰ, as Od. 2. 218 εἰ μέν κεν ἀκούσω, ἦ τ᾽ ἂν τλαίην, cp. 11. 104, 110., 12. 137.   But the general rule is to let the subordinate Clause follow the Mood of the governing Verb : hence the so-called ʻAttractionʼ of the Optative.

306.] Clauses with ὡς, ὅπως, ἵνα and the Opt. are either Final or Object Clauses (not Conditional in Homer, see the note at the end of this section).

(1) In Final Clauses the Opt. may be used either (a) to

indicate that the consequence is not immediate or certain (the governing Verb having a present or future meaning), or (b) because the governing Verb is an Opt., or (c) a Secondary Tense. Thus we have the Opt.—

(a) After a Present, &c. in the principal Clause; especially when the Clause bears a *negative* meaning (so that the occasion is necessarily imaginary):—

Il. 1. 343 οὐδέ τι οἶδε νοῆσαι ἅμα πρόσσω καὶ ὀπίσσω,
ὅππως οἱ παρὰ νηυσὶ σόοι μαχέοιντο Ἀχαιοί.

(μαχέοιντο however is not a good Homeric form, and makes an intolerable hiatus: read probably μαχέονται, cp. § 326, 3).

Od. 2. 52 οἳ πατρὸς μὲν ἐς οἶκον ἀπερρίγασι νέεσθαι
Ἰκαρίου, ὥς κ' αὐτὸς ἐεδνώσαιτο θύγατρα.

But also after an affirmative Clause:—

Od. 23. 134   ἡγείσθω φιλοπαίγμονος ὀρχηθμοῖο,
ὥς κέν τις φαίη γάμον ἔμμεναι ἐκτὸς ἀκούων
= *so that any one who happens to hear may think &c.*

12. 156 ἀλλ' ἐρέω μὲν ἐγὼν ἵνα εἰδότες ἤ κε θάνωμεν
ἤ κεν ἀλευάμενοι θάνατον καὶ κῆρα φύγοιμεν
(the Opt. of the less emphatic alternative, § 275, b).

17. 249 τόν ποτ' ἐγὼν ἐπὶ νηὸς ἐϋσσέλμοιο μελαίνης
ἄξω τῆλ' Ἰθάκης, ἵνα μοι βίοτον πολὺν ἄλφοι
(ποτέ indicates a *distant* occasion).

13. 401 κνυζώσω δέ τοι ὄσσε πάρος περικαλλέ' ἐόντε,
ὡς ἂν ἀεικέλιος πᾶσι μνηστῆρσι φανείης (so 16. 297).

24. 532 ἴσχεσθε .. ὥς κεν .. διακρινθεῖτε (leg. διακρινθῆτε?).

(b) After an Optative, either of *wish* or of *expectation:* especially in the Odyssey, as—

Od. 14. 407   τάχιστά μοι ἔνδον ἑταῖροι
εἶεν, ἵν' ἐν κλισίῃ λαρὸν τετυκοίμεθα δόρπον.

15. 537 τῷ κε τάχα γνοίης .. ὡς ἄν τίς σε .. μακαρίζοι.

So Od. 18. 369., 20. 81 : and *à fortiori* after an implied *prohibition*—

Od. 3. 346 Ζεὺς τό γ' ἀλεξήσειε .. ὡς ὑμεῖς .. κίοιτε
Zeus avert that you should go &c.

(c) After a Past Tense—a use of which it is needless to give examples.

Regarding the use of κεν and ἄν, it is to be observed that—

1. The Opt. with ἵνα and ὅπως is always pure.

2. The Opt. with ὡς takes κεν or ἄν in a few places where there is clear reference to a single occasion, as in Od. 2. 52

(quoted above), Il. 19. 331, Od. 17. 362; and in the combinations ὡς ἄν τις (Od. 15. 538), ὥς κέν τις (Od. 23. 135).

(2) The corresponding Object Clause with ὡς and ὅπως is found (a) after Verbs of *trying, considering how*, &c. as—

Il. 2. 3 ἀλλ᾽ ὅ γε μερμήριζε κατὰ φρένα ὡς ᾿Αχιλῆα
τιμήσει᾽ ὀλέσαι δὲ κτλ.

The reading τιμήσει᾽ is supported by Ven. A, which has τιμήσηι (τιμήσει εὐκτικόν Schol. A. B.) : all other authorities have τιμήσῃ, and all have ὀλέσῃ.

Il. 9. 181 πειρᾶν ὡς πεπίθοιεν (*bade them try how to persuade*).
    21. 137 ὥρμηνεν δ᾽ ἀνὰ θυμὸν ὅπως παύσειε (so 24. 680).
Od. 14. 329 ὅππως νοστήσει᾽ ᾿Ιθάκης ἐς πίονα δῆμον.

This reading is proved (against νοστήσῃ of the MSS.) by the parallel Od. 19. 298 ὅππως νοστήσειε φίλην ἐς πατρίδα γαῖαν. Cp. also Od. 9. 420., 11. 479.

In one place ὡς with the Opt. follows a Verb of *saying*, viz. in Od. 24. 237 (μερμήριξε) εἰπεῖν ὡς ἔλθοι καὶ ἵκοιτ᾽ εἰς πατρίδα γαῖαν *to tell how he had come*. This is the only Homeric instance of ὡς with the Opt. in *oratio obliqua*. The next is H. Ven. 215 εἶπεν δὲ ἕκαστα, ὡς ἔοι ἀθάνατος κτλ.

An example of ὅπως and the Opt. with iterative meaning (nearly=ὅτε, § 308, 1, *d*) occurs in Hesiod, Theog. 156 καὶ τῶν μὲν ὅπως τις πρῶτα γένοιτο πάντας ἀποκρύπτασκε. This use is to be classed as Conditional, like the corresponding uses of ὡς and ὅπως with the Subj., § 285, 3.

307.] Clauses with ἕως (ἧος) and ὄφρα. These also are Final in character : *i. e.* the Conjunction has the meaning *till the time that*, hence (commonly) *in order that*,—not *while, so long as*.
The notion of *time* is distinct in—

Od. 12. 437 νωλεμέως ἐχόμην ὄφρ᾽ ἐξεμέσειεν ὀπίσσω
        until it should vomit forth again (so 12. 428., 20. 80).

Od. 23. 151 εἴρυσθαι μέγα δῶμα διαμπερὲς ἧος ἵκοιτο
        till he should come (so 5. 386., 9. 376).

It is indistinct, or lost, in the ordinary use of ὄφρα, as—

Il. 6. 170 δεῖξαι δ᾽ ἠνώγει ᾧ πενθερῷ ὄφρ᾽ ἀπόλοιτο.
Od. 12. 427 ἦλθε δ᾽ ἐπὶ Νότος ὦκα, φέρων ἐμῷ ἄλγεα θυμῷ,
        ὄφρ᾽ ἔτι τὴν ὀλοὴν ἀναμετρήσαιμι Χάρυβδιν
        to the end that I should measure again &c.

and with ἕως in Od. 4. 799 πέμπε δέ μιν . . ἧος Πηνελόπειαν παύσειε κλαυθμοῖο, and other places in the Odyssey (5. 386., 6. 80., 19. 367).

The corresponding form of Object Clause with these Conjunctions may be traced in one instance of each, viz. Il. 4. 465 λελιημένος ὄφρα τάχιστα τεύχεα συλήσειε, and Od. 19. 367 ἀρώμενος ἧος ἵκοιο. Here, after a Verb of *wishing*, the meaning *until* passes into the simple *that*.

With ἕως and ὄφρα the Opt. is nearly always pure : but we have ὄφρ' ἂν in Od. 17. 298 (*until*), 24. 334 : and ἕως κεν in—

Od. 2. 77 τόφρα γὰρ ἂν κατὰ ἄστυ ποτιπτυσσοίμεθα μύθῳ
      χρήματ' ἀπαιτίζοντες, ἕως κ' ἀπὸ πάντα δοθείη,

where there is a stress on the *particular* time contemplated. So—

Il. 15. 69 ἐκ τοῦ δ' ἄν τοι ἔπειτα παλίωξιν παρὰ νηῶν
      αἰὲν ἐγὼ τεύχοιμι διαμπερές, εἰς ὅ κ' Ἀχαιοὶ
      Ἴλιον αἰπὺ ἕλοιεν (the only instance with εἰς ὅ).

The similar uses of ἔστε, ἄχρι, μέχρι are post-Homeric.

The chief instance of ὄφρα with an Opt. following a Fut. or Subj. is Il. 7. 339 πύλας ποιήσομεν .. ὄφρα .. ὁδὺς εἴη. But the example is open to doubt, partly because there may be a Subj. εἴη (see § 80), partly because the line also occurs (7. 349) where the governing Verb is an Imperfect, and it may have been wrongly inserted in v. 339. In other places—as Il. 7. 72, Od. 5. 378., 15. 51., 22. 444—where some editions have Opt. forms, the Subj. is to be restored. It is true that the Opt. is found after the Future with other Conjunctions, to express remoteness or uncertainty ; but a word which literally means *till the time that* could not naturally be used to express a *remote* end or consequence.

308.] Clauses with ὅτε, ὁπότε, &c. Most Clauses of this kind are essentially—

(1) Conditional. The Verb of the principal Clause may be—

(*a*) An Optative of *wish :* as—

Il. 21. 428 τοιοῦτοι νῦν πάντες, ὅσοι Τρώεσσιν ἀρωγοί,
      εἶεν ὅτ' Ἀργείοισι μαχοίατο (cp. Il. 18. 465, &c.).

(*b*) An Optative of *expectation :* as—

Od. 13. 390 καί κε τριηκοσίοισιν ἐγὼν ἄνδρεσσι μαχοίμην
      σὺν σοί, πότνα θεά, ὅτε μοι πρόφρασσ' ἐπαρήγοις.

Il. 14. 247 Ζηνὸς δ' οὐκ ἂν ἔγωγε Κρονίονος ἄσσον ἱκοίμην,
      οὐδὲ κατευνήσαιμ' ὅτε μὴ αὐτός γε κελεύοι.

(*c*) A Future : in one place, viz. Il. 13. 317 αἰπύ οἱ ἐσσεῖται .. νῆας ἐνιπρῆσαι ὅτε μὴ αὐτός γε Κρονίων ἐμβάλοι κτλ., where the speaker does not wish to imply the fulfilment of the condition.

In Od. 24. 343 ἔνθα δ' ἀνὰ σταφυλαὶ παντοῖαι ἔασιν, ὁππότε δὴ Διὸς ὧραι ἐπιβρίσειαν the Present ἔασιν is open to suspicion, because all the rest of the description is in the past tense ; with which the Opt. is in harmony. In Il. 4. 263 ἔστηχ' ὥς περ ἐμοί, πιέειν ὅτε θυμὸς ἀνώγοι the Opt. is read by most MSS. It may be regarded as an Opt. of the *remoter* event (§ 305, *c*), depending on πιέειν, which is an Inf. of *purpose* (Goodwin § 555). But La Roche reads ἀνώγῃ.

(*d*) A Past Tense, generally of an event which happens repeatedly or habitually, as—

Il. 1. 610 ἔνθα πάρος κοιμᾶθ' ὅτε μιν γλυκὺς ὕπνος ἱκάνοι.

21. 265 ὁσσάκι δ᾽ ὁρμήσειε κτλ. *as often as he started &c.*
Od. 8. 87 ἦ τοι ὅτε λήξειεν .. ἔλεσκεν (iterative).
So with ὅτε after πρίν, in Il. 9. 486 οὐκ ἐθέλεσκες .. πρίν γ᾽ ὅτε
δὴ .. ἄσαιμι=*you would only .. when &c.*: cp. § 297.
In these cases the Opt. after a past tense answers to the pure
Subj. after a Present, § 289, 2, *a.* In one place the Opt. with
ὅτε represents the Subj. with ὅτε κεν, viz. in Od. 20. 138 ἀλλ᾽ ὅτε
δὴ κοίτοιο καὶ ὕπνου μιμνήσκοιτο, ἡ μὲν δέμνι᾽ ἄνωγεν ὑποστορέσαι
δμωῇσι *bade them spread the couch against the time when he should
bethink him &c.*
In this group of uses the Opt. is pure, except in—

Il. 9. 524 οὕτω καὶ τῶν πρόσθεν ἐπευθόμεθα κλέα ἀνδρῶν
ἡρώων, ὅτε κέν τιν᾽ ἐπιζάφελος χόλος ἵκοι,

where the κέν may be accounted for by the change from the
Plural to the Singular: cp. § 283, *b, c.*

(2) After a Past Tense of a Verb of *waiting* ὁπότε with the
Aorist Opt. forms a kind of Object Clause; as Il. 7. 415 ποτιδέγ-
μενοι ὁππότ᾽ ἄρ᾽ ἔλθοι *waiting for (the time) when he should come;*
so Il. 9. 191., 18. 524, and (after μένοντες) 4. 334. Cp. § 289 (1).

309.] Clauses with ἐπεί. The few examples of this use show
the same varieties as with ὅτε. Thus, (*a*) after another Opt.—

Il. 9. 304 νῦν γάρ χ᾽ Ἕκτορ᾽ ἕλοις, ἐπεὶ ἂν μάλα τοι σχεδὸν
ἔλθοι.
24. 226 αὐτίκα γάρ με κατακτείνειεν Ἀχιλλεὺς
ἀγκὰς ἑλόντ᾽ ἐμὸν υἱόν, ἐπὴν γόου ἐξ ἔρον εἵην.
Od. 4. 222 ὃς τὸ καταβρόξειεν, ἐπὴν κρητῆρι μιγείη, κτλ.

(*b*) After a Present, in the statement of a supposed consequence—
Od. 24. 254 τοιούτῳ δὲ ἔοικας, ἐπεὶ λούσαιτο φάγοι τε,
εὐδέμεναι (*such a one as would sleep after that &c.*).

(*c*) After a Past tense, in the iterative sense:—
Il. 24. 14 ἀλλ᾽ ὅ γ᾽ ἐπεὶ ζεύξειεν κτλ., Od. 2. 105 (=19. 150.,
24. 140) ἐπὴν δαΐδας παραθεῖτο (*v. l.* ἐπεί).

The use of ἄν is intelligible in the first of these passages (Il. 9.
304), since it refers to an event in the immediate future;
perhaps also in Il. 24. 227, after an Opt. of *concession.* But as
to the form ἐπήν see § 362.

310.] πρίν. The peculiar way of expressing a condition by a
Negative followed by πρίν (§ 297) is transferred to the past, the
Subj. becoming an Opt., in one passage—
Il. 21. 580 οὐκ ἔθελεν φεύγειν πρὶν πειρήσαιτ᾽ Ἀχιλῆος.

The Optative with εἰ, &c.

311.] **Optative with εἰ—Conditional Protasis.** The Clause with εἰ expresses a *supposition*, made in order to lead up to the Clause which expresses the *expected consequence :* as—

Od. I. 163 εἰ κεῖνόν γ' Ἰθάκηνδε ἰδοίατο νοστήσαντα,
πάντες κ' ἀρησαίατ' ἐλαφρότεροι πόδας εἶναι κτλ.

Il. 7. 129 τοὺς νῦν εἰ πτώσσοντας ὑφ' Ἕκτορι πάντας ἀκοῦσαι,
πολλά κεν ἀθανάτοισι φίλας ἀνὰ χεῖρας ἀείραι.

The Clause with εἰ may follow the other, as—

Il. 22. 20 ἦ σ' ἂν τισαίμην, εἴ μοι δύναμίς γε παρείη.

The apodosis is generally given by the Opt. with κεν, as in the examples quoted : but we may have the Subj. with κεν, the Future, or the Present.   In such cases there is some change of tone between Protasis and Apodosis : as Il. 11. 386 εἰ μὲν δὴ ἀντίβιον σὺν τεύχεσι πειρηθείης, οὐκ ἄν τοι χραίσμησι κτλ., where the Subj. is more peremptory than the Opt. : cp. Od. 17. 539 and (Fut.) Il. 10. 222.   So with the εἰ-Clause following the other, as Il. 9. 388 κούρην δ' οὐ γαμέω, οὐδ' εἰ ἐρίζοι *I shall not wed the maiden* (and would not) *even if she rivalled &c.;* cp. Il. 2. 488, Od. 17. 539.   The instances of the Opt. following a Present are nearly all in the Odyssey : 1. 414 οὔτ' οὖν ἀγγελίη ἔτι πείθομαι εἴ ποθεν ἔλθοι, also 7. 52., 14. 56.   In these cases the Present has the force of a general statement (see Goodwin, §§ 409–501).   So when the Verb is understood, as—

Il. 9. 318 ἴση μοῖρα μένοντι καὶ εἰ μάλα τις πολεμίζοι.

Od. 8. 138 οὐ γὰρ ἔγωγέ τί φημι κακώτερον ἄλλο θαλάσσης
ἄνδρα γε συγχεῦαι, εἰ καὶ μάλα καρτερὸς εἴη
no matter if he is very strong (= *even if he should be*).

The combination ὡς εἰ (or ὡς εἴ τε) expresses supposition for the purpose of *comparison ;* the principal Clause being in a past Tense, as—

Il. 2. 780 οἱ δ' ἄρ' ἴσαν ὡς εἴ τε πυρὶ χθὼν πᾶσα νέμοιτο
(cp. Il. 11. 467., 22. 410, Od. 9. 314., 10. 416, 420., 17. 366).

Or else negative—

Il. 11. 389 οὐκ ἀλέγω ὡς εἴ με γυνὴ βάλοι ἠὲ πάϊς ἄφρων.

The use of εἰ with the Opt. in the iterative sense (*if ever, whenever*), which is common in later Greek, is not Homeric : the only passage which might be quoted as an example is—

Il. 24. 768 ἀλλ' εἴ τίς με καὶ ἄλλος ἐνὶ μεγάροισιν ἐνίπτοι . .
ἀλλὰ σὺ τόν γ' ἐπέεσσι παραιφάμενος κατέρυκες.

312.] Optative with εἰ—Wish. The Conditional Protasis, when used without an Apodosis, becomes a form of expressing *wish* :—

Il. 15. 569 Ἀντίλοχ', οὔ τις σεῖο νεώτερος ἄλλος Ἀχαιῶν,
οὔτε ποσὶν θάσσων οὔτ' ἄλκιμος ὡς σὺ μάχεσθαι·
εἴ τινά που Τρώων ἐξάλμενος ἄνδρα βάλοισθα.

So Il. 10. 111., 16. 559., 24. 74. More frequently a wish is introduced by εἰ γάρ or αἰ γάρ, as in—

αἰ γάρ, Ζεῦ τε πάτερ καὶ Ἀθηναίη καὶ Ἄπολλον, κτλ.

Such a wish is sometimes used as a form of asseveration, as—

Il. 18. 464 αἰ γάρ μιν θανάτοιο δυσηχέος ὧδε δυναίμην
νόσφιν ἀποκρύψαι, ὅτε μιν μόρος αἰνὸς ἱκάνοι,
ὥς οἱ τεύχεα καλὰ παρέσσεται

i. e. fair arms shall be his as surely as I wish I could save him from death : so Il. 8. 538, Od. 9. 523 : and ironically—

Od. 21. 402 αἰ γὰρ δὴ τοσσοῦτον ὀνήσιος ἀντιάσειεν,
ὡς οὗτός ποτε τοῦτο δυνήσεται ἐντανύσασθαι.

Here also we must place the wishes expressed by εἴθε or αἴθε, which have generally the character of hopeless *regret:* as εἴθ' ὡς ἡβώοιμι κτλ. It may be noted that in the Odyssey *wish* is not expressed by εἰ except in the combinations εἰ γάρ and εἴθε.

A *wish* is often followed by a Clause expressing an expected consequence of its fulfilment ; as—

Il. 2. 371 αἰ γάρ, Ζεῦ τε πάτερ . .
τῷ κε τάχ' ἠμύσειε πόλις Πριάμοιο ἄνακτος.

Od. 7. 331 Ζεῦ πάτερ, αἴθ' ὅσα εἶπε τελευτήσειεν ἅπαντα
Ἀλκίνοος· τοῦ μέν κεν ἐπὶ ζείδωρον ἄρουραν
ἄσβεστον κλέος εἴη.

So we should probably punctuate—

Il. 13. 485 εἰ γὰρ ὁμηλικίη γε γενοίμεθα τῷδ' ἐπὶ θυμῷ·
αἶψά κεν ἠὲ φέροιτο μέγα κράτος ἠὲ φεροίμην.

Or we may take αἶψά κεν κτλ. closely with the preceding line, and then it becomes the Apodosis to a Conditional clause. Other examples of this ambiguity are given in § 318.

313.] Optative with εἰ κεν—Conditional Protasis. This is a comparatively rare form ; it can generally be explained in accordance with the other uses of κεν :—

Il. 5. 273 εἰ τούτω κε λάβοιμεν ἀροίμεθά κε κλέος ἐσθλόν
if (*as I propose*) *we take them, we should &c.*
(But perhaps we should read τούτω γε.)

9. 141 εἰ δέ κεν Ἄργος ἱκοίμεθ' Ἀχαιϊκόν κτλ.
if (as a further step) *we reach Argos &c.*

Il. 23. 591 ἵππον δέ τοι αὐτὸς
δώσω, τὴν ἀρόμην· εἰ καί νύ κεν οἴκοθεν ἄλλο
μεῖζον ἐπαιτήσειας, ἄφαρ κέ τοι αὐτίκα δοῦναι
βουλοίμην if (after that) you demand more &c.

Od. 2. 76 εἴ χ᾽ ὑμεῖς γε φάγοιτε, τάχ᾽ ἄν ποτε καὶ τίσις εἴη
if (as I say is better, see v. 74) you devour, then &c.

See also Il. 2. 123., 8. 196, 205., 13. 288., 23. 592, Od. 2. 246.,
12. 345., 13. 389., 19. 590. And with the Clause with εἰ following the other—

Il. 6. 49 τῶν κέν τοι χαρίσαιτο πατὴρ ἀπερείσι᾽ ἄποινα,
εἴ κεν ἐμὲ ζωὸν πεπύθοιτ᾽ ἐπὶ νηυσὶν Ἀχαιῶν.

So Il. 1. 60., 10. 381 ; cp. Od. 7. 315., 8. 353, and the use of οὐδ᾽
εἴ κεν not even in case, Il. 9. 445., 19. 322., 22. 220.

There is one instance of the Opt. with εἰ—ἄν, viz.

Il. 2. 597 εἴ περ ἂν αὐταὶ Μοῦσαι ἀείδοιεν.

314.] Opt. with εἰ—Final and Object Clauses. These are
generally found after a past Tense in the Principal Clause ; e.g.—

Il. 2. 97 κήρυκες βοόωντες ἐρήτυον, εἴ ποτ᾽ ἀϋτῆς
σχοίατ᾽, ἀκούσειαν δὲ κτλ. (in view that they should &c.)

Od. 4. 317 ἤλυθον, εἴ τινά μοι κληηδόνα πατρὸς ἐνίσποις
I have come in case you may tell me some &c.

With Verbs of seeking, trying, desiring, &c. the Clause with εἰ
has the character of an Object Clause : as—

Il. 4. 88 Πάνδαρον ἀντίθεον διζημένη εἴ που ἐφεύροι
seeking in the hope of finding (= seeking to find).

So Il. 12. 333, Od. 13. 415., 22. 381.

With Verbs of telling, knowing, seeing, thinking, &c. this idiom
is almost confined to the Odyssey ; e.g.—

Od. 1. 115 ὀσσόμενος πατέρ᾽ ἐσθλὸν ἐνὶ φρεσίν, εἴ ποθεν ἐλθὼν
μνηστήρων τῶν μὲν σκέδασιν κατὰ δώματα θείη

i.e. with the thought in his heart, whether his father would
come and scatter the suitors: cp. 5. 439., 9. 317, 421., 18. 375.

Od. 12. 112 εἰ δ᾽ ἄγε δή μοι τοῦτο, θεά, νημερτὲς ἐνίσπες
εἴ πως τὴν ὀλοὴν μὲν ὑπεκπροφύγοιμι Χάρυβδιν
tell me as to the hope that I may escape &c.

In a few places an Object Clause of this kind follows a present
Tense :—

Od. 2. 350 ὃν σὺ φυλάσσεις
κεῖνον ὀϊόμενον τὸν κάμμορον εἴ ποθεν ἔλθοι.

14. 119 Ζεὺς . . οἶδε . . εἴ κέ μιν ἀγγείλαιμι ἰδών.

20. 224 ἀλλ᾽ ἔτι τὸν δύστηνον ὀΐομαι εἴ ποθεν . . θείη.

So in the only example of the kind found in the Iliad :—

Il. 11. 792 τίς δ' οἶδ' εἴ κέν οἱ σὺν δαίμονι θυμὸν ὀρίναις ;
The pure Optative is used in all the places quoted, except the
two in which εἴ κεν follows οἶδε (Il. 11. 792, Od. 14. 119). In
these the structure is the same as in the corresponding *independent* Clauses (§ 300). That is to say, the phrase τίς οἶδεν εἰ is
treated as a mere 'perhaps' (Lat. *nescio an*).

An Opt. in a Final Clause depending upon a Subj. is perhaps to be found
in Od. 5. 471 εἰ δέ κεν .. καταδράθω εἴ με μεθείη (so all MSS. : μεθήῃ Bekk.). Cp.
§ 293.

History of the Subjunctive and Optative.

315.] Uses in Independent Clauses. The uses of the Subj.
and Opt. in independent Clauses have been shown to fall in each
case into two main groups. In one set of meanings the Mood
expresses *desire on the part of the speaker ;* to this belong the Subj.
of *command* and *prohibition*, and the Opt. of *wish*. In the other
the Mood is a kind of Future ; the Subj. being an emphatic or
confident Future (like our Future with *shall*), the Opt. a softened
Future, expressing expectation, or mere admission of possibility
(the English *may* or *should*).

These two sets of meanings may be called the 'quasi-Imperative,' and the 'quasi-Future.' We must remember however that
they are not always clearly separable, but are connected by transitional or intermediate uses : such as (*e. g.*) the Subj. which expresses *necessity* (§ 277), and the Opt. of *concession* (§ 299, *d*).

316.] Uses in Subordinate Clauses. Passing over for the
present the question whether the quasi-Imperative or the quasi-
Future use is to be regarded in each case as representing the
original meaning of the Mood, we proceed to consider the uses in
Subordinate Clauses. Here the main distinction is that between
'Final' and 'Conditional,' if these terms are used with some
latitude : especially if we rank with the Final Clauses not only
those which distinctly express the *end* or purpose of an action,
but also all Clauses which are referred to the time of the governing Verb. It is true that this distinction does not always apply ;
e. g. to the Subj. in—

Δαναῶν ὀλοφυρόμεθ' αἰχμητάων,
οἵ κεν δὴ κακὸν οἶτον ἀναπλήσαντες ὄλωνται·

or to the Opt. in—

ἀλλὰ πολὺ μεῖζον ..
μνηστῆρες φράζονται, ὃ μὴ τελέσειε Κρονίων.

For there the Relative Clause is in sense a *parenthesis*, and is
construed accordingly as an independent Sentence. Again, in—

ἔσσεται ἦμαρ ὅτ' ἄν ποτ' ὀλώλῃ κτλ.

φρασσόμεθ' ἠὲ νεώμεθ' ἐφ' ἡμέτερ' ἠὲ μένωμεν.

δείδιε γὰρ μὴ λαιμὸν ἀποτμήσειε κτλ.

and generally in *Object* Clauses, the Subordinate Clause does not
express *end ;* but the time from which it is regarded as spoken is
fixed by the governing Verb, in the same way that the time of a
true Final Clause is fixed by the action of which it gives the end.
For the present purpose, accordingly, there are two kinds of
Clause to be considered, (1) Final and Object Clauses, and (2)
Conditional Clauses.

Regarding the meaning of the Subjunctive and Optative in
Final Clauses there can be little doubt. The Subj. in most
instances follows either a First Person (Present or Future), or an
Imperative : that is to say, it expresses the immediate purpose
with which the speaker announces his own action, or commands
the action of others.   Hence, by a natural transference, it comes
to express the purpose of another person (viz. the Subject of the
Principal Clause). Similarly the Opt., whether as the Mood of
wish or of *expectation,* comes to express a wish or expectation not
now felt, but spoken of. Again, by virtue of its character as a
softened or less confident Future, it naturally expresses a *purpose*
that does not lie within the speaker's own sphere of action or
direct influence.

It should be noticed, too, that the relation which we imply by
the term ʻFinal Clause' may exist without grammatical Subordination, *i. e.* without a Particle such as ἵνα or ὡς to introduce
the clause. Thus in Il. 6. 340 ἀλλ' ἄγε νῦν ἐπίμεινον ἀρήϊα τεύχεα
δύω the meaning would not be altered by saying ἐπίμεινον ἵνα δύω.
So in Il. 18. 121–125 νῦν δὲ κλέος ἀροίμην καὶ . . στοναχῆσαι
ἐφείην, γνοῖεν δ' ὡς δὴ δηρὸν ἐγὼ πολέμοιο πέπαυμαι : the last wish
is evidently also the *result* hoped for from the fulfilment of the
preceding wishes (so that γνοῖεν δέ = ὡς γνοῖεν).

In Conditional Clauses, on the other hand, the condition or
supposition is not subordinated to the time of the governing
Verb, but is made from the *present* point of view of the speaker.
The question arises : What is the original force of the Subj. and
Opt. in this use ?

In the case of the Subj. we naturally look to the quasi-Imperative use. It is common to use the Imperative as a way of
stating a supposition ; as when we say ʻlet it be so,' meaning ʻif
it is so ' (cp. Latin *cras petito, dabitur*). This view is confirmed
by the fact that negative Conditional Clauses take μή, not οὐ :
that is to say, they are felt to be akin to *prohibition* rather than
denial. Thus ὃς μὴ ἔλθῃ literally means not ʻwho *will* not come '

(ὃς οὐκ ἂν ἔλθῃ), but 'who *shall* not come,' *i. e.* whom we are not to suppose coming.

Similarly we may understand the Opt. in these Clauses as the Mood of *concession*; 'admitting this to be so': and so in a negative sentence, ὃς μὴ ἔλθοι 'whom I agree to suppose not coming.' For the choice of the Mood does not depend on the greater or less *probability* of the supposition being true, but on the *tone* in which it is made—on the degree of *vividness*, as Mr. Goodwin says, with which it is expressed (*Moods and Tenses*, § 455).

It may be objected that on this view we ought to have εἰ οὐ, not εἰ μή, whenever the Verb is in the Indicative. But there is no difficulty in supposing that μή was extended to the Indicative on the analogy of the Clauses with the Subj. and Opt.; just as μὴ ὤφελον is an extension from the common use of μή in wishes. And this is strongly supported by the circumstance that in fact εἰ οὐ with the Indicative occurs several times in Homer:—

Il. 15. 162 εἰ δέ μοι οὐκ ἐπέεσσ' ἐπιπείσεται κτλ. (so 178).

20. 129 εἰ δ' Ἀχιλεὺς οὐ ταῦτα θεῶν ἐκ πεύσεται ὀμφῆς.

24. 296 εἰ δέ τοι οὐ δώσει ἑὸν ἄγγελον κτλ.

Od. 2. 274 εἰ δ' οὐ κείνου γ' ἐσσὶ γόνος κτλ.

See also Il. 4. 160, Od. 12. 382., 13. 143. On the other hand, in the very few examples of εἰ οὐ with a Subj., the οὐ goes closely with the Verb, viz. Il. 3. 289 (οὐκ ἐθέλωσιν), 20. 139 (οὐκ εἴωσι). On the whole, therefore, it is probable that the Subj. in Conditional Clauses represents the tone of *requirement* in which the speaker *asks us to suppose* the condition to be true: and that the Opt. implies *concession*, or willingness to make the supposition involved.

317.] **Original meaning.** Whether the use of the Subj. as an emphatic Future was derived from its use to express Will, or *vice versa*, and whether the Optative originally expressed *wish* or *supposition*, are questions which take us back to a very early period in the history of Indo-European speech. The two Moods are found in the same uses (generally speaking) in Homer and in the Veda: the formation of these uses therefore belongs in the main to the period before the separation of the different languages,—to the period, indeed, when the original parent language was itself in course of formation. The problem therefore is one on which comparison of the earliest forms of the known Indo-European languages can hardly throw any light. It is as though we were asked to divine whether the use of *shall* in commands (*thou shalt not kill*) or in predictions (*ye shall see me*) is the older, without recourse to earlier English, or to other Germanic languages. Some considerations of a general character may however be suggested :—

(*a*) The Subj. is strongly differentiated from the Imperative by its Person-Endings, and especially by the existence of a First Person.

(*b*) In most languages it will be found that the Imperative meaning is expressed in more than one way. Thus in Sanscrit we find the Imperative

U

proper, the Injunctive, the Subj., and the Optative : in Greek the Imper., the Subj. and certain uses of the Future. The reason of this is evident. Variety in the expression of will and wish is one of the first needs of human society. The form which has been appropriated to express *command* is unsuitable to courteous *request*, still more unsuitable to humble *entreaty*. Accordingly other forms are used, precisely because they are not Imperatives. In time these acquire a quasi-Imperative character, and fresh forms are resorted to as the same want of a non-Imperative mode of expression is again perceived.

(c) The use of the Secondary Endings in the Optative points to the con-clusion that in its origin it was a Mood of past time. The tendency to use a past Tense in wishes, and in some kinds of suppositions, may be amply illustrated from English and other modern languages.

(d) The uses with οὐ go far to show that the quasi-Future sense of the Subj. and Opt. is at least as primitive as the quasi-Imperative sense. If the strong negation οὐ γένηται is derived by gradual change of meaning from a *prohibition*, the appearance of οὐ is difficult to explain.

(e) The use of the Subj. as an Imper. may be compared to the Attic use of the Future in a 'jussive' sense, and in Final Clauses to express purpose (Goodwin, p. 373). The change from an expression of will to one of expectation is one to which it would be much more difficult to find a parallel.

318.] **Conditional Protasis with εἰ.** The derivations that have been pro-posed for the Particle εἰ or αἰ are too uncertain to furnish ground for any theory as to the manner in which the Conditional Protasis may have been formed. The question arises for us on the passages in which εἰ with the Opt. is used to express a wish. Thus in εἴ τις καλέσειε *I pray some one to call* we may take the Clause as Conditional, with a suppressed Apodosis (καλῶς ἂν ἔχοι or the like). Or we may follow L. Lange in holding that the Clause is not Subordinate at all, the Particle εἰ being originally a kind of affirmative Interjection, used to introduce expressions of wish and supposition ; and we can thus explain the ordinary Complex Conditional Sentence as made up of two originally independent Clauses, viz. (1) a *wish* or *supposition*, introduced by εἰ, and (2) an assertion of the consequence to be expected from its being realised. On this theory the Clause of Wish introduced by εἰ is not an in-complete Sentence, derived from a Complex Sentence by omission of the Apodosis, but is one of the elements from which the Complex Sentence was itself developed.

The latter of these views has *a priori* the advantage of deriving the complex from the simple : and it has some apparent support in Homeric usage. We find in Homer—

(1) Wish, standing alone :—

> ὡς ἀπόλοιτο καὶ ἄλλος ὅτις τοιαῦτά γε ῥέζοι.

(2) Wish followed by an independent Clause expressing expectation of a consequence :—

> Od. 15. 180 οὕτω νῦν Ζεὺς θείη, ἐρίγδουπος πόσις Ἥρης·
> τῷ κέν τοι καὶ κεῖθι θεῷ ὣς εὐχετοῴμην.

> Il. 13. 55 σφῶϊν δ' ὧδε θεῶν τις ἐνὶ φρεσὶ ποιήσειεν,
> αὐτώ θ' ἑστάμεναι κρατερῶς καὶ ἀνωγέμεν ἄλλους·
> τῷ κε καὶ ἐσσύμενόν περ ἐρωήσαιτ' ἀπὸ νηῶν.

(3) Wish, with εἰ, εἰ γάρ, εἴθε, &c., but without 'Apodosis' :—

    Il. 4. 189 αἲ γὰρ δὴ οὕτως εἴη, φίλος ὦ Μενέλαε.

    11. 670 εἴθ᾽ ὡς ἡβώοιμι, βίη δέ μοι ἔμπεδος εἴη, κτλ.

(4) Wish, with εἰ, εἰ γάρ, εἴθε, &c., followed by a Clause of Consequence :—

    Il. 7. 157 εἴθ᾽ ὡς ἡβώοιμι, βίη δέ μοι ἔμπεδος εἴη·

        τῷ κέ τάχ᾽ ἀντήσειε κτλ.

    Od. 15. 536 αἲ γὰρ τοῦτο, ξεῖνε, ἔπος τελέσειε Κρονίων·

        γνοίης χ᾽ οἵη ἐμὴ δύναμις καὶ χεῖρες ἕπονται.

(5) Supposition, with εἰ, followed by a Clause of expectation :—

    Il. 7. 129 τοὺς νῦν εἰ πτώσσοντας ὑφ᾽ Ἕκτορι πάντας ἀκούσαι,

        πολλά κεν ἀθανάτοισι φίλας ἀνὰ χεῖρας ἀείραι.

The similarity in these examples is manifest. The type in the first four sets consists of a Clause of Wish, either alone (1 and 3) or followed by a Clause of Consequence (2 and 4). Again, (5) only differs from (4) in punctuation, so to speak : the two Clauses are taken together, and thus the εἰ-Clause is no longer an independent *supposition*, but is one made with a view to the *consequence* expressed in the Clause with κεν. And this, it is contended, was the result of a gradual process, such as we find whenever parataxis passes into hypotaxis.

319.] **Final Clauses with εἰ.** An argument for Lange's view of the original force of εἰ is found in the use in Final Clauses, such as εἶμι εἴ κε πίθηται. The meaning here is essentially different from that of the Conditional sentence *I go if he listens;* and on the ordinary hypothesis, that εἰ originally expressed a condition, it is difficult to account for the two uses. But if εἰ is a mere interjection, introducing wish or supposition, it is intelligible that the Clause should be Conditional or Final, as the context may determine.

320.] **The formula εἰ δ᾽ ἄγε**, with the varieties εἰ δ᾽ ἄγετ᾽ (Il. 22. 381) and εἰ δέ (Il. 9. 46, 262), is often used in Homer to introduce an Imperative or Subjunctive (§ 275). It has generally been supposed to be elliptical, standing for εἰ δ᾽ ἐθέλεις ἄγε, or the like. And εἰ δ᾽ ἐθέλεις is actually found with an Imperative in a few places : Il. 19. 142 εἰ δ᾽ ἐθέλεις ἐπίμεινον, Od. 16. 82., 17. 277 (cp. 3. 324). It has been pointed out, however, by Lange, in his dissertation on this question,* that εἰ δ᾽ ἐθέλεις is only found where it introduces a distinct *second alternative*. Thus in Od. 16. 82 the context is : 'I will send the stranger wherever he desires ; or if you choose (εἰ δ᾽ ἐθέλεις) take him into your house.' So Od. 3. 323 ἀλλ᾽ ἴθι νῦν σὺν νηΐ . . εἰ δ᾽ ἐθέλεις πεζός κτλ. But with εἰ δ᾽ ἄγε this is not the case. We find it at the beginning of a speech ; as—

    Il. 6. 376 εἰ δ᾽ ἄγε μοι, δμωαί, νημέρτεα μυθήσασθε.

    Od. 2. 178 ὦ γέρον, εἰ δ᾽ ἄγε νῦν μαντεύεο κτλ. : so Il. 16. 697., 17. 685,

        Od. 12. 112., 22. 391., 23. 35.

Or in the Apodosis of a Conditional sentence, as—

    Od. 4. 831 εἰ μὲν δὴ θεός ἐσσι, θεοῖό τε ἔκλυες αὐδῆς,

        εἰ δ᾽ ἄγε μοι κτλ. : so Il. 22. 379–381.

Or to express an appeal which is *consequent* upon something just said : as—

    Il. 1. 301 τῶν οὐκ ἄν τι φέροις ἀνελὼν ἀέκοντος ἐμεῖο·

        εἰ δ᾽ ἄγε μὴν πείρησαι (ay, come now and try) : cp. Il. 8. 18.

---

* *De formula Homerica* εἰ δ᾽ ἄγε *commentatio*, Lipsiae 1873.

            U 2

Il. 1. 523   ἐμοὶ δέ κε ταῦτα μελήσεται ὄφρα τελέσσω·
          εἰ δ' ἄγε τοι κεφαλῇ κατανεύσομαι (so come, I will nod my head).

23. 579   εἰ δ' ἄγ' ἐγὼν αὐτὸς δικάσω, καί μ' οὔ τινά φημι
          ἄλλον ἐπιπλήξειν Δαναῶν· ἰθεῖα γὰρ ἔσται·
          'Αντίλοχ', εἰ δ' ἄγε δεῦρο . . ὄμνυθι κτλ.
          come I will be judge myself . . so come, Antilochus, take this oath :
          see also Od. 1. 271., 9. 37., 21. 217., 24. 336.

Hence, Lange argues, it is probable that εἰ does not express condition, but has
an interjectional character (cp. Latin eia age` : and if so it may be the same
with the use in Clauses expressing wish.

321.] Conclusion. Notwithstanding these arguments, the common explanation of the εἰ-Clause of wish (as primarily a Clause of supposition)
seems to be the more probable one.* For—

(1) The uses of εἰ present a marked correspondence with those of the
Relative and its derivatives. Note especially the use of ὅτε μή as almost
exactly = εἰ μή.

(2) The analogy εἶτα : εἰ :: ἔπειτα : ἐπεί makes it likely that εἰ was
originally temporal. The fact that εἶτα is not Homeric takes something from
the force of this argument.

(3) The use of alternative forms of wish, and the use of some form of
supposition to express wish, are phenomena which can be exemplified from
many languages : cp. the Latin o si, German wenn, wenn nur, &c. And ellipse
of the apodosis occurs with εἰ-clauses of other kinds ; see § 324.*

(4) The εἰ-clause, whether of supposition or of wish, is specifically Greek,
whereas the chief meanings of the Optative—wish, concession, supposition—
are much older, being common to Greek and Sanscrit. Hence the εἰ-clause
was formed at a time when the Opt. of wish had long been established in
use. The presumption surely is that the εἰ-clause, when it came to be used
as a form of wish, was a new way of expressing wish. It would probably
be adopted at first as a less direct form, suited for wishes couched in a
different tone (as εἴθε is confined to hopeless wish).

(5) The only use of εἰ not obviously expressive of supposition is that which
is seen in the isolated phrase εἰ δ' ἄγε, of which Lange has given an exceedingly probable analysis. Possibly however the εἰ of εἰ δ' ἄγε is not the same
word as εἰ if, but an interjection, like εἶεν and Latin eia. We may go further,
and point out that the δέ of εἰ δ' ἄγε has been shown by Lange himself
to be out of place, hence the true form may be εἰ' ἄγε, like Latin eia age.

It may be observed, in conclusion, that the question of the εἰ-clause is
quite distinct from the question of the original meaning of the Optative. It
is possible to combine Lange's theory of εἰ with Delbrück's earlier view
of the Optative as originally the Mood of wish,† but Lange himself does not
do so. He regards the εἰ-clause of supposition (Fallsetzung) as developed
independently of the εἰ-clause of wish. His main thesis is that εἰ does not

---

* This is also the conclusion maintained by Mr. Goodwin, who discusses
the question very fully in the new edition of his Moods and Tenses (pp. 376 ff.).

† This view was proposed in Delbrück's Syntaktische Forschungen (vol. i. p. 13),
but is withdrawn in his recent work (Altindische Syntax, § 172).

imply a correlative particle, or an apodosis (καλῶς ἄν ἔχοι or the like), so that the two meanings of εἰ γένοιτο—*suppose it happened* and *would that it happened*—belong to originally distinct meanings of the Opt. γένοιτο. That is to say, the development of εἰ *if* with various Moods—Opt., Subj., Indic.—was parallel to an entirely distinct development of interjectional εἰ with the Opt. of wish.

322.] **Homeric and Attic uses.** The main difference between Homer and later writers in regard to the Moods may be said to be that the later uses are much more restricted. Thus the Subj. is used by Homer in Principal Clauses of every kind—Affirmative and Negative, as well as Prohibitive, Interrogative, &c. In Attic it is confined to the Prohibitive use with μή, and the idiomatic 'Hortatory' and 'Deliberative' uses.

Again, in Subordinate Clauses the important Homeric distinction between the 'pure' Subj. and the Subj. with ἄν or κεν is almost wholly lost in Attic. In Clauses of Conditional meaning, whether Relatival, Temporal, or introduced by εἰ, the Subj. with ἄν has become the only generally allowable construction: the pure Subj. being confined to a few instances in poetry. With the Optative, on the other hand, an equal uniformity has been attained by the loss of the use with ἄν or κεν. In short, of the four distinct Homeric constructions—

1. ὃς ἔλθῃ (ὅτε ἔλθῃ, εἰ ἔλθῃ, &c.)
2. ὃς ἄν (or ὅς κεν) ἔλθῃ (ὅτ' ἄν ἔλθῃ, ἐὰν ἔλθῃ, &c.)
3. ὃς ἔλθοι (ὅτε ἔλθοι, εἰ ἔλθοι, &c.)
4. ὃς ἄν (or ὅς κεν) ἔλθοι (ὅτ' ἄν ἔλθοι, ἐὰν ἔλθοι, &c.)

the language dropped the first and last: with the result that as ἄν always accompanied the Subj. and was absent from the Opt., it ceased to convey a distinct meaning, independent of the meaning given by the Mood. In other words, the use became a mere idiom. The change, though apparently slight, is very significant as an evidence of linguistic progress.

In regard to Final Clauses the most noticeable point is the use of the Relative with a Subjunctive. In this respect Homeric Greek agrees with Latin: while in later Greek the Subj. was replaced, generally speaking, by the Future Indicative. It is also worth observing here that in Homer, as has been said (§ 316), the Final Clause in the great majority of instances expresses the speaker's own purpose, not a purpose which he attributes to a person spoken of: see §§ 280, 281, 285, 286. In other words, the subordination of the Clause to the governing Verb does not often go so far as to put the Third Person for the First (e. g. φράσσεται ὥς κε νέηται = *he will consider—* '*how am I to return*'). The further license by which a past purpose is thought of as if still present—so that the Subj. is used instead of the Opt.—is not Homeric (§ 298).

Modal Uses of the Indicative.

323.] **The Indicative** is primarily the Mood of *assertion:* from which it is an easy step to the use in Negative and Interrogative sentences. It is also used in Greek (as in other languages) to express mere *supposition:* thus we have εἰ in a Conditional Protasis with all Tenses (εἰ ἦν, εἰ ἔστι, εἰ ἔσται),

where there need be no implication either for or against the truth
of the supposition thus made.   Further, the Indicative may be
used in certain cases in a Conditional Apodosis, expressing an
imaginary *consequence*.   Again, it may be used in Final and
Object Clauses referring to the past or to the future.   All such
uses, in which the Indicative does not *assert*, may be called
Modal Uses.

The tendency of language appears to be to extend the Modal Uses of the
Indicative, and consequently to diminish the range of the other Moods.   It
is found possible, and more convenient, to show the modal character of
a Clause by means of Particles, or from the drift of the context, without
a distinct Verbal form.   It will be seen, on comparing the Homeric and Attic
usage, that the Indicative has encroached in several points upon the other
Moods.

324.]   Conditional Clauses (Apodosis). The Secondary Tenses
or Tenses of *past time* (Aor. Impf. and Plupf.), are used with κεν
or ἄν to express a supposed consequence : as—

   Il. 4. 420 δεινὸν δ' ἔβραχε χαλκὸς ἐπὶ στήθεσσιν ἄνακτος
           ὀρνυμένου· ὑπό κεν ταλασίφρονά περ δέος εἷλεν
           fear would have seized even the stout-hearted.

This way of speaking of a conditional event ordinarily implies
that the condition on which it depended was not fulfilled.   For
if (*e. g.*) the assertion ἦλθεν *he came* is true, we can hardly ever
have occasion to limit it by saying ἦλθεν ἄν *he came in that case*.
Hence a Past Tense with κεν or ἄν naturally came to be used
where the event in question had not happened, owing to the
non-fulfilment of the condition.

The rule does not apply to events that occur *repeatedly*, or on no particular
occasion ; for there is no contradiction in saying of such an event that it
happened when a condition was fulfilled.   Hence the use in the *iterative* sense
(as Hdt. 3. 119 κλαίεσκε ἂν καὶ ὀδυρέσκετο, Thuc. 7. 71 εἴ τινες ἴδοιεν . . ἀνεθάρση-
σάν τε ἂν κτλ.).   This use, however, is not Homeric.   In Od. 2. 104 ἔνθα κεν
ἠματίη μὲν ὑφαίνεσκεν has slender authority, most MSS. reading ἔνθα καί.
Another supposed instance is—

           Od. 18. 263 ἵππων τ' ὠκυπόδων ἐπιβήτορας, οἵ κε τάχιστα
                   ἔκριναν μέγα νεῖκος κτλ.,

where the commentators (Fäsi, Ameis, Merry) take ἔκριναν as a 'gnomic'
Aorist.   The words as they stand can only mean 'who would most speedily
have decided mighty strife' (so Goodwin, § 244) : but this does not suit the
context.   The difficulty is best met by reading οἵ τε : cp. § 283, *b*.

An exceptional use of a different kind is—

           Od. 4. 546 ἢ γάρ μιν ζωόν γε κιχήσεαι, ἤ κεν Ὀρέστης
                   κτείνεν ὑποφθάμενος.

Here κεν marks the alternative (§ 283, *n*. 2) : *either you will find him alive or* (*in
the other case*) *Orestes has killed him* (i. e. *must have killed him*).   Thrown into

a Conditional form the sentence would be : 'if you do not find him alive, then Orestes has killed him.' So with an Infinitive—

Il. 22. 108   ἐμοὶ δὲ τότ' ἂν πολὺ κέρδιον εἴη
ἄντην ἢ 'Αχιλῆα κατακτείναντα νέεσθαι
ἠέ κεν αὐτῷ ὀλέσθαι ἐϋκλειῶς πρὸ πόληος.

In the Protasis κεν with the Indicative occurs only once, viz. Il. 23. 526 εἰ δέ κ' ἔτι προτέρω γένετο δρόμος (see Leaf's note *a. l.*). This may be compared with the occasional use of κεν with εἰ and an Opt. (§ 313). The rarity of the use with an Indic. need not be felt as a difficulty: cp. the oracle in Hdt. 1. 174 Ζεὺς γάρ κ' ἔθηκε νῆσον εἴ κ' ἐβούλετο, also Erinna, fr. 4, 4, and Ar. Lys. 1098 (Hartung, ii. p. 240).

In later Greek the Imperfect with ἄν may express either a continuous action which *would have occurred* at some past time, or an action (continuous or momentary) which *would have been occurring* at the moment of speaking. The latter of these uses, as Mr. Goodwin points out (§ 435), is not Homeric. He sees an approach to it in Il. 24. 220 εἰ μὲν γάρ τίς μ' ἄλλος ἐκέλευεν *were it any one else who bade me*. Another may be found in Od. 20. 307 καί κέ τοι ἀντὶ γάμοιο πατὴρ τάφον ἀμφεπονεῖτο ἐνθάδε (*if you had struck the stranger*) *your father would have had to busy himself here with your burial in place of wedding*: cp. also Od. 4. 178 καί κε θάμ' ἐνθάδ' ἐόντες ἐμισγόμεθ', οὐδέ κεν ἡμέας ἄλλο διέκρινεν.

The Impf. without ἄν or κεν may express what *ought to have been*, if the meaning of *fitness, obligation*, &c. is given by the Verb or Predicate. Thus we have Od. 20. 331 κέρδιον ἦεν *it would have been better*. So in Attic with ἐχρῆν, ἔδει, and similar words.

The Opt. with ἄν or κεν, as we have seen (§ 300, *c*), is not unfrequently used in Homer with the same meaning as the Aor. or Impf. with ἄν has in later Greek. This is one of the points in which the use of the Indicative gained on that of the Optative.

324.*] **Ellipse of the Apodosis.** We may notice here the cases in which εἰ with an Indic. or Subj. is not followed by a corresponding Clause expressing the *consequence* of the supposition made. This occurs—

(*a*) When two *alternative* suppositions are made, the second being the one upon which the speaker wishes to dwell : as Il. 1. 135 εἰ μὲν δώσουσι γέρας .. εἰ δέ κε μὴ δώωσιν, ἐγὼ δέ κεν αὐτὸς ἕλωμαι *if they give* (there is nothing to be said), *but if not*, &c.

(*b*) When the consequence is sufficiently *implied* in the εἰ-Clause : as Il. 6. 150 εἰ δ' ἐθέλεις καὶ ταῦτα δαήμεναι *if you wish to be told this* (I will do so): Il. 7. 375 αἴ κ' ἐθέλωσι παύσασθαι

if they wish to cease (let them): Od. 21. 260 ἀτὰρ πελέκεάς γε καὶ
εἴ κ᾽ εἰῶμεν ἅπαντας ἑστάμεν: Il. 19. 147., 20. 213., 21. 487, Od.
4. 388., 15. 80.

(c) When the speaker prefers to *suggest* the consequence in an
indirect way: as Il. 1. 580 εἴ περ γάρ κ᾽ ἐθέλῃσιν Ὀλύμπιος ἀστερο-
πητὴς ἐξ ἑδέων στυφελίξαι, ὁ γὰρ πολὺ φέρτατός ἐστιν *if he wishes*
(he will), *for he is strong enough;* Il. 14. 331., 21. 567, Od. 3. 324.

There is a similar omission of the apodosis in Causal Clauses
with ἐπεί at the beginning of a speech, as Il. 3. 59 Ἕκτορ, ἐπεί
με κατ᾽ αἶσαν ἐνείκεσας: Il. 6. 382 Ἕκτορ, ἐπεὶ μάλ᾽ ἄνωγας κτλ. ;
Il. 13. 68, 775, Od. 1. 231., 3. 103, 211. The full form appears
in Il. 6. 333 ἐπεί με κατ᾽ αἶσαν ἐνείκεσας . . τοΰνεκά τοι ἐρέω.

In such sentences as εἰ δ᾽ ἐθέλεις . . δαήμεναι some commentators obtain an
apodosis by taking the Inf. as equivalent to an Imperative : ' if you wish,
then learn &c.' But this is exceedingly forced, and indeed impossible in
some places, *e. g.* Il. 7. 375, Od. 21. 260. Elsewhere the apodosis is *forgotten*
(anacoluthon) ; so after εἰ in Il. 22. 111, after ἐπεί in Il. 18. 101, Od. 4. 204.,
6. 187, 262., 8. 236., 17. 185.

325.] **Past Tense by 'Assimilation.'** When a Past Tense
relating to an event which has not happened is followed by a
Subordinate Clause, the Verb of the Subordinate Clause may
also be in a Past Tense (the event which it expresses being
equally imaginary): as—

Il. 6. 345 ὥς μ᾽ ὄφελ᾽ ἤματι τῷ ὅτε . .
οἴχεσθαι προφέρουσα κακὴ ἀνέμοιο θύελλα,
ἔνθα με κῦμ᾽ ἀπόερσε κτλ.

and so v. 350 ἀνδρὸς ἔπειτ᾽ ὤφελλον . . ὃς ἤδη κτλ., and Od. 1. 218:
also the use with πρίν, Od. 4. 178 οὐδέ κεν ἡμέας ἄλλο διέκρινεν . .
πρίν γ᾽ ὅτε δὴ θανάτοιο μέλαν νέφος ἀμφεκάλυψεν *nothing would
have parted us before the dark cloud of death had wrapped us round.*

This idiom is the same in principle as the use of Past Tenses
in Final Clauses, which is common in Attic with ἵνα and ὡς: as
Soph. O. T. 1393 τί μ᾽ οὐ λαβὼν ἔκτεινας εὐθύς, ὡς ἔδειξα μή ποτε
κτλ. *that so I might never have shown &c.* When the context has
once shown that we are dealing with a purely imaginary event,
the Indicative serves to carry on the train of suppositions. The
Indic. is similarly used in an Object Clause after a Verb of
fearing, as δείδω μὴ δὴ πάντα θεὰ νημερτέα εἶπεν.

326.] **Future Indicative.** The following points have to be
noticed :—

1. Homer not unfrequently uses κεν with the Future, the
effect being (as with the Subj.) to indicate a limitation or condition : as—

Il. 1. 139 ὃ δέ κεν κεχολώσεται *and he (if I do so) will be angry.*

Il. I. 522 ἀλλὰ σὺ μὲν νῦν αὖτις ἀπόστιχε μή τι νοήσῃ
    Ἥρη· ἐμοὶ δέ κε ταῦτα μελήσεται (*to me, as my part*).

4. 76 καί κέ τις ὧδ᾽ ἐρέει *in such case men will say.*

This use of κεν is chiefly found after δέ, as Il. 1. 139., 6. 260., 8.
419., 14. 267, &c.: and in Relative Clauses, as Il. 12. 226., 17.
241., 22. 70, Od. 5. 36., 8. 318., 16. 438: perhaps with ὅτε, Il.
20. 335 ὅτε κεν συμβλήσεαι unless we read συμβλήεαι as 2 Aor.
Subj. (Dindorf, *Thes. Ling. Gr. s. v. βάλλω*). Cp. the use of κεν
with the Subj., § 275, *b*.

The Future with ἄν is very rare: see Il. 9. 167., 22. 66.

2. The use of the Future with the force of a *gentle Imperative*
has been ascribed to Homer, but without sufficient ground.
Where it appears to take the place of an Imperative it will be
found in reality to express the *indifference* of the speaker; as —

Il. 6. 70 ἀλλ᾽ ἄνδρας κτείνωμεν· ἔπειτα δὲ καὶ τὰ ἕκηλοι
    νεκροὺς ἂμ πεδίον συλήσετε τεθνηῶτας
    then you can (if you like) strip the dead of their arms.

20. 137 ἡμεῖς μὲν καθεζώμεσθα . . πόλεμος δ᾽ ἄνδρεσσι
    μελήσει (we will leave war to men).

The forms οἴσετε and ἄξετε, which are sometimes given as instances of this
use, do not belong to the Future, but are Imperatives of an Aorist (§ 41).

3. The Future is occasionally found in Final Clauses with
nearly the force of the Subj.: viz. with the Conjunctions ὅπως in
Od. I. 57 θέλγει ὅπως Ἰθάκης ἐπιλήσεται *charms so that he may
forget Ithaca,* also in Il. 1. 344 (if with Thiersch we read ὅππως
μαχέονται Ἀχαιοί for the anomalous μαχέοιντο), and with ὄφρα,
as —

Il. 8. 110 Τρωσὶν ἐφ᾽ ἱπποδάμοις ἰθύνομεν, ὄφρα καὶ Ἕκτωρ
    εἴσεται κτλ. (so Il. 16. 242, Od. 4. 163., 17. 6).

So with μή, Il. 20. 301 μή πως καὶ Κρονίδης κεχολώσεται, Od. 24.
544.

The Future with κεν in Relative Clauses sometimes appears to
express *end*, as in Il. 1. 174 πάρ᾽ ἔμοιγε καὶ ἄλλοι οἵ κέ με τιμήσουσι:
cp. 2. 229., 23. 675, Od. 8. 318., 16. 438. So without κεν in Il.
24. 154, Od. 14. 333. In all these places, however, as in the
corresponding uses of the Subj. (§ 282), and Opt. (§ 304), it is
difficult to say how far the notion of *end* is distinctly expressed:
in other words, how far the future action is subordinated to that
of the main Verb.

4. The use of the Future in *Object Clauses* (common in Attic
after Verbs of *striving,* &c.) may perhaps be seen in Il. 12. 59
μενοίνεον εἰ τελέουσι, also Od. 5. 24., 13. 376.

It is sometimes impossible to decide whether a form is a Future or
an Aorist Subj.: *e. g.* in Od. 1. 269 σὲ δὲ φράζεσθαι ἄνωγα ὅπως κε μνηστῆρας

ἀπώσεαι, where the Verb may be a Future, as in the places now quoted, or a Subj., according to the commoner Homeric construction. So in Il. 10. 44, 282., 17. 144.

The use of the Future in Final Clauses is probably later than that of the Subjunctive. In general, as we have seen, the Subj. is akin to the Imperative, and therefore expresses the speaker's *purpose* directly, by its own force; whereas the Fut. Ind. properly expresses *sequence*. Thus θέλγει ὡς λάθηται literally means 'charms so that he *shall* forget': θέλγει ὅπως λήσεται 'charms so that he will forget.' The same conclusion seems to follow from the rule that ὅπως and ὄφρα may be used with a Future, but not ὡς or ἵνα (Goodwin, § 324). For ὡς *in the manner that* fits a direct purpose better than ὅπως *in some such manner that*, or ὄφρα *till the time that*. It would seem probable, then, that in Final Clauses the Future is a less emphatic and positive expression of end. Thus when Achilles prays ⟨Il. 16. 242⟩, 'embolden him so that Hector will know,' the Future conveys a shade of indifference, as though Hector's knowledge were the natural consequence rather than the direct object. And so in Il. 1. 175 οἵ κέ με τιμήσουσι *who will (I presume) honour me.*

5. In Clauses with εἰ the Future is chiefly used of events regarded as necessary, or as determined by some power independent of the speaker: as—

Il. 14. 61 ἡμεῖς δὲ φραζώμεθ' ὅπως ἔσται τάδε ἔργα,
   εἴ τι νόος ῥέξει (*if wit is to be of any avail*).

17. 418 εἰ τοῦτον Τρώεσσι μεθήσομεν (*if we are going to &c.*).

So Il. 1. 61, 294., 5. 350., 12. 248, 249., 13. 375., 15. 162., 24. 57, Od. 2. 115.

We may compare the Conditional Relative Clause—

Il. 23. 753 ὄρνυσθ' οἳ καὶ τούτου ἀέθλου πειρήσεσθε
   rise, ye that will make trial of this contest.

And with κεν—

Il. 15. 213 αἵ κεν ἄνευ ἐμέθεν .. πεφιδήσεται κτλ.

So Il. 2. 258., 5. 212., 17. 588, Od. 15. 524.

The Imperative.

327.] The Homeric uses of the Imperative present little or no difficulty. We may notice the use in *concession*, ironical or real:—

Il. 4. 29 ἔρδ', ἀτὰρ οὔ τοι πάντες ἐπαινέομεν θεοὶ ἄλλοι.

The forms ἄγε and ἄγετε are often combined with other Imperatives for the sake of emphasis: and sometimes ἄγε is treated as indeclinable, and used where the context requires a Plural; as—

Il. 2. 331 ἀλλ' ἄγε μίμνετε πάντες κτλ. (so 1. 62., 6. 376, &c.). Similarly ἴθι is a kind of Interjection in Il. 4. 362 ἀλλ' ἴθι, ταῦτα δ' ὄπισθεν ἀρεσσόμεθ' κτλ.: and so we have βάσκ' ἴθι (like εἴπ' ἄγε). And δεῦτε *hither!* is evidently an Imperative: cp. Il. 14. 128 δεῦτ' ἴομεν πόλεμόνδε. The corresponding 2 Sing. doubtless enters into the formation of δεῦρο; but it is not clear how that word is to be analysed.

328.] Prohibition. The Aorist Imperative is very rarely used with μή : examples are—

Il. 4. 410 τῷ μή μοι πατέρας ποθ᾽ ὁμοίῃ ἔνθεο τιμῇ
       (so Od. 24. 248 σὺ δὲ μὴ χόλον ἔνθεο θυμῷ).

   18. 134 σὺ μὲν μή πω καταδύσεο μῶλον Ἄρηος.

Od. 16. 301 μή τις ἔπειτ᾽ Ὀδυσῆος ἀκουσάτω.

Il. 16. 200 μὴ λελαθέσθω.

For the rule which is the complement of this one, forbidding the use of the Present Subj. with μή, see § 278 *fin.*

Regarding the origin of this curious idiom a very probable conjecture has been made by Delbrück (*Synt. Forsch.* iv. p. 120). In the Veda it has been shown by Grassmann that the prohibitive Particle *mâ* is never found with the forms of the Imperative proper, but only with the so-called 'spurious Conjunctive' or 'Injunctive.' Hence it may be inferred that the Imperative was only used originally in *positive* commands, not in prohibitions. Again, it appears that in Sanscrit the Imperative is nearly confined to the Present Tense : and in Greek the forms of the First Aor. Imper. (κλέψον, Mid. κλέψαι) are certainly of late origin. The fine distinction which is made, in the Imperative as well as in other Moods, between the continuous action expressed by the Present Stem and the momentary action expressed by the Aorist belongs to the specific development of Greek. Accordingly Delbrück suggests that the extension of the Imperative to express prohibition took place at a time when the Aorist Imperative had not come into general use : and hence it was only carried into the Present Tense. In other words, the form μὴ κλέπτε came into use in pre-historic Greek as an extension of the positive κλέπτε, and superseded μὴ κλέπτῃς : but μὴ κλέψῃς kept its ground, because the form κλέψον did not then exist. This account of the idiom seems much more probable than any attempt to explain it on psychological grounds.

CHAPTER XIII.

The Particles.

329.] Under the term *Particles* it is convenient to group together a number of words that are mainly used to show the relations between other words, and between Clauses. In respect of this office they are akin to the various syllables or letters used as Endings : and with them go to constitute what are called the 'formal elements' of the language, in contradistinction to the roots or stems which compose its 'matter.'

The Particles which connect successive Clauses in any way form the *Conjunctions.* As such they may be distinguished, according to the nature of the connexion which they indicate, as *Copulative* (καί, τε, ἠδέ, &c.), *Adversative* (δέ, ἀλλά, αὐτάρ), *Disjunctive* (ἤ—ἤ), *Conditional* (εἰ, ἄν, κεν), *Illative* (ἄρα, δή, οὖν), *Causal* (γάρ), &c.

Those Particles, again, which affect single Clauses may either serve to show the character of the whole Clause (as Affirmative, Interrogative, Conditional, &c.), or to influence particular words in it. We cannot, however, make a satisfactory classification of the Particles on the basis of these uses, because some of them are employed in several distinct ways: and moreover they enter into various combinations in which they often acquire new meanings. It will be best therefore to take them separately, beginning with the most familiar.

καί.

330.] The uses of καί are in the main the same in all periods of Greek. It is (1) a Copulative Conjunction, conveying the idea of *addition* to what has preceded: Ζηνὶ φόως ἐρέουσα καὶ ἄλλοις *to Zeus and the others besides:* ὡς ἄρ' ἔφη καὶ κτλ. *thus he spoke and thereupon &c.:* and (2) a strengthening or emphasising Particle meaning *also, even, just:* as—

Il. 1. 63 ἢ καὶ ὀνειροπόλον *or even a dream-prophet.*

3. 176 τὸ καὶ κλαίουσα τέτηκα *which is the very reason that I am wasted with weeping.*

It is especially used with words that imply *comparison*, increase or diminution, extension of time or the reverse, &c.; as καὶ ἄλλος *another* (not this only), καὶ αὐτός *himself* (as well as others): καὶ πάλαι *long ago* (not merely now), καὶ αὖθις *another time* (if not now), καὶ μάλα, καὶ λίην (in a *high* degree, not merely in an *ordinary* degree): so with Comparatives, καὶ μεῖζον, καὶ ῥίγιον, &c. Both terms of a comparison may be strengthened in this way; as—

Il. 1. 81 εἴ περ γάρ τε χόλον γε καὶ αὐτῆμαρ καταπέψῃ,
ἀλλά τε καὶ μετόπισθεν κτλ.

Notice, too, the use at the beginning of an Apodosis, esp. with Adverbs of *time*, as—

Il. 1. 477 ἦμος δ' ἠριγένεια φάνη ῥοδοδάκτυλος ἠώς,
καὶ τότ' ἔπειτ' κτλ.

καί precedes the word which it emphasises, but is sometimes separated from it by other Particles, enclitic Pronouns, &c.: as Il. 1. 213 καί ποτέ τοι τρὶς τόσσα (not merely compensation but) *three times as much:* 2. 292 καὶ γάρ τίς θ' ἕνα μῆνα μένων *a man who stays even one month.* So 7. 281 καὶ ἴδμεν ἅπαντες (= ἴσμεν καὶ πάντες).

καὶ εἰ and εἰ καί. The combination καὶ εἰ indicates that the *whole* condition is an extreme one : *even on the supposition that*—. But with the order εἰ καί the καί emphasises particular words : εἰ καὶ μάλα καρτερός ἐστι *even if he is* (I will go so far as to say) *very strong.* Hence εἰ καί usually implies that the supposition is more or less true.

TE.

331.] The enclitic τε has two main uses which it is essential to distinguish ; besides one or two special uses of less importance.

(*a*) As a Conjunction τε connects clauses and single words. It is especially used when a new fact or new object is to take its place *pari passu* with what has been already said : κύνεσσιν οἰωνοῖσί τε πᾶσι *to dogs and birds as well:* αἳ πᾶσι κακὸν Τρώεσσι γένοντο οἳ τ᾽ αὐτῷ *which were a bane to all the Trojans, and to himself* (equally). This meaning is given still more distinctly by the Correlative τε—τε : thus we have the pairs ἀνδρῶν τε θεῶν τε, δῆμός τε πόλις τε, κλαγγῇ τ᾽ ἐνοπῇ τε, &c. and the pairs of Clauses expressing *simultaneous* action, such as—

ἂψ τ᾽ ἀνεχώρησεν, ὦχρός τέ μιν εἷλε παρειάς.

Hence τε—τε sometimes marks that two things are *mutually dependent* : ὀλίγον τε φίλον τε=‘not less dear because small,’ λυσόμενός τε θύγατρα φέρων τ᾽ ἀπερείσι᾽ ἄποινα=‘bringing vast ransom for the deliverance of his daughter’: Il. 5. 359 κόμισαί τέ με δός τέ μοι ἵππους.

The combinations τε—καί and τε—ἠδέ (or ἰδέ) are also common in Homer, and not sensibly different in meaning from τε—τε : as—

ᾤμωξέν τ᾽ ἄρ᾽ ἔπειτα καὶ ὣ πεπλήγετο μηρώ.
χλαῖνάν τ᾽ ἠδὲ χιτῶνα.

As to the *place* of τε the general rule is that it follows the first word in the Clause. Hence when standing first in the pair τε—τε it does not always follow the word which it couples : *e. g.* Il. 6. 317 ἐγγύθι τε Πριάμοιο καὶ Ἕκτορος *near both Priam and Hector ;* Il. 5. 878 σοί τ᾽ ἐπιπείθονται καὶ δεδμήμεσθα ἕκαστος (cp. 2. 136, 198., 4. 505., 7. 294-5).

The use of τε as a Particle of *transition* (to begin a fresh sentence after a pause) is not Homeric, though common in later Greek. This may indicate that the use as a connecting Particle was originally confined to the Correlative τε—τε (Delbrück, *Synt. Forsch.* iv. p. 145).

332.] (*b*) In its other use—which is distinctively Homeric— τε serves to mark an assertion as *general* or *indefinite.* Hence it is found in *gnomic* passages : as—

Il. 1. 218 ὅς κε θεοῖς ἐπιπείθηται, μάλα τ᾽ ἔκλυον αὐτοῦ.

9. 509 τὸν δὲ μέγ᾽ ὤνησαν καί τ᾽ ἔκλυον εὐξαμένοιο.

Od. 6. 185 μάλιστα δέ τ᾽ ἔκλυον αὐτοί.

Il. 16. 688 ἀλλ' αἰεί τε Διὸς κρείσσων νόος ἠέ περ ἀνδρῶν.

19. 221 αἶψά τε φυλόπιδος πέλεται κόρος (cp. Od. 1. 392).

Hes.Th.87 αἶψά τε καὶ μέγα νεῖκος ἐπισταμένως κατέπαυσε.

So in many short maxims, such as ῥεχθὲν δέ τε νήπιος ἔγνω—στρεπτοὶ δέ τε καὶ θεοὶ αὐτοί. In *similes* it is very common, and is often repeated in the successive Clauses ; *e.g.*—

Il. 4. 482   ὁ δ' ἐν κονίῃσι χαμαὶ πέσεν, αἴγειρος ὥς,
ἥ ῥά τ' ἐν εἰαμενῇ ἕλεος μεγάλοιο πεφύκη
λείη, ἀτάρ τέ οἱ ὄζοι ἐπ' ἀκροτάτῃ πεφύασι·
τὴν μέν θ' ἁρματοπηγὸς ἀνὴρ αἴθωνι σιδήρῳ
ἐξέταμ', ὄφρα κτλ.

16. 156   οἱ δὲ λύκοι ὣς
ὠμοφάγοι, τοῖσίν τε περὶ φρεσὶν ἄσπετος ἀλκή,
οἵ τ' ἔλαφον κεραὸν μέγαν οὔρεσι δῃώσαντες
δάπτουσιν· πᾶσιν δὲ παρήϊον αἵματι φοινόν·
καί τ' ἀγεληδὸν ἴασιν ἀπὸ κρήνης μελανύδρου
λάψοντες γλώσσῃσιν ἀραιῇσιν μέλαν ὕδωρ
ἄκρον, ἐρευγόμενοι φόνον αἵματος· ἐν δέ τε θυμὸς
στήθεσιν ἄτρομός ἐστι, περιστένεται δέ τε γαστήρ.

So where the meaning is frequentative :—

Od. 4. 102 ἄλλοτε μέν τε γόῳ φρένα τέρπομαι (cp. 5. 55., 12. 64).

Il. 19. 86 καί τέ με νεικείεσκον (20. 28, Od. 5. 331, &c.).

So Il. 1. 521 νεικεῖ καί τέ μέ φησι κτλ. *and says* (habitually) *that I &c.* : cp. 9. 410., 17. 174, Od. 1. 215., 4. 387., 10. 330., 17. 25. Hence it is used of *names*, as Il. 1. 403 ἄνδρες δέ τε πάντες (καλέουσι), 2. 814., 5. 306, &c. ; of characteristic attributes, as—

Il. 2. 453 οὐδ' ὅ γε Πηνειῷ συμμίσγεται . .
ἀλλά τέ μιν καθύπερθεν ἐπιρρέει ἠΰτ' ἔλαιον.

5. 340 ἰχώρ, οἷός πέρ τε ῥέει μακάρεσσι θεοῖσι.

And generally of any fixed condition of things, as Il. 4. 247 ἔνθα τε νῆες εἰρύατ' εὔπρυμνοι: 5. 477 οἵ πέρ τ' ἐπίκουροι ἔνειμεν: 15. 187 τρεῖς γάρ τ' ἐκ Κρόνου εἰμὲν ἀδελφεοί (a fact of permanent significance) : 22. 116 ἥ τ' ἔπλετο νείκεος ἀρχή. It may be laid down as a general rule that τε in the combinations μέν τε, δέ τε, καί τε, γάρ τε, ἀλλά τε, and the like, is not a Conjunction, and does not affect the meaning of the Conjunction which it follows.

In a Conditional sentence of gnomic character the τε is often used in both members, as—

Il. 1. 81 εἴ περ γάρ τε χόλον γε καὶ αὐτῆμαρ καταπέψῃ,
ἀλλά τε καὶ μετόπισθεν ἔχει κότον.

The use with the Article and the different forms of the Relative has been already discussed in the chapter on the Pronouns (see §§ 263, 266). It was there pointed out that τε is used when the Clause serves to describe a *class*, as—

ἄγρια πάντα, τά τε τρέφει οὔρεσιν ὕλη.
ῥεῖα δ᾽ ἀρίγνωτος γόνος ἀνέρος ᾧ τε Κρονίων κτλ.

or to express a permanent characteristic, as—

γῆρας καὶ θάνατος, τά τ᾽ ἐπ᾽ ἀνθρώποισι πέλονται.
χόλος, ὅς τ᾽ ἐφέηκε πολύφρονά περ χαλεπῆναι.
Λωτοφάγων, οἵ τ᾽ ἄνθινον εἶδαρ ἔδουσιν.

So ὥς τε, ὅτε τε, ἵνα τε, ἔνθα τε, ὅσος τε, οἷός τε, ὡς εἴ τε, &c. Of these ὥς τε (or ὥστε) and οἷός τε, with the adverbial ἅτε and ἐφ᾽ ᾧ τε, are the only forms in which this use of τε has remained in Attic Greek. ἐπεί τε, which is regular in Herodotus, is rare in Homer: see Il. 11. 87, 562., 12. 393.

Further, the Indefinite τις is not unfrequently strengthened in its meaning (*any one*) by τε (cp. Latin *quisque*):—

Il. 3. 12 τόσσον τίς τ᾽ ἐπιλεύσσει ὅσον τ᾽ ἐπὶ λᾶαν ἵησιν.

14. 90 σίγα, μή τίς τ᾽ ἄλλος .. ἀκούσῃ (so Od. 19. 486).

So καὶ γάρ τίς τε, καὶ μέν τίς τε, and in Relative Clauses, ὅς τίς τε, ὅτε τίς τε, ὥς τίς τε, &c.: also ἤν τίς τε (Od. 5. 120).

Notice also the use with the disjunctive ἤ after a Comparative, in Od. 16. 216 ἀδινώτερον ἤ τ᾽ οἰωνοί. This is akin to the use in similes. So in Il. 4. 277 μελάντερον ἠΰτε πίσσα *blacker than pitch*. The true reading is probably ἠέ τε, as was suggested by Bekker (*H. B.* i. p. 312): see however Buttmann, *Lexil.*, *s. v.* ἠΰτε. On ἤ τε—ἤ τε *either—or* see § 340.

The two uses of τε may sometimes be distinguished by its place in the sentence. Thus τε is a Conjunction in Il. 2. 522 οἵ τ᾽ ἄρα *and who*— (cp. εἴ τ᾽ ἄρα, οὔτ᾽ ἄρα), and in Il. 23. 277 ἀθάνατοί τε γάρ εἰσι κτλ.; also in the combinations οὔτε τις, μήτε τις. With the indefinite τε we should have the order ἄρα τε, γάρ τε, τίς τε. Both uses may even occur in the same clause; as Il. 5. 89 τὸν δ᾽ οὔτ᾽ ἄρ τε γέφυραι ἐεργμέναι ἰσχανόωσιν.*

The places in which τε appears to be used in statements of single or definite facts can generally be corrected without difficulty. In several places δέ τ᾽ (οὐδέ τ᾽, μηδέ τ᾽) has crept into the text instead of δ᾽ ἔτ᾽. Thus we find—

Il. 1. 406 τὸν καὶ ὑπέδεισαν μάκαρες θεοὶ οὐδέ τ᾽ ἔδησαν
    (Read οὐδ᾽ ἔτ᾽,—*they no longer bound, gave up binding*).

2. 179 ἀλλ᾽ ἴθι νῦν κατὰ λαὸν Ἀχαιῶν μηδέ τ᾽ ἐρώει.
    (Read μηδ᾽ ἔτ᾽ with four of La Roche's MSS.).

11. 437 οὐδέ τ᾽ ἔασε
    (Read οὐδ᾽ ἔτ᾽ with the *Lipsiensis*, and so in Il. 21. 596).

---

* The account now given of the uses of τε was suggested (in substance) by Dr. Wentzel, whose dissertation (*Ueber den Gebrauch der Partikel τέ bei Homer*, Glogau, 1847) appears to have been overlooked by subsequent writers.

Il. 23. 474 αἱ δέ τ᾽ ἄνευθεν

(Read αἱ δ᾽ ἔτ᾽ with the *Townleianus*).

Similarly we should read οὐδ᾽ ἔτ᾽ in Il. 15. 709., 17. 42., 21. 248., 22. 300., 23. 622, 730., 24. 52, Od. 12. 198. In such a matter manuscript authority is evidently of no weight, and it will be found that the MSS. often have δέ τ᾽ where the editors have already corrected δ᾽ ἔτ᾽ (*e.g.* in Il. 1. 573., 2. 344., 12. 106, Od. 2. 115., 11. 380., 21. 186., 24. 401). In Il. 11. 767 the editions have νῶϊ δέ τ᾽ ἔνδον, but all MSS. νῶϊ δὲ ἔνδον: so perhaps we may correct Il. 21. 456 νῶϊ δέ τ᾽ ἄψορροι κίομεν. Perhaps ἔτι should be restored in Il. 16. 836 σὲ δέ τ᾽ ἐνθάδε γῦπες ἔδονται, Od. 15. 428 πέρασαν δέ τε δεῦρ᾽ ἀγαγόντες.

Two isolated Epic uses remain to be noticed :—

(1) After an Interrogative in the combination τ᾽ ἄρα, τ᾽ ἄρ : as—

Il. 1. 8 τίς τ᾽ ἄρ σφωε θεῶν ἔριδι ξυνέηκε μάχεσθαι ;

18. 188 πῶς τ᾽ ἄρ᾽ ἴω μετὰ μῶλον; (so πῇ τ᾽ ἄρ Il. 13. 307).

Od. 1. 346 μῆτερ ἐμή, τί τ᾽ ἄρα φθονέεις κτλ.

The ancient grammarians regarded ταρ as a single enclitic Particle (so Herodian, Schol. Il. 1. 65). As the force of the τε seems to have merged in the compound, this is probably right : just as γ᾽ ἄρ having become a single Particle is written γάρ. But if so, we must also recognise the form ταρα.

(2) With ἦ in strong Affirmation : as ἦ τ᾽ ἐφάμην *I did indeed think*. This may originally belong to the same head as the indefinite use: ἦ τε = *surely anyhow*. But a distinct force of the τε is no longer perceptible.

The Latin *que*, which is originally identical with τε, shows the same separation into two main uses. In the use as a Conjunction the agreement between τε and *que* is close. It is less so in the other use, chiefly because τε in Homer is still a distinct word, whereas *que* in Latin is confined to certain combinations, viz. *at-que, nam-que* (cp. καί τε, ἀλλά τε, γάρ τε, &c.), *ita-que*, the Indefinite *quisque* (with the corresponding forms *ubique, quandoque, uterque*, &c.), and the Relative *quicunque*. The two uses are also united in the Sanscrit *ca*, which as a connecting Particle agrees closely with τε, and is also found after the Indefinite *kas*, especially in the combination yáḥ káç ca (ὅς τίς τε). See Delbrück, *Synt. Forsch.* iv. p. 144, *A. S.* § 284.

δέ.

333.] The chief use of the Adversative Particle δέ is to show that a Clause stands in some *contrast* to what has preceded. Ordinarily, however, it merely indicates the continuation of a narrative (*i.e.* shows that the new fact is not *simultaneous*). It is especially used to introduce a parenthesis or subordinate statement (whereas τε introduces something parallel or coordinate : *e. g.*—

νοῦσον ἀνὰ στρατὸν ὦρσε κακήν, ὀλέκοντο δὲ λαοί,
οὕνεκα κτλ.

Here a prose writer would say ὀλεθρίαν, or ὥστε ἀπόλλυσθαι τὸν
λαόν, or ὑφ᾽ ἧς ὁ λαὸς ἀπώλλυτο, &c. So—

    'Αντίλοχος δὲ Μύδωνα βάλ᾽, ἡνίοχον θεράποντα,
    ἐσθλὸν Ἀτυμνιάδην, ὁ δ᾽ ὑπέστρεφε μώνυχας ἵππους,
    χερμαδίῳ ἀγκῶνα τυχὼν μέσον.

I. e. 'struck him as he was turning the horses.'

δέ is nearly always the *second* word in the Clause. It is occasionally put after (1) a Preposition and Case-form, as ἐπ᾽ αὐτῶν
δ᾽ ὠμοθέτησαν, or (2) an Article and Numeral, as τῇ δεκάτῃ δ᾽ κτλ.:
but not after other combinations. Hence καὶ δέ, as Il. 7. 113
καὶ δ᾽ Ἀχιλεύς *and even Achilles* (never καὶ Ἀχιλεὺς δέ, as in later
Greek).

334.] δέ of the Apodosis. While δέ generally stands at the
beginning of a new independent Sentence, there are certain uses,
especially in Homer, in which it marks the beginning of the
principal Clause after a Relatival, Temporal or Conditional
Protasis. This is found where there is an *opposition* of some
kind between the two members of the Sentence : e. g.—

Il. 4. 261 εἴ περ γάρ τ᾽ ἄλλοι γε κάρη κομόωντες 'Αχαιοὶ
        δαιτρὸν πίνωσιν, σὸν δὲ πλεῖον δέπας κτλ. (so 12. 245).

  5. 260 αἴ κέν μοι πολύβουλος 'Αθήνη κῦδος ὀρέξῃ
        ἀμφοτέρω κτεῖναι, σὺ δὲ . . ἐρυκακέειν κτλ.

Od. 7. 108 ὅσσον Φαίηκες περὶ πάντων ἴδριες ἀνδρῶν
        νῆα θοὴν ἐνὶ πόντῳ ἐλαυνέμεν, ὡς δὲ γυναῖκες
        ἱστὸν τεχνῆσσαι (cp. Od. 14. 178, 405., 18. 62).

With οὐ and μή, giving οὐδέ, μηδέ, as—

Il. 5. 788 ὄφρα μὲν ἐς πόλεμον πωλέσκετο δῖος 'Αχιλλεύς,
        οὐδέ ποτε Τρῶες κτλ.

  6. 58   μηδ᾽ ὅν τινα γαστέρι μήτηρ
        κοῦρον ἐόντα φέροι, μηδ᾽ ὃς φύγοι.

Od. 1. 16 ἀλλ᾽ ὅτε δὴ ἔτος ἦλθε . . οὐδ᾽ ἔνθα κτλ.

  10. 17 ἀλλ᾽ ὅτε δὴ καὶ ἐγὼ ὁδὸν ᾔτεον . . οὐδέ τι κεῖνος κτλ.

This use, which was called by the ancient grammarians the δέ
ἀποδοτικόν, or ' δέ of the apodosis,' has been variously explained
by scholars.

  1. In many places the Clause introduced by this δέ stands in a
double opposition, first to the immediate protasis, and then to a
preceding sentence. Thus in—

Il. 2. 716 οἳ δ᾽ ἄρα Μηθώνην . . ἐνέμοντο,
        τῶν δὲ Φιλοκτήτης ἦρχεν κτλ.

Philoctetes is opposed as commander to the people of Methone,
and the whole statement is opposed to the previously mentioned
peoples with their commanders. So in a period composed of two
pairs of correlated Clauses, as—

> Il. 1. 135 ἀλλ' εἰ μὲν δώσουσι γέρας . .
> εἰ δέ κε μὴ δώωσιν, ἐγὼ δέ κεν αὐτὸς ἕλωμαι.
> 9. 508 ὃς μέν τ' αἰδέσεται κούρας Διὸς ἆσσον ἰούσας,
> τὸν δὲ μέγ' ὤνησαν καί τ' ἔκλυον εὐχομένοιο·
> ὃς δέ κ' ἀνήνηται καί τε στερεῶς ἀποείπῃ,
> λίσσονται δ' ἄρα ταί γε Δία κτλ.

Here the δέ of the last Clause appears to carry on the opposition
of the second pair to the first, and so to repeat the δέ of its own
protasis. This use of δέ in apodosis to repeat or carry on the opposition of the whole sentence is regular in Attic; e.g. Xen.
Anab. 5. 6, 20 εἰ δὲ βούλεσθε . . πλοῖα δ' ὑμῖν πάρεστι : Isocr. 4. 98
ἃ δ' ἐστὶν ἴδια . . ταῦτα δ' ἐμὸν ἔργον ἐστὶν εἰπεῖν (Kühner, § 533,
2). It has been regarded as the key to the Homeric usage now
in question : * but this would compel us in many cases to give
different explanations of uses to which the same explanation is
evidently applicable. For instance, in the four lines last quoted,
if we account for the δέ of λίσσονται δ' ἄρα κτλ. as a repetition of
the δέ of its protasis ὃς δέ κ' κτλ., how do we treat the δέ of the
first apodosis (τὸν δὲ κτλ.)? The two forms are essentially
similar.

2. The δέ of the Apodosis is commonly regarded as a survival
from a period in which the Relative Clause or Conditional Protasis was not yet subordinate, so that the Apodosis, if it followed
the other, still needed or at least admitted of a connecting
Particle. Such an explanation is attractive because it presents
us with a case of the general law according to which the complex
sentence or period is formed by the welding together of originally
distinct simple sentences.† It is to be observed, however, that
the phenomenon in question is not necessarily more than a particular use of δέ. The survival may be, not of a paratactic form
of sentence, but only of a use of δέ where it is not a Conjunction. Such a use has been already seen in the Particle καί.
In the correlation ἀλλ' ὅτε δή—καὶ τότε δή we need find nothing

---

* So in the first edition of this book, following the discussion of Nägelsbach
in his *Anmerkungen zur Ilias* (p. 261 and p. 271, ed. 1834). The Excursus on
the subject was omitted in later editions. For the view adopted in the text
the author is indebted almost wholly to Dr. R. Nieberding, *Ueber die paratak-
tische Anknüpfung des Nachsatzes in hypotaktischen Satzgefügen, insbesondere bei Homer*,
Gross-Glogau, 1882.

† On the danger of explaining the Syntax of complex sentences by
recourse to a supposed survival of paratactic structure there is a timely warning
given by Brugmann, *Gr. Gr.* § 203.

more than the ordinary use of καί with the meaning *also, even ;* that is to say, it emphasises the *sequence* of the apodosis, just as it often emphasises single words or phrases. Similarly δέ may have been used to mark the *adversative* character of an apodosis.

3. These points may be illustrated by the parallel between καί *also, even* and οὐδέ or μηδέ=*not even, also not.* In this use δέ is clearly not a Conjunction, but merely serves to mark the natural opposition between the negative and some preceding affirmation (expressed or implied). Thus it is closely akin to the use in apodosis, the difference being only that it belongs to a single word rather than a Clause.

4. It is a confirmation of this view that among the cases of δέ in the apodosis we never find one in which the protasis is introduced by the corresponding μέν.* Where this is apparently the case it will be found that the μέν refers forward, not to the δέ of the immediate apodosis, but to a new sentence with δέ or some equivalent Particle : *e.g.*—

Il. 2. 188 ὅν τινα μὲν βασιλῆα καὶ ἔξοχον ἄνδρα κιχείη,
τὸν δ᾿ ἀγανοῖς ἐπέεσσιν κτλ.
ὃν δ᾿ αὖ δήμου τ᾿ ἄνδρα ἴδοι κτλ.

where the correspondence is not ὃν μέν—τὸν δέ—, but ὃν μέν—ὃν δ᾿ αὖ—. See also Il. 9. 508, 550., 12. 10., 18. 257., 20. 41, Od. 9. 56., 11. 147., 19. 329.

It has been observed that when the Protasis is a Relative Clause, δέ of the Apodosis is generally found after a Demonstrative. The only exceptions to this rule are, Il. 9. 510 ὃς δέ κ᾿ ἀνήνηται . . λίσσονται δ᾿ ἄρα ταί γε κτλ., and Il. 23. 319 ἀλλ᾿ ὃς μέν θ᾿ ἵπποισι . . ἵπποι δὲ πλανόωνται κτλ. (Schömann, *Opusc. Acad.* ii. p. 97.)

335.] **Enclitic δέ.** There are two uses which may be noticed under this heading :—

(1) The δε of ὅ-δε, τόσοσ-δε, τοιόσ-δε is properly an Enclitic (as the accent shows).

The form τοῖσ-δεσι or τοῖσ-δεσσι may be a trace of an inflected Pronoun akin to δέ (related to it perhaps as τις to τε) ; or it may be merely a form created by the analogy of other Datives in -εσσι, -εσι.

(2) The δε which is suffixed to Accusatives expressing *motion to* is generally treated as an Enclitic in respect of accent : as οἴκόνδε, πόλεμόνδε. The ancient grammarians, however, wrote δέ as a distinct orthotone word, hence οἶκον δέ, πόλεμον δέ, &c. (but οἴκαδε, φύγαδε were made exceptions).

---

* Nieberding, *op. cit.* p. 4.

It seems likely that the -δε of these two uses is originally the same. The force in both cases is that of a *local* Adverb. Whether it is to be identified with the Conjunction δέ is a further question.

ἀλλά, αὐτάρ, ἀτάρ, αὖ, αὖτε.

336.] The remaining Adversative Particles do not need much explanation.

ἀλλά and αὐτάρ are used (like δέ) in the apodosis, especially after a Clause with εἴ περ : as—

    Il. 1. 81 εἴ περ γάρ τε . . ἀλλά τε (cp. 8. 153., 19. 164).
    22. 390 εἰ δὲ θανόντων περ . . αὐτὰρ ἐγὼ κτλ.

αὐτάρ and ἀτάρ express a slighter opposition than ἀλλά, and accordingly are often used as Particles of transition ; *e.g.* in such formulae as ὡς οἱ μὲν . . αὐτὰρ κτλ. A similar use of ἀλλά may be seen with Imperatives; as ἀλλ' ἴθι, ἀλλ' ἄγε μοι τόδε εἰπέ, and the like. It is evident that the stronger Adversative is chosen where greater *liveliness* of tone is to be conveyed.

337.] αὖ and αὖτε (*again, on the contrary*) have nearly the same force as αὐτάρ, but do not begin the sentence : hence νῦν αὖ, τίς δ' αὖ, τίπτ' αὖτε, &c.: and so in correspondence to μέν or ἦ τοι, as Il. 4. 237 τῶν ἦ τοι . . ἡμεῖς αὖτε κτλ. They also serve to mark the apodosis of a Relative or Conditional Clause, as Il. 4. 321 εἰ τότε κοῦρος ἔα, νῦν αὖτέ με γῆρας ὀπάζει. Thus they have the two chief uses of δέ.

Originally, doubtless, αὖ meant *backwards*, but in Homer this sense is only found in the form αὖτις : though perhaps it survives in the sacrificial word ἀνέρυσαν.

The form ὅμως is later, the Homeric word being ἔμπης.

ὅμως is usually read in Il. 12. 393 ὅμως δ' οὐ λήθετο χάρμης, and Od. 11. 565 ἔνθα χ' ὅμως προσέφην. In both places however the Scholia indicate that the word was anciently circumflexed by some authorities.

ἦ.

338.] The Particle ἦ at the beginning of a sentence gives it the character of a strong *affirmation* :—

    Il. 1. 240 ἦ ποτ' Ἀχιλλῆος ποθὴ ἵξεται *be sure that one day &c.*

So, with an ironical tone,—

    Il. 1. 229 ἦ πολὺ λώϊόν ἐστι κατὰ στρατὸν εὐρὺν Ἀχαιῶν
        δῶρ' ἀποαιρεῖσθαι κτλ.

It is often used *interrogatively*, esp. in questions of surprise indignation, irony, &c. : as—

    Il. 2. 229 ἦ ἔτι καὶ χρυσοῦ ἐπιδεύεαι κτλ.

15. 504 ἢ ἔλπεσθ' ἢν νῆας ἕλῃ κορυθαίολος Ἕκτωρ
      ἐμβαδὸν ἵξεσθαι κτλ. (do you really hope &c.).

Od. 3. 312 ἢ οὐχ ἅλις ὡς κτλ. (is it not—?=surely it is) : cp.
      § 358, c.

Occasionally, in short parenthetical sentences, ἦ has a *concessive*
force, *it is true that*, hence *and yet, although* : as—

Il. 3. 214 παῦρα μέν, ἀλλὰ μάλα λιγέως, ἐπεὶ οὐ πολύμυθος,
      οὐδ' ἀφαμαρτοεπής· ἦ καὶ γένει ὕστερος ἦεν.

7. 393 οὔ φησιν δώσειν· ἦ μὴν Τρῶές γε κέλονται (§ 344).

11. 362 ἐξ αὖ νῦν ἔφυγες θάνατον, κύον· ἦ τέ τοι ἄγχι
      ἦλθε κακόν (so 18. 13).

22. 280 ἦ τοι ἔφην γε (=*though I did think;* so 22. 280).

The question whether ἦ (or ἤ) can be used to introduce a Dependent Interrogative depends upon a few passages. Bekker favours ἤ in this use, and
reads accordingly, *e. g.* Il. 1. 83 σὺ δὲ φράσαι ἤ με σαώσεις. The majority of the
editors recognise it in three or four places :—

Il. 8. 111 εἴσεται ἤ καὶ ἐμὸν δόρυ μαίνεται κτλ.

Od. 13. 415 ᾤχετο πευσόμενος μετὰ σὸν κλέος, ἤ που ἔτ' εἴης.

16. 137 ἀλλ' ἄγε μοι τόδε εἰπὲ καὶ ἀτρεκέως κατάλεξον,
      ἤ καὶ Λαέρτῃ αὐτὴν ὁδὸν ἄγγελος ἔλθω.

19. 325 πῶς γὰρ ἐμεῦ σύ, ξεῖνε, δαήσεαι, ἤ τι γυναικῶν
      ἀλλάων περίειμι ;

In all these places, however, there is manuscript support for εἰ, and so La
Roche reads in the two last. For the use of εἰ with the Subj. see § 294, with
the Opt. § 314. It is difficult to derive the use of ἤ which Bekker supposes
either from the emphatic ἦ, or from the disjunctive ἠέ or ἤ (*Hom. Bl.* p. 59).
In any case there is no sufficient ground for deserting the MSS.

ἦ is often combined more or less closely with other Particles :
as ἦ τε (§ 332, 2), ἦ μάν, &c. (§§ 343–5), ἦ τοι (or ἤτοι), ἤδη (for
ἦ δή), and the correlative ἠμέν—ἠδέ. In these combinations ἦ
strengthens the other Particle. Note that—

ἠμέν—ἠδέ are used of slightly opposed things, especially when
alternation is implied : as—

Od. 2. 68 λίσσομαι ἠμὲν Ζηνὸς Ὀλυμπίου ἠδὲ Θέμιστος,
      ἥ τ' ἀνδρῶν ἀγορὰς ἠμὲν λύει ἠδὲ καθίζει·

i. e. 'assembles and dissolves again in turn' (Lat. *tum—tum*).
Cp. Il. 8. 395 ἠμὲν ἀνακλῖναι . . ἠδ' ἐπιθεῖναι : and so Il. 7. 301,
Od. 1. 97., 8. 383, and probably Il. 6. 149 ἠμὲν φύει ἠδ' ἀπο-
λήγει. The original emphasis may sometimes be traced, as in
the formula Il. 14. 234 ἠμὲν δή ποτ' ἐμὸν ἔπος ἔκλυες ἠδ' ἔτι καὶ
νῦν πείθευ *surely you have heard me before, and even so listen now.*

ἠδέ is also used (=*and*) without a preceding ἠμέν : but not to
begin a fresh sentence. Cp. § 331 *fin.* for the similar use of τε.

339.] ἦ after τί, ἐπεί. In most editions of Homer we find the

forms τίη (or τιή) and ἐπειή, which are evidently τί, ἐπεί with a
suffix -η of an affirmative or emphasising kind.

The ancient grammarians seem generally to have considered
this η as a distinct word. They lay down the rule that after
ἐπεί it is circumflexed, after τί oxytone. The form ἐπεὶ ἦ is
supported by the fact that it is chiefly found in the combination
ἐπεὶ ἦ πολὺ κτλ. (Il. 1. 169., 4. 56, 307, &c.); also with μάλα (Il.
1. 156 ἐπεὶ ἦ μάλα πολλὰ μεταξὺ κτλ., Od. 10. 465 ἐπεὶ ἦ μάλα
πολλὰ πέπασθε, cp. ἦ μάλα, Il. 17. 34), and καί (Il. 20. 437, Od.
16. 442).

The case of τί is different. There is no ground for writing
τί ἦ (like ἐπεὶ ἦ). The form τί ἤ, which is adopted by the most
recent editors on the authority of the ancients, is not satisfactory.
If this ἤ was originally the affirmative ἦ, the change of accent
would indicate that it had lost its character as a separate word.
And this is confirmed by the combination τί ἦ δὲ σὺ κτλ. (Il. 6.
55, &c.), which as now written is contrary to the general rule
for the place of δέ. Moreover the ancients were not unanimous
on the point, since Trypho wrote τίη in one word (Apollonius,
de Conj. p. 523).

It may be observed that the opinion of the grammarians as to
τίη has more weight than in the case of ἐπεὶ ἦ, since τίη and ὁτιή
were Attic. We may suspect therefore that the accentuation
ἐπεὶ ἦ rests on mere inference.

With τίη is to be placed the emphatic Nom. τύν-η *thou*, a form
which occurs in the Iliad only (cp. the Doric ἐγών-η).

<h3 style="text-align:center">ἠέ, ἤ.</h3>

340.] ἠέ and ἤ are used in Homer as equivalent forms of the
same Particle: which is (1) Disjunctive (*or*) and (2) used after
Comparatives (*than*).

The use of the Correlative ἠέ (ἤ)—ἠέ (ἤ)=*either—or* is also
common in Homer: as Il. 1. 504 ἢ ἔπει ἢ ἔργῳ: 3. 239 ἢ οὐχ
ἑσπέσθην .. ἢ δεύρω μὲν ἔποντο κτλ.

When a question is asked in a disjunctive form, the accent of
the Particle ἠέ, ἤ is thrown back, *i. e.* it is written ἦε or ἦ :—

Il. 13. 251 ἦέ τι βέβληαι, βέλεος δέ σε τείρει ἀκωκή,
         ἦέ τευ ἀγγελίης μετ᾿ ἔμ᾿ ἤλυθες ;

Od. 4. 362 ᾽Αντίνο᾿, ἤ ῥά τι ἴδμεν ἐνὶ φρεσίν, ἦε καὶ οὐκί ;

So when the first part of the question is not introduced by
a Particle; Il. 10. 534 ψεύσομαι ἢ ἔτυμον ἐρέω ; *shall I speak
falsehood or the truth ?* Od. 1. 226 εἰλαπίνη ἦε γάμος ; cp. 4. 314,
372. Indeed the first half of the sentence need not be interrogative ; as Od. 21. 193 ἔπος τί κε μυθησαίμην, ἢ αὐτὸς κεύθω ;

I would say a word ; or shall I keep it to myself ? (so perhaps Il. 14. 190).

One of the members of a disjunctive question may be itself Disjunctive : *e. g.*—

Il. 6. 377 πῇ ἔβη Ἀνδρομάχη λευκώλενος ἐκ μεγάροιο ;
ἠέ πῃ ἐς γαλόων ἢ εἰνατέρων ἐϋπέπλων,
ἦ ἐς Ἀθηναίης ἐξοίχεται κτλ.

Here ἢ εἰνατέρων offers an alternative for γαλόων, but the main question is between these two alternatives on one side and ἐς Ἀθηναίης κτλ. on the other.

Most editors of Homer recognise an *interrogative* use of the form ἦε, but erroneously.* The questions in which ἦε is found are all *disjunctive,* so that we must write ἠέ—ἦε (Il. 6. 378., 13. 251., 15. 735., 16. 12, 13, 17, Od. 1. 408., 2. 30., 11. 399). In—

Od. 13. 233 τίς γῆ ; τίς δῆμος ; τίνες ἀνέρες ἐγγεγάασιν ;
ἦ πού τις νήσων εὐδείελος, ἠέ τις ἀκτὴ | κεῖθ' κτλ.

ἦ που means *surely methinks:* the sense being, 'what land is this? It must be some island or else promontory.' Hence we should read ἠέ in the last clause, not ἦε (as Ameis, &c.).

ἠέ or ἤ=*than* is found after Comparatives ; also after Verbs implying comparison, as βούλομαι *I prefer,* φθάνω *I come sooner.*

The correlative ἤ τε—ἤ τε appears in three places, viz. Il. 9. 276 ἤ τ' ἀνδρῶν ἤ τε γυναικῶν (where it seems to be=ἠμέν—ἠδέ), 11. 410 ἤ τ' ἔβλητ' ἤ τ' ἔβαλ' ἄλλον, and 17. 42 ἤ τ' ἀλκῆς ἤ τε φόβοιο (where however Aristarchus read ἠδ'—ἠδέ). The single ἤ τε occurs with the meaning *or* in Il. 19. 148 ἤ τ' ἐχέμεν παρὰ σοί : and with the meaning *than* in Od. 16. 216 (§ 332). Considering the general difficulty of deciding between εἰ and ἤ in the text of Homer, we cannot regard the form ἤ τε as resting on good evidence : see the next section.

341.] Dependent Interrogative Clauses. A Disjunctive question after a Verb of *asking, saying, knowing,* &c. is generally expressed by the Correlatives ἠέ (ἤ)—ἦε (ἤ) : as—

Od. 1. 174 καί μοι τοῦτ' ἀγόρευσον ἐτήτυμον, ὄφρ' ἐΰ εἰδῶ,
ἠὲ νέον μεθέπεις, ἦ καὶ πατρώϊός ἐσσι κτλ.

Il. 2. 99 τλῆτε φίλοι καὶ μείνατ' ἐπὶ χρόνον, ὄφρα δαῶμεν,
ἦ ἐτεὸν Κάλχας μαντεύεται, ἦε καὶ οὐκί.

Other examples have been given in the account of the Subjunc-

---

* This has been well shown by Dr. Praetorius, in a dissertation to which I am largely indebted (*Der homerische Gebrauch von ἤ (ἠέ) in Fragesätzen,* Cassel, 1873). The rule as to the accentuation in a disjunctive question rests upon the unanimous testimony of the ancient grammarians, and is now generally adopted. The MSS. and the older editors give ἦέ or ἤ only.

tive (§ 280) and the Optative (§ 302). In general it will be seen that these Dependent Clauses are the same in form as the corresponding direct questions.

In a very few instances the first member of a sentence of this kind is without ἠέ (ἤ): as—

Od. 4. 109 οὐδέ τι ἴδμεν | ζώει ὅ γ᾽ ἦ τέθνηκε (4. 837., 11. 464). So Il. 10. 544 εἴπ᾽ ἄγε . . ὅππως τούσδ᾽ ἵππους λάβετον, καταδύντες ὅμιλον Τρώων, ἢ τίς σφωε πόρεν κτλ., Od. 4. 643.

The combination εἰ—ἦε (ἤ) is often found in the MSS. of Homer; see Il. 2. 367., 8. 532, Od. 4. 28, 712, 789., 16. 238, 260., 17. 308., 18. 265., 24. 217. La Roche (following Bekker) reads ἤ—ἦε (ἤ) in all these places.

The common texts have in one place εἴ τε—ἦε,

Il. 2. 349 γνώμεναι εἴ τε ψεῦδος ὑπόσχεσις ἦε καὶ οὐκί.

In this instance, if the reading is right, there is a slight irregularity : the speaker beginning as if he meant to use εἴ τε—εἴ τε, and changing to the familiar ἦε καὶ οὐκί. But the best MSS. have εἴ τε—εἴ τε.

A change of construction may also be seen in Od. 24. 235-8 μερμήριξε . . κύσσαι καὶ περιφῦναι . . ἦ πρῶτ᾽ ἐξερέοιτο *he debated about embracing &c., or should he first ask &c.*

μάν, μήν, μέν.

342.] The three words μάν, μήν, μέν agree so nearly in meaning and usage that they are to be regarded as etymologically connected, if not merely varieties of the same original form. The two former (with the long ā, η) express strong affirmation (= *surely, indeed,* &c.). The shorter form μέν is also originally a Particle of affirmation, but has acquired derivative uses of which the chief are : (1) the concessive use, preparing us for a Clause with an Adversative δέ, αὐτάρ, ἀλλά, &c. : and (2) the use in the second of two Clauses with the meaning *yet, nevertheless.*

Taking the generally received text of Homer, we find that μάν occurs 24 times, and that there are only two places in which it is not followed by a vowel. The exceptions are, Il. 5. 895 ἀλλ᾽ οὐ μάν σ᾽ ἔτι δηρὸν ἀνέξομαι ἄλγε᾽ ἔχοντα, where μάν may be due to the parallel Il. 17. 41 ἀλλ᾽ οὐ μὰν ἔτι δηρὸν ἀπείρητος πόνος ἔσται, and Il. 5. 765 ἄγρει μάν οἱ (*i. e.* ϝοι) ἔπορσον κτλ. (cp. Il. 7. 459 ἄγρει μὰν ὅτ᾽ ἂν κτλ.). On the other hand μήν, which occurs 10 times, is followed by a consonant in every place except Il. 19. 45 καὶ μὴν οἱ τότε γ᾽ εἰς ἀγορὴν ἴσαν. These facts have not yet been satisfactorily explained. Bekker in his second edition (1858) wrote μήν throughout for μάν, and sought to distinguish μήν and μέν as far as the metre allowed according to Attic usage (*H. B.* pp. 34, 62). Cobet on the contrary proposed to restore μέν for μήν (*Misc. Crit.* p. 365), and so far as these two forms are concerned his view is probable enough. But how are we to explain the peculiar facts as to μάν? We can hardly account for it except as a genuine Homeric form, and such a form must have been used before consonants as well as vowels. If so, we can only suppose that an original μάν was changed into μέν whenever it came before a consonant, and preserved when the metre made this corruption impossible.

It is to be observed also that μάν and μήν are almost confined to the Iliad, in which μάν occurs 22 times and μήν 7 times. In the Odyssey μάν is found twice, viz. in 11. 344., 17. 470, and μήν three times, in 11. 582, 593., 16. 440 (= Il. 23. 410). It appears then that μέν is the only form which really belongs to the language of the Odyssey. Consequently the substitution of μέν for μάν in the Iliad may have taken place very early. The change of μέν to μήν probably belongs to the later period when μήν had been established in Ionic and Attic prose.

343.] μάν has an affirmative and generally a hortatory or interjectional force: as in ἄγρει μάν *nay come!* (Il. 5. 765., 7. 459), and ἦ μάν, οὐ μάν, used when a speech begins in a tone of surprise, triumph, or the like ; as—

Il. 2. 370 ἦ μὰν αὖτ' ἀγορῇ νικᾷς, γέρον, υἷας 'Αχαιῶν.

12. 318 οὐ μὰν ἀκληεῖς Λυκίην κάτα κοιρανέουσιν
ἡμέτεροι βασιλῆες (cp. 4. 512., 13. 414., 14. 454, &c.).

An approach to the force of an emphatic *yet* appears in—

Il. 8. 373 ἔσται μὰν ὅτ' ἂν αὖτε φίλην γλαυκώπιδα εἴπῃ·

and in ἀλλ' οὐ μάν (Il. 5. 895., 17. 41, 418, &c.), μὴ μάν (Il. 8. 512., 15. 476., 22. 304).

344.] μήν with a hortatory force occurs in Il. 1. 302 εἰ δ' ἄγε μήν πείρησαι *come, do but try.* The combination ἦ μήν is affirmative (rather than merely *concessive*),—not so much admitting as insisting upon an objection or reply : Il. 2. 291 ἦ μὴν καὶ πόνος ἐστί *it is true enough that there is toil:* 7. 393 ἦ μὴν Τρῶές γε κέλονται *I assure you that the Trojans bid him:* 9. 57 ἦ μὴν καὶ νέος ἐσσί *we must remember that you are young.* In καὶ μήν it emphasises the fact introduced by καί : Il. 19. 45 καὶ μὴν οἳ τότε γ' εἰς ἀγορὴν ἴσαν *observe that even these then went.*

345.] μέν is very common in Homer. The original simply affirmative force appears especially in the combinations ἦ μέν, καὶ μέν, and the like, in which it is indistinguishable in sense from μήν.*

ἦ μέν is regularly used in *oaths*, and is even found with an Inf. in *oratio obliqua*, as Il. 1. 76 καί μοι ὄμοσσον ἦ μέν μοι . . ἀρήξειν. So in a strong asseveration, as Il. 7. 97 ἦ μὲν δὴ λώβη τάδε γ' ἔσσεται *this will really be a foul shame,* Od. 19. 235 ἦ μὲν πολλαί γ' αὐτὸν ἐθηήσαντο γυναῖκες *you may be sure that many women gazed with wonder at it.* In these and similar passages μέν

---

* On the uses of μέν see the dissertation of Carl Mutzbauer, *Der homerische Gebrauch der Partikel* **MEN**, Köln, 1884–86.

strengthens a purely affirmative ἦ, and there is no sense of *contrast*. The adversative use may be perceived, as with the simple ἦ (§ 338) and ἦ μήν, when a speaker insists on his assertion as true along with or in spite of other facts: *e.g.* in Od. 10. 64 πῶς ἦλθες, Ὀδυσεῦ; τίς τοι κακὸς ἔχραε δαίμων; ἦ μέν σ' ἐνδυκέως ἀπεπέμπομεν *surely we sent you on your way with due provision:* and in the common form of reproach, Il. 11. 765 ὦ πέπον, ἦ μὲν σοί γε Μενοίτιος ὧδ' ἐπέτελλε (cp. 5. 197., 9. 252). So with ironical emphasis, Il. 3. 430 ἦ μὲν δὴ πρίν γ' εὔχε' κτλ. *why surely you boasted &c.*, cp. 9. 348.

The corresponding negative form μὴ μέν occurs in formal oaths (§ 358, *b*), and with the Opt. in a sort of imprecation in Od. 22. 462 μὴ μὲν δὴ καθαρῷ θανάτῳ ἀπὸ θυμὸν ἐλοίμην κτλ. (cp. μὴ μάν). Denial insisted upon in view of some state of things is expressed by οὐ μέν, as Il. 4. 372 οὐ μὲν Τυδέϊ γ' ὧδε φίλον πτωσκαζέμεν ἦεν (*why do you shrink?*) *surely Tydeus did not.*

The form καὶ μέν answers closely to the Attic καὶ μήν, which is used to call attention to a fact, especially as the ground of an argument; as Il. 18. 362 καὶ μὲν δή πού τις μέλλει βροτὸς κτλ. *a mortal, remember, will accomplish his will:* (*much more a great goddess*): Il. 1. 269 καὶ μὲν τοῖσιν ἐγὼ μεθομίλεον (*these were the mightiest of men*): *yes, and I was of their fellowship.* Sometimes the fact is first indicated, then dwelt upon in a fresh clause with καὶ μέν: Il. 9. 497 στρεπτοὶ δέ τε καὶ θεοὶ αὐτοί, . . καὶ μὲν τοὺς θυέεσσι κτλ. *even gods may be moved* . . *they are indeed turned from their anger by sacrifice &c.*: cp. 24. 488, Od. 7. 325., 14. 85. Similarly when a new point in the narrative is reached: as Il. 6. 194 καὶ μέν οἱ Λύκιοι τέμενος τάμον *yes and* (besides what the king gave) *the Lycian people made him a τέμενος* (cp. 6. 27., 23. 174., 24. 732).

The adversative sense—*but yet, but surely*—is chiefly found after a negative, μέν being used either alone or in combination with an adversative Conjunction (ἀλλά, ἀτάρ): as—

Il. 1. 602 δαίνυντ', οὐδέ τι θυμὸς ἐδεύετο δαιτὸς ἐΐσης
οὐ μὲν φόρμιγγος *nor yet the phorminx.*

2. 703 οὐδὲ μὲν οὐδ' οἳ ἄναρχοι ἔσαν, πόθεόν γε μὲν ἀρχόν.

Od. 15. 405 οὔ τι περιπληθὴς λίην τόσον, ἀλλ' ἀγαθὴ μέν.

Il. 6. 123 οὐ μὲν γάρ ποτ' ὄπωπα . . ἀτὰρ μὲν νῦν γε κτλ.

Also after a question—

Il. 15. 203 ἦ τι μεταστρέψεις; στρεπταὶ μέν τε φρένες ἐσθλῶν.

With the Article μέν is sometimes used to bring in a parenthesis, which may be simply affirmative, or indicate some opposition:—

Il. 1. 234 ναὶ μὰ τόδε σκῆπτρον, τὸ μὲν οὔ ποτε φύλλα καὶ

ὄζουs φύσει (= by this sceptre, even as it shall
never &c.).

5. 892 μητρόs τοι μένος ἐστὶν ἀάσχετον, οὐκ ἐπιεικτόν,
   Ἥρηs, τὴν μὲν ἐγὼ σπουδῇ δάμνημ' ἐπέεσσι
   she is indeed one whom I can hardly tame.

Cp. Il. 10. 440., 15. 40., 16. 141. A less emphatic use (merely
to bring out a new point in the story) is not uncommon : as Il.
2. 101 ἔστη σκῆπτρον ἔχων, τὸ μὲν κτλ.: cp. Il. 18. 84, 131., 23.
328, 808, Od. 9. 320, 321. Further, the interposed statement
may have a double reference, a corresponding Clause with δέ or
αὐτάρ serving to resume the narrative : as—

   Il. 8. 256 ἀλλὰ πολὺ πρῶτος Τρώων ἕλεν ἄνδρα κορυστήν,
   Φραδμονίδην Ἀγέλαον· ὁ μὲν φύγαδ' ἔτραπεν ἵππους,
   τῷ δὲ μεταστρεφθέντι κτλ. (so ibid. 268–271).

Again, the return to the main story after a digression may be
marked by a similar form : e.g. in Od. 6. 13 (after a parenthetical
account of the Phaeacians and Alcinous) τοῦ μὲν ἔβη πρὸς δῶμα
κτλ. now it was to his house that she went: cp. Od. 9. 325.

TOI.

346.] The enclitic τοι seems properly to express a *restricted*
affirmation, generally qualifying a preceding statement : *at least,
yet surely,* &c. It is especially used of a *concession*, whether
made by the speaker or claimed from the person addressed : as
Il. 4. 405 ἡμεῖς τοι πατέρων μέγ' ἀμείνονες εὐχόμεθ' εἶναι: 5. 801
Τυδεύς τοι μικρὸς μὲν ἔην δέμας, ἀλλὰ μαχητής *Tydeus, you must
admit, &c.*: 5. 892 μητρός τοι μένος ἐστὶν ἀάσχετον *I admit (as an
excuse)*: 8. 294 οὐ μέν τοι ὅση δύναμίs γε πάρεστι παύομαι: cp. 5.
873., 6. 211., 10. 250, Od. 2. 280, &c. So again in maxims,
Od. 2. 276 παῦροι γάρ τοι παῖδες κτλ. *few children, it must be said,*
&c. : Il. 23. 315 μήτι τοι δρυτόμος κτλ. *it is by understanding, after
all, that the woodman &c.* : Od. 9. 27 οὔ τοι ἔγωγε ἧς γαίης δύναμαι
κτλ. *I cannot, when all is said, &c.*: Il. 22. 488, Od. 8. 329, &c.

τοι is combined in Homer with Adversative Particles, as αὐτάρ
τοι, ἀλλά τοι (Il. 15. 45, Od. 18. 230); and with μέν (but not
closely, as in the later μέντοι *but*). So with the Affirmative ἦ in
ἦ τοι (or ἤτοι), which expresses a restricted concession (Il. 1. 140,
211., 5. 724, &c.). But the combinations καίτοι *and yet*, τοίνυν
so then, and the Disjunctive ἤτοι *either, or*, are post-Homeric.

τοι has the first place in the sentence in the compound τοιγάρ,
which is used to begin speeches ; as Il. 1. 76 τοιγὰρ ἐγὼν ἐρέω *so
then I will speak*. It is generally used with the First Person,
and has a kind of apologetic force (= *I will say, since I must
speak*). In Attic it survives in the compounds τοιγάρτοι, τοι-
γαροῦν : and the same meaning is commonly expressed by τοίνυν.

It has sometimes been thought that τοι is originally the same as the Dat. of σύ, meaning 'I tell you' or the like. The orthotone τοιγάρ (or τοὶ γάρ, as some MSS. read) is difficult to explain on this view. It has also been explained as the Locative of τό : cp. the Dat. τῷ = in that case, therefore. Or it may be from the same stem as τις and τε (as Kühner holds, § 507) : cp. που (δή που) = somehow, thence surely. But the Loc. of this stem exists already in the form ποῖ whither.

ἄρα, γάρ.

347.] The Adverb ἄρα properly means *fittingly, accordingly* (root ἀρ- *to fit*). The forms ἄρ and ῥα seem to be varieties produced by difference of stress, answering to the different values which the Particle may have in the sentence. Of these ἄρ retains its accent, but ῥα, the shortest form, is enclitic.

The ordinary place of ἄρα is at the beginning of a Clause which expresses what is *consequent* upon something already said. But occasionally it follows a Participle in the same Clause, as in the formula ἦ τοι ὅ γ' ὡς εἰπὼν κατ' ἄρ' ἕζετο (cp. Il. 2. 310., 5. 748).

It is to be observed, however, that ἄρα may indicate a *reason* (as well as a consequence) : that is to say, we may go back from a fact to the *antecedent* which falls in with and so *explains* it. *E. g.* Il. 1. 429 χωόμενον κατὰ θυμὸν ἐϋζώνοιο γυναικός, τήν ῥα . . ἀπηύρων *whom (and this was the reason of his anger) they had taken away.* So in the combinations ὅς ῥα, ἐπεί ῥα, ὅτι ῥα, οὕνεκ' ἄρα = *because (and this is the explanation)* : also in γάρ ῥα, as Il. 1. 113 καὶ γάρ ῥα Κλυταιμνήστρης προβέβουλα.

ἄρα is also found in the first of two correlative Clauses, as—

εἴ τ' ἄρ' ὅ γ' εὐχωλῆς ἐπιμέμφεται εἴ θ' ἑκατόμβης.

ὡς ἄγαγ' ὡς μήτ' ἄρ τις ἴδῃ μήτ' ἄρ τε νοήσῃ.

The parallel form of the sentence enables us to regard the first Clause, by anticipation, as falling in with and completing the second.

The Attic ἆρα is unknown to Homer. Whether it is identical with ἄρα seems doubtful. It is worth while noticing that ἆρα answers in usage to the Homeric combination ἦ ῥα (*is it then—?*).

348.] The Causal Particle γάρ is originally a compound of γε and ἄρα, but the two elements have so completely united into a new whole that the fresh combination γάρ ῥα is found in Homer.

γάρ serves to indicate that the Clause in which it is used is a *reason* or *explanation*, usually of something just mentioned or suggested : as τῷ γὰρ ἐπὶ φρεσὶ θῆκε θεὰ λευκώλενος Ἥρη· κήδετο γὰρ Δαναῶν, κτλ. Thus it follows the *sequence of thought*—by which we go back from a consequent to an antecedent—whereas ἄρα more commonly (though not always) indicates the sequence of the facts themselves.

Compare the double use of ὅ, ὅτι, ὅ τε (1) to express a cause, (2) to express a consequent used as an argument (cp. τοίου γὰρ καὶ πατρός, ὃ καὶ πεπνυμένα βάζεις, and other examples in § 269). To understand the ordinary use of γάρ we have only to suppose that when a speaker was going back upon an *antecedent* fact, he generally used the combination γε ἄρα (γ' ἄρ, γάρ), rather than the simple ἄρα. The principle of this usage is that a causal relation may be indicated by a distinction of emphasis, such as γε would express (as indeed γε alone sometimes has a distinctly *causal* force).

As subordinate or exceptional uses, we have to note the following :—

1. The use of γάρ to introduce a mere explanation, which became very common in Attic (*e. g.* Thuc. 1. 8 μαρτύριον δέ· Δήλου γὰρ κτλ.) and may be traced back to Homer. Thus—

Il. 8. 147 ἀλλὰ τόδ' αἰνὸν ἄχος κραδίην καὶ θυμὸν ἱκάνει·
  Ἕκτωρ γάρ ποτε φήσει κτλ.

This idiom—by which the Clause with γάρ becomes a kind of Object-Clause, in apposition to a Pronoun—may be compared with the use of ὅτι and οὕνεκα with the meaning *that*, instead of *because*: see §§ 268, 269. In both cases the language does not clearly distinguish between the *ground* of a fact (which is properly a separate and prior fact), and a mere *analysis*, or statement of circumstances in which a fact consists.

2. The inversion (as it may be regarded) by which the Clause with γάρ precedes the fact explained ; as—

Il. 2. 802 Ἕκτορ, σοὶ δὲ μάλιστ' ἐπιτέλλομαι ὧδέ γε ῥέξαι·
  πολλοὶ γὰρ κατὰ ἄστυ μέγα Πριάμου ἐπίκουροι,
  ἄλλη δ' ἄλλων γλῶσσα πολυσπερέων ἀνθρώπων·
  τοῖσιν ἕκαστος ἀνὴρ σημαινέτω (Il. 13. 736., 23.
      890, Od. 1. 337., 9. 319., 10. 174, 190, 226,
      383., 11. 69., 12. 154, 208, 320, &c.).

Here the speaker begins by stating something that leads up to his main point. Sometimes, especially when the reason is stated at some length, the main point is marked as an inference by τῷ *so, therefore*: as—

Il. 7. 328 πολλοὶ γὰρ τεθνᾶσι κάρη κομόωντες Ἀχαιοί,
  τῶν νῦν αἷμα κελαινὸν . .
  331 τῷ σε χρὴ πόλεμον μὲν ἄμ' ἠοῖ παῦσαι Ἀχαιῶν.

So Il. 13. 228., 15. 739., 17. 221, 338., 23. 607; there is no instance in the Odyssey.

When the Clause with γάρ precedes, it may be opposed to the preceding context: hence the γάρ may be combined with adversative Conjunctions, as—

Il. 12. 326 νῦν δ' ἔμπης γὰρ κῆρες ἐφεστᾶσιν θανάτοιο . .
  ἴομεν κτλ. (cp. Il. 7. 73., 17. 338., 24. 223).

Od. 14. 355   ἀλλ' οὐ γάρ σφιν ἐφαίνετο κέρδιον εἶναι
μαίεσθαι προτέρω· τοὶ μὲν πάλιν αὖτις ἔβαινον
νηὸς ἐπὶ γλαφυρῆς (cp. Od. 19. 591).

ἀλλά—γάρ also occurs without a subsequent Clause :—

Od. 10. 201 κλαῖον δὲ λιγέως, θαλερὸν κατὰ δάκρυ χέοντες·
ἀλλ' οὐ γάρ τις πρῆξις ἐγίγνετο μυρομένοισι.

Here it has the force of ' but be that as it may,' ' but the truth
is ' (Riddell, *Dig.* § 147). That is, ἀλλά—γάρ meets what has
preceded not by a simple opposition, but by one which consists in
going back to a *reason* for the opposite : which may be enough
to convey the speaker's meaning.

In these uses of γάρ the peculiarity is more logical than grammatical. The γάρ (or rather the ἄρα contained in it) indicates
that the Clause gives a *reason* or *explanation,* which the speaker
chooses to mention before the consequent or thing to be explained.
The use only strikes us because the English *for* is restricted to
causal clauses placed in the more natural order.

With δέ—γάρ and ἀλλά—γάρ it is incorrect (as Riddell shows,
l. c.) to treat the Clause with γάρ as a parenthesis (writing *e.g.*
νῦν δ'—ἔμπης γὰρ κτλ.). The Clause so introduced is always in
opposition to the preceding context, so that the δέ or ἀλλά has its
full force.

3. After the Relative ὅς, ἥ, ὅ : as—

Il. 12. 344 ἀμφοτέρω μὲν μᾶλλον· ὃ γάρ κ' ὄχ' ἄριστον ἁπάντων
εἴη (so Il. 23. 9, Od. 24. 190).

Od. 1. 286 (Μενέλαος) ὃς γὰρ δεύτατος ἦλθεν (cp. 17. 172).

So with ὡς γάρ=*for thus,* and ἵνα γάρ (Il. 10. 127).

These are generally regarded as instances of the original use of
ὅς as a Demonstrative (§ 265). But it is only the use of γάρ that
is peculiar; or rather, this is only another case in which γάρ is
not translated by *for.* It will be seen that ὃς γάρ may always be
replaced by ὃς ἄρα without changing the sense.

4. In abrupt *questions,* and expressions of *surprise :* as—

Il. 1. 123 πῶς γάρ τοι δώσουσι γέρας μεγάθυμοι Ἀχαιοί ;
why, how are the Greeks to give you a prize?

18. 182 Ἶρι θεά, τίς γάρ σε θεῶν ἐμοὶ ἄγγελον ἧκε ;

1. 293 ἦ γάρ κεν δειλός τε καὶ οὐτιδανὸς καλεοίμην κτλ.
why, I should be a coward &c.

So in the formulae of *wish,* εἰ γάρ, αἲ γάρ, &c. In all such cases
the γάρ seems to be mainly interjectional. Properly it implies
that the speaker is taking up the thread of a previous speech,
and as it were continuing the construction : the new Clause being
one that gives a reason, or affects to do so ironically. Particles
so used easily acquire an irrational character. We may compare

the use of δέ and τ' ἄρα in questions, ὥς in expressions of *wish*,
ἀλλά before an imperative (§ 336): also the English use of *why*,
well, and similar pleonasms.

οὖν, δή, νυ, θην.

349.] οὖν in Homer does not properly express *inference*, or even
consequence (like ἄρα). Its use is to affirm something with reference to other facts, already mentioned or known ; hence it may
generally be represented by a phrase such as *after all, be this as it
may*, &c. E. g.—

Il. 2. 350 φημὶ γὰρ οὖν *for I do declare that &c.*

Od. 11. 350 ξεῖνος δὲ τλήτω, μάλα περ νόστοιο χατίζων,
    ἔμπης οὖν ἐπιμεῖναι ἐς αὔριον (*nevertheless to wait*).

Like ἄρα, it is used to emphasise correlative Clauses, but only
with the negative οὔτε—οὔτε and μήτε—μήτε : as—

Od. 6. 192 οὔτ' οὖν ἐσθῆτος δευήσεαι οὔτε τευ ἄλλου.

Il. 16. 97 αἲ γάρ.. μήτε τις οὖν Τρώων . . μήτε τις Ἀργείων, κτλ.
    (so Il. 8. 7., 17. 20., 20. 7, Od. 1. 414., 2. 200.,
    11. 200., 16. 302., 17. 401).

The combination γ' οὖν (not to be written γοῦν in Homer)
occurs only twice, with the meaning *in any case:*—

Il. 5. 258 εἰ γ' οὖν ἕτερός γε φύγῃσι *if one of the two does
    (after all) escape.*

16. 30 μὴ ἐμέ γ' οὖν οὗτός γε λάβοι χόλος
    (cp. 19. 94 κατὰ δ' οὖν ἕτερόν γε πέδησεν).

As an emphatic Particle of *transition* οὖν is found in μὲν οὖν (Il.
9. 550, and several times in the Odyssey), much more frequently
in the combinations ἐπεὶ οὖν, ὡς οὖν. In these an approach to the
illative force may perhaps be observed.

350.] δή is properly a *temporal* Particle, meaning *now, at
length* (Lat. *jam*): hence it implies arriving at a result, as ἐξ οὗ
δὴ τὰ πρῶτα διαστήτην *from the time that the point was reached
when they quarrelled :* εἰ δή *if it has come to this that*, and so *if
finally, if really*. With Superlatives it expresses that the highest
stage has been reached, as Il. 1. 266 κάρτιστοι δὴ κεῖνοι κτλ. *these
were quite (finally) the mightiest*. So in questions, πῶς δή *how has
it come to be that—; and prohibitions, μὴ δή do not go so far as to—.

δή may begin a sentence in Homer, as Il. 15. 437 Τεῦκρε πέπον,
δὴ νῶϊν ἀπέκτατο πιστὸς ἑταῖρος : and often in the combinations
δὴ τότε (*tum vero*), and δὴ γάρ. The original meaning is best
seen in these forms (where δή is emphatic), and in ἤδη (for ἤ δή),
and ἐπεὶ δή.

As δή is one of the words which unite with a following vowel, so as to form one syllable, it is sometimes written δ', and so is liable to be confused with δέ. This occurs especially in the combinations δὴ αὖ, δὴ αὐτός, δὴ οὕτως : as Il. I. 131 μὴ δὴ οὕτως, 340 εἴ ποτε δὴ αὖτε, 10. 385 πῇ δὴ οὕτως, 20. 220 ὃς δὴ ἀφνειότατος κτλ. So in εἰ δ' ἄγε the sense generally requires δή : see § 321.

Note that δῆτα, δῆθεν (cognate or derivative forms) are post-Homeric ; as also are the combinations δήπου, καὶ δή.

351.] νυ is obviously a shortened form of νῦν *now*. It is used as an affirmative Particle (like δή, but somewhat less emphatic), especially in combinations such as ἦ ῥά νυ, καί νύ κε, οὔ νυ, μή νυ, ἐπεί νυ, and after Interrogatives, as τίς νυ *who now*, τί νυ *why now* (see Od. I. 59–62).

The form νυ is exclusively Epic : νυν (ῠ), which is used by Attic poets (Ellendt, *Lex. Soph.* ii. p. 183) appears in Il. 10. 105 ὅσα πού νυν ἐέλπεται, and Il. 23. 485 δεῦρό νυν, ἢ τρίποδος κτλ. : but it is probably not Homeric.

In Il. 10. 105 the sense is distinctly temporal, and accordingly we should probably read νῦν ἔλπεται. The temporal sense also suits Il. 23. 485, where moreover there is a variant δεῦρό γε νῦν τρίποδος, found in the Scholia on Aristophanes (Ach. 771, Eq. 788).

352.] θην is an affirmative enclitic, giving a mocking or ironical force, like the later δήπου and δῆθεν (which is perhaps originally δή θην) : as Il. 2. 276 οὔ θήν μιν πάλιν αὖτις ἀνήσει θυμὸς ἀγήνωρ *his bold spirit will not I imagine impel him again*: Il. 13. 620 λείψετέ θην οὕτω γε *methinks in this fashion you will leave &c.* It is only Epic.

περ.

353.] The enclitic Particle περ is evidently a shorter form of the Preposition πέρι, which in its adverbial use has the meaning *beyond, exceedingly* (§ 185). Accordingly περ is *intensive*, denoting that the word to which it is subjoined is true in a high degree, in its fullest sense, &c. : *e. g.*—

Il. 23. 79 λάχε γεινόμενόν περ *was my fate even from my birth*.

Od. 1. 315 μή μ' ἔτι νῦν κατέρυκε λιλαιόμενόν περ ὁδοῖο.

8. 187 στιβαρώτερον οὐκ ὀλίγον περ.

Il. 2. 236 οἴκαδέ περ σὺν νηυσὶ νεώμεθα
(= *let us have nothing short of return home*).

8. 452 σφῶϊν δὲ πρίν περ τρόμος ἔλλαβε φαίδιμα γυῖα
even beforehand trembling seized your knees.

13. 72 ἀρίγνωτοι δὲ θεοί περ *gods, surely, are easily known*.

Od. 4. 34 αἴ κέ ποθι Ζεὺς | ἐξοπίσω περ παύσῃ ὀϊζύος.

So with Relatives, ὅς περ *the very one who,* ὡς ἔσεταί περ (Attic ὥσπερ καὶ ἔσται) *just as it will be,* ὅτε περ *just when.* Also εἴ περ *even if,* and ἠέ περ or ἤ περ *even than.*

Usually, however, περ implies a sense of opposition; *i. e.* it emphasises something as true *in spite of* a preceding assertion: as οὔ τι δυνήσεαι ἀχνύμενός περ *thou wilt not be able, however much vexed,* πολέες περ ἐόντες *many as they are,* πίνοντά περ ἔμπης *even though drinking,* &c.; and with Substantives, Il. 20. 65 τά τε στυγέουσι θεοί περ *which even the gods* (gods though they are) *dread.* So Il. 1. 353 ἐπεί μ’ ἔτεκές γε, μινυνθάδιόν περ ἐόντα *since you are my mother, short-lived though I am.* Or it may imply compensation for the *absence* of something else: Il. 1. 508 ἀλλὰ σύ πέρ μιν τῖσον *do thou honour him* (since Agamemnon will not); 17. 121 αἴ κε νέκυν περ Ἀχιλλῆϊ προφέρωμεν γυμνόν· ἀτὰρ τά γε τεύχε’ κτλ.

The intensive καί and περ are often used with the same word or phrase: as καὶ ὀψέ περ *even though late,* καὶ πρὸς δαίμονά περ *even though it were against a higher power,* καὶ πεζός περ ἐών *though only on foot:* εἰ δὲ καὶ Ἕκτορά περ φιλέεις, &c. So with οὐδέ *not even,* as οὐδὲ θεοί περ *not even the gods,* οὐδ’ ὥς περ *not even so,* οὐδέ νυ σοί περ *not even to you.*

The combination καί περ (or καίπερ) occurs in Homer in one place only, viz. Od. 7. 224 καί περ πολλὰ παθόντα.

When καί precedes a word followed by περ, it is always = *even* (not *and*). Hence in Il. 5. 135 καὶ πρίν περ μεμαώς means *even though formerly eager,* and is to be taken with the preceding line, not with the succeeding δὴ τότε μιν κτλ. Thus there is no anacoluthon, as is generally assumed.

γε.

354.] γε is used, like περ, to emphasise a particular word or phrase. It does not however *intensify* the meaning, or insist on the fact as *true,* but only calls attention to the word or fact, distinguishing it from others: *e. g.*—

Il. 1. 81 εἴ περ γάρ τε χόλον γε καὶ αὐτῆμαρ καταπέψῃ,
ἀλλά τε καὶ μετόπισθεν ἔχει κότον.

Here γε shows that the word χόλος is chosen in order to be contrasted with κότος. So too—

Il. 2. 379 εἰ δέ ποτ’ ἔς γε μίαν βουλεύσομεν, οὐκέτ’ ἔπειτα κτλ.
(if we could ever *agree,* instead of contending).

Again, where an idea is repeated—

Il. 5. 350 εἰ δὲ σύ γ’ ἐς πόλεμον πωλήσεαι, ἦ τέ σ’ ὀίω
ῥιγήσειν πόλεμόν γε.

Cp. also Il. 1. 299 ἐπεί μ’. ἀφέλεσθέ γε δόντες *since you have but*

Y

taken away what you gave (where we should rather emphasise
δόντες): Od. 4. 193 οὔ τοι ἔγωγε τέρπομ' ὀδυρόμενος .. νεμεσσῶμαί
γε μὲν οὐδὲν κλαίειν κτλ. *I do not take pleasure in lamenting, but
yet I do not say that I* complain *of a man weeping &c.* : 9. 393 τὸ
γὰρ αὖτε σιδήρου γε κράτος ἐστί *that is the strength of iron* (*in particular*) : 10. 93 οὐ μὲν γάρ ποτ' ἀέξετο κῦμά γ' ἐν αὐτῷ, οὔτε μέγ'
οὔτ' ὀλίγον, λευκὴ δ' ἦν ἀμφὶ γαλήνη *no wave at all* (nothing that
could be *called* a wave) *rose in it,* &c.

So too γε emphasises a word as a strong or appropriate one,
or as chosen under the influence of feeling (anger, contempt,
&c.). As examples may be quoted, Od. 9. 458 τῷ κέ οἱ ἐγκέφαλός
γε .. ῥαίοιτο κτλ. : 17. 244 τῷ κέ τοι ἀγλαΐας γε διασκεδάσειεν ἀπά-
σας : Il. 7. 198 ἐπεὶ οὐδ' ἐμὲ νήϊδά γ' οὕτως ἔλπομαι κτλ. So in the
phrase εἴ ποτ' ἔην γε, which means *if he lived at all,* and thus is
a form of asseveration ; *e.g.* Il. 3. 180 δαὴρ αὖτ' ἐμὸς ἔσκε κυνώ-
πιδος εἴ ποτ' ἔην γε *he was my brother-in-law if he was anything,*
i. e. that he was so is as sure as that there was such a person.

γε is common with the Article (§ 257, 2) and the Personal
Pronouns (so that it is usual to write ὅγε, ἔγωγε as one word),
also with ὅδε, οὗτος, κεῖνος, and the corresponding Adverbs
ὧδε, τότε, &c. It serves chiefly to bring out the contrast which
these Pronouns more or less distinctly imply. Similarly with
words implying comparison, as ἄλλος and ἕτερος, πρίν, πάρος, &c.
When a special emphasis is intended, Homer usually employs
περ, as Od. 1. 59 οὐδέ νυ σοί περ ἐντρέπεται φίλον ἦτορ *not even are
you moved* (who are especially bound to care for Ulysses). So too,
as Nauck has pointed out (*Mél. gr.-rom.* iv. 501), πάρος γε
means *before* (*not now*), while πάρος περ means *even before* (*not
merely now*). Hence in Il. 13. 465 ὅς σε πάρος γε γαμβρὸς ἐὼν
ἔθρεψε the γε of the MSS. is right ; and so we should read (with
A against other MSS.) Il. 17. 587 ὃς τὸ πάρος γε μαλθακὸς
αἰχμητής, but (again with A) in Il. 15. 256 ὅς σε πάρος περ
ῥύομαι.

In a Conditional Protasis (with ὅς, ὅτε, εἰ, &c.), γε emphasises
the condition as such : hence εἴ γε *if only, always supposing that* ;
cp. Od. 2. 31 ἤν χ' ὑμῖν σάφα εἴποι, ὅτε πρότερός γε πύθοιτο *which
he would tell you, if and when he had been first to hear it.* On the
other hand, εἴ περ means *supposing ever so much,* hence *if really*
(Lat. *si quidem*). So when πρίν expresses a condition (§ 297) it
takes γε, as Il. 5. 288 πρίν γ' ἢ ἕτερόν γε πεσόντα κτλ.

οὐ, μή.

355.] οὐκί, οὐκ, οὐ. The full form οὐκί occurs in the formula
ἠὲ καὶ οὐκί or *else not* (Il. 2. 238, &c.), and one or two similar
phrases : Il. 15. 137 ὅς τ' αἴτιος ὅς τε καὶ οὐκί, and Il. 20. 255
πόλλ' ἐτεά τε καὶ οὐκί.

The general use of οὐ is to *deny* the predication to which it is attached (while μή *forbids* or *deprecates*). In some instances, however, οὐ does not merely negative the Verb, but expresses the *opposite* meaning : οὔ φημι is not *I do not say*, but *I deny, refuse ;* οὐκ ἐῶ *I forbid*, &c. (Krüger, § 67, 1, 1).

The uses of οὐ in Subordinate Clauses, and with the Infinitive and Participle, will be best treated along with the corresponding uses of μή (§§ 359, 360).

According to Delbrück (*Synt. Forsch.* iv. p. 147) the negative Particle was treated originally like the Prepositions, *i.e.* it was placed immediately before the Verb, and closely connected with it : as in the Latin *ne-scio, ne-queo, nolo*, and in some parallel Slavonic forms. The same relation appears in the accent of οὔ φημι, and in the use of οὐ in the combinations οὐκ ἐθέλω, οὐκ ἐάω, &c., in which οὐ is retained where general rules would require μή (§ 359).

356.] οὐδέ, μηδέ. These forms are generally used as negative *connecting* Particles (*but not, and not*). Sometimes however they have a strengthening or emphatic force, corresponding to the similar use of καί in affirmative sentences ; as Il. 5. 485 τύνη δ' ἕστηκας, ἀτὰρ οὐδ' ἄλλοισι κελεύεις *you stand still (yourself)*, *and (what is more) do not call on the others to fight :* and in combination with περ, as Il. 4. 387 ἔνθ' οὐδὲ ξεῖνός περ ἐὼν κτλ. So καὶ ὅς *even he*, οὐδ' ὅς *not even he*, &c.

οὐδείς is originally an emphatic form (like the later οὐδὲ εἷς). In Homer the Neut. οὐδέν is occasionally found, sometimes as an emphatic Adverb, = *not at all*, as Il. 1. 244 ὅ τ' ἄριστον Ἀχαιῶν οὐδὲν ἔτισας (so Il. 1. 412., 16. 274., 22. 332, 513., 24. 370, Od. 4. 195., 9. 287) : sometimes as a Substantive, *nothing at all* (Nom. and Acc.), as Od. 9. 34 ὡς οὐδὲν γλύκιον *no single thing is sweeter* (cp. 18. 130., 22. 318). The adjectival use is found with ἔπος (Od. 4. 350., 17. 141), also in Il. 10. 216 τῇ μὲν κτέρας οὐδὲν ὁμοῖον, and perhaps Il. 22. 513 οὐδὲν σοί γ' ὄφελος (where οὐδέν may be adverbial). The Gen. Neut. appears in the Compound οὐδενός-ωρος *worth nothing* (Il. 8. 178). The Masc. occurs only in the phrase τὸ ὃν μένος οὐδενὶ εἴκων (Il. 22. 459, Od. 11. 515).

The form μηδείς is post-Homeric, except the form μηδέν, which occurs only in Il. 18. 500 ὁ δ' ἀναίνετο μηδὲν ἑλέσθαι.

357.] Double negation. This characteristic feature of Greek is caused by the tendency to *repeat* the negative Particle with any word or phrase to which the negation especially applies : as Il. 1. 114 ἐπεὶ οὔ ἑθέν ἐστι χερείων, οὐ δέμας κτλ. *since she is not inferior—not in form* &c. The emphatic οὐδέ and μηδέ are chiefly used in this way : as οὐ μὰν οὐδ' Ἀχιλεὺς κτλ. *no, not even Achilles* &c. : Il. 2. 703 οὐδὲ μὲν οὐδ' οἱ ἄναρχοι ἔσαν : Od. 8. 280 τά γ'

οὔ κέ τις οὐδὲ ἴδοιτο, οὐδὲ θεῶν μακάρων: Il. 6. 58 μηδ' ὅν τινα
γαστέρι μήτηρ κοῦρον ἐόντα φέροι μηδ' ὃς φύγοι.

358.] μή is commonly used (as we should expect) with the
Moods expressive of *command* or *wish*, viz. the Imperative, the
Subjunctive and the Optative. These uses having been discussed (§§ 278, 281, 299, 303, &c.), it only remains to notice
some idiomatic uses in which μή is found with the Mood of
simple *assertion* or *denial*.

With the **Indicative** μή is used in Homer—

(*a*) In the phrase μὴ ὤφελλον (or ὤφελον) *would that I had not
&c.* Logically the μή in this idiom belongs to the following
Infinitive (cp. § 355).

(*b*) In *oaths*, to express solemn or impassioned denial:—

Il. 10. 329 ἴστω νῦν Ζεὺς αὐτός, ἐρίγδουπος πόσις Ἥρης,
μὴ μὲν τοῖς ἵπποισιν ἀνὴρ ἐποχήσεται ἄλλος
(*I swear that no one else shall ride &c.*).

15. 36 ἴστω νῦν τόδε γαῖα . . .
41 μὴ δι' ἐμὴν ἰότητα Ποσειδάων ἐνοσίχθων | πημαίνει.

In this use μή denies by *disclaiming* (as it were) or protesting
against a fact supposed to be within the speaker's power (=*far
be it from me that &c.*). We should probably add—

Il. 19. 258 ἴστω νῦν Ζεὺς πρῶτα κτλ.
μὴ μὲν ἐγὼ κούρῃ Βρισηΐδι χεῖρ' ἐπένεικα,

where the MSS. have ἐπενεῖκαι. The Indic. form was restored
conjecturally by Stephanus.

(*c*) After ἦ, to express incredulity, &c.:—

Od. 6. 200 ἦ μή πού τινα δυσμενέων φάσθ' ἔμμεναι ἀνδρῶν
(*surely you do not suppose it is any enemy !*)

9. 405 ἦ μή τίς σευ μῆλα βροτῶν ἀέκοντος ἐλαύνει;
ἦ μή τίς σ' αὐτὸν κτείνει δόλῳ ἠὲ βίηφι;
(*surely no one is driving off your sheep ? &c.*)

This is the common type of 'question expecting a negative
answer,' viz. a strong form of denial uttered in a hesitating or
interrogative tone. Compare the quasi-interrogative use of ἦ
(§ 338) to indicate surprise or indignation.

(*d*) After Verbs of *fearing* which relate to a past event:—

Od. 5. 300 δείδω μὴ δὴ πάντα θεὰ νημερτέα εἶπεν.

Here, as with the Subj. (§ 281, 1), the Clause with μή passes into
an Object-Clause. The difference is that the Indicative shows
the event to be past.

So perhaps Od. 13. 216 μή τί μοι οἴχονται *I fear they are gone* : but the better
reading is οἴχωνται, the Subj. being understood as in Il. 1. 555 μή σε παρείπῃ

lest she have persuaded thee (*i. e.* prove to have persuaded); cp. Od. 21. 395
μὴ κέρα ἶπες ἔδοιεν *lest worms should* (*be found to*) *have eaten* (§ 303, 1). Cp. Matth.
xvi. 5 ἐπελάθοντο ἄρτους λαβεῖν *they found that they had forgotten* (Field's *Otium
Norvicense*, Pt. 3, p. 7).

The use of the Past Indicative after Verbs of *fearing* is closely parallel to the
use in Final Clauses, noticed in § 325. While the Clause, as an expression of
the speaker's mind about an event—his fear or his purpose—should have
a Subj. or Opt., the sense that the happening of the event is matter of past
fact causes the Indicative to be preferred. Cp. the Modal uses noticed in
§§ 324-326, and the remark in § 323 as to the tendency in favour of the
Indicative.

The essence of these idioms is the combination of the imperative *tone*—shown in the use of μή—with the Mood proper to a
simple assertion. The tendency to resort to the form of *prohibition* in order to express strong or passionate *denial* may be
seen in the use of μή with the Optative in *deprecating* a supposition (§ 299, *e*), and of μή with the Subj. in *oaths*, as Od. 12.
300., 18. 56.

359.] Conditional Clauses. The rule which prescribes μή as
the negative Particle to be used in every Clause of Conditional
meaning does not hold universally. In Homer—

(*a*) When the Verb is a Subjunctive or Optative μή is used:
the very few exceptions being confined to οὐκ ἐθέλω (Il. 3. 289.,
15. 492) and οὐκ ἐάω (Il. 20. 139), which are treated almost as
Compounds (§ 355). Cp. the use of οὐκ ἐθέλω in Final Clauses,
as Il. 5. 233 μή . . ματήσετον οὐδ᾽ ἐθέλητον κτλ.

(*b*) With the Relatives ὅς, ὅσος, &c. when the Verb is an
Indicative οὐ is generally used; as—

   Il. 2. 143 πᾶσι μετὰ πληθύν, ὅσοι οὐ βουλῆς ἐπάκουσαν.
   Od. 3. 348 ὥς τέ τευ ἢ παρὰ πάμπαν ἀνείμονος ἠὲ πενιχροῦ,
              ᾧ οὔ τι χλαῖναι κτλ. (a general description).

   Il. 2. 338 νηπιάχοις, οἷς οὔ τι μέλει κτλ. (so 7. 236., 18. 363).
The only clear instance of μή is Il. 2. 301 ἐστὲ δὲ πάντες μάρτυροι,
οὓς μὴ κῆρες ἔβαν θανάτοιο φέρουσαι, where the speaker wishes to
make an *exception* to what he has just said. In Od. 5. 489 ᾧ μὴ
πάρα γείτονες ἄλλοι we may supply either εἰσί or ἔωσι: the latter
is found in the similar cases Od. 4. 164., 23. 118. But Hesiod
uses μή with the Indic.; see Theog. 387, Op. 225.

(*c*) With εἰ and the Indicative οὐ is used when the Clause
with εἰ precedes the Principal Clause: as—

   Il. 4. 160 εἴ περ γάρ τε καὶ αὐτίκ᾽ Ὀλύμπιος οὐκ ἐτέλεσσε,
and similarly in Il. 9. 435., 15. 213, Od. 19. 85, and the (eight)
other places quoted in § 316. But when the Clause with εἰ follows the other, μή is used, as in the sentences of the form—

   Il. 2. 155 ἔνθα κεν . . νόστος ἐτύχθη | εἰ μὴ κτλ.

The only instance in which this rule fails seems to be—

Od. 9. 410 εἰ μὲν δὴ μή τίς σε βιάζεται οἶον ἐόντα,
νοῦσόν γ' οὔ πως ἔστι Διὸς μεγάλου ἀλέασθαι.

Here μή τις may be used rather than οὔ τις in order to bring out more clearly the misunderstanding of the Οὖτις of Polyphemus.

This curious law was pointed out by A. R. Vierke, in a valuable dissertation *De μή particulae cum indicativo conjunctae usu antiquiore* (Lipsiae, 1876). With regard to the ground of it, we may observe that a Clause with εἰ in most cases precedes the apodosis ; and this is probably the original order. When it is inverted it may be that the use of μή instead of οὐ has a prohibitive character, as though the condition were added as an afterthought, *in bar* of what has been already said. In any case the inversion throws an *emphasis* on the Clause, which would account for the preference for μή ; see § 358.

360.] Infinitive and Participle. It appears from comparison with the forms of negation in the oldest Sanscrit that the negative Particles were originally used only with *finite Verbs*. The negation of a Noun was expressed by forming it into a Compound with the prefix *an-* or *a-* (Greek ἀν-, ἀ-): and the Infinitives and Participles were treated in this respect as Nouns. The first exception to this rule in Greek was probably the use of οὐ with the Participle—a use which is well established in Homer.

οὐ with the Infinitive is used in Homer (as in Attic) after Verbs of *saying, thinking, knowing*, &c. (§ 237); as in Il. 16. 61 ἦ τοι ἔφην γε οὐ πρὶν μηνιθμὸν καταπαυσέμεν κτλ. : Od. 5. 342 δοκέεις δέ μοι οὐκ ἀπινύσσειν.

This use however is to be compared with that noticed above (§ 355), in which an οὐ which belongs in sense to the Infinitive is placed before the governing Verb ; as οὔ φησιν δώσειν *he says he will not give*. Sometimes the Homeric language seems to hesitate between the two forms, or to use them indifferently : compare (e. g.) Il. 12. 106 οὐδ' ἔτ' ἔφαντο σχήσεσθ' κτλ. and (a few lines further) l. 125 ἔφαντο γὰρ οὐκέτ' 'Αχαιοὺς σχήσεσθ' κτλ. Occasionally the negative is used with the Verb and repeated with the Infinitive :—

Il. 17. 641 ἐπεὶ οὔ μιν ὀίομαι οὐδὲ πεπύσθαι (cp. 12. 73).

Od. 3. 27 οὐ γὰρ ὀίω | οὔ σε θεῶν ἀέκητι γενέσθαι κτλ.

It may be conjectured that the use of οὐ with the governing Verb is the more ancient ; the use with the Infinitive is obviously the more logical.

361.] μή with the Infinitive and Participle. The Homeric uses of this kind are few and simple in comparison with those of later Greek.

The **Infinitive** when used for the Imperative (§ 241) naturally takes μή instead of οὐ : as Il. 4. 42 μή τι διατρίβειν τὸν ἐμὸν χόλον, ἀλλά μ' ἐᾶσαι.

An Infinitive which stands as Object of a Verb of *saying*, &c. takes μή when it expresses *command* or *wish*: as Il. 3. 434 παύεσθαι κέλομαι μηδὲ κτλ. *I bid you stop and not &c.* (so 9. 12): Od.

1. 37 ἐπεὶ πρό οἱ εἴπομεν ἡμεῖς μήτ' κτλ. *we told him before not to &c.* So Od. 9. 530 δὸς μὴ 'Οδυσσῆα . . ἱκέσθαι *grant that Ulysses may not come.*

Again, a dependent Infinitive takes μή in *oaths*, as Il. 19. 176 ὀμνυέτω . . μή ποτε τῆς εὐνῆς ἐπιβήμεναι κτλ. *let him swear that he never &c.*; cp. Od. 5. 184 ἴστω νῦν τόδε γαῖα . . μή τί σοι αὐτῷ πῆμα κακὸν βουλευσέμεν ἄλλο, and Il. 19. 258 (but see § 358 *b*). So generally after Verbs of *promising*, &c. as Il. 14. 45 ὥς ποτ' ἐπηπείλησεν . . μὴ πρὶν κτλ. *threatened that he would not &c.*; Il. 18. 500 ὁ δ' ἀναίνετο μηδὲν ἑλέσθαι *refused to accept anything* (see Mr. Leaf's note *a. l.*). This use of μή is evidently parallel to the use with the Indicative, § 358. Compare also Il. 19. 22 οἵ' ἐπιεικὲς ἔργ' ἔμεν ἀθανάτων μηδὲ βροτὸν ἄνδρα τελέσσαι, where the μή may be emphatic (*such as we must not suppose any mortal to have made*).* Or this may be an instance of the use of μή in Relative Clauses containing a *general description* (§ 359, *b*).

The use of μή with the Participle appears in one Homeric instance :—

Od. 4. 684 μὴ μνηστεύσαντες μηδ' ἄλλοθ' ὁμιλήσαντες
ὕστατα καὶ πύματα νῦν ἐνθάδε δειπνήσειαν.

Here μή belongs to ὁμιλήσαντες, and expresses a *wish :* 'may they (after their wooing) have no other meeting, but sup now for the last time.' For the parenthetical μνηστεύσαντες and the repetition of the negative with ἄλλοτε, cp. the parallel place Od. 11. 613 μὴ τεχνησάμενος μηδ' ἄλλο τι τεχνήσαιτο.

κεν *and* ἄν.

362.] The Particles κεν and ἄν, as we have seen, are used to mark a predication as *conditional*, or made with reference to a particular or *limited* state of things : whereas τε shows that the meaning is *general*. Hence with the Subj. and Opt. κεν or ἄν indicates that an event holds a *definite* place in the expected course of things : in other words, κεν or ἄν points to an *actual occurrence* in the future.†

κεν is commoner in Homer than ἄν. In the existing text κεν occurs about 630 times in the Iliad, and 520 times in the Odyssey : while ἄν (including ἤν and ἐπήν) occurs 192 times in

---

* This would be akin to the later use with Verbs of *belief*. As to the Verbs which take μή see Prof. Gildersleeve in the *Am. Jour. Phil.* vol. i. p. 49.

† ' Im Allgemeinen steht das Resultat durchaus fest : κεν beim Conjunctiv und Optativ weist auf das Eintreten der Handlung hin' (Delbrück, *Synt. Forsch.* i. p. 86). This view is contrary to the teaching of most grammarians (see especially Hermann on Soph. O. C. 1446). It will be found stated very clearly in an article in the *Philological Museum*, vol. i. p. 96 (Cambridge 1832).

the Iliad and 157 times in the Odyssey. Thus the proportion is more than 3 : 1, and is not materially different in the two poems.

It is part of Fick's well known theory that ἄν was unknown in the original Homeric dialect (see Appendix F): and a systematic attempt to restore the exclusive use of κεν in Homer has been made by a Dutch scholar, J. van Leeuwen,* who has proposed more or less satisfactory emendations of all the places in which ἄν now appears. It is impossible to deny the soundness of the principles on which he bases his enquiry. When the poems were chiefly known through oral recitation there must have been a constant tendency to modernise the language. With Attic and Ionic reciters that tendency must have led to ἄν creeping into the text, sometimes in place of κεν, sometimes where the pure Subj. or Opt. was required by Homeric usage. Evidence of this kind of corruption has been preserved, as Van Leeuwen points out, in the *variae lectiones* of the ancient critics. Thus in Il. 1. 168 ἐπεί κε κάμω is now read on the authority of Aristarchus ; but ἐπὴν κεκάμω and ἐπήν κε κάμω were also ancient readings, and ἐπήν is found in all our MSS. Similarly in Il. 7. 5 Aristarchus read ἐπεί κε κάμωσιν, and the MSS. are divided between ἐπεί κε and ἐπήν κε (or ἐπὴν κεκ.). There is a similar variation between the forms ἤν and εἴ κε (or αἴ κε) in the phrases αἴ κ᾿ ἐθέλησθα, αἴ κ᾿ ἐθέλησι, &c. Thus in Il. 4. 353 (=9. 359) the MSS. nearly all have—

ὄψεαι ἢν ἐθέλησθα καὶ αἴ κέν τοι τὰ μεμήλῃ,

but αἴ κ᾿ ἐθέλησθα, which gives a better rhetorical effect, is found in Il. 8. 471 ὄψεαι αἴ κ᾿ ἐθέλησθα (so all MSS., ἢν ἐθ. as a *v. l.* in A), also in Il. 13. 260., 18. 457, Od. 3. 92, &c. Similarly in Il. 16. 453 ἐπεὶ δὴ τόν γε λίπῃ the *v. l.* ἐπήν is given by good MSS. (D, G, L, and as a variant in A). And the line Il. 11. 797 Μυρμιδόνων, αἴ κέν τι φόως Δαναοῖσι γένηαι is repeated in Il. 16. 39 with the variation ἤν που for αἴ κεν. In such cases we can see the intrusion of ἄν actually in process.

Again, the omission of ἄν may be required by the metre, or by the *indefinite* character of the sentence (§ 283): *e. g.* in Il. 15. 209 ὁππότ᾿ ἂν ἰσόμορον ἐθέλῃσι both these reasons point to ὁππότε Ϝισόμορον κτλ. So in Il. 2. 228 εὖτ᾿ ἂν πτολίεθρον ἕλωμεν read εὖτε πτ., and in Od. 11. 17 οὔθ᾿ ὁπότ᾿ ἂν στείχῃσι read οὔθ᾿ ὁπότε (ὅτε κε, which Van Leeuwen proposes in these two places, is not admissible, since the reference is general).

Several reasons combine to make it probable that the forms ἤν

---

* *De particularum κέν et ἄν apud Homerum usu* (*Mnemosyne*, xv. p. 75). The statistics given above are taken from this valuable dissertation.

and ἐπήν are post-Homeric. The contraction of εἰ ἄν, ἐπεὶ ἄν is contrary to Homeric analogies (§ 378*), and could hardly have taken place until ἄν became much commoner than it is in Homer. Again, the usage with regard to the order of the Particles excludes the combinations ἦν δέ, ἦν περ, ἦν γάρ—for which Homer would have εἰ δ' ἄν, εἴ περ ἄν, εἰ γὰρ ἄν (§ 365). Again, ἦν cannot properly be used in a *general* statement or simile, and whenever it is so used the metre allows it to be changed into εἰ: e.g. in Il. 1. 166 ἀτὰρ ἦν ποτε δασμὸς ἵκηται: Od. 5. 120 ἦν τίς τε φίλην ποιήσετ' ἀκοίτην (ἤ τίς τε in several MSS.): Od. 11. 159 ἦν μή τις ἔχῃ εὐεργέα νῆα: Od. 12. 288 ἦν πως ἐξαπίνης ἔλθῃ: Il. 20. 172 ἦν τινα πέφνῃ (in a simile). Similar arguments apply with even greater force to ἐπήν. Of the 48 instances there are 18 in general sentences, and several others (Il. 4. 239., 16. 95, Od. 3. 45., 4. 412., 5. 348., 11. 119., 15. 36., 21. 159) in which the reference to the future is so indefinite that ἐπεί with a pure Subj. is admissible. It cannot be accidental that in these places, with one exception (Od. 11. 192), ἐπήν is followed by a consonant, so that ἐπεί can be restored without any metrical difficulty. On the other hand, in 13 places in which ἐπήν is followed by a vowel the reference is to a definite future event, and accordingly we may read ἐπεί κ'. In the combination ἐπὴν δή, which occurs seven times, we should probably read ἐπεὶ δή, or in some places ἐπεί κεν (as in Od. 11. 221). The form ἐπειδάν occurs once, in a simile (Il. 13. 285): hence we should read ἐπεὶ δή (not ἐπεί κεν, as Bekker and Nauck, or αἴ κεν as Menrad).

The distinction between general statements and those which refer to an actual future occurrence has hardly been sufficiently attended to in the conjectures proposed by Van Leeuwen and others. Thus in Od. 5. 121 ἦν τίς τε φίλον ποιήσετ' ἀκοίτην (in a general reflexion) Van Leeuwen would read αἴ κέν τίς τε: and in Od. 12. 288 ἦν πως ἐξαπίνης ἔλθῃ he proposes αἴ κέ που. So in Il. 6. 489, Od. 8. 553 ἐπὴν τὰ πρῶτα γένηται (of the lot of man) he bids us read ἐπεί κε. If any change is wanted beyond putting ἐπεί for ἐπήν, the most probable would be ἐπεί τε: see § 332. On the other hand he would put ἐπεί for ἐπήν in such places as Od. 1. 293 αὐτὰρ ἐπὴν δὴ ταῦτα τελευτήσῃς τε καὶ ἔρξῃς (cp. Od. 5. 363., 18. 269), where a definite future occasion is implied, and consequently ἐπεί κεν (which he reads in Od. 4. 414) would be more Homeric. In Od. 6. 262 αὐτὰρ ἐπὴν πόλιος ἐπιβήομεν we should perhaps read ἐπεί κε πόλεος (◡–): see § 94, 2.

In a few places the true reading may be εἰ or ἐπεί with the Opt.: as Od. 8. 511 αἶσα γὰρ ἦν ἀπολέσθαι, ἐπὴν πόλις ἀμφικαλύψῃ (ἐπεὶ .. ἀμφικαλύψαι, as in Il. 19. 208 we should read ἐπεὶ τισαίμεθα): Od. 21. 237 (=383) ἦν δέ τις .. ἀκούσῃ μή τι εὐράζε προβλώσκειν (εἰ δέ τις .. ἀκούσαι): Il. 15. 504., 17. 245., 22. 55, 487.

The form ὅτ' ἄν occurs in our text in 29 places, and in 22 of these the metre admits ὅτε κ' (χ'), which Van Leeuwen accordingly would restore. The mischief however must lie deeper. Of the 22 places there are 13 in which ὅτ' ἄν appears in the leading clause of a simile (ὡς δ' ὅτ' ἄν—), and in three others (Il. 2. 397, Od. 11. 18., 13. 101) the sense is general; so that ὅτε κ' is admissible in six only (Il. 7. 335, 459., 8. 373, 475, Od. 2. 374., 4. 477). It cannot be an accident that there are so many cases of ὅτ' ἄν where Homeric usage requires the pure Subj., and no similar cases of ὅτε κεν: but for that very reason we cannot correct them by reading ὅτε κ'. Meanwhile no better solution has been proposed, and we must be content to note the 16 places as in all probability corrupt or spurious.

It is one thing, however, to find that ἄν has encroached upon κεν in Homer, and another thing to show that there are no uses of ἄν which belong to the primitive Homeric language.

The restoration of κε(ν) is generally regarded as especially easy in the combination οὐκ ἄν, for which οὔ κεν can always be written without affecting either sense or metre. The change, however, is open to objections which have not been sufficiently considered. It will be found that οὐκ ἄν occurs 61 times in the ordinary text of Homer: while οὔ κεν occurs 9 times, and οὔ κε 7 times. Now of the forms κεν and κε the first occurs in the Iliad 272 times, the second 222 times. Hence, according to the general laws of probability, οὔ κεν and οὔ κε may be expected to occur in the same proportion: and in the ordinary text this is the case (9 : 7). But if every οὐκ ἄν were changed into οὔ κεν, there would be 70 instances of οὔ κεν against 7 of οὔ κε. This clearly could not be accidental: hence it follows that οὐκ ἄν must be retained in all or nearly all the passages where it now stands.* And if οὐκ ἄν is right, we may infer that the other instances of ἄν with a negative —22 in number—are equally unassailable.

Another group of instances in which ἄν is evidently primitive consists of the dactylic combinations ὅς περ ἄν, ᾗ περ ἄν, εἴ περ ἄν. Van Leeuwen would write ὅς κέ περ, &c.; but in Homer περ usually comes immediately after the Relative or εἰ, and before κεν (§ 365). Similarly οὐδὲ γὰρ ἄν (Il. 24. 566) and τόφρα γὰρ ἄν (Od. 2. 77) cannot be changed into οὐδέ κε γάρ, τόφρα κε γάρ, since the order γάρ κεν is invariable in Homer. In these uses, accordingly, ἄν may be defended by an argument which was inapplicable to οὐκ ἄν, viz. the impossibility of making the change to κεν.

The same may be said of the forms in which ἄν occurs under the ictus of the verse, preceded by a short monosyllable (⏑ –́), as—

Il. 1. 205 ᾗς ὑπεροπλίῃσι τάχ' ἄν ποτε θυμὸν ὀλέσσῃ.

Od. 2. 76 εἴ χ' ὑμεῖς γε φάγοιτε, τάχ' ἄν ποτε καὶ τίσις εἴη.

Il. 9. 77 τίς ἂν τάδε γηθήσειε (so τίς ἄν, Il. 24. 367, Od. 8. 208., 10. 573).

---

* It will be seen that the argument is of the same kind as that by which it was shown above (§ 283 b) that τε must have been often changed into κε. The decisive fact in that case was the excessive occurrence of κε: here it is the absence of any such excess which leads us to accept the traditional text.

Il. 4. 164 ἔσσεται ἦμαρ ὅτ' ἄν ποτ' κτλ. (cp. 1. 519., 4. 53., 6. 448., 9. 101).

8. 406 ὄφρ' εἰδῇ γλαυκῶπις ὅτ' ἂν ᾧ πατρὶ μάχηται (=420).

So καὶ ἄν and τότ' ἄν (see the instances, § 363, 2, c), σὺ δ' ἄν (Il. 6. 329), ὃς ἄν (Od. 21. 294, cp. Od. 4. 204., 18. 27, Il. 7. 231). In this group, as in the last, we have to do with recurring forms, sufficiently numerous to constitute a *type*, with a fixed rhythm, as well as a certain tone and style.

The combination of ἄν and κεν in the same Clause is found in a very few places, and is probably not Homeric. In four places (Il. 11. 187, 202, Od. 5. 361., 6. 259) we have ὄφρ' ἂν μέν κεν κτλ., where the place of ἄν is anomalous (§ 365). For οὔτ' ἄν κεν (Il. 13. 127) we should probably read οὔτ' ἄρ κεν, and so in Od. 9. 334 τοὺς ἄρ κε (or rather οὓς ἄρ κε) καὶ ἤθελον αὐτὸς ἑλέσθαι (cp. Il. 7. 182 ὃν ἄρ' ἤθελον αὐτοί). In Od. 18. 318 ἤν περ γάρ κε should be εἴ περ γάρ κε (*supra*).

363.] Uses of κεν and ἄν. It will be convenient, by way of supplement to what has been said in the chapter on the uses of the Moods, (1) to bring together the chief exceptions to the general rule for the use of κεν or ἄν in Subordinate Clauses; and (2) to consider whether there are any differences of meaning or usage between the two Particles.

1. In Final Clauses which refer to what is still future, the use of κεν or ἄν prevails (§§ 282, 285, 288, 293, 304). But with certain Conjunctions (especially ὡς, ὅπως, ἵνα, ὄφρα) there are many exceptions: see §§ 285–289, 306–307. When the purpose spoken of is not an actual one, but either past or imaginary, the Verb is generally ' pure.'

In Conditional Clauses the Subj. and Opt. generally take κεν or ἄν when the governing Verb is in the Future, or in a Mood which implies a future occasion (Imperative, Subjunctive, Optative with κεν or ἄν). On the other hand in similes, maxims, and references to frequent or *indefinite* occasions, the Particle is not used. But—

(a) Sometimes the pure Subj. is used after a Future in order to show that the speaker avoids referring to a particular occasion: cp. Il. 21. 111 ἔσσεται ἢ ἠὼς ἢ δείλη ἢ μέσον ἦμαρ ὁππότε .. ἕληται, and the examples quoted in § 289, 2, a and § 292, a.

(b) In our texts of Homer there are many places in which κεν or ἄν is used although the reference is *indefinite*: but the number is much reduced if we deduct the places in which it is probable that κε (or κ') has crept in instead of τε (τ'): see § 283, b. The

real exceptions will generally be found where a Clause is added
to restrict or qualify a general supposition already made :—

Il. 3. 25　　　μάλα γάρ τε κατεσθίει, εἴ περ ἂν αὐτὸν
σεύωνται (*even in the case when &c.*).

Od. 21. 293 οἶνός σε τρώει μελιηδής, ὅς τε καὶ ἄλλους
βλάπτει, ὃς ἄν μιν χανδὸν ἔλῃ (in the case of him
who takes it greedily).

So Il. 6. 225., 9. 501, 524., 20. 166, Od. 15. 344., 19. 332
(§§ 289, 292, 296). In these places we see the tendency of the
language to extend the use of κεν or ἄν beyond its original limits,
in other words, to state indefinite cases as if they were definite—
a tendency which in later Greek made the use of ἄν universal in
such Clauses, whether the event intended was definite or not.

The change is analogous to the use of the Indicative in a general Conditional
protasis ; when, as Mr. Goodwin expresses it, 'the speaker refers to one of
the cases in which an event *may* occur as if it were the only one—that is,
he states the general supposition as if it were particular' (*Moods and Tenses*,
§ 467). The loss of the Homeric use of τε, and the New Ionic use of ὁ ἡ τό
as a Relative with indefinite as well as definite antecedents, are examples of
the same kind.

2. Up to this point the Particles κεν and ἄν have been treated
as practically equivalent. There are however some differences of
usage which remain to be pointed out.

(*a*) In *Negative* Clauses there is a marked preference for ᾽ν.
In the ordinary text of the Iliad ἄν is found with a negative 53
times (nearly a third of the whole number of instances), κεν is
similarly used 33 times (about one-twentieth). The difference is
especially to be noticed in the Homeric use of the Subj. as a kind
of Future (§§ 275, 276). In affirmative clauses of this type κεν
is frequent, ἄν very rare : in negative clauses ἄν only is found.

(*b*) κεν is often used in two or more successive Clauses of a
Sentence: *e.g.* in both protasis and apodosis, as—

Il. 1. 324 εἰ δέ κε μὴ δώῃσιν, ἐγὼ δέ κεν αὐτὸς ἕλωμαι κτλ.

In Disjunctive Sentences, as—

Il. 18. 308 στήσομαι, ἤ κε φέρῃσι μέγα κράτος ἤ κε φεροίμην.

Od. 4. 692 ἄλλον κ᾽ ἐχθαίρῃσι βροτῶν, ἄλλον κε φιλοίη.

And in parallel and correlative Clauses of all kinds :—

Il. 3. 41 καί κε τὸ βουλοίμην καί κεν πολὺ κέρδιον εἴη.

23. 855 ὃς μέν κε βάλῃ . . ὃς δέ κε μηρίνθοιο τύχῃ, κτλ.

Od. 11. 110 τὰς εἰ μέν κ᾽ ἀσινέας ἐάᾳς νόστου τε μέδηαι,
καί κεν ἔτ᾽ εἰς Ἰθάκην κακά περ πάσχοντες ἵκοισθε·
εἰ δέ κε σίνηαι κτλ.

ἄν, on the other hand, is especially used in the *second* of two parallel or connected Clauses : as—

Il. 19. 228 ἀλλὰ χρὴ τὸν μὲν καταθάπτειν ὅς κε θάνῃσι ..
  ὅσσοι δ' ἂν πολέμοιο περὶ στυγεροῖο λίπωνται κτλ.

Od. 19. 329 ὃς μὲν ἀπηνὴς αὐτὸς ἔῃ καὶ ἀπηνέα εἰδῇ ..
  ὃς δ' ἂν ἀμύμων αὐτὸς ἔῃ κτλ.

So Il. 21. 553 εἰ μέν κεν .. εἰ δ' ἂν κτλ.; Il. 3. 288 ff. εἰ μέν κεν εἰ δέ κε—εἰ δ' ἂν (the last an alternative to the second).

The only instance of ἄν in two parallel Clauses is—

Od. 11. 17 οὔθ' ὁπότ' ἂν στείχῃσι πρὸς οὐρανὸν ἀστερόεντα
  οὔθ' ὅτ' ἂν ἂψ ἐπὶ γαῖαν κτλ.

and there we ought to read ὁπότε στείχῃσι, according to the regular Homeric use of the Subj. in *general* statements (§ 289, 2, *a*).

(*c*) There are several indications of the use of ἄν as a more *emphatic* Particle than κεν. Thus the combination ἦ τ' ἄν *surely in that case* occurs 7 times in the Iliad, ἦ τέ κεν only twice. Compare the force of καὶ ἄν in—

Il. 5. 362 (=457) ὃς νῦν γε καὶ ἂν Διὶ πατρὶ μάχοιτο

Od. 6. 300 ῥεῖα δ' ἀρίγνωτ' ἐστί, καὶ ἂν πάϊς ἡγήσαιτο.

So Il. 14. 244 ἄλλον μέν κεν .. ῥεῖα κατευνήσαιμι, καὶ ἂν ποταμοῖο ῥέεθρα Ὠκεανοῦ *I would put any other to sleep, even Oceanus, &c.*

Cp. also τότ' ἄν (*then indeed, then at length*), in—

Il. 18. 397 τότ' ἂν πάθον ἄλγεα θυμῷ.

  22. 108 ἐμοὶ δὲ τότ' ἂν πολὺ κέρδιον εἴη κτλ.

  24. 213 τότ' ἂν τιτὰ ἔργα γένοιτο.

Od. 9. 211 τότ' ἂν οὔ τοι ἀποσχέσθαι φίλον ἦεν.

And τίς ἄν (*quis tandem*) in Il. 9. 77 τίς ἂν τάδε γηθήσειεν; Il. 24. 367 τίς ἂν δή τοι νόος εἴη; Od. 8. 208 τίς ἂν φιλέοντι μάχοιτο; Od. 10. 573 τίς ἂν θεὸν οὐκ ἐθέλοντα κτλ.

The general effect of these differences of usage between the two Particles seems to be that ἄν is used either in an *adversative* sense—with a second or opposed alternative—or when greater *emphasis* has to be expressed.

This account of the matter is in harmony with the predominance of ἄν in negative sentences. When we speak of an event as *not happening* in certain circumstances, we generally do so by way of contrast to the *opposite* circumstances, those in which it will happen; as οὐκ ἄν τοι χραίσμῃ κίθαρις *the lyre will not avail you* (viz. *in battle—whatever it may do elsewhere*).

The *accent* of the Particles must not be overlooked as a confirmation of the view now taken. Evidently ἄν is more likely to convey emphasis than the enclitic κεν. We may find an analogy

in the orthotone and adversative δέ, which stands to τε and the
correlated τε—τε somewhat as we have supposed ἄν to stand to
κεν and κεν—κεν.

364.] **Original meaning of ἄν and κεν.** The identity of the Greek ἄν with
the Latin and Gothic *an* has been maintained with much force and ingenuity
by Prof. Leo Meyer. The following are some of the chief points established
by his dissertation.*

1. The Latin *an* is used by the older poets in the second member of a
disjunctive question, either direct, as *egone an ille injurie facimus?* or indirect,
as *utrum scapulae plus an collus calli habeat nescio* (both from Naevius). The use
in single questions is a derivative one, and properly implies that the question
is put as an alternative : as—

Plaut. Asin. 5. 1, 10 credam istuc, si te esse hilarum videro. AR. An tu
me tristem putas? *do you then think me (the opposite, viz.) sad?*

Amph. 3. 3, 8 derides qui scis haec dudum me dixisse per jocum. SO. an
illut joculo dixisti? equidem serio ac vero ratus.

In these places † we see how *an* comes to mean *then on the contrary, then in the
other case, &c.* So in Naevius, eho an vicimus? *what then, have we conquered?*

2. In Gothic, again, *an* is used in questions of an adversative character :
as in Luke x. 29 *an hvas ist mis nêhvundja* ('he willing to justify himself, said :
and who is my neighbour?' John xviii. 37 *an nuh thiudans is thu* 'art thou a
king then?'

3. These instances exhibit a close similarity between the Latin and the
Gothic *an*, and suggest the possibility of a Disjunctive Particle (*or, or else*)
coming to express recourse to a second alternative (*if not, then —*), and so
acquiring the uses of the Greek ἄν. This supposition, as Leo Meyer goes on
to show, is confirmed by the Gothic *aiththau* and *thau*, which are employed
(1) as Disjunctive Particles, *or, or else*, and (2) to render the Greek ἄν, chiefly
in the use with the Past Indicative. Thus we have, as examples of *aiththau*—

Matth. v. 36 ni magt ain tagl hveit aiththau svart gataujan *thou canst not
make one hair white or black.*

Matth. ix. 17 aiththau distaurnand balgeis (*neither do men put new wine into
old bottles) else the bottles break.*

John xiv. 2 niba vêseina, aiththau qvêthjau *if it were not so, I would have told
you* [= it is not so, *else* I would have told you].

John xiv. 7 ith kunthêdeith mik, aiththau kunthêdeith &c. *if ye had known
me, ye should have known &c.*

Similarly *thau* is used (1) to translate ἤ in double questions, as in Matth.
xxvii. 17 *whom will ye that I release unto you, Barabbas or* (thau) *Jesus?* and
after a Comparative (= *than*): frequently also (2) in a Conditional Apodosis,
esp. to translate ἄν with Past Tenses, as —

Luke vii. 39 sa ith vêsi praufêtus ufkunthedi thau *this man, if he were a
prophet, would have known.*

---

* 'AN *im Griechischen, Lateinischen und Gothischen*, Berlin 1880. The parallel
between the Greek ἄν and the Gothic *thau* and *aiththau* was pointed out by
Hartung (*Partikeln*, ii. p. 227).

† Taken from Draeger's *Historische Syntax*, i. p. 321, where many other
examples will be found.

Sometimes also with the Present (where there is no ἄν in the Greek),—the meaning being that of a solemn or emphatic Future :—

Mark xi. 26 ith jabai jus ni aflêtith, ni thau . . aflêtith *if ye do not forgive neither will . . forgive* (οὐδὲ . . ἀφήσει).

Matth. v. 20 ni thau qvimith (*except your righteousness shall exceed &c.*) *ye shall in no case enter &c.* (οὐ μὴ εἰσέλθητε).

This use evidently answers to the Homeric κεν or ἄν with the Subj. and Fut. Ind.: ni thau qvimith = οὐκ ἂν ἔλθητε, ni thau aflêtith = οὐδ' ἂν ἀφήσει.

4. If now we suppose that ἄν, like *aiththau* and *thau*, had originally two main uses, (1) in the second member of a Disjunctive sentence (= *else, or else*), and ·(2) in the Conditional apodosis (= *in that case rather*), we can explain the Gothic and Latin *an* from the former, the Greek ἄν from the latter. The idiomatic 'ellipse' in ἦ γὰρ ἄν . . ὕστατα λωβήσαιο *else you would outrage for the last time* will represent an intermediate or transitional use. We can then understand why ἄν should often accompany negatives, and why it should be used in the *latter* Clause of a sentence. The main difference of the two uses evidently is that in the first the Clauses are co-ordinate, in the second the Clause with ἄν is the apodosis or principal Clause. Thus the two uses are related to each other as the two uses of δέ (1) as an adversative Conjunction, (2) in the apodosis.

5. The use of ἄν in Final Clauses may be illustrated by that of *thau* in Mark vi. 56 bêdun ina ei thau . . attaitôkeina παρεκάλουν αὐτὸν ἵνα κἂν . . ἄψωνται *that they might touch if it were but &c.* With ἵνα, ὡς, &c. ἄν may have had originally the same kind of emphasis as κἄν in this passage : 'that in any case,' 'that if no more then at least &c.' The use in a Conditional Protasis *following* the Principal Clause may be compared with Luke ix. 13 niba thau . . bugjaima (*we have no more*) *except we should buy* (= unless indeed we should buy).

The Particle κε(ν) is found in Æolic, in the same form as in Homer (see Append. F), and in Doric, in the form κα. It is usually identified with the Sanscrit *kam*, which when accented means *well* (*wohl, gut, bene*), and as an enclitic appears to be chiefly used with the Imperative, but with a force which can hardly be determined (Delbrück, *A. S.* pp. 150, 503). A parallel may possibly be found in the German *wohl*, but in any case the development of the use of κε(ν) is specifically Greek.

Order of the Particles and Enclitic Pronouns.

365.] The place of a Particle in the Homeric sentence is generally determined by stricter rules than those which obtain in later Greek : and similar rules are found to govern the order of the enclitic Pronouns and Adverbs.

1. The two enclitics περ and γε, when they belong to the first word in a clause, come before all other Particles. Hence we have the sequences εἴ περ γάρ—εἴ περ ἄν—τοῦ περ δή—·πόθεόν γε μέν, &c. Exceptions are to be found in Il. 9. 46 εἰς ὅ κέ περ Τροίην διαπέρσομεν (read perhaps εἰς ὅτε περ), Il. 7. 387 εἴ κέ περ ὔμμι . . γένοιτο, Od. 3. 321 ὅθεν τέ περ, Il. 8. 243 αὐτοὺς δή περ ἔασον.

2. μέν and δέ, also τε in its use as a *connecting* word, come before other Particles. Hence we have οἱ δὲ δή—εἰ δέ κεν—ἐγὼ δέ κέ τοι—εἰ δ' ἄν—οὐ μὲν γάρ—οὔτε κε—οὔτ' ἄρα, &c.

μέν may be placed later when it emphasises a particular word, or *part* of a clause, especially in view of a following clause with δέ, as Il. 9. 300 εἰ δέ τοι 'Ατρείδης μὲν ἀπήχθετο .. σὺ δ' ἄλλους περ κτλ., Od. 4. 23., 11. 385., 18. 67, &c.; and in such collocations as σοὶ δ' ἦ τοι μὲν ἐγὼ κτλ., ἔνθ' ἦ τοι τοὺς μὲν κτλ. Cp. also Od. 15. 405 οὔ τι περιπληθὴς λίην τόσον, ἀλλ' ἀγαθὴ μέν.

The form ὄφρ' ἂν μέν κεν is probably corrupt, see § 362 *ad fin.*

3. Of the remaining Particles γάρ comes first: as ἦ γάρ κε—τίς γάρ κε—εἴ περ γάρ κε—τόφρα γὰρ ἄν—ὡς γάρ νύ τοι, &c. Among the other Particles note the sequences καί νύ κεν—ἐξ ἄρα δή—ὁππότε κεν δή—ἦ ῥά νυ—τίς τοί νυ. But ἄρα is sometimes put later in the clause, as ὡς εἰπὼν κατ' ἄρ' ἕζετο, cp. Il. 5. 748 Ἥρη δὲ μάστιγι θοῶς ἐπιμαίετ' ἄρ' ἵππους.

τε in its *generalising* use comes after other Particles: hence δέ τε—μέν τε—γάρ τε—ἀλλά τε—δ' ἄρα τε—ὅς ῥά τε—οὔτ' ἄρ τε—οὔ νύ τε.

4. The Indefinite τις and the corresponding Adverbs, που, πως, πω, ποτε, &c. follow the Particles. Hence we have ὅτε κέν τις—αἴ κέν πως—ὅτ' ἄν ποτε—ὅν ῥά τις—δή που—νύ που—ἦ πού τί σε, &c.

But τε follows τις (§ 332), as in καὶ γάρ τίς τε, ὅς τίς τε. And sometimes ὅς τις is treated as a single word, as in ὅν τινα μέν (Il. 2. 188), ὅς τις δέ (Il. 15. 743), ὅς τίς κε (Il. 10. 44, Od. 3. 355). Similarly we find εἴ ποτε in the combination εἴ ποτε δή, as well as the more regular εἰ δή ποτε.

τις sometimes comes later, as Il. 4. 300 ὄφρα καὶ οὐκ ἐθέλων τις κτλ., especially after a Gen. which it governs, as Il. 13. 55 σφῶϊν δ' ὧδε θεῶν τις κτλ.; cp. also Il. 22. 494 τῶν δ' ἐλεησάντων κοτύλην τις τυτθὸν ἐπέσχεν, and Od. 21. 374.

So ποτε, as in Il. 4. 410 τῷ μή μοι πατέρας ποθ' ὁμοίῃ ἔνθεο τιμῇ, Il. 6. 99 οὐδ' 'Αχιλῆά ποθ' ὧδε κτλ., Il. 10. 453, Od. 2. 137. In these places ποτε seems to be attracted to an emphatic word. Cp. που in Il. 12. 272, ποθεν in Od. 18. 376.

5. The enclitic Personal Pronouns come after the Particles and Pronouns already mentioned: οὔ ποτέ με—ἦ πή με—οὐδέ νύ πώ με—οὐ γάρ πώ ποτέ μοι—ἐγὼ δέ κέ τοι—ἐπεὶ ἄρ κέ σε—ὁππότε κέν μιν—αἴ κέν πώς μιν—οὐ γάρ πώ σφιν—ἦ πού τίς σφιν, &c.

Sometimes however an enclitic form follows the emphatic Pronoun αὐτός: as Il. 5. 459 αὐτὰρ ἔπειτ' αὐτῷ μοι ἐπέσσυτο, Il. 22. 346 αἲ γάρ πως αὐτόν με κτλ.

Occasionally an enclitic is found out of its place at the end of

a line which has the bucolic caesura : Il. 3. 368 οὐδ' ἔβαλόν μιν
(v. l. οὐδ' ἐδάμασσα), 5. 104 εἰ ἐτεόν με, 7. 79 ὄφρα πυρός με, 11.
380 ὡς ὄφελόν τοι : so with τις, Il. 4. 315 ὡς ὄφελέν τις ; and
without bucolic caesura, Il. 17. 736 ἐπὶ δὲ πτόλεμος τέτατό σφιν.

6. The negative Particles οὐ and μή, which regularly begin the
clause, are often put later in order that some other word may be
emphasised, and in that case the Indefinite τις, ποτε, &c. follow
οὐ or μή : as μετάλλησάν γε μὲν οὔ τι (for οὐ μέν τι μετάλλησάν γε),
κείνοισι δ' ἂν οὔ τις (for οὐ δ' ἄν τις κείνοισι), σὺ δὲ μή τι, τὸ μὲν
οὔ ποτε, &c. Similarly κεν and ἄν are attracted to the negation,
as in πληθὺν δ' οὐκ ἂν ἐγώ (for οὐδ' ἂν ἐγὼ πληθύν), and when the
negative is repeated, as in οὐδὲ γὰρ οὐδέ κεν κτλ. : cp. Od. 15. 321
ὁρηστοσύνῃ οὐκ ἄν μοι ἐρίσσειε βροτὸς ἄλλος.

7. The place of the enclitic is perhaps explained by the pause
of the verse in Od. 15. 118 ὅθ' ἑὸς δόμος ἀμφεκάλυψε | κεῖσέ με
νοστήσαντα, Od. 14. 245 αὐτὰρ ἔπειτα | Αἴγυπτόνδε με κτλ. (unless
we read κεῖσ' ἐμέ, Αἴγυπτόνδ' ἐμέ, cp. Od. 16. 310); and so in—

Il. 1. 205 ἧς ὑπεροπλίῃσι τάχ' ἄν ποτε θυμὸν ὀλέσσῃ.

1. 256 ἄλλοι τε Τρῶες μέγα κεν κεχαροίατο θυμῷ.

5. 362 Τυδείδης, ὃς νῦν γε καὶ ἂν Διὶ πατρὶ μάχοιτο.

22. 108 ὡς ἐρέουσιν· ἐμοὶ δὲ τότ' ἂν πολὺ κέρδιον εἴη.

Od. 1. 217 ὡς δὴ ἐγώ γ' ὄφελον μάκαρός νύ τευ ἔμμεναι υἱός.

The second half of the line is treated as a fresh beginning of a
sentence.

Without assuming that the Homeric usage as to the place of Particles and
Enclitics is invariable, we may point out that in several places where these
rules are violated the text is doubtful on other grounds. Thus —

Il. 3. 173 ὡς ὄφελεν θάνατός μοι ἀδεῖν. Read ὥς μ' ὄφελεν θάνατος Ϝαδέειν :
for the elision μ(οι) cp. Il. 6. 165 ὅς μ' ἔθελεν φιλότητι μιγήμεναι (§ 376).

Il. 6. 289 ἔνθ' ἔσαν οἱ πέπλοι κτλ. Read ἔνθα Ϝ' ἔσαν (see § 376). Similarly
in Il. 20. 282 κὰδ δ' ἄχος οἱ χύτο Van Leeuwen reads κὰδ δέ Ϝ' ἄχος χύτο.

Od. 1. 37 ἐπεὶ πρό οἱ εἴπομεν ἡμεῖς. Bekker would omit πρό (Hom. Bl. ii. 21).

Od. 2. 327 ἐπεί νύ περ ἵεται αἰνῶς (read νύ τε Ϝίεται ?).

Od. 15. 436 ὅρκῳ πιστωθῆναι ἀπήμονά μ' οἴκαδ' ἀπάξειν. Omit μ'.

Od. 11. 218 ἀλλ' αὕτη δίκη ἐστὶ βροτῶν, ὅτε κέν τε θάνωσιν, with v. l. (in
five MSS.) ὅτε τίς κε θάνῃσιν. Read ὅτε τίς τε θάνῃσιν (§ 289 ad fin.).

Il. 20. 77 τοῦ γάρ ῥα μάλιστα ἓ θυμὸς ἀνώγει : so Aristarchus, but the other
ancient reading was μάλιστά γε.

Il. 21. 576 εἴ περ γὰρ φθάμενός μιν ἢ οὐτάσῃ κτλ. : for μιν the 'city-editions'
had τις, but neither word is needed.

Od. 7. 261 (= 14. 287) ἀλλ' ὅτε δὴ ὄγδοόν μοι ἐπιπλόμενον ἔτος ἦλθεν : Dind.
reads ὀγδόατον, to avoid the unusual synizesis. Read ἀλλ' ὅτε δή μ' ὄγδωον :
an earlier ὄγδωος (= Lat. octāvus) is almost necessary to account for ὄγδοος
(Brugmann, M. U. v. 37).

Z

Il. ϝ. 273 εἰ τούτω κε λάβοιμεν κτλ.   For κε (without meaning here) read γε.

Il. 14. 403 ἐπεὶ τέτραπτο πρὸς ἰθύ οἱ.   The sense seems to require πρὸς ἰθύν
in the direction of his aim, cp. πᾶσαν ἐπ' ἰθύν *for every aim*, ἀν' ἰθύν *straight onwards*
(Il. 21. 303, Od. 8. 377).

Il. 24. 53 μὴ . . νεμεσσηθέωμέν οἱ ἡμεῖς.   Read-θήομεν, omitting οἱ.

A less strict usage may be traced in the 10th book of the Iliad : cp. l. 44
ἥ τίς κεν, 242 εἰ μὲν δὴ ἑταρόν γε κελεύετέ μ' αὐτὸν ἐλέσθαι, 280 νῦν αὖτε μάλιστά
με φίλαι, 344 ἀλλ' ἐῶμέν μιν, 453 οὐκέτ' ἔπειτα σὺ πῆμά ποτ' ἔσσεαι.   The subject,
however, needs more detailed investigation.

CHAPTER XIV.

Metre and Quantity.

The Hexameter.

366.] The verse in which the Homeric poems are composed—
the *heroic hexameter*—consists of six *feet*, of equal length, each of
which again is divided into two equal parts, viz. an accented
part or *arsis* (on which the rhythmical beat or *ictus* falls), and an
unaccented part or *thesis*.   In each foot the arsis consists of one
long syllable, the thesis of one long or two short syllables ;
except the last thesis, which consists of one syllable, either long
or short.

The fifth thesis nearly always consists of two short syllables,
thus producing the characteristic − ∪ ∪ − ⌣ which marks the
end of each hexameter.

The last foot is probably to be regarded as a little shorter than
the others, the time being filled up by the pause at the end of
the verse.   The effect of this shortening is heightened by the
dactyl in the fifth place, since the two short syllables take the
full time of half a foot.

367.] **Diaeresis and Caesura.**   Besides the recognised *stops*
or pauses which mark the separation of sentences and clauses
there is in general a slight pause or break of the voice between
successive words in the same clause, sufficient to affect the
rhythm of the verse.   Hence the rules regarding *Diaeresis* and
Caesura.

By **Diaeresis** is meant the coincidence of the division between
words with the division into feet.   The commonest place of
diaeresis in the hexameter is after the fourth foot: as—

ἡρώων αὐτοὺς δὲ ἑλώρια | τεῦχε κύνεσσιν.

This is called the *Bucolic Diaeresis.*

Caesura (τομή) occurs when the pause between two words falls within a foot, so as to 'cut' it into two parts. The caesura which separates the arsis from the thesis (so as to divide the foot equally) is called the *strong* or *masculine* caesura : that which falls between the two short syllables of the thesis is called the *weak* or *feminine* or *trochaic* caesura.

The chief points to be observed regarding caesura in the Homeric hexameter are as follows :—

1. There is nearly always a caesura in the third foot. Of the two caesuras the more frequent in this place is the trochaic (τομὴ κατὰ τρίτον τροχαῖον), as—

　　ἄνδρα μοι ἔννεπε Μοῦσα | πολύτροπον ὃς μάλα πολλά.

The strong caesura, or 'caesura after the fifth half-foot' (τομὴ πενθημιμερής), is rather less common : as—

　　μῆνιν ἄειδε, θεά, | Πηληϊάδεω Ἀχιλῆος.

In the first book of the Iliad, which contains 611 lines, the trochaic caesura of the third foot occurs in 356, and the corresponding strong caesura in 247.*

On the other hand, there must be no diaeresis after the third foot; and in the few cases in which the third foot lies wholly in one word there is always a strong caesura in the fourth foot (τομὴ ἐφθημιμερής), as—

　　ὅς κε θεοῖς ἐπιπείθηται | μάλα τ' ἔκλυον αὐτοῦ
　　Ἥρη τ' ἠδὲ Ποσειδάων | καὶ Παλλὰς Ἀθήνη.

The division between an enclitic and the preceding word is not sufficient for the caesura in the third foot : hence in Od. 10. 58 we should read—

　　αὐτὰρ ἐπεὶ σίτοιό τ' | ἐπασσάμεθ' ἠδὲ ποτῆτος

not σίτοιό τε πασσάμεθ' (as La Roche).

The remaining exceptions to these rules are—

Il. 1. 179 οἴκαδ' ἰὼν σὺν νηυσί τε σῆς καὶ σοῖς ἑτάροισι,

which is an adaptation of the (probably conventional) form σὺν νηΐ τ' ἐμῇ καὶ ἐμοῖς ἑτάροισι (1. 183). We may help the rhythm by taking νηυσί τε σῆς closely together, so as to avoid the break in the middle of the line.

Il. 3. 205 ἤδη γὰρ καὶ δεῦρό ποτ' ἤλυθε δῖος Ὀδυσσεύς.

Il. 10. 453 οὐκέτ' ἔπειτα σὺ πῆμά ποτ' ἔσσεαι Ἀργείϊσι.

Where ποτέ, as an enclitic, is in an unusual place in the sentence (§ 365, 4), but it is perhaps in reality an emphatic 'one day.' Similarly, in—

Il. 3. 220 φαίης κε ζάκοτόν τέ τιν' ἔμμεναι ἄφρονά τ' αὔτως,

τινα may be slightly emphatic. Or should we read τὸν ἔμμεναι ?

Il. 15. 18 ἦ οὐ μέμνῃ ὅτε τ' ἐκρέμω ὑψόθεν, ἔκ τε ποδοῖϊν.

We may read ὅτε τε κρέμω : but possibly the peculiar rhythm is intentional, as being adapted to the sense.

---

* In this calculation no lines are reckoned twice, short monosyllables being taken either with the preceding or the following word, according to the sense.

2. Trochaic caesura of the fourth foot is very rare, and is only found under certain conditions, viz.—

(1) when the caesura is preceded by an enclitic or short monosyllable (such as μέν, δέ, &c.); as—

καί κεν τοῦτ' ἐθέλοιμι Διός γε διδόντος ἀρέσθαι.

(2) when the line ends with a word of four or five syllables; as—

αὐτὰρ ὁ μοῦνος ἔην μετὰ πέντε κασιγνήτῃσι.

πολλὰ δ' ἄρ' ἔνθα καὶ ἔνθ' ἴθυσε | μάχη πεδίοιο.

The commonest form of this kind of caesura (especially in the Iliad) is that in which these two alleviations are both present; as—

Θερσῖτ' ἀκριτόμυθε, λιγύς περ ἐὼν ἀγορητής.

The first fifteen books of the Iliad contain eleven instances of trochaic caesura in the fourth foot, of which seven are of this form.

In Il. 9. 394 the MSS. give—

Πηλεύς θήν μοι ἔπειτα γυναῖκα | γαμέσσεται αὐτός.

But we should doubtless read, with Aristarchus,—

γυναῖκά γε μάσσεται αὐτός.

Similarly we should probably read τὰ δέ μ' οὐκ ἄρα μέλλον ὀνήσειν (Il. 5. 205, &c.), instead of ἔμελλον: and conversely θαλερὴ δ' ἐμιαίνετο χαίτη (Il. 17. 439), and ῥαφαὶ δ' ἐλέλυντο ἱμάντων (Od. 22. 186), instead of μιαίνετο, λέλυντο. In Od. 5. 272 we may treat ὀψὲ δύοντα as one word in rhythm. But it is not easy to account for the rhythm in Od. 12. 47 ἐπὶ δ' οὔατ' ἀλεῖψαι ἑταίρων.

The result of these rules evidently is that there are two chief breaks or pauses in the verse—the *caesura* in the third foot, and the *diaeresis* between the fourth and fifth—and that the *forbidden* divisions are the diaeresis and caesura which lie nearest to these pauses. Thus—

Best caesura $-\,\smile\smile\,-\,\smile\smile\,-\,\smile\,|\,\smile\,-\,\smile\smile\,-\,\smile\smile\,-\,-$
Worst diaeresis $-\,\smile\smile\,-\,\smile\smile\,-\,\smile\smile\,|\,-\,\smile\smile\,-\,\smile\smile\,-\,-$

Again—

Best diaeresis $-\,\smile\smile\,-\,\smile\smile\,-\,\smile\smile\,-\,\smile\smile\,|\,-\,\smile\smile\,-\,-$
Worst caesura $-\,\smile\smile\,-\,\smile\smile\,-\,\smile\smile\,-\,\smile\,|\,\smile\,-\,\smile\smile\,-\,-$

It is also common to find a diaeresis with a slight pause after the first foot; cp. the recurring ὡς φάτο, ὡς ἔφατ', ὡς ὅ γε, αὐτὰρ ὁ, and forms of address, as τέκνον, δαιμόνι', ὦ φίλοι, ὦ πόποι, &c. Hence the occasional hiatus in this place, as Il. 2. 209 ἠχῇ, ὡς κτλ., Il. 1. 333 αὐτὰρ ὁ ἔγνω ᾗσιν ἐνὶ φρεσί.

368.] **Spondaic verses.** The use of a spondee in the fifth place occurs most commonly in verses which end with a word of four or more syllables, as—

στέμματ' ἔχων ἐν χερσὶν ἑκηβόλου 'Απόλλωνος.

"Αρεϊ δὲ ζώνην, στέρνον δὲ Ποσειδάωνι.

It is also found with words of three long syllables, as—

τῷ δ' ἤδη δύο μὲν γενεαὶ μερόπων ἀνθρώπων.

And once or twice when the last word is a monosyllable: as νωμῆσαι βῶν (Il. 7. 238), ἑστήκει μείς (Il. 19. 117).

A spondee in the fifth place ought not to end with a word. Hence we should correct the endings ἠῶ δῖαν &c. by reading ἠόα, and δήμου φῆμις (Od. 14. 239), by restoring the archaic δήμοο. In Od. 12. 64 the words λὶς πέτρη at the end of the line are scanned together.

Words of three long syllables are very seldom found before the Bucolic diaeresis. Examples are:—

Il. 13. 713 οὐ γάρ σφι σταδίη | ὑσμίνη | μίμνε φίλον κῆρ.

Od. 10. 492 ψυχῇ χρησομένους | Θηβαίου | Τειρεσίαο.

The rarity of verses with this rhythm may be judged from the fact that it is never found with the oblique cases of ἄνθρωπος (ἀνθρώπων &c.), although these occur about 150 times, and in every other place in the verse: or with ἀλλήλων &c., which occur about 100 times.

Syllabic Quantity—Position.

369.] The quantity of a syllable—that is to say, the time which it takes in pronunciation—may be determined either by the length of the vowel (or vowels) which it contains, or by the character of the consonants which separate it from the next vowel sound. In ancient technical language, the vowel may be long by its own *nature* (φύσει), or by its *position* (θέσει).

The assumptions that all long syllables are equal, and that a long syllable is equal in quantity to two short syllables, are not strictly true of the natural quantity in ordinary pronunciation. Since every consonant takes *some* time to pronounce, it is evident that the first syllables of the words ὄφις, ὀφρύς, ὀμφή, ὄμβρος are different in length; and so again are the first syllables of Ὦτος, ὤτρυνον. Again, the diphthongs ῃ, ηυ, &c. are longer than the single vowels η, ω, &c., and also longer than the diphthongs ει, ευ, οι, ου. In short, the poetical ' quantities' must not be supposed to answer exactly to the natural or inherent length of the syllables. The poetical or metrical value is founded upon the natural length, but is the result of a sort of compromise, by which minor varieties of quantity are neglected, and the syllables thereby adapted to the demands of a simple rhythm.

It has been shown, however, that the general rule of Position rests upon a sound physiological basis. 'The insertion of a consonant may be regarded as equivalent in respect of time to the change of a short vowel into a long one.' Brücke, *Die physiologischen Grundlagen der neuhochdeutschen Verskunst*, p. 70 ; quoted by Hartel).

370.] Position. The general rule is that when a short vowel is followed by two consonants the syllable is long.

Regarding this rule it is to be observed that—

(1) Exceptions are almost wholly confined to combinations of a Mute (esp. a *tenuis*) with a following Liquid. But even with these combinations the general rule is observed in the great majority of the instances.

(2) Most of the exceptions are found with words which could not otherwise be brought into the hexameter : such as Ἀφροδίτη, Ἀμφιτρύων, βροτῶν, τράπεζα, προσηύδα, &c.

(3) The remaining exceptions are nearly all instances in which the vowel is separated by Diaeresis from the following consonants : as Il. 18. 122 καί τινὰ Τρωϊάδων, 24. 795 καὶ τά γε χρυσείην.

The chief exceptions in Homer are as follows * :—

τρ : in Ἀμφιτρύων, ἐτράφην (Il. 23. 84—but see the note on § 42 in the Appendix, p. 390), τετράκυκλον (Il. 24. 324), φαρέτρης (Il. 8. 323), Ὀτρυντεύς (Il. 20. 383-4) ; and in ἀλλότριος (unless we scan -ιος, -ιου, &c.).

Before τράπεζα, τρίαινα, τρίτη (τριήκοντα, &c.), τραπείομεν (τράπουτο, προ-τραπέσθαι, &c.), τράγους, τροποῖς, τρέφει (Od. 5. 422., 13. 410), τροφοῦ (Od. 19. 489), τρέμον (Od. 11. 527).

Before a diaeresis, καί τινα Τρωϊάδων (Il. 18. 122).

πρ : in ἀλλοπρόσαλλος (Il. 5. 831) ; before προσηύδα, πρόσωπον, προΐκτης, πρόσω, and other Compounds of πρό and πρός (προκείμενα, προσαίξας, &c.); also before πρὸς ἀλλήλους, πρὸ ἄστεος, and one or two similar phrases (cp. Il. 13. 799., 17. 726).

Before Πριαμίδης (Il.), πρίν (Il. 1. 97 οὐδ' ὅ γε πρίν κτλ., cp. 19. 313, Od. 14. 334., 17. 597) ; πρῶτος (Od. 3. 320., 17. 275), προσφάσθαι (Od. 23. 106).

κρ : in δακρύοισι (Od. 18. 173), δακρυπλώειν (Od. 19. 122), ἐνέκρυψε (Od. 5. 488), κεκρυμμένα (Od. 23. 110).

Before Κρονίων, Κρόνου παῖς, κραταιός, Κραταιΐς, κράτος μέγα (Il. 20. 121), κράνεα, κρυφηδόν, κραδαίνω, κρατευτάων, κρεῶν.

Add Il. 11. 697 εἵλετο κρινάμενος ; Od. 8. 92 κατὰ κράτα (κὰκ κρᾶτα ?), 12. 99 δέ τε κρατί.

βρ : in βροτός and its derivatives, as ἀβρότη, ἀμφίβροτος : also before βραχίων.

δρ : in ἀμφι-δρυφής (Il. 2. 700), and before δράκων, Δρύας, δρόμους. Also Il. 11. 69 τὰ δὲ δράγματα (unless we read δάργματα, as Hartel suggests).

θρ : in ἀλλό-θροος (Od. 1. 183, &c.), and before θρόνων, &c. and θρασειάων. Also in Il. 5. 462 ἡγήτορι Θρηκῶν.

---

* They are enumerated by La Roche, *Homerische Untersuchungen*, pp. 1-41, with his usual care and completeness.

φρ: in Ἀφροδίτη : and Od. 15. 444 ἡμῖν δ᾽ ἐπι-φράσσετ᾽ ὄλεθρον. Cp. Hes. Op. 655 προπεφραδμένα.

χρ: before χρέος or χρέως (Od. 8. 353) : and in Il. 23. 186 ῥοδόεντι δὲ χρῖεν, Il. 24. 795 καὶ τά γε χρυσείην.

τλ: in σχετλίη (Il. 3. 414), which however may be scanned - -.

κλ: in Πάτροκλε (Il. 19. 287), ἐκλίθη (Od. 19. 470—should perhaps be read ἑτέρωσε κλίθη), προσέκλινε (Od. 21. 138, 165—read perhaps πρόσκλινε or ἔκλινε) : and before Κλυταιμνήστρη, Κλεωναί, κλύων, κληδών, κλιθῆναι (Od. 1. 366). Also, in Od. 12. 215 τύπτετε κληΐδεσσιν, 20. 92 τῆς δ᾽ ἄρα κλαιούσης.

πλ: in the Compounds τειχεσι-πλῆτα (Il. 5. 31, 455), πρωτό-πλοος, προσέπλαζε (Od. 11. 583—read perhaps πρόσ-πλαζε) : before Πλάταια, πλέων sailing, πλέων more (Il. 10. 252), πλέον full (Od. 20. 355). Add Il. 9. 382 (= Od. 4. 127) Αἰγυπτίας, ὅθι πλεῖστα (with v. l. ᾗ πλεῖστα, cp. Od. 4. 229), and Il. 4. 329 αὐτὰρ ὁ πλησίον.

χλ: in Od. 10. 234 καὶ μέλι χλωρόν, 14. 429 ἀμφὶ δὲ χλαῖναν.

To these have to be added the very few examples of a vowel remaining short before σκ and ζ : viz. —

σκ: before Σκάμανδρος, σκέπαρνον (Od. 5. 237., 9. 391), σκίη (Hes. Op. 589).

ζ: before Ζάκυνθος (Il. 2. 634, Od. 1. 246, &c.), Ζέλεια (Il. 2. 824, &c.).

στ: before στέατος in Od. 21. 178, 183—unless it is a case of Synizesis.

A comparison of these exceptions will show that in a sense we are right in attributing them to metrical necessity. There are comparatively few instances in which the two consonants do not come at the beginning of a word of the form ⏑ –, so that the last syllable of the preceding word must be a short one. On the other hand, the extent to which neglect of position is allowed for metrical convenience is limited, and depends on the *natural quantity* of the consonants in question, *i. e.* the actual time occupied by their pronunciation. Sonant mutes (*mediae*) are longer than surd mutes (*tenues*); gutturals are longer than dentals or labials; and of the two liquids λ is longer than ρ. Thus shortening is tolerably frequent before πρ and τρ, less so before κρ, πλ, κλ, θρ, χρ. With other combinations of mute and liquid, as φρ, βρ, δρ, and with σκ and ζ, it seems to be only admitted for the sake of words which the poet was absolutely compelled to bring in : such as Ἀφροδίτη, Σκάμανδρος, Ζάκυνθος, βροτός, with its compounds, &c. No exceptions are found before γρ, γλ, φλ, κν, κμ, or any combination other than those mentioned. In short, the harshness tolerated in a violation of the rule usually bears a direct relation to its necessity. It was impossible to have an Iliad without the names Aphrodite and Scamander, but these are felt and treated as exceptions.

The word ἀνδρότης, which appears in the fixed ending λιποῦσ᾽ ἀνδρότητα καὶ ἥβην, should probably be written ἁδρότης. As the original μρ of βροτός becomes either μβρ (as ἄ-μβροτος, φθισί-μβροτος), or βρ (as νὺξ ἀ-βρότη, ἀμφί-βροτος), so νρ might become νδρ (as ἀνδρός), or δρ. So perhaps Ἐνναλίῳ ἀνδρεϊφόντῃ should be Ἐνναλίῳ ἀδριφόντῃ (⏑ ⏑ – –) : cp. ἀνδρε-φόνος (Hdn. ap. Eustath. 183, 6).

The plea on which a short vowel is allowed before Σκάμανδρος and σκέπαρνον may be extended, as Fick points out (*Bezz. Beitr.* xiv. 316), to some forms of σκίδνημι now written without the σ, viz. *κέδασθεν* (Il. 15. 657), κεδασθέντες, &c. Metrical necessity, however, would not justify the same license with σκίδναται (ἐπικίδναται Il. 2. 850, &c.), ἐ-σκίδνατο, ἐ-σκέδασσε (for which ἐσκέδασε is available).

Neglect of Position is perceptibly commoner in the Odyssey than in the Iliad. Apart from cases in which the necessities of metre can be pleaded, viz. proper names and words beginning with ⌣ -, it will be found that the proportion of examples is about 3 : 1. It will be seen, too, that some marked instances occur in Books 23 and 24 of the Iliad. In Hesiod and the Homeric Hymns the rule is still more lax. Thus in Hesiod a vowel is allowed to be short before κν (Op. 567, Fr. 95), and πν (Theog. 319). In the scanty fragments of the Cyclic poets we find πέπρωται (Cypria), πᾶτρί (Little Iliad), Ἀγχίσαο κλυτὸν κτλ. (*ibid.*), ἄκριβέα (Iliupersis).

371.] Lengthening before ρ, λ, μ, ν, σ, δ. There are various words beginning with one of these letters (the liquids ρ, λ, μ, ν, the spirant σ, and the *media* δ), before which a short final vowel is often allowed to have the metrical value of a long syllable. Initial ρ appears always to have this power of lengthening a preceding vowel ; but in the case of the other letters mentioned it is generally confined to certain words. Thus we have examples before—

λ, in λίσσομαι, λήγω, λείβω, λιγύς, λιαρός, λιπαρός, λίς, λαπάρη, λόφος, and occasionally in a few others : but not (*e. g.*) in such frequently occurring words as Λύκιος, λέχος, λείπω.

μ, in μέγας, μέγαρον, μοῖρα, μαλακός, μέλος, μελίη, μάστιξ, μόθος : but not (*e. g.*) μάχομαι, μένος, μέλας, μάκαρ, μῦθος.

ν, in νευρή, νέφος, νιφάς, νύμφη, νότος, νηητός, νύσσα : once only before νηῦς (Il. 13. 472) : not before νέκυς, νόος, νέμεσις, &c.

σ, in σεύω, σάρξ : once before σύ (Il. 20. 434), and once before συφεός (Od. 10. 238).

δ, in δέος, δεινός, δεί-σας &c. (Stem δϜει-), δήν, δηρόν (§ 394).

This lengthening, it is to be observed, is almost wholly confined to the syllables which have the metrical ictus : the exceptions are, πολλὰ λισσομένη (Il. 5. 358, so Il. 21. 368., 22. 91), πυκνὰ ῥωγαλέην (Od. 13. 438, &c.), πολλὰ ῥυστάζεσκεν (Il. 24. 755). Further, it is chiefly found where the sense requires the two words to be closely joined in pronunciation : in particular—

(1) In the final vowel of Prepositions followed by a Case-form : as ἐπὶ ῥηγμῖνι, ποτὶ λόφον, ὑπὸ λιπαροῖσι, κατὰ μοῖραν, ἐνὶ μεγάρῳ, κατὰ μόθον, διὰ νεφέων, ἀπὸ νευρῆφιν, κατὰ συφεοῖσιν, κατὰ δεινούς, ἐπὶ δηρόν, and similar combinations.

(2) In fixed phrases : ὥς τε λίς (Il. 11. 239., 17. 109., 18. 318), κλαῖον δὲ λιγέως (Od. 10. 201, &c.), ἀπήμονά τε λιαρόν τε (Il. 14. 164, &c.), καλή τε μεγάλη τε, εἶδός τε μέγεθός τε, Τρῶες δὲ μεγά-

θυμοι, τρίποδα μέγαν, Πηλιάδα μελίην, ὥς τε νιφάδες, σὺν δὲ νεφέεσσι κάλυψε, ὅτε σεύαιτο, οὔ τι μάλα δήν, and the like.

These facts lead us to connect the lengthening now in question with the peculiar *doubling of the initial consonant* which we see in Compounds, as ἀπο-ρρίπτω, ἐΰ-ρροος, ἄ-ρρηκτος, τρί-λλιστος, ἐΰ-μμελίης, ἀγά-ννιφος, ἐπι-σσεύω, ἐΰ-σσελμος, ἀ-δδεής: and after the Augment (§ 67), as ἔ-ρριψα, ἔ-ρρηξα, ἔ-ρρεον, ἐ-λλίσσετο, ἔ-μμορε, ἔ-ννεον, ἔ-σσευα, ἔ-δδεισα (so the MSS., but Aristarchus wrote ἔδεισα). The words and stems in which this doubling occurs are in the main the same as those which lengthen a preceding final vowel : and the explanation, whatever it be, must be one that will apply to both groups of phenomena.

With most of these words the lengthening of a preceding vowel (or doubling of the consonant, as the case may be) is optional. But there is no clear instance in Homer of a short vowel remaining short before the root δϜει- (*e.g.* in the 2 Aor. δίον, the 1 Aor. ἔδεισα, the Nouns δέος, δεινός, δειλός, even the proper names Δεισήνωρ, &c.), or the Adverb δήν. The same may be said of ῥάκος, ῥήγνυμι, ῥύομαι, ῥητός, ῥίπτω, ῥίον, also μαλακός, μελίη, νιφάς. Lengthening is also the rule, subject to few exceptions, with λίσσομαι, λόφος, νέφος, νευρή, ῥινός, ῥόος, ῥάβδος, ῥίζα, and some others (La Roche, *H. U.* pp. 47 ff.).

372.] Origin of the lengthening.* The most probable account of the matter is that most of the roots or stems affected originally began with *two consonants*, one of which was lost by phonetic decay. Thus initial ρ may stand for Ϝρ (as in Ϝρήγ-νυμι), or σρ (as *σρέω, Sanscrit *sravāmi*): λίς is probably for λϜίς (with a weaker Stem than the form seen in λέϜ-ων): υἱός is for συνός (Sanscr. *snushā*): νιφ-άς goes back to a root *sneibh* (Goth. *snaivs*, snow): μοῖρα is probably from a root *smer*: σέλμα is for σϜέλμα (Curt. *s. v.*): and δει- in δει-νός &c. is for δϜει- (cp. δεί-δοικα for δέ-δϜοικα). It is not indeed necessary to maintain that in these cases the lost consonant was pronounced at the time when the Homeric poems were composed. We have only to suppose that the *particular combination* in question had established itself in the usage of the language before the two consonants were reduced by phonetic decay to one. Thus we may either suppose (*e.g.*) that κατὰ ῥόον in the time of Homer was still pronounced κατὰ σρόον, or that certain combinations—κατα-σρέω, ἐΰ-σροος, κατὰ σρόον, &c.—passed into κατα-ρρέω, ἐΰ-ρροος, κατὰ ῥρόον (or κατᾱ ῥόον). There are several instances in which a second form of a word appears in combinations of a fixed type. Thus we have

---

* On this subject the chief sources of information are, La Roche, *Homerische Untersuchungen* (pp. 49–65); Hartel, *Homerische Studien* (Pt. i. pp. 1–55); and Knös, *De Digammo Homerico Quaestiones* (Pt. iii. 225 ff.).

the form πτόλις, in ποτὶ πτόλιος, Ἀχιλλῆα πτολίπορθον, &c.: πτόλεμος, in μέγα πτολέμοιο μεμηλώς, ἀνὰ πτολέμοιο γεφύρας. Similarly a primitive γδοῦπος survives in ἐρί-γδουπος (also ἐρί-δουπος), ἐ-γδούπησε: and γνόος in ἀ-γνοέω. Cp. also the pairs σμικρός and μικρός, σκίδναμαι and κίδναμαι, σῦς and ῦς, ξύν and σύν. It is at least conceivable that in the same way the poet of the Iliad said μοῖραν and also κατὰ σμοῖραν, μειδιάων but φιλο-σμειδής, δὴν ἦν at the beginning of a line, but μάλα δϜήν at the end: and so in other cases.

It is true that the proportion of the words now in question which can be proved to have originally had an initial double consonant is not very great. Of the liquids, the method is most successful with initial ρ, which can nearly always be traced back to vr or sr. And among the words with initial ν a fair propor-tion can be shown to have begun originally with σν (νευρή, νυός, νιφάς, νέω, νύμφη). The difficulty is partly met by the further supposition that the habit of lengthening before initial liquids was extended by analogy, from the stems in which it was originally due to a double consonant to others in which it had no such etymological ground. This supposition is certainly well founded in the case of ρ, before which lengthening became the rule.

373.] **Final ι of the Dat. Sing.** The final ι of the Dat. (Loc.) **Sing.** is so frequently long that it may be regarded as a 'doubtful vowel.' The examples are especially found in lines and phrases of a fixed or archaic type:—

ἦ ῥα, καὶ ἐν δεινῷ σάκεϊ ἔλασ' ὄβριμον ἔγχος.

οὕτω που Διὶ μέλλει ὑπερμενέϊ φίλον εἶναι (thrice in the Il.).

τὸ τρίτον αὖθ' ὕδατι (Od. 10. 520., 11. 28).

αὐτοῦ πὰρ νηΐ τε μένειν (Od. 9. 194., 10. 444).

ἤλυθον εἰκοστῷ ἔτεϊ ἐς κτλ. (6 times in the Od.).

So in Αἴαντι δὲ μάλιστα, Ὀδυσσῆϊ δὲ μάλιστα, &c. and the fixed epithet Διὶ φίλος. Considering also that this vowel is rarely elided (§ 376), it becomes highly probable that ῑ as well as ῐ was originally in use.†

It is an interesting question whether these traces of -ῑ as the ending of the Homeric Dat. are to be connected with the occasional -ῑ of the Locative in the Veda (Brugmann, *Grundr.* ii. § 256, p. 610). The Vedic lengthening appears to be one of a group of similar changes of quantity which affect a short final vowel, and which are in their origin rhythmical, since they generally serve to prevent a succession of short syllables (Wackernagel, *Das Dehnungsgesetz der griechischen Composita*, p. 12 ff., quoted by Brugmann *l. c.*). The same thing may evidently be said of the Homeric -ῑ in many of the cases quoted, as

† The priority in this as in so many inferences from Homeric usage belongs (as Hartel notices) to H. L. Ahrens (*Philologus*, iv. pp. 593 ff.).

πατέρι, σάκεϊ, ἔτεϊ. Hence it is probable that the lengthening dates from the Indo-European language, and is not due in the first instance to the requirements of the hexameter. But in such a case as 'Οδυσσῆϊ it may be that the Greek poet treats it as a *license*, which he takes advantage of in order to avoid the impossible quantities ◡ – – ◡ (cp. ὀϊζυρώτερος for the unmetrical ὀϊζυρότερος).

374.] Final α. The metrical considerations which lead us to recognise -ῑ in the Dat. Sing. might be urged, though with less force, in favour of an original -ᾱ as the ending of the Neut. Plur. We have—

Il. 5. 745 (= 8. 389) ἐς δ' ὄχεα φλόγεα ποσὶ βήσετο.

8. 556 φαίνετ' ἀριπρεπέα, ὅτε κτλ.

11. 678 (Od. 14. 100) τόσα πώεα οἰῶν (v. l. μήλων).

20. 255 πόλλ' ἐτεά τε καὶ οὐκί.

21. 352 τὰ περὶ καλὰ ῥέεθρα.

23. 240 ἀριφραδέα δὲ τέτυκται.

24. 7 ὅποσα τολύπευσε.

Od. 9. 109 ἄσπαρτα καὶ ἀνήρωτα.

10. 353 πορφύρεα καθύπερθ'.

12. 396 ὀπταλέα τε καὶ ὠμά.

14. 343 ῥωγαλέα, τὰ καὶ αὐτός.

23. 225 ἀριφραδέα κατέλεξας.

In the majority of these instances, however, the final α is preceded by the vowel ε, from which it was originally separated by a spirant (ὄχε-σ-α, πορφύρε-ϟ-α). Cp. Il. 1. 45 ἀμφηρεφέα τε φαρέτρην, 5. 576 Πυλαιμένεα ἐλέτην, 5. 827 Ἄρηᾱ τό γε, 14. 329 Περσῆᾱ πάντων, Od. 1. 40 ἐκ γὰρ Ὀρέσταο τίσις. As two successive vowels are often found to interchange their quantity (βασιλῆα, βασιλέᾱ), so perhaps, even when the first vowel retains its metrical value, there may be a slight transference of quantity, sufficient to allow the final vowel, when reinforced by the *ictus*, to count as a long syllable. Cp. § 375, 3.

The scanning ἔᾱ (in Il. 4. 321 εἰ τότε κοῦρος ἔα νῦν κτλ., cp. 5. 887, Od. 14. 352) may be explained by transference of quantity, from ᾖα.

375.] Short syllables ending in a consonant are also occasionally lengthened in arsis, although the next word begins with a vowel : as—

οὔτε ποτ' ἐς πόλεμον ἅμα λαῷ θωρηχθῆναι.

αἴθ' ὄφελες ἄγονός τ' ἔμεναι κτλ.

χερσὶν ὑπ' Ἀργείων φθίμενος ἐν πατρίδι γαίῃ.

The circumstances under which this metrical lengthening is generally found differ remarkably, as has been recently

shown,* from those which prevail where short final vowels are
lengthened before an initial consonant. In those cases, as we
saw (§ 371), the rule is that the two words are closely connected,
usually in a set phrase or piece of epic commonplace. In the
examples now in question the words are often separated by the
punctuation : and where this is not the case it will usually be
found that there is a slight pause. In half of the instances the
words are separated by the penthemimeral caesura, which always
marks a pause in the rhythm. Further, this lengthening is
only found in the syllable with the *ictus*. The explanation,
therefore, must be sought either in the force of the *ictus*, or in
the pause (which necessarily adds something to the time of a
preceding syllable), or in the combination of these two causes.

In some instances, however, a different account of the matter
has to be given : in particular—

(1) With ὥς following the word to which it refers : as Il. 2.
190 κακὸν ὥς (∪ – –), and so θεὸς ὥς, κύνες ὥς, ὄρνιθες ὥς, ἀθάνατος ὥς, &c. In these instances the lengthening may be referred to the original palatal ι or *y* of the Pronoun (Sanscr. *yas*,
yā, *yad*=ὅς, ἥ, ὅ). It is not to be supposed that the actual
form ιώς existed in Homeric times : but the habit of treating
a preceding syllable as long by Position survived in the group
of phrases. Others explain this ὥς as 'Fώς (Sanscr. *sva*-), comparing Gothic *své* 'as' (Brugmann, *Gr. Gr.* § 98) ; or σώς (§ 108, 3).

(2) In the case of some words ending with -ις, -ιν, -υς, -υν,
where the vowel was long, or at least ' doubtful,' in Homer.

In βλοσυρῶπις and ἦνις the final syllable is long before a
vowel even in thesis. So the ι may have been long in θοῦρις (cp.
the phrase θοῦριν ἐπιειμένος ἀλκήν) : and traces of the same
scansion may be seen in the phrases ἔρις ἄμοτον μεμαυῖα, Διὶ μῆτιν
ἀτάλαντος, although ἔρῐς, μῆτῐς are more common.

Final -υς (Gen. -υος) is long in Feminine Substantives (§ 116,
4), as ἰθύς *aim* (ῡ in thesis, Il. 6. 79., 21. 303), πληθύς (Il. 11.
305), ἀχλύς (Il. 20. 421), ἰλύς (Gen. -ῠος), βρωτύς (Od. 18. 407)
and other Nouns in -τύς : also in the Masc. ἰχθύς, νέκυς, βότρυς
(βοτρῠδόν), and perhaps πέλεκυς (Il. 17. 520).

(3) Where the vowel of the final syllable is preceded by
another, especially by a long vowel ; as οἰκῆας ἄλοχόν τε (Il. 6.
366), Ἀχιλλῆος ὀλοὸν κῆρ (Il. 14. 139), ὃς λαὸν ἤγειρα (Od. 2. 41),
δμῶες ἐνὶ οἴκῳ (Od. 11. 190), πλεῖον ἐλέλειπτο (Od. 8. 475), χρεῖος
ὑπαλύξαι (with *v. l.* χρείως, Od. 8. 355): and so in νῆας (ᾱ, Il. 2.
165., 18. 260), νηός (Od. 12. 329), Τρῶες (Il. 17. 730), βοός (Il. 11.
776), also Ἄρηα, Περσῆα, and the other examples given in § 374.

In such cases there is a tendency to lengthen the second

---

* By Hartel, in the *Homeric Studies* already quoted, i. p. 10.

vowel, as in the Attic forms βασιλέᾱ, ᾿Αχιλλέως, &c. In Homer we may suppose that the second of the two vowels borrows some of the quantity of the other, so that *with the help of the ictus* it can form the arsis of a foot. Actual lengthening of the second vowel may be seen in Homer in the form ἀπ-ήωρος *hanging loose* (cp. μετ-ήορος and the later μετ-έωρος) also in δυσαήων (Gen. Plur. of δυσαής).

(4) In the Ending -οιϊν of the Dual, as ὤμοιϊν (Il. 13. 511., 16. 560, Od. 6. 219), ἵπποιϊν, σταθμοῖϊν: also in νῶϊν, σφῶϊν. We may compare the doubtful ι of ἡμῖν, ὑμῖν, and the two forms of the Dat. Plur. in Latin (-bŭs, -bīs). Similarly there are traces of ῑ in μίν (Il. 5. 385., 6. 501., 10. 347., 11. 376, &c.). In the case of -οιϊν and -ωϊν the account given under the last head would apply.

In a few places it appears as though the 3 Plur. of Secondary Tenses in -ν (for -ντ) were allowed to be long: as ἔφαν ἀπιόντες (Od. 9. 413), καὶ κύνεον ἀγαπαζόμενοι (Od. 17. 35, &c.), &c. This is confined (curiously enough) to the Odyssey and the Catalogue of the Ships. In the latter it occurs seven times: in the Odyssey eleven times, in the rest of the Iliad once (7. 206).

Elision, Crasis, &c.

376.] A final vowel cut off before a word beginning with a vowel is said to suffer *Elision* (ἔκθλιψις): as μυρί᾿ ᾿Αχαιοῖς ἄλγε᾿ ἔθηκε. Whether an elided vowel was entirely silent, or merely slurred over in such a way that it did not form a distinct syllable, is a question which can hardly be determined.

The vowels that are generally liable to elision are α, ε, ο, ι. But—

(1) The ο of ὁ, τό, πρό is not elided.

Final -ο is not elided in the Gen. endings -οιο, -αο, and very rarely in the Pronouns ἐμεῖο, &c. This however may be merely because the later forms of these endings, viz. -ου, -εω, -ευ, took the place of -οι᾿(ο), -ά᾿(ο), -ει᾿(ο) when a vowel followed. In the case of āο this supposition is borne out by the fact that -εω is often found before a vowel, as Πηληϊάδεω ᾿Αχιλῆος (l. Πηληϊάδα᾿): and by the rarity of the contraction of εο to ευ (§ 378*). There is less to be said for elision of -ο in the ending -οιο. That ending in Homer is archaic (§ 149), therefore the presumption is against emendations which increase the frequency of its occurrence. And the cases of -ου remaining long before hiatus are not exceptionally common (Hartel, *H. S.* ii. 6).

(2) The ι of τί, περί is not elided in Homer; regarding ὅτι see § 269. But περί is elided in Hesiod: as περοίχεται, περίαχε.

(3) The -ι of the Dat. Sing. is rarely elided; but see § 105, 1. Exceptions are to be seen in Il. 4. 259 ἠδ᾿ ἐν δαίθ᾿ ὅτε κτλ.; 5. 5

ἀστέρ' ὀπωρινῷ κτλ.; Il. 3. 349., 10. 277., 12. 88., 16. 385., 17. 45, 324., 23. 693., 24. 26, Od. 5. 62, 398., 10. 106., 13. 35., 15. 364., 19. 480. The ι of the Dat. Plur. is often elided in the First and Second Declensions, and in the forms in -σσι of the Third Declension. On the other hand, elision is very rare in the forms in -εσι, -ᾱσι, -ῡσι, &c.

The diphthong -αι of the Person-Endings -μαι, -σαι, -ται, -νται, -σθαι is frequently elided : as βούλομ' ἐγώ, κείσοντ' ἐν προθύροισι, πρὶν λύσασθ' ἑτάρους. But not the -αι of the 1 Aor. Inf. Act. or of the Inf. in -ναι : hence in Il. 21. 323 read τυμβοχόῃς, not the Inf. τυμβοχοῆσ'.

The diphthong -οι of the enclitic Pronouns μοι and σοι (τοι) is elided in a few places : Il. 6. 165 ὅς μ' ἔθελεν φιλότητι μιγήμεναι οὐκ ἐθελούσῃ; 13. 481 καί μ' οἴῳ ἀμύνετε (so Od. 4. 367); 17. 100 τῷ μ' οὔ τις νεμεσήσεται : also Il. 1. 170., 9. 673., 13. 544., 23. 310, 579, Od. 1. 60, 347., 23. 21 (Cobet, Misc. Crit. p. 345). Other instances may be recovered by conjecture : thus in Il. 3. 173 ὡς ὄφελεν θάνατός μοι ἀδεῖν should probably be ὥς μ' ὄφελεν θάνατος ἀδέειν (§ 365); and in Il. 24. 757 νῦν δέ μοι ἐρσήεις Van Leeuwen reads νῦν δέ μ' ἐερσήεις.

In the case of the enclitic οἱ ('Foι) elision involved the disappearance of the Pronoun from the later text. In Il. 6. 289 (= Od. 15. 105) ἔνθ' ἔσαν οἱ πέπλοι the original was probably ἔνθα 'F'(οι) ἔσαν (cp. Od. 15. 556 ἔνθα οἱ ἦσαν ὗες). In Il. 5. 310 (= 11. 356) ἀμφὶ δὲ ὄσσε κελαινὴ νὺξ ἐκάλυψε read ἀμφὶ δέ 'F'. In Od. 9. 360 ὡς φάτ', ἀτάρ οἱ αὖτις, where some MSS. have ὡς ἔφατ', αὐτάρ οἱ αὖτις, read αὐτάρ 'F'.*

377.] Crasis. When a final vowel, instead of being elided, coalesces with the initial vowel of the next word, the process is termed *Crasis*.

The use of Crasis in Homer is limited. It is seen in οὕνεκα and τοὔνεκα, also in τἆλλα for τὰ ἄλλα (Il. 1. 465, &c.), καὐτός for καὶ αὐτός (in Il. 6. 260., 13. 734, Od. 3. 255., 6. 282—the three last being passages where κ' αὐτός for κε αὐτός is inadmissible), and χἠμεῖς for καὶ ἡμεῖς (Il. 2. 238). In these cases either Crasis or Elision is required by the metre. Most texts also have ὥριστος, οὑμός (Il. 8. 360), ωὑτός for ὁ αὐτός (Il. 5. 396), κἀγώ, τὠμῷ, τἠμῇ: also προὔ- for προ-ε- (in προὔφαινε, προὔχούσας, &c.). But since the full forms ὁ ἄριστος, &c. are equally allowed by the

---

* J. van Leeuwen, *Mnemos.* xiii. 188 ff. Of the numerous other emendations of this kind which he proposes few are positively required. The style of Homer constantly allows an unemphatic Pronoun to be supplied from the context. Moreover, he frequently proposes to insert enclitics in a part of the sentence in which they seldom occur (§ 365). It would be difficult (*e.g.*) to find a parallel for ἐπεί μ' ἀφέλεσθέ 'Fε δόντες or χειρὶ δὲ νεκταρέου Fεανοῦ 'F' ἐτίναξε λαβοῦσα.

metre we cannot but suspect that the spelling with Crasis may be due to later usage. The forms κἀκεῖνος, κἀκεῖσε, &c. (for καὶ κεῖνος, &c.) are certainly wrong, as ἐκεῖνος is not the Homeric form.

378.] Synizesis is the term used when the two coalescing vowels are written in full, but 'sink together' (συνιζάνω) into one syllable in pronunciation.

The Particle δή unites with the initial vowel of a following vowel, especially with αὖ, αὐτός and οὕτως (§ 350); also with Ἀντιμάχοιο (Il. 11. 138), ἀφνειότατος (Il. 20. 220), ἄγρην (Od. 12. 330).

Synizesis is also found with ἦ, in the combination ἦ οὐχ (Il. 5. 439, &c.), ἦ εἰς ὅ κεν (Il. 5. 466), ἦ εἰπέμεναι (Od. 4. 682); with ἐπεὶ οὐ (Od. 4. 352, &c.); with μὴ ἄλλοι (Od. 4. 165); and in—

Il. 17. 89 ἀσβέστῳ· οὐδ' υἱὸν λάθεν Ἀτρέος : where we may perhaps read ἀσβέστῳ· οὐδ' υἷα λάθ' Ἀτρέος.

18. 458 υἱεῖ ἐμῷ ὠκυμόρῳ (one or two MSS. give υἷ' ἐμῷ).

Od. 1. 226 εἰλαπίνη ἦε γάμος κτλ.

In Il. 1. 277 Πηλείδη ἔθελ', and Od. 17. 375 ὦ ἀρίγνωτε the case is different : a *short* vowel is absorbed in a preceding long one.

Other examples of Synizesis are to be found in the monosyllabic pronunciation of εα, εο, εω, both in Verbs (§ 57) and Nouns (§ 105, 3). It will be seen that in the cases now in question (apart from some doubtful forms) an E-sound (η, ει, ε) merges in a following α or ο.

The term Synizesis may also be applied to the monosyllabic pronunciation of the vowels in Αἰγυπτίη (Od. 4. 229), &c. σχετλίη (Il. 3. 414), Ἱστίαια (Il. 2. 537). It has been thought that in these cases the ι was pronounced like our *y* : but this is not a necessary inference from the scansion. In Italian verse, for instance, such words as *mio, mia* count as monosyllables, but are not pronounced *myo, mya*. For πόλιος (∪ – in Il. 2. 811., 21. 567) it is better to read πόλεος (§ 107) ; and for πόλιας (Od. 8. 560, 574) πόλῑς. The corresponding Synizesis of υ is generally recognised in the word Ἐνυαλίῳ (commonly scanned υα in the phrase Ἐνυαλίῳ ἀνδρεϊφόντῃ) : but see § 370 *ad fin.*

378.*] Contraction. The question of the use of contracted forms has been already touched upon in connexion with the different grammatical categories which it affects : see §§ 56, 81, 105. It will be useful here to recapitulate the results, and to notice one or two attempts which have been made to recover the original usage of Homer in this respect.*

---

* See especially J. van Leeuwen, *Mnemosyne*, Nov. Ser. xiii. p. 215, xiv. p. 335 : and Menrad, *De contractionis et synizeseos usu Homerico* (Monachii, 1886).

1. Contraction is most readily admitted between similar sounds, or when the second is of higher vowel pitch, *i. e.* higher in the scale ο, ω, α, η, ε. Thus we have many instances with the combinations εε, οο, αε, οε; few with εα, αω, αο, still fewer with εω, εο.

2. In most cases in which contraction is freely admitted we find that the sound which originally separated the vowels was the semi-vowel *i̯* or *y*. In case of the loss of σ it is comparatively rare; with ϝ it is probably not Homeric at all (§ 396). Hence (*e. g.*) although it is common with the combinations εε, εει in most Verbs in -εω (§ 56), it is not found in χέω (χέϝ-ω) and is extremely rare in τρέω (τρέσ-ω, see § 29, 6). But it is admitted with loss of σᵢ̯, as in the Gen. ending -ου from -οσιο (-οι̯ο, -οο), and the Verbs in -εω from stems in -εσ, as νεικέω (νεικεσ-ι̯ω).

(*a*) On these principles we should expect the 2 Sing. endings -εαι, -εο, -ηαι, -αο (for -εσαι, &c.) to remain uncontracted; and this view is borne out on the whole by the very careful investigation made by J. van Leeuwen. Omitting the Verbs in -αω and -εω we find that there are about 522 occurrences of these endings, and that of these 434 present uncontracted forms: while in 66 instances the contracted syllable comes before a vowel, so that it can be written with elision of -αι or -ο (*e.g.* Il. 3. 138 κεκλήσε' ἄκοιτις, for κεκλήσῃ: Il. 9. 54 ἔπλε' ἄριστος, for ἔπλευ). In the case of -εο this mode of writing finds some support in the MSS.: *e.g.* ψεύδε' (Il. 4. 404), παύε' (Il. 9. 260, Od. 1. 340), εὔχε' (Il. 3. 430, Od. 4. 752), also ἔπε', read by Aristarchus in Il. 10. 146 (ἔπευ MSS.). Against these 500 instances there are only 22 exceptions, 7 in the Iliad and 15 in the Odyssey, some of which can be readily corrected. Thus Il. 4. 264 (=19. 139) ὄρσευ πόλεμόνδε should be ὄρσο πτόλεμόνδε (Nauck): in Il. 2. 367 γνώσεαι δ' εἰ omit δὲ (Barnes): in Il. 24. 434 for ὅς με κέλῃ read ὃς κέλεαι, and so in Od. 4. 812., 5. 174. In Od. 18. 107 for ἐπαύρῃ read the Act. ἐπαύρης (Van L.): as in Il. 1. 203 we may retain ἴδης (so the MSS.; Ar. ἴδῃ,—but the corruption lies deeper). The greater frequency of instances in the Odyssey (and in book xxiv of the Iliad) is hardly enough to indicate a difference of usage within the Homeric age.

(*b*) In the corresponding forms of Verbs in -αω and -εω there is a concurrence of three vowels, which in our text are always reduced to two syllables, either by contraction, as in αἰδεῖο, μυθεῖαι, νεῖαι, μνάᾳ, or by hyphaeresis (§ 105), as μυθέαι, αἴρεο, ἔκλεο, πώλεαι (Od. 4. 811). A single vowel appears in πειρᾷ for πειρά-εαι, ἡρῶ for ἡρά-εο. The metre requires αἰδεῖο, αἴρεο, ἔκλεο, πώλεαι; for πειρᾷ it allows πειράαι (becoming πειρά' in Il. 24. 390, 433, Od. 4. 545). The isolated form ὄρηαι (Od. 14. 343) for ὁρά-εαι should perhaps be ὁρᾶαι or ὁράᾳ. If the ending is in its original form it belongs to the Non-Thematic conjugation (§ 19): another example may be found in ὁρῆτο (or ὄρητο), read by Zenodotus in Il. 1. 56.

(*c*) In the Future in -εω (for -εσω) contraction is less frequent than in the Present of Verbs in -εω (-ει̯ω or -εσι̯ω). Forms such as ὀλεῖται, καμεῖται, μαχεῖται, ὀμεῖται, κομιῶ, κτεριῶ, κτεριοῦσι, evidently could not otherwise come into the verse. In Il. 17. 451 σφῶϊν δ' ἐν γούνεσσι βαλῶ we may read βάλω (Fick).

Il. 4. 161 ἔκ τε καὶ ὀψὲ τελεῖ we should take τελεῖ as a Present. The remaining exceptions are, κτενεῖ in Il. 15. 65, 68 (probably an interpolation), κατακτενεῖ in Il. 23. 412, and ἐκφανεῖ in Il. 19. 104.

(d) Similarly in the declension of stems in -εσ the ending -εες is rarely contracted. In the phrase φαίνονται (or φαίνεσθαι) ἐναργεῖς (Il. 20. 131, Od. 7. 201., 16. 161) Fick happily reads ἐναργές, to be taken as an adverb. The same remedy is applicable in Il. 9. 225 δαιτὸς μὲν ἐΐσης οὐκ ἐπιδευεῖς, and Il. 13. 622 ἄλλης μὲν λώβης τε καὶ αἴσχεος οὐκ ἐπιδευεῖς, where the Nom. Plur. is unexplained : read οὐκ ἐπιδευές *there is no lack*.

(e) The contraction of εο to ευ is rare in the Gen. of stems in -εσ (§ 105, 3), but frequent in the Pronominal Genitives ἐμεῦ (μευ), σεῦ, εὗ, τεῦ. Here again, however, we are struck by the number of cases in which we can substitute the forms in -ειο or -εο, with elision of -ο. In our MSS. the elision actually occurs in ἐμεῖ' (Il. 23. 789, Od. 8. 462) and σεῖ' (Il. 6. 454, also Hom. H. xxxiv. 19). In Il. 17. 173 νῦν δέ σευ ὠνοσάμην Zenodotus is said to have read νῦν δέ σε, i.e. probably νῦν δέ σε'. The full forms in -ειο or -εο occur 121 times, and may be restored without elision 9 times, with elision 56 times. To these we should add the instances in which we may put the form *μεο (6 times) or με' (19 times). There remain altogether fifty-five exceptions, which are discussed by J. van Leeuwen (*Mnemos.* xiii. 215). In the phrase κέκλυτέ μευ, which occurs 19 times, he would read μοι, according to the Homeric construction (§ 143, 3). So in the formula κέκλυτε δὴ νῦν μευ, Ἰθακήσιοι (5 times in the Odyssey), where however we are tempted to restore ἐμεῖ' (cp. Il. 3. 97 κέκλυτε νῦν καὶ ἐμεῖο). He suggests putting the Dat. for the Gen. also in Od. 10. 485 οἵ μευ φθινύθουσι φίλον κῆρ, Od. 15. 467 οἵ μευ πατέρ' ἀμφεπένοντο, Od. 16. 92 ἦ μάλα μευ καταδάπτετ' ἀκούοντος φίλον ἦτορ. In the last passage it is needless to alter the Gen. ἀκούοντος (§ 243, 3, d), and we may even read in Il. 1. 453 ἐμοὶ πάρος ἔκλυες εὐξαμένοιο (cp. Il. 16. 531 ὅττι οἱ ὦκ' ἤκουσε μέγας θεὸς εὐξαμένοιο). The substitution of the Dat. seems the most probable correction in various places where Leeuwen proposes other changes : Od. 4. 746 ἐμεῦ δ' ἕλετο μέγαν ὅρκον (cp. Il. 22. 119 Τρωσὶν δ' αὖ . . ὅρκον ἕλωμαι), Il. 2. 388 ἱδρώσει μέν τευ τελαμὼν ἀμφὶ στήθεσφι, Il. 22. 454 αἱ γὰρ ἀπ' οὔατος εἴη ἐμεῦ ἔπος (cp. 18. 272) ; also Il. 1. 273., 9. 377., 16. 497., 19. 185., 20. 464., 24. 293, 311, 750, 754, Od. 5. 311., 9. 20., 13. 231., 19. 108., 24. 257 ; and perhaps Il. 19. 137 καί μευ φρένας ἐξέλετο Ζεύς (unless the με of some MSS. is right), so Il. 9. 377 and Il. 9. 335. In Od. 19. 215 νῦν μὲν δὴ σεῦ, ξεῖνε, ὀΐω πειρήσεσθαι εἰ κτλ. Leeuwen restores the Acc. σέ (as in Il. 18. 600). In Od. 17. 421 (=19. 77) we may perhaps read καὶ ὅτι κεχρημένος ἔλθοι (ὅτί as in Il. 20. 434 οἶδα δ' ὅτι σὺ μὲν κτλ.). The remaining exceptions are Il. 5. 896 ἐκ γὰρ ἐμεῦ γένος ἐσσί, Il. 23. 70 οὐ μέν μευ ζώοντος ἀκήδεις, Il. 24. 429 δέξαι ἐμεῦ πάρα, and Il. 1. 88 οὔ τις ἐμεῦ ζῶντος κτλ., where the contraction ζῶντος and the Dat. Plur. κοίλῃς before a consonant are also suspicious (Fick, *Ilias*, p. xvii).

(f) The contraction of οα, οε (from οσ-α, οσ-ε) is doubtful in the Nouns in -ω and -ως (§ 105, 6), but appears in the forms of the Comparative, viz. ἀμείνω, ἀρείω, ἀρείους, κακίους, πλείους, and μείζω (Hesiod). The uncontracted forms in -οα, -οες do not occur, since the metre allows either -ω, -ους or else the later -ονα, -ονες. But in such a phrase as ἀμείνω δ' αἴσιμα πάντα (where Nauck reads ἀμείνονα) we may suspect that ἀμείνοα was the original form.

(g) Vowels originally separated by ϝ are so rarely contracted that instances in our text must be regarded with suspicion. Thus ἄκων (ἀ-ϝέκων) should

always be ἀέκων : ἄτη (ἀϜάτη) may be written ἀάτη except in Il. 19. 88
φρεσὶν ἔμβαλον ἄγριον ἄτην (where the use of ἄγριον as a Fem. is also anomalous,
§ 119). In Il. 3. 100., 6. 356., 24. 28 (where ἄτης comes at the end of the line)
the better reading is ἀρχῆς. κοῖλος may be κόϊλος (cp. Lat. *cavus*), except
in Od. 22. 385. εἶδον (ἔ-Ϝιδον) may be εἴδον, except in four places (Il. 11. 112.,
19. 292, Od. 10. 194., 11. 162). πολέας (Acc. Plur. of πολύς) is not uncommon,
but should probably be πολῦς (§ 100) : πολέων occurs once (Il. 16. 655). Other
instances with Nouns in -vs and -evs are rare (Nauck, *Mél. gr.-rom.* iii. 219 ;
Menrad, p. 60). The Fem. in -εῖα is not contracted from -εϜϊα, -εΐα but comes
directly from -εϜια. So οἱός, οἱῶν for ὀϜ̣-ός, ὀϜ̣-ῶν (cp. ὄεσσι for ὀϝ̣-εσσι), and
δῖος for δίϜ-ιος. ἕως and τέως, which occur several times in our text, are
nearly always followed by a Particle (μέν, περ, &c.), which has evidently
been inserted for the sake of the metre (ἕως μέν for ἧος, &c.). For ἀλλοειδέα
in Od. 13. 194 we should doubtless read ἀλλο-ϊδέα (§ 125, 2).

εἴρυσα may be from ἔ-Ϝρυσα (but see Schulze in *K.Z.* xxix. 64) : as to ἴαχον,
which has been supposed to stand for εἴαχον, from ἐ-ϜίϜαχον, see § 31, 1.

The most important example of contraction notwithstanding Ϝ is the word
πάϊς (παῖς, παιδός, &c.). Other words which present the same difficulty are :
ἄσε (Od. 11. 61), ἄσατο (Il. 19. 95)—in both places Nauck would read ἄασε—
ἀθλοφόρος (Il. 9. 266., 11. 699), ἀθλεύων (Il. 24. 734), ἆθλον (Od. 8. 160), ἄσαμεν
we slept (Od. 16. 367), ἐᾷ (Il. 5. 256) and other forms of ἐάω (Il. 10. 344., 23. 77,
Od. 21. 233), νέα (Od. 9. 283), ῥέα (Il. 12. 381., 17. 461., 20. 101, 263), κρέα
(Od. 9. 347), χεῖσθαι (Od. 10. 518), τιμῆντα (Il. 18. 475), τεχνῆσσαι (Od. 7. 110),
ἥλιος (Od. 8. 271), ἐωσφόρος (Il. 23. 226), πλέων (Od. 1. 184), τεθνεῶτι (Od. 19.
331), πεπτεῶτα, -τας (Il. 21. 503, Od. 22. 384), βεβῶσα (Od. 20. 14), νόου (Il. 24.
354), καιρουσσέων (Od. 7. 107), the compounds of ἐννέα—ἐννῆμαρ, ἐννέωρος·
ἐννεόργυιος—and the proper names Εὐρύκλεια ᾿Αντίκλεια (-κλέεια Nauck).
Some of these may be disposed of by more or less probable emendation :
others occur in interpolated passages (*e. g.* ἥλιος in the Song of Demodocus) :
others (as πλέων, τεθνεώς) may be explained by the loss of Ϝ before ω, ο (§ 393).
On the whole they are too few and isolated to be of weight against the
general usage of Homer.

The general result of the enquiry seems to be that the harshness of a synizesis or a contraction is a matter admitting of
many degrees. With some combinations of vowels contraction
is hardly avoided, with others it is only resorted to in case of
necessity. We have already seen that the rules as to lengthening
by Position (§ 370) are of the same elastic character. And as there
is hardly any rule of Position that may not be overborne by the
desire of bringing certain words into the verse, so there is no
contraction that may not be excused by a sufficiently cogent
metrical necessity. Thus the synizesis in such words as Ἰστίαια,
Αἰγυπτίους, χρυσέοισι stands on the same footing as the neglect
of Position with Σκάμανδρος or σκέπαρνον : and again the synizesis in τεμένεα, ἀσινέας, or the contraction in πονεύμενος, ἀμφι-
βαλεῦμαι is like the shortening of a vowel before προσηύδα,
or the purely metrical lengthening of a short vowel (§ 386).

On the same principles harshness of metre may be tolerated
for the sake of a familiar phrase : *e.g.* the hiatus ἄφθιτα αἰεί in

Il. 13. 22 (ἄφθιτον ἀεί in Il. 2. 46, 186., 14. 238). So when the formula καί μιν φωνήσας ἔπεα κτλ. is used of a goddess (Il. 15. 35, 89) it becomes καί μιν φωνήσασα ἔπεα. Again the harsh lengthening in μέροπες ἄνθρωποι (Il. 18. 288, at the end of the line) is due to the familiar μερόπων ἀνθρώπων.

Hiatus.

379.] Hiatus is a term which is used by writers on metre in more than one sense. It will be convenient here to apply it to every case in which a word ending with a vowel or diphthong is followed by a word beginning with a vowel, and the two vowel-sounds are not merged together (as by elision, crasis, &c.) so as to form one syllable for the metre.

It would be more scientific, perhaps, to understand the word Hiatus as implying that the two vowels are separated by a break or stoppage of vocal sound, so that the second begins with either the rough or the smooth ' breathing.' Thus it would be opposed to every form of *diphthong* (including *synizesis*), the characteristic of which is that the two vowels are slurred together, by shifting the position of the organs without any perceptible interruption of the current of breath. This definition, however, might exclude the case of a long vowel or diphthong shortened before an initial vowel (as τὴν δ' ἐγὼ οὐ, where the final ω seems to be partly merged in the following ου). Again when a final ι or υ comes before a vowel without suffering elision, it is probable that the corresponding ' semi-vowel ' (= our *y* or *w*) is developed from the vowel-sound, and prevents complete hiatus.

380.] **Long vowels before Hiatus.** The general rule is that a long final vowel or diphthong coming before a vowel forms a short syllable in the metre. This shortening is very common in Homer: cp. Il. 1. 299 οὔτε σοὶ οὔτε τῷ ἄλλῳ, ἐπεὶ κτλ., where it occurs in three successive feet.

But the natural quantity may be retained before hiatus when the vowel is in the arsis of the foot, as Ἀτρείδη Ἀγαμέμνονι, ὅς κ' εἴποι ὅτι κτλ. And in a few instances a long vowel or diphthong is allowed to remain long in thesis, as Il. 1. 39 Σμινθεῦ· εἴ ποτέ τοι κτλ.

The readiness with which long syllables are allowed before hiatus varies with the several long vowels and diphthongs; partly also it depends on the *pauses* of the sense.

The long diphthongs (as they may be called), viz. ῃ and ῳ, are the most capable of resisting the shortening influence of hiatus; next to them are ευ and ου, and the long vowels η and ω: while ει, οι and αι are at the other end of the scale. A measure of this may be gained by observing how often each of these terminations is long before a vowel, and comparing the number with the total number of times that the same termination occurs. Thus it appears that out of every 100 instances of final ῳ, it is long before hiatus about 23 times. Similarly final -η is long 19 times, -ευ 6·7 times, -ου 6 times, -η 5·7 times, -ω 4 times, -ει 1·8 times, -οι 1·6 times, and -αι only 1·3 times. Thus hiatus after ῳ and η is scarcely avoided, while after ει, οι and αι it is very rare.

In a large proportion of the instances in which a long vowel retains its quantity before hiatus it will be found that the hiatus coincides with a division either in the sense or the rhythm. Of the examples in the arsis of the foot, more than half occur before the penthemimeral caesura, where there is almost always a pause: while in thesis the same thing is chiefly found to occur either after the first foot, as Il. 2. 209 ἠχῇ, ὡς ὅτε κτλ., Od. 11. 188 ἀγρῷ, οὐδὲ κτλ.; or after the fourth foot (in the Bucolic diaeresis).

381.] Shortening of diphthongs before Hiatus. Regarding the nature of the process by which a diphthong before hiatus was reduced to the time or metrical value of a short syllable two probable views have been maintained.

1. Curtius holds that whenever long syllables are shortened by the effect of hiatus something of the nature of *Elision* takes place. Thus η and ω lose the second half of the vowel sound, while αι, ει, οι lose the ι. In support of this he points to the facts of Crasis: thus καὶ ἐγώ in becoming κἀγώ may be supposed to pass through the stage κα ἐγώ.

2. According to an older view, which has been revived and defended with great ingenuity by Hartel,* the ι or υ in a diphthong is turned into the corresponding spirant; so that καὶ ἐγώ becomes κα-ι̯-εγώ, and ἐκ Πύλου ἐλθών becomes ἐκ Πύλο-ϝ-ελθών.

It is certainly in favour of this latter supposition that it does not oblige us to suppose the frequent elision of the two vowels which in general are the least liable to be elided. The explanation however is not a complete one. It does not account for the shortening of η and ῳ, which on the principle assumed by Hartel would become ηι̯, ωι̯. On the whole it seems most probable that the shortening in question was effected, for diphthongs as well as for simple long vowels, by a process in which ancient grammarians would have recognised rather 'Synizesis'—viz. the slurring of vowels together without complete loss of any sound—

---

* *Homerische Studien*, iii. pp. 7 ff.

than either Elision or Contraction. And this conclusion is supported by the general tendencies of the Ionic dialect, which was especially tolerant of hiatus, and allowed numerous combinations of vowels, such as εα, εο, εω, εοι, to have the value either of one syllable or two.*

382.] Hiatus after short syllables. The vowels which are not liable to elision may generally stand before hiatus: thus we find ζωστῆρι ἀρηρότι (§ 376, 3), πρὸ ὁδοῦ, πρὸ Ἀχαιῶν, αὐτὰρ ὁ ἐμμεμαώς, ἑτάροιο ἐνηέος, and the like.

Hiatus is also tolerated occasionally in the pauses of the verse:

(1) In the trochaic caesura of the third foot: as—

Il. 1. 569 καί ῥ' ἀκέουσα καθῆστο, ἐπιγνάμψασα κτλ.

Od. 3. 175 τέμνειν, ὄφρα τάχιστα ὑπὲκ κτλ.

(2) In the Bucolic diaeresis: as—

Il. 8. 66 ὄφρα μὲν ἠὼς ἦν καὶ ἀέξετο ἱερὸν ἦμαρ.

Od. 2. 57 εἰλαπινάζουσιν πίνουσί τε αἴθοπα οἶνον.

The vowel of the Person-endings -το, -ντο seems to be especially capable of standing before hiatus in these places. It appears in more than a fourth of the whole number of instances given by Knös (pp. 42–45).

Hiatus in the Bucolic diaeresis is commoner in the Odyssey than in the Iliad, in the proportion 2 : 1. Hiatus after the vowel ε is also comparatively rare in the Iliad: Knös reckons 22 instances (many of them doubtful), against 40 in the Odyssey. It is worth notice that in both these points books xxiii and xxiv of the Iliad agree with the Odyssey, also that book xxiv of the Odyssey contains an unusual number of instances of hiatus, both legitimate (ll. 63, 215, 328, 374, 466) and illegitimate (ll. 209, 351, 430).

Illegitimate hiatus, like other anomalies, may be diminished by emendation. Thus in Od. 5. 135 ἠδὲ ἔφασκον we may read ἠδέ ϝ' ἔφασκον: in 5. 257 ἐπιχεύατο ὕλην we may insert ἄρ', on the model of Il. 5. 748 ἐπεμαίετ' ἄρ' ἵππους. But in Il. 13. 22 ἄφθιτα αἰεί must stand because ἄφθιτος αἰεί is a fixed phrase. It is unlikely, then, that Hiatus was ever absolutely forbidden in Epic verse.

Doubtful Syllables.

383.] Besides the cases in which the metrical value of a syllable may be made uncertain by its place in a particular verse—*i. e.* by the circumstances of Position, Hiatus, Ictus, &c. —there are many instances in which the 'natural' quantity of the vowel appears to be indeterminate.

---

* The use of εο for ευ in Ionic inscriptions shows, not indeed that ευ and εο were identical in pronunciation, or that εο was a true diphthong, but certainly that εο was very like ευ, and might be monosyllabic *in scansion.* Probably monosyllabic εο (when it was not a mere error for ευ) stood to ευ as the Synizesis εα, εω, εοι, &c. to the contracted η, ω, οι. See Erman in *Curt. Stud.* v. 292 ff.

Under the heading of 'doubtful vowels' should be classed, not only the words in which the same letter may stand either for a long or a short vowel, as Ἄρης, ἀνήρ, but also those in which the change is shown by the spelling, *i. e.* in which a short vowel interchanges with a long vowel or diphthong: as νεός and νηός, ὄνομα and οὔνομα, &c. And with these variations, again, we may place, as at least kindred phenomena, the doubtful syllables which arise from the interchange of single and double consonants: Ὀδυσσεύς and Ὀδυσεύς, Ἀχιλλεύς and Ἀχιλεύς. As we speak of doubtful vowels, these might similarly be called 'doubtful consonants.'

In all such words the variation of quantity may either mean that there were two distinct forms between which the poet had a choice, or that the quantity as it existed in the spoken language was in fact intermediate. The former case would usually arise when a vowel or syllable which had come to be short in the spoken language was allowed to retain its older quantity as a poetical archaism. In the latter case the poet could give the syllable either metrical value; or (as in so many instances) he might treat the syllable as ordinarily short, but capable of being lengthened by the *ictus*, or by the pauses of the verse.

384.] Doubtful vowels appear to rise chiefly in two ways:—
' (1) By the shortening of a long vowel or diphthong before a vowel: viz.—

ᾱ, in ἵλαος (ᾱ in Il. 1. 583, ᾰ in Il. 9. 639., 19. 178).

η, in the oblique cases of νηῦς (except the Dat. νηΐ) and of several Nouns in -ευς, as Πηλῆος, Πηλέος: the forms ἥαται and ἔαται (ἧμαι): ἀφήῃ and ἀφέῃ (§ 80); ἠΰς and ἐΰς, ληϊστοί and λεϊστή (Il. 9. 408); perhaps also in Θρήϊκες, δήϊος, ἥϊα, which shorten η when the case-ending is naturally long (Θρηΐκων, δηΐων, ἠΐων, &c. scanned ∪ ∪ –, unless we suppose contraction or synizesis).

ῑ, in ἱερός, κονίη, λίην: Comparatives in -ιων: Patronymics, as Κρονίων: ἵομεν, ἵημι (ἀφίει, &c.), ἰαίνω, and Verbs in -ιω, as τίω, ὀΐω (§ 51, 1): probably also in the abstract Nouns in -ιη, the ι being treated as long in ὑπεροπλίη, προθυμίη, ὑποδεξίη, ἀτιμίη, ἀκομιστίη.

ῡ, in Verbs in -υω (§ 51, 4).

ω, in ἥρωος (– ∪ ∪ in Od. 6. 303): ἥρῳ, *leg.* ἥρωϊ (Il. 7. 453).

αι, in ἀεί for αἰεί, ἔμπαιος (– ∪ ∪ in Od. 20. 379), and the Compound χαμαιεῦναι, χαμαιευνάδες: also Verbs in -αιω, as ἀγαιόμενος and ἀγάασθε, κέραιε and κεράασθε, ναῖον and νάει, νάουσι.

ει, in ὠκέα, βαθέης (for ὠκεῖα, βαθείης) : Adjectives in -ειος, as χάλκειος and χάλκεος : ῥεῖα and ῥέα : πλεῖον, &c. and πλέονες : βείομαι and βέομαι (§ 80), and many Verbs in -εω (§ 51, 3).

οι, in ὀλοός and ὀλοιός ; also οἶος (‿ ‿), as in Il. 13. 275 οἶὸ' ἀρετὴν οἷός ἐσσι, cp. Il. 18. 105, Od. 7. 312., 20. 89.

ευ, in δεύομαι and δέομαι, ἔχευα and ἔχεα, ἠλεύατο and ἀλέασθαι.

υι, in υἱός (Il. 4. 473., 5. 612, &c.).

The Gen. endings -άων, -εων fall under this head, if -εων represents an older Ionic -ηων.

In some cases of this kind our texts have ει where it is probable that the original vowel was η : so in πλεῖος *full* (Attic πλέως from πλῆος), χρεῖος *debt* and χρειώ *need* (from χρη-, χρᾰ-). See Appendix C.

Sometimes ει has taken the place of ευ before another vowel, as in the Verbs θέω, πνέω, πλέω, χέω, κλέω (§ 29, 3), also in λείουσι, Dat. Plur. of λέων (λεύων or λέϝων), and perhaps in the Pf. εἴωθα (cp. ἐνέθωκε Hesych.), εἰοικυῖαι (Il. 18. 418). Similarly ᾱ may stand for αυ, as φάεα *eyes* (φαυ-), ἀήρ (cp. αὔρα) and other derivatives of ἄϝημι (ἀλιάής, ἀκρ-αής), ἀέσαμεν *we slept* (ἰαύω), ἀασάμην (ἀϝάτη), and probably μεμαότες, ἄϊον, ἀείδω, Ἄϊδος. We even find οι for ου (from οϝ), in οἰετέας for ὀ-ϝετέας *of like age* (Il. 2. 765), πνοιή for πνοϝή: cp. ὄϊες (‿ ‿ ‿ in Od. 9. 425).

η for ευ may perhaps be seen in ἠείδης, ἠείδει (ἐ-ϝείδεας, -εε) : but see the explanation suggested in § 67, 3.

Interchange of quantity is occasionally found : στέωμεν, κτέωμεν, φθέωμεν for στήομεν, &c. (§ 80) : ἕως and τέως (if these forms are Homeric) for ἧος and τῆος. So the Gen. ending -εω, for -ᾱο (-ηο).

(2) By compensatory lengthening, of—

ε to ει, in ξεῖνος (ξένϝος) but ξενίη, κεινός and κενός, πεῖραρ and πέρας (ἀπειρέσιος), εἴνατος, εἵνεκα.

ο to ου, μοῦνος (but μονωθείς Il. 11. 470) ; οὖρος (*a watcher*) but ὀρ-άω : οὔρεα and ὄρος (ὄρϝος ?).

ᾰ in παρέχῃ (παρ-σέχω), Od. 19. 113 ; ῠ in συνεχές, Il. 12. 26.

Under this head we should place double forms arising by Epenthesis, as ἔταρος and ἑταῖρος (for ἑταρ-ιος) : ἐνί, ἐν and εἰν. But ἀπερείσιος *boundless* should be ἀπερήσιος, from *πέρη (πέρην).

Other variations, of which no general account can be given, are seen in Ἄρης, ἀνήρ, ἀμάω *I reap* (ᾱ generally in the simple Verb, ᾰ in the compounds) ; φίλος (ῑ in φίλε κασίγνητε) ; ἄτιτος and τῑτός ; ὕδωρ, ἀντικρύ ; δύο and δύω, δεῦρο and (once) δεύρω, Διόνυσος and Διώνυσος. The chief cases of a doubtful vowel being long without the help of the ictus are, ἀρή, ἀλῶναι (ἀλόντε with ᾱ in Il. 5. 487), πρίν, ἱμάς, πιφαύσκω.

385.] **Double consonants,** causing doubtful syllables: chiefly— σσ, in the First Aorist (§ 39, 1), and Dat. Plur. (§ 102); also ὅσσος, μέσσος, νεμεσσάω (where σσ=τι̯), Ὀδυσσεύς. So for ἴσασι (– – ◡) we should write ἴσσασι (for ἴδ-σασι, § 7, 3). λλ, in Ἀχιλλεύς. κκ, in πελέκκῳ (κκ=κϝ ?), cp. πέλεκυς. As to ππ and ττ, in ὅππως, ὅττι, &c. see § 108, 2.

386.] **Metrical licence.** In a few cases the use of a vowel as long appears to be merely due to the necessities of the metre. Such are:—

α in ἀθάνατος, ἀκάματος, ἀπονέεσθαι, ἀποδίωμαι, ἀγοράασθε.

ε in ἐπίτονος (Od. 12. 423), ζεφυρίη (Od. 7. 119).

ι in Πριαμίδης, διά (in διὰ μὲν ἀσπίδος κτλ. Il. 3. 357, &c.).

υ in θυγατέρες (Il. 2. 492, &c.), δυναμένοιο (Od. 1. 276, &c.).

In these cases there is every reason to believe that the vowel was naturally short, and the lengthening must therefore be regarded as a necessary *licence*, to be compared with the neglect of Position before Σκάμανδρος, &c. (§ 370), or the synizesis of Αἰγυπτίη and Ἱστίαια (§ 378 *fin.*). The diphthong of εἰαρινός (ἔαρ), εἰρεσίη, οὐλόμενος, οὔνομα, Οὐλύμποιο, is of the same nature. The ου of πουλύς perhaps began in compounds in which it was required by the metre, as πουλυβότειρα, &c., and was extended to the simple word. It is apparently a poetical form only (but see H. W. Smyth, *Vowel System,* p. 98).

Similarly a short vowel between two long syllables is some-times treated as long: as in ἠγάασθε (Od. 5. 122), Ἡρακληείη (properly -κλεειη), Ὀϊκλείης (Od. 15. 244). So τετράκυκλος is scanned – – – ◡ in Od. 9. 242, but ◡ ◡ – ◡ in Il. 24. 324.

Vocatives.

387.] The short final syllable of the Vocative appears in several places as a metrically long syllable: as—

Il. 4. 155 φίλε κασίγνητε, θάνατον κτλ. and so 5. 359: also Il. 19. 400 Ξάνθε τε καὶ Βάλιε, 21. 474 νηπύτιε, Od. 3. 230 Τηλέμαχε.

4. 338 ὦ υἱὲ Πετεῶο κτλ.

18. 385 ὄρσο Θέτι τανύπεπλε: so Od. 24. 192 Λαέρταο πάϊ.

14. 357 Πόσείδαον ἐπάμυνε: so Il. 24. 569., Od. 8. 408, &c.

23. 493 Αἶαν Ἰδομενεῦ τε.

The reason may be found (as Hartel thinks*) in the nature of the Vocative as an interruption of the natural flow of a sentence. It is very possible, however, that the Nominative ought to be read in these places : see § 164.

The Digamma.

388.] In seeking to arrive at general conclusions as to the rules and structure of the Homeric hexameter, it was necessary to leave out of sight all the words whose metrical form is uncertain on account of the possible or probable loss of an initial consonant. It is time to return to this disturbing element of the enquiry.

The scholars who first wrote on this subject had few materials for their investigations outside of the Homeric poems. To them, therefore, the 'Digamma' was little more than a symbol—the unknown cause of a series of metrical anomalies. In the present state of etymological knowledge the order of the enquiry has been to a great extent reversed. It is known in most cases which of the original sounds of the Indo-European languages have been lost in Greek, and where in each word the loss has taken place. Hence we now come to Homer with this knowledge already in our possession. Instead of asking what sounds are wanting, we have only to ask whether certain sounds, of whose former existence we have no doubt, were still living at the time when the poems were composed, and how far they can be traced in their effect on the versification.

389.] **Nature of the evidence from metre.** The questions which are suggested by the discovery in Homer of traces of a lost ' Digamma' cannot be answered without some reference to the very exceptional circumstances of the text.

Whatever may be the date at which writing was first used in Greece for literary purposes, there can be no doubt that the Homeric poems were chiefly known for some centuries through the medium of oral recitation, and that it was not till the time of the Alexandrian grammarians that adequate materials were brought together for the study and correction of the text. Accordingly when these scholars began to collect and compare the manuscripts of Homer, they found themselves engaged in a problem of great complexity. The various readings, to judge from the brief notices of them preserved in the *Scholia*, were very numerous; and they are often of a kind which must be attributed to failure of memory, or the licence of oral recitation, rather than to errors of transcription. And the amount of

---

* *Homerische Studien*, i. p. 64.

interpolation must have been considerable, if there was any ground
for the suspicions so often expressed by the ancient critics.

It follows from these circumstances that an attempt to restore
the lost F throughout the text of Homer cannot be expected to
succeed. Such an attempt necessarily proceeds on the assumption that the text which we have is sound as far as it goes, or
that it is so nearly right that we can recover the original by
conjecture. With an imperfect text the process can only be
approximate. We may be satisfied if the proportion of failure
is not greater than the history of the text would lead us to
expect.

The loss of the F-sound, moreover, must have been itself a
cause of textual corruption. It led to irregularities of metre,
especially to frequent hiatus, and there would be a constant
tendency to cure these defects by some slight change. The
insertion of the ν ἐφελκυστικόν was almost a matter of course
(see however § 391). The numerous alternative forms used in
the poetical language, and the abundance of short Particles such
as γε, τε, ῥα, &c. made it easy to disguise the loss of F in many
places. We cannot be surprised, therefore, if we have often to
make the reverse changes.

A few instances will serve to show the existence in pre-Alexandrian times
of corruption arising from the tendency to repair defects of metre.

In Il. 9. 73 the MSS. have πολέεσσι δ' ἀνάσσεις, Aristarchus read πολέσιν
γὰρ ἀνάσσεις. Both are evidently derived from πολέσιν δὲ ἀνάσσεις (i. e.
Ϝανάσσεις), corrected in two different ways.

In Il. 13. 107 the MSS. have νῦν δ' ἕκαθεν, the reading of Aristarchus : but
Zenodotus and Aristophanes had νῦν δὲ ἕκας (i. e. Ϝέκας).

In Il. 9. 88 the reading of Aristarchus was τίθεντο δὲ δόρπα ἕκαστος : other
ancient sources had δόρπον (the reading of most MSS.).

In Il. 14. 235 πείθεν, ἐγὼ δέ κέ τοι εἰδέω χάριν ἤματα πάντα, the order χάριν
εἰδέω was preferred by Aristarchus.

Two very similar instances are—

Il. 5. 787 κάκ' ἐλέγχεα, εἶδος ἀγητοί (Ar. ἐλεγχέες).

9. 128 γυναῖκας ἀμύμονα ἔργα ἰδυίας (Ar. ἀμύμονας).

In Od. 5. 34 ἤματί κ' εἰκοστῷ . . ἵκοιτο the 'common' texts of Alexandrian
times (αἱ κοινότεραι) omitted the κ', which is not necessary, and may have
been inserted in imitation of ἤματί κε τριτάτῳ κτλ. (Il. 9. 363).

In Od. 1. 110 οἱ μὲν ἄρ' οἶνον ἔμισγον some MSS. omit ἄρ'. So in Od. 3. 472
most MSS. have οἶνον οἰνοχοεῦντες (vulg. ἐνοινοχ.).

In Od. 2. 331., 8. 174., 13. 125 the ε of αὖτε is elided before a word with F.
But in each case there is MS. authority for reading αὖ.

In Od. 8. 526 the MSS. are divided between ἀσπαίροντ' ἐσιδοῦσα and ἀσπαί-
ροντα ἰδοῦσα.

It should be observed that the argument from these instances is equally
good, whether the readings ascribed to Zenodotus, Aristarchus, &c. are
conjectures made by them, or were derived (as is more probable) from older
sources. They equally serve to illustrate the process by which traces of an

original ϝ were liable to be gradually effaced. And it is not likely that there was any deliberate attempt to emend Homer on metrical grounds. It is enough to suppose that the metre helped to determine the preference given (consciously or unconsciously) to one or other of the existing variants.

390.] Words with initial ϝ. The former existence of the ϝ in a given Homeric word may be inferred either from its appearance in some other dialect of Greek, or (where this kind of evidence fails) from the corresponding forms in the cognate languages. Thus an original ϝείκοσι is supported by the forms ϝίκατι and ϝείκατι on Doric and Boeotian inscriptions, by the Laconian βείκατι (given by Hesychius), and again by Latin *viginti*, Sanscrit *viṃçati*, &c.: an original ϝέσπερος by the form ϝεσπαρίων on a Locrian inscription, as well as by Latin *vesper*: original ϝιδεῖν, ϝοῖδα, &c. by ϝίστορες on inscriptions, γοῖδα and γοίδημι in Hesychius (erroneously so written, as Ahrens showed, for ϝοῖδα and ϝοίδημι), and also by Latin *video*, Sanscrit *vedmi*, *veda*, Engl. *wit*, &c. We do not, however, propose to discuss the external evidence, as it may be called, by which the loss of an initial ϝ is proved, but only to consider the degree and manner in which the former existence of such a letter can be shown to have affected the versification of Homer. For this purpose it will be enough to give a list of the chief words in question, and in a few cases a statement, by way of specimen, of some of the attempts made to restore the ϝ to the text.*

ἄγνυμι.
The initial ϝ is to be traced by the hiatus in Il. 5. 161 ἐξ αὐχένα ἄξῃ, Il. 8. 403 κατά θ' ἄρματα ἄξω (similar phrases in 8. 417., 23. 341, 467); less decisively by the lengthening of the final -ιν of the preceding word in Il. 4. 214 πάλιν ἄγεν ὀξέες ὄγκοι. The evidence against an initial consonant is very slight. In Od. 19. 539 πᾶσι κατ' αὐχένας ἦξε we should read αὐχέν' ἔαξε (Bekk.), understanding the Singular distributively (§ 170). In Il. 23. 392 for ἵππειον δέ οἱ ἦξε may be read ἵππειόν οἱ ἔαξε.

---

* The first systematic attempt to restore the digamma was made by Heyne in his edition of the Iliad (1802). It was based upon Bentley's manuscript annotations, of which Heyne had the use. The first text with restored ϝ was published by Payne Knight (1820). Much was done by the thorough and methodical *Quaestiones Homericae* of C. A. J. Hoffmann (Clausthal, 1842–48). The ϝ was again printed in the text of Bekker's second edition (Bonn, 1858). The light of the comparative method was brought to bear upon it by Leskien (*Rationem quam I. Bekker in restituendo digammo secutus est examinavit Dr. A. Leskien*, Lipsiae, 1866). The most complete treatise on the subject is that of Knös (Upsaliae, 1872). The most important contributions, in addition to those mentioned, have been made by Leo Meyer (*K. Z.* xviii. 49), and by W. Hartel (*Hom. Stud.* iii). Most of the conjectures given in this chapter come from one or other of these sources.

ἄναξ (ἄνασσα, ἀνάσσειν).

The words of this group occur in Homer about 300 times, and in about 80 instances they are preceded by a final short vowel which would ordinarily be elided. This calculation does not include the phrase ἶφι ἀνάσσειν, or the numerous examples of hiatus after the Dat. Sing. in -ι and the Genitives in -οιο, -ειο, -āο.*

The cases in which a slight correction of the text is needed to make room for the ϝ are as follows :—

Il. 1. 288 πάντεσσι δ' ἀνάσσειν (read πᾶσιν δέ).

9. 73 πολέεσσι δ' ἀνάσσεις (read πολέσιν δέ, § 389).

2. 672 Χαρόποιό τ' ἄνακτος (read Χαρόπου τε).

7. 162 (=23. 288) πρῶτος μὲν ἄναξ (read perhaps πρώτιστα).

15. 453 κροτέοντες· ἄναξ (read κροτέοντε, the Dual).

16. 371 (=507) λίπον ἅρματ' ἀνάκτων (read ἅρμα, § 170).

523 σύ πέρ μοι, ἄναξ, τόδε καρτερὸν ἕλκος ἄκεσσαι (read με).

23. 49 ὄτρυνον, ἄναξ (read ὄτρυνε, the Pres. Imper.).

517 ὅς ῥά τ' ἄνακτα (read ὅς τε or ὅς ῥα).

Od. 9. 452 ἢ σύ γ' ἄνακτος (omit γ').

17. 189 χαλεπαὶ δέ τ' ἀνάκτων (omit τ').

21. 56 (=83) τόξον ἄνακτος (read τόξα).

The Imperfect ἤνασσε, which occurs five times, can always be changed into ἐάνασσε. The remaining passages are :—

Il. 19. 124 σὸν γένος· οὗ οἱ ἀεικὲς ἀνασσέμεν Ἀργείοισιν (a verse which is possibly interpolated).

20. 67 ἔναντα Ποσειδάωνος ἄνακτος (in the probably spurious θεομαχία).

24. 449, 452 ποίησαν ἄνακτι.

Od. 14. 40 ἀντιθέου γὰρ ἄνακτος κτλ.

395 εἰ μέν κεν νοστήσῃ ἄναξ.

438 κύδαινε δὲ θυμὸν ἄνακτος.

24. 30 ἧς περ ἄνασσες.

ἄρνα (ἄρνες, &c.).

The ϝ is supported by three instances of hiatus, viz. Il. 4. 158 αἱμά τε ἀρνῶν, 4. 435 ὄπα ἀρνῶν, 8. 131 ἠΰτε ἄρνες : and by the metrical length given to the preceding syllable in Il. 3. 103 ἐς δίφρον ἄρνας, 16. 352 λύκοι ἄρνεσσι.

The passages which need correction are—

Il. 3. 103 οἴσετε δ' ἄρν' (the δέ is better omitted).

119 ἠδ' ἄρν' ἐκέλευεν (read ἰδὲ ἄρν').

22. 263 οὐδὲ λύκοι τε καὶ ἄρνες (omit τε).

Od. 4. 86 ἵνα τ' ἄρνες ἄφαρ κεραοὶ τελέθουσι (omit τ').

9. 226 ἐρίφους τε καὶ ἄρνας.

* For a complete analysis of the examples in the Iliad see Dawes, *Miscellanea Critica*, Sect. IV.

Note, however, that the evidence for Ϝ is confined to the Iliad, and that the derivative ἀρνειός shows no trace of it.

ἄστυ.

The presence of an initial consonant is shown by hiatus in nearly 80 places. In two places the text is uncertain : Il. 24. 320 ὑπὲρ ἄστεος (but διὰ ἄστεος in the Bankes papyrus, and several MSS.), Od. 3. 260 ἑκὰς ἄστεος (ἑκὰς Ἄργεος in most MSS.).

Two passages admit of the easiest correction :—

Il. 3. 140 ἀνδρός τε προτέροιο καὶ ἄστεος (read προτέρου).

15. 455 τοὺς μὲν ὅ γ᾽ Ἀστυνόμῳ (omit γε or μέν).

Two remain, viz.—

Il. 11. 733 ἀμφίσταντο δὴ ἄστυ (ἀμφέσταν Bekk.).

18. 274 νύκτα μὲν εἰν ἀγορῇ σθένος ἕξομεν ἄστυ δὲ πύργοι (ἕξετε Bekk.).

The changes made by Bekker in these places are not improbable, but are hardly so obvious as to exclude other hypotheses.

ἔαρ, εἰαρινός.

Hiatus is found in Il. 8. 307 νοτίῃσί τε εἰαρινῇσι, and a short final syllable is lengthened in Od. 19. 519 ἀείδῃσιν ἔαρος. In the phrase ὥρῃ ἐν εἰαρινῇ we should doubtless omit the ἐν, as in Od. 5. 485 ὥρῃ χειμερίῃ (Bentl.).

εἴκοσι.

The Ϝ appears in ἀνὰ εἴκοσι (Od. 9. 209), and the combination καὶ εἴκοσι (which occurs 9 times, including the compounds with δυωκαιεικοσι-).

In Il. 11. 25 χρυσοῖο καὶ εἴκοσι read χρυσοῦ : and in the combination τε καὶ εἴκοσι (in three places) omit τε. In the recurring ἤλυθον εἰκοστῷ ἔτεϊ κτλ. Bekker reads ἦλθον ἐεικοστῷ (Cobet well compares Od. 23. 102 ἔλθοι ἐεικοστῷ κτλ.). On Od. 5. 34 ἤματί κ᾽ εἰκοστῷ κτλ. see § 389.

εἴκω.

Two instances of hiatus indicate Ϝ, in Il. 24. 100, 718, besides many places in which the word is preceded by a Dat. Sing., as οὐδένι εἴκων, κάρτεϊ εἴκων.

Two places may be easily corrected : Il. 4. 509 μηδ᾽ εἴκετε (read μὴ εἴκετε, with asyndeton, as Od. 24. 54 ἴσχεσθ᾽ Ἀργεῖοι, μὴ φεύγετε), and 12. 48 τῇ τ᾽ εἴκουσι (omit τε). In Od. 12. 117 for θεοῖσιν ὑπείξεαι read θεοῖς ὑποείξεαι (Bekk.) There remains Il. 1. 294 εἰ δὴ σοὶ πᾶν ἔργον ὑπείξομαι.

ἔοικα, ἐΐσκω, εἴκελος.

The Ϝ of ἔοικα appears from hiatus in 46 instances (not counting the numerous places in which it follows a Dative in -ι). The adverse instances are 11 in number, besides the form ἐπ-έοικε (which occurs 11 times). The corresponding Present εἴκω is generally recognised in Il. 18. 520 ὅθι σφίσιν εἶκε λοχῆσαι *where it suited them to be in ambush.* The form ἐΐσκω has hiatus before

366 METRE. [390.

it in 3 places, but twice rejects Ϝ (Od. 9. 321., 11. 363). The
adjective εἴκελος or ἴκελος usually needs an initial consonant (except Il. 19. 282, Od. 11. 207).

It seems probable that this is the same word as εἴκω *to yield*. The notion of
giving way easily passes into that of *suiting* or *fitting*, hence *conforming to*,
resembling.

ἑκών, ἕκητι, ἕκηλος.

Hiatus indicating Ϝ is found in 22 places (not reckoning οὔ τι
ἑκών Il. 8. 81, &c.).

In Od. 4. 649 for αὐτὸς ἑκών we may read αὐτὸς ἐγών (cp. Od. 2. 133, where
both these forms are found in good MSS.). In Od. 17. 478 ἔσθι᾽ ἕκηλος two
MSS. have ἔσθ᾽ (*i. e.* ἔσθε). The remaining exceptions are; with ἑκών, Il. 23.
434, 585, Od. 5. 100 (where we may read τίς κε, or perhaps τίς δὲ ἑκὼν . .
διαδράμοι; the Opt. without ἄν being used as in negative Clauses, § 299 *f*):
with ἕκηλος, Il. 8. 512, Od. 2. 311 (ἐϋφραίνεσθ᾽ ἐΰκηλον Bekk.).

ἑκάς, ἕκατος, &c.

Traces of Ϝ are to be seen in the hiatus νῦν δὲ ἑκάς (Il. 5. 791.,
13. 107), ἀλλὰ ἑκάς (Od. 15. 33), οὐδὲ ἐκηβολίαι (Il. 5. 54): and
in the lengthening in Ἀπόλλωνος ἑκάτοιο (Il. 7. 83., 20. 295),
ἐϋπλόκαμος Ἑκαμήδη, &c.

The exceptions are, Il. 1. 21, 438., 17. 333., 20. 422., 22. 15,
302, Od. 7. 321—mostly admitting of easy correction.

ἕκαστος.

The original Ϝ of this word (recently found on a Locrian
inscription, see *Curt. Stud.* ii. 441 ff.) is traced by means of
hiatus in 115 places. The adverse instances, however, are about
50 in number, and the proportion that can be removed by
emendation is not so large as in most cases (see L. Meyer, *K. Z.*
viii. 166. About a fourth of the exceptions appear in the recurring phrase μένος καὶ θυμὸν ἑκάστου.

The form ἑκάτερθε shows slight traces of initial Ϝ in Od. 6. 19 σταθμοῖϊν
ἑκάτερθε, 11. 578 γῦπε δέ μιν ἑκάτερθε, 22. 181 τὼ δ᾽ ἔσταν ἑκάτερθε. It is preceded by elision in Il. 20. 153 (omit ῥ᾽), and in Il. 24. 273, Od. 7. 91 (omit δ᾽).

εἴλω (ἔλσαι, ἐάλην), ἁλῶναι, ἅλις.

The Ϝ is shown by hiatus in Il. 1. 409 ἀμφ᾽ ἅλα ἔλσαι: 16. 403
ἧστο ἀλείς (and five other examples of this Tense, viz. Il. 5. 823.,
21. 571, 607., 22. 308, Od. 24. 538): Il. 18. 287 κεκόρησθε ἐελμένοι: Il. 12. 172 ἠὲ ἁλῶναι (so 14. 81), Il. 21. 281 εἵμαρτο ἁλῶναι
(so Od. 5. 312., 24. 34), Il. 81. 495 τῇ γε ἁλώμεναι. Before
ἅλις hiatus occurs in about 12 places: cp. also Il. 23. 420 εἰνά-
τερες ἅλις ἦσαν.

In Il. 21. 236 κατ᾽ αὐτὸν ἅλις ἔσαν some MSS. read ἔσαν ἅλις, and at l. 344
the same transposition may be made. The only other instance against Ϝ is
Il. 17. 54 ὅθ᾽ ἅλις ἀναβέβρυχεν (ἀναβέβροχεν Zenod.), where Bentley read ὃ ἅλις
ἀναβέβροχεν.

ἑλίσσω, εἰλύω.

Before ἑλίσσω hiatus is found in four places, and the recurring phrases καὶ ἕλικας βοῦς and εἰλίποδας ἕλικας βοῦς point in the same direction. The only exceptions are Od. 12. 355 βοσκέσκονθ᾽ ἕλικες κτλ., and Il. 18. 401 γναμπτάς θ᾽ ἕλικας.

It is probable that in many places the forms ἐλέλικτο, ἐλελίχθη, &c. are old errors for ἐϜέλικτο, ἐϜελίχθη, &c.: see Dawes, *Misc. Crit.* 177 : also Heyne on Il. 1. 530.

Traces of Ϝ in εἰλύω should perhaps be recognised in Od. 5. 403 (ἐρευγόμενον, εἴλυτο) and 15. 479 σάκεσιν εἰλυμένοι: cp. Il. 20. 492 φλόγα εἰλυφάζει. In Il. 18. 522 ἵζοντ᾽ εἰλυμένοι it is easy to read ἵζον (as Bekker). The Aor. Part. ἐλυσθείς has no Ϝ : but it may be from a different Verb-stem (see Buttm. *Lexil.* s. v. εἰλύω).

ἔλπω (ἔολπα).

The initial Ϝ of this word is proved by 10 instances of hiatus (including καὶ ἐλπίδος, Od. 16. 101., 19. 84). The Perfect ἔολπα also shows traces of Ϝ in the reduplicated syllable, viz. in Od. 2. 275., 3. 375., 5. 379.

In Il. 8. 526 εὔχομαι ἐλπόμενος should be εὔχομ᾽ ἐελπόμενος (Hoffm.) or perhaps (as Zenodotus read) ἔλπομαι εὐχόμενος. In four places Ϝέλπω can be restored by very slight corrections :—

Il. 15. 701 Τρωσὶν δ᾽ ἔλπετο (Τρωσὶ δέ Heyne).

18. 194 ἀλλὰ καὶ αὐτὸς ὅδ᾽, ἔλπομ᾽ (αὐτὸς ἐέλπομ᾽ Heyne).

Od. 2. 91 (= 13. 380) πάντας μέν ῥ᾽ ἔλπει (omit ῥ᾽).

Two others are less easy ; Il. 15. 539 πολέμιζε μένων, ἔτι δ᾽ ἔλπετο (μένων δ᾽ ἔτι ἔλπετο Bentl.), and Il. 24. 491 ἐπί τ᾽ ἔλπεται (καὶ ἔλπεται Bentl.). The passages which tell against ϜέϜολπα are Il. 20. 186 χαλεπῶς δέ σ᾽ ἔολπα τὸ ῥέξειν (read σὲ ἔολπα), 21. 583 μάλ᾽ ἔολπας (μάλα ἔλπε᾽ Hoffm.), 22. 216 νῶι γ᾽ ἔολπα (omit γ᾽), Od. 8. 315., 24. 313.

ἔπος, εἰπεῖν.

The Ϝ of ἔπος is supported by about 26 instances of hiatus, and a much larger number in which preceding syllables are lengthened (as in the common line καί μιν ἀμειβόμενος ἔπεα κτλ.).

Of the apparent exceptions, about 35 are removed by reading ἔπεσσι for ἐπέεσσι (as in Il. 5. 40 χειρὸς ἑλοῦσ᾽ ἐπέεσσι προσηύδα, read ἑλοῦσα ἔπεσσι). This is justified by the fact that in similar words (esp. βέλος) the form in -εεσσι is less frequent than that in -εσσι. A group of 11 may be corrected by scanning ἔπεα as a disyllable (⌣ –) in the formula φωνήσασα ἔπεα πτερόεντα προσηύδα. Another small group of exceptions is formed by phrases such as Od. 4. 706 ὀψὲ δὲ δή μιν ἔπεσσιν κτλ., where perhaps ἐ may be put for μιν. There remain two instances in the Iliad (5. 683., 7. 108) and seven in the Odyssey (11. 146, 561., 14. 509., 15. 375., 16. 469., 17. 374., 24. 161).

In εἰπεῖν the Ϝ is proved by about 80 instances of hiatus, besides lengthening such as we have in the forms ὧδε δέ τις εἴπεσκε, ὡς ἄρα οἱ εἰπόντι, &c. The exceptions number about 35.

Of these exceptions 10 are found in the recurring line ὄφρ' εἴπω τά με θυμὸς ἐνὶ στήθεσσι κελεύει. It has been suggested as possible that εἴπω has here taken the place of an older ἔπω (Ϝέπω), or ἔσπω (cp. ἔσπετε). This supposition would of course explain other instances of neglected Ϝ, as Il. 1. 64., 11. 791, Od. 1. 10, 37, &c.

ἔρδω, ἔργον, &c.

The Verb ἔρδω is preceded by hiatus in two clear instances, Il. 14. 261, Od. 15. 360. In Il. 9. 540 πόλλ' ἔρδεσκεν there is an ancient *v. l.* ἔρρεζεν. In Il. 10. 503 ὅτι κύντατον ἔρδοι we may read κύντατα. But there are several instances on the other side in the Odyssey (viz. 1. 293., 5. 342, 360., 6. 258., 7. 202., 8. 490., 11. 80).

The reduplicated form ἔοργα (for ϜέϜοργα) is preceded by hiatus in 7 places. Instances on the other side are, Il. 3. 351 ὅ με πρότερος κάκ' ἔοργε (where the Aor. ἔρεξεν is more Homeric, cp. § 28), 21. 399 ὅσσα μ' ἔοργας (ὅσσα ἔοργας Ambr.), 22. 347 οἷά μ' ἔοργας (here also με may be omitted), Od. 22. 318 οὐδὲν ἐοργώς (read οὔ τι, cp. § 356).

The Noun ἔργον, with its derivative ἐργάζομαι, occurs in Homer about 250 times, and the Ϝ is required to prevent hiatus in about 165 places. There are about 18 instances against Ϝ.

εἴρω, ἐρέω.

The Ϝ of εἴρω is required by hiatus in the three places where it occurs, viz. Od. 2. 162., 11. 137., 13. 7 ; that of ἐρέω by about 50 instances of lengthening (such as ἀλλ' ἔκ τοι ἐρέω, ὥς ποτέ τις ἐρέει, and the like), against which are to be set three instances of elision (Il. 4. 176., 23. 787, Od. 12. 156).

ἕννυμι, εἷμα, ἐσθής.

The Ϝ is shown by hiatus in more than 80 places, including the instances of the Perfect Mid. (εἷμαι, ἔσσαι, &c., see § 23, 5). The contrary instances are of no weight. The superfluous ῥ' may be omitted in ἐπεί ῥ' ἔσσαντο (three places), and τ' similarly in Od. 14. 510., 24. 67. This leaves Il. 3. 57, Od. 6. 83., 7. 259.

ἐμέω.

The Ϝ (which is inferred from Lat. *vomo*) may be restored by reading ἐϜέμεσσε for ἀπέμεσσε (Il. 14. 437) and αἷμα Ϝεμέων, or possibly Ϝέμων (L. Meyer), for αἷμ' ἐμέων (Il. 15. 11).

ἕσπερος.

Hiatus occurs in six places, after the Prepositions ποτί (Od. 17. 191) and ἐπί. There are no instances against Ϝ.

ἔτος.

The Ϝ is supported by the lengthening of the preceding syllable in five places, such as Il. 24. 765 ἐεικοστὸν ἔτος ἐστί.

In the only adverse instance, Il. 2. 328 τοσσαῦτ' ἔτεα, we may read and scan τοσσαῦτα ἔτεα, as in the case of ἔπεα (*supra*).

ἰάχω, ἰαχή, ἠχή.

The F in ἰάχω and ἰαχή is chiefly indicated by 23 instances of a peculiar hiatus, viz. after a naturally short final vowel in arsis; as ἣ δὲ μέγα ἰάχουσα, ἡμεῖς δὲ ἰάχοντες, γένετο ἰαχή, and the like. There are 3 instances of lengthening by Position. The F is also proved by αὐίαχος (=ἀ-ϜίϜαχος) *without a cry*. The exceptions are confined to the Aor. or Impf. ἴαχον (ῐ), which never admits F in Homer: see § 31, 1, *note*.

The derivative ἠχήεις follows hiatus in two places (Il. 1. 157, Od. 4. 72): elsewhere in Homer ἠχή only occurs at the beginning of the line. The compound δυσ-ηχής (πολέμοιο δυσηχέος, Il. 2. 886, &c.) is best derived from ἄχος (see Wackernagel, *Dehnungsgesetz*, p. 42).

ἰδεῖν, οἶδα, εἶδος.

In the different forms of the Second Aor. ἰδεῖν the F is shown by upwards of 180 instances of hiatus, and about 12 instances of lengthening of a short syllable. The Indicative (εἶδον in Attic) is nearly always a trisyllable (*i. e.* ἔϜιδον) in Homer. On the other side we have to set nearly 50 instances of neglected F, about half of which are susceptible of easy emendation (such as putting ἰδεῖν for ἰδέειν, omitting superfluous δέ, and the like).

In the Perfect οἶδα there are about 125 instances of hiatus, against 24 which need emendation. Of these, however, only about seven or eight present any difficulty. The proportion is much the same with the other forms, as εἴδομαι, εἴσομαι, &c., and the Nouns εἶδος (11 instances of hiatus, two adverse), ἴστωρ, ἰδρείη, εἴδωλον, &c.

ἴον (ἰόεις, ἰοδνεφές).

The F is supported by hiatus in Od. 4. 135., 9. 426, and is nowhere inadmissible.

ἴς, ἶφι (ἴφια), ἶνες.

These words, with the derived proper names Ἰφιάνασσα, Ἴφιτος, &c., show F in about 27 places, while seven or eight places need slight emendation. ἴφθιμος, which shows no trace of F, is probably from a different root.

ἴσος.

The F is traced in about 30 instances of hiatus; the adverse passages being 8 or 9 in number. In three of these, containing the phrase ἀτεμβόμενος κίοι ἴσης (Il. 11. 705, Od. 9. 42, 549) the form ἴσης should perhaps be changed to αἴσης *share*. Or we may recognise the Æolic form of the word, viz. ἴσσα (Fick, *Odyssee*, p. 20). The other places are easily corrected.

ἴτυς, ἰτέη.

The Ϝ is shown by hiatus (Il. 4. 486, Od. 10. 510). The Particle τε may be left out before καὶ ἰτέαι in Il. 21. 350.

οἶκος.

The Ϝ is required in 105 places by hiatus, in 14 by the lengthening of a short syllable. About 25 places are adverse.

οἶνος.

The Ϝ is required by hiatus in nearly 100 places. The adverse places are about 20 (including the names Οἰνεύς and Οἰνόμαος).

391.] Words with initial σϝ ('ϝ). Since the change of initial σ into the rough breathing must have been much earlier than the loss of Ϝ, it may be presumed that words which originally began with σϝ were pronounced at one time with the sound 'ϝ (= our *wh*). The following are the chief examples in Homer:—

ἕο, οἷ, ἕ, ὅς, &c.

The Ϝ is proved by hiatus in upwards of 600 instances, by lengthening of a preceding short syllable in 136 instances. There are also about 27 places in which a short vowel in arsis is lengthened before it: as ἀπὸ ἕο, προτὶ οἷ ($\cup$ – –), θυγατέρα ἥν, πατέρι ᾧ, &c. About 43 places do not admit Ϝ without some change ; of these 30 are instances of the Possessive ὅς.

This Pronoun is noticeable as the only word in which the original Ϝ is recognised in the spelling of our texts. The moveable -ν is not used before the forms οἷ, ἕ : thus we have δαίε οἱ, ὥς κέ οἱ, &c. ; and, similarly, οὔ οἱ, οὐ ἕθεν (not οὔχ οἱ, οὐχ ἕθεν). This rule is observed not only in Homer but also in the later Elegiac and Lyric poets, and even the lyrical parts of Tragedy (Soph. El. 195, Trach. 650). It does not apply, however, to the forms of the Possessive ὅς.

When the forms 'ϝε, 'ϝοι suffer elision (§ 376), the word is reduced to 'ϝ' and consequently disappears from our texts. Thus in Il. 24. 154 ὅς ἄξει κτλ. it is plain from the parallel l. 183 ὅς σ' ἄξει that the original was ὅς 'ϝ' ἄξει (Bekker, *Hom. Bl.* i. 318). Other corrections of the kind are :—

Il. 1. 195 πρὸ γὰρ ἧκε, read πρὸ δέ 'ϝ,' as in l. 208 πρὸ δέ μ' ἧκε.

    4. 315 ὡς ὄφελέν τις ἀνδρῶν ἄλλος ἔχειν, read ὥς 'ϝ.'

    16. 545 μὴ ἀπὸ τεύχε' ἕλωνται, read μή 'ϝ' (Cobet, *Misc. Crit.* 265).

Od. 5. 135 ἠδὲ ἔφασκον θήσειν ἀθάνατον, read ἠδέ 'ϝ.'

Examples of the restoration of 'ϝ(οι) will be found in § 376.*

---

* The whole subject is fully treated by J. van Leeuwen, *Mnemos.* xiii. 188 ff. from whom these emendations are taken.

ἀνδάνω, ἡδύς, ἦδος.

The F appears in 12 or 15 instances of hiatus, and in the 2 Aor. form εὔαδε (for ἔϝαδε). The exceptions are, Il. 3. 173 ὡς ὄφελεν θάνατός μοι ἀδεῖν (read ὥς μ' ὄφελεν θάνατος ἀδέειν, see § 365) and 6 places with ἡδύς, two of which (Il. 4. 131, Od. 19. 510) may be easily emended. The Substantive ἦδος occurs chiefly in the phrase ἔσσεται ἦδος, where ἔσται may perhaps be read.

ἔθος, ἦθος.

The F is indicated by the hiatus κατὰ ἤθεα (Od. 14. 411). In μετά τ' ἤθεα καὶ νομὸν ἵππων (Il. 6. 511., 15. 268) the τε is better omitted. The Pf. εἴωθα or ἔωθα probably had no initial F, since σF- would give in reduplication σεσF- or ἐσF- (not σFεσF-).

ἑκυρός.

The only place bearing on the question before us is Il. 3. 172 φίλε ἑκυρέ, where the metre points to an initial consonant.

ἕξ.

The F may be traced by hiatus in Il. 5. 270 τῶν οἱ ἐξ κτλ., by lengthening in Il. 24. 604, Od. 10. 6. Adverse instances are Il. 23. 741, Od. 3. 115, 415., 14. 20.

ἔτης.

The F appears from hiatus in seven places, and can always be restored. The word is probably formed from the pronominal stem σFε- (so that it is=*unus e suis*).

392.] F inferred from metre. A few words may be added here which in all probability had initial F, though the traces of it in the metre are not supported by independent evidence.

ἀραιός.

The hiatus in three places indicates the loss of a consonant.

ἔθνος (perhaps akin to ἔθος, ἦθος).

Hiatus precedes in 12 places, and there is only one instance on the other side, viz. Il. 11. 724 τὰ δ' ἐπέρρεον ἔθνεα πεζῶν (where ἐπέρρεε is better, see § 172).

ἐρύω, ἔρρω.

Hiatus is found before ἐρύω *to draw* in 14 places (not counting those which are indecisive, such as ξίφος ὀξὺ ἐρυσσάμενος, or ἐπ' ἠπείροιο ἔρυσσαν), and preceding short syllables are lengthened in 17 places. There are 17 instances against F, one of the strongest being Il. 1. 141 νῆα μέλαιναν ἐρύσσομεν (=Od. 8. 34., 16. 348). The Verb ῥύομαι *to protect* is unconnected with ἐρύω.

The Verb ἔρρω (probably Lat. *verro*) shows hiatus in the phrase ἐνθάδε ἔρρων (Il. 8. 239., 9. 364); cp. ἀπό-ερσε, ἀπο-έρσειε.

ἤνοψ.

The word occurs six times (counting the proper name Ἦνοψ), and except in one place (where it begins the line) always requires an initial consonant.

ἦρα.

In the phrase ἐπὶ ἦρα φέρειν : referred to the root *var* meaning to *choose* or *wish*.

ἠρίον.

The only instance of this word (Il. 23. 126 μέγα ἠρίον) is in favour of initial F.

ἵεμαι.

An initial consonant is shown by hiatus in 23 places (ὁ δὲ ἵετο, οἴκαδε ἱεμένων, &c.) : there are four adverse places, viz. Il. 18. 501, Od. 2. 327., 10. 246., 14. 142. It is not connected with ἵημι, but is to be referred to root *vī*, meaning to *aim at, wish* (L. Meyer, *Bezz. Beitr.* i. 301).

Ἴλιος.

An initial consonant is indicated in about 50 places ; the number of adverse instances is 14. The derivation of this important word is unknown.

Ἶρος, Ἶρις.

These words may be connected with εἴρω *to tell.* If so, the F of Ἶρις is to be traced in ὠκέα Ἶρις (19 times), ὡς ἔφατ', ὦρτο δὲ Ἶρις (three times), βάσκ' ἴθι, Ἶρι κτλ. ; that of Ἶρος, Od. 18. 73, 334 (but not always, see vv. 38, 56, 233).

393.] Loss of F in Homer. The chief instances in which loss of an original F can be shown to have taken place in the language of Homer fall under the following rule :—

When the original initial F is followed by the vowels o, ω, or the diphthong ου, it produces no effect on the metre of Homer.

The following are words to which this rule will apply * :—

ὁράω, οὖρος (and οὐρεύς) *a watcher* ; ὄρεσθαι *to watch.* The original F (Germ. *wahr-*) will account for the forms ἑώρων and ἐπί-ουρος, but there are no traces in the *metre* of such forms as Fοράω, &c.

ὄρος *mountain* (cp. Βορέας), and ὀρθός *upright*, which may be from the same root (cp. the Laconian Ἄρτεμις Βωρθία). There is only one instance of hiatus (viz. Od. 3. 290 ἴσα ὄρεσσιν).

ὄρτυξ (Sanscr. *vartakas a quail*) appears in the name Ὀρτυγίη, which does not admit F (Od. 5. 123).

---

* See an article by Leo Meyer, *K. Z.* xxiii. pp. 49 ff.

ὄχος *chariot* (Lat. *veho*); ὄχλος (lit. *movement, tossing*), ὀχλέω *to disturb* (cp. ὀχλεύς and Lat. *vectis*); ὀχθέω (Lat. *vehe-mens*). A trace of Ϝ appears in the form συνεοχμός (Il. 14. 465).

ὄψ, ὄσσα, ὀμφή *voice*. The traces of Ϝ are, one instance of hiatus before ὄπα (Od. 11. 421), two of lengthening of a short syllable (Il. 18. 222, Od. 12. 52), and one or two phrases such as ἀμειβόμεναι ὀπὶ καλῇ, &c.; while there are three undoubtedly adverse places (Il. 11. 137., 21. 98, Od. 5. 61). In the case of ὀμφή the evidence is clear against Ϝ; in ὄσσα it is indecisive.

οὐρανός (Sanscr. *varuṇas*).

οὐλαί *coarsely ground barley*, connected with the root Ϝελ-, meaning *to roll*, &c. Neither this word nor the derivative οὐλοχύται admits Ϝ.

οὐλαμός *crowd, press of battle*, shows traces of initial Ϝ in Il. 20. 379 ἐδύσετο οὐλαμὸν ἀνδρῶν and the phrase ἀνὰ οὐλαμὸν ἀνδρῶν (Il. 4. 251, 273., 20. 113). It does not occur except in these places.

οὐτάω, ὠτειλή *wound*: cp. ἄ-ουτος *unwounded*, and the form γατάλαι in Hesychius.

ὠθέω (ἐώθεον, ἔωσα), root *vadh to beat*.

ὦνος *price*, Impf. ἐωνούμην (Sanscr. *vasnas*, Lat. *vēnum*).

Other words which may have originally had initial Ϝ are, ὅρκος (cp. ἐπί-ορκος), ὀνίνημι (ἐρι-ούνιος), ὄιγνυμι (ἀνα-οίγεσκον, ἀνέῳγε, &c.), ὀπυίω, ὄκνος, οὐρή, &c. (L. Meyer, *l. c.*). However this may be, none of them show traces of Ϝ in Homer. There remain the forms of the Possessive ὅς to which the rule would apply, viz. οὗ, ὅν, ᾧ, ὧν, οὕς. Hiatus is found before ὅν in 18 places (before ὅνδε δόμονδε seven times, ὃν κατὰ θυμόν six times, in προτὶ ὅν four times), οὕς twice (Il. 2. 832., 11. 330), οὗ once (Od. 15. 358). On the other hand there are 22 places in which the forms in question do not admit Ϝ. The significance of this proportion appears when we know that in the case of the remaining forms of the Possessive ὅς the places with hiatus number 50, the adverse instances 8, and that with the forms of the Personal Pronoun (ἕο, οἷ, &c.) the proportion is 728 to 19. It seems probable, therefore, that in the forms οὗ, ὅν, &c. the Ϝ was no longer pronounced, though *traces* of the former pronunciation remained (as in the case of οὐλαμός and ὄψ). Similarly in English the sound of *w* is lost before the vowel *o* in *who, whom, whose*, but retained in *which, what*, &c.

The retention of Ϝ before the diphthong οι, as in οἷ, οἷο, οἷς, also in οἶκος and οἶνος, may indicate that o before ι had not its ordinary sound, but one approaching to ε (possibly like French *eu*). This agrees with the fact that οι and **v** were afterwards identical in sound, and that in the modern language both are = ι.

Words with initial **v** are not found in Homer with ϝ ; but we cannot in this case speak of the loss of ϝ—the combination ϝv having been *originally* impossible.

The remaining instances in which loss of ϝ may be assumed in Homeric words are few, and for the most part open to question.

ἕλκω, root *valk* or *vlak* (Knös, following Curtius) : ϝ is perhaps seen in κατὰ ὦλκα (Il. 13. 707., Od. 18. 375). This account of the word separates it from Lat. *sulcus*.

ἑλεῖν, ἕλωρ, possibly to be connected with Lat. *vollur* the bird of *prey*. The instances of hiatus before ἕλωρ are hardly enough to prove ϝ.

ἕλος, from which the name Velia is said by Dionysius Hal. (*Arch.* I. 20) to be derived, has no ϝ in Homer (Il. 2. 584, 594., 20. 221, Od. 14. 474). The ϝ of this word is also wanting in the Cyprian dialect (Deecke and Siegismund, *Curt. Stud.* vii. 249).

Ἦλις, Ἠλεῖος is without ϝ in Homer : ϝαλήϊοι is the form found on Elean and Laconian inscriptions.

ἧλος (Lat. *vallus*) rejects ϝ in Il. 11. 29 ἐν δέ οἱ ἧλοι : the two other places where it occurs prove nothing.

ἰδίω, ἱδρώς (root *svid*) : the σϝ is lost in Homer.

ἴκω, ἱκνέομαι : the derivation from the root *viç* is quite uncertain.

ἱστίη (Lat. *Vesta*) : the forms ἀν-έστιος, ἐφ-έστιος show that the ϝ is lost in Homer (as also in the Laconian, Locrian, and Boeotian dialects, see § 404).

394.] Initial δϝ. This combination is to be recognised in two groups of words :—

δϝει- (δϝι-), ἔδεισα (so Ar.), δέος, δεινός, δειλός, &c.

A short vowel is frequently lengthened before these words, as Il. 1. 515 οὔ τοι ἔπι δέος, Il. 11. 37 περὶ δὲ Δεῖμός τε Φόβος τε, Od. 5. 52 ὅς τε κατὰ δεινούς, Od. 9. 236 ἡμεῖς δὲ δείσαντες.

The cases in which a vowel is allowed to count as short before the δ of this root are extremely few : Il. 8. 133 βροντήσας δ᾽ ἄρα δεινόν, Od. 12. 203 τῶν δ᾽ ἄρα δεισάντων (read ἄρ) ; Il. 13. 165 ἀπὸ ἕο δεῖσε δέ. There remain only Il. 13. 278 ἔνθ᾽ ὅ τε δειλὸς ἀνήρ (read ἔνθ᾽ ὅς τε δειλός), Il. 15. 626, and the forms ὑποδείσατε (Od. 2. 66), δεδίασι (Il. 24. 663), ἀδεής (Il. 7. 117).

δήν, δηρόν, δηθά.

In δήν the ϝ is required in the phrases οὔ τι μάλα δήν, οὐδ᾽ ἄρ᾽ ἔτι δήν, &c. ; there are no contrary instances. In δηρόν it is traced in two places, Il. 9. 415 (ἐπὶ δηρὸν δέ μοι αἰών), Od. 1. 203 : but is more commonly absent (οὐκέτι δηρόν, &c.). The instances of δηθά do not show anything.

It is to be observed that except in ἔδεισα the original δϝ does not lengthen a vowel without the ictus. Compare the rule as to initial ϝ lengthening a short syllable by Position, § 391.

395.] Initial ϝρ, &c. The metrical value of an initial ῥ which represents ϝρ differs in the several words. It has always the effect of a double consonant in ῥήγνυμι, ῥίπτω, ῥάκος, ῥυ- (in ῥυτός, &c.), ῥη- (in ῥητός, ῥητήρ), and nearly always in ῥινός (except Od. 5. 281), ῥίζα (Od. 9. 390). But lengthening is optional in ῥέζω, ῥιγέω, ῥεῖα : thus we have ἔρρεξα and ἔρεξα (in 27 places) ; ἵπποι δὲ ῥέα (Il. 8. 179), but ἔνθα κε ῥεῖα κτλ. ; ἐρρίγησαν, but ὣς φάτο ῥίγησεν δὲ κτλ. As to ῥ- standing for an older σρ-, and the other letters (λ, μ, ν) which lengthen a preceding short vowel, see § 371.

396.] ϝ not initial. The metrical tests by which initial ϝ is discovered generally fail us when the sound occurs in the middle of a word. Loss of ϝ may be shown either (1) by the contraction or synizesis of two vowels originally separated by it, or (2) by the shortening of the first of two such vowels. We have seen that the instances of contraction and synizesis are too rare or doubtful to prove much (§ 378*, 4). The cases in which hiatus is indicated by the shortening of a vowel are somewhat more important. In the declension of νηῦς the forms νεός, νέες, νεῶν, νέεσσι, νέας (§ 94, 1) cannot be derived phonetically from νηϝός, &c., unless we suppose loss of ϝ to have taken place. The same applies to the double forms of Nouns in -ευς, as Πηλῆος and Πηλέος, &c. Unless the short vowel is explained on some other hypothesis (e. g. by variation in the stem, as in Ζεύς and βοῦς, § 106, 2), we must suppose that ϝ had ceased to be sounded in the middle of a word. The loss of ϝ would also explain the metathesis of quantity in ἕως for ἧος in Od. 2. 79 (see § 171, 1), τέως for τῆος in Il. 19. 189 αὖθι τέως ἐπειγόμενος (where G. Hermann read αὐτοῦ τῆος), Il. 24. 658, Od. 18. 190 : but this, as these instances show, is even rarer than synizesis in these words, and is almost certainly post-Homeric.

Compound Verbs usually recognize ϝ, as ἀπο-ειπών, δια-ειπέμεν, also with apocope παρ-ειπών (ᾱ), &c. Exceptions are : ἀπ-ειπέμεν (Od. 1. 91), ἀπ-ειπόντος (Il. 19. 75), δί-ειπε (Il. 10. 425), πᾶρ-είπῃ (Il. 1. 555) : κατ-είρυσται (Od. 8. 151., 14. 332., 19. 289) : ἐσ-ίδεσκε, ἐσ-ιδέσθην, ἐσ-ιδοῦσα, ἐκκατ-ιδών, ἐπ-ιδόντα : ἐπ-έοικε (11 places) : ὑπείξομαι (Il. 1. 294, Od. 12. 117). In some of these forms metrical necessity may be pleaded ; thus ἐπι-ϝέϝοικε and ἐπ-ϝέϝοικε, κατα-ϝιδών and κατ-ϝιδών (‒ ◡ ‒) are alike impossible in the hexameter. Hence we may suppose a *licence* by which (as in the case of φρ, βρ, &c. § 370) the combinations νϝ, τϝ, πϝ, did not ‘make Position.’ The instances to which this excuse does not apply are very few.

On the other hand there are several examples of words in which ϝ between two vowels, or between a vowel and a liquid (ρ or λ), is *vocalised* as υ ; αὐίαχοι (ἀ-ϝίϝαχοι), αὐέρυον, ἀγαυός, ταλαύρινος (ταλά-ϝρινος), εὔαδε, ἔχευα, ἀλεύασθαι, δεύομαι, εὔληρα, ἀπούρας (§ 13), ἀκονή. It is very possible that many more such forms were to be found in the original text: cp. § 384, 1.

397.] Loss of initial σ and ι (ϳ). The traces of these sounds in the metre of Homer are chiefly of interest for the purpose of comparison with the facts relating to F.

The effects of initial σ may be seen in a few cases of the non-elision of prepositions: ἐπι-άλμενος (Lat. *salio*), ἀμφί-αλος (Lat. *sal*), ἀμφί-επον (Lat. *sequor*), κατα-ἴσχεται (ἴσχω for σίσχω), and the lengthening in πάρέχῃ (Od. 19. 113) and σύνεχές (Od. 9. 74). Hiatus is also found twice before ὕλη (Il. 14. 285, Od. 5. 257), once before ὕπνος (Od. 10. 68), and 18 times before ἐός (mostly in the principal caesura). These instances however are too few to prove anything.

Initial ι or ϳ is chiefly traced in the Adverb ὥς, which when used after the Noun to which it refers is allowed to lengthen the final syllable: as θεὸς ὥς, ὄρνιθες ὥς, &c. (so in 36 places). On the other hand there are nearly as many places which do not admit an initial consonant: as κτίλος ὥς (Il. 3. 196), λέονθ' ὥς (Il. 11. 383., 12. 293., 16. 756), θεὸς δ' ὣς κτλ. Probably therefore no spirant was heard, and the lengthening of the syllable before ὥς was a mere 'survival' or traditional rule (§ 375, 1).

398.] Summary. According to the computation of Prof. Hartel there are 3354 places in which the effect of the Digamma can be traced on the metre of Homer. In 2324 places its presence is shown by hiatus after a short vowel (*i. e.* it prevents elision); in 359 places it justifies the lengthening of a short syllable ending in a consonant, in other words, it helps to make 'Position;' in 164 places it follows a long vowel or diphthong which is without ictus: in 507 places it follows a long vowel or diphthong with ictus. It is further to be noticed that in many places a short final vowel in arsis is lengthened before the F: see especially the instances given under ἕο (§ 390), and ἰάχω (§ 389).* On the other hand there are 617 places where the F is neglected. Short vowels suffer Elision before it in 324 places: it fails to lengthen by Position after another consonant in 215 places: and long vowels or diphthongs are shortened before it in 78 places. Also the power to lengthen by Position is confined, except in the case of the enclitic ἕο, οἱ, to lengthening of syllables which have the ictus.

399.] Theories of the F. The main question which arises on these facts evidently is: How can the great number of passages

---

* A short vowel is also lengthened with ictus before ἔπος (Od. 10. 246), ἔρξαν (Od. 14. 411), and in the Compounds ἀπο-ειπών (Il. 19. 35) and ἀπο-έρσῃ, ἀπο-έρσειε (Il. 21. 283, 329).

in which the F affects the metre of Homer be reconciled with the not inconsiderable number of passages in which it is neglected? The scholars who first became aware of the traces of a lost letter in Homer assumed that in the original form of the poems this letter, or at least the consonantal sound for which it afterwards stood, was consistently used—that it was in fact one of the ordinary sounds of the language—; and accordingly they directed their efforts to restoring it to the text. This was the principle on which Bentley made his famous series of emendations: and which was carried out by Bekker in his edition of 1858. Of late years, however, different views of the matter have been taken. Leskien seems to have been the first to maintain that the passages which do not admit F are not necessarily corrupt or spurious, but are to be regarded as evidence of an original fluctuation in the use of the sound. His view is adopted and defended by Curtius (*Grundz.* p. 560, 5th ed.). Prof. Hartel has more recently put forward a theory which agrees with that of Curtius in treating the apparent neglect of the F as part of the original condition of the text. But he ascribes this neglect, not to irregularity in the use of the sound, but to the intermediate half-vowel character of the sound itself.

400.] If we are not satisfied that the F had the value of an ordinary consonant at the time when the Homeric poems were produced (or when they received their present form), we may explain the influence which it has on the metre in several ways.

Hypothesis of alternative forms. We may suppose that each word that originally had initial F was known to Homeric times in two forms, an older form with the F—confined perhaps to the archaic or poetical style—and a later in which F was no longer heard. Just as the poet could say either σῦς or ὗς, either πόλις or πτόλις, either τελέσσαι or τελέσαι, so he may have had the choice between Fάναξ and ἄναξ, ῾Fηδύς and ἡδύς, &c.

In order to test the probability of this hypothesis, let us take a few common words of different metrical form, and which show no trace of F, the words Ἄρης, ἄριστος, ἔγχος, ἦμαρ, ὅμιλος, ὀφθαλμός, ὕδωρ, ὕπνος. These words, with their immediate derivatives, occur in the Iliad 1022 times; and the places that would not admit an initial consonant number 684, or just two-thirds of the whole. Again, take some of the commonest words with F, ἄναξ, ἄστυ, ἔργον, οἶκος, and the Aorist ἰδεῖν. These occur in the Iliad 685 times, and the exceptions are hardly 50, or about one-fourteenth. Compared with the other proportion this surely proves that the recognition of the F in these words was not arbitrary, but was the rule in Homeric verse.

401.] Explanation from fixed phrases, &c. The traces of F may also be ascribed to the conventional phrases of the early epic style. The word ἄστυ, for example, is found very frequently in the combinations προτὶ ἄστυ, ἀνὰ ἄστυ, κατὰ ἄστυ, &c.; but these do not prove the pronunciation Fάστυ for Homeric times any more than (e. g.) ἐπιεικής proves an Attic ἐπιϝεικής. Such phrases, it may be said, were handed on ready-made, with a fixed metrical value, and served as models for fresh combinations, in which the hiatus was retained as part of the familiar rhythm.

This explanation is inadequate, for the following reasons :—

(1) The instances of F are not confined to the commonest words, or to frequently recurring phrases. Thus it is found in ἴον *a violet*, ἴτυς *the felloe of a wheel*, ἰτέη *a willow*, ἄρνες *lambs*. And it is used (generally speaking) in all the different forms of each Verb or Noun, whether of common occurrence or not (ἰδεῖν as well as ἰδέειν, ἴϝεσι as well as ἴς and ἴφι, &c.).

(2) The other cases in which tradition can be shown to have had the effect of retaining older phrases and combinations are not really parallel. In the Homeric Hymns the F can be clearly traced : but the proportion of instances which do not admit F is markedly different. Taking the words already used as examples, viz. ἄναξ, ἄστυ, ἔργον, οἶκος, ἰδεῖν, we find them in the Hymns 152 times, while the F is neglected in 36 places, or nearly one-fourth of the whole. Again if we look at the words which begin with ο, as οὐλαμός, ὄψ, &c. (§ 393), we find similar conditions. The traces of F are undoubted, but do not predominate as with ἄναξ or ἄστυ. Other examples may be seen in the traces of the double consonants, σρ, σλ, σν, Fρ discussed in § 371. Compare the free use of alternate forms, as ἔρεξα and ἔρρεξα, προ-ρέω and ἐπιρρέω, with the almost invariable recognition of δF in δέος, δείσας, &c. We seem to be able to draw a broad distinction between the *predominating* influence of the F in Homer and the arbitrary or occasional influence of the older forms in other cases. And these other cases, we may conclude, give us a measure of the force of tradition in such matters, while in the case of the Homeric F the effect is due to its retention as a living sound.

(3) A further argument in favour of F as a real sound in Homer has been derived from the places in which ʻϜε, ʻϜοι suffer elision (§ 391); see Leaf's note on Il. 24. 154. The argument has much force, and would be conclusive if we could assume that an elided vowel was not sounded at all.

402.] **Hiatus &c. as a survival.** Another supposition, akin to the last discussed, is that in the words which originally had initial F the ordinary effects of an initial consonant remained after the sound itself was no longer heard. Such a phenomenon would be by no means without parallel in language. In French, for instance, elision is not allowed before certain words beginning with *h*, as *le héros, la hauteur,* though the *h* is no longer pronounced. Similarly, then, it may be held that the facts of Homeric metre only prove the habit or rule of treating certain words as if they began with ϝ.

On the other side it may be urged that the *h* of *héros, hauteur,* &c. is only traced in one way, viz. by hiatus, and that only in a small number of combinations; whereas the ϝ not only protects hiatus, but also makes Position. Moreover the retention of a traditional usage of this kind is very much easier in an age of education. Anomalies which would naturally disappear in a few years are kept alive by being taught to successive generations of children. It seems difficult to believe that the ϝ would have kept its present place in the memory of the poets unless it were familiar, either to the ear as a present sound, or to the eye as a letter in the written text.

403.] Explanation from the nature of the ϝ. The theory recently advanced by Prof. Hartel is one to which it is difficult to do justice in a short statement. The careful re-examination which he has made of the metrical facts has convinced him that the influence of the ϝ is not occasional or arbitrary, but in the strictest sense universal in Homer. He does not however regard the passages in which the ϝ appears to be neglected as corrupt or spurious, but explains them on the theory that the ϝ in Homer has not the full value of an ordinary consonant: comparing it, for instance, not with the initial V of Latin, but with the sound which that letter has in the combination QV.

Hartel's chief argument is that hiatus after short vowels is the most common of the metrical facts pointing to a lost ϝ, and especially that it is much commoner than lengthening by Position, the numbers being 2995 and 359 respectively. But the force of this argument depends in the case of each word on the metrical form: thus before a word of iambic form the syllable must be short, hence we may find hiatus, but not lengthening: before an anapaest the reverse holds good. If (using Hartel's list) we take the instances in which ϝ is followed in the verse by two short syllables—the words being ἄγεν, ἅλις, ἔαρος, ἕλικες (with ἑλίκωπες, &c.), ἔπος, ἐρύω, ἔτος, ἰαχή, ἴδον—we shall find that they number 415, and the ϝ makes Position in 98. But this is not materially different from the proportion which will be found to obtain in the case of any common word of the same metrical form (such as πόλεμος).

404.] ϝ in other Greek dialects. It seems desirable here to say something of the uses of the Digamma which are found on the older inscriptions of the chief Doric and Æolic dialects.

The forms preserved on these inscriptions do not indeed prove anything directly as to the Homeric digamma. We cannot infer from them, for instance, that the symbol Ϝ was ever used in any written copies of the poems, or that the sound which it represented in other dialects was known to the Homeric language. But they may serve by way of analogy to direct our conjectures on these questions.

The most striking examples of Ϝ are found on the inscriptions of Corinth and its colony Corcyra (as Ϝεκάβα, ϜιόλαϜος, Ϝίφιτος, ΔϜεινίας, ΑἴϜας, ΞένϜων, ΞενϜάρεος, ὄρϜος, ΤλασίαϜο, &c.). With these may be placed the Argive inscriptions (in one of which occurs ΔιϜί), and the few Laconian inscriptions. In the older monuments of these dialects initial Ϝ is never wanting; but omission in the body of the word is occasionally found, as in Δαΐφοβος and Πολυξένα (on the same Corinthian vase), and several names ending in -κλῆς (for -κλέϜης), and -λας (for -λαϜος). The scanty Phocian inscriptions yield the important forms Ϝέξ, αἰϜεί, κλέϜος, with no early examples of omission; and the little known Pamphylian dialect is equally constant, so far as it has been made out. The Locrian dialect shows more decided indications of falling off in the use of the digamma. On the inscriptions of that dialect (discussed by Prof. Allen in Curt. Stud. iii. 207 ff.) we find it in Ϝαστός, Ϝέκαστος, Ϝεκών, Ϝέτος, Ϝεσπάριος, Ϝοῖκος and its compounds (ἐπίϜοικος, &c.), also in καταιϜεί, ϜεϜαδηκότα: but not in δαμιωργός, ξένος, ἐννέα, Ὀπώντιος (for original ὈποϜέντιος). The only initial Ϝ which is wanting is in the word ἱστίαι (we may compare the Laconian and Homeric ἐφέστιος). Similarly in the older Elean inscriptions initial Ϝ is regular (Ϝάργον, Ϝέπος, Ϝράτρα, &c.); and we have also ἘρϜαοῖοι (people of Heraea?), ἐϜέρεν (prob. an Infinitive), but ξένος, Διός without Ϝ. In the great inscription of Gortyn initial Ϝ appears in Ϝός (suus), Ϝίν (= Ϝοῖ), Ϝέκαστος, Ϝεκάτερος, Ϝέρξαι, Ϝεργασία, Ϝῆμα (εἶμα), Ϝεῖπαι, Ϝοικεύς, Ϝοῖνος, Ϝίκατι, Ϝεξήκοντα, and is only lost in ὠνά, ὠνάω (before ω, § 393). The Ϝ is also found in Compounds, as ἐνϜοικῇ, προϜειπάτω, δυοδεκαϜετίες, and in the body of the word ϜισϜόμοιρος, but disappears between vowels, as in λάω (Gen. of λᾶος a stone), αἰεί, παιδίον, the oblique Cases of Nouns in -υς and -ευς (υἱέες, Ϝοικέα, δρομέες, &c.), and the contracted words ἄτα (ἀϜάτη) and ᾶς (for ἆϜος, = ἕως). It is also lost before ρ, as in ἀπορρηθέντι.*

A somewhat later stage in the use of Ϝ is well exemplified by the numerous Boeotian inscriptions. In these the general rule is that initial Ϝ is retained: the only word from which it is regularly absent is ἕκαστος. On the other hand the only instances of

---

* Baunack, Die Inschrift von Gortyn, pp. 37–39, 68.

Ϝ in the body of a word are, the compound ϜικατιϜέτιες (εἰκοσι-
ετέες), and a group of derivatives of ἀείδω (αὐλαϜϙδός, τραγα-
Ϝϙδός, &c.). The same rule applies to the Arcadian inscriptions,
which however are too few to be of importance. The further
progress of decay may be seen in the Doric dialect of Heraclea,
of which a specimen remains in the well known *Tabulae Hera-
cleenses* (of the 4th cent.). We there find Ϝέξ, Ϝέτος, Ϝίϙιος, Ϝίκατι
and the compound ἐγ-Ϝηληθίωντι (=ἐξ-ειληθῶσι), but ἕκαστος,
ἴσος, ἀφ-ερξόντι, πενταέτηρίς, ἐργάζομαι, οἰκία, ῥήτρα : from which
it follows that the use of Ϝ even as an initial sound must have
been fluctuating. ˙A similar condition of at least partial loss of
Ϝ is found in inscriptions of Melos.

If we do not confine our view to the *character* Ϝ, but look to
the other indications of the sound which it represented, the most
important evidence is that furnished by the Cyprian inscriptions.
The forms which they yield belong, generally speaking, to an
earlier period of the language than is known from alphabetical
inscriptions. Yet the use of the sounds answering to Ϝ is not
uniform : we have ΔιϜός and Διός, βασιλέϜος and βασιλέος.

An original Ϝ is represented by β in several parts of Greece,
especially Laconia, Elis, Crete : but probably the β is merely a
graphical substitute for Ϝ. It is found in the inscriptions of later
times, when β was probably = our *v*.

The substitution of υ for Ϝ is characteristic of the Æolic of
Lesbos, as εὔιδε (for ἔϜιδε), αὐώς, δεύομαι, ἐνδευής (=ἐνδεής). In
these forms the Ϝ is vocalised ; cp. Homeric αὐίαχος (=ἀ-Ϝίαχος),
εὔαδε, ταλαύρινος.

. It is necessary here to notice a group of uses of the Ϝ in which
it seems to have been developed from a neighbouring vowel (υ or
ο). The vowel usually precedes, as in Laconian ἐδήϙοϜας, ἐδήϙοϜε,
Corcyrean ἀριστεύϜοντα, Boeotian ΕὐϜαρα, βακευϜαι, Cyprian
ΕὐϜέλθων, ΕὐϜαγόρω, κατεσκεύϜασε : but we also find ΤλασίαϜο
(Corcyr.), ΓίλγαϜος (Cypr.), ΤιμοχάριϜος (Cypr.), Ϝότι (Locr.).
So perhaps the Boeotian αὐλαϜϙδός, τραγαϜϙδός, &c. (see above).
With the former instances we might compare Italian *Genŏva,
Padŏva* (for Genua, Padua) ; with the latter the *u* of Italian
uomo, uopo, the *w* of *whole*, the provincial English *wuts* for *oats*,
&c. With Ϝότι we should compare the form ΝαϜπάκτιος, also
Locrian. Both are exceptional, and indeed must be considered
as mere errors :* but they help to show how near Ϝ was to a
pure vowel sound. It is evident that this redundant Ϝ, growing

---

* The ordinary form Ναύπακτος occurs on the inscription 19 times, the
form with ΝαϜ- only once. Similarly against the single instance of Ϝότι are
to be set 2 instances of ὅτι, and 5 others of the Relative ὅς, in the older
Locrian inscription. See Allen in *Curt. Stud.* iii. p. 252 ; Brugmann, *ibid.* iv.
p. 133, n. 57 : Tudeer, *De digammo*, p. 45.

out of the vowel υ or ο, is a parallel phenomenon to the loss of Ϝ
before these vowels which was noticed above as a characteristic
of Homer (§ 393).

405.] Ϝ in Ionic. There remains the interesting question
whether the existence of the Ϝ in Ionic can be traced in
inscriptions. The evidence appears to be as follows (Tudeer,
De digammo &c. pp. 5 ff.) :—

(1) The form AϜΥΤΟ (= αὐτοῦ) on a Naxian inscription of
the end of the 6th century B.C. But, as has been pointed out,*
the Ϝ of ἀϜυτός indicates at most a special way of pronouncing
the υ, and is to be compared with the erroneous ΝάϜπακτος noticed
above.

(2) The name of the city of Velia, which was founded by
exiles from Phocaea (Ϝέλεα *marshes;* but see § 393).

(3) The forms ϜΙΟ, ΓΑΡΥϜΟΝΕΣ, ΟϜΑΤΙΕΣ—all proper names
—on vases found in Magna Graecia, and supposed to have come
from Chalcis in Euboea, or one of its Italian colonies.

It is inferred by Tudeer (*l. c.*) that the Ϝ must have been a
living sound in the Ionic dialect of Euboea at the time when the
colonies of Chalcis were sent to Magna Graecia, *i. e.* probably in
the 8th century B.C. On the other hand, since there is no
example on the inscriptions of Euboea itself, the sound does not
seem to have survived there down to the date of the earliest
examples of writing, viz. the 6th century B.C. Hence Tudeer
puts the loss of the Ϝ in Ionic Euboea at some time between the
8th and the 6th centuries.

It has been recently pointed out by P. Kretschmer (*K. Z.* xxxi.
285) that the Ionic change of ᾱ to η cannot be placed very early.
The name Μῆδοι underwent the change,—the original ᾱ appears
in the form Μᾱδοι on the monument of Idalion—and the Medes
must therefore have become known to the Ionians before it was
completed. The Persian names which reached Ionia later—
Δᾱρεῖος, Μιθριδάτης, &c.—retain their ᾱ. Similarly the old
Carian Μίλατος became the Ionic Μίλητος. Hence the Ionic η
is later than the contact of Ionians with the nations of Asia
Minor. Now the anomalous η after ρ in the Attic κόρη and δέρη
is to be explained from the older forms κόρϜη, δέρϜη (cp. κόρρη
from κόρση). Consequently the loss of Ϝ in Attic must be later
than the change of ᾱ to η, and *a fortiori* later than the Ionian
migration. This inference is confirmed by the ο of the Comparatives κενότερος and στενότερος, pointing as it does to the forms

---

* By Brugmann, *Curt. Stud.* iv. p. 132, n. 55, and Tudeer, p. 7.

κενϝός, στενϝός (since the lengthening of the ε, as in Ionic κεινός, στεινός, never took place in Attic).

The former use of ϝ as a letter in all Greek alphabets is shown by its use as a numeral, and also by the existence of the first non-Phoenician letter, Υ. The addition of Υ, which was the earliest made, and perhaps contemporaneous with the introduction of the alphabet, shows that the Greeks felt the need of a vowel distinct from the labial spirant Vau. Otherwise the Phoenician Vau would have served for the vowel υ, just as the Yod was taken for the vowel ι. And as there is no Greek alphabet without Υ, it follows that the consonant ϝ was equally universal.*

Combining these inferences with the independent evidence furnished by the metre, we may arrive at some approximate conclusions regarding the value of ϝ in the Ionic of Homer.

(*a*) Initial ϝ had the value of a consonant, except before ο or ω (§ 393).

(*b*) δϝ was retained, not only at the beginning of a word (§ 394), but also in ἔδϝεισα, δέδϝια, &c. : we can hardly suppose compensatory lengthening in these forms.

(*c*) ϝ between vowels is more doubtful (§ 396). Since initial ϝ was lost as early as Homer before ο or ω, it probably vanished before most Case-endings of the Second Declension, and before the -ος, -ων of the Third Declension. Thus for λαϝός, &c. we should have λαός, λαοῦ, &c. (but ϝ possibly in λαϝοί, λαϝοῖσι): and again ἡδύς, ἡδέος, ἡδέϝι, &c., Πηλεύς, Πηλῆος, Πηλῆϝι, &c. Then other Cases might follow the analogy of the Gen. Sing. and Plur., and so drop the ϝ altogether. However this may be, it is clear that ϝ between vowels was generally lost much earlier than ϝ at the beginning of the word (cp. Italian *amai* for *amavi*, &c.). The absence of contraction proves little, as we see from the Attic χέω, ἔχεα, ἔχεε, &c. At the same time we occasionally find a partial survival of ϝ in a vocalised form, making a diphthong with the preceding vowel (§ 396).

---

* As the Vau is written Ψ on the Moabite Stone, it has been suggested that it was the source of the Greek Υ. It seems not improbable that the letters ϝ and Υ were at first only two forms of Vau, appropriated in course of time to the consonant ϝ and vowel υ,—just as our *u* and *v* come from the two uses of Latin V. If this is so, the place of Υ at the end of the then alphabet is significant, as showing the importance attached to the original order of the letters. See Roberts, *Greek Epigraphy*, § 11 : Taylor, *The Alphabet*, ii. p. 82.

APPENDIX.*

C. On η and ει in Homer.

THIS seems the most convenient place for a short statement of the question as to the spelling of the Subjunctives formed from Stems in -η, and of some other forms about which similar doubts have arisen.

1. In the case of Stems in which -η represents an older -ā the MSS. usually have ει before ο, ω, but η before ε, η. Thus in the Subj. of ἔβην, ἔστην we find βείω, στείωσι, &c., but βήῃς, στήετον, &c. There are one or two exceptions: καταβήομεν once in A (Il. 10. 97), ἐπιβήομεν in good MSS. of the Odyssey (6. 262., 10. 334). Aristarchus however wrote περιστήωσ' in Il. 17. 95 (where all the MSS. have περιστείωσ'), and βήομαι in Il. 22. 431 (where the MSS. have either βείομαι or βίομαι): from which it may be inferred that he wrote η in all similar forms.

2. In the Subjunctives from Stems in -η (the short Stem ending in -ε), the MSS. always have ει before ο, ω, and usually before ε, η. Thus we find θείω, θείῃς, θείῃ, and less commonly θήῃς, θήῃ, &c. But Aristarchus wrote θήῃς, θήῃ, &c., and so in all similar cases, δαμήῃ, σαπήῃ, &c. As to θείω, δαμείω, &c., no express statement of his opinion has been preserved. If we may argue from this silence, we should infer that the question had not arisen, and therefore that with these Stems the spelling -εω, -ειομεν, &c. was anciently universal.

3. The spelling with ει appears in some forms of the Aor. ἔκηα (for ἔκηυα, see § 15), esp. κείομεν, κείαντες, κείαντο, κειάμενοι, κακ-κεῖαι; also in the Pf. Part. τεθνειώς, and the 3 Plur. forms εἵαται, εἵατο, ἀκαχείατο. Aristarchus certainly wrote ἔκηα, τεθνηώς: and the form ἥαται (for ἥσ-αται) is supported by ancient authority (Eust. Od. 20. 354.)

4. In the declension of Stems in -εεσ (for -εϝεσ-) we sometimes find η throughout, as Ἡρακλῆς, Ἡρακλῆϊ, Ἡρακλῆα, sometimes η before ει and ι, but ει before α, ο, ω: as ἀκληεῖς, ζαχρηεῖς, but ἀκλειῶς, εὔκλειας, εὔρρειος, ζαχρειῶν. So δείους, σπείους, but σπῆϊ, σπήεσσι. In all these cases, however, the uncontracted εε should probably be substituted for η or ει (§ 105, 15). In χέρῃϊ, χέρηες, χέρεια (Aristarchus and most MSS.) the origin of the long vowel is not quite certain (§ 121).

---

* The matter contained in the Appendix to the first edition under the headings A, B, D and E has now been incorporated with the body of the work.

5. The Attic -εω- in πλέως, κρεω-φάγος, χρεωκοπέω points to original πλῆος, κρῆας, χρῆος, instead of the usual πλεῖος, κρείας, χρεῖος. And ἕως, τέως are for ἦος, τῆος (not εἵως, as in the MSS.).

6. So Attic -εᾱ points to -ηα, and accordingly we should have φρῆαρ, στῆαρ (instead of φρεῖαρ, &c.); and similarly ὄνηαρ.

The rule adopted by Bekker and La Roche is phonetic. They write ει before ο, ου, ω, α, but η before ε, ει, η, ι. Thus they give στείω, στήῃς; θείω, θήῃς; ἧμαι, εἵαται: and so on. This rule, however, is purely empirical.

On the other hand the scholars who look at the question as an etymological one are inclined to prefer η in all the instances in question. They hold that if (e. g.) we find the strong Stem θη- in τίθη-μι, θή-σω, ἔθηκα, &c., it must also be found in the Subjunctive. And they point out that in this and similar cases there is a special reason for distrusting, not only the extant MSS. (which are admittedly liable to error from itacism), but also the statements of the ancient grammarians, so far at least as they may be regarded as founded upon MSS. of the 4th century B.C. The older alphabet, which was used in Athens down to 400 B.C., employed the same character E for three distinct sounds, viz. the short ε, the long η, and (in many words) the diphthong ει. This would not lead to practical difficulty with a living language, but in the case of Homeric forms there was nothing to prevent confusion except the metre, and (it may be) the traditional pronunciation of the rhapsodists. There is therefore no good ground for believing that the spelling even of the 4th century B.C. could be trusted to decide between η and ει *in any form which was then obsolete.*

The substitution of ει for η, however, is not a matter of chance, but depends on the circumstance that in later Greek ει represented a single long vowel of the same quality as the short ε (probably a close e, such as French ê), while η was of different quality (a more open e, French è). Accordingly when Homeric η passed into ε in Attic, as in τεθνηώς, τεθνεώς, there was a special tendency to make the archaic long vowel (which the metre requires) as like as possible to the ε of the living speech. So the forms στήω, βήω, θήω, στήομεν, &c. would be liable to change their η to ει under the influence of the New Ionic στέω, στέωμεν, &c.; and so too ἦος, τῆος became εἵως, τείως from the influence of ἕως, τέως. We may even suppose that η first became ε, and this ε was afterwards lengthened to fit the metre,— just as Wackernagel supposes ὁράω to have been changed to ὁρόω through the intermediate form ὁρῶ (§ 55).

C C

A similar account is to be given of the forms which exhibit ει for ευ or εϝ, as πνείει *breathes,* θείειν *to run,* χείη (Subj.) *shall pour,* πλείοντες *sailing,* κλείουσι *celebrate* (§ 29, 3). The original Present is preserved in σεύω and δεύομαι, cp. the Aorists ἔχευα, ἠλεύατο. When -ευω passed into -εϝω and then -εω, the ε was lengthened by the force of the metre, and became ει. So the ει of κείαντες (for κηύαντες or κήαντες, from καίω) is to be attributed to the Attic 1 Aor. Part. κέας. But the Verbs in -ειω (§ 51, 3), or some of them, may be Verbs in -ηω: *e.g.* ὀκνήω, like Æolic ποθήω, ἀδικήω.

It is probable that in the same way the ᾱ of φάεα (Plur. of φάος), ἀήρ, ἀείδω, ἄασε, ἄϊον, ἄεσα, ἄορ, ἀλιαής, ζαής, &c. represents αυ. The lengthening cannot well be merely metrical, as in ἀθάνατος &c. (§ 386).

In some cases ει takes the place of an ε which was long by Position: as δείδοικα for δέδϝοικα, and perhaps εἶδαρ for ἔδ-ϝαρ.

The readiness to put ει for ε, especially before a vowel, appears in Ionic inscriptions of the 4th century B.C. where we find (*e.g.*) the forms δειόμενον, δείηται, δείωνται, ἐννεία, ἱδρύσειως, πόλειως, and Genitives in -κλειους (H. Weir Smyth, *The Vowel System of the Ionic Dialect,* in the *Trans. of the Am. Phil. Ass.* xx. p. 74: G. Meyer, *Griech. Gr.²* § 149). It is worth observing that these inscriptions belong to the same period as the MSS. in which, as we gather from the criticism of Aristarchus, such forms as τεθνειῶτας, στείωσι, βείω, &c. first found their way into the text.

F. *Fick's theory of the Homeric dialect.*

The theory put forward by Aug. Fick in his two works on Homer (*Die homerische Odyssee in der ursprünglichen Sprachform wieder-hergestellt,* 1883: *Die homerische Ilias nach ihrer Entstehung betrachtet und in der ursprünglichen Sprachform wiederhergestellt,* 1886) admits of being stated in a very few words. He holds that the poems (with certain exceptions) were originally composed in an Æolic dialect; that some three centuries later (about 540 B.C.) they were translated into Ionic; and that in this process every Æolic word for which there was no metrically equivalent form in Ionic was simply left unchanged. Thus, in his view, was formed the Epic dialect of literature,—a dialect mainly Ionic, but with a considerable admixture of Æolic forms.

The arguments which Fick advances in favour of this theory are not entirely linguistic. The scene of the Iliad, he reminds us, is laid in Æolis; the heroes and legends are largely those of the Æolic race; the parts of Ionia which tradition connects with Homer adjoin Æolic settlements; and Smyrna, which figures in some of the oldest traditions as his birthplace, was for a time an Æolic city. Now if the poems were first composed in some Æolic district of the north-west of Asia Minor, and passed thence to Ionia, they would take an Ionic form; and, as the result of the supremacy of Ionia in art and literature, that form, though full of anomalies and half-understood archaisms, would naturally hold its ground as the accepted text of Homer, and become the standard to which later poets, both of the Homeric and the Hesiodic school, would be obliged to conform.

The linguistic arguments upon which Fick chiefly relies are as follows:

1. The Ϝ or 'digamma,' which is required by the metre of Homer, is an Æolic letter, unknown to the earliest extant Ionic. Moreover the vocalisation of the Ϝ seen in a number of Homeric words (αὐίαχος and the like, § 396) is characteristically Æolic: cp. the Æolic εὔιδε (for ἔ-ϝιδε), αὔηρ (for ἀϝήρ), αὐάτα (=ἄτη), &c. The prothetic ἐ- of ἔεδνα (ἔ-ϝεδνα), ἐείκοσι, ἔέργω, &c. is also Æolic.

In order to prove that Ϝ never existed in Ionic Fick appeals to the Ionic inscriptions, and the early Ionic poets. This evidence, however, does not go back beyond the 7th century B.C., and therefore proves nothing for the original language of Homer. As we have seen (§ 405), there is reason to believe that the loss of Ϝ in the Ionic dialect was subsequent to the first settlements of Ionians in Asia.

2. The Æolic accent and breathing are found in a number of Homeric words. Thus the barytone accent appears in the Nominatives in -ă (as μητίετα, &c.), in the Perfect forms ἀκάχησθαι, ἀκαχήμενος, ἀλάλησθαι, ἀλαλήμενος, ἐγρήγορθαι, also in ἀπούρας, ζάης, ἄλλυδις, πόποι; the smooth breathing in ἆλτο (ἐπ-άλμενος), ἔμμορε, ὑββάλλειν, ἤμβροτον, ἦμαρ, ἄμαξα, ἄμυδις, ἀμόθεν, ἦμος, ἐπ-ίστιον, αὐτ-όδιον (ὁδός); and both peculiarities in the Pronouns ἄμμες and ὔμμες.

The answer is suggested by Fick himself,—though he makes it apply to a small part only of these forms.* It is that the accent and breathing of the Æolic words in Homer was determined by the

---

* 'Für ὔμμες, ὔμμιν, ὔμμε und ὑββάλλειν mag die psilose aus dem äolischen dialect erschlossen sein, in den übrigen fällen liegt wohl ächte überlieferung vor' (Odyssee, p. 12). Where is the evidence of any such tradition? Whenever the grammarians have to do with a form which was obsolete or archaic in their time, they are evidently quite at a loss.

living Æolic dialect. Let us take the form ἄμμι(ν) as a typical
instance. Fick holds that the Æolic ἄμμῐ(ν) was adopted by the Ionic
reciters and preserved with all its Æolic features—the double μ, the
smooth breathing, the barytone accent—for several generations,
because the Ionic ἡμῖν is metrically different (‒ ‒ instead of ‒ ◡).
The alternative is to suppose that the original Homeric language had
a form with short ῐ—as in Doric ἀμῐν—and that in later times,
when this form had gone out of use, the Æolic ἄμμι(ν) took its place
in the text. Such a substitution is eminently natural. The rhapsodists were doubtless familiar with the Æolic Pronouns, and their
adoption of the form ἄμμι(ν) was simply putting the known in place of
the unknown. In the case of ὔμμι(ν) and ὐββάλλειν Fick himself takes
this view. But if the form ὔμμι(ν) was maintained by the influence
of contemporary Æolic, we need go no further for an explanation of
the whole group of forms of which it is the type.

3. Several of the inflexional forms of Æolic are more or less frequent in Homer, and their occurrence, according to Fick, is subject to
a law which holds almost without exception, viz. that the Æolic form
is used (1) whenever the corresponding Ionic form is different in
quantity, and therefore is not admitted by the metre, and (2) when
the word itself is wanting in Ionic. In either case the simple substitution of Ionic for Æolic was impossible. On the other hand the
Ionic of Homer can be translated back into Æolic without encountering
any difficulty of the kind.

The forms to which Fick applies his argument are: the Fem. Voc.
in -ᾰ (νύμφᾰ), the Gen. in -οιο (-οο), -ᾱο, -άων : the Dat. Plur. in
-εσσι(ν): the Gen. of Pronouns in -θεν : the forms ἄμμες, ἄμμιν, ὔμμες,
ὔμμιν, ὔμμε : the Pres. in -άω, -ηω (-ειω), -ωω : the Inf. in -μεναι and
-μεν : the Pf. Part. in -ων (as κεκλήγων for κεκληγώς) : the Nouns in
-ᾱος, -ᾱων (λαός, ὀπάων, διδυμάων, and many proper names); θεά,
Ναυσικάα, and some proper names in -ειᾱ, -ειᾱς (in Ionic -ης). Other
Æolic words in Homer are γέλος (γέλως), πλέες (πλέονες), πίσυρες (Ion.
τέσσερες), ἤμβροτον (ἤμαρτον)—all metrically different from the Ionic
form. In several instances the corresponding Ionic form would have
suited the metre, but was not in use ; so θεά (Ionic only θεός), πολυ-
πάμων (Æol. πέπαμαι=κέκτημαι), ἔμμορε (in Ionic only Middle εἵμαρμαι),
ἐννῆμαρ, ἐννοσίγαιος, ἀργεννός, ἐρεβεννός. So ὅππως was retained because
the Ionic form was ὅκως, never ὅκκως : and ὅππως again led to the
retention of ὅπως.

In order to determine how far these forms are proofs of an Æolic

Homer, it is necessary to distinguish between those which are specifically Æolic, *i.e.* Æolic modifications of a common original, and those which are simply the older forms, which Ionic and other dialects modified each in its own way. To the latter class belong the Gen. endings -οιο (Indo-Eur. *-osyo*), -āο, -āων (New Ion. -εω, -εων), the Voc. in -ἄ, the Inf. in -μεναι, -μεν. These are forms which would be found everywhere in Greece, if we could trace the different dialects far enough back. They are 'Æolic' only because they were retained in Æolic (among other dialects), but were altered or lost in Attic and Ionic. The same may be said of the endings of the Pronouns ἄμμες, &c. They appear also in the corresponding Doric forms ἁμές, ὑμές, Dat. ἁμίν, ὑμίν, Acc. ἁμέ, ὑμέ. In these cases, then, we only know that a form is *archaic*, not that it belongs to any one dialect.*

On the other hand there are some forms to which this account does not apply. The Dat. Plur. in -εσσι is not proved to be 'Pan-hellenic,' and is certainly less primitive than the form in -σι (§ 102). The case stands thus : Ionic has only -σι, Æolic only -εσσι, in Homer both are found (-εσσι being rather less frequent). Therefore, says Fick, the language of Homer is Æolic,—not the later Æolic, in which every Dat. Plur. ended in -εσσι, but an earlier, in which -εσσι had begun to take the place of -σι. The same may be said *mutatis mutandis* of the Genitives ἐμέθεν, σέθεν, ἔθεν, and the Participles κεκλήγων, κεκόπων (§ 27). The argument here has greater weight than in the case of Pan-hellenic inflexions, but it is not conclusive. The forms now in question are not confined to Æolic : they appear occasionally in Doric, and in the dialects of northern Greece. There was therefore a general tendency towards these forms, and the dialect of Homer may have shared in this tendency without being thereby proved to be non-Ionic.

In the case of the Genitives in -οιο and the Voc. in -ἄ the argu-ment may be pressed somewhat further. The forms -οιο and -ου, which are found together in Homer, represent different steps of a phonetic process (-οιο, -ο͜ο, -οο, -ου): therefore they cannot have subsisted together in any spoken dialect, and -οιο in Homer must be an archaism, preserved by literary tradition. This conclusion is

---

* Undue stress has been laid upon the variety of forms of the Infinitive in Homer : *e. g.* θέμεναι, θέμεν, θεῖναι. Originally there were as many Infinitive endings as there were different ways of forming an abstract Substantive. In Vedic Sanscrit, where the Infinitive is less developed than in Greek, the variety of formation is much greater (Whitney, § 970).

confirmed by the Homeric use of the ending (§ 149, 3). If then
Fick is right in regarding -οιο in Alcaeus as taken from the living
Æolic of Lesbos (*Odyssee*, p. 14), it follows that Lesbian retained a
form which had died out of the supposed old Æolic of Homer's time.
Again, the Fem. Voc. in -ᾰ appears to be regular in Lesbian Æolic :
whereas in Homer it is found only in the isolated νύμφᾰ. This is
therefore another point in which historical Æolic is more primitive
than Homer. The argument would apply also to the Gen. in -ᾱο and
-ᾱων, if it were certain that -εω and -εων belong to the original
Homeric language.

4. Among the forms now in question there are many instances of
ᾱ for which Ionic must have had η, and which therefore—Fick argues
—cannot have come to Homer from Ionic. Such are, the Gen. in -ᾱο,
-ᾱων, which must have appeared in Old Ionic as -ηο, -ηων, whence
New Ionic -εω, -εων : the Participles πεινάων, διψάων : the Nouns in
-ᾱος, -ᾱων : the word θεά, and some proper names, Ἑρμείας, Αἰνείας,
Ῥεία, Φεία, Ναυσικάα : the words λᾶας, ἀήρ (Gen. ἠέρος), δαήρ (§ 106, 1),
τετρ-άορος (Od. 13. 81), perhaps also the Perfects ἔᾱδώς, ἔᾱγα (§ 22, 1).
The normal change to η appears in νηῦς (νηός for νηϝός, &c.), νηός
temple, ἠώς, ἠέλιος, παρ-ήορος, δήιος (Æol. δάϝιος), κληΐς, ῥηΐδιος, πηός.
Against the Nouns in -αων we can only set the single form παιήων.

In the first place, it is very probable (as has been shown in § 405),
that the Ionic of Homer's time still had the sound of ᾱ in all these
forms. This however is not a complete answer to Fick. We have
to explain how this primitive ᾱ was retained in these particular cases,
when the change of ᾱ to η took place generally in the dialect. For
we can hardly suppose that the change of -ᾱο, -ᾱων to -ηο, -ηων (on the
way to -εω, -εων) could have been made in the spoken language
without extending to the recitation of poetry.

The true answer seems to be that the retention of ᾱ in Homer was
due, generally speaking, to the influence of the literary dialects,
especially Attic and Æolic.

Let us take the case of λαός (λᾱϝός), which in some ways is typical.
The Ionic form ληός is quoted from Hipponax (fr. 88 Bergk), and is
preserved, as Nauck acutely perceived (*Mél. gr.-rom.* iii. 268), in the
Homeric proper names Λήϊτος, Λειώκριτος (for Ληόκριτος), and Λειώδης
(Ληο-ϝάδης). Fick supposes that when Homer was translated into
Ionic the form ληός had become antiquated, and accordingly, as λεώς
was metrically different, λαός was retained. If so, however, the
proper names would *à fortiori* have remained in their Æolic form

(Λᾶῖτος, Λαόκριτος), just as the older form *θέρσος for θάρσος is preserved in the names Θερσίτης, Θερσίλοχος, Ἁλιθέρσης, Πολυθερσείδης, &c. For in a proper name a stem is comparatively isolated, and thus may escape the influence of later usage. It follows that there was a time when ληός was the proper Homeric form. Why then do we find λαός in our text? Doubtless because it was the established form in Old Attic, and in other dialects familiar to the rhapsodists of the 6th and 5th centuries. In the case of so common a word this influence was sufficient to change ληός back into λαός, or (it may be) to prevent the change to ληός from taking place.*

The same considerations apply to ἶλᾶος, the form ἴληος occurring on a metrical inscription (Epigr. Kaib. 743, quoted by Nauck, *Mél. gr.-rom.* iv. 579): and to the name Ἀμφιάρᾶος, for which Ἀμφιάρηος was read by Zenodotus (Schol. Od. 15. 244), and is found in the MSS. of Pindar. So we find in Il. 11. 92 Βιήνορα (MSS.), Βιάνορα (Aristarchus); in Il. 14. 203 Ῥείης (MSS.), Ῥείας (Ar. Aristoph.); in Il. 13. 824 βουγᾶϊε (Ar. and MSS.), βουγήϊε (Zenod.); in Il. 18. 592 Ἀριήδνη (Zenod. — for Ἀριάδνη?); in Od. 13. 81 τετράοροι, but elsewhere in Homer συνήοροs, παρήοροs. These variations show that the question between ᾱ and η was often unsettled even in Alexandrian times †. On the same principle Fick would read Ποσειδήωνος in Archilochus (fr. 10), comparing the month Ποσιδηϊῶν (Anacr. fr. 6).

As a negative instance, we may notice the case of ἕως and τέως. These go back to a primitive Greek ἇϝος, τᾶϝος, which would become in Old Ionic ἦος, τῆος, in New Ionic and Attic ἕως, τέως. The existence in Homer of such metrical deformities as ἕως ὁ ταῦθ' ὥρμαινε is proof that later usage had the strongest influence on the formation of the text.

The ᾱ of Genitives in -ᾱο and -ᾱων (for -ᾱσων) stands on a somewhat different footing, since the loss of the intervening spirant is much more ancient. Hence it is possible that the change to an *E*-sound took place after the ᾱ in these endings had been shortened,

---

* The occurrence of λαός in Callinus (i. 18) and Xenophanes (ii. 15) shows that it became the usual Epic form from a very early time.

† Note however that Zenodotus sometimes gave η for ᾱ where the true Ionic form had ᾱ: thus he read ὁρῆτο for ὁρᾶτο (Il. 1. 198), κρητός for κρατός (Il. 1. 530). Perhaps βουγήϊος and Ἀριήδνη fall under this head: and ὄρηαι, which stands in our text (Od. 14. 343), is to be placed with ὀρῆτο. The most probable account of these forms surely is that they are 'hyper-Ionic,' *i.e.* are produced by the habit of regarding η as in every case the Ionic equivalent of Attic ᾱ. On this view they are parallel to the hyper-Doric forms which are produced by indiscriminately turning Attic η into ᾱ.

in other words, that the steps were -āo, -ăω, -εω and -āων, -ăων, -εων
(not -āo, -ηo, &c.). It is also not improbable that the shortening had
taken place in the time of Homer, so that -āo and -āων were then
archaic (as -οιο almost certainly was). There are 54 instances of the
Gen. Plur. Fem. in -εων (-ῶν) in Homer, against 306 in -āων (Menrad,
pp. 36, 38). Considering the strength of tradition in such matters
we may infer that the vowel was doubtful in quantity, if not actually
short, in the spoken language of the time. As to -āo see § 376, 1.
Now if the forms in -āo and -āων were then archaic, they might be
exempted, by the force of a poetical tradition, from the general phonetic law or tendency which turned ā into η in the Ionic dialect.
And the influence of Old Attic and other literary dialects which
retained the ā would operate the more decisively. However this may
be, it is clear that the causes which retained the ā of λαός, ναός,
παράορος, ξυνάορος, δᾶος, παός, πέπᾱμαι in the Old Attic of tragedy, may
have operated at an earlier time in favour of -āo and -āων.

The question between ă and ε in the later form of these endings
would naturally be settled by the example of Ionic in favour of -εω,
-εων : but it is worth noticing that the result has not been the same
in the Gen. of Neuters in -ăς (§ 107, 3). Here the Ionic ε appears in
Homer in the declension of οὖδας, κῶας, κτέρας, but not in γήρα-ος,
δεπά-ων, τερά-ων. The tendency to uniformity works much more
powerfully on a large class of words, such as the Nouns in -ā (-η),
than on a small group, like the Neuters in -ăς. But the survival
of -ăος, -ăων in the latter makes it probable that -ăω, -ăων were at
one time the Homeric forms, anterior to -εω, -εων.*

A singular problem is presented by the ā in the two forms πεινάων
(Acc. πεινάοντα) and διψάων, as to which see § 55, 8. As these verbs
belong to the small group in which contraction gives η instead of ā,
it seems at first sight strange that they should be the only examples
of -āων in the Participle. But the connexion between the two
phenomena appears when we consider that the contraction in πεινῇς,
&c. implies the steps āε > ηε > η. consequently that the exceptional
feature in it is precisely the retention of the long vowel. Thus it
remains only to explain the combination āω, āo, which in Ionic
should become ηω, ηo.

---

* The fact that -εω and -εων are scanned with synizesis, except in θυρέων
and πυλέων, is unimportant. Obviously an ending such as -εων can only
be scanned ◡ – when it is preceded by one, and not more than one, short
syllable. It will be found that θύρη and πύλη are the only Nouns in -η which
fulfil this condition.

5. In his earlier work on the Odyssey Fick recognised both ἄν and κεν as Homeric; but subsequently he came to the conclusion that ἄν is everywhere due to the Ionic translators (*Ilias*, p. xxiii). His main argument is that of the 43 instances of ἄν in the Ionic poets (Archilochus, &c.) there are not more than 21 in which it could be changed into κεν (κε, κ') without affecting the metre, whereas in Homer the change can be made in a much larger proportion of cases. The inference is that in making the change in Homer we are restoring the original form. But his induction is far too narrow. In the first three books of Apollonius Rhodius there are 46 instances of ἄν, and only 13 in which it cannot be changed into κε(ν). Again in Æschylus (excluding chorus) there are 212 instances of ἄν, of which 73 are unchangeable. In the *Œdipus Tyrannus* the number is 31 out of 107. In the Iliad, without counting ἤν and ἐπήν, the instances of unchangeable ἄν are 43 out of 156. This is nearly the same proportion; and we admit that in a few cases ἄν has replaced an original κεν. Moreover it has been already shown, on quite independent grounds, that the combination οὐκ ἄν is Homeric (§ 362). There can be little doubt, therefore, that while κε(ν) is distinctive of Æolic, as ἄν of Ionic and Attic, the Homeric dialect possessed both Particles. It may seem strange that κε(ν), which is commoner than ἄν in Homer, should have died out of Ionic. On the other hand ἄν was the more emphatic Particle, and the desire of emphasis is a frequent cause of change in the vocabulary of a language.

It may be objected that we have still to explain the remarkable coincidence on which Fick's argument rests, viz. the fact that in so many cases the non-Ionic forms are precisely those which are different in metrical value from the Ionic equivalents. The answer is that the same coincidence would be found with *archaisms* of any dialect. It is only the metre of Homer (generally speaking) that has preserved or could preserve such things. Why do we find (*e.g.*) στῆομεν, στῆετε, but στῆῃς, στῆῃ, στῆωσι (not στῆεις, στῆει, στῆουσι)? Evidently because the metre admits the modernised forms in the latter case, not in the former. Thus all words or inflexions which do not belong to the New Ionic or Attic dialect, be they Old Ionic or Old Æolic, will be found to be metrically different from the later forms.

It has been sought thus far to show that phenomena which Fick explains by supposing a translation from Æolic into New Ionic may be equally well accounted for, partly by the changes which must have taken place within the Attic-Ionic dialect itself, and partly by the influence of the post-Homeric spoken language. We may now consider what Homeric peculiarities cannot be explained on Fick's principles, and may therefore be held to turn the scale in favour of the alternative view.

(a) The Dual is wanting in the earliest Æolic, whereas it is in living use in Homer, and also in Attic down to the 5th century B.C. It is true, as Fick urges, that the loss of the Dual may have taken place in Æolic between the 9th and the 7th centuries. But the gap thus made between the earliest known Æolic and the supposed Æolic of Homer is a serious weakening of his case.

(b) The moveable -ν is unknown in Æolic, as also in New Ionic. Fick strikes it out whenever it is possible to do so, but is very far from banishing it from the text. Thus in the first book of the Iliad he has to leave it in ll. 45, 60, 66, 73, 77, &c.

(c) The psilosis which Fick introduces (ἀπίη for ἀφίει, &c.) is common to Æolic and New Ionic. Why then does it not appear in Homer?

(d) The forms of the type of ὁράω, ὁρόωντες, &c. (§ 55) are not accounted for by Fick's theory. This is recognised by Fick himself (Odyss. p. 2). He adopts the view of Wackernagel, supposing that the Attic forms ὁρῶν, ὁρῶντες were introduced into the recension of Pisistratus, and that these were afterwards made into ὁρόων, ὁρόωντες to fit the metre. This view is doubtless in the main correct. Setting aside the mythical 'recension of Pisistratus,' and putting in its place the long insensible influence of Attic recitation upon the Homeric text, we obtain a probable account of ὁράω, and of much besides. But it can hardly be reconciled with a translation into New Ionic about 540 B.C. It is uncertain, indeed, whether the New Ionic form was ὁρέω or ὁρῶ (see H. Weir Smyth, Vowel-system &c. p. 111); but the argument holds in either case. If the form was ὁρέω (as is made probable by the Homeric ὁμόκλεον, &c. § 55, 10), that form is metrically equivalent to the original, and on Fick's theory would have been adopted. If it was ὁρῶ, which is metrically different, then on Fick's theory the original Æolic would have been retained.

(e) The forms ἕως and τέως, as has been already noticed, have crept into the text in spite of the metre; on Fick's theory the original ἆος and τᾶος must have been preserved.

(*f*) Many Attic peculiarities may be noted : οὖν for ὦν (which Aristarchus counted among the proofs that Homer was an Athenian) : πῶς, πότε, &c. for κῶς, κότε, &c. : the two Genitives δείους and σπείους (for δέεος, σπέεος) : Neuters in -ας, Gen. -αος (instead of -εος) : ἄρσην (for Æolic and Ionic ἔρσην) : τέσσαρες for Ionic τέσσερες ; κρείσσων, μείζων for κρέσσων, μέζων. Cp. also ἔᾱγα (Ionic ἔηγα), and ἑᾱδότα (§ 22, 1), for which Ionic analogy would require ἐηδότα.

(*g*) The Æolic forms ἄμμι(ν), ὔμμι(ν) are not used quite consistently : thus we find the form ἄμμιν in three places (Il. 13. 379., 14. 85, Od. 12. 275), but ἡμῖν in three others (Od. 8. 569., 11. 344., 17. 376). On Fick's theory ἧμιν, if it was an Ionic form, would have been adopted. Again ὔμμιν is occasionally used where ὑμῖν is admitted by the metre (Il. 10. 380, Od. 4. 94., 20. 367).

Several of these arguments may be met by admitting an *Atticising* tendency, subsequent to the Ionicising which Fick supposes. Some such Attic influence clearly was exerted, and also an Æolic influence (as Fick allows in the case of ὔμμες). But if the Ionic Homer only dates from 540 B.C., what room is there for these other processes ? And if we suppose a *modernising* process, as wide in place and time as the knowledge of Homer, but in which Attic and Ionic naturally predominated, what ground is left for an original Æolic element ?

(*h*) The Iterative forms in -εσκον (§ 48) appear to be characteristic of Homer and also of later Ionic. This is one of the points—in the nature of the case not numerous—in which the Ionic character of Homer is guaranteed by the metre.

Another point of this kind is the use of μέν in ἦ μέν, καὶ μέν, and other combinations where Attic would have μήν (§ 345). On the other side it may be said that the retention of μάν (see § 342) was due to the want of the form μήν in Ionic. But if μάν were an original Æolic form we should expect on Fick's theory to find it in the older parts of the Odyssey as well as in the Iliad.

Other words which show a difference of quantity between the Homeric and the Æolic forms are : Πρίαμος (Æol. Πέρραμος), τρίτος (Æol. τέρτος), κᾱλός (Æol. κᾰλος, see Meyer, *G. G.* § 65).

The ancients supposed that Homer of set purpose employed a mixture of dialects. Modern scholars have condemned this notion as uncritical, but have generally held that his language is a poetical and conventional one, a *Sängersprache*, never used in actual speech. It may be allowed that there is a measure of truth in both these views, provided that we distinguish between the dialect of the time of Homer and the 'Epic' of our texts. For—

1. Even in the time of Homer there was doubtless an element of conventionality in the style and vocabulary, and even in the grammatical forms of poetry. Such phrases as μερόπων ἀνθρώπων, νήδυμος (or ἥδυμος) ὕπνος, ἀνὰ πτολέμοιο γεφύρας, are used with little or no sense of their original meaning, but evidently as part of a common poetical stock. Doubtless the Gen. in -οιο was already poetical, perhaps also the Gen. in -āo and in -āων. These forms then were genuinely Homeric, but not part of the living speech of the time.

2. Many primitive Homeric forms were lost in Ionic and Attic, but survived elsewhere in Greece. These seemed to the ancients to be borrowed from the dialects in which they were known in historical times, and thus gave support to the notion of a mixture of dialects.

3. The poems suffered a gradual and unsystematic because generally unconscious process of modernising, the chief agents in which were the rhapsodists, who wandered over all parts of Greece and were likely to be influenced by all the chief forms of literature. In this way forms crept in from various dialects,—from Ionic, from Lesbian Æolic, and from Attic. The latter stages of this process may be traced in the various readings of the ancient critics, and even in our MSS., in which a primitive word or form is often only partially displaced by that of a later equivalent. The number of instances of this kind may be materially increased as the MSS. of Homer become better known.

Other Notes and Corrections.

§ 23, 5 (p. 27). With the instances here given we may place the Cretan καταϝελμένοι, which occurs in the inscription of Gortyn with the meaning *gathered together, assembled* (cp. Homeric ἐελμένοι *crowded*). Baunack however takes it for καταϝηλμένοι, supposing loss of ϝ and contraction from καταϝεϝελμένοι.

§ 27 (p. 30). The Present ἀκούω *I hear* appears to be originally a Perfect which has gone through the process here exemplified. The true Present form is ἀκεύω, which survived in Cyprus (ἀκεύει· τηρεῖ Κύπριοι) and Crete (*Law of Gortyn*, ii. 17). Hence the Attic ἀκήκοα (for ἀκ-ήκοα), and presumably also an earlier form *ἄκοα, formed like ἄνωγα, and passing into ἀκούω as ἄνωγα passed into ἀνώγω. This explains the use of ἀκούω with the Perfect meaning (§ 72, 4), which accordingly is not quite parallel to the similar use of πυνθάνομαι, μανθάνω, &c. Other Homeric examples are διώκω (§ 29), in which the want of reduplication may be original (§ 23, 5), and ἰλήκω (§ 22, 9, b.). The form ἥκω, which is probably of this nature, occurs in our MSS. of Homer (Il. 5. 473., 18. 406, Od. 13. 325., 15. 329), but Bekker substituted the undoubtedly Homeric ἴκω (La Roche, H. T. 287).

The form ἐνένιπε rebuked, which occurs several times in Homer (usually with the variants ἐνένιπτε and ἐνένισπε), should perhaps be placed here. It is usually classed as a Reduplicated Aorist (so Curt. Verb. ii. 26), but there is no analogy for this, and the Homeric passages do not prove that it is an Aorist. The ῑ of the stem may be due to the influence of the Pres. ἐνίπτω and the Noun ἐνιπή (cp. § 25, 3). Buttmann acutely compared it with ἐπέπληγον, which is evidently related to πλήσσω and πληγή as ἐνένιπον to ἐνίπτω (ἐνίσσω) and ἐνιπή. The reduplication is of the type of ἐρέριπτο.

§ 42 (p. 44). The Aor. ἐτράφην, which occurs four times in our texts of the Iliad, is probably post-Homeric. In Il. 2. 661 for the vulgate τράφη ἐν (μεγάρῳ) nearly all MSS. have τράφ' ἐνί. If this is right we should doubtless read τράφ' ἐνί in the two similar places, Il. 3. 201 and 11. 222. In Il. 23. 84 the MSS. have ἀλλ' ὁμοῦ ὡς ἐτράφην περ, with the v. l. ἐτράφημεν: the quotation in Æschines (Timarch. 149) gives ὡς ὁμοῦ ἐτράφεμέν περ, from which Buttmann (Ausf. Sprachl. ii. 307) restored ὡς δ' ὁμοῦ ἐτράφομέν περ. On the other hand the Thematic ἔτραφον occurs with intransitive or passive meaning in Il. 5. 555., 21. 279 (where ἔτραφ' is the only possible reading), and in the recurring phrase γενέσθαι τε τραφέμεν τε. The variation in the MSS. (including the vox nihili ἐτράφεμεν) is sufficient evidence of the comparative lateness of the forms of ἐτράφην. Buttmann's reading (adopted by Nauck) is supported by the apodosis in l. 91 ὡς δὲ καὶ ὀστέα κτλ. See Christ (Proll. p. 115) to whom I am indebted for the reference to Buttmann.

§ 62 (p. 56). The derivative verbs in -αζω are often frequentative or intensive, but with a tone of contempt: e. g. μιμνάζω I loiter, ἀλυσκάζω I shirk, πτωσκάζω I cower (stronger than πτώσσω, cp. Il. 4. 371 τί πτώσσεις, τί δ' ὀπιπεύεις πολέμοιο γεφύρας; οὐ μὲν Τυδεῖ γ' ὧδε φίλον πτωσκαζέμεν ἦεν): ἀκουάζομαι I please myself with hearing (Il. 4. 343 δαιτὸς ἀκουάζεσθον, Od. 13. 9 ἀκουάζεσθε δ' ἀοιδοῦ): so νεύω and νευστάζω (Il. 20. 162), μίγνυμι and μιγάζομαι (Od. 8. 271), ῥίπτω and ῥιπτάζω, ἐρύω and ῥυστάζω, εἰλύω and εἰλυφάζω.

§ 67 (p. 61). With ἐήνδανον compare the Aor. form ἔηξα (for ἔαξα), preserved in the text of Zenodotus in Il. 13. 166 (ξυνέηξε for ξυνέαξε) and 257 (κατεήξαμεν for κατεάξαμεν). In this case the change to η did not make its way into the vulgate—perhaps because the form ἦξα, which suggested it, was a rarer word than ἤνδανον.

§ 71 (p. 63). The use of the Present stem to express *relative* time is well exemplified by the following sentence from an early Attic inscription : εἰσπραξάντων αὐτοὺς οἱ ἡρημένοι, συνεισπραττόντων δὲ αὐτοῖς καὶ οἱ στρατηγοί (Meisterhans, § 48 a.).

§ 72, 2, n. 2 (p. 64). In the Law of Gortyn ἄγω and φέρω are employed where the Aor. is the usual tense : see especially i. 12 αἰ δ' ἀννίοιτο μὴ ἄγεν if he deny that he has taken away (Baunack, *Die Inschrift von Gortyn*, p. 79).

§ 77 (p. 66). Some valuable remarks on this and similar uses of the Aor. Part. are to be found in an article by Mr. Frank Carter in the *Classical Review* (Feb. 1891, p. 4). He observes that it is really a *timeless* use, *i.e.* that the speaker does not wish to indicate a relation in time between the action of the Participle and that of the finite verb. The Participle expresses a predication, but one which is only a part or essential circumstance of that which the verb expresses. See below, on § 245, 1.

§ 80 (p. 68). As to the MS. authority for some forms of the Pf. Subj. see § 283, a.

§ 92 (p. 79). The Nominative is used for the Vocative in the case of oxytones in -ων, and all Nouns in -ην (Brugmann, *Grundr.* ii. § 206, p. 544).

§ 99* (p. 84). To the examples of metaplastic Neut. Plur. used with collective meaning add ἕσπερα evening-time (Od. 17. 191), νεῦρα sinews (used in Il. 16. 316 of *one* bowstring), πλευρά side (Il. 4. 468), παρειά cheeks (Neut. Plur. in Il. 22. 491 according to Aristarchus). It may be suspected that ἐρετμά oars belongs to this group, since the Sing. in later Greek is always ἐρετμός, and a Neut. ἐρετμόν is contrary to analogy, and only rests on the phrase εὐῆρες ἐρετμόν (Od.), for which we can read εὐῆρε' ἐρετμόν.

§ 102 (p. 86). It appears that the stems in -ā originally formed a Loc. Plur. in -ās (as well as -āsu and -āsi) : hence Lat. *forās, aliās, devās* (Inscr.). Hence it is possible that the few Homeric forms in -αις or -ης which cannot be written -ησ' represent this -ās (Brugmann, *Grundr.* ii. § 358, p. 704).

§ 110 (p. 95). The question between πάντῃ and πάντη cannot be

decided, as Joh. Schmidt supposes (*Pluralb.* p. 40), by the circumstance that the final vowel is frequently shortened before another vowel
in Homer. It is true, as was observed by Hoffmann (*Quaest. Hom.* i.
p. 58, quoted by Schmidt *l. c.*), that final η is oftener shortened than
final ῃ. In the first four books of the Iliad and Odyssey, as Hartel
shows (*Hom. Stud.* ii. p. 5), -η is shortened 41 times, -ῃ 19 times:
and further examination confirms this ratio. But, as Hartel also
points out, -η occurs in Homer about three times as often as -ῃ:
consequently the shortening of -η is *relatively* more frequent.

§ 116, 4 (p. 109). For ἡδὺς ἀϋτμή in Od. 12. 369 we may read
ἡδὺς ἀϋτμήν, as suggested by Baumeister on Hom. H. Merc. 110.

§ 116, 5 (p. 109). ὑγιής has been explained as a Compound, viz. of
the prefix *su-* (*su-manas*, &c.) and a stem from the root *jyâ* (Saussure,
Mém. Soc. Ling. vi. 161).

§ 117 (p. 110). Adjectives in -ιος are often used with some of the
meaning of a Comparative, *i. e.* in words which imply a contrast
between two sides: as in ἑσπέριος *evening* and ἠοῖος or ἠέριος *morning*,
ἡμάτιος *day* and νύχιος *night*, ἄγριος (cp. ἀγρότερος), θεῖος (cp. θεώτερος),
ἅλιος (opposed to *dry land*), νότιος, ζεφύριος (opp. to *north* and *east*),
δαιμόνιος, ξείνιος, δούλιος. The suffix serves to form a kind of softened
Superlative in ἐσχάτιος and ὑστάτιος, lit. ' of the last': and the same
analogy yields ὀσσάτιος from ὅσσος, a formation like Lat. *quantulus.*
The Comparative force of -ιος, -ιος in the Pronouns is noticed by
Brugmann (see § 114, p. 101).

§ 121 (p. 115 *foot*). The ω of σοφώτερος, &c. has lately been discussed by J. Wackernagel (*Das Dehnungsgesetz der griech. Composita*,
pp. 5 ff.). He treats it along with the ω which we find in ἑτέρωθι,
ἑτέρωσε, ἀμφοτέρωθεν, &c., also in ἱερωσύνη, and shows that if we derive
it from a Case-form in -ω (as κατωτέρω from κάτω, &c.), we have still to
explain the rhythmical law according to which ω and ο interchange:
for a law which governed common speech in all periods cannot have
arisen merely from the needs of the hexameter. Accordingly he
connects the phenomenon with a rhythmical lengthening of final
short vowels (among others of the final ι of the Locative, see § 378),
which is found in Vedic Sanscrit.

λαρώτατος (Od. 2. 350) points to a Homeric form λαερός, which we
can always substitute for λαρός. It is probably for λασ-ερός from
λασ- *desire*: see Curtius, *Grundz*, p. 361 (5th edit).

§ 125, 8 (p. 121). This peculiar lengthening in the second member
of a Compound has been explained by Wackernagel (*Dehnungsgesetz*,

pp. 21 ff.) as the result of a primitive contraction, or Crasis, with the
final vowel of the first part : e. g. ὁμώνυμος for ὁμο-ονυμος. The chief
argument for this view is that the lengthening is only found in stems
beginning with a vowel—a fact which can hardly be accounted for on
any other supposition. Such cases as δυσώνυμος, in which no contraction can have taken place, may be extensions by *analogy* of the
original type. It is to be understood of course that the contraction
was governed by different laws from those which obtain in the Greek
which we know. The chief rule is that the resulting long vowel is
fixed by the *second* of the two concurrent vowels : ὁμήγυρις for ὁμο-
αγυρις, πεμπώβολον for πεμπε-οβολον, &c. Whether this was a primitive
phonetic rule, or partly due to the working of analogy, it finds an
exact parallel in the Temporal Augment, which must have been due
to the influence of a prefix ἐ- upon the initial vowel of the verb-stem.
We may compare also the Subjunctive forms δύναμαι, τίθηντι, &c. (§ 81).
Thus the later contraction, as in σκηπτοῦχος, Λυκοῦργος, stands in the
same relation to the older forms now in question as εἶχον, &c. (with ει
for εε) to ἥλασα, ὤμοσα, &c.

The primitive Indo-European 'sandhi,'—crasis of the final vowel
of one word with the initial vowel of the next,—was generally given
up in Greek, and the system of *elision* took its place. In Compounds
we constantly find elision of a short final vowel along with the
lengthening (which is then a mere survival) : as ἐπ-ήρατος, ἀμφ-ήριστος,
φθισ-ήνωρ (cp. φθισί-μβροτος). But lengthening does not take place
if the vowel is long by position (e. g. ἑτερ-αλκής, Ἀλέξ-ανδρος, ἀναιδής),
which seems to indicate that the preservation—though not the origin
—of the lengthened stem was a matter of rhythm (as in σοφώ-τερος).
Other exceptions to the rule of lengthening may be variously explained.
In some cases, as Wackernagel suggests (p. 51), an initial short
vowel may have been retained from the original formation : as in the
ancient Compounds βωτιάνειρα (ἀντιάνειρα, κυδιάνειρα), ἀργιόδοντες, εὐρύοπα,
εὐρυάγυια, where the metre stood in the way of lengthening by analogy.
More generally it is a mark of lateness : e. g. in the forms compounded
with παν-, as παν-άποτμος, παν-αφῆλιξ, παν-αώριος, Παν-αχαιοί, and with
Prepositions, as ἐν-αρίθμιος, ὑπεναντίος (p. 55). Such words as αἰν-
αρέτης (Il. 16. 31), λαβρ-αγόρης (Il. 23. 479), ἀν-όλεθρος (Il. 13. 761
τοὺς δ᾽ εὑρ᾽ οὐκέτι πάμπαν ἀπήμονας οὐδ᾽ ἀνολέθρους), ἀνάποινον (Il. 1. 99),
δυσ-αριστοτόκεια (Il. 18. 54), have all the appearance of being of the
poet's own coinage.

On the view here taken the lengthening in ὠλεσίκαρπος and the similar cases given at the end of the section must be otherwise explained. It is probably of the kind noticed in § 386.

§ 170 (p. 159). Another example of the distributive use of the Singular is Od. 13. 78 ἀνερρίπτουν ἅλα πηδῷ *they threw up the salt sea (each) with his oar-blade.* So in the recurring phrase of the Odyssey ἅλα τύπτον ἐρετμοῖς we should probably read ἐρετμῷ (§ 102), which may be similarly distributive. Or we may take ἐρετμός in a collective sense, *oarage.*

§ 173, 2 (p. 162). For the use of the Dual with a large number which contains the numeral δύο, cp. πεντακοσίαις εἴκοσι δυοῖν δραχμαῖν in an Attic inscription of the 5th century (Meisterhans, p. 45, 4). This is a good parallel to Od. 8. 35, 48 κούρω δύω καὶ πεντήκοντα.

§ 198 (p. 180). Notice under this head the use of ἐπί with a Comparative, Od. 7. 216 οὐ γάρ τι στυγερῇ ἐπὶ γαστέρι κύντερον ἄλλο *nought else is more shameless with* (when you have to do with) *a hungry belly,* = more shameless than the belly. So Hdt. 4. 118 οὐδὲν ἐπὶ τούτῳ ἔσται ἐλαφρότερον.

§ 241 (p. 206). In Il. 17. 155 it is better to take οἴκαδ᾽ ἴμεν with ἐπιπείσεται, leaving the apodosis to be understood : ‘ if any one will be persuaded to go home (let him do so), &c.’ Thus the sentence is of the type exemplified in § 324* b.

§ 245, 1 (p. 212). The Aor. Part. in such a sentence as εἰ ἴδοιμι κατελθόντα seems to be ‘ timeless,’ meaning *if I were to see him go down* (Goodwin, § 148). Mr. Carter, in the article quoted above, ranks ἐς ἠέλιον καταδύντα as an instance of timeless use in an attributive sense. It should be observed, however, that there is a distinction between a Participle which expresses a *single* action or event (however timeless), and one which has become a mere adjective, as in περιπλομένου ἐνιαυτοῦ, &c. (§ 243, 1). Thus ἐς ἠέλιον καταδύντα means *to the setting of the sun* (not *to the setting sun*): and so with the other examples given in § 245, 1. It is otherwise perhaps with Od. 1. 24 οἱ μὲν δυσομένου Ὑπερίονος οἱ δ᾽ ἀνιόντος, where the place of sun-set—not of a particular sun-set—is intended.

§ 297 (p. 269). In the Law of Gortyn πρίν κα with the Subj. is repeatedly used after an affirmative principal clause : see Baunack, *Die Inscrift von Gortyn,* p. 82.

§ 324*, b, c. The omission of the principal Verb in passages of this kind (especially when it is suggested by an Infinitive in the protasis) finds a perfect parallel in the Law of Gortyn : iii. 37 κόμιστρα αἴ κα λῇ δόμεν ἀνὴρ ἢ γυνά, ἢ Fῆμα ἢ δυώδεκα στατῆρανς ἢ δυώδεκα στατήρων χρῆος,

D d

πλίον δὲ μή (sc. δότω) *if man or wife choose to give payment for nurture, let him or her give a garment or twelve staters or something of the value of twelve staters, but not more*: cp. the other places quoted by Baunack, *Die Inschrift von Gortyn*, p. 77. This shows that the usage must have been well established in Greek prose from an early period.

§ 338 (p. 309). In Il. 3. 215 most MSS. have εἰ καὶ γένει ὕστερος ἦεν, but ἢ καί is found in the two Venetian (AB) and the Townley and Eton MSS. The scholia show that the ancients knew nothing of εἰ, and only doubted between ἤ (in the sense of *if*) and ἦ.

§ 348, 4 (p. 318). In Il. 18. 182 one of the editions of Aristarchus had τίς τάρ σε (for τίς γάρ σε). Cobet adopts this, and would read τάρ for γάρ in the similar places Il. 10. 61, 424, Od. 10. 501., 14. 115., 15. 509., 16. 222 (*Misc. Crit.* p. 321). In the two last passages Bekker had already introduced τ' ἄρ into his text.

§ 370 (p. 342). To the instances of shortening before -βρ- should be added ἀβροτάξομεν (Il. 10. 65), which is a derivative verb from the stem which we have in the two forms ἁμαρτ- and ἁ(μ)βροτ- (cp. ἤμβροτον). The appearance of ρο instead of ρα (for ɼ) is Æolic.

§ 405 (p. 382). A parallel to the Naxian ΑϜΥΤΟ has now been found in the form ΑϜΥΤΑΡ on an Attic inscription of the VIth cent. B. C. (see J. van Leeuwen, *Mnemos.* xix. 21). Further instances of Chalcidian Ϝ (Ϝοικέων, σαϜοῖ?) are given by Roberts, *Epigraphy*, p. 204.

---

§ 69 (p. 62). In an article on the Augment in Homer in the last number of the *Journal of Philology* (xix. p. 211 ff.), Mr. Arthur Platt has shown that, in the case of the Aorist, the choice between the augmented and the unaugmented form is largely determined by the sense in which the tense is used. In the common historical or narrative use the augment is often wanting; but in the uses which we may call *non-narrative*—the use for the *immediate past* (§ 76), and the *gnomic* use (§ 78)—the augmented form prevails. With the gnomic use the rule appears to be especially strict. This is obviously a valuable extension and generalisation of the facts observed by Koch. In the case of the Imperfect there seems to be a preference for unaugmented forms in continuous narrative ; but the difference is much less marked. Mr. Platt gives some good reasons for believing that the number of unaugmented forms was originally greater than it is in our text. In this we find a fresh example of the modernising process to which the poems were subjected from a very early time.

INDEX I.

OF HOMERIC FORMS.

N.B. The figures refer to the *sections*.
Compound verbs are not indexed if the same form of the simple verb occurs.

E e

ψευδάγγελος 124 d.
ψευδέσσι 116 (5).
ψεύδονται 29 (3).

ὧδε 108, 110.
ὠδύσατο 39 (1).
ὠθέω 393.
ὠίγνυντο 17.
ὤϊξα 67.
ὠίσθη 44.
ὦκα 110.
ὠκύς 114.

ὠλεσίκαρπος 124 c, 125.
ὤλετο 31 (5).
ὤμνυε 18.
ὤνατο 11.
ὦνος 393.
ὠνοσάμην 78.
ὦπα 107 (2).
Ὠρείθυια 125 (8).
ὤρετο 31 (4).
ὤριστος 377.
ὠρμήθη 44.
ὦρσα 39 (3), 40.

ὦρτο 40.
ὥς (Demonstr.) 265.
ὡς 375 (1), 397; (use)
  235, 267, 285, 306.
ὡς εἰ 295, 312.
ὥσασκε 49.
ὦσι 81.
ὡσί 107 (2).
ὥς τε 235, 285 (3) a.
ωὑτός 377.
ὤφελον ⎫
ὤφελλον ⎭ 33.

POST-HOMERIC FORMS

(including Hesiodic, Ionic and Attic forms quoted.)

αἴνημι 12.
αἰσθέσθαι 32 (2), 34.
αἰῶ (Acc.) 107.
ἁμαρτίνοος 126.
ἀνδράποδον 107 (1).
ἄνωγμεν 25 (1).
ἀπέφατο 13.
ἆρα 347.
ἀρήρεται (Subj.) 80.
ἀρηρυῖα 26 (3).

βάθος 114.
βεβρῶτες 26 (4).
βλαστεῖν 34.

γεγονώς 26 (4).
γοῦν 349.

δέδοιγμεν 25 (1).
δῆθεν, δῆτα 350.
διδόασι 7.
δικεῖν 34.

ἑαυτῇ 108.
ἔδον (2 Aor.) 7, 15.
ἔθεν (2 Aor.) 7, 15.
εἶ (2 Sing.) 5.
εἴληφα 23 (2).
εἴξασι 7 (3).
εἶτα 318.

ἐκεῖ 109.
ἔοιγμεν 25 (1).
ἐπέφυκον 68 (1).
ἐπίσχε 88.
ἐρήρισται 23 (3).
ἔρρωγα 22 (1).
ἔρσην App. F (ƒ).
ἔρωτα (Acc.) 107.
ἐτεύχθην 43.
ἔχθομαι 31 (7).

ἦν (1 Sing.) 12.
ἦς, ἦστε 12.

θιγεῖν 34.

ἷκτο 40.
ἵλαμαι 16.

καίτοι 346.
κανεῖν 34.
κᾱλός App. F (h .
κέκοφα 24 (2).
κέκραγα 28, 31 (1).
κεκρύφαται 24 (2).
κέκτημαι 23 (2).
κλύω 31 (4).
κρύφα 110.
κτίννυμι 17.

μέντοι 346.
μηδείς 356.

οἴδαμεν, οἴδασι 24 (1).
ὅμως 337.
ὅσσοισι 107 (1).

πάθος 114.
πῖθι 32 (1).
πίτνω 17.
πλέως 384.
πόλευς 94 (2).

σχές 5.

τανύπτερος 126.
τεθηλυῖα 26 (3).
τεθνηκώς 26 (4).
Τερψιχόρη 124 c.
τέτοκα 22 (8).
τιθέασι 7.
τοίνυν 346.

ὑμνείω 51 (3).

φερέοικος 124 d.
φερεσσακής 124 f.
φρασί 106 (3).

χρέα 105 (4).

ὦν (οὖν) App. F (ƒ).
ὡς (Prep.) 228.

INDEX II.

OF SUBJECTS.

N.B.—The figures refer to the *sections*.

Ablative : the Ending -ως 110, 160 : Ablatival Genitive 146, 152, 153 : with Prepositions 178, cp. περί 188 (1), παρά 192, ὑπό 204 (1), (3), ἀνά 209, κατά 213 (1), ὑπέρ 219, ἐξ 223, ἀπό 224, πρό 225 : -φι(ν) 156 : -θεν 159.

Accentuation : the Verb 87 : Compound Verbs 88 : Inf. and Part. 89 : Nom. Sing. in -ᾰ 96 : Acc. in -ιν 97 : Case-forms 111 : the Vocative 112 : Primary Nouns 115 : Compounds 128 : Prepositions 180 : the Reflexive Pronoun 253 (2) : ἀνύω, ἐρύω (Fut.) 64 : -δε 335 : ἐπειή, τιή or τίη 339 : ἠέ—ἦε 340.

Accusative : Singular 97 : Plural 100 : Adverbial 110, 133–6 : in Compounds 124 f. : Internal Object 132 ff. : 'part affected' 137, 139 (3) : Time and Space 138 : with Adjectives 139 : External Object 140 : Acc. *de quo* 140 (3), 237 (2), 245 (2) : of the *terminus ad quem* 140 (4) : Double Acc. 141 : Whole and Part 141 : with Prepositions 178 : with παρέξ 227 : with the Infinitive 237, cp. 240 : with a Participle 245 : ὅ, ὅτι, ὅ τε 269, 270 : with -δε 335.

Adjective 165 : Adverbial uses 134 : predicative 162 : Gender 166 : Participle 243 : the Article with Adjectives 260 : in -ύς 116 (4) : in -ης 116 (5) : in -εος, -ρος, -ιμος, -ινος, -εις, -ικός 117 : -αλέος, -άλιμος, -εινός (-εννός), -διος, -δανος 118 : Comparison of Adjectives 121, 122.

Adverbs 90 : Adverbial Suffixes 109, 110, 160 : use of Neuter Pronouns 133 : Neuter Adjectives 134, 139 (1) : other Accusatives 135–139 : -θεν 159 : -ως 160 : -ως in the Predicate 162 (5) *a* : adverbial use of Prepositions 175, 176 : see esp. ἀμφί, πέρι, πάρα, μέτα, ἔπι, ὕπο, προτί, ἀνά, ἔνι, πρό, and cp. 227 : Relative Adverbs 267 : ὅ, ὅτι, ὅ τε 269, 270.

Æolic : Verbs in -μι 12, 19 : Opt. in -σεια 83 (3) : Opt. in -φην, -οιην 19, 83 : Nom. Sing. Masc. in -ᾰ 96 : ἄορ, ἦτορ 114 : κεν 364 : ν for ϝ 404 : Fick's Theory, App. p. 486 ff. πίσυρες 130 (3) : ἀβροτάξομεν App. p. 402.

Anacoluthon 163, 243 (3) *d*, 353.

Anaphoric Pronouns 247 : ὅδε 249 : κεῖνος 250 : οὗτος 251 : αὐτός 252 : ἕο, &c. 253 : ὁ ἡ τό 256.

Antecedent to Relative : definite 262 : omitted 267 (2), (3) : attracted by the Rel. 267 (4) : attracting the Rel. 267 (5) : τό 269.

Aorist 13–15 : Thematic 31–34 : Reduplicated 36 : in -ᾰ 37 : Sigmatic or Weak 39, 40 : in -σε (ο) 41 : in -ην 42 : in -θην 43 : meaning 21, 44, 75–8, cp. 298 : Aor. Inf. after πρίν and πάρος 236.

Apocope of Prepositions 180*.

Apodosis : Ellipse of 324*, δέ in apodosis 334.

Archaic forms : in Composition 124 *b* : Gen. in -οιο 149 : in -οο 98, 368 : forms in -φι(ν) 154 : αὐέρυσαν 337 : false archaism 82, 83, 158 *fin.*, 216.

INDEX III.

CHIEF PASSAGES REFERRED TO.

THE END.